Server+ Guide to Advanced Hardware Support

James I. Conrad

Proud Sponsor of

CompTIA®

Server+™ Certification Program

COURSE
TECHNOLOGY

THOMSON LEARNING

Australia • Canada • Mexico • Singapore • Spain • United Kingdom • United States

COURSE TECHNOLOGY
THOMSON LEARNING

Server+ Guide to Advanced Hardware Support

by James I. Conrad is published by Course Technology

Senior Product Manager:
Lisa Egan

Managing Editor:
Stephen Solomon

Development Editor:
Deb Kaufmann

Marketing Manager:
Toby Shelton

Associate Product Manager:
Elizabeth Wessen

Editorial Assistant:
Janet Aras

Manuscript Quality Assurance:
John Bosco

Manufacturing Coordinator:
Alexander Schall

Book Production:
Brooke Albright, Trillium Project
Management

Cover Production:
Elena Montillo, Production Editor

Cover Design:
Steve Deschene and Julie Malone

Compositor:
GEX Publishing Services

Disclaimer
Course Technology reserves the right to revise this publication and make changes from time to time in its content without notice.

ISBN 0-619-06202-9

BRIEF
Contents

TABLE OF
Contents

CHAPTER EIGHT
Configuring a Network Operating System

Introduction

Server+ Guide to Advanced Hardware Support takes you beyond generic PC repair and administration into the world of high-end PC servers. This book will enable you to feel confident when talking with businesspeople as well as technical people about the many features and technologies of server administration and hardware. It will also help you make wise decisions concerning how your business career is linked to server management. If you are planning a technical career, consider this book the foundation of your education about servers.

This book provides support in preparation for CompTIA's Server+ Certification examination. This new, vendor-neutral certification focuses on server hardware, configuration, administration, and troubleshooting. Obtaining certification increases your ability to gain employment and improve your salary. To get more information on Server+ Certification and its sponsoring organization, the Computing Technology Industry Association, visit their web site at *www.comptia.org*.

FEATURES

To ensure a successful learning experience, this book includes the following pedagogical features:

- **Learning Objectives:** Every chapter opens with a list of learning objectives that sets the stage for you to absorb the lessons of the text.
- **Appealing Art Program:** The text is full of diagrams, drawings, screen captures, and photographs that make the many server technologies easy to follow and understand.
- **Step-by-Step Procedures:** The book has step-by-step instructions that you can easily follow for hands-on experience on all aspects of working with servers, including upgrading and repairing server hardware, configuring the network to which servers connect, and configuring and installing server operating systems along with their various applications and services.

 Tip icons highlight additional helpful information related to the subject being discussed.

 Caution icons highlight potential pitfalls and dangers of which you should be aware.

Note icons highlight additional information about the subject being discussed.

■ **End-of-Chapter Material:** The end of each chapter includes the following features to reinforce the material covered in the chapter:

- **Chapter Summary:** A bulleted list is provided that gives a complete but brief summary of the chapter.

- **Key Terms:** A list of all new terms and their definitions.

- **Review Questions:** To test knowledge of the chapter, review questions cover the most important concepts of the chapter.

 Hands-on Projects help you apply the knowledge gained in the chapter.

 Case Projects present scenarios that will help you develop server planning, troubleshooting, and optimization techniques relevant to the material in each chapter.

■ **CoursePrep® Software Server+ Test Preparation CD-ROM:** 50 test preparation questions, powered by MeasureUp©, simulate the testing environment so you can practice for exam day.

Before using this book, you should have moderate computer experience and at least a basic understanding of most PC terms and technologies. Many readers might already have a previous certification, such as CompTIA A+ or Network+ certification, but they are not prerequisites. After completing the book, you will have mid-level to upper-level knowledge of server administration and technology. After becoming Server+ certified, you will be able to fulfill the roles of job titles such as:

■ Service manager

■ Technician

■ Systems engineer/administrator

■ Help desk staff

■ Service and repair professional

■ System analyst and integrator

■ PC support specialist

■ Network engineer/administrator/analyst/architect/manager/specialist

For instructors using this book in a classroom environment, the following teaching materials are available on the Instructors Resource Kit CD-ROM:

Electronic Instructor's Manual: The Instructor's Manual that accompanies this textbook includes a list of objectives for each chapter, detailed lecture notes, suggestions for classroom activities, discussion topics, and additional projects and solutions.

ExamView®: This textbook is accompanied by ExamView, a powerful testing software package that allows instructors to create and administer printed, computer (LAN-based), and Internet exams. ExamView includes hundreds of questions that correspond to the topics covered in this text, enabling students to generate detailed study guides that include page references for further review. The computer-based and Internet testing components allow students to take exams at their computers, and also save the instructor time by grading each exam automatically.

PowerPoint Presentations: This book comes with Microsoft PowerPoint slides for each chapter. These are included as a teaching aid for classroom presentation. They can be made available to students on the network or printed for classroom distribution.

ACKNOWLEDGMENTS

A special thanks to Stephen Solomon for offering this book to me, and to Lisa Egan, the Senior Product Manager, whose dedication to this book appears on every page. Thanks, Lisa, for your guidance through our very tight deadline schedule. Thanks to Deb Kaufmann, the Development Editor, for your humor, encouragement, and top-notch professionalism all along the way. I could never have made this book what it is without you. Thanks to Robert (Mac) McMullen, Michael Shannon, and Stephen Brown, who contributed their extensive server and networking knowledge to this book. Thanks to the artists who rendered my chicken-scratch drawings into high-quality, illuminating graphics.

Writers always need other eyes to review their work, and for this book I had several reviewers whose extensive experience and knowledge were very helpful. I know that you all have very demanding full-time jobs that required you to make sacrifices to help with this book. Thanks to the reviewers and technical editors:

John Anderson	AND-R Companies
Tina Ashford	Macon State College
Randol Larson	Estrella Mountain Community College
Don Locke	Center for Disease Control
Bob Pierson	Northwestern Michigan College
Clint Saxton	Hewlett-Packard
Mike Woznicki	ExecuTrain

A very special thanks goes to Bob Pierson, whose networking and server knowledge is unbelievable.

DEDICATION

All my love to my wife, Jana, an author herself. You never once complained about late nights and time away from family. Thanks to my three children (Kenley, Marina, and Cooper), who, even though I work in a home office, had to do without me for months while I was behind the locked door. Thanks to all of you for your prayers.

James I. Conrad (MCSE, MCP+I, Server+) is a full-time author who has written several books on networking and Microsoft Windows products, and is President of Accusource Computer Consulting, Inc., a company that hires contract writers for technical publications. James has taught seminars to thousands of IT professionals in the United States and Europe, and continues to teach with trainAbility of Scottsdale, AZ, a premier Windows 2000 and Windows Exchange training organization.

PHOTO CREDITS

Figure #	Credit Line
1-9	Courtesy of Seagate Technology
2-14	Courtesy of Liebert Corporation open front
3-1	Courtesy of Intel Corporation
3-6	Courtesy of Intel Corporation
4-16	Courtesy of Hewlett-Packard Company
4-25	Courtesy of Dell Computer Corporation
6-8	Courtesy of FLOTRON, Inc. www.flotron.com
7-19	Photo courtesy of Eclipse Enterprises, Inc.
7-20	Photo Courtesy of Eclipse Enterprises, Inc.
7-21	Photo Courtesy of Eclipse Enterprises, Inc.
7-22	Products courtesy of UNICOM Electric, Inc., City of Industry, CA
7-23	Products Courtesy of UNICOM Electric, Inc., City of Industry, CA
10-1	Courtesy of StorageTek
10-2	Courtesy of StorageTek

COMPUTER REQUIREMENTS

You can perform several of the Hands-on Projects on a personal computer, but you will see as you go that a standard PC might not be sufficient for some of the server projects. The course assumes you will have access to:

- **Windows 2000 Server** or **Advanced Server installation CD.** Most projects use Windows 2000.
- **Red Hat Linux version 7.0 or better.** Although Linux is not included in the Hands-on Projects, you should install and familiarize yourself with the Linux interface and tools.
- **Novell NetWare version 5.1 or better CD**
- **Two or more servers.** For most projects requiring two computers, you could substitute one of the servers for any Windows computer.

 Suggestion for instructors. Install Windows 2000 and image the hard drive using imaging software or tape backup software. After completing projects, you can restore the server(s) to the original configuration by restoring the image.

- **Microsoft Internet Explorer 4.0 or better, or Netscape Navigator.** Some Hands-on Projects require Internet access. You can download a copy of Internet Explorer from *www.microsoft.com/windows/ie/* and Netscape Navigator from *www.netscape.com.*
- **A server rack at least 24 U in height, and any rack-mountable server** or other network device such as a hub or switch.
- **A motherboard** capable of at least two processors.
- **A redundant, hot-swappable power supply**
- **A UPS**
- **A KVM** (keyboard, video, mouse) device
- **A PDU**
- **A scrap hard disk with the cover removed** (for easy observation of internal parts)
- **Two IDE hard disks and a 40-pin, 80-conductor IDE cable**
- **An IDE host adapter** (unless the motherboard has an IDE connection)
- **A Windows 98 boot floppy**
- **A blank floppy**
- **Two or three SCSI hard drives and a compatible SCSI cable**
- **A SCSI host adapter**
- **A SCSI terminator** compatible with the above SCSI equipment

- **An ESD grounding kit** consisting of a wrist strap with alligator clip and grounding mat
- **A digital multimeter**
- **Two identical processors**, one already installed on the motherboard
- **At least one memory module compatible with the motherboard**
- **A PCI network card with older (but compatible drivers)** that will be updated via the Web
- **Four or more RJ-45 jacks** per student
- **Six feet or more of Cat 5 cable** per student
- **Diagonal cutters**
- **RJ-45 crimper**
- **A hub**
- **A tape backup drive and compatible tape media**

Visit Our World Wide Web Site

Course Technology publishes a full array of Networking and CompTIA certification products. For more information, go to **http://www.course.com/networking**.

1

DEFINING A SERVER

After reading this chapter and completing the exercises, you will be able to:

♦ Differentiate between peer-to-peer and client-server networking models

♦ Identify server functions and benefits

♦ Identify characteristics that distinguish server hardware from client hardware

♦ Identify three main types of servers

The server is the single most critical element of most networks. This fact becomes very evident when a server fails. If a user's computer fails, it affects only that user. However, if a server fails, it can affect hundreds or thousands of users and disrupt an organization's business operations. In server planning, you must be able to determine if the network needs a server (or an additional server) and what server capabilities are required. What kind of hardware will meet the anticipated needs? How will you justify the initial and maintenance expense of server equipment? In order to make these decisions, you should know what to look for in a server. This chapter starts with the most basic network model—a simple network without a server—and defines the benefits of adding a server. You will also learn the characteristics that distinguish a user's computer from a server, and what distinguishes various server types from one another.

DOES YOUR NETWORK NEED A SERVER?

Before you delve into planning and installing a server, consider if you really need a server. This might seem like an odd statement to place in the first chapter of a book on servers, but it is a legitimate one. If your organization is small (perhaps 12 or fewer workgroup computers), users only occasionally share printers, files, or applications, and security is not a major concern, then it is possible to network all the computers together without a server. For example, users in a small, family-run construction company probably already trust one another and only need to print invoices or checks to a shared printer from time to time. The company does not require a database, and the construction managers create job estimates on their own laptop PCs, which only occasionally connect to the network. In this case, it is of little use to implement a server.

Conversely, most organizations (even small ones) can benefit from adding one or more servers to the network. Some of the benefits include enhanced security, improved performance, centralized file storage, centralized administration, and a central location from which to run applications. For example, the owner of a small real-estate office installs a high-speed Internet connection so that real-estate agents can research land values and receive email from clients. Also, the owner wants each agent to enter sales records into a company database. A server could include special software to protect office users and the company database from malicious Internet users and provide a central location to store the company database.

After determining the need for a server, you must also determine "how much" server you need. Will the server support dozens, hundreds, or thousands of users? Do you require extremely high performance? Some servers offer features and performance comparable to common desktop personal computers, some are extremely powerful and cost hundreds of thousands of dollars, and others fall somewhere in the middle.

COMPARING PEER-TO-PEER AND CLIENT-SERVER MODELS

A **network** is a collection of two or more computers connected with wired transmission media such as network cable or with wireless radio or infrared signals, and it usually includes other devices such as printers. A **network device** is any device connected to the network for purposes of communicating with other network devices. (A network device is also known as a **host** in most networks.) Cumulatively, the network devices form what is known as a **local area network (LAN)**—a collection of computers in close proximity to one another on a single network (see Figure 1-1). A LAN includes a single cable to which all computers connect, or more commonly, each device has its own network cable, each of which converges to a central **hub** or **switch**. You can use a network cable to join multiple hubs together, but the entire collection of hubs still constitutes a single network. A LAN can be one of two basic networking models: peer-to-peer or client-server. Expanding upon a LAN, a **wide area network (WAN)** involves multiple, geographically distant LANs connected to one another across relatively great distances. For example, an organization's LAN in Seattle connected to the same organization's LAN in Phoenix constitutes a WAN.

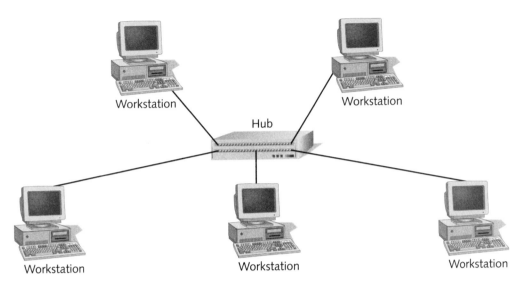

Figure 1-1 A simple LAN connected to a hub

Peer-to-Peer

A network does not necessarily require a server. A **peer-to-peer network** is a network of computers with no logon server to verify the identity of users. (Although a peer-to-peer network might include a file server that stores files for the users, this is seldom the case.) This model is called a peer-to-peer network because each network device has an equal (peer) level of authority. Computers in a peer-to-peer network are usually common desktop computers, otherwise known as **workstations**, and are generally equipped with only enough hardware to service the needs of a single user. Most peer-to-peer networks use the file and printer sharing capability of Microsoft Windows 95/98/ME/NT/2000 to share network resources. A **network resource** (sometimes called only a "resource") is an object that users can access across the network. Common examples of network resources include printers, files, and folders (see Figure 1-2).

Although the file and printer sharing capability of a peer-to-peer network can service a small network, it can also limit network growth. For example, Microsoft Windows 95, 98, NT Workstation, and 2000 Professional limit inbound concurrent network connections to 10. This means that if 10 users are already accessing a folder, an additional attempt to access the folder will fail because the limit of connections has already been reached. This limitation restricts the size and growth capacity of peer-to-peer networks.

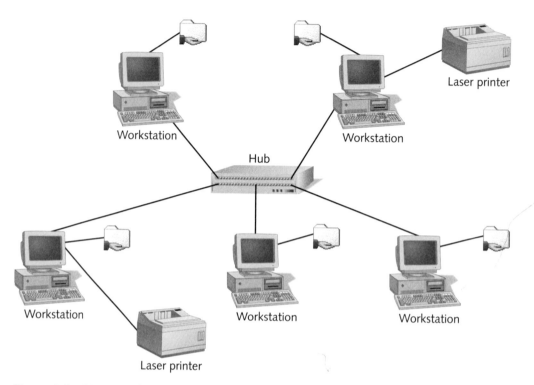

Figure 1-2 Users on the LAN can share folders, files, and printers

 Peer-to-peer networks function best when individual users seldom access one another's files. If user A accesses a file on user B's workstation, then saves the file to user A's local hard disk, it causes confusion when attempting to locate the most up-to-date version of a file.

Peer-to-peer networks also lack file security. Windows 95/98/ME shares folders (and hence the files contained in the folders) with password protection. A password can be easily compromised and, at best, is only as secure as the operating system. Most desktop client operating systems are designed with minimal security. For example, any passerby can boot up a Windows desktop client and, whether logging on to the network or not, access local resources on the entire local hard disk.

Windows NT or 2000 workstations in a peer-to-peer configuration, on the other hand, require you to create a user account that has a username and password in order to log on locally. Access to folders or individual files can be specified for designated users. If a user attempting to access your shared files across the network does not have valid credentials for the shared files, he or she is denied access. Although Windows NT or 2000 is inherently more secure than Windows 95/98/ME password security, a peer-to-peer network requires you to store user accounts on each workstation.

For example, suppose you, Shelly, and Karl all have Windows NT 4.0 workstations in a peer-to-peer network. You want to share a folder with Shelly, and Karl also wants to share a folder with Shelly. Both you and Karl must create a user account for Shelly on your respective workstations, and Shelly's username and password must be exactly the same. If Karl changes the password for Shelly's user account on his machine and you don't, then Shelly's credentials will be inconsistent and she will not be able to access resources where her password is different than the one she used to log on (see Figure 1-3). The root of this problem is that there is no centralized location in which to store user accounts, a significant weakness of the peer-to-peer network. Managing users and resources without centralized user account management can quickly become a time-consuming nightmare.

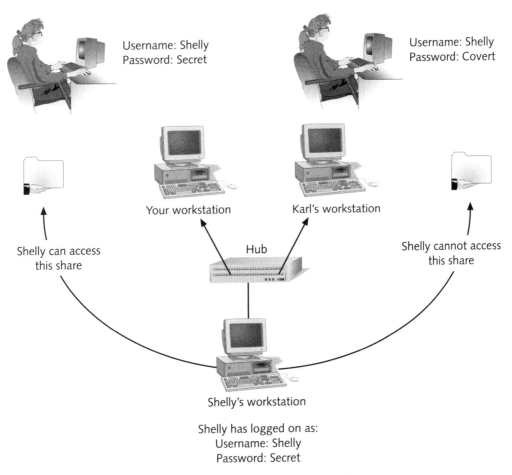

Username: Shelly
Password: Secret

Username: Shelly
Password: Covert

Your workstation

Karl's workstation

Shelly can access
this share

Hub

Shelly cannot access
this share

Shelly's workstation

Shelly has logged on as:
Username: Shelly
Password: Secret

Figure 1-3 Inconsistent user accounts can cause access problems

A peer-to-peer network is simple to configure, but it is limited in terms of expandability, features, services, and security. Many small networks are peer-to-peer networks because the organizations they serve do not require (or cannot afford) the benefits of a server, or there is insufficient technical expertise to administer a server. A peer-to-peer network:

- Usually involves a small number of computers (around one dozen or less)
- Has limited growth potential
- Has decentralized file management, user accounts, and overall management
- Offers minimal security
- Is simple to configure
- Is typically the least expensive option

Client-Server

The **client-server** networking model has most of the benefits of the peer-to-peer network model and potentially none of its weaknesses. The client-server network begins with a LAN and one or more servers, but it can also encompass a more complicated network configuration such as a WAN.

A **server** usually possesses more processing power, RAM, and hard disk capacity than workstation computers on the LAN. The server also has a server **network operating system (NOS)** such as Microsoft Windows NT or 2000, Linux, IBM OS/2, or Novell NetWare. A server running a NOS provides file and printer sharing, centralized file storage, administration, security, services, and significantly more stability than desktop operating systems.

At a basic level, simply installing a server into an existing peer-to-peer network changes the network model to a client-server network (see Figure 1-4). Workstations in the client-server network request and receive services (access to files, printers, or applications, for example) from the server—hence the term **client**. The server serves the client—hence the term server.

Although users at the workstations can save files on their local hard disks, it may be more practical to save files on the server so that all users have a central location to access files. A server in the role of storing files on behalf of network clients is commonly referred to as a **file server**. A file server also offers other advantages, including:

- *Version control:* Using a file server helps to avoid the situation in which differing versions of a file are saved on various workstations.
- *Backup:* Network administrators can back up data files centrally on the file server as opposed to hunting for and individually backing up the data on each user's workstation.
- *Security:* Network administrators can centrally audit file resources to see if unauthorized persons have tried to gain access to them. Also, administrators can configure security settings on the files instead of users, improving the chances that sensitive files will be well protected.

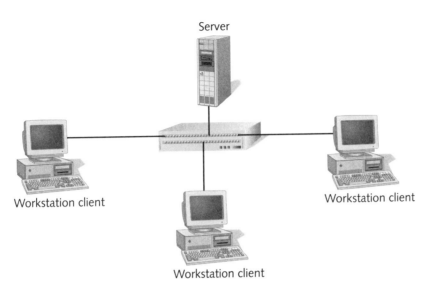

Figure 1-4   A client-server network

- *Availability:* The file server is usually placed in a well-connected location to increase the availability of file resources. Because of the stability of the NOS and the use of redundancy, the server is less likely to be subject to outages or downtime. (**Redundancy** is the ability to continue providing service when something fails. For example, if a hard disk fails, a redundant hard disk can continue to store and serve files.) In addition, the server remains on 24/7, so it is always available to clients, as opposed to a computer in a peer-to-peer network in which resources are only available when the user turns on the computer.

- *Integrity:* NOS file systems protect the integrity of their files by using special logs and error correction that can repair a damaged file on the fly or issue an alert to an administrator.

Because a NOS is capable of hundreds or thousands of simultaneous connections, servers can significantly increase the size and growth potential of a network. Some servers can even handle millions of simultaneous connections provided the server hardware and network bandwidth can match the demand.

A server in the client-server network model:

- Possesses more processing power, RAM, and hard disk capacity than typical workstations

- Uses a NOS such as Microsoft Windows NT, Windows 2000, Linux, IBM OS/2, or Novell NetWare

- Provides a central file storage location

- Is capable of many more simultaneous connections than a workstation

- Offers security features such as logon authentication
- Provides centralized administration

All these benefits are the result of server implementation in the network. In addition to these features, servers offer several other functions and benefits.

SERVER FUNCTIONS AND BENEFITS

The server's impact on the network varies depending upon which of its many features you choose to implement. Even adding a single server to a peer-to-peer network adds benefits to the network in terms of services, security, performance, storage capabilities, access to applications, and centralized management. These features add up to more cost effectiveness, efficiency, and productivity.

Services

A **service** is a function of the NOS that provides various server functions and benefits to the network. For example, a company web server could host many services. When a user accesses the web site by typing a Uniform Resource Locator (URL) into a web browser, the Domain Name System (DNS) service translates the URL into a unique number that identifies the server that contains the web pages. When the user views the web page, he or she might want to leave a message for someone at the site by clicking a link that sends an email message. The email functionality requires an email service. If the user purchases products from the web site and wants to view his or her account information, a service checks the user's username and password so that only that user can view the account. Yet another service could filter and monitor all traffic from the user's network to and from the Internet for security purposes. In most networks, these services are probably distributed among several servers for purposes of redundancy and performance.

 Specific services are addressed in more detail in later chapters.

Security

Protecting the network against unauthorized access is a significant challenge. Though you want to grant network access to users, you do not want to allow them free reign on the network and its resources. Conversely, too many restrictions will be counterproductive. The administrator must permit a level of access that is only as much as the user needs.

Authentication

Security starts with **authentication**, which verifies a person's identity based on their credentials entered at logon (usually a username and password). As an authenticator, the server is an authority in the network, negating the concept of a peer-to-peer network in which all computers are equal. Once authenticated by the server, the user gains general access to the network for which the server is responsible. Thereafter, when the user attempts to access network resources, the authorized user account is compared against a list of users or groups with access to those resources. If the user account is on the list, the NOS grants access. This process of verifying that the user has the ability to access the resource is known as **authorization** (see Figure 1-5).

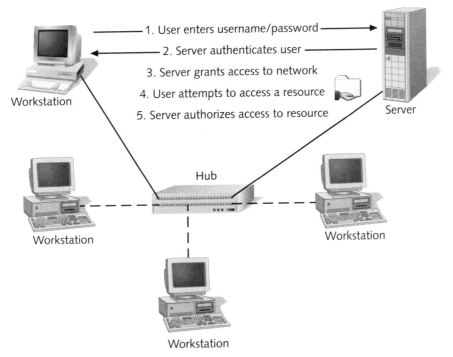

Figure 1-5   The server authenticates users and authorizes access to network resources

In a server environment, authentication better protects network resources than password protection in a peer-to-peer network. Each user account is stored on the server only, mitigating the need to create user accounts on each workstation. Recall that in a peer-to-peer environment, when a user wants to share a folder, he or she must protect it with a password or have sufficient administrative rights to create user accounts for those who want to access it. In a client-server environment, instead of using a password or creating user accounts, permission to access the folder can be granted by the user (or an administrator) to a list of users or groups of users on the server. The administrator creates the users and groups, and it is not necessary to grant administrative rights to individual users. Figure 1-6 shows a list of users (shown with a single head icon) and groups (shown with a double head icon) on a Windows 2000 Server computer.

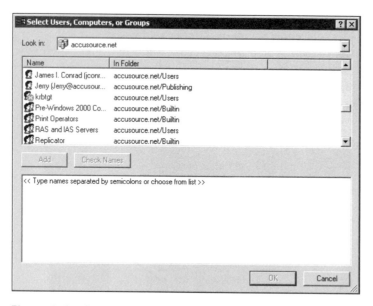

Figure 1-6   Granting access to users or groups

For added security, consider using emerging technologies such as smart cards to authenticate users (see Figure 1-7). A smart card includes an encrypted certificate, and the user typically inserts the card into a reader attached to the computer and enters a password or personal identification number (PIN). Because it requires both the physical card and a password or PIN, the smart card protects against unauthorized persons using stolen passwords. Similarly, a SecurID card synchronizes with the computer to generate a randomized pattern of six-digit numbers displayed in a timed sequence; you enter what is displayed along with a PIN as your password and you are granted access based on this "one-time" password. This "something you have and something you know" authentication is similar to smart cards, but insertion into a reader is not required.

1. User inserts smart card into smart card reader

2. User enters a logon password or PIN

Figure 1-7   Smart card authentication provides a high level of security

Permissions

Authentication verifies the user's identity, and authorization compares that identity against a list of users or groups that are permitted to access resources such as files. Once a user accesses a resource, however, there is the further question of what that user can do with that resource. That is what permissions are about. **Permissions** specify the degree to which a user or group can access or alter a resource. For example, an administrator could set permissions on a folder for individual users or for groups. Who should be able to read but not change the folder contents? Who should be able to access the folder and change permissions? It could be extremely problematic if permission were given to the wrong users or groups to access sensitive information. Consider what would happen if everyone on a company network were able to read the Salaries.xls spreadsheet! To avoid this kind of trouble, administrators assign specific permissions to individuals or groups of individuals. For example, the administrator might assign permissions to the Human Resources department that allows the ability to read and change the Salaries.xls spreadsheet, assign read permissions to managers, and deny permissions to all other users. The NOS permits the administrator to assign these very specific permissions for resources, as shown in Figure 1-8.

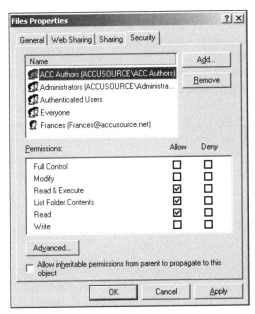

Figure 1-8   The NOS (Windows 2000 in this case) allows you to configure specific permissions

Of course, even on a peer-to-peer network, a user can set (perhaps unwise) permissions on a workstation resource. However, because a server centralizes resources, it makes monitoring those resources more efficient. Compare monitoring permissions individually on 10 computers in a peer-to-peer network with monitoring permissions for tens or hundreds of workstations on a single server.

Security Boundaries

Closely associated with security, authentication, and permissions is the issue of security boundaries, which delineate where a user can "go" in the network. In a large enterprise, administrators do not want an employee in Los Angeles to be able to access a resource in Hong Kong only because they work for the same company and are connected to the same network. To control user access, administrators can use security boundaries such as the domain model of Windows NT 4.0. Users in the Los Angeles domain can access resources only in the Los Angeles domain. Similarly, users in the Hong Kong domain cannot access resources in the Los Angeles domain. However, the administrator of each respective domain can manually allow access between the domains using what is known as a **trust**. Windows 2000 also uses a domain system, except that it implements automatic trusts between domains—administrators do not have to manually create a trust.

Performance

Because a server typically has significantly more powerful processors, more hard disks, and greater storage capacity than a workstation, it can perform tasks on behalf of the workstation, improving overall performance and freeing the workstation to perform other tasks. For example, a special-effects technician creating a video clip can use the server to render the clip instead of using his or her own local workstation. High-end servers that provide better performance can also cost several times more than a low-end workstation. It is more financially feasible to purchase a $20,000 server to service 10 special-effects technicians than it is to spend $3,000 to upgrade each technician's individual workstation (for a total of $30,000). In this simple example, the administrator saves the organization $10,000 by using a server instead of upgrading individual workstations.

Processor

Three primary factors—clock speed, data bus, and cache—contribute to the effective speed of the processor (CPU).

- **Clock speed** is the number of cycles the processor can execute in a single second, measured in millions of cycles per second, or megahertz (MHz). Instructions executed by the processor require a certain number of cycles, so the more cycles the processor can handle per second, the faster it operates, or "thinks." Current processors are also **superscalar**—that is, they can execute more than one instruction in a single clock cycle.

 The processor operates at a speed in MHz that is a multiplier of the bus speed. For example, a 700 MHz processor multiplies a 100 MHz bus speed times seven.

- **Data bus** refers to the number of data bits that can pass into or out of the processor in a single cycle. Data bus width is typically 32 bits. Think of a 32-lane highway over which data travels. Some new processors offer 64-bit bandwidth, equivalent to a 64-lane data highway. Because of other internal engineering modifications, a 64-bit processor utilizes its resources more efficiently than a 32-bit processor and is, therefore, more than twice as fast. Data bus width and RAM have a direct relationship such that a 64-bit processor can also utilize 4,294,967,296 times more memory than a 32-bit processor (assuming that the 64-bit architecture extends throughout the entire system).

- **Cache** is memory that exists on or near the processor itself but is separate from main system memory (RAM). Processor cache stores recently accessed data from the hard disk or RAM. When the same information must be retrieved at a later time, the system can access instructions stored in the cache more quickly than the system can retrieve information from the hard disk or RAM. Also, the cache anticipates what the processor will request next and fetches it in advance, hoping that it has guessed correctly. (Intel claims that 90 percent of the time, the cache guesses correctly.)

Although clock speed, data bus, and cache are components of both servers and workstations, servers are typically more powerful in each respect. Also, servers often utilize **symmetric multiprocessing (SMP)**, which is the simultaneous use of multiple processors on the same server. SMP results in a corresponding increase in performance such that two processors are about twice as fast as one, four processors are about twice as fast as two, and so forth.

 With multiple processors, you can also set processor affinity or *asymmetric multiprocessing* so that a processor is dedicated to a specific task of your choosing. For example, you could dedicate one processor to performing a complex scientific calculation while the other processor performs other server functions.

Hard Disk

Workstations and servers both store programs and data on hard disks. However, server hard disks are often optimized for high performance and **throughput**—a measure of the quantity of data sent or received in a second. For example, a 100 MBps throughput sends or receives at a maximum of 100 MB per second. In most computers, the hard disk is the slowest component and, therefore, a bottleneck that inhibits the overall performance of the system. Typically, the processor and memory can function thousands of times more quickly than the hard disk and often must wait for the hard disk to read or write data before performing other tasks. The following characteristics contribute to improving hard disk performance:

- Servers are capable of implementing multiple hard disks while addressing them as a single logical disk. For example, drive E might appear to the NOS and users as a single drive. However, an administrator can use special hardware or software to implement several disks at once that act as a single drive E, thus reducing or eliminating a hard disk bottleneck. As a rough approximation, you could utilize two hard disks to double the performance of the logical disk. (Multiple use of disks in this manner is known as "striping" and is addressed in more detail in Chapter 5.)

- A **buffer** (or read cache) on a hard disk is memory that functions similarly to cache on a processor. When the hard disk retrieves data, it can store part of the data in a buffer. Later, the CPU can request the same data and it will be retrieved from the buffer, which is many times faster than mechanically retrieving it from the hard disk. Also, because data tends to be stored sequentially on the disk, a buffer can automatically read the next sequential data on the hard disk in anticipation that it might be needed soon after. An optimized workstation hard disk might have between 512 KB and 2 MB of buffer, while a hard disk optimized for server use might have 4 MB.

- **Access time** (also called "seek time") is the time it takes for the hard disk drive head, which reads or writes data on the platter, to arrive at the location of the data. Access time depends upon the spin rate of the hard disk. Most workstation hard disks spin at 5400 or 7200 revolutions per minute (rpm). Server hard disks usually spin at 7200, 10,000, or 15,000 rpm or higher. The faster the disk spins, the more quickly the required data can arrive under the disk drive head. Access times for lower-end workstation hard disks are around 9 or 10 milliseconds (ms), and high-end server hard disks can be as low as 4.5 ms.

- The disk drive **interface** is the hardware connecting the drive to the computer motherboard. The interface is perhaps the most important factor in hard disk performance. At the low end, the workstation interface is usually an Advanced Technology Attachment (ATA), considered synonymous with the Enhanced IDE (EIDE) interface, of which there are several types. Generally, workstation interfaces can read data from the hard disk at between 33 and 100 MBps and can connect up to four hard disks (two disks per channel). Server interfaces such as Small Computer Systems Interface (SCSI) can read data at around 100 MBps and support up to 15 hard disks.

ATA interfaces are making great strides in performance such that they can be utilized in some servers to provide very good performance at an exceptionally low cost compared to high-end SCSI controllers.

In addition to the performance factors that distinguish server processors and hard disks, storage capacity is significantly greater on servers than on workstations.

Storage Capabilities

Network servers require more hard disk storage space than typical workstations in order to serve files and applications. A file server must have enough disk space available to store files for all users. Because most workstations have less storage space than a server, users could fill up their available local hard disk space over time. By storing files on the file server, an administrator can more feasibly monitor available hard disk space than he or she could by monitoring disk space on each workstation. Should low disk space occur on the server, the administrator could use any of several methods to add hard disks on the fly without any disruption in service. This is made possible by **hot-plug** or **hot-swap** capability, which means that you can add or remove a device without first powering down the computer.

Software programs are available that can monitor each user workstation's disk space individually and notify administrators of low disk space. In addition, these programs (as well as Windows 2000) can restrict the amount of disk space available for each user on both the local workstation and the file server. However, it is better to minimize administration by using the same software to monitor a few file servers.

Access to Applications

Network applications are server-based programs that run in memory and on the processor on behalf of other servers or clients. Running applications on the server (referred to as **back-end applications**) minimizes or eliminates the processing, storage, and memory requirements for each individual client. Instead, the client computer runs a front-end application requiring much less overhead. (A **front-end application** is an application running on the client that retrieves information processed by a back-end application.) For example, it is much more effective to run most larger databases on a high-powered server than on client workstations. Even with multiple users running the database and performing queries at once, the server can usually outperform the same tasks on a workstation, because each workstation does not have to download the entire database across the network.

Let's say an organization has a relatively small database of 20 MB stored on a file server. Without using an application server, users at each workstation access the database file and run the database application locally. This means that each user accessing the database must download the entire 20 MB database, as illustrated in Figure 1-9. This is quite taxing on network bandwidth and requires users to wait for the download to complete. However, with an application server, the back-end database application and file stay on the server. If each record is 1 KB in size, and a user runs a query against the database with 30 matches, the client downloads only a 30 KB result as requested by the client's front-end database application (Figure 1-10).

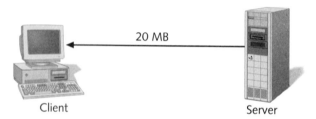

Figure 1-9   The entire database downloads to the client

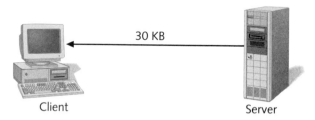

Figure 1-10   Only the database query results download to the client

There are several reasons for the performance gains with an application server, including the use of multiple processors, increased RAM, and fast hard disks on the server. Also, downloading only query results instead of the entire database greatly reduces the burden on network bandwidth. Examples of network applications and services include:

- *Database applications:* Programs such as Microsoft SQL 7 or SQL 2000 perform many of the functions and provide the benefits mentioned in the previous paragraph. Primarily, application databases benefit from the server in its role as a data warehouse (a storage location for extremely large databases) and from the server's processing power.

- *Email services:* Users can, to some degree, utilize Internet email with little if any involvement from the network administrator. However, an email server allows the administrator to perform management functions such as monitoring, virus scanning, forwarding, integration with directory services, clustering, security management, **failover** (an alternate system that takes over for a failed system), redundancy, and so forth. Many email servers go beyond email services to provide collaboration with users' calendars and videoconferencing.

- *Network management software:* This varies greatly from one product to another. Administrators of smaller networks might not require network management software, but larger networks require some sort of management software to manage client software distribution and licensing, monitor user activity, monitor and manage network traffic, back up and restore data, manage Internet services, integrate with other server operating systems, and more. Network management software is particularly useful because it can email or page the administrator when there is a problem with a server. Examples of network management software include Microsoft SMS, Computer Associates Unicenter TNG, and IBM Tivoli.

■ *Remote access:* Even when away from their desk or office, users require access to the LAN. When a user is away from the local network, he or she is a **remote user**. Many remote users telecommute from home or connect to the LAN from another office (Figure 1-11). Remote access makes this possible in two primary ways. First, the user can use a modem to dial into the network. The remote access server also has a modem dedicated to remote access purposes, and receives the user's call. Once the connection is complete, the user experiences the same network access as when locally present and connected to the LAN (except that network connectivity is only as fast as the modem, usually between 14.4 and 53 Kbps depending on phone line conditions). Second, faster remote access connections such as digital subscriber line (DSL) are replacing the modem-to-modem connection from client to server because they are faster and always on. However, traveling users generally continue to use a modem to connect (from a hotel room, for example).

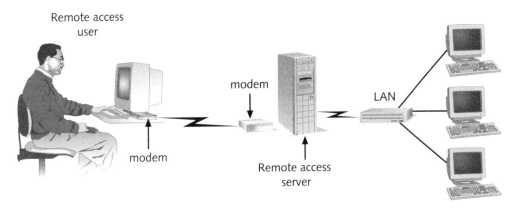

Figure 1-11   Remote users have the same network access as local users

■ *Virtual private networks:* Users can also connect to the network over a **virtual private network (VPN)**, which is a highly secured network connection that makes eavesdropping from unauthorized persons nearly impossible. This connection can take place over the first connection type, a modem. Increasingly, however, users utilize an existing public Internet connection to establish the VPN connection. For example, a telecommuter with a high-speed Internet connection to his or her home office can establish a VPN connection to the corporate LAN and experience virtually the same security as if locally connected to the LAN. Windows 2000 utilizes routing and Remote Access Server (RAS) and Novell NetWare utilizes Network Access Server (NAS) to provide remote access.

Centralized Management

Any time the network grows beyond two or three dozen users, the administrator's role can become more reactive than proactive. That's because he or she must continually go from one computer to the next, troubleshooting applications, helping users find their files, and so forth. Although adding a server does not eliminate these tasks, its centralized management capabilities can certainly contribute to reducing overall administration.

Centralized management means that administrators can administer servers from one place instead of traversing frantically from one end of the building or campus to the other fixing problems. With the proper NOS options enabled or network management software installed on a server, an administrator can browse a user's hard disk from the administrator's own computer to help them find the files they are looking for. Or if a user is experiencing difficulty using a program, the administrator can view the user's desktop without leaving his or her own seat. Sharing applications from the server also reduces administration because the administrator can install, troubleshoot, and upgrade applications from a single server location rather than on each individual client.

 Managing applications on a single server reduces administration, but it also provides a single point of failure. If the server fails or the application stops functioning correctly, all network users are affected. Consider having a redundancy plan. For example, multiple servers hosting the application can allow users to continue using the application should one of the servers fail (Figure 1-12). Clustering is an example of **fault tolerance**, which allows for continued service despite failure of a server or component.

Cost Effectiveness

While you, as the network administrator, see obvious benefits for installing a server, it might not be up to you. Much of the time, some combination of management, accountants, or both determine what they think is best for the network strictly on the basis of how much something costs. So when you propose adding a modest $8,000 to the budget for a server and applications for your LAN of 30 users, be prepared for the possibility of a knee-jerk reaction and a resounding no.

Increasingly, administrators must show the money sense in the budgets they propose, and in fairness to an organization's financial affairs, they should. As you prepare to propose new server equipment, know that well-planned servers eventually recoup their initial expense and continued operation in long-term cost savings and increased productivity. The following sections illustrate the savings in several important areas.

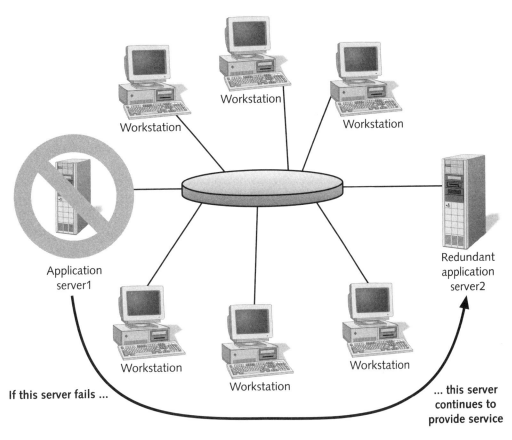

Figure 1-12   Clustering ensures continued service to clients

Storage

Workstations in many organizations are several years old. Applications, operating systems, and data files on the workstations grow larger, but the hard disks do not. It would be much more cost effective to install centralized storage on a server for all the users. Although the price per megabyte on high-performance server hard disks might be higher than that of a workstation, you can save time (and hence money) by performing a single hard disk upgrade on the server instead of upgrading each workstation's hard disk. Upgrading individual user's hard disks might also involve the sometimes tricky process of moving the existing operating system, applications, and data to the new drive without disruption or loss of current settings.

 Sometimes you cannot avoid transferring the contents of the user's current hard disk to a new one. The best way to perform this operation safely is to use software designed for this purpose. Several products from third parties allow you to do this. For example, PowerQuest's Drive Image Pro 4.0 can duplicate one hard disk to another.

Processors and Memory

As operating systems and applications become increasingly complex, workstations require more processing power and RAM. Individual workstation upgrades quickly become cost prohibitive. However, you can upgrade one or more servers and transfer the memory and processing burden to the server, as in the case of a large database. Also, to avoid the costly operating system and hardware upgrade for client computers, you can leave the existing operating system and hardware, and make the workstations thin clients. A **thin client** (similar to a dumb terminal) receives its operating system environment, including applications and data, from the server (Figure 1-13). The server does all the work, and the client sends the input from the keyboard and monitor and receives the output to the monitor. For example, users could boot to Microsoft Windows 3.11 at the workstation and connect to the server to run the Windows 2000 operating system as the primary environment. Microsoft Windows NT Server 4.0, Terminal Server Edition, Microsoft Windows 2000 Server, and Citrix MetaFrame provide thin client services. Novell's ZENworks integrates with and enhances thin client services to provide powerful administrative tools and to better manage the user desktop.

 Be careful: If you plan to move to a thin client solution, the network utilization will increase significantly. You might have to anticipate this and increase available bandwidth prior to moving to thin clients.

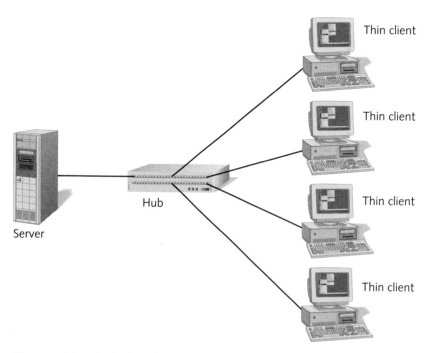

Figure 1-13   Each thin client receives its desktop environment from the server

Savings, Efficiency, and Productivity

Efficiency and productivity are difficult to quantify and vary from one organization to the next. Most managers and accountants to whom administrators must defend their budgets already understand that computers are generally cost effective. When proposing to add server equipment or software, you must demonstrate that the addition saves money, increases efficiency and productivity, or both.

For example, what would it cost a corporation to lose its customer database to a competitor? A company with an Internet connection exposes itself to unauthorized access to the world at large. Intruders who succeed in invading your network might not do anything harmful, but administrators must plan for the worst in case someone destroys, steals, or alters data. An administrator can add a **firewall**, which protects the internal LAN from the public Internet and is placed between the LAN and the Internet (Figure 1-14). By protecting the network, a firewall saves the company from potential financial and productivity losses. A firewall can be either a hardware or software solution. In a server context, it is a server with special software. For example, Novell offers BorderManager as its software firewall.

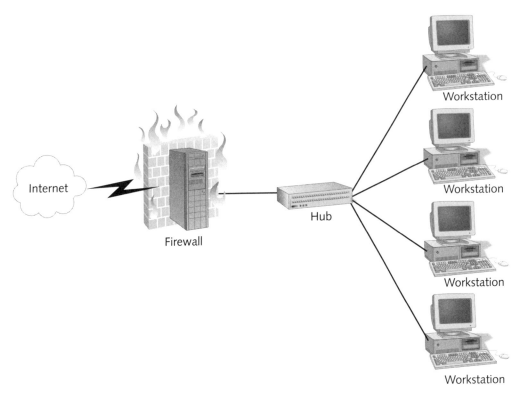

Figure 1-14   A firewall protects user workstations from the Internet

CLASSES OF SERVERS

Having established the need for a server in several contexts, you must also determine what type of server is appropriate for your organization. A poorly chosen server might be more expensive and more powerful than current and future needs require, or it might be woefully inadequate, necessitating the purchase of more equipment at a less efficient cost factor. For example, if an administrator purchased a single PC server capable of supporting two processors, and after installation discovers that it cannot meet the processing demands placed upon it, he or she must purchase another system. In this case, it might have been less expensive to purchase a single midrange server with support for four or more processors in the first place.

Although the Server+ certification focuses primarily on PC servers, a brief discussion of the mainframe, minicomputer, and midrange computer classes provides you with a broader understanding of other server types. In addition, it helps to know something about mainframes because administrators often connect PC servers to them.

PC Servers

Basically, a PC server uses Intel-compatible complex instruction set computing (CISC) processors, as opposed to reduced instruction set computing (RISC) processors from vendors such as Sun Microsystems or IBM. At the low end, a PC server can be a workstation-level computer in terms of its hardware. For example, a small insurance company with 12 desktop PC workstations has a need for a file and logon server. The company could install a NOS on one of the existing PCs and suddenly the PC becomes a server, and the network changes from a peer-to-peer LAN to a client-server network. The fact that the "server" has only desktop PC-level hardware does not change the fact that it is a server, and in this small LAN, more powerful hardware is unnecessary.

On the high end, a PC server can involve significantly more powerful hardware; therefore, it has a much larger case than a standard PC workstation. (For purposes of this book, assume that the server is a high-end server unless stated otherwise.) The server case also provides much more space for expansion and requires more components, such as extra power supplies.

Other characteristics of a high-end server include:

- *Hot-pluggable PCI slots:* Peripheral component interface (PCI) slots store various adapters such as disk controllers, video cards, and network adapters. A desktop PC workstation would require you to shut down the computer before adding or removing adapters. A server with hot-pluggable PCI slots allows you to add or remove adapters while the server is on. This is a very useful feature in mission-critical operations where you cannot afford the extra minutes required to shut down and restart the server. Some servers offer this functionality by allowing you to shut down individual PCI slots without powering down the entire system.

1

- *Hot-swappable hard disks:* These allow you to quickly remove hard disks without powering down the system (see Figure 1-15). They are useful for quick emergencies that occur when it's time to upgrade a hard disk or replace a failed one.

- *Power supply:* Servers usually have two or three power supplies to power the additional component slots and drives, and to provide redundancy. If one power supply fails, the system can usually continue to operate until you replace it with another hot-swappable power supply (Figure 1-16).

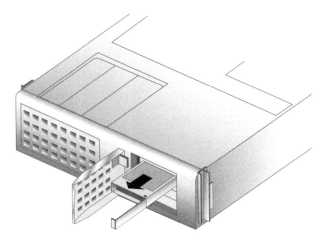

Figure 1-15   Hot-swapping hard disks

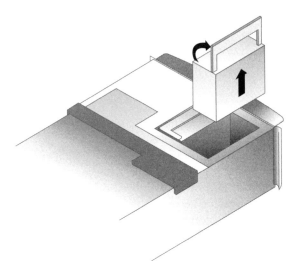

Figure 1-16   Hot-swapping a power supply

- *Cooling fans:* Redundant hot-swappable cooling fans help ensure that the system does not overheat if one of the fans fails, because the other fan(s) can continue operating until you hot-swap the failed fan for a new one. This is a critical element to maintaining server uptime. (**Uptime** is the continued operation of the overall server or specific components such as the hard disk, depending upon the context.) An overheated system can quickly burn out or reduce the life of the components, especially the processor, which is the hottest component of the system.

- *Expandability:* Servers have more PCI slots and drive bays, and are modularly designed so that you can easily add or remove the components (Figure 1-17).

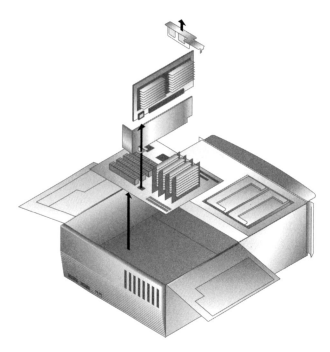

Figure 1-17   Servers are modular to facilitate adding and removing parts

- *Heavy-duty chassis:* The **chassis** is the metal frame to which the motherboard is attached and which forms the case structure. A server chassis is much heavier than a workstation chassis and often weighs about 75 lbs, including the case and components. It is heavier because the metal is of a heavier gauge, and the case is often larger to accommodate more internal components, such as more hard disks. After adding all internal equipment (drives, power supplies, and so on), the server can weigh over 170 lbs!

- *Rack mountable:* For many servers, when you order the server you can specify a **tower** (upright, free-standing case) or a **rack** configuration. The rack mount consolidates space because you can stack several servers and other network equipment in the same floor space, offering good **density** (Figure 1-18).

Figure 1-18   A rack stacks servers and equipment in a small floor space

Mainframe or "Big Iron"

A **mainframe** is a large and extremely powerful computer. Nearly all computers in the 1960s were mainframes and usually filled an entire room. IBM was one of the first mainframe pioneers and continues to lead the mainframe market today with its S/390 and ZSeries 900 systems. Mainframe computers are colloquially known as "big iron" in reference to their size and power. The term "mainframe" becomes less definitive as minicomputers become increasingly powerful and some mainframes become smaller in size. However, there are several characteristics that continue to distinguish a mainframe:

- *Size:* It's just plain big. Many of the newest mainframes boast a relatively small size compared to their predecessors, and require about 20 square feet of floor space, and weigh over 2000 lbs.

- *Cost:* Mainframe prices are in the range of "if you have to ask how much, you can't afford it." Mainframes are still in the range of at least several hundred thousand dollars.

- *Processors:* Mainframes nearly always use multiple processors—up to 32 for Intel-based machines. Also, mainframes frequently use proprietary RISC-based processors that usually run a version of UNIX. Although the processors in a mainframe might be comparable to a PC in terms of MHz, a PC processor is busy delivering data to and from its peripherals. This is very time consuming in terms of clock cycles. The mainframe utilizes mechanisms to offload I/O and avoid the negative impact on performance.

- *Bus speed:* No computer can be any faster than its main board (or motherboard) bus speed. While a PC server might have a speed of 100 MHz, a mainframe might have significantly higher bus speed, which when multiplied with its SMP capability can provide blazing processing performance.

- *Memory:* Mainframes can have upward of 96 GB of main memory. Also, mainframes have extremely well-engineered cache and memory architecture, providing very high efficiency and performance.

- *Storage:* Mainframe disk storage is capable of storing hundreds of GB or a terabyte (TB) or more. Typically, large quantities of storage are external to the server.

- *Durability:* Mainframe hardware circuitry design detects and corrects errors, and it can anticipate and alert administrators of impending problems. Some mainframes can generate a list of parts that need replacement at the next regular maintenance. **Mean time between failure (MTBF)** is the anticipated lifetime of a computer (or one of its components). Mainframes often have MTBF of about 20 years. While it is difficult to specify PC server MTBF, it is usually a fraction of that of a mainframe.

The Minicomputer or Midrange Computer

Minicomputer characteristics lie somewhere between the desktop workstation and the mainframe computer. The minicomputer is sometimes known as the **midrange computer**. This is an extremely broad range, with distinction between midrange and PC blurring at the low end, and between midrange and mainframe at the high end. The first minicomputer was the Digital Equipment Corporation (DEC) PDP-1, which cost $20,000 in 1959 and was not as large as a mainframe but was still quite sizable. Compared to mainframes costing millions of dollars, the price tag was extremely attractive. However, the PDP series was not considered successful until the mass-produced PDP-8 in 1965, which was a tabletop-size unit. Minicomputers also offer an advantage compared to mainframes in that they require significantly less floor space and weigh less.

This book and the CompTIA Server+ Certification focus on PC servers.

CHAPTER SUMMARY

◻ A peer-to-peer network is a collection of networked computers with no logon server to verify the identity of users. This model is called a peer-to-peer network because each network device has an equal (peer) level of authority. Peer-to-peer networks have limited growth potential because client workstations are limited to 10 concurrent inbound network connections. Peer-to-peer networks have weaknesses in regard to security and file version consistency, and there is no centralized location on which to store user accounts.

❏ The client-server network begins with a LAN and one or more servers. The client-server network can also encompass a more complicated network configuration such as multiple, geographically distant LANs connected to one another across a relatively great distance, known as a wide area network (WAN).

❏ A server possesses more processing power, RAM, and hard disk capacity than workstation computers on a LAN. The server also has a server network operating system (NOS) such as Microsoft Windows NT or 2000, Linux, IBM OS/2, or Novell NetWare. A server running a NOS provides file and printer sharing, centralized file storage, security, and other network services.

❏ Three primary factors—clock speed, data bus, and cache—contribute to the effective speed (performance) of the processor or CPU. Servers generally have higher-performance CPUs than workstations, which means they have greater clock speed, bandwidth, and cache. Servers also may utilize symmetric multiprocessing (SMP), the simultaneous use of multiple processors on the same server.

❏ Servers are capable of implementing multiple hard disks while addressing them as a single logical disk, which reduces or eliminates hard disk bottlenecks. Server hard disks also utilize buffers and interfaces that can easily support multiple hard disks. By storing files on the file server, an administrator can more feasibly monitor available hard disk space than he or she could by monitoring disk space on each workstation.

❏ Network applications are server-based programs that run in memory and on the processor on behalf of other servers or clients. Running the application on the server minimizes or eliminates the processing, storage, and memory requirements for each client.

❏ Centralized management consolidates administration of user workstations and other servers to a single location.

❏ Increasingly, administrators must justify the budgets they propose. Well-planned servers eventually recoup their initial expense and continued operation in long-term cost savings and increased productivity.

❏ Different classes of servers include PC servers, mainframes, and minicomputer or midrange servers. A PC server generally uses Intel-compatible complex instruction set computing (CISC) processors as opposed to reduced instruction set computing (RISC) processors from vendors such as Sun or IBM. Characteristics of a high-end server include hot-pluggable PCI slots, hot-swappable hard disks, redundant power supplies, redundant cooling fans, high expandability, a heavy-duty chassis, and rack mount capability.

Key Terms

access time — The time it takes for the hard disk drive head to arrive at the location of the data. Access time depends upon the spin rate of the hard disk.

authentication — Verification of a person's identity based on their credentials (usually a username and password).

authorization — Verification that an authenticated user is permitted to access a network resource.

back-end application — Applications that run on the server on behalf of the client.

buffer (or **read cache**) — On a hard disk, memory that stores part of the data read from the hard disk. Later, the CPU can request the same data and it will be retrieved from the buffer, which is many times faster than mechanically retrieving it from the hard disk.

cache — Memory that assists performance by storing frequently used data for fast access. Processors and hard disks use cache, and cache is separate from main system memory (RAM).

centralized management — The ability to administer a given system from a single location instead of disparate locations.

chassis — The metal frame to which the motherboard is attached and which forms the case structure.

client — A network workstation that requests and receives service from the server.

client-server — A network that begins with a LAN and one or more servers. The client-server network can also encompass a more complicated network configuration such as multiple, geographically distant LANs connected to one another across a relatively great distance known as a wide area network (WAN).

clock speed — The number of instructions the processor can execute in a single instruction, measured in megahertz (MHz)—which is one million cycles per second. Instructions sent to the processor require a certain number of cycles, so the more cycles the processor can handle per second, the faster it operates, or "thinks."

clustering — Redundant servers hosting the same application for the purpose of fault tolerance. If one of the servers fails, the remaining server(s) continues to serve the application to the network.

data bus — The number of bits the processor can execute in a single instruction. Bandwidth is typically 32 bits. Some new processors offer 64-bit bandwidth.

density — A term used with equipment racks that describes consolidation of space because you can stack several servers and other network equipment into the rack in the same floor space.

failover — An alternate system that takes over for a failed system.

fault tolerance — Continued service despite failure of a server or component.

file server — A server that provides a central location to store files for network clients.

firewall — A hardware or software solution that protects internal LAN users from the public Internet.

1

front-end application — An application running on the client that retrieves information processed by a back-end application.

host — A network device (usually a computer) in a TCP/IP network.

hot-plug (or **hot-swap)** — Add or remove a device without first powering down the computer.

hub — A network device that connects network cables together in a central, star configuration. Passive hubs simply make the connections, and active hubs (multiport repeaters) regenerate the signal to increase the distance it can travel.

interface — The hardware connecting the drive to the computer motherboard.

local area network (LAN) — A collection of computers in close proximity to one another on a single network.

mainframe — The most powerful level of computer classification, mainframes are extremely large and powerful computers. Also known as "big iron."

mean time between failure (MTBF) — The anticipated lifetime of a computer or one of its components.

midrange computer (or **minicomputer)** — A broad computer classification that lies somewhere between desktop workstation and mainframe computer.

network — A collection of two or more computers connected with transmission media such as network cable or wireless means, such as radio or infrared signals. Usually includes other devices such as printers.

network applications — Server-based programs that run in memory and on the processor on behalf of other servers or clients.

network device — Any device connected to the network for purposes of communicating with other network devices. (A network device is also known as a host in most networks.)

network operating system (NOS) — Provides file and printer sharing, centralized file storage, security, and various services. Primary examples of a NOS include Microsoft Windows NT or 2000, Linux, IBM OS/2, or Novell NetWare.

network resource — An object users can access from across the network, such as printers, files, and folders.

peer-to-peer network — A collection of networked computers with no logon server to verify the identity of users. Each network device has an equal (peer) level of authority.

permissions — The configured level of access applied to a resource. For example, if a user can read a file but not change the file, then they have read-only permission.

rack — A cabinet that houses stacked network equipment, storage, and servers. A rack can store multiple items in the same floor space.

redundancy — The ability to continue providing service when something fails. For example, if a hard disk fails, a redundant hard disk can continue to store and serve files.

remote user — A user connected to the LAN from a geographically distant location, usually over a modem or virtual private network (VPN).

server — A computer with more processing power, RAM, and hard disk capacity than typical workstations. A server has a server NOS such as Microsoft Windows NT or Novell NetWare, and provides file and printer sharing, centralized file storage, security, and various services.

services — A function of the NOS that provides server features to the network.

superscalar — A processor architecture that allows a processor to execute more than one instruction in a single clock cycle.

switch — Similar to a router in that it segments a network, and similar to a hub in that it connects network cables together in a central, star configuration. Switches forward traffic at very high speeds.

symmetric multiprocessing (SMP) — The simultaneous use of multiple processors on the same server.

thin client — A computer that receives its operating system environment, including applications and data, from the server.

throughput — A measure of the quantity of data sent or received in a second.

tower — An upright, free-standing computer case.

uptime — The continued operation of the overall server or specific components.

virtual private network (VPN) — A highly secured network connection over an otherwise unsecured network such as the Internet.

wide area network (WAN) — Multiple, geographically distant LANs connected to one another across a relatively great distance.

workstation — Desktop computer with only enough hardware to service the needs of a single user at a time. Synonymous in most contexts with PC, desktop computer, or client.

REVIEW QUESTIONS

1. A network is:

   a. at least a dozen computers on one network cable

   b. any context in which the server and client can communicate with one another

   c. a collection of two or more computers connected with transmission media

   d. two or more computers that are in close proximity to one another

2. Which of the following are true of LANs and WANs? (Choose all that apply.)

   a. A LAN involves networked computers in close proximity to one another.

   b. A WAN involves at least one Internet connection.

   c. A LAN is a linked area network involving two or more sites.

   d. A WAN involves two or more geographically separate LANs connected to one another.

3. Which of the following is true of a peer-to-peer network?

    a. It is limited to no more than one logon server.

    b. It is limited to no more than one file server.

    c. No logon server is present.

    d. No server of any kind is present.

4. Why not use Microsoft Windows NT or Windows 2000 workstations to create user accounts instead of a server?

    a. There is no support for complex passwords.

    b. There is no support for encrypted passwords.

    c. More administration is necessary. Each workstation must match the username and password exactly for users to gain access to resources.

    d. Each workstation must copy the username and password to the other workstations.

5. Which of the following is not a server NOS?

    a. Linux

    b. IBM OS/2

    c. Windows Millennium Edition

    d. Novell NetWare

6. Which of the following is not a feature of a NOS?

    a. email

    b. resource sharing

    c. security

    d. multiple simultaneous connections

7. How does a smart card increase network security?

    a. It provides a better online shopping experience.

    b. You cannot enter the building without it.

    c. The user must possess the smart card to log on.

    d. Users do not need to use a password.

8. What is the difference between authentication and authorization?

    a. Authentication verifies the identity of the user and authorization permits access to resources.

    b. Authorization verifies the identity of the user and authentication permits access to resources.

    c. Authentication validates computers and authorization validates users.

    d. Authentication and authorization are the same thing.

9. You recently discovered that some users are changing their own salaries by accessing the Salaries.xls file. What should you do?

   a. Change the user's password.

   b. Change the permissions on the Salaries.xls file.

   c. Deny users permission to log on to the file server.

   d. Fire the users.

10. Why wouldn't a wise administrator allow users to store data files on their own workstations? (Choose all that apply.)

   a. Users might not assign prudent permissions to their files.

   b. Backing up the files is more difficult.

   c. Workstations might require a hard disk upgrade to store the files.

   d. A workstation operating system might not permit sufficient simultaneous network connections for shared files.

11. Which of the following does not contribute to the effective speed of the processor?

   a. clock speed

   b. cache

   c. voltage of the power supply

   d. data bus

12. Hard disk and processor cache provides which of the following benefits?

   a. fast access to recently accessed data

   b. long-term storage

   c. on-the-fly data backup

   d. increase in main system RAM

13. How does SMP benefit the performance of a server?

   a. Multiple hard disks aggregate read/write performance.

   b. Additional cache improves data access.

   c. Multiple processors increase processor performance.

   d. Multiple computers provide clustering in case of server failure.

14. The most likely bottleneck in most computers is:

   a. the processor

   b. the hard disk

   c. the main memory

   d. the cache memory

15. Access time is dependent upon:

    a. how fast the processor can issue instructions to the hard disk

    b. the number of platters the hard disk uses

    c. the disk drive interface

    d. how fast the hard disk spins

16. Several server components offer hot-swap capability, which is:

    a. the ability to replace a hardware server in the rack in less than five minutes

    b. a temperature problem that requires immediate replacement of a processor when it overheats

    c. the ability to distribute processing tasks between two processors

    d. the ability to replace a hardware component without first turning off server power

17. Which one of the following statements is true of an application server?

    a. Applications run on the clients, freeing the server resources to perform more complex tasks.

    b. Applications run on the server, improving responsiveness for the clients.

    c. Applications run on the server, increasing network traffic.

    d. Application installation files are located on the server and installed on the client.

18. Which of the following provides thin client services?

    a. Novell Network Access Server

    b. Windows NT 4.0 or Windows 2000 remote access server

    c. Citrix MetaFrame

    d. any workstation operating system

19. Which of the following characterize a PC server?

    a. CISC processors

    b. RISC processors

    c. extremely heavy

    d. utilizes a FEP

20. Which of the following characterize a mainframe?

    a. the largest classification in terms of size

    b. hard disk storage up to hundreds of GB

    c. utilize a single extremely powerful RISC-based processor

    d. usually cost less than $100,000

HANDS-ON PROJECTS

Each chapter of this book contains hands-on projects in which you can verify and practice concepts, techniques, and other information discussed in the main text. These projects are intended to give you direct experience and to reinforce your learning. Plan to create a lab journal or a running word-processed document so that you can record your findings as you perform each project. The lab journal or word-processed document will be a valuable study aid.

Project 1-1

Most desktop operating systems such as Windows 9x (referring to Windows 95, 98, or ME) allow only a limited number of simultaneous connections to a shared resource. This can be extremely limiting in networks of a dozen or more users. In this project, you will create a share and observe the connection limitations of a peer-to-peer operating system.

1. From the Windows 9x computer, double-click **My Computer**.

2. Double-click the **C:** drive.

3. Right-click in a blank location of the window, and from the context menu, click **New**, and then click **Folder**.

4. Type *YourName***Share** as the name of the folder.

5. Right-click your new folder and click **Sharing** from the context menu.

The Sharing option is only available in the context menu if the "allow others access to my files" option has been enabled in File and Printer Sharing.

6. In the Sharing dialog box, click the **Shared As** radio button.

7. Click **OK**.

8. Close all open windows.

9. Double-click **Network Neighborhood**, and browse other computers. Notice that others now have shared folders that you can access.

10. Double-click a specific computer as determined by your instructor. If you have 11 or more students, the eleventh simultaneous connection will fail to connect.

11. Close all open windows.

Project 1-2

A server does not offer the same limitations as a workstation desktop operating system. In this project, your instructor will add a server. Then, you will access the server and add a file. In contrast to the peer-to-peer model, the client-server model allows multiple simultaneous connections.

1. The instructor adds a server to the network.

2. The instructor creates a share called ClassShare.

3. As per the instructor's direction, double-click **Network Neighborhood** to locate the server, and locate the share.

4. Notice that more than 10 users can connect to the server share.

5. Create a text file named *YourName* inside the shared folder, enter some text in the file, and then save and close the file.

6. Leave the Network Neighborhood windows open for Hands-on Project 1-3.

7. In your lab journal or word-processed file, list some of the benefits of accessing shared files from a server instead of a workstation.

Project 1-3

In this project, you will see how servers can adjust security settings by adjusting shared permissions. Your instructor will change permissions on the share you accessed earlier. Observe how this affects your level of access.

1. Double-click the file you created in Project 1-1.

2. Make changes to the file and attempt to save it. You cannot save the file because the instructor changed the permissions so that you can only read (not write to) the file.

3. Close all open windows and applications.

Project 1-4

Administering servers requires you to keep abreast of current servers and equipment. If an organization wants you to add a server, you must generally have a grasp of what is available and how much it might cost. If an organization wants you to improve its current network, you must know what kind of equipment you can add, and if you should add or replace servers.

The web sites listed in these projects and throughout the book are usually the vendor's home pages, because specific web pages might be outdated by the time you read this. Go to the vendor's home page and follow general steps to arrive at the requested locations.

Use your web browser to visit *www.dell.com*. Look for a server for medium-size to large businesses and answer the following questions in your lab journal or word-processed document:

1. What appears to be the most powerful server Dell offers?

2. What is the maximum number of processors this server can use?

3. What components are hot-pluggable?

4. Is the server rack mount only or can you get it in both rack and tower configurations?

5. How much does it cost?

6. What are a few of the server's features that cause it to stand out?

7. Would you consider this server to be a PC server, a midrange server, or a mainframe?

Project 1-5

This time, you will visit a different web site and notice a difference in equipment.

Use your web browser to visit *www.unisys.com*. Look for the server content on the site, and answer the following questions:

1. What appears to be the most powerful server Unisys offers?

2. What is the maximum number of processors this server can use?

3. What components are hot-pluggable?

4. How much does the server weigh?

5. How much does it cost? (Prices might not be available because you usually must request a salesperson to bid a price for you.)

6. What are a few of the server's features that cause it to stand out?

7. Would you consider this server to be a PC server, a midrange server, or a mainframe?

Project 1-6

The focus of this book is to prepare students for the CompTIA Server+ exam. Although this book addresses the exam objectives, you should also view them at CompTIA's web site. These steps direct you to specific links. If the links have changed, attempt to locate the same general area.

1. Browse to *www.comptia.org*.

2. Click the **Certification** link. You see several certifications such as A+, Network+, and Server+.

3. Click the link for **Server+**. What kind of experience does CompTIA expect that candidates for the Server+ exam will have?

4. Notice that several vendors support the Server+ certification. Who are some of the vendors?

5. Some portions of the Server+ certification have a greater emphasis than others. Name three certification objectives that have the greatest emphasis.

6. Which other certifications does CompTIA recommend as prior experience for the Server+ exam?

CASE PROJECTS

1. Stan, the owner of a local vending machine supplier, calls upon your services to assist with their network of 14 desktop PCs. Stan has little, if any, knowledge about computers and even less about networks and servers, but he knows that all his PCs run Windows 98. Stan is concerned about security because he wants to allow Internet access to each desktop, but he is afraid of possible security risks. All his customers call in their orders when they need something, but Stan wants to eventually allow customers to use the web to place orders. Stan has limited financial resources to contribute to this, and does not expect to hire new employees or significantly expand his business over the next two or three years. Does Stan have a peer-to-peer or client-server network? What can you recommend to Stan to help him accomplish his objectives?

2. Andie, a stockbroker at a local stock brokerage, calls you to assist with their network. The brokerage is an office of about 100 users, each with workstations. A high-speed dedicated line connects the brokerage to the main headquarters in another city. The brokerage also has high-speed Internet access. The problem is, the computer that directly connects to the Internet connection failed a few days ago. The network administrator was on a sailing vacation and unreachable, so someone with little computing knowledge decided to plug the incoming line from the Internet directly into the company's rack of hubs. Nobody seemed to mind because all users were immediately productive and access to the Internet resumed. Now, Andie notices that several files on her Windows 98 computer are missing. She cannot find them in the Recycle Bin and is sure she did not delete them. Some of her client files have missing data, and others appear to have been tampered with. Other stockbrokers at the office are complaining of the same problems. What can you do to help? What is the most likely cause of these problems? What would have been the best course of action when the server connected to the Internet failed? What was the purpose of the server connected to the Internet?

2

SERVER PLANNING

After reading this chapter and completing the exercises, you will be able to:

♦ Determine the most appropriate server solution for a given business purpose
♦ Plan for user demands on the server
♦ Consider interoperability among operating systems
♦ Optimize server placement
♦ Diagram server plans
♦ Plan the server environment
♦ Plan physical site readiness
♦ Implement sound physical server security practices

The administrator must choose the most appropriate server solution for his or her business environment while also providing adequately for user demand and usage of the server. Sometimes, the administrator's choices involve other mitigating factors such as providing for interoperability between operating systems.

Server administration does not end after the server purchase. You must also place server equipment in optimal locations for both accessibility and disaster prevention. Planning the placement should be documented with accurate and up-to-date diagrams. Server locations must be environmentally fit so that heat, dust, and humidity do not adversely affect server uptime. Finally, the administrator must arrange for the best security available to protect both the hardware investment and the intellectual property that the server data represents.

DETERMINING THE BUSINESS PURPOSE

As discussed in Chapter 1, the network administrator must have a business sense of how a server plan directly benefits the organization financially, or indirectly in terms of improving efficiency or productivity. It is obviously the responsibility of the network administrator to obtain necessary network equipment and servers. However, going a step beyond this basic responsibility by contributing to the bottom line of the business will also contribute to your value in the marketplace. Increasingly, organizations see somebody who not only "knows a lot about computers," but also knows how to get the most value for every dollar spent in servicing the network.

Although each organization differs in what benefits its business, the following questions provide a common starting point as you consider if and how a server or servers can improve your organization's business and support its goals.

Do We Really Need This Server Right Now?

As an administrator responsible for thousands (and sometimes millions) of dollars worth of equipment, your IT budget can be substantial. However, you must take server purchases seriously and proceed cautiously, just as if you had a minimal budget. Although this book does not intend to force a financial philosophy, carefully weighing the need for a server against its costs can sometimes help your standing as an administrator. For example, most publicly-traded companies watch the timing of quarterly expenses very carefully. If the company is experiencing less than stellar performance in the quarter, it might not be the best time to propose a large equipment purchase, especially if the purchase is not urgent (i.e., not particularly time-sensitive). You might wait until the beginning of a more promising quarter and attempt to push through equipment approval before anyone has a chance to get nervous!

Conversely, there is little reason to pause before purchasing a vital server. For example, if an email server experiences a catastrophic failure, you would want to replace it (or the failed component) immediately and without apology, because email is a highly utilized function of most organizations and used nearly every second of the workday. In this case, the email server purchase is urgent, and failure to purchase it would negatively impact your standing as an administrator.

In between the urgent and nonurgent equipment purchase comes the "we really could use that pretty soon" purchase. This might be something that does not immediately affect daily productivity or profitability, but for which you can provide reasonable justification. These types of purchases might optimize an existing server plan or proactively save money in the long run. For example, let's say you have a growing research division that is vital to your company's success. The research division can get by on the equipment it currently has, but you often hear about slow access to large user files on the department file server. The network has plenty of available bandwidth and acceptable network utilization, so network issues do not seem to be a problem. (**Bandwidth** is the transmission capacity of the network. For example, most Ethernet networks can transmit at 10 Mbps or 100 Mbps. **Network utilization** is the percentage of bandwidth in use during a given period of time.) However, you have confirmed that the file server is overutilized. Your solution is to purchase an additional file server to provide **load balancing** by distributing the files between the file servers, effectively halving the burden on the original file server. An additional benefit of load balancing is **failover**—if one of the servers fails, the remaining server(s) continue to provide service. Although you might not be able to specify the exact long-term savings, you can probably present an obvious case for improved productivity and redundancy with the additional file server.

 You could also do several other things to increase responsiveness when users access files, such as optimizing external storage or adding more hard disks. These types of solutions are discussed in more detail in later chapters.

Is the Expense of the Server Offset in Savings?

Suppose that your research division also has an office in Denver. You find that researchers in Denver often download large files from file servers in your local research division. The WAN link that connects these two offices is a high, ongoing expense because subscription charges accrue according to usage. (A WAN link is the telecommunications connection that links the various networks that comprise your WAN.) The WAN link is **oversubscribed** (bandwidth utilization is so high that it slows network access), so you want to reduce its usage. In this case, consider adding a file server to the Denver research office that periodically **synchronizes** (updates two or more copies of the same file so that they are the same) with your location's research division. By controlling when this synchronization occurs, you can save bandwidth and lower subscription costs. As an added benefit, the Denver researchers obtain faster access to their file resources. In this case, you can easily justify the addition of the Denver file server against the savings of the oversubscribed WAN link.

Is the Timing of a Server Purchase Appropriate?

Even if budgeting and financial resources are not a concern, the administrator must continue to be careful about the timeliness of a purchase. For example, you might delay the purchase of a new server with the fastest and latest processor even though you require more processing power. If you do not urgently need that much speed now or in the near future, consider other possibilities. For example, if the existing server supports SMP, and you have room for an additional processor, add another processor instead of purchasing an entire server. You might also consider purchasing a server with a processor that is a step or two below the latest and greatest—prices often come down after the release of a new processor.

Is Sufficient Expertise Available to Operate and Maintain the Server?

Sometimes an organization needs a server but does not have anyone available to run and maintain the equipment. This is particularly true in the case of a WAN where multiple, geographically distant locations make it impossible for a network administrator to be everywhere at once. This situation is difficult in that you must supply the server needs of the organization, yet the server cannot run and maintain itself. Although you will probably have to go ahead and provide the server, you might have to budget additional funding to hire outside support services for that office or to fund travel expenses for you to physically visit the server.41

While software exists that allows you to remotely operate a server from your location, such software cannot perform every function. For example, software cannot perform physical actions on the server, such as replacing a power supply.

ANTICIPATING USER DEMAND

It's essential to remember that *the network or systems administrator provides a service to users*. Remembering this responsibility affects the administrator's perspective and job performance. Some administrators find humor in belittling the end user. However, you will be a better administrator if you take the user (a little more) seriously. For example, in asking for a faster Internet connection, users might not understand that they are really asking for another high-speed Internet line and associated equipment costing thousands of dollars per month. The request might or might not be valid. The administrator often helps others (such as members of management) to determine which requests are valid.

The network administrator's job is to ensure that users can perform their jobs in an efficient, timely manner. To do this, he or she may need to wear many "hats," from educator to technician to business manager. The needs in each networking environment vary. However, the following questions might help you as a starting point in servicing user needs.

How Many Users Will Connect to the Server?

This is perhaps the most relevant issue in providing a server for user access. If you anticipate only a few users, you could use virtually any kind of server for general purposes, such as a desktop PC server. However, if you expect frequent access to the server from a large number of users, a more capable midrange computer might be more appropriate with the fastest network card that your network design supports. For example, a large corporation with a company intranet might have several midrange computers serving as intranet web servers. (Multiple web servers providing the same web content are collectively referred to as a **web farm**.)

A **network interface card (NIC)** is the computer's adapter card that connects to the network and through which network communication takes place. Consider installing two or more NICs in highly utilized servers. This multiplies the effective network I/O to and from the server by the number of NICs you install. For example, three NICs provide three times the network I/O capacity of a single NIC, provided the network bandwidth is not oversubscribed.

What Is the Nature of the User Access?

You might have only a few dozen users who, because of their access needs, require a more powerful server than hundreds of users with a different type of access requirement. For example, a few dozen users frequently performing complex and demanding queries on a very large database might require a server with significant storage and processing power. However, hundreds of users requiring a simple logon server probably do not need a significantly powerful server. Later in this book you will learn more about various services and applications, some of which require more powerful hardware than others.

Should Users Be Able to Access the Server Directly?

Some servers are not designed for direct user access. For example, in a Transmission Control Protocol/Internet Protocol (TCP/IP) network, a Dynamic Host Configuration Protocol (DHCP) server assigns unique identification to each computer on the network. This function requires minimal processing, memory, and hard disk storage, and a fairly bland server in terms of power can probably service hundreds of computers. This type of server requires no direct access on the user's part. As a rule, assume that users do not require direct server access and take measures to prevent such access unless you know users or groups of users who require a specific level of access. Also, user access to the server should only be from workstations across the network; users should never log on locally to a server.

PLANNING FOR INTEROPERABILITY

Many network environments use multiple operating systems across their servers and clients (see Figure 2-1). Reasons for this mixture vary. Perhaps two companies with differing operating systems merge, or a particular application only works with one NOS but you want to use the features of another NOS. The administrator must ensure that different operating system platforms can operate with one another and that the user experience is not disrupted. Ideally, the user has no idea that two or more operating systems are in use.

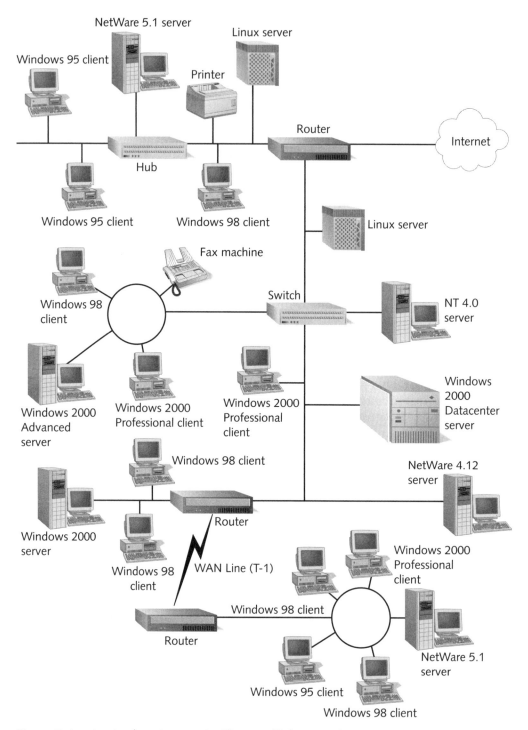

Figure 2-1 A mixed environment utilizes multiple operating systems

Sometimes an organization utilizes multiple operating systems because of a gradual evolution within the company. Perhaps the organization started out with UNIX application servers and Windows 95 workstations, but later added Novell NetWare file and print servers for users to store and print files. (**UNIX** usually operates on more expensive RISC-based processors. **Linux** is a version of UNIX and operates on PCs in addition to Alpha RISC-based processors and PowerPC processors.) The expensive UNIX hardware platform became less attractive compared to a less expensive PC computing platform, so PC servers running Windows NT 4.0 and Linux were added. Later, the organization upgraded client computers to Windows 2000 Professional and the UNIX hardware platform to PC servers running Linux. Regardless of the path an organization takes to arrive at its current constellation of operating systems, the network administrator must ensure that all operating systems interoperate as seamlessly as possible.

Operating system vendors have come to realize that no one operating system will meet every need, and they have produced various patches and other software to allow interoperability. For example, a Windows NT 4.0 logon server and a NetWare file and print server may have to interoperate. In this case, you probably want users to log on to the Windows NT 4.0 server as usual and access files on the NetWare server. Users should not be required to log on to the NetWare server separately if you want seamless interoperability. Instead, users access resources on the file and print server without any awareness that it is a NetWare server. Microsoft includes Gateway Services for NetWare with Windows NT 4.0 (see Figure 2-2). This product allows users to access NetWare resources through the Windows NT 4.0 computer. Whatever network environment you find yourself in, research the various operating system combinations and find the resources that allow the best interoperability.

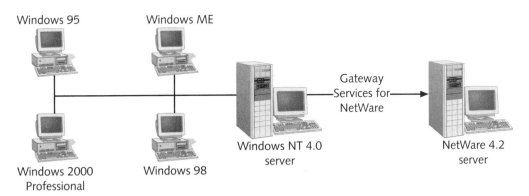

Figure 2-2   Gateway Services for NetWare allows access to the NetWare server

Consider protocol incompatibilities in the mixed environment as well. Continuing the previous interoperability scenario involving Windows NT 4.0 and NetWare, realize that Windows NT 4.0 installs TCP/IP by default, and NetWare often uses IPX/SPX (Internet Packet eXchange/Sequenced Packet eXchange). These two protocols are incompatible. For interoperability purposes, you would probably install both TCP/IP and IPX/SPX on the Windows NT 4.0 server. Then, the Windows NT 4.0 server can internally translate from IPX/SPX to TCP/IP (and vice versa) as messages travel to and from the NetWare server (Figure 2-3).

 Adding Gateway Services for NetWare automatically installs IPX/SPX on the Windows NT 4.0 server.

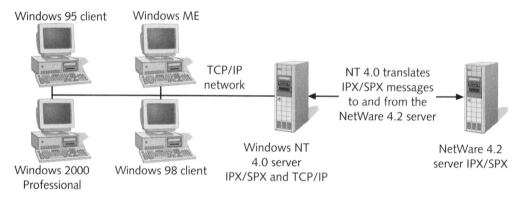

Figure 2-3   Using TCP/IP and IPX/SPX, Windows NT 4.0 can communicate in both protocols

Prior to adding another operating system to your network design, be sure to test for possible incompatibilities. For example, perhaps your UNIX system uses a custom-designed database. If you plan to install Windows 2000 Server, it will not be able to use the same application. You will either choose a different database product or pay to port the application to the Windows platform.

Also consider the interoperability of network operating systems with client workstation operating systems. For example, if you install a NetWare server in a LAN that uses Windows 98 computers, can the Windows 98 computers access all the benefits of the NetWare server? In fact, they cannot do so using the Microsoft Client for NetWare Networks software that is included with Windows 98. In order to utilize the powerful features of Novell Directory Services (NDS), Windows 98 clients must download and install the Novell Client v3.3 for Windows 95/98 from Novell (Figure 2-4). (**Novell Directory Services (NDS)** is an example of a directory service, a hierarchical data-base of network resources that allows users from anywhere in the enterprise to access resources throughout the organization. Microsoft Active Directory is another example of a directory service.) An **enterprise** is a geographically dispersed network under the jurisdiction of one organization. It often includes several different types of networks and computer systems from different vendors.

2

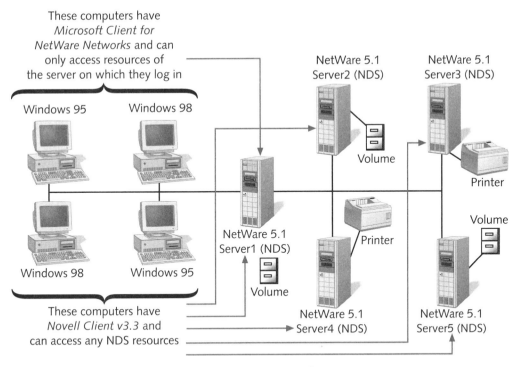

These computers have
*Microsoft Client for
NetWare Networks* and can
only access resources of
the server on which they log in

Windows 95   Windows 98

NetWare 5.1
Server2 (NDS)

NetWare 5.1
Server3 (NDS)

Volume

Printer

Volume

NetWare 5.1
Server1 (NDS)

Printer

Windows 98   Windows 95

Volume

These computers have
Novell Client v3.3 and
can access any NDS resources

NetWare 5.1
Server4 (NDS)

NetWare 5.1
Server5 (NDS)

Figure 2-4   Novell Client v3.3 for Windows 95/98 allows access to NDS

TIP

You might also consider using the NDS Authentication Services (NDS-AS) 3.0 download from Novell to allow users to log on to NDS transparent from virtually any other operating system platform. NDS-AS transparently redirects the user credentials to the NDS database for authentication and authorization. Other vendors also use credential redirection, known as a **single sign-on**.

Caution

If you decide to convert from one NOS to another, be aware that the user and group accounts are incompatible between operating systems. For example, if you want to convert from NetWare to Windows NT, the NetWare accounts are not readable by the Windows NT operating system. However, most NOS vendors offer a migration tool that allows you to separately convert the accounts.

SERVER PLACEMENT

No matter how good your business sense, ability to meet user demands, or skills in server interoperability, a service outage and lengthy recovery significantly impact the business of the organization. One of the most critical issues in server planning is assessing the physical location at which you plan to install the servers. An improper server environment can result in severe problems later on. Installing a server involves much more than finding an empty space, plugging it in, and installing the operating system. You must also place the server so that it serves network users in the best possible way. In a global enterprise, also consider factors such as site links and bandwidth utilization within and between networks.

For example, you might be from the United States and accustomed to reliable, high-speed WAN links. However, many locales have slower or less reliable connections. A WAN link connects a **site**, which consist of the LAN(s) on either side of a WAN connection. Figure 2-5 illustrates a WAN with two sites and two site links.

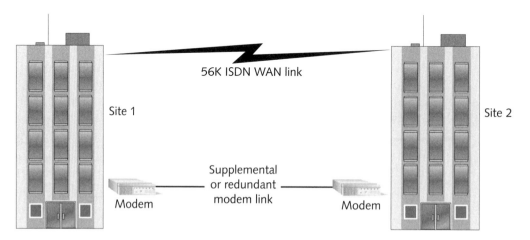

Figure 2-5   Two sites utilize a WAN link and a modem link

If the WAN link is slow but is the fastest type available in that locale, consider adding an additional WAN link of the same type. For example, the best available connection at some locations might be a 56 Kbps ISDN (Integrated Services Digital Network) from the telephone company. The advantage of an ISDN connection is that you can either leave it in an always-on state or have it dial out to another site on demand (which is useful if the telco charges for connection time). Also, an ISDN line usually provides clean, consistent data transmission. If this single connection is too slow, you might be able to combine two ISDN channels and double the speed, or add a dial-up modem connection to increase bandwidth during peak times (again refer to Figure 2-5). The dial-up connection can also provide redundancy in case the ISDN line fails.

Server placement within your WAN has an impact on network service and response to user requests. First, let's look at server placement within a site, and then at server placement for connecting sites.

Intra-Site Server Placement

Intra-site communication refers to communication between hosts within a single site, often over a LAN. Within the site, you should determine the best location in the building and on the network to place the server. Even a high-powered server's performance can flounder if the server is poorly placed. Although most network connections in a LAN are high-speed and well-connected, you should still carefully place the server in the most efficient location possible. Most networks represent a progression of growth both technologically and physically over a period of years. As a result, a network might have some locations that offer better connectivity than others. Figure 2-6 shows a network that originally started with a 4 Mbps network. As the network grew, a new section utilized a 10 Mbps network. Later, a 100 Mbps section was added. However, the servers remain in the 4 Mbps section.

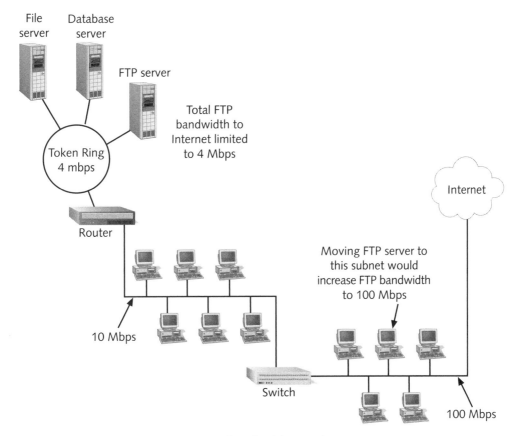

Figure 2-6   A network with various bandwidth speeds

Users on the 4 Mbps network seldom complain of bandwidth speed connecting to the servers because they have never experienced speeds faster than 4 Mbps. Users on the 10 Mbps network complain more often, and users on the 100 Mbps network complain every day about slow service from the servers because those users can compare 10 or 100 Mbps speed to 4 Mbps speed. The connection speed problem compounds with outside sources accessing the servers. For example, if one of the 4 Mbps servers were a **File Transfer Protocol (FTP)** server, the effectiveness of the server file transfer would be severely limited. It would be better to move the servers from the 4 Mbps network to a faster section, or to redesign the network so that all sections are at 100 Mbps.

Though these seem like simple solutions, in some environments making these changes could be a difficult task for several reasons. Perhaps the 4 Mbps network is large, and it requires a significant equipment investment to upgrade all equipment, including hubs and the NICs, on all servers and clients. Even if it were impractical to upgrade the 4 Mbps network, you would still want to move the servers. Moving a server might also prove to be problematic if the higher-speed networks do not have the physical facilities necessary for such a move—such as if a server room or closet were not available. If servers were added to the 10 or 100 Mbps networks that replicate data with servers on the 4 Mbps network, then the 4 Mbps network would experience even higher bandwidth utilization, limiting the effective shared connection speed for all other network hosts.

 A 4 Mbps network is typical of earlier Token Ring networks; 10 Mbps and 100 Mbps networks are typical of current Ethernet networks.

Inter-Site Server Placement

Inter-site communication refers to communication between hosts in different sites, often over a WAN link. Servers communicating over a WAN link also require you to determine the best connection method to optimize your bandwidth. When planning inter-site network communication across a WAN, you should generally place the servers that directly communicate across the WAN in closest physical and logical proximity to the WAN link. This makes sense because it reduces the number of variables between the WAN link and the server. In addition, placing the server as close as possible to the WAN link helps ensure that the server receives the maximum available bandwidth from the WAN.

If you place the server further away from the WAN link, you increase the number of possible problems. For example, additional hubs, switches, or **routers** (network devices that divide the network into separate parts usually known as **subnets** and forward network traffic to appropriate destinations) each add a potential point of failure in the data path between the WAN and the server. For example, in Figure 2-7 a Windows NT 4.0 domain controller is moved closer to the actual WAN connection, removing potential intermediate points of failure. Also, placing the server further away from the WAN link slows down network performance, because data traveling from the WAN must compete with other network traffic that occurs within the LAN.

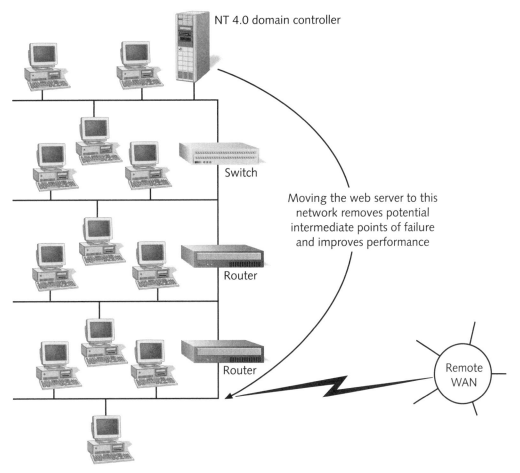

NT 4.0 domain controller

Switch

Moving the web server to this
network removes potential
intermediate points of failure
and improves performance

Router

Router

Remote
WAN

Figure 2-7 Inter-site server placement can improve availability and performance

CREATING THE NETWORK DIAGRAM

A network diagram is a physical and/or logical representation of the network, and is also known as a network map. You create a network diagram to design a network, keep a record of the network, or assist in changing or troubleshooting a network. You can draw a network map by hand, but regardless of your artistic skills, you should use special software designed to create a network diagram (see Figure 2-8). As a technician, you will find it much easier to trace problems if you have a diagram of what the network looks like. For example, if you visit a large network and you have little knowledge of its physical or topological structure, attempting to physically locate a failed server might be difficult without a network diagram.

The network diagram also provides a record and justification for why an organization decided to use specific servers, why the servers are placed in their specific location, and helps to logically determine a course of action in making a change to the network design and in troubleshooting.

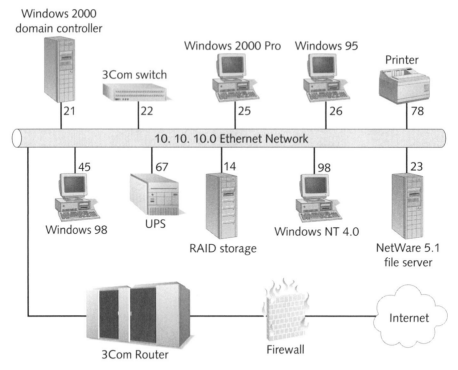

Figure 2-8   Network diagram (Visio)

Many companies use programs such as Visio 2000 to create network diagrams. Visio 2000 includes several predrawn images of various types of computers and network equipment. Using drag and drop, you can whip up a dream network in no time. If the network design changes, you can drag and drop the changes directly on the diagram and the rest of the network adjusts accordingly.

PLANNING PHYSICAL SITE READINESS

The physical server environment is one of the most critical aspects in determining where to place servers. In fact, you might have to significantly modify a particular room to ensure that the conditions are optimal for server reliability and uptime. Variances in the physical environment can also affect the lifetime of the server and its components. The two most significant factors affecting the health of a server are temperature and humidity. Other elements about the site's physical readiness include floor space, power availability, and the possibility of a fire or flood.

The physical site plan for your server room is foundational to the success of your network. However, you cannot plan a new server room yourself, regardless of how much you know about servers and networking. Several key planning considerations require the involvement of an architect, electrical and mechanical engineers, and a general contractor. For example, you probably do not want to design a fire suppression system on your own. For that, you would use a mechanical engineer to ensure the best possible solution for your environment and to avoid liability on your part and that of your organization. Also, these professionals can ensure that the server room installation complies with federal OSHA requirements and local building codes.

Temperature

Servers run hot. When you consider individual factors that contribute to the server heating and put them all into a single box, temperature problems quickly compound themselves. The hottest element is and will probably always be the processor(s) (Figure 2-9). The processor consists of around 40 million tiny transistors, each charged with electricity, albeit a small amount at about 1.7–3.5 volts. (A **transistor** is an electronic device that opens or closes, or turns on or off to provide a logic gate or switch, and provides the "thinking" capability of the processor.) Maximum temperature tolerance for the processor is about 185° Fahrenheit (85° Celsius); however, you should never allow the temperature to get this high. Fans and other cooling measures dedicated to the processor help to keep the temperature at 90–110° F (32–44° C). If you have an SMP system with multiple processors, potential temperature problems multiply accordingly.

Other hot components in the system are the hard drives, which on a server often have cooling fans of their own, and the motherboard. Internal components in the server collectively contribute to the overall heat of the server room. The increased heat in the air results in warmer air entering the server and aggravates the heat issue, which is why the server room should have dedicated air conditioning.

Figure 2-9   Processors can be very hot; cool processors to 90–110°F (32–44°C)

Generally, a series of fans inside the case helps keep the system cool and achieves maximum effectiveness if the ambient (i.e., surrounding) room temperature is also cool. In order to provide cool ambient temperature, keep the air conditioning in the server room as cool as possible. To compromise between human comfort and cooling server equipment, you can usually keep the server room temperature between 68 and 72° F (20–22° C). However, be sure to keep the temperature at a constant setting, because temperature fluctuations cause expansion and contraction of server components, shortening the server's life span.

Because equipment in the server room generates heat disproportionate to the heat level in the rest of the office, setting a thermostat in general areas cannot adequately cool the server room. A thermostat set at 70° F (21° C) for general areas will allow significantly higher temperatures in the server room. Therefore, it is important to provide an independent air-conditioning system and thermostat in the server room. If the budget allows, also consider installing two air-conditioning units and thermostats in the same server space for redundancy (Figure 2-10). If one unit fails, the other should be able to cool the room.

 Unless the site is in an extremely cold natural environment, you will seldom need to provide heat to the server room—it provides plenty of heat on its own.

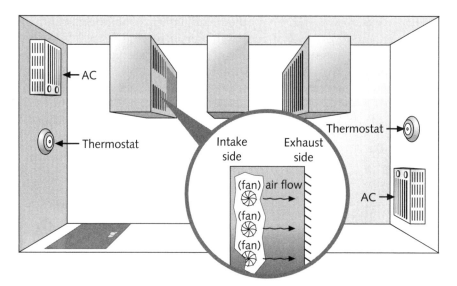

Figure 2-10   Use separate thermostats and air conditioners in addition to internal equipment fans to cool equipment

Regardless of the ambient room temperature and adequacy of server cooling fans, the server cannot adequately cool itself unless you provide good airflow to the server. This is an often-overlooked factor for a number of reasons. For example, server rooms often lack adequate space. As administrators cram more equipment into the server room, they are often forced to shove equipment closer to the wall to create more usable floor space. Or, someone receives a new carton of equipment and, for lack of a better place, simply places it in front of the server rack—unaware of the fact that he or she has just blocked the ventilation slots to the server. Space in front of and behind the server or server rack is critical. According to most specifications, about three feet of clearance is required both in front of and behind the rack (Figure 2-11).

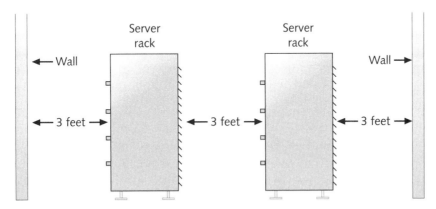

Figure 2-11   Allow three feet in front of and behind server equipment

Air Quality

While air quality sounds like a health-related issue for people, it is also an important issue for server equipment. Air quality in a server context means that the air must be clean and as free as possible from dust particles. Rooms designed to house server equipment often have added filtration beyond the usual air filters installed in the general-purpose HVAC (heating, ventilation, and air conditioning) system.

Excessive dust in the air directly relates to the previously discussed issue of temperature. A layer of dust effectively becomes insulation on server components. Insulation is fine for a home, where you want to keep heat inside, but it's *not* fine on server components, where you want to prevent heat as much as possible. Also, dust particles can adversely affect moving parts such as floppy and hard disks. Dust accumulation can also present a fire hazard. Take regular measures to clean dust off of all server components, regardless of air cleanliness. Add supplemental air filtration to any server room that does not already have it.

Remember that dust begets more dust. Passersby or air movement from the HVAC system easily disturbs a layer of dust. While you as the administrator are responsible for maintaining dust-free components, a cleaning service can remove dust in general areas. There are contractors who specialize in cleaning controlled environments, such as your server room, using highly trained crews. An example is Data Clean Corporation (see Hands-on Project 2-4).

Contact any reputable commercial HVAC or mechanical company to assess the air quality in your server room and make recommendations. Many organizations are large enough to require their own on-site facilities engineers, who might also be a good source of information on air filtration.

Several server components—such as the power supply fans, supplemental cooling fans, server racks and cabinets, and hard disks—might also include supplemental filters. For example, a force-filtered server uses one or more filtered fans to supply main internal airflow throughout the server. Other cooling fans inside the server only draw upon this filtered air, creating a **positive pressure** environment (Figure 2-12). In server rooms that are extremely sensitive to dust, you can also install an adhesive pad in front of the server room door that collects dust particles from the bottom of shoes as people enter the room.

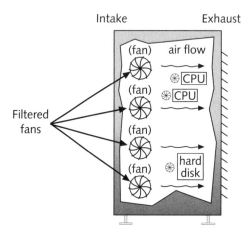

Figure 2-12 A positive pressure environment helps ensure clean air inside the server

Humidity

Humidity factors vary widely depending upon the physical location of the site. For example, the desert climate of Phoenix is not as likely to present the same humidity issues as the rain-soaked climate of Seattle. Humidity affects the health of electronic server components because a drier environment presents a greater occurrence of electrostatic discharge. **Electrostatic discharge (ESD)** is static electricity that can damage, destroy, or shorten the life of the server's electrical components. Many servers specify operating allowances between 20 percent and 80 percent **noncondensing relative humidity** (noncondensing means there is no moisture accumulation, such as on the outside of a cold glass). However, you should strive to humidify or dehumidify the air as needed to keep the humidity range between 40 percent and 60 percent.

High humidity presents the possible problem of condensation on equipment, which could obviously drip onto electronic components and generate significant damage—not to mention an electrocution and fire hazard to personnel. Even high-humidity environments do not normally cause condensation unless the temperature changes drastically—perhaps due to an HVAC outage. Higher humidity can create corrosion on metal components such as adapter cards and memory chips, and accelerate deterioration of magnetic media such as tape backups and floppy disks. Few environments contend with high humidity because both heating and air conditioning automatically remove humidity. However, you might find higher levels of humidity in basements or other subterranean locations, or environments that do not have a quality HVAC system in place.

If humidity is too high or too low, HVAC companies can offer a variety of solutions to add or remove humidity. Typically, HVAC modifications add humidity to the air that flows from the heating or air-conditioning unit. Utilize a dehumidification solution from the HVAC company as well. For economic reasons, you might be tempted to utilize a household dehumidifier in smaller server rooms. However, I cannot recommend these units for at least two reasons. First, these units are designed to cycle on and start dehumidifying based on a humidity threshold setting. When the unit powers on, it might cause a brief dip in power level if it is on the same circuit as server equipment (more on power later in this chapter). Second, these units usually remove the humidity from the air by condensing it into water in a pan. The pan must be emptied regularly—an overflowing pan threatens safety (slick floors) in addition to electrical hazards.

 TIP Look for equipment manufacturers that specialize in equipment that addresses the special air-conditioning, filtration, and humidity requirements of a server room (try Hands-on Project 2-5). Figure 2-13 shows a self-contained Liebert air-conditioning system that fits nicely into the corner of an existing server room, and filters air for dust control.

Figure 2-13   An air conditioning unit controls temperature, humidity, and dust
(*www.liebert.com*)

Flooring

In a server room, flooring is much more than a location on which to place equipment. Flooring can have a direct effect on the health of your servers, particularly in respect to the risk of ESD and the efficiency of cooling. In practical terms, flooring also affects where you put cable and smoke alarms. Choose from either a flat floor or a raised floor—each has its own characteristics and advantages.

A flat floor usually involves commercial-grade floor tiles on top of concrete. Check with your architect for floor tiles that can withstand the pressure of heavy server equipment and are static-resistant. Inevitably, some equipment will scar or crack tiles, which is not a functional issue if the damage is only cosmetic. To plan for future equipment additions and rearrangements in the server room, be sure to request extra replacement tile. Also consider no-wax flooring to avoid the time-consuming and messy job of stripping and applying wax, in addition to the regular maintenance of machine buffing, which can generate a flurry of dust. Avoid carpet because it can retain dust and presents a static risk despite manufacturers' best efforts to make static-resistant carpet.

A flat floor requires you to place cable, power lines, and HVAC ducts inside walls and above ceiling tiles between the actual ceiling and the dropped ceiling—a space known as the **plenum** (Figure 2-14). Running cable in the plenum might not always be possible (for example, in an older building that does not have a plenum area).

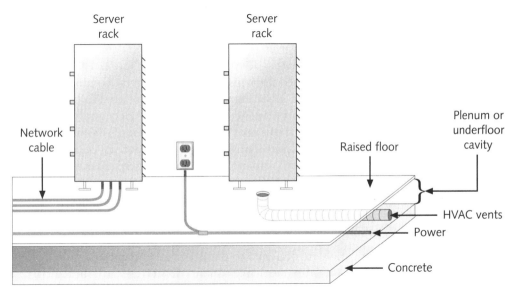

Figure 2-14   The plenum is useful for cable runs HVAC vents, and power lines

A raised floor attaches to supports that provide a subfloor between the concrete floor and the floor panels (see Figure 2-15). This space (also called a plenum or under-floor cavity) serves the same purpose as the plenum in the ceiling—you can run cables, power lines, and HVAC vents in this space.

Gasses and smoke emitted by burning cable can be noxious, so in both the plenum and subfloor, you must use plenum-rated cable (coated with a Teflon-like material) to limit the spread of flame and smoke.

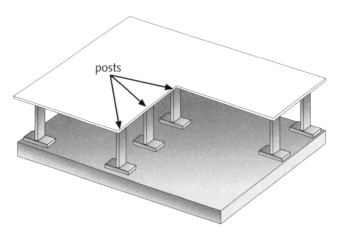

Figure 2-15 A raised floor rests on posts and provides plenum space

The depth of the subfloor varies from one design to another, but it usually involves 2-foot-by-2-foot panels 11 inches above the concrete. (You can adjust the height using different sized supports.) Raised floor installations were quite common in the era of large mainframes, and then became less common as more compact PC-based servers played a larger role. Server rooms became smaller as organizations decentralized from a very large room containing all servers to multiple smaller server rooms. Now, many organizations use a datacenter to house space-consuming equipment or consolidate contents of departmental server closets into a single, centralized, larger server room. (**Datacenter** is a term with two meanings, depending upon the context. It can refer to a consolidation of the majority of computer systems and data into a main location, or it can refer to one or more very powerful servers optimized as database servers—sometimes configured with as many as 32 processors. This context references the former.)

Heavy-duty floor panels are designed to withstand an enormous amount of weight (over 1000 lbs each) and are often steel filled. Some floors use an I-beam construction for added stability at the edges of the panel. These panels can be very heavy, weighing up to 45 lbs each, and require a floor puller with suction cups to lift them off the supports (Figure 2-16). The floor surface is specially coated to reduce ESD.

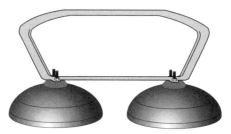

Figure 2-16 A floor puller uses suction cups to remove floor panels

TIP When running cable in either the ceiling or floor plenum, consider using cable trays or other cable organizers to prevent a tangled mess and minimize future troubleshooting efforts. Also consider pulling the cable through a conduit to minimize interference with other mechanical equipment and to make replacing cable more feasible should the need arise.

Raised floors (Figure 2-17) offer excellent grounding to avoid ESD. Many designs ground each supporting post and offer grounding points for server racks, cabinets, or other equipment. You can place HVAC vents beneath cabinets or racks to force cooled air up through the equipment. A cabinet usually includes at least one 10-inch (25.5-cm) fan (and several supplemental fans) at the top to draw cool air through the opening at the bottom and expel warm air at the top.

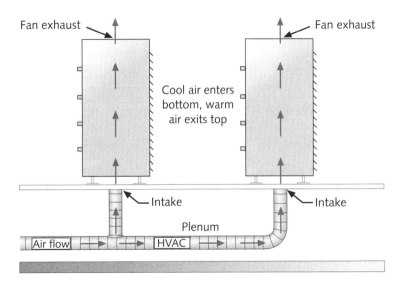

Figure 2-17   Raised floors can assist the cooling of server cabinets and racks

 Note In a flat floor environment, the cooling system can be reversed. You might place the rack or cabinet directly beneath a cooling vent so that cool air enters through the top and warm air exits through the bottom.

Coordinate raised floor installations with your architects, engineers, and general contractors. Raised floor materials are available from many vendors. For a good start on the physical installation of raised floors and server rooms in general, visit the following web sites:

- *www.beanfield.com*
- *www.accessfloorsystems.com*
- *www.compucraftconstruction.com*

As a safety precaution, place highly visible signs in areas where you remove a tile to access the subfloor, as shown in Figure 2-18.

Figure 2-18   Warn others of an open floor

POWER

Designing an appropriate power solution for the server room is one of the trickiest considerations and should fall almost completely to the electrical engineers. Just tell the engineers what you want and the level of redundancy you require, and depend upon them to provide the solution. When providing planning objectives to the engineers, be sure to consider the factors of availability, quality, and susceptibility to electromagnetic interference.

Availability

Three power sources provide power to the server room: the main power supply, the uninterruptible power supply (UPS) for temporary power, and backup generator power for extended, system-wide outages. Make sure to request dedicated circuits to the server room that are separate from the building's main power supply. Calculate the total power the current equipment requires, including servers, monitors, routers, hubs, and switches. Add to this calculation anticipated amperage requirements for future expansion, and ask the electrical engineers to oversupply the power requirements just to be sure. (Also make sure to install plenty of easy-to-reach electrical outlets.)

TIP Although you should rely on an electrical engineer to design server room power, you might also want to keep on hand the IEEE (Institute of Electrical and Electronic Engineers) publication *IEEE Recommended Practice for Powering and Grounding Sensitive Electronic Equipment* (ISBN 0-7381-1660-2). This book is also known as the "emerald book" in reference to its cover color, and provides complex electrical information such as reducing electrical noise and ensuring proper grounding. You might find it hard to locate in retail stores, but you can obtain it from *www.ieee.org.*

Administrators can probably determine what kind of UPS to use; however, the engineer should plan main power and backup generator power. The purpose of the UPS and backup generator is to provide redundancy, ensuring that power is available at all times. The UPS (more details in Chapter 3) supplies power temporarily while administrators perform a graceful shutdown of server equipment. Otherwise, the sudden loss of power to the server can be extremely damaging to the operating system, applications, and open data files. Figure 2-19 shows a typical power configuration for a server room.

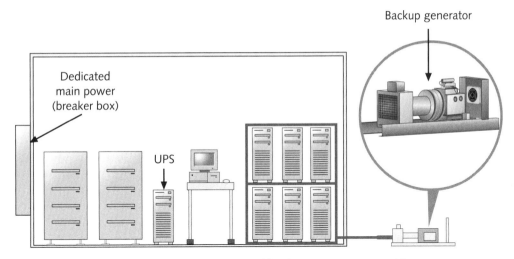

Figure 2-19   Main power, UPS systems, and backup generator provide power to the server room

Backup generators can be extremely expensive depending upon the amount of power they provide. Some generators cost about $250,000 and require a facility of their own, separate from the main building. Backup generators operate for as long as diesel fuel or natural gas is available. You will still need UPS systems because it usually takes about 15 seconds for the generator to start up and supply power. Of course, only organizations that absolutely require 24/7 operation would opt for such an expensive generator, which might also provide main power to the rest of the organization.

Make sure to request a "phase protector" in the backup generator system. Otherwise, the backup generator might confuse the UPS, causing it to continue to supply and eventually drain battery power.

Quality

Clean power extends the life of the server and its components. "Clean power" means the absence of surges, spikes, dips, or poor grounding, which can lead to short circuits, tripped electrical breakers, and possibly damage to equipment or people. Use a receptacle tester (also known as a polarity tester, Figure 2-20) to test receptacles for power and grounding, especially in older buildings that might have questionable electrical wiring.

Figure 2-20   The receptacle tester verifies power and ground wiring

Request that the electrical engineer provide a connection to the earth ground in the server room. The earth ground of a home typically connects to the plumbing outside that provides water into the home. In a commercial building, electrical engineers usually design the earth ground to utilize a rod that is driven deep into the ground (Figure 2-21).

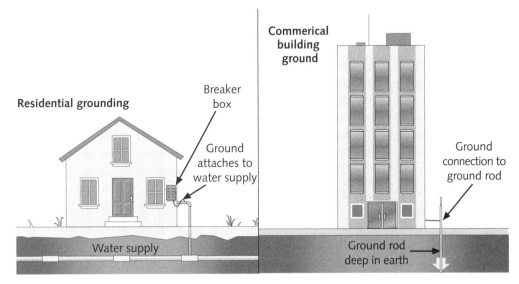

Figure 2-21   A commercial earth ground is a rod forced deep into the earth

The electrical engineer takes measures to ensure clean power, but the administrator also ensures clean power to the server by using good surge protectors, UPS systems, and possibly line conditioners, which supplement power in the event of a brownout and/or minimize electromagnetic interference (EMI).

Electromagnetic Interference

EMI is a byproduct of electricity and can disrupt or corrupt data traveling along network cable as well as disrupt other electrical equipment. Design data cable routes to and from the server room so that they avoid electrical equipment such as fluorescent lights, heavy electrical equipment, motors, and so forth. Make sure your electrical engineer is aware of the types of other equipment (such as heavy manufacturing equipment) in your organization so that he or she can design around potential EMI pitfalls. Shielded twisted-pair (STP) network cable includes a foil inner jacket, adding a level of protection against EMI (Figure 2-22); however, you should avoid EMI sources when possible.

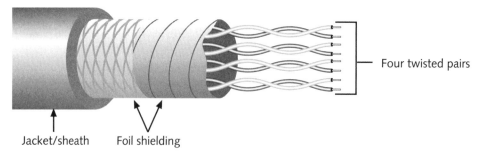

Four twisted pairs

Jacket/sheath   Foil shielding

Figure 2-22   STP cable includes a foil inner jacket to protect against EMI

Because servers and associated equipment are electrical devices, they also produce a level of EMI. While most equipment manufacturers take precautions to minimize the production of EMI, a certain level is unavoidable. If you find that certain server equipment exhibits strange, intermittent problems that do not seem to be associated with a specific component or the NOS, try moving the equipment to a different location where there might be less EMI from surrounding equipment. Also be sure to cover any open drive bays and expansion slots, and leave covers attached to servers when you are not servicing them. Otherwise, these exposures can radiate EMI.

If a situation arises in which you need to shut off a breaker, the description next to the breakers might be blank, incomplete, vague, or just plain wrong. Verify that you are about to switch off the correct breaker so that you do not inadvertently shut down other systems. You can use a circuit breaker finder, which is actually two pieces. The first piece (the transmitter) plugs into an electrical outlet on the circuit you wish to shut off (see Figure 2-23a). The second piece (the receiver) emits a tone when you physically pass it over the correct breaker (see Figure 2-23b).

(a)   (b)

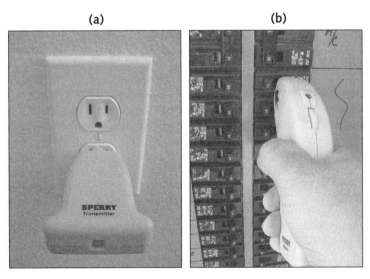

Figure 2-23   The circuit breaker finder locates the correct circuit breaker

DISASTER PLANNING

Disaster planning requires a significant budgetary outlay for the relatively unlikely possibility that a natural disaster, building defect, or other unexpected occurrence takes place. However, in the event that a disaster does occur, you will be glad for every penny spent in planning. Much of this book teaches disaster planning in various respects, such as the typical hard disk failure; however, this chapter focuses on planning the server room to be as resilient as possible in case of fire or flood.

Fire Detection and Suppression

A fire presents an obvious threat to people and equipment. Most buildings are built (or remodeled) according to relatively stringent OSHA regulations and local building codes. As a result, people sometimes dismiss the threat of a fire. However, alert administrators must remain keenly aware of the possibility of a fire (particularly an electrical fire) in both planning and daily operations. If there is a single location at which a fire is most likely, it is probably a single room filled with complex electrical equipment. That's right—the server room.

First, in the event of a developing fire, you must ensure that people in the server room are notified of the danger. Smoke alarms serve this purpose, and commercially available alarms can alert emergency services and people within the organization in addition to setting off an audible alarm. While most smoke detectors are in the ceiling, they can also be in the subfloor in a raised floor design. If they are in the subfloor, you should mark the surface of the floor panel above the smoke detector with adhesive signs, so that if it goes off you can more easily find it when it's time to reset or maintain it.

In years past, halon was the primary fire suppressant in server rooms because water has an obvious negative impact on electronics. Essentially, a fire is a chemical chain reaction. Halon breaks the chain reaction by substituting hydrogen atoms with halogen atoms. Halon leaves little or no residue and does not cause electrical short circuits. However, some suspect that halon can cause corrosion on computer components. Because halon is harmful to the earth's ozone layer, the Environmental Protection Agency (EPA) has banned the production of new halon, although you can purchase recycled halon. Because halon is being phased out, you might want to choose a different chemical fire suppressant. Consult EPA's list of halon substitutes at *www.epa.gov/ozone/title6/snap/halonreps.html.* Unfortunately, converting to another fire-protection chemical involves more than replacing the gas canisters—you must replace the entire system. Whatever product you use to extinguish fire, consider that you might also need an emergency ventilation system to expel gasses from the suppressing chemicals or burnt objects.

If you choose to supplement the chemical extinguisher, consider using a dry system instead of a water sprinkling system. A dry system uses water but only fills the pipes when there is a fire, ensuring that a damaged or leaking sprinkler head does not harm equipment. When a fire alarm trips, the pipes fill with water. Then, heat sensors release water from only areas of the room that indicate heat caused by fire. This prevents the unnecessary release of water in areas where there is no fire threat. Also, when the fire is extinguished, the sprinkler head can automatically close to prevent excess water release. Consider including floor drains for quick removal of water. Make sure the drains include a backflow prevention system so that sewer water backups do not flood the server room.

Flood Considerations

In a flood, there is good news and bad news. The bad news is that there is not much you can do to prevent a flood. The good news is, at least you have less planning to do. Depending upon the cause, you might be able to prevent some types of flooding. For example, you could avoid placing the server room in locations where plumbing runs above or below the floor. A burst pipe could cause immense damage to server equipment. Also, remember to request floor drains with a backflow prevention system to prevent sewer backups into the server room while allowing fire sprinklers or other sources of water to evacuate.

If the flood is caused by a natural disaster, placing the server room as centrally as possible and away from exterior walls might allow other rooms to absorb the brunt of the initial water flow, although it may eventually reach the server room. General plumbing principles dictate that your floor drains seldom work when a large-scale flood is in progress. Your flood disaster plan will primarily determine the best way to minimize damage and move equipment quickly, instead of trying to avoid the flood. In an evacuation plan, move anything storing data first—file servers and backup tapes in particular. A well-planned system design calls for redundant copies of data, so you probably have off-site copies of your data. However, off-site copies are usually not as recent as local copies. Even though the servers are expensive, they are replaceable—whereas the organization's data is probably not replaceable. Remember that much server equipment is extremely heavy and cannot be lifted by a single individual. Also, some server NOSs feature built-in redundancy. For example, the Windows 2000 Active Directory automatically replicates its database between domain controllers.

Be certain that your server equipment is adequately covered by an insurance policy.

USING SPACE EFFECTIVELY

In addition to technical issues relating to servers and networking, other factors can affect your server planning. Some factors might be specific to your organization, and others might be common to most situations, as in the following list:

- *Choose a central location:* If you have a choice (as in new construction), try to locate the server room centrally (Figure 2-24). A central location makes it easier to provide good connectivity to the rest of the network and saves cabling costs. Try to design Internet and WAN traffic to and from your organization so that it flows freely and with as few intermediary devices as possible (switches or routers, for example).

- *Consolidate space:* The best way to get the most bang for the buck out of server floor space is to use racks and cabinets. (A cabinet is similar to a rack, except that it has a locked enclosure and cooling fans.) That way, you can store several pieces of equipment in a single horizontal floor space (Figure 2-25).

- *Restrict foot traffic:* Place the server room in a low-traffic area to minimize the risk of unauthorized access. Sometimes there are exceptions to this rule. For example, I recently visited a very large server manufacturer in Silicon Valley that displays parts of a server room through a window to a busy hallway. I didn't ask why they did this, but it seemed obvious that the company was proudly displaying its products to employees.

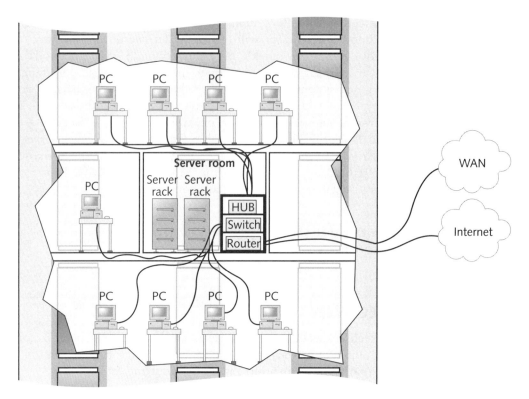

Figure 2-24 Centralize the server room for accessibility and reduced cable costs

- *Avoid exterior windows and walls:* Place the server room away from exterior building windows and walls for environmental and security purposes. In event of inclement weather, exterior windows might leak wind or rain, and sunlight contributes unwelcome warmth to the server room. A window that displays your server equipment to the outside world presents a security risk because someone can surmise much about your network design by viewing the equipment. Also consider that an evildoer could break the window and access the server room.

- *Be prepared to budget extra financing for server room design:* A server room is expensive. It requires expensive equipment and special design considerations. If you are responsible for budgeting the server room, bear this in mind and warn management in advance. As a general rule, you can multiply the cost per square foot of the building's general office space times four to arrive at the cost of server room space.

2

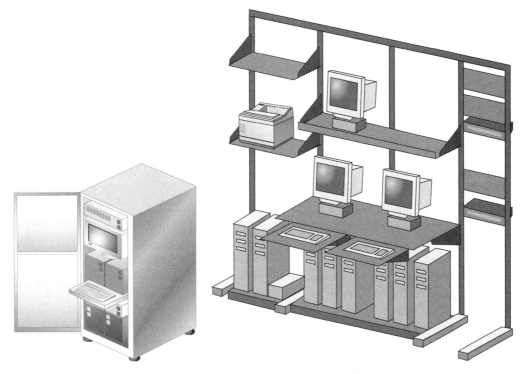

Figure 2-25   Cabinets and racks permit more equipment in the same space

PLANNING A SECURE LOCATION

Administrators of larger corporations are responsible for hundreds of millions and even billions of dollars worth of vital company data, such as customer databases, company secrets, accounting records, confidential employee records, and scores of other types of information—not to mention the value of the server equipment. Even if the organization is small, protecting company assets is still the administrator's vital concern. Securing the server room protects both the physical assets and the information stored on the servers. Although electronic security is designed to protect against hackers, viruses, malicious Internet users, and the like, physical security protects the actual server facility and equipment.

Physical security can be sophisticated, but it is not complicated. It is as simple as physical security has always been for everything from precious documents to currency—place the valuables in a safe and lock it. The server room is really a very large safe, and you as an administrator are responsible for ensuring that it is not accessed by unauthorized people. In fact, I know of a corporate contractor to the United States government that runs a server and a few highly secure workstations in a steel vault.

All other security measures are only as effective as the level of physical security. You might have extremely restrictive permissions and detailed auditing records on who can access company payroll records. While hackers are always a threat over the Internet or internal network, anyone with physical access to the server can utilize special utilities that allow access to the data stored on the hard disk even though they are not authorized for such access. For example, a utility known as NTFSDOS allows the user to boot the server from an MS-DOS floppy and gain complete control of the NT file system on an otherwise secure hard disk. Monitoring security starts with your own IT staff.

I Have Seen the Enemy ...

And it is your own IT staff! A common source of company loss is employees, especially in the server room where there are a great many valuables. Instead of "borrowing a few paperclips," employees in the server room can "borrow a few memory DIMMs!" It is not up to me to tell you who to trust or to question your character judgment—just don't trust anybody. Sometimes, a security breach could be an innocent oversight—perhaps a new administrator provided a tour of the new server room to unauthorized outside persons. Or the security breach could be a deliberate, mean-spirited attack. Perhaps a disgruntled IT employee might want to seek revenge against the company before leaving for another job and, using his or her administrative privileges, destroys company data. It is wise to assume that anybody can steal or damage company assets—so implement sound security measures to remove or reduce such opportunities.

 Always log off before leaving your computer. Otherwise, any passerby can access the local computer and network with the same authority you have, and any trace of improper activity will be logged to your account. Operating systems such as Windows NT or Windows 2000 allow you to lock your computer, requiring a password to unlock. Also consider logging on under only a general user account with no specific administrative privileges, and log on with administrative rights only when you need to perform administrative actions.

Restricting Access to the Server Room

As discussed earlier in this chapter, you should place the server room in an area that has minimal traffic. This minimizes the opportunity to access the server room and makes unwelcome visitors more obvious. Also, be very discriminating when determining who should see the server room. It is not a good practice to provide tours of the server room, even to employees of the organization. Next, make sure that the door you place on the server room is a solid, heavy, secure door made of solid wood, steel, or steel clad with a

2

heavy-duty lock. The type of lock you choose depends upon the level of security you want or can afford. A simple keyed lock might be sufficient; however, most organizations probably want more controlled access, such as the following:

- *Keypad:* Enter a number into an electronic keypad to unlock the door. This number might be a shared number that all IT staff knows, or it might be unique for each user. You should reset the number on a regular basis to ensure the secrecy of the number. A keypad provides minimal security because a passerby might be able to see a number as the user enters it.

- *Card scanners:* Issue authorized persons a card that is read by a scanner at the entrance to the server room. The cards are available in a number of formats. Some have embedded magnetic data that uniquely identifies the user. Others are smart cards that have digital certificates with metal contacts read by the scanner. These are nearly impossible to duplicate. Administrators can set conditions on the cards so that they grant access to the room only at certain times—to prevent employees from sneaking into the server room and performing malicious deeds when no one else is around, for example. When the scanner reads the card, an electronic lock unlocks the door for a few seconds. One of the only drawbacks to this system is that people tend to lose, misplace, borrow, or steal the access cards. Provide a written policy to your staff that specifies penalties for missing access cards. Also make sure that employees always wear the access card. Most cards include a photograph of the person, helping to ensure that only the person to whom the card was issued uses it.

- *Bio-recognition:* This is an emerging technology that verifies a person's identity based upon physical identifiers such as fingerprints, retinal scans, voice imprints, or some combination thereof.

For maximum security, require some combination of access methods. For example, employees might insert a smart card into a reader and also type a password. This method would ensure that the card was not stolen.

Monitoring Access to the Server Room

Despite your best security efforts, unauthorized persons might still find a way to access the server room, or authorized users might damage the server room. If such unfortunate occurrences take place, utilize a method of record keeping that allows you to know which persons were present at the time of the deed. Some of the following methods monitor access to your server room:

- *Sign-in:* Clearly the least secure method, a sign-in sheet depends upon the honor system, and persons that are a security risk are unlikely to be "honorable." A sign-in system should implement one or both of the next two methods that follow.

- *Security guard:* Because of the high cost associated with staffing a facility with a 24/7 security guard, this option might not be practical for all environments. However, a security guard adds an observer to unauthorized security breaches and is useful for quick apprehension and prevention as well as adding a visible level of deterrence. A security guard might also check contents of all bags going into the server room.

- *Video surveillance:* Video surveillance captures activity in the server room or at the server room door 24/7. Some facilities keep video tapes indefinitely, but most rotate tapes on at least a seven-day schedule. Be sure to replace tapes periodically, because older, worn tapes do not provide a clear image. Video surveillance is only as good as the area it covers. If you cover the server room, be sure to also cover wiring closets, areas where you store backup tapes, and so forth.

- *Logs:* Most controlled access methods such as scanners or electronic keypads keep logs that show who entered the server room and when. In addition, you can configure the NOS to track certain resources so that if someone attempts to access a resource (whether successfully or unsuccessfully), a log records the name of the logged-on user and time and date of access.

In securing the server room, do not forget to also secure other sensitive, physically accessible areas. You should, for example, secure patch panels and wiring closets, which provide a point of convergence for network cabling, making it easier to manage. In seconds, someone could access an exposed patch panel and start ripping out cable, causing considerable damage to network operations. Also, place backup media in secured data storage areas to prevent stolen tapes. In the IT context, your organization is not the server room; it is the data. Stolen tapes are a severe security risk. Secure the telco room, which is the access point for telephone communications and often shares its connections with a WAN or Internet connection.

Further secure the contents of the server room by placing locks on server equipment. For example, most server cabinets require a lock, and you can optionally lock individual components of the server rack. One reason for rack-mounted equipment is easy portability from one rack to another. However, you do not want someone easily porting the equipment into a backpack or briefcase. Do not leave spare parts lying around—secure them in a locked cabinet as well, and record parts with serial numbers.

CHAPTER SUMMARY

- ❏ Increasingly, organizations are looking for network administrators who not only have computer and network expertise, but also know how to get the most value for every dollar spent in servicing the network.

- ❏ Ask the following questions about server needs: Do we really need this server right now? Is the expense of the server offset in savings? Is the timing of a server purchase appropriate? Is there sufficient expertise available to run and service the server?

❑ Ask the following questions about fulfilling user requirements: How many users will connect to the server? What is the nature of user access? Should users be able to access the server directly? As a rule, assume that users do not require direct server access and take measures to prevent such access unless you know users or groups of users that require a specific level of access. Also, user access to the server should only be from workstations across the network; users should never log on locally to a server.

❑ In planning for interoperability, the administrator must ensure that operating system platforms can interoperate with one another and that the user experience is not disrupted.

❑ Installing a server involves much more than finding an empty space, plugging it in, and installing the operating system. You must also place the server so that it serves users in the network design in the best possible way. In a global enterprise, also consider factors such as the site links and bandwidth utilization within and between networks.

❑ A network diagram is a physical and/or logical representation of the network, also known as a network map. You create a network diagram to design a network, keep a record of the network, or assist in changing or troubleshooting a network.

❑ Physical site readiness is one of the most critical aspects in determining where to place servers, and involves controlling temperature, humidity, and dust.

❑ Keeping server equipment cool requires adequate airflow and redundant air conditioners that are independent of general-use air conditioners.

❑ Good server room air quality requires efficient filtration both in the HVAC system as well as in the ventilation of the internal server components. Filtration prevents a buildup of dust, which contributes to overheating.

❑ High humidity can lead to condensation with sudden temperature changes and accelerates buildup of corrosion on metal components. Low humidity increases the risk of ESD.

❑ Use static-resistant, commercial-grade floor tiles in the server room. Avoid carpet, which increases the risk of ESD. A flat floor requires a ceiling plenum to run cable, power, and HVAC.

❑ A raised floor design allows for a floor plenum and provides excellent grounding to avoid ESD. HVAC vents in the floor provide excellent cooling when directed up through server racks.

❑ There are three sources of power to the server room: the main power, the uninterruptible power supply (UPS) for temporary situations, and the backup generator power for extended, system-wide outages. Clean power extends the life of the server and its components. "Clean power" means the absence of surges, spikes, dips, or poor grounding, which can lead to short circuits, tripped electrical breakers, and possibly damage to equipment or people. Electromagnetic interference (EMI) is a byproduct of electricity, can disrupt or corrupt data traveling along network cable, and can disrupt other electrical equipment.

❑ While smoke detectors provide a warning for fire, chemical extinguishers suppress the fire without damaging equipment. When using chemical extinguishers, be sure to also provide quick ventilation to expel the chemicals after the fire. Alternatively, a "dry" extinguishing system uses water but only fills the pipes when there is a fire.

❑ Strategically place plumbing away from the server room ceiling and floor, and make sure floor drains include backflow preventers.

❑ In an evacuation plan, move anything storing data first—file servers and backup tapes in particular. Even though the servers are expensive, they are replaceable, whereas the organization's data is probably not replaceable.

❑ In using space effectively, consider the following factors: Choose a central location, consolidate space, restrict foot traffic, avoid windows and walls, and prepare to budget extra financing for server room design.

❑ It's important to physically secure the server room and important networking equipment. A common source of company loss is the employees, especially in the server room, where there is a lot of valuable data and equipment. In addition to a solid locked door, consider controlled access methods such as keypads, card scanners, and bio-recognition devices. Also, monitor access to the server room using a sign-in sheet, security guard, video surveillance, and logs. Further secure the contents of the server room by locking server racks and cabinets.

KEY TERMS

bandwidth — The transmission capacity of the network. For example, most Ethernet networks can transmit 10 Mbps or 100 Mbps.

datacenter — A term with two meanings, depending upon the context. It can refer to a consolidation of the majority of computer systems and data into a main location, or it can refer to one or more very powerful servers optimized as database servers—sometimes configured with as many as 32 processors.

electrostatic discharge (ESD) — Static electricity that can damage, destroy, or shorten the life of the server's electrical components.

enterprise — A geographically dispersed network under the jurisdiction of one organization. It often includes several different types of networks and computer systems from different vendors.

failover — If one server fails, the remaining server(s) continue to provide service.

File Transfer Protocol (FTP) — A TCP/IP protocol that manages file transfers. Usually used to download files over the Internet.

inter-site communication — Communication between hosts in different sites, such as over a WAN link.

intra-site communication — Communication between hosts within a single site, often over a LAN.

Linux — A version of UNIX that operates on PCs as well as Alpha RISC and PowerPC platforms.

load balancing — Distributing a network role between two or more servers.

network interface card (NIC) — The workstation's adapter card that connects to the network and through which network communication takes place.

network utilization — The percentage of bandwidth in use in a given period of time.

noncondensing relative humidity — Absence of moisture accumulation, such as on the outside of a cold glass.

Novell Directory Services (NDS) — A hierarchical database of network resources that allows users from anywhere in the enterprise to access resources throughout the organization, as opposed to logging on to a single server and accessing only resources available from that server.

oversubscribe — A network connection with network utilization that exceeds an acceptable baseline for the available network bandwidth. The network utilization has a direct relationship to network bandwidth: the higher the network bandwidth, the lower the network utilization.

plenum — The space between the dropped ceiling tiles and the actual ceiling, or the space between the raised floor surface and the concrete.

positive pressure — The internal environment of a server case or cabinet that utilizes one or more filtered fans to supply main internal airflow throughout the server. Internal server fans only draw upon this filtered air.

router — A device that divides the network into separate parts and forwards network traffic to appropriate destinations.

single sign-on — A single logon that allows transparent access to multiple servers. For example, a single sign-on might allow you to log on to a NetWare server and pass the logon credentials to an NT 4.0 server as well.

site — The LAN(s) on either side of a WAN connection.

subfloor — A space between the concrete floor and the floor tiles; also known as the plenum.

subnet — A division in the network useful for limiting network traffic to a particular location; also known as a segment in many contexts.

synchronize — The process of making data in one location consistent with data in another location. Synchronization is necessary to ensure that user accounts, for example, are consistent from one logon server to another. Synchronization also applies to items such as data files.

transistor — An electronic device that opens or closes, or turns on or off to provide a logic gate or switch. Transistors provide the "thinking" capability of the processor.

uninterruptible power supply (UPS) — A device that supplies power temporarily to allow administrators to perform a graceful shutdown of server equipment. Otherwise, the sudden loss of power to the server can be extremely damaging to the operating system, applications, and open data files.

UNIX — An open server operating system that allows vendors to specially modify it to their servers. UNIX usually operates on more expensive RISC-based processors.

WAN link — The telecommunications connection that links the various networks that comprise parts of a wide area network (WAN).

web farm — Multiple web servers providing the same web content.

REVIEW QUESTIONS

1. You have a very limited budget, but the email server failed. What should you do?

   a. Replace the failed server or the failed component(s).

   b. Convert the corporation to Internet mail only.

   c. Use paper memoranda until you have more money.

   d. Use a user's workstation as an email server.

2. What does load balancing do?

   a. distributes a network role between two or more servers

   b. evenly distributes server weight on a raised floor

   c. evenly distributes power load between breakers

   d. evenly distributes WAN traffic between multiple links

3. Bandwidth is:

   a. a measure of electromagnetic interference

   b. the percentage of network utilization in a given period of time

   c. the average amount of data that can be transmitted in a given period of time

   d. the transmission capacity of the network

4. Network utilization is:

   a. the transmission capacity of the network

   b. the number of hosts on the network as a percentage of the maximum allowed number of hosts on the network

   c. the percentage of bandwidth in use in a given period of time

   d. the amount of bandwidth required to upload or download a large file

5. Which of the following would be a reasonable justification to add a more expensive, higher-bandwidth WAN link?

   a. The existing WAN link is oversubscribed.

   b. The existing WAN link is undersubscribed.

   c. The existing WAN link is used only for nightly synchronization.

   d. to increase the number of users that can log on across the WAN link

6. The administrator provides what to the users?

   a. a service

   b. endless ridicule

   c. only what the user asks for

   d. troubleshooting expertise when users damage their computers

7. Which of the following could be good reasons for using differing operating systems? (Choose two.)

   a. merging of two companies with different operating systems

   b. Some users like one type of NOS while others like another.

   c. It is better to have separate user logons to each operating system to improve security.

   d. You require the features of a particular operating system and you also have an application that only works on another operating system.

8. Linux is a version of:

   a. NetWare

   b. OS/2

   c. Windows

   d. UNIX

9. You should put the server room:

   a. on the bottom floor of a multiple-story building

   b. on the top floor of a multiple-story building

   c. furthest away from the incoming WAN and Internet links

   d. as centrally as possible

10. Why would you want to create a network diagram? (Choose all that apply.)

    a. to express yourself artistically

    b. to assist in locating equipment when you need to troubleshoot

    c. to use as a tool to justify your budgetary expenditures

    d. so users know which servers are closest to them

11. Why is a server room hotter than other rooms in the building?

    a. Electrical components generate heat.

    b. It is hotter by design to reduce humidity.

    c. Optimum placement by exterior windows allows heat from sunlight.

    d. It is designed to make people uncomfortable.

12. Besides fans in server equipment and cabinets, what can you do to keep the server room cool?

    a. Prop the server room door open at all times.

    b. Add one or more dedicated air conditioners to the server room.

    c. Add oscillating fans wherever possible.

    d. Open a window.

13. Why is a lack of adequate humidity detrimental to the server room?

    a. It increases EMI.

    b. It might cause electronic circuitry to crack.

    c. It causes expansion and contraction of server components.

    d. It increases chances of ESD.

14. Why is dust in the server room a problem?

    a. Dust accumulation creates an unprofessional appearance.

    b. Dust acts as an insulator, increasing heat problems.

    c. Dust particles can adversely affect moving parts.

    d. Dust is no more a problem in the server room than it is in other rooms.

15. A positive pressure environment:

    a. provides filtered air to internal server cooling fans

    b. encourages people to do good deeds

    c. forces filtered air into the server room at a greater rate than it escapes

    d. is a server room condition that occurs when temperature, humidity, and dust control are all within acceptable parameters

16. High humidity can cause:

    a. mold spores on server components

    b. increased occurrences of ESD

    c. increased occurrences of EMI

    d. corrosion on metal components

17. A raised floor is advantageous for which of the following reasons? (Choose all that apply.)

    a. makes the ceiling closer, thereby easier to service the ceiling plenum

    b. excellent grounding to avoid ESD

    c. provides plenum space for cables, power, and HVAC

    d. handy plenum space for storing spare parts

18. Why should you use a UPS even if you already have a reliable backup generator?

   a. The backup generator can only run for a few minutes.

   b. The backup generator might not provide clean power, and the UPS can condition the power as necessary.

   c. Backup generators normally serve the general building, not the server room.

   d. The backup generator requires about 15 minutes to start—the UPS provides power in the mean time.

19. Why might you choose to install a dry system for fire suppression?

   a. to avoid water in event of a broken or leaking sprinkler head

   b. to avoid rust

   c. to reduce the weight of pipes in the plenum

   d. to avoid use of harmful chemical-based fire-suppression systems

20. In case of a flood, what should you first attempt to move to a safe location?

   a. the mainframe

   b. spare parts

   c. anything storing company data

   d. the Chia Pet

HANDS-ON PROJECTS

 Web links in projects were accurate at the time this book was published. If you notice discrepancies, look for similar links and follow the same general steps.

Project 2-1

Three departments have specific network problems, as shown in Table 2-1. You intend to solve the problems with the equipment shown. However, your budget is extremely slim and you will have to request additional funding to purchase equipment. Your supervisor asks you to prioritize each item. In the Proposed Equipment column, write the number 1, 2, or 3 to represent the highest priority (1), second highest (2), and the lowest (3).

Table 2-1   Priorities of Proposed Equipment

Department	Problem	Proposed Equipment
Data Processing	Slow response in processing user queries; however, functionality is 100%.	New server with four processors
Administration	Email server is heavily utilized and frequently stops responding. Day-to-day operations heavily dependent on email.	Two new clustering email servers
Research & Development	Approaching full disk space. You predict it might take a few more weeks before a critical shortage occurs.	New file server

Project 2-2

Using your web browser, access *www.novell.com*. This is an exceptionally well-designed site in most respects, and in your career as a network administrator, you should be able to use it to find information fairly quickly. Locate and read about the Client 4.8 for Windows NT/2000 download.

1. Describe how this download helps Microsoft Windows NT/2000 and Novell NetWare to interoperate.

2. Look for a note to Innoculan users—what does it say? (Innoculan is a virus-detection utility.) What should you do to remedy the problem with Innoculan?

Project 2-3

NTT India is an Internet and intranet solutions company. NTT hosts web sites for their clients on their servers. Of course, the servers must have significant uptime and failover protection. Access *www.nttindia.com,* click the Servers link, and answer the following questions:

1. What operating system does NTT use?

2. What components on their servers are hot-swappable?

3. Describe the force-filtered cooling of NTT servers.

4. What type of redundant power system does NTT use?

5. What temperature does NTT maintain in their server room?

6. How does NTT control access to the server room?

Project 2-4

Data Clean Corporation provides cleaning services for controlled environments such as server rooms. Using your web browser, access *www.dataclean.com*. Click the services link, read the web page, and then answer the following questions:

1. Why is it important to have the floor plenum cleaned?
2. What is important about cleaning the floor surfaces?

Project 2-5

The Liebert Corporation provides a variety of environmental control solutions. Using the Liebert web page, find information about air conditioning and airflow.

1. Using your web browser, access *www.liebert.com*.
2. Click the **Computer Rooms** link.
3. Click the **Precision Cooling** link. The Computer Rooms page displays a Precision Cooling column.
4. Click the **precision air conditioning** link.
5. Scroll down to the High Capacity section, and click the **Deluxe System 3–60Hz** link.
6. Under Support Documents, click **Brochure (4pg) – Upflow Applications (R 11/98) – 23KB** and read the document (click **Next** at the bottom to access all the pages).
7. On the second page, which of the airflow methods is specifically designed for a raised floor?
8. Exit the web site and your browser.

Project 2-6

Because halon is being phased out, consider other alternatives for chemical fire-extinguishing needs, such as those manufactured by DuPont.

1. Access *www.dupont.com/fire*.
2. Play the AVI video clip link **Burning Heptanet 10B Pan Extinguished by FE-36**. Although FE-36 is used in portable hand-held fire extinguishers, its effectiveness in extinguishing a fire is similar to the effect of other chemical extinguishers. (Note: this video clip is 1.5 MB, so if your Internet connection is slow, you might have to be patient.)
3. From the *www.dupont.com/fire* page, click the **Alternatives** link (*www.dupont.com/fire/products/index.html*).
4. Click the link for FE-13. What are a few reasons that FE-13 would be good for use in server rooms?

CASE PROJECTS

1. You have started a new job as the manager of network administration for a medium-sized company in Phoenix. This company has had several managers in your position through the years, and each one has favored one operating system over another. As a result, you have several Intel CISC-based computers running several versions of Linux, NetWare 4.2, NetWare 5.1, Windows NT 4.0, and one server running IBM OS/2. Desktop workstations run Windows 95, Windows 98, Windows NT 4.0 Workstation, and IBM OS/2. The company's other office is located in San Francisco and is only a satellite office with no servers. The users in the San Francisco office complain that they must use a dial-up connection to access the Linux server at your office. Your first assigned task is to standardize the entire environment as much as possible. In your opinion, Windows 2000 is easiest from the end-user perspective and also provides effective management tools. What can you do to standardize the operating systems while resolving the San Francisco users' complaint about using a dial-up connection to your office?

2. In your first week on the job described in Case Project #1, you find that there isn't a server room. Instead, as the company grew, each department added their own servers in utility or storage closets. You know that because a server room was not designed into the original building plans, you might not be able to install the server room of your dreams. However, there is a centrally located break room that is not used much because the company has a new cafeteria. You have permission to use this room and have hired a construction company to provide architects and engineers who will help you migrate all servers to the central location. What kinds of requests in terms of physical site conditions, power supplies, disaster planning, and security will you make to the architects and engineers?

3

MOTHERBOARD ARCHITECTURE, PROCESSORS, MEMORY, AND BIOS

> **After reading this chapter and completing the exercises, you will be able to:**
>
> ♦ Explain various motherboard buses
> ♦ Describe how clock frequency affects performance
> ♦ Identify common server processors
> ♦ Identify various types of memory
> ♦ Configure the BIOS and identify common server configuration items

The motherboard provides the system "bus," the transportation medium for data to and from processors, memory, peripherals, and input/output (I/O) devices. Knowing about these server components (and those in Chapter 4) helps you to make educated decisions in the server equipment you procure. The motherboard—sometimes referred to as the system board or backplane—is the "mother of all circuit boards." The processor(s), memory, buses, adapter cards, I/O ports, mass storage—just about every component in the system—are connected directly or indirectly to the motherboard. The various hardware components attached to the motherboard require basic management using a **BIOS (basic input/output system)**, which identifies and confirms correct hardware installation and configuration.

Most readers of this book have had at least some experience with personal computers and might already understand many of the basic hardware components. However, when addressing hardware relating to servers, you must be careful to change perspective. Not only is server hardware more powerful in many respects, but it also includes different features and functions than you might find in a PC.

This chapter outlines the most important factors in assessing server components to help you make informed server purchasing decisions. For budgetary purposes, you might be more interested in building a server on your own instead of purchasing a preassembled server. Although Chapter 6 explains how to install major components, I strongly recommend that you purchase servers as much as possible as pretested turnkey solutions (configured hardware and operating system ready to run right out of the box) from major server vendors. Technicians acquainted with PC workstations might be tempted to use their technical expertise to assemble their own server systems. However, server availability is a high priority, and even the best technician cannot responsibly guarantee the same system uptime as major PC server vendors such as Dell, Compaq, and Hewlett-Packard (HP), which offer server systems with between 99.9% and 99.999% uptime. (Server technicians colloquially refer to this as a certain number of nines. For example, 99.999% uptime is referred to as "five nines" and equals about five minutes of downtime per year.) Some vendors even promise financial compensation if your server fails.

GET ON THE BUS

The bus is to the server what a highway is to a transportation system. The **bus** provides the data path to and from server components such as the processor and memory on the motherboard, the foundation of the computer. The motherboard attaches to the chassis and includes slots, sockets, and other connections for server components. A foundational architectural factor of the motherboard and its components is the bus width, in bits. Motherboard bus width corresponds to individual data wires that transmit data. The more wires a component such as the motherboard has, the more data it can transmit in a given period of time. Current motherboard data bus architecture is either 32 bits wide or 64 bits wide, which you could equate with a 32- or 64-lane data "highway." Of course, the 64-bit data highway will be able to deliver twice the data in the same amount of time as a 32-bit data highway. As this section will explain, a motherboard includes a front side bus, sometimes a back side bus, and three primary I/O expansion buses: Industry Standard Architecture (ISA), Extended ISA (EISA), and Peripheral Components Interconnect (PCI). The speed of each bus is dependent upon the motherboard clock frequency.

Clock Frequency

Each bus and every device that connects to the motherboard bus depends on the clock frequency of the motherboard. **Clock frequency** (sometimes called the clock speed, cycle, or clock cycle) is the number of times in one second that an electrically charged quartz crystal located on the motherboard vibrates (oscillates). Clock frequency is measured in megahertz, a hertz equaling one cycle per second and "mega" meaning million. If a motherboard has a clock frequency of 66 MHz, then it cycles 66 million times per second. (Most new motherboards have a bus clock speed of 100 or 133 MHz.) The importance of the clock speed is that the processor requires at least one cycle (and usually more cycles) for each instruction that it executes. Therefore, the more times the motherboard clock cycles, the more instructions the processor can perform per second. An 800 MHz Pentium processor has about 800

3

million opportunities per second to perform an action, subtracting wait states in which the processor uses empty clock cycles to wait for another instruction or hardware function to complete. Other system components, such as buses attached to expansion slots, also depend upon the clock cycle to determine the speed with which they operate.

 You can increase the computing speed of the processor by increasing voltage to the processor, thereby improving performance. This procedure is known as **overclocking**, a risky process in terms of overall stability and increased temperature. I do not recommend overclocking production servers, but if you want to experiment (at your own risk) on a spare PC, first check into specific overclocking instructions and precautions at *www.tomshardware.com* and *www.overclockers.com*.

This chapter makes no attempt to explain every type of bus, peripheral, and port, because many simply do not apply to current technology or to servers. (Examples include VESA and MCA buses and game ports.) However, several buses apply to PC servers, in particular PCI buses, which are explained in this chapter.

Chipset Function

In early personal computers, the entire system and its components operated on one bus and ran at 4.77 MHz. This fact seems unimportant until you consider the dramatic changes in bus speeds in the computing industry. Various hardware components require differing bus speeds in order to perform well. Faster components can run without waiting for slower devices to complete their tasks, because the devices operate in an independent bus context. If all components continued to run on a single bus as in early PCs, the resulting bottlenecks would significantly defeat computing efficiency.

Using different buses in the system requires a way to divide the motherboard into separate parts. The **chipset** (see Figure 3-1) is a group of motherboard chips that operate at the same speed as the motherboard clock and provide the boundary that divides one bus from another and controls the flow of bus data. Choosing a motherboard is mostly choosing a chipset.

Figure 3-1   The chipset is identified directly on the chip

Although I do not intend to recommend a specific manufacturer over another, I will direct you to Intel's web site at *http://support.intel.com/support/motherboards/server,* which displays a current listing of server motherboards/chipsets. Intel is the primary manufacturer of PC-based server boards, and regardless of the name on the server case, most PC server vendors use Intel chipsets. Other vendors also make chipsets that are compatible with Intel processors, but again, they tend to be low-cost alternatives and often focus on the desktop computer market. I do not address chipsets geared toward desktop client computers, although a small organization can use a desktop PC as an inexpensive entry-level server. For our purposes throughout the remainder of this book, only systems supporting two or more processors shall be considered servers unless stated otherwise. Also, I do not address other chipsets such as those designed for AMD processors because AMD tends to focus on desktop computers with the exception of the AMD Sledgehammer (see the section on processors in this chapter), which is developing a following in the Linux community. Nevertheless, AMD provides excellent low-cost, high-speed processors and is making significant headway into the desktop PC market. For more about AMD products, visit *www.amd.com* and also refer to Course Technology's *Enhanced A+ Guide to Managing and Maintaining Your PC* (ISBN 0-619-03433-5) by Jean Andrews (*www.course.com/pcrepair*).

Hierarchical Bus

PC-based bus systems use what is known as a **hierarchical bus**, because several buses actually comprise the (collective) "bus," each running at different speeds and with the slower buses hierarchically structured beneath the faster buses. Dividing the bus into the front side bus, PCI bus, and ISA buses allows slower components to operate without negatively impacting the faster components. (There is also a back side bus, which we

3

will discuss later.) Intel architecture utilizes a North Bridge, South Bridge, and Super I/O chipset (see Figure 3-2) to divide the PCI bus from fastest to slowest and facilitate communication between buses in the order listed:

- **Front side bus**—A 64-bit data pathway that the processor uses to communicate with main memory and the graphics card through the North Bridge chipset. The **North Bridge** chipset divides the processor bus from the PCI bus, and manages data traffic between the South Bridge (see below) and between components on the front side bus and PCI bus. This core bus runs at motherboard clock speed. The front side bus is also known by several other names, including processor bus, memory bus, and system bus.

- **PCI bus**—A 32-bit data pathway for high-speed I/O for expansion adapter cards, USB, and IDE ports. The CMOS (defined later in this chapter) and system clock also connect to the PCI bus. The PCI bus connects to both the North Bridge and the South Bridge. The **South Bridge** separates the PCI bus from the ISA bus. (See more about the PCI bus later in this chapter.)

- **ISA bus**—A 16-bit data pathway for slower expansion adapter cards and the floppy disk, mouse, keyboard, serial and parallel ports, and the BIOS via a Super I/O chip, which mitigates the need for a separate expansion card for each of the aforementioned items. The South Bridge connects to the ISA bus, which is the end of the hierarchical bus chain. (More about ISA follows.)

It might be helpful for you to know the throughput capabilities of the following types of ports and buses, because many times you will need to transfer data through these ports, even as a temporary solution. For example, you might need to transfer diagnostic data from one server to another or to a laptop through a special serial cable known as a **null modem cable**. This type of cable uses special crossed wires to simulate a modem presence, allowing data to travel between the two hosts. In addition, many devices such as UPS systems are now connecting to the server via a USB port instead of a serial port, and new external hard disk storage devices can connect through a FireWire (IEEE 1394) port. Table 3-1 shows the various interfaces and their maximum throughput from the slowest to the fastest.

Table 3-1   Throughput Capabilities of Ports and Buses

Port or Bus	Maximum Throughput
Serial	230 or 460 Kbps with a 16650 UART*
Parallel	500 KBps to 2MBps with ECP**
USB 1.1	12 Mbps
USB 2.0	480 Mbps
IEEE 1394 (FireWire)	200 Mbps (though future specifications will go as high as 1 Gbps)
SCSI-3 (Ultra320)***	320 MBps

 * UART is Universal Asynchronous Receiver/Transmitter, a special serial port chip that increases throughput.
 ** ECP is Enhanced Capabilities Port, a high-speed, bidirectional parallel port.
*** See more about SCSI in Chapter 5.

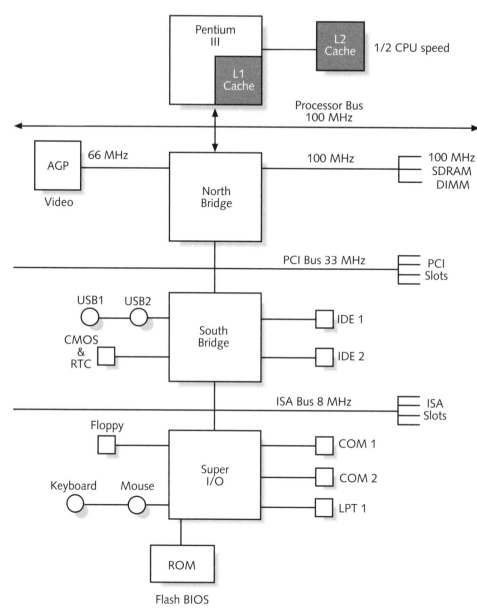

Figure 3-2   Typical North Bridge/South Bridge motherboard architecture

Accelerated Hub Architecture

Intel implements a new hub architecture to replace the tried-and-true North Bridge/South Bridge architecture, which connects the various buses described above through the PCI bus. The **accelerated hub architecture** connects buses to the system bus independently through a dedicated interface to the PCI bus, yielding throughput of up to 266 MBps—twice as much throughput as 33 MHz PCI. The independent buses do not share the PCI bus, thus increasing PCI bus bandwidth available to PCI-connected devices. Also, the hub architecture improves traffic throughput between slower I/O buses and the system bus.

In an accelerated hub architecture (see Figure 3-3), the North Bridge is called the **Graphics Memory Controller Hub (GMCH)**, and the South Bridge is called the **I/O Controller Hub (ICH)**. This architecture allows devices directly connected to the ICH (such as high-speed ATA-66 and ATA-100 disk controllers and USB 2.0 interfaces) much greater throughput.

North Bridge/South Bridge architecture is common on Intel 44*X* series chipsets, such as the 440LX, and the accelerated hub architecture is the current architecture in Intel 8*XX* series chipsets, such as the 840NX.

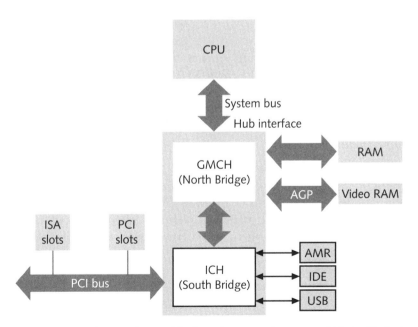

Figure 3-3   The accelerated hub architecture improves I/O traffic between slower I/O buses and the faster system bus

BUS INTERFACES

The front side bus, ISA bus, and PCI bus are only useful if there is a way to connect devices to each respective bus. The front side bus uses a slot or socket on the motherboard to connect the processors and memory. The ISA and PCI buses use expansion slots. Although PCI is quickly becoming the only slot available on new motherboards, you might still see the older ISA/EISA slots on some motherboards, so we briefly discuss them as well.

ISA

Industry Standard Architecture (ISA) was originally the AT (advanced technology) bus, developed by IBM (not to be confused with the AT motherboard). Devices connect to an ISA bus through an ISA expansion slot, which is 16 bits wide and accommodates both 16-bit devices and older 8-bit devices. The ISA bus operates at only 8.33 MHz and is capable of transfer speeds up to 8 MBps. This performance seems slow compared to the clock speed of the motherboard. However, most ISA devices (a modem, for example) are even slower, so the slot performance does not hinder performance of the ISA device. You might see some older servers with ISA expansion slots, but newer server motherboards (and workstations or home computers) do not usually include them. Motherboards still include the ISA bus (not the expansion slots) to accept a Super I/O chip as the means to connect slower devices such as the serial and parallel port, floppy controller, keyboard, and mouse.

EISA

The 32-bit **Extended ISA (EISA)** bus provides backward compatibility with older ISA devices and a maximum bandwidth of about 33 MBps. Even though EISA performance is better than ISA, most motherboards do not include EISA buses any more because most manufacturers engineer devices that are compatible with the better-performing PCI bus interface.

PCI

The purpose of the **Peripheral Components Interface (PCI) bus** is to interface high-speed devices with the system bus so that slower devices do not create a bottleneck. For example, an older computer with a 16-bit ISA, 8 MHz video card would create a significant bottleneck for the rest of the system (mostly the processor) because it can only transfer a maximum of 8 MBps, and would use clock cycles that could otherwise be used by other devices. The processor would have to wait for the ISA video card to complete its task before being able to use the system bus. Using the bridge or hub architecture, faster PCI devices can use the PCI bus, reducing or removing the bottleneck. Continuing the video card example, a PCI video card uses a 32-bit 33 MHz card for much faster performance and better throughput at 132 MBps. Other devices such as network cards and hard disk controllers can also take advantage of this improved performance.

As for usability, one of the most significant benefits of PCI is that a Plug and Play operating system such as Windows 95 or later can automatically detect and assign system resources to new devices. Other buses such as ISA required BIOS configuration and/or manual configuration of jumpers and switches on devices. PCI 2.2 is the current specification of PCI, and PCI-X is soon to supercede it (see below).

The most authoritative web site on PCI is *www.pcisig.com*. However, you can only view limited information unless you either pay a fee for each download or pay a hefty annual membership fee. This site is geared toward developers who need to know specific electrical details about PCI so that they can develop products using the PCI architecture.

The PCI standard is compatible not only with PC platforms, but also with Macintosh, Sun, and Alpha platforms using platform-specific chipsets.

PCI-X

PCI-X (**PCI-eXtended**) is actually Addendum 1.0 to the PCI 2.2 specification. The basic advantage to PCI-X is simple: much higher bandwidth and correspondingly higher performance. PCI-X utilizes 64 bits and up to 133 MHz, yielding a maximum bandwidth of 1064 MBps. Devices that are designed according to the PCI-X standard will be able to utilize the full maximum available bandwidth, provided no other processes or devices contend for the same bandwidth. Also, relaxed ordering arranges real-time audio and video instructions in an efficient order instead of the first in/first out (FIFO) method of previous PCI versions.

Relaxed ordering could be a significant advantage if you use servers to deliver multimedia content to the web, for example.

Other efficiency enhancements to the PCI-X bus help to free up bandwidth and reduce wait states, with the net result of a nearly tenfold performance increase over 32 bit, 33 MHz PCI. Motherboard designers divide the PCI-X bandwidth in one of several slot combinations for each PCI-X bus segment: one 133 MHz slot, two 100 MHz slots, or four 66 MHz slots. Table 3-2 shows PCI and PCI-X performance statistics.

Table 3-2 PCI Performance

Data Path Width (bits)	Bus Speed (MHz)	Max Bandwidth (MBps)
32	33	133.33
32	66	266.66
64	33	266.66
64	66	533.33
64	133 (PCI=X)	1066.66 (PCI=X)

Bus Mastering

Most devices utilize the processor to control the flow of information through the bus. As a result, a processor laden with the task of controlling requests from various devices is not as available to process more important productivity functions, slowing down overall performance. In PCI architecture, hardware designers can use **bus mastering** to bypass the processor and directly access memory, resulting in an overall increase in processor performance. Bus mastering is actually a form of direct memory access (DMA) known as first-party DMA. "First party" refers to the device directly controlling memory access, and compares to a third-party DMA transfer using a motherboard DMA controller. Also, bus mastering devices can communicate among themselves over the bus without CPU intervention. Video adapters and disk controllers commonly utilize bus mastering.

PCI Interrupts

Devices issue requests for system resources using an ISA-based interrupt request. An **interrupt request (IRQ)** is an electrical signal that obtains the CPU's attention in order to handle an event immediately, although the processor might queue the request behind other requests. Most devices utilize one of several IRQs on the motherboard. However, there are a limited number of available interrupts, and the number of devices is often greater than the available IRQs. The BIOS utilizes the PCI bus to assign special **PCI interrupts** to PCI devices using the designation INTA#, INTB#, INTC#, and INTD# (sometimes known simply as #1-#4). Single-function PCI cards always receive INTA# according to PCI specifications. Chips or cards with multiple functions can receive assignments for INTB# through INTD# as needed. The PCI interrupts map to one of four corresponding ISA IRQs, usually IRQ 9-12. For example, if you have three single-function PCI cards, they all receive INTA#; however, each device still requires a unique ISA IRQ mapping. Functionally, the result is not that much different than if each device was a standard ISA device in the first place, because each device still receives unique, nonshareable IRQs. The benefit of the PCI interrupt appears when no more ISA IRQ addresses are available. With no more available IRQs, the PCI interrupt utilizes another PCI function known as **PCI steering**, in which the PCI interrupt assigns two or more PCI devices the same ISA IRQ.

PCI Hot Swap

PCI hot swap, otherwise known as **PCI hot plug**, means that you can add, remove, or replace PCI devices without first powering down the server. Note that even though it sounds like you can just take off the cover and rip out a card, many devices and PCI slots require you to follow specific steps. For example, most servers require you to turn off the power to the slot using management software (as with many Dell and HP systems) or using a switch or button (as with Compaq systems) before removing the device (see Figure 3-4). The power switch is often a button located near the actual slot. After you turn off the power to the slot, then remove and replace a card, you can turn the power back on. If the NOS is Plug and Play compatible (such as Windows 2000), it should be able to detect the new device and load (or request) the appropriate drivers. Hot swapping is truly a lifesaver in servers that require 24/7 operation.

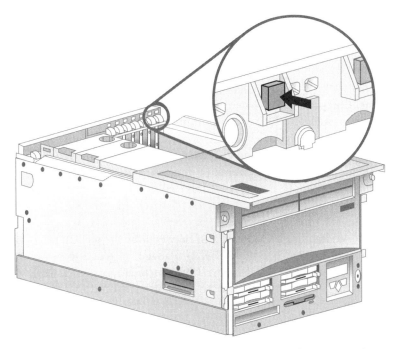

Figure 3-4 To turn off power to a PCI slot, use a button (as shown) or management software

Peer PCI Bus

The **peer PCI bus** is usually a server-specific function that both increases available PCI bandwidth and expands the number of PCI expansion cards from the usual limit of four with a minimal impact on overall system bus bandwidth. This architecture usually involves dual peer PCI buses and two North Bridges, which connect to a primary PCI bus and a secondary PCI bus. PCI expansion slots connect to each respective PCI bus and are either integrated into the motherboard or installed as add–on daughtercards. Many motherboards use this expanded functionality not only to increase the number of expansion slots, but also to offer flexible PCI bus width and speed. For example, Bus #1 could offer four standard 32-bit 33 MHz PCI slots, while Bus #2 offers two additional 64-bit 66 MHz PCI slots, and devices in both buses can simultaneously access their respective buses. Peer PCI slots allow the administrator to load balance the system. For example, if you have two high-speed network cards for which you expect a great deal of traffic, you could place each one on a separate PCI bus to balance the load. That way, they can each handle I/O without waiting for the other to complete a task on the PCI bus. You can extend the same load-balancing benefits to other devices such as high-throughput SCSI controllers. High-end servers such as the HP Netserver running Windows 2000 Datacenter Server offer up to 32 processors and 96 PCI slots!

Compare peer PCI slots with the bridged PCI bus, in which an additional PCI-to-PCI bridge is inserted below the North Bridge. This only increases the number of available slots, but does not offer better PCI load balancing because all expansion slots actually use a common data path to the system bus. In the peer PCI architecture, separate buses independently communicate with the system bus for more efficient load balancing.

I2O

Intelligent Input/Output (I2O) is an initiative to improve I/O performance via an I2O processor and driver model. The I2O driver communicates with the I2O processor, which is located on the device itself, as a separate add-in card, or integrated into the motheboard. Even on the PCI bus, which is designed to relieve traffic from the system bus, frequent PCI interrupts to the processor slow overall performance. With I2O, devices intelligently perform much of the processing function on their own. Also, I2O devices can communicate among themselves when necessary instead of using the processor to manage their communication. The I2O driver utilizes a "split driver" model in which the Operating System Module (OSM) handles I/O interaction between the device and the operating system, and the Hardware Device Module (HDM) manages interaction between hardware controllers and I2O-compatible devices. The I2O specification goes a long way toward developing a common standard that hardware and software vendors can use to simplify and reduce the costly, time-consuming process of driver development. Most I2O-enabled devices are network cards or storage devices because they typically require the highest I/O levels in the system. The I2O specification can work with OS/2, but don't expect to see great strides in I2O technology on the OS/2 platform. Windows NT 4.0 initially offered no participation with I2O; however, Windows 2000 and NetWare 5.x fully support the I2O specification.

The latest I2O specification (2.0) includes several new features, the most significant of which are:

- 64-bit addressing accommodates increased memory capabilities for newer CPUs.

- Hot-plug capability lets you change the adapter without shutting down the entire system.

■ Direct memory access (DMA) allows direct access to memory instead of first utilizing the processor. High-speed I2O RAID disk controllers in particular benefit from DMA.

Accelerated Graphics Port (AGP)

3

The **Accelerated Graphics Port (AGP)** is designed to relieve the system bus and CPU of traffic and processing. Producing graphics is a very complex function, requiring memory usage and significant processing power. In the past, graphics functions used portions of main memory and depended on the main CPU to process much of the graphics load. Later, as video adapters matured, they performed much of their own graphics processing by adding memory chips and onboard processors specially designed for graphics functions. Nevertheless, the graphics card would frequently request attention from the system bus and the processor.

The AGP specification introduced in 1996 utilizes a single AGP slot on standard motherboards, and further relieves the processor and system bus of video burdens. The slot is brown in color and fits only AGP cards—so you can't accidentally insert any other type of card into the slot.

 TIP The AGP specification (*www.agpforum.org*) lists a known problem with AGP cards coming loose from the sockets. Because they are set further away from the back of the computer than other slots, there is a tendency for AGP cards to loosen from vibration, as might occur during shipment. When you receive a new system with an installed AGP card, be sure to firmly reseat the card. Some vendors also include an additional AGP retention device.

The initial specification offered both a 1X and 2X mode, representing a performance multiplier of 2, doubling the effective clock speed of a 1X card. Later, a 4X mode appeared; however, most cards are still produced at the 2X speed. There is also an AGP Pro spec, which uses a longer slot and more pins for higher voltage. In November 2000 the AGP 8X was introduced, but at this writing there are no cards available for it. Table 3-3 shows AGP performance statistics.

Table 3-3 AGP Performance

AGP Mode	Effective Clock Speed MHz (AGP Mode x 66 MHz)	Throughput (MBps)
1X	66	266
2X	133	533
4X	266	1066
8X	533	2133

AGP has an immediate and obvious benefit to overall system performance; however, AGP provides the greatest benefit to graphics-intensive computing, such as PC gaming, computer-aided drafting (CAD), graphic design, and other high-end graphics applications. Some servers come with AGP, particularly dual-processor machines that could just as easily serve as high-end graphics workstations. High-end servers normally do not include AGP because it is not necessary and adds a potential point of failure. Manufacturers try to ensure highest availability for servers by not including complex graphics features. You are not likely to be playing PC games on the server, so there is really no need for AGP graphics. High-end servers usually include a motherboard-integrated video adapter at 1024 × 768 screen resolution and only 256 colors. By graphics standards, this is video from the late 1980s. However, its simplicity avoids potential graphics problems on the server. Also, it does not matter from the administrator's perspective that the graphics are unimpressive, because most day-to-day server administration is actually done remotely on a desktop PC workstation (which probably does have snazzy graphics).

PROCESSORS

It is not within the scope of this book to exhaustively describe every processor known to the PC world, starting with the 8088 pioneer of the Intel platform and finishing with the latest Pentium. You should, however, be aware of the characteristics of common processors found in servers today. Another reason for not covering earlier processors is that you are less likely to find older processors in servers, because administrators tend to update server processing power more frequently than desktop workstation processors. This makes sense because business applications and data on servers become larger and more complex much faster than on desktops, and because server performance affects multiple users. Therefore, a server upgrade yields a higher return on investment than a workstation upgrade, which benefits only a single user. Also, this section focuses on Intel processors for good reasons. First, PC servers by definition involve Intel or Intel-based processors. Otherwise, they would be something like a RISC processor. Also, you will find Intel processors in more PC servers. An Intel competitor, AMD, also makes Intel-compatible processors. However, AMD largely aims its efforts at cost-effective desktop PCs and workstations. We will discuss AMD to some degree in relation to servers because its latest product, a 64-bit processor, is aimed at high-end workstations and low-end servers. In fact, Compaq has started to make servers using the AMD processor.

Processor Speed

Processor speed is a measure in MHz of the number of opportunities per second that the processor can execute an action. Recall that each clock cycle represents an opportunity for the processor to do something. The processor architecture design uses a multiplier methodology to provide the processor's speed. For example, a Pentium III 600 MHz processor installed on a motherboard with a system bus speed of 100 MHz uses a multiplier of 6 (100 MHz system bus speed × multiplier factor of 6 = 600).

Cache Memory

Cache memory is a small amount of memory that stores recently or frequently used program code or data, reducing the latency involved in retrieving data from RAM or disk. Cache memory appears in a number of places on the server, including the hard disk, CD-ROM, and processor. Processors use two types of cache memory: L1 (level 1) and L2 (level 2).

L1 Cache

L1 cache is a small amount of memory (usually 32–64 KB) that provides extremely fast access to its data because of its proximity to the processor and because it runs at the same speed as the processor itself—not at the speed of the motherboard. For example, a Pentium III 850 running on a 100 MHz motherboard utilizes an L1 cache that also runs at 850 MHz, not 100 MHz. L1 cache provides an advantage to system performance, because the processor can access data directly from the L1 cache instead of having to fetch the data from memory, which is slower, or from the hard disk, which is painfully slower. Also, if the data in the L1 cache is the result of a processing action such as a complex calculation, retrieval from the L1 cache conserves valuable processor utilization because a recalculation is not necessary. While the size of the cache seems too small to be of any use, it is a great benefit because frequently used chunks of code or data are constantly served from extremely fast L1 cache.

L2 Cache

L2 cache provides the same basic benefits as L1 cache, but it is larger, ranging from 256 KB to 2 MB. In the past, L2 cache was not stored on the processor die, but was instead stored on a separate chip inside the processor housing. This orientation is known as **discrete L2 cache**. The data path used to access the L2 cache was called the **back side bus**, and it ran at half the processor speed. For example, a Pentium III 450 MHz processor utilizes a 512 KB L2 cache running at 225 MHz. Some Pentium III 500's run a 512 KB L2 cache at half the processor speed and some run a 256 KB L2 cache at full processor speed. Most processors after the Pentium III 500 locate the L2 cache directly on the processor die (similar to the L1 cache) and run it at full processor speed. This **Advanced Transfer Cache (ATC)** is 256 bits wide and eliminates the need for a back side bus.

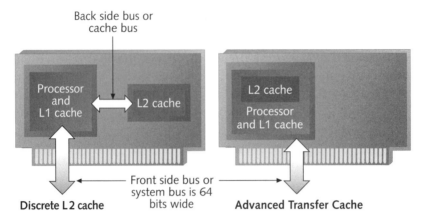

Figure 3-5   Older architectures separate the L2 cache from the processor (discrete L2 cache), while newer processors include L2 cache on the same die (ATC)

Server Processors

In existing servers, you are likely to find processors no slower than Pentium II 233 MHz or Pentium Pro 200 MHz. Servers also utilize an additional processor model not typically found in home or standard desktop PCs—the Pentium II Xeon and Pentium III Xeon (pronounced "zeon"; see Figure 3-6). Xeon processors differ from standard Pentium II or III models in the following respects:

- Type of enclosure
- Cache size
- Cache speed
- Amount of addressable memory
- SMP (symmetric multiprocessing)

Figure 3-6   The Intel Pentium III Xeon

The Xeon uses a Slot 2 single-edge contact (SEC) enclosure and is larger than a Pentium III in order to accommodate the internal board with more L2 ATC memory—up to 2 MB of error checking and correction memory (see more about error correcting code (ECC) later in this chapter). The Xeon uses a 256-bit data path to the L2 cache—a four-fold improvement over the standard Pentium II/III 64-bit data path. On the Xeon, both the L1 and L2 cache can run in parallel, offering simultaneous access and further reducing latency. The Xeon increases the number of fill buffers, the interface between the CPU and main memory, from four to eight, and increases bus queue entries, which hold outstanding bus and memory operations, from four to eight.

 The Xeon processor and 2 MB cache add up to 140 million transistors! This fact is more than novelty, because with more transistors comes more heat, so you will have to ensure adequate cooling for this processor.

The amount of memory that the processor can use is a factor of the processor bit width and motherboard chipset. Typically, the processor can address more memory than the motherboard allows. A 32-bit processor can address 4 GB of memory (2^{32} = 4,294,967,296 bytes, or 4 GB). In the home desktop and corporate workstation, you are unlikely to find a motherboard with physical space and chipset design to allow for this much memory. Server processor design, however, is changing to allow substantial amounts of addressable memory by modifying the motherboard and/or chipset. Intel Pentium II Xeon and later processors let the processor utilize 36 bits to address memory using Intel's

Physical Address Extension (PAE) feature, allowing up to 64 GB of addressable memory (2^{36} = 68,719,476,736, or 64 GB). While even 4 GB sounds like an immense amount of memory (and it is), large, real-time server applications such as online transaction processing (OLTP) and e-commerce require large amounts of data to reside in RAM for fast access.

A Pentium III motherboard configuration accepts either single or dual processors. A Xeon SMP configuration can use up to four processors, though by adding another processor bus (often called a **mezzanine bus**), eight processors are possible, and some manufacturers engineer buses that can use up to 132 processors (though four or eight is more common).

A dual-processor system is known as "2-way," four processors as "4-way," eight processors as "8-way," and so on.

Except for the differences outlined earlier, Xeon processors at the core are no different than Pentium II/III brethren of the same speed. If your server needs do not include significant caching power and more than two processors, you can save a substantial amount of money by using the fastest available Pentium III instead of the Xeon.

Characteristics of Intel Pentium server processors appear in Table 3-4.

Table 3-4   Intel Server Processors

Processor	Processor Speed (MHz)	L1 Cache (KB)	L2 Cache (KB)	System Bus Speed (MHz)
Pentium Pro	200	16	256, 512, 1 MB	60, 66
Pentium II	233, 266, 333, 350, 366, 400, 450	32	256, 512	66, 100
Pentium II Xeon	400, 450	32	512, 1 MB, 2 MB	100
Pentium III	400, 450, 500, 533, 550, 600, 650, 667, 700, 733, 750, 800, 850, 866, 933, 1 GHz, 1.3 GHz	32	256, 512	100, 133
Pentium III Xeon	550, 600, 667, 733, 800, 866, 933, 1 GHz	32	256, 1 MB, 2 MB	100, 133

Notably absent from Table 3-3 and the general discussion to follow is the Celeron processor, because it is designed for the low-cost home PC market. Intel reduces the cost by utilizing a smaller cache and cheaper packaging, although the core Celeron II/III is the same core as the basic Pentium II/III. Also absent are the Classic (original) Pentium and the Pentium MMX because it is unlikely that you will find these in servers—although MMX video technology is still present in server processors. The Pentium 4 processor offers significant performance benefits over the Pentium III; however, it is not capable of SMP and is geared toward the high-end workstation or demanding home user. Intel plans to release an SMP-capable Pentium 4 Xeon (code name "Foster") at 1.7 GHz.

64-Bit Processors

As with motherboard buses and adapter cards, the bit width on a processor correlates to the amount of data that it can transmit. Each bit corresponds to a wire connector through the socket or slot for data transmission between the processor and the motherboard. Most Pentium processors function internally at 64 bits, and then the data results are passed on to the 32-bit external bus interface.

Most server processors use 32-bit bus interfaces, but new processors from Intel and AMD are 64-bit processors both internally and externally. Although these processors are not in final form at this writing, they are likely to affect the future of PC server computing very soon.

Intel Itanium

The 64-bit Intel Itanium using Intel's IA-64 technology represents a departure from the 32-bit x86 Intel architecture, and performs optimally with 64-bit operating systems (Windows 2000 will be ported to 64 bit) and applications. Co-developed with HP, the Itanium depends upon new compiler technology. (A **compiler** translates a high-level programming language into the lowest language the computer can understand, machine language.) In addition, 32-bit applications running on the Itanium processor utilize the Itanium's hardware emulation to adapt the 32-bit instructions for the 64-bit architecture. Because of the translation process, 32-bit applications will usually run more slowly on the IA-64 than on fast 32-bit Pentium III Xeon processors. The Itanium processor runs on Intel's upcoming 460GX chipset.

One of the reasons many large organizations will migrate to the Itanium 64-bit platform (IA-64) is not so much the core processor speed as the 64-bit memory addressability. With 64 bits, the processor can address up to 18 billion GB (2^{64} = 18,446,744,073,709,551,616 bytes). This seems like an absurd amount of memory, but at least it doesn't appear as if there will ever be a memory ceiling again, and memory-hungry applications such as databases will make good use of any available memory. In addition to a large L2 cache, the Itanium also supports a 2 or 4 MB Level 3 motherboard cache (much like L2 cache before ATC).

The IA-64 architecture uses Explicitly Parallel Instruction set Computing (EPIC), allowing the processor to simultaneously process as many as 20 operations. New motherboard designs will take advantage of IA-64 architecture to also allow handling of up to 64 bits of data at a time. This type of functionality will be an especially powerful feature when applying 64-bit processing to encryption schemes such as RSA encryption/decryption. Intel estimates that an IA-64 processor will outperform the fastest RISC-based processors by a factor of eight or more.

AMD Sledgehammer

The AMD Sledgehammer (built on the AMD Athlon core) is also a 64-bit processor, but there is otherwise little similarity between the Itanium and the Sledgehammer (or "Hammer"). AMD decided to extend Intel's original x86 architecture in the Hammer design with AMD's new x86-64 architecture. In fact, 32-bit operating systems and applications can run on the Hammer without complicated hardware emulation, resulting in minimal performance overhead. This strategy could prove to be a wise marketing move for AMD, because few enterprises will be able to switch all operating systems and applications to 64-bit overnight. The Hammer allows organizations to gradually merge 64-bit functionality into their existing framework. Unfortunately, Microsoft has committed to creating 64-bit operating systems and applications only for the Intel IA-64 platform, not the AMD x86-64 platform. The Linux community, however, already has a 64-bit version of Linux under way, and Sun Microsystems has also announced that it will port Solaris UNIX to the x86-64 platform. AMD is developing a new Lightning Data Transport (LDT) system bus with throughput as high as 6.4 GBps.

MEMORY

Many types of memory have been available in PCs and servers over the past few decades, but this section describes only the types of memory most likely to be found in servers today. Desktop PCs and servers share many of the same memory characteristics, but servers often have additional memory features, such as registered memory and ECC memory. Several **dynamic RAM (DRAM)** memory chips are installed on a printed circuit board (PCB), which is collectively referred to as a module. DRAM is dynamic random access memory—referred to as dynamic because the information requires continuous electrical refresh, or else the data can become corrupt or lost.

SIMM Modules

You will probably find SIMMs (single inline memory modules) only on older servers. The original SIMM was 8 bits wide (plus one optional parity bit) and used 30 pins to connect to its slot on the motherboard. However, you won't find these older modules in servers. Instead, you are more likely to find SIMMs with a data path of 32 bits (plus four optional parity bits) with 72 pins (see Figure 3-7). The physical SIMM module has gold or tin contacts at the bottom. Although the contact appears both on the front and back, it is really a single contact (hence the *single* in SIMM).

Be careful not to identify a memory module as a SIMM because it has memory chips on one side only or a DIMM (see later in this chapter) because it has memory chips on both sides. It is the contacts on the bottom that differentiate a SIMM from a DIMM.

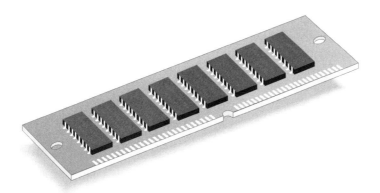

Figure 3-7   A 72-pin SIMM

SIMMs are rated according to the time it takes to retrieve data from memory in nanoseconds (ns), which is one billionth of a second. The typical SIMM is 50 ns, 60 ns, or 70 ns, and older SIMMs can be 80 ns. Even memory running at 60 ns is currently considered slow in light of faster SDRAM DIMMs, described later in this chapter.

EDO

SIMMs and early DIMMs (see next topic) are known for the Extended Data Out (EDO) RAM technology (sometimes called "hyper page mode"), which relates to locations in memory known as memory addresses. A memory address references rows and columns. Instead of providing only the exact location requested, EDO can send the entire row address so that subsequent references to the same row require only a column lookup, saving time. This functionality is the same as an older technology known as Fast Page Mode (FPM) RAM, and also adds the ability to eliminate a 10 ns delay prior to issuing the next requested memory address.

DIMM Modules

DIMMs (dual inline memory modules) dramatically improve memory performance over SIMMs by expanding the module to 64 bits (nonparity) or 72 bits (parity or ECC) using 168 pins (see Figure 3-8). The contacts on both sides of the module are separate (hence the *dual* in DIMM). Recall that the more bits available for the data, the more data that can be processed in a given period of time. Because a DIMM uses 64 bits (instead of 32, like a SIMM), it yields a performance increase.

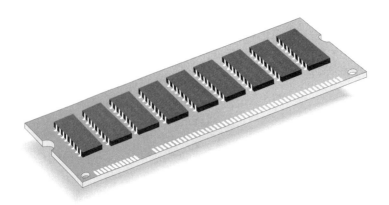

Figure 3-8 A 168-pin DIMM

SDRAM

Closely associated with a DIMM is **SDRAM (synchronous dynamic RAM)**, because a DIMM is the physical platform of SDRAM. SDRAM removes the FPM and EDO DRAM signal-controlled bottleneck that emerged as buses faster than 66 MHz appeared. At 60–80 ns, the processor would request information faster than memory could serve it over the bus. SDRAM operates at clock speed; if the system bus is 100 MHz, then SDRAM matches that frequency, which functionally operates at about 10 ns. SDRAM memory is referred to with a PCXXX, where XXX is the bus speed for which the memory is designed. For example, PC100 refers to memory designed with a rated speed for use in 100 MHz motherboards. However, manufacturers actually make SDRAM run at 125 MHz on a 100 MHz bus for added margin because of extremely tight nanosecond timing. SDRAM is also available at 133 MHz at about 7.5 ns. Expect even faster SDRAM to match increasing speeds of newer buses. To identify the speed in nanoseconds upon visual inspection of the memory chip, look at the digits at the end of the product number. You should see 10 for 10 ns, 8 for 8 ns, and so on. Table 3-5 shows common SDRAM speeds.

Table 3-5 SDRAM Speed

Speed in ns	Manufactured Speed in MHz	Rated Speed in MHz
15	66	PC66
10	100	PC66
8	125	PC100
7.5	133	PC133

RDRAM

RDRAM (Rambus DRAM) is an invention of Rambus Technology. Rambus does not actually manufacture memory, but it developed the technology and charges royalties against memory manufacturers. RDRAM memory chips fit on a narrow, 16-bit-wide RIMM memory module. (RIMM is not an acronym; it's a Rambus-patented name). RDRAM provides extremely fast 800 MHz internal clock speed on a 400 MHz bus, because data is transferred on both the leading and trailing edge of each clock cycle. This adds up to 1.6 GB throughput (16 bits $\times$ 800 MHz / 8 = 1.6 GB). Intel has expressed the most interest in RDRAM, making it the memory of choice in the 820 chipset for PC desktop platforms, the 850 series for Pentium 4 platforms, and the 840 chipset for high-end workstation and server platforms. However, because of the licensing royalty and tight production tolerances, other chipsets (such as AMD-based chipsets) avoid RDRAM, preferring DDR SDRAM instead (see next topic). The RDRAM data path must travel through each RIMM from beginning to end, which adds a delay when data exits the modules. Compare this to DIMMs, with parallel connections to the motherboard, which allow independent data throughput for each DIMM. Because of the unique data circuit of RDRAM, empty RIMM sockets must be filled with a C-RIMM, a device that has no memory but provides continuity to complete the memory data path. The RIMM is uniquely identifiable because you cannot see the actual memory chips, as with other memory types. Instead, an aluminum sheath known as a "heat spreader" covers the RDRAM to help diffuse high heat levels brought on by the fast access and transfer speeds.

 This fact won't help you run your servers, but it's interesting that RDRAM has been around long before its implementation in the PC—it started as proprietary memory for the Nintendo 64!

DDR SDRAM

Double data rate SDRAM (DDR SDRAM) is the next generation of SDRAM, and also uses a 64-bit DIMM with future plans for a 128-bit DIMM. DDR SDRAM (or SDRAM II), like SDRAM, is synchronous with the system clock. However, DDR SDRAM transfers data twice per clock cycle, similar to RDRAM, but at a lower cost because DDR SDRAM is an open standard charging no royalties. If the bus is 133 MHz, DDR SDRAM transfers data at 266 MHz. In addition, it retains the data pathway of DIMMs, offering faster data transfer from the actual DIMM to the bus with parallel construction, as opposed to the continuity requirement of RDRAM.

Table 3-6 summarizes the memory technology of the various types of RAM.

Table 3-6   RAM Memory Technologies

Memory Technology	Calculation of Throughput	Data Throughput
RDRAM	16 bits × 400 MHz /8	800 MBps
RDRAM	16 bits × 800 MHz /8	1.6 GBps
SDRAM on 100 MHz bus	64 × 100 MHz /8	400 MBps
SDRAM on 133 MHz bus	64 × 133 MHz /8	532 MBps
DDR SDRAM on 133 MHz bus	64 bits × 266 MHz	1064 MBps
DDR SDRAM on 166 MHz bus	128 bits × 332 MHz	2656 MBps

Interleaving

Interleaving allows memory access between two or more memory banks and/or boards to occur alternately, minimizing wait states. For interleaving among banks on the same board, you must completely fill the first bank, and then completely fill the second bank with memory that is identical in size and speed. For example, if you have two banks of memory with four slots each, Bank A and Bank B, and Bank A has 256 MB RAM in each slot totaling 1 GB, then Bank B must have exactly the same memory configuration (see Figure 3-9).

If you use larger memory configurations, such as with servers that have separate dedicated memory boards, you can interleave not only among banks on a board, but also among the boards. This configuration also requires you to configure RAM pairs identically. To interleave boards, each pair on one board must exactly match the corresponding pair on the other board (see Figure 3-10). See more about your vendor's specific interleaving requirements. For example, HP has several other considerations for their Netserver Lxr8000 servers (*www.netserver.hp.com*—search for board-to-board interleaving)

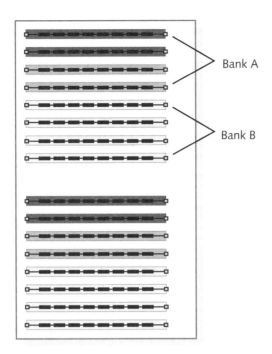

Figure 3-9   Interleaving between banks of memory—Bank A and Bank B must be filled identically

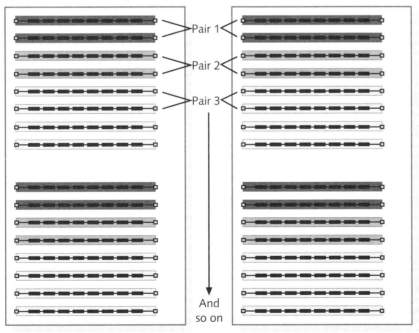

Figure 3-10   Interleaving between boards of memory—corresponding pairs between boards must be filled identically

Interleaving configurations are described in an X-way format, where X is the number of interleaved banks in use. For example, if you have two memory boards with two memory banks, you have four-way interleaving (2 boards $\times$ 2 banks = 4-way).

Buffered and Registered Memory

Buffered memory is a function of FPM or EDO memory, and is an older memory technology. The purpose of both buffered and **registered memory** (which is more common in current computers) is to re-drive (amplify) the signal entering the module. Buffered or registered modules, which have a synonymous function, also assist the chipset in handling the larger electrical load when the system has a lot of installed memory, allowing the module to include more memory chips, which is one reason that servers often use registered modules. (With desktop PCs, SIMMs are likely to be unbuffered, because the chipset manages the buffering function.) You find registered memory on servers or high-end workstations, but rarely on a desktop PC. Registered memory also enacts a deliberate pause of one clock cycle in the module to ensure that all communication from the chipset arrives properly. Registered memory is useful on heavily loaded server memory, and was designed for SIMMs containing 32 or more chips.

Error Correcting Code (ECC)

Servers commonly use **error correcting code (ECC)** SDRAM. Although error correction is more expensive and involves a slight performance penalty, it is well worth it on a server, where data integrity is critical and other high-performing system components help make up for memory latency. ECC calculates check bits and appends them to the data during memory writes. For memory reads, ECC decodes the appended check bits and compares the write and read check bits. If there is a discrepancy in the check bits, then an error has occurred, and the NOS can be notified. If only a single bit error occurs, ECC can correct the error, but ECC cannot correct the more rare 2-, 3-, or 4-bit errors (multiple bit errors).

 Some complex forms of ECC can detect and correct multiple bit errors, but at this point they are not common.

To find out more about specific memory modules, or to order memory for your servers, check the following web sites:

- *www.crucial.com*
- *www.micron.com*
- *www.kingston.com*
- *www.pny.com*

CMOS, BIOS, AND POST

The computer needs to have a way of finding its bearings—that is, it requires a means to locate, identify, and configure the various hardware components in the system. Hardware settings apply to two basic stages: first when you turn on the system, and second when the NOS loads. The NOS detects and/or applies configured resources to system hardware. This section addresses how the CMOS, BIOS, and POST relate to configuring and detecting hardware when the system is powered on.

CMOS

The **CMOS** is a complimentary metal oxide semiconductor that includes a small amount of memory, the purpose of which is to store the BIOS settings such as the boot order (floppy, CD-ROM, hard disk, and so forth), hard disk configuration, power management settings, and more (see next topic). The CMOS can store data for as long as power is available. The power supply provides power when the system is on, and a small, nonrechargeable, metal oxide battery (similar to a watch battery) supplies power when the server is off. Unlike desktop PCs, servers are usually powered on continuously except for regular maintenance, hardware upgrades, and troubleshooting when you must necessarily power off. Typical batteries can last for more than five years on desktop PCs, and somewhat longer on servers since the battery charge naturally dissipates as a matter of time instead of actual use. Server replacement might precede battery replacement, so sometimes battery life is not an issue. However, you should stock a few of the most common batteries in use on your servers just in case. You identify the specific battery in use by reading the identification stamped into the battery surface. Batteries near the end of their life usually lose time on the real time clock, so you should replace batteries on systems with slowing time.

 Older systems copied BIOS settings into a small portion of main memory for faster access. This was known as shadow RAM, which is no longer implemented.

BIOS

The **Basic Input/Output System (BIOS)** is a series of software programs that is the lowest-level interface between the hardware and the operating system. The BIOS programming is stored on a **flash BIOS** memory chip, also known as **EEPROM (electrically erasable programmable read-only memory)**. The administrator can configure the BIOS programming to suit his or her needs and preferences, and the configuration is stored in the CMOS, which is powered by a small battery that retains the settings even when the power fails or is turned off. As its name implies, the BIOS is a series of input and output configuration settings for peripherals, adapters, and on-board components. Phoenix Software, Award Software, and American Megatrends Inc. (AMI) create most base BIOS programming, though individual server manufacturers often add modifications to provide functionality with their specific hardware. Phoenix

Technologies acquired Award Software in late 1998, so a newer system will usually use either a Phoenix or an AMI BIOS. The BIOS controls all of the hardware on the system board and acts as a bridge for various NOS hardware drivers.

Note We generally consider the BIOS to be only the programming stored in flash BIOS memory, but in reality, it's also collectively on various other hardware and adapters, such as a network or sound card. SCSI controllers, for example, often have their own BIOS programming.

Accessing CMOS Settings

Most of the time, when you turn on the power, the display tells you a specific key or keyboard combination to press in order to access the BIOS settings in CMOS. Typically, this is F1, F2, Esc, Del, or some combination of Ctrl+Alt (such as Ctrl+Alt+Shift, Enter, Esc, or S). Compaq computers usually use F10. A simple instruction such as "Press F2 to enter settings" often appears on the screen. Several manufacturers display a manufacturer-promoting splash screen that would prevent you from seeing such instruction, although pressing the Esc key often removes it.

TIP In the unusual instance that the display does not indicate a method for accessing the BIOS, you can trick the system into allowing you to access the BIOS by pressing and holding virtually any key immediately after you power on the computer. The BIOS will often interpret your action as a keyboard problem and provide an opportunity for you to access the BIOS.

When the system powers on, a procedure known as the **POST (power-on self-test)** verifies functionality of motherboard hardware. If the settings do not match, one or more beeps occur. Check system documentation to interpret the meaning of beep codes, which usually also accompany an on-screen error notification code. During the POST, if a device has its own BIOS such as a video card or SCSI card, the POST allows the device to perform its own diagnostics and then resumes when the diagnostics are finished. The POST checks the following:

- Video card and monitor
- CPU stepping (specific incremental version of the CPU)
- CPU model and speed
- BIOS version
- RAM
- Keyboard (which it enables)
- Various ports such as USB, serial, and parallel
- Floppy and hard disk drives
- Disk controllers using separate BIOS
- CD-ROM or DVD-ROM

- Sound cards
- Operating system (which it finds and loads)

 TIP Sometimes you want to see exactly what the POST is displaying on the screen, but it often blinks by very quickly. To freeze the screen, press the Pause key.

3

Protecting the CMOS

Protecting the CMOS for both the server and workstation is an important security precaution. For example, anyone with physical access to the server could access the BIOS settings in CMOS to ensure that the system can boot from a floppy disk. Then, after booting from an MS-DOS or Windows 98 boot floppy, he or she could gain access to local hard disks and steal, alter, destroy, or otherwise damage data or the operating system. Protecting the CMOS first involves physical security (as addressed in Chapter 2), and then applying a password to the CMOS. The BIOS menu system is usually easily navigable, and you should be able to locate where to designate a password for the BIOS settings in CMOS. The CMOS usually includes two levels of password protection: a password to access and change the BIOS configuration, intended to prevent the curious from viewing the CMOS settings, and a password to boot the system. After setting the password(s), be sure to record and store them in a secure location.

In the event that you cannot find a server's CMOS password, you have no choice but to reset the CMOS, which clears password settings in addition to any configuration settings. Reset the CMOS in one of two ways. First, use jumper pins to short the battery circuit to the CMOS. To find the exact jumper pins, refer to the motherboard manufacturer's manual. In absence of a manual, you can also search for labeling on the circuit board. Usually the label is something like CPW (clear password), RPW (reset password), or the unmistakable "Short here to clear CMOS." Without battery power, BIOS settings drain from the CMOS, and the password resets to the original null (none) password setting. Second, you can simply remove the battery for a few seconds to clear the BIOS configurations, and then replace it. Either way, when you reboot, there will be no password required to boot or access BIOS settings.

 TIP Some motherboards have capacitors that retain electricity and could continue to power the CMOS for hours, even without a battery. In this case, you might have to leave the battery out for a day or so. To resume POST, press the spacebar.

 Caution Whenever possible, be sure you first back up the BIOS settings either by writing them down or using a utility (such as CMOS.ZIP) that can print settings or save them to a floppy disk. Once you reset the CMOS, the recorded settings can prevent guesswork in reconfiguring the BIOS settings.

If you clear the BIOS settings, the operating system, hardware devices, or system preferences such as power conservation settings might not function as expected. Although a BIOS maker provides the basic BIOS, the server manufacturer has likely shipped the computer with default settings. Without these default settings, items such as the hard disk might not be accessible, making a boot impossible. After resetting the CMOS (or after you replace a dead battery), navigate the menu system to locate a setting that restores default settings to get back to a workable starting point.

Fortunately, the BIOS interacts with several hardware components to automatically configure settings, as in the hard disk configuration and memory detection.

Common BIOS Settings

It would be impractical to list all common BIOS settings from all manufacturers. A general list of configuration categories usually revolves around the system time/date, hard and floppy disks, disk controller (IDE), keyboard, processor(s), memory, ISA/EISA/PCI expansion buses, system resources (IRQ, DMA, etc.), serial/parallel ports, and boot configuration. However, you should know some common features that you are more likely to find on a server than a workstation. After you access the BIOS settings in CMOS, use the menu system to navigate to various settings (see Table 3-7). The BIOS menu system varies from one manufacturer to the other, and a BIOS from a particular BIOS maker might be different from one machine to the next because server manufacturers often modify the menu system for uses specific to their computers.

Table 3-7 Common BIOS Settings

Feature	Description
Ultra DMA settings	Configures the high-throughput UDMA disk controller.
Processor	On a server, displays information about processor stepping (version) and L2 cache size. You can view the settings for each of the installed processors and test each one.
PCI bus mastering	Enables/disables devices as PCI bus masters and sets the number of clock cycles that a device can master on a PCI bus during a single transaction.
RAM testing	Selects the degree to which the system tests the installed memory (e.g., each 1 MB, 1 KB, or each byte boundary).
Memory scrubbing	Allows capable chipsets to automatically detect and correct single-bit memory errors.

Table 3-7   Common BIOS Settings (continued)

Feature	Description
Security	Allows the system to boot as usual, but prevents use of keyboard or mouse until the correct password is entered. Included on many servers, this secure boot mode also requires the password to boot from a floppy or CD-ROM. Some vendors secure the power and reset switches, which also require a password to use. You can usually configure a hot-key combination or countdown timer that places the server back in secure mode.
Management port	Specifies a serial port to which you can connect another device (a laptop, for example) to externally diagnose the server—even with the server turned off. You can configure management port settings such as whether a password is required to use the port, the connection type (port or modem), and so forth.
Logging	Logs system events in a small segment of nonvolatile memory.
Management interrupt	Allows system management to issue a **non-maskable interrupt (NMI)**, which takes priority over standard interrupt requests. An NMI is useful to stop the system or issue a message in the event of critical events such as failing memory.
General hardware information	Displays hardware information such as part and serial numbers for the board, chassis, and system.
I2O drives	Allows you to specify the maximum number of I2O drives that will be assigned a DOS drive letter, usually one or four.

Most servers also include an additional management utility that provides similar management to that seen in the BIOS, except using a manufacturer-specific interface and settings. The settings are usually saved in BIOS, but settings can go beyond basic BIOS settings. For example, Intel's System Setup Utility also allows you to save **field replaceable unit (FRU)** information. (An FRU is a system with replaceable CPU, CMOS, CMOS battery, RAM, and RAM cache.) Typically, the management utility is a DOS-based utility run from floppy disk(s) or a CD-ROM. In some server types, however, these devices are not replaceable without sending the server to the manufacturer.

You should not use power management features in the NOS or in the BIOS. Servers generally need to be running 24/7, and you do not want to add latency to the server. However, power savings to the monitor are usually OK.

CHAPTER SUMMARY

❐ A motherboard includes a front side bus, sometimes a back side bus, and three primary I/O expansion buses: Industry Standard Architecture (ISA), Extended ISA (EISA), and Peripheral Components Interconnect (PCI). Newer motherboards include only the PCI expansion bus. The speed of each bus is dependent upon the motherboard clock frequency.

❏ The front side bus connects to RAM, and the back side bus connects to L2 cache.

❏ Clock frequency (sometimes called the clock speed, cycle, or clock cycle) is the number of times in one second that an electrically charged quartz crystal located on the motherboard vibrates (oscillates). Clock frequency is measured in mega-hertz, a hertz equaling one cycle per second and "mega" meaning million.

❏ Using different buses in the system requires a way to divide the motherboard into separate parts. The chipset operates at the same speed as the motherboard clock and provides the boundary that both divides one bus from another (using a North Bridge and a South Bridge or the more current hub architecture) and controls the flow of bus data. Choosing a motherboard is mostly choosing a chipset.

❏ PC-based bus systems use what is known as a hierarchical bus, because several buses actually comprise the (collective) "bus," each running at different speeds and with the slower buses hierarchically structured beneath the faster buses. Dividing the bus into the front side bus, PCI bus, and ISA bus allows slower components to operate without negatively impacting the faster components.

❏ The accelerated hub architecture connects buses to the system bus indepen-dently through a dedicated hub interface to the PCI bus, yielding throughput of up to 266 MBps—twice as much throughput as 33 MHz PCI. The indepen-dent buses do not share the PCI bus—increasing PCI bus bandwidth available to PCI-connected devices.

❏ Devices connect to an ISA bus through an ISA expansion slot, which is 16 bits wide and accommodates both 16-bit devices and older 8-bit devices. The ISA bus only operates at 8.33 MHz and is capable of transfer speeds up to 8 MBps.

❏ The 32-bit EISA bus is backward compatible with older ISA devices and pro-vides maximum bus bandwidth of about 33 MBps.

❏ The purpose of the PCI bus is to interface high-speed devices with the system bus so that slower devices do not bottleneck the system. The PCI bus also allows the processor to access L2 cache while simultaneously transferring data to and from other parts of the system.

❏ PCI-X utilizes 64 bits and up to 133 MHz, yielding a maximum bandwidth of 1064 MBps.

❏ In PCI architecture, hardware designers can create a device using bus mastering that is able to bypass the processor and directly access memory, resulting in an overall increase in processor performance. Bus mastering is actually a form of direct memory access (DMA) known as first-party DMA.

❏ The benefit of the PCI interrupt appears when no more ISA IRQ addresses are available. Then, with no more available IRQs, the PCI interrupt utilizes another PCI function known as PCI IRQ steering, in which the PCI interrupt assigns two or more PCI devices the same ISA IRQ.

3

❐ Although PCI hot swap (or hot plug) allows you to add, remove, or replace a device without first powering down the server, most servers still require you to power off the specific PCI slot using a button, switch, or software.

❐ The peer PCI bus is usually a server-specific function that both increases available PCI bandwidth and expands the number of PCI expansion cards from the usual limit of four with minimal impact on overall system bus bandwidth. This architecture usually involves dual peer PCI buses and two North Bridges, which connect to a primary PCI bus and a secondary PCI bus.

❐ I2O (Intelligent Input/Output) is an I/O design initiative that allows improved I/O performance via an I2O processor using the I2O driver model. With I2O, devices intelligently perform much of the processing function on their own instead of relying on the CPU.

❐ The design of the Accelerated Graphics Port (AGP) is to relieve the system bus and CPU of traffic and processing.

❐ Many servers come with AGP, particularly dual-processor machines that could just as easily serve as a high-end graphics workstation. However, high-end servers normally do not include AGP because it is not necessary.

❐ High-end servers usually include motherboard-integrated 1024 × 768 display adapters and only 256 colors.

❐ Processor speed is a measure in MHz of the number of opportunities per second that the processor can execute an instruction. The processor architecture design uses a multiplier methodology to provide the processor's speed.

❐ Cache memory is a small amount of memory that stores recently or frequently used program code or data, reducing latency. Cache memory appears in a number of places on the server including the hard disk, CD-ROM, and the processor. Processors use two types of cache memory: L1 (level 1) and L2 (level 2).

❐ L1 cache is a small amount of memory (usually 32–64 KB) and provides extremely fast access to its data because of its proximity to the processor and because it runs at the same speed as the processor itself—not the speed of the motherboard.

❐ L2 cache provides the same basic benefit as L1 cache, except that it is a larger cache, ranging from 256 KB to 2 MB. In the past, the L2 cache was not stored on the processor die, but was instead stored on a separate chip inside the processor housing. This orientation is known as discrete L2 cache. The data path used to access the L2 cache was called the back side bus, and it ran at half the processor speed.

❐ Most processors after the Pentium III 500 locate the L2 cache directly on the processor die (similar to the L1 cache) and run it at full processor speed. This is known as Advanced Transfer Cache (ATC), is 256 bits wide, and eliminates the need for a back side bus.

❑ Intel Xeon processors differ from standard Pentium II or III models in the following respects: type of enclosure, cache size, cache speed, addressable memory, and SMP.

❑ Intel Pentium II Xeon and later processors let the processor utilize 36 bits to address memory using Intel's Physical Address Extension (PAE) feature, allowing up to 64 GB addressable memory (2^{36} = 68,719,476,736, or 64 GB).

❑ Xeon SMP configuration can use up to four processors, though by adding another processor bus often called a mezzanine bus, eight processors are possible, and many manufacturers engineer buses that can use up to 132 processors (though four or eight processors are more common).

❑ A dual-processor system is known as 2-way, four processors as 4-way, eight processors as 8-way, and so on.

❑ The 64-bit Intel Itanium using Intel's IA-64 technology represents a departure from the previous 32-bit x86 Intel architecture, and performs optimally with 64-bit operating systems (Windows 2000 will be ported to 64 bit) and applications.

❑ Because of the translation process from 32 to 64 bits, 32-bit applications will usually run more slowly on the IA-64 than on fast 32-bit Pentium III Xeon processors.

❑ With 64 address bits, the Itanium processor can address up to 18 billion GB.

❑ The IA-64 architecture uses Explicitly Parallel Instruction set Computing (EPIC), allowing the processor to simultaneously process as many as 20 operations.

❑ AMD decided to extend Intel's original x86 architecture in the Hammer design with AMD's new x86-64 architecture.

❑ 32-bit operating systems and applications can continue to run on the Hammer without complicated hardware emulation, resulting in minimal performance overhead.

❑ You will probably find SIMMs (single inline memory modules) on older servers, if at all. The physical SIMM module has gold or tin contacts at the bottom. Although the contact appears both on the front and back, it is really a single contact (hence the *single* in SIMM).

❑ The typical SIMM is 50 ns, 60 ns, or 70 ns, and older SIMMs can be 80 ns.

❑ Instead of providing only the exact location requested, EDO can send the entire row address so that subsequent references to the same row only require a column lookup, saving time.

❑ DIMMs (dual inline memory module) dramatically improve memory performance over the SIMM predecessor by expanding the module to 64 bits (nonparity) or 72 bits (parity or ECC). The contacts on both sides of the module are separate (hence the *dual* in DIMM).

❑ SDRAM operates at clock speed; if the system bus is 100 MHz, then SDRAM matches that frequency, which functionally operates at about 10 ns.

3

❐ RDRAM memory chips fit on a narrow, 16-bit-wide RIMM memory module.

❐ RDRAM provides extremely fast 800 MHz internal clock speed on a 400 MHz bus, because data is transferred twice during each clock cycle. This adds up to 1.6 GB throughput (16 bits × 800 MHz / 8 = 1.6 GB).

❐ Because of the unique data circuit of RDRAM, empty RIMM sockets must be filled with a C-RIMM, a device that has no memory but provides continuity to complete the memory data path.

❐ Double data rate SDRAM (DDR SDRAM) is the next generation of SDRAM, and also uses a 64-bit DIMM with future plans for a 128-bit DIMM.

❐ Interleaving allows memory access between two or more memory banks and/or boards to occur alternately, minimizing wait states. Memory must be installed in exactly the same configuration between banks/boards.

❐ The purpose of both buffered and registered memory is to re-drive (amplify) the signal entering the module.

❐ Buffered or registered modules also assist the chipset in handling the larger electrical load when the system has a lot of installed memory, allowing the module to include more memory chips, which is one reason that servers often use registered modules.

❐ Registered memory enacts a deliberate pause of one clock cycle in the module to ensure that all communication from the chipset arrives properly.

❐ Servers commonly use error correcting code (ECC) SDRAM. Although error correction is more expensive and involves a slight performance penalty, it is well worth it on a server, where data integrity is critical and other high-performing system components help make up for memory latency.

❐ If only a single bit error occurs, ECC can correct the error, but ECC cannot correct the more rare 2-, 3-, or 4-bit errors (multiple bit errors).

❐ The CMOS is a complimentary metal oxide semiconductor that includes a small amount of memory, the purpose of which is to store the BIOS settings.

❐ The power supply provides power to CMOS when the system is turned on, and a small, nonrechargeable, metal oxide battery (similar to a watch battery) supplies power when the server is turned off.

❐ The data stored in the CMOS is the BIOS settings. As its name implies, the BIOS is a series of input and output configuration settings for peripherals, adapters, and on-board components.

❐ Most of the time, when you turn on the power, the display tells you a specific key or keyboard combination to press in order to access the BIOS settings.

❐ When the system powers on, a procedure known as the POST (power on self-test) verifies functionality of the motherboard hardware.

❐ Protecting the BIOS for both the server and workstation is an important security precaution.

❐ The BIOS usually includes two levels of password protection: a password to access and change the BIOS configuration, intended to prevent the curious from so much as viewing the BIOS, and a password to boot the system. In the event that you cannot find a server's BIOS password, you have no choice but to reset the BIOS, which clears password settings in addition to any configuration settings.

❐ Reset the CMOS BIOS settings using jumpers or removing the battery.

❐ Most servers also include an additional management utility that provides similar management as seen in the BIOS, except using manufacturer-specific interface and settings.

KEY TERMS

Accelerated Graphics Port (AGP) — A high-speed graphics port that relieves the system bus and CPU of video-processing traffic.

accelerated hub architecture — Connects buses to the system bus independently through a dedicated hub interface to the PCI bus, yielding throughput of up to 266 MBps.

Advanced Transfer Cache (ATC) — L2 cache located on the processor die and running at full processor speed.

back side bus — The data path used to access L2 cache.

BIOS (basic input/output system) — A series of input and output configuration settings for peripherals, adapters, and on-board components.

buffered memory — Re-drives (amplifies) signals entering the memory module.

bus — Set of wires or printed circuits that provides the data path to and from the processor, memory, hard disk, adapters, and peripherals.

bus mastering — A technology that allows devices to bypass the processor and directly access memory, resulting in an overall increase in processor performance. Bus mastering devices can also communicate among themselves without processor intervention. Bus mastering is actually a form of direct memory access (DMA).

bus queue entries — A Pentium Xeon technology that holds outstanding bus and memory operations.

bus width — The number of individual data wires that transmit data. The more wires the component such as the motherboard has, the more data it can transmit in a given period of time.

cache memory — A small amount of memory that stores recently or frequently used program code or data.

3

chipset — Circuitry that provides motherboard features and organizes the various buses.

clock speed — The number of times in one second that the electrically charged quartz crystal located on the motherboard vibrates (oscillates). Also known as clock cycle, clock frequency, frequency, or cycle.

CMOS — Complimentary metal oxide semiconductor that includes a small amount of memory, the purpose of which is to store the BIOS settings.

compiler — Translates high-level programming language into the lowest language the computer can understand, machine language.

DDR SDRAM (double data rate SDRAM) — Transfers data twice per clock cycle, similar to RDRAM, but at a lower cost because DDR SDRAM is an open standard charging no royalties.

discrete L2 cache — L2 cache located inside the processor housing but not on the processor die.

dynamic RAM (DRAM) — Main memory referred to as dynamic because the information requires continuous electrical refresh, or else the data can become corrupt or lost.

error correcting code (ECC) — Circuitry on the memory chip that uses check bits to verify the integrity of memory and corrects single bit errors.

EEPROM (electrically erasable programmable read-only memory) — A chip that stores the BIOS programming. EEPROM has been mostly superceded by a similar memory known as flash BIOS.

Extended ISA (EISA) — An evolution of ISA, the EISA bus provides backward compatibility with older ISA devices and provides maximum bus bandwidth of about 33 MBps.

field replaceable unit (FRU) — A system with replaceable CPU, CMOS, CMOS battery, RAM, and RAM cache.

fill buffers — The interface between the CPU and main memory.

flash BIOS — BIOS memory that can be reprogrammed without having to remove the chip. Instead, you download and run a program that updates the BIOS.

front side bus — A 64-bit data pathway that the processor uses to communicate with L1 cache, main memory, and the graphics card through the North Bridge chipset.

Graphics Memory Controller Hub (GMCH) — Replaces the North Bridge in newer chipsets, providing higher data throughput.

hierarchical bus — Various portions of the bus running at different speeds, with the slower buses hierarchically structured beneath the faster buses.

Industry Standard Architecture (ISA) — A bus interface that connects ISA devices to the ISA bus, which is 16 bits wide and accommodates both 16-bit devices and older 8-bit devices. The ISA bus only operates at 8.33 MHz and is capable of transfer speeds up to 8 MBps.

Intelligent Input/Output (I2O) — An I/O design initiative that allows improved I/O performance via an I2O processor using the I2O driver model.

interleaving — A process that allows memory access between two or more memory banks and/or boards to occur alternately, minimizing wait states.

interrupt request (IRQ) — An electrical signal that obtains the CPU's attention in order to handle an event immediately, although the processor might queue the request behind other requests.

I/O Controller Hub (ICH) — Replaces the South Bridge in newer chipsets, allowing higher data throughput.

ISA bus — A 16-bit data pathway for slower expansion adapter cards and the floppy disk, mouse, keyboard, serial and parallel ports, and the BIOS via a Super I/O chip, which mitigates the need for a separate expansion card for each of the aforementioned items.

L1 cache — A small amount of memory (usually 32–64 KB) that provides extremely fast access to its data because of its proximity to the processor and because it runs at the same speed as the processor itself—not at the speed of the motherboard.

L2 cache — Provides the same basic benefits as L1 cache, but it is larger, ranging from 256 KB to 2 MB.

mezzanine bus — An add-on bus used to increase the number of processors in a single system.

motherboard — The heart of the computer, which attaches to the chassis and includes slots, sockets, and other connections for server components.

non-maskable interrupt (NMI) — An interrupt that takes priority over standard interrupt requests. An NMI is useful to stop the system or issue a message in event of critical events or failures such as failing memory.

North Bridge — A chipset element that divides the processor bus from the PCI bus and manages data traffic to and from the South Bridge, and components on the FSB and PCI bus.

null cable modem — A special cable that uses special crossed wires to simulate a modem presence, allowing data to travel between two hosts without an actual modem or network connection.

overclocking — Increasing the speed of the motherboard clock and/or the CPU to accelerate the clock speed, which can yield a performance increase. Not recommended on servers because of the higher risk associated with higher temperatures and a reduction in overall stability.

PCI hot swap (PCI hot plug) — The ability to add, remove, or replace PCI devices without first powering down the server.

PCI interrupts — Assignment of a designation to PCI devices that represent an actual ISA IRQ. The main benefit with PCI interrupts is that if no more IRQ addresses are available, PCI can use PCI steering to assign two or more PCI devices the same ISA IRQ.

PCI steering — Using PCI interrupts to assign two or more PCI devices the same ISA IRQ.

PCI-X (PCI-eXtended) — A 64-bit addendum to PCI 2.2 utilizing 64 bits and up to 133 MHz.

peer PCI bus — A bus architecture that increases available PCI bandwidth and expands the number of PCI expansion cards from the usual limit of four with a minimal impact on overall system bus bandwidth. This architecture usually involves dual peer PCI buses and two North Bridges, which connect to a primary PCI bus and a secondary PCI bus.

Peripheral Components Interface (PCI) bus — A 32-bit data pathway for high-speed I/O for expansion adapter cards, USB, and IDE ports. The CMOS and system clock also connect to the PCI bus. The PCI bus connects to both the North Bridge and the South Bridge.

Physical Address Extension (PAE) — Intel technology that allows the processor to utilize 36 bits to address up to 64 GB of memory.

POST (power-on self-test) — Verifies functionality of motherboard hardware.

RDRAM (Rambus DRAM) — Memory manufactured under license to Rambus. RDRAM is very fast, transferring data on both leading and trailing clock cycles.

registered memory — Memory that re-drives (amplifies) signals entering the memory module. Registered memory also enacts a deliberate pause of one clock cycle in the module to ensure that all communication from the chipset arrives properly. Registered memory is useful on heavily loaded server memory, and was designed for SIMMs containing 32 or more chips.

South Bridge — A chipset element that divides the PCI bus from the ISA bus.

synchronous dynamic RAM (SDRAM) — Memory that operates at system clock speed.

REVIEW QUESTIONS

1. What is the main data transportation medium in the server?

    a. the PCI bus

    b. the motherboard

    c. the ISA bus

    d. ECC memory

2. How does the bus bit width affect data throughput?

    a. A wider bus results in less data throughput.

    b. Bus width does not affect data throughput.

    c. A wider bus results in more data throughput.

    d. A wider bus accepts higher voltage, allowing for overclocking.

3. If a server offers uptime of five nines, how many minutes per year might it be down?

    a. five minutes

    b. five increments of nine minutes each

    c. nine increments of five minutes each

    d. 59 minutes

4. How does clock frequency affect server performance?

   a. Each clock cycle represents a period of latency during which components cannot perform actions.

   b. Each clock cycle represents an opportunity for a component to perform an action.

   c. Only the processor, not clock frequency, affects performance.

   d. Slowing clock frequency means you should replace the CMOS battery soon.

5. What is the function of a chipset?

   a. manage data traffic and separate buses

   b. perform mathematical functions on behalf of the processor

   c. cache data to accelerate performance

   d. provide electrical continuity between the CPU and memory

6. What is a hierarchical bus?

   a. a bus that is the latest in a series of buses based on the same technology

   b. multiple motherboards in the same server

   c. a motherboard that uses a mezzanine bus to expand memory and/or processors

   d. the structuring of slower buses beneath faster buses

7. Which of the following motherboard buses is the fastest?

   a. ISA bus

   b. front side bus

   c. PCI bus

   d. USB

8. Which of the following buses are likely to be phased out on server boards?

   a. ISA bus

   b. PCI bus

   c. USB

   d. EISA bus

9. What is bus mastering?

   a. the ability of a device to bypass the processor and directly access memory

   b. a description of the system bus

   c. a description of the North Bridge's control over the system bus

   d. the ability of the GMCH to direct traffic between the processor and memory

10. How is a PCI interrupt beneficial?

   a. It allows PCI devices to have a priority when directing interrupt requests to the processor.

   b. It arbitrates between two PCI devices contending for processor time.

c. It allows PCI IRQ steering to assign two or more devices the same IRQ.

d. It divides a single PCI bus into two separate, faster PCI buses.

11. What do most servers require you to do before performing a PCI hot swap?

a. Shut down the server power.

b. Shut down power on the PCI slot.

c. Reboot the server.

d. Place the server in sleep mode.

12. What is the purpose of I2O? (Choose all that apply.)

a. improve I/O performance

b. simplify driver development

c. provide a wider I/O bus

d. provide a faster I/O bus

13. Why is AGP not included on some servers?

a. AGP is incompatible with the Intel Xeon processor.

b. Servers include a separate, independent bus to handle video.

c. Servers do not require high-performance graphics functionality.

d. AGP places too many demands on the processor.

14. What is the purpose of L1 and L2 cache?

a. to supplement main memory in low memory conditions

b. to store recently or frequently accessed data to reduce latency

c. short-term storage in case of data corruption

d. to cache data streams from the ISA bus

15. Which of the following characteristics does not differentiate the Intel Pentium III Xeon from the Pentium III?

a. enclosure type

b. cache size

c. cache speed

d. core clock speed

16. Which of the following is an advantage of the Intel Itanium?

a. direct compatibility with 32-bit operating systems and applications

b. Windows 2000 will be ported to 64 bits, taking advantage of the wider data path.

c. support for up to eight processors

d. cost-effective alternative to the Pentium III

17. What differentiates a SIMM from a DIMM?

    a. Contacts on either side of a SIMM are actually the same—on a DIMM, they are separate.

    b. You can only install one SIMM, but you install DIMMs in pairs.

    c. A DIMM has buffering, but a SIMM does not.

    d. A SIMM has registers, but a DIMM does not.

18. What makes SDRAM faster than standard DRAM?

    a. SDRAM operates at PCI speed.

    b. DRAM operates at bus speed.

    c. SDRAM operates at bus speed.

    d. They are the same speed.

19. Why is DDR SDRAM faster than standard SDRAM?

    a. DDR SDRAM transfers data twice per clock cycle.

    b. DDR SDRAM is not faster; it only has a wider data path.

    c. SDRAM can only run at half bus speed.

    d. SDRAM is only 32 bits wide.

20. Why do servers use ECC memory?

    a. increase performance

    b. increase latency

    c. increase data reliability

    d. purge memory in case of data errors

21. How does the BIOS relate to the CMOS?

    a. CMOS is the configuration programming that is stored in BIOS.

    b. CMOS stores BIOS configuration settings.

    c. BIOS and CMOS both provide I/O configuration settings for hardware.

    d. BIOS is an error-correcting utility for the CMOS.

22. What two benefits do BIOS passwords offer?

    a. ability to disable the power switch

    b. ability to prevent access to the operating system

    c. ability to prevent access to BIOS settings

    d. ability to prevent booting

HANDS-ON PROJECTS

Web links in projects were accurate at the time this book was published. If you notice discrepancies, look for similar links and follow the same general steps.

3

Project 3-1

In this project, you will observe a motherboard and answer several questions about it. Your instructor should have a motherboard for you to view. If possible, it should be at least a dual-processor motherboard.

Look at the motherboard provided by your instructor, and answer the following questions:

1. What chipset does the motherboard use?
2. How many processors can the motherboard accept?
3. What company makes the BIOS?
4. What kind of battery powers the CMOS?
5. Is there an AGP slot?

Project 3-2

In this project, you will access information on the Internet to describe information about Intel's server motherboards.

Using your Internet browser, access *http://support.intel.com/support/motherboards/server*. Intel makes bare motherboards for sale to system integrators (computer system manufacturers), listed under Boxed Server Boards. Intel also makes systems that are assembled motherboards, cases, and several components, listed under Server Platforms. Click **SBT2 Boxed Server Board** at the left. Answer the following questions:

1. How many processors does this board support?
2. What kinds of processors are supported?
3. What kind of memory is used?
4. What is the maximum amount of memory supported?
5. Click the **Supported Processors** chart. What is the fastest supported processor?
6. Click the **Technical Notes** link, and open the document titled **Microsoft Windows 2000 Advanced Server and 4GB or greater memory installed**. What must you do in order for Windows 2000 Advanced Server to recognize 4 GB or more of RAM?

Project 3-3

In this project, you find out how to access your BIOS settings and view some of its configurations.

1. Boot your server and observe what appears on the screen as the POST takes place. List what you see as best you can. You might need to reboot a couple of times (or try pressing the Pause key) as some of the information flashes quickly on screen.

2. What key would you press to access BIOS settings?

Project 3-4

In this project, you use the BIOS menu to find configuration information.

1. Boot your server and access the BIOS configurations.

2. Using the menu system, answer the following questions:

   a. How much memory is installed in the computer?

   b. How large is the hard disk?

   c. In what order does the BIOS search for bootable media?

3. Attempt to exit the BIOS configuration. You are prompted to save your settings. Choose to discard the changes.

Project 3-5

In this project, you will see a visual demonstration of how the Intel chipset architecture works.

1. Access the Intel web site at *http://developer.intel.com/design/chipsets*.

2. Under **Server**, click the link to the **Intel 840 Chipset**.

3. Under the **Spotlight** heading, click **840 Chipset Architecture Demo**, and play the video. Be sure to click each of the links on the right-hand side of the window.

4. Is the chipset a North Bridge/South Bridge? If not, what chipset is it?

5. How many processors can the chipset use?

6. What kind of processors does it use?

7. What type of memory does this chipset use?

Project 3-6

In this project, you learn how to quickly access additional information about memory.

1. Access the Kingston Technology Company web site at *www.kingston.com*.

2. Click the link for **Educational Tools**.

3. Click the link for **Memory Bits**.

4. Click several topics at the left to research more about memory.

5. Return to the home page, and click the **Memory Configurator** link. Locate the correct memory for the Compaq ProLiant 8500. What is the largest single memory module Kingston makes for this server? How much does it cost? (Click **Add to Basket** to find out.)

CASE PROJECTS

1. KidHelp, a nonprofit charity, asks you to donate your expertise to help them with their growing organization's network. (You are a notable humanitarian, so of course you agree to help.) The network has grown from a peer-to-peer network of six users to about 50 regular users. Somewhere in the growth path, somebody donated a NetWare 3.11 server, the main purpose of which is as a file and print server, which is configured as follows:

   - One Classic Pentium 60 MHz

   - 16 MB RAM

   - One 780 MB hard disk

   - One CD-ROM drive

   KidHelp has biannual fundraisers in which 250 volunteers answer phones and write down donation information, which someone later enters into a spreadsheet. A larger charity has donated their 500 MB SQL database of donors to KidHelp, and KidHelp wants to add their own donors to the SQL database and use it during the next fundraiser. KidHelp has asked you to upgrade the hardware and NOS with the following objectives:

   - Upgrade somewhat ahead of current needs to increase the length of time necessary for the next upgrade.

   - Use two processors.

   - Utilize a motherboard with a fast, high-throughput network and SCSI adapters.

   - Utilize a memory solution that would allow for more memory chips per module so that as the database grows, it can still be loaded completely into memory. Also, the memory should automatically correct errors.

   - Optionally, upgrade the NOS to another version of NetWare or to Windows 2000.

   What kind of server hardware would you suggest?

2. Your pager alerts you that a network card has failed on one of your file and print servers. You want to replace the NIC immediately, except that because you recently used most of your spare NICs in some new servers, you only have one left. Unfortunately, this NIC is from a different manufacturer than the original one, and usually requests a different IRQ—one that is in use by the AGP video card. Also, you would like to replace the NIC without shutting off the server. What steps should you take to replace the NIC? What PCI technologies help to make this NIC replacement smooth and why?

4

SERVER POWER AND RACK INSTALLATION

> **After reading this chapter and completing the exercises, you will be able to:**
>
> ♦ Identify features of server power supply
>
> ♦ Correctly implement an uninterruptible power supply (UPS)
>
> ♦ Plan optimum placement of equipment in a server rack
>
> ♦ Configure a keyboard, video, mouse (KVM) console
>
> ♦ List tips for installing equipment in racks

Power is an obvious requirement for a server, and this chapter shows you how server-level power supplies differ from standard desktop workstation power supplies. While a server power supply typically has a respectable mean time between failure (MTBF) of around two million hours, power to the office building does not. Many factors can cause power to fail to the server room, and you should prepare server room equipment for such an event with one or more devices that can temporarily provide power.

The byproduct of powering the server is the generation of heat. Fans are the primary method of protecting server components from overheating. It's almost impossible to install too many fans in the server, rack, or cabinet, and this chapter shows you various types of fans and how to strategically place them. This is especially important in the rack, where multiple server devices compound heating issues. Installing server equipment in the rack is a strategic process that requires planning in terms of power, heat, and weight distribution. In fact, the server rack often has so many installed servers that it is impractical to attach a separate keyboard, monitor, and mouse to each server. In that case, you will need to use a single keyboard, monitor, and mouse to switch between numerous servers.

SUPPLYING POWER TO THE SERVER

Obviously, without power you don't have a working server. Selecting a server with the type of power supply you need and ensuring its continued operation through the use of an uninterruptible power supply (UPS) is the first step in ensuring solid uptime percentages.

Power Supply

On the most basic level, an entry-level server probably has one power supply of at least 330 watts (W), whereas most workstations are probably as low as 145 W. A high-end, 8-way server probably provides between two and four power supplies rated between 375 W and 750 W each. The power supply, also known as the **power supply unit (PSU)**, attaches to the server chassis. Low-end servers and high-end workstations might not have hot-swappable and/or redundant power supplies. This means that in order to replace the power supply, you must remove the server case cover and disconnect power supply connectors to the motherboard, hard disks, floppy disks, and CD-ROMs before removing the screws attaching the PSU to the chassis and lifting out the power supply. This type of power supply installation is no different from the procedure on a typical desktop workstation because the chassis includes space for only a single, non-hot-swappable PSU. Well-configured servers, on the other hand, offer at least two hot-swappable power supplies. You can replace one of the power supplies without turning off the server (see Figure 4-1).

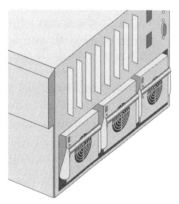

Figure 4-1   Redundant power supply units

Typically the server can operate acceptably with only a single PSU. The second power supply provides load balancing to reduce demands placed on a single PSU, as well as failover in case one of the power supplies fails. Often, a server includes three power supplies—two to provide continuous power and a third on standby in case one of the first two fails. Server management software and warning lights on the server should alert you to failed or unstable power supplies, usually indicated by a fan that does not spin at appropriate levels (see Figure 4-2).

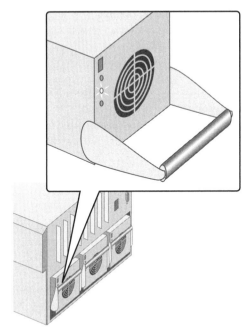

4

Figure 4-2   Most PSUs include a warning light that notifies you of problems

If one PSU fails, a standby comes online automatically and without interruption in service. (Some server configurations such as the Intel AD450NX server platform include support for an optional fourth PSU.) Because most networks require server availability 24/7, PSU failover is critical to a true server-level configuration. Also, the hot-swappable power supply does not require separate connectors for hard disks, CD-ROMs, the motherboard, and so forth. A hot-swappable PSU has sockets that plug directly into the power system of the server, which supplies power cables to server components. The power cord does not attach directly to the PSU (which would require a separate power cord for each PSU). Instead, a single power inlet serves all power supplies. Specific steps to replace a power supply are given in Chapter 6.

Many servers offer **N+1** expandability for critical components, particularly the processor and the PSU. "N" is a variable that refers to the quantity of a given component installed in a system, such as two power supplies. The "+1" refers to a spare component. For example, a server with three power supplies might be referred to as 2+1, in which two power supplies provide ongoing power while an additional power supply provides redundancy. N+1 can also refer to a chassis designed with space to accommodate additional components.

Each PSU requires a large fan to dissipate the heat generated by the power supply. While desktop workstation power supplies also have a fan, the server PSU often uses variable fan speed, which increases or decreases based upon the amount of heat the PSU thermistor detects. A **thermistor** is an internal thermostat that increases or decreases fan speed based on heat levels.

Calculating Server Power Requirements

Before calculating power requirements, make sure that the power from the building to the server room is sufficient to service your equipment. Although most building outlets are 110 volts (V), like household power outlets, server rooms usually also have 208/220 V outlets to accommodate the high power demands of larger servers with multiple power supplies and racks full of equipment. As part of your server room design, make sure the electrical engineers provide plenty of 208 V outlets for present and future needs. In a rack configuration, a **power distribution unit** (**PDU**), similar in function to a household "power strip" but with much higher capacity, often plugs into the 208 V outlet and supplies power to internal rack components (see more about racks later in this chapter). Server power supplies automatically detect the voltage of the power source and adjust as needed.

When a high-powered server or rack power is turned on, a sudden, temporary surge of power to the system takes place (known as **inrush power**). To account for this, be sure that the electrical engineer not only knows the amperage requirements for equipment that is up and running, but also accounts for inrush power, usually at least 20 amps (A) per PDU. Otherwise, you won't be able to power up a rack of equipment all at once without tripping the breaker.

Calculating the power supply needs for a server requires you to know how much power the motherboard, processor, internal adapters, and peripherals require. The power supply in the server can probably handle additional components without any problems; however, if you fill all expansion slots and drive bays, you might exceed power supply ratings. Though some components might list power requirements on the device or with its documentation, power requirements for other components might be difficult to locate. In that case, I recommend that you err on the safe side and calculate based on the maximum wattage allowed for a given type of device. Table 4-1 is a starting point.

Some devices might list volts, watts, amps, or combinations thereof. Use the information you gather to calculate power according to the following formula:

$$watts = volts \times amps$$

(This formula involves slight rounding, but should suffice for calculating general power requirements.) For example, a PCI slot requiring 5 V of 5 A current would require 25 W.

Computer components require positive power voltages in +3.3, +5, and +12 V. For example, a hard disk requires +12 V, and the processor usually requires +3.3 V. You might also find a negative power voltage of –5 V for backward compatibility with the ISA bus. The motherboard can be designed to supply negative voltages if the power supply does not. Assume all voltages in this book to be positive unless stated otherwise.

Table 4-1   Approximate Wattage Requirements

4

Component	Wattage Requirement
ATX motherboard (without CPU or RAM)*	30 W
RAM (approx. 10 W per 128 MB)	40 W for 512 MB
Pentium III 750 MHz	25 W
Floppy drive	5 W
IDE 50X CD or 10X DVD	25 W
4X AGP	30 W
PCI Card (5 W each)	30 W for six cards
IDE 5400 RPM drive**	10 W
IDE 7200 RPM drive	15 W
SCSI 7200 RPM drive	25 W
SCSI 10000 RPM drive	40 W

* 30 W represents a single, basic motherboard. Motherboard power requirements vary greatly depending on whether the server uses riser or mezzanine boards, which in turn require additional power.

** Hard drives require much more power during the spinup phase: 7200 RPM IDE drives require up to 30 W, and 10,000 RPM drives up to 40 W. Power requirements listed include **drive logic**, which is the circuitry included in the floppy or hard drive that interfaces with the disk controller. Many current hard drives are much more efficient in power requirements than the drives listed here.

Add the total power requirements for all server components, and subtract the total number from the power rating for the power supply. You should have plenty of power to spare, preferably about 6%, if you want the system to be as reliable as possible. If available power is marginal, you might consider moving certain components to other servers if possible, or upgrading the power supply.

Older computers use a paddle switch located on the power supply to turn on the computer. More recent servers and workstations use a remote power switch, which runs cables from the power source connecting leads to connectors on the switch. Be sure that if you are working inside the case with these wires, you disconnect the power cable first because the wires carry 110 V AC at all times. Accidentally touching the ends of the leads together might result in an unpleasant shock.

Uninterruptible Power Supply

An uninterruptible power supply (UPS) temporarily supplies power using batteries to the **load equipment** (anything connected to the UPS that draws power, usually servers and possibly other network equipment) in the event of a power outage. The UPS also supplements power in case of a brownout, where utility power continues but is below acceptable operating voltages.

A UPS typically provides backup power in that the load equipment constantly receives power from one or more backup batteries. The batteries receive a constant charge from utility power. If the utility power fails, the batteries continue to provide power just as they always have, minus the battery-charging function from utility power. The primary purpose of a UPS is not to continue normal operations for the entire duration of a brownout or power failure. Instead, the UPS provides a few minutes of power to give administrators enough time to send network messages to users (giving them time to save and close files) and gracefully shut down the server using normal procedures in the NOS. Otherwise, users can lose data from open files and the NOS can become corrupt or unstable.

 In a Microsoft Windows environment, you can notify connected users individually or as a group. For example, at a command prompt you could enter "NET SEND /USERS Save Files Now and Log Off!" (Of course, sending users a message only applies if the power outage is limited to the server room.)

Power protection systems fall under three major architectures, as shown in Table 4-2.

Table 4-2 UPS Architectures

UPS Type	Function	Advantages	Disadvantages
Standby/Offline	A transistor momentarily switches a large transformer, which stores a small amount of power, before transferring power to the UPS battery. These UPS systems are better suited for home PCs, workstations, and so forth	• Low cost • Energy efficient—only converts DC current to AC during blackout or brownout	• No long-term brownout operation because battery power only lasts a few minutes • Provides minimal noise filtering on incoming power—does not regenerate power • Output power variance—can pass voltages outside normal levels up to +/-20%

Table 4-2   UPS Architectures (continued)

UPS Type	Function	Advantages	Disadvantages
Line Interactive	Similar to Standby/Offline, but adds automatic voltage regulation to stabilize power levels during brownouts and overvoltages without using battery power. Used in PC desktops as well as smaller servers, and usually provides up to 3 kilovolt/amps (kVA).	• Only nominally more expensive than Standby/Offline • Saves battery power by not operating during brownouts or overvoltages, instead using Automatic Voltage Regulation (AVR) circuits • Efficient energy use—only converts DC current to AC during blackout or brownout	• Provides minimal noise filtering on incoming power—does not regenerate power • Output power variance—can pass voltages outside normal levels up to +/−10%
Online/Double Conversion	AC utility power enters UPS where the rectifier converts to DC and then back to AC out to the load equipment. This conversion process cleans the power stream to near perfection. Used for higher-end, mission-critical servers, and is commonly used where more than 3 kVA is required*	• Precision output to within 2% of normal levels • No switchover time because load equipment already operates through the continuously charged battery • Extremely clean power output	• Reduced energy efficiency because the AC/DC/AC conversion reduces efficiency to about 85% • Expense—though costs are coming down, Online/Double Conversion UPS systems are still the most expensive

* Extremely large power requirements over 3000 VA often require a huge amount of space, and might be centrally located with specially wired UPS-supported building circuits or power distribution strips.

 Several sources recommend that you do not purchase **standby power supply (SPS)** equipment, which detects an interruption in line power and switches to a transformer to bridge the period of time it takes to switch to battery power. This is no longer an issue, as it was in the 1980s and '90s, because the quality of UPS equipment and server power supplies can easily survive the momentary transition without ill effects. The switch might take 2–4 ms, while power supplies can usually handle a 100–200 ms pause.

Understanding UPS Operation

The following description and Figure 4-3 describe what takes place during normal operation of an online UPS when utility power is at normal, uninterrupted levels:

1. The UPS receives AC power.

2. The UPS uses a rectifier to convert AC power to DC power.

3. Some DC power is siphoned off to charge the battery.

4. An inverter converts DC power back to clean, nearly perfect AC power.

5. Power passes through the transformer to the load equipment.

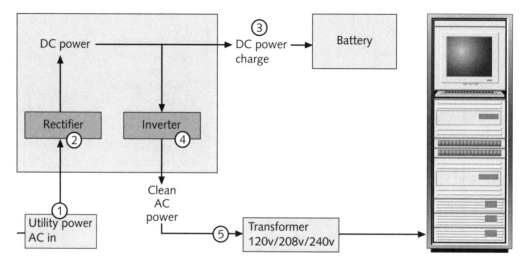

Figure 4-3   Normal online operation

The following steps and Figure 4-4 describe what takes place during a power failure:

1. Because there is no AC in, the battery discharges DC power to the inverter.

2. The inverter converts DC power to clean, nearly perfect AC power.

3. Power passes through the transformer to the load equipment.

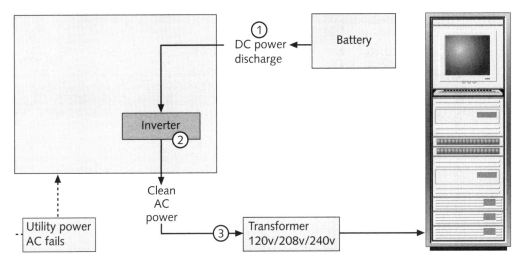

Figure 4-4   Battery operation

UPS Software

UPS software such as American Power Conversion (APC) PowerChute can also assist the administrator by automatically shutting down the server and safely storing data that might otherwise be lost. The UPS connects to a port on the server (usually a serial or USB port) and sends a message to the server when backup functionality activates. The message serves as a trigger to the software, which begins to perform administratively pre-determined functions such as data backup and system shutdown. Many UPS manufac-turers are including increasingly sophisticated administrative software that goes beyond these basic functions. For example, Tripp-Lite offers software that allows you to remotely manage UPS systems of most major manufacturers from an Internet connection.

Failover for the UPS

Backup batteries eventually fail or lose their ability to retain a charge. Server-level UPS systems usually also offer N+1 functionality that allows you to replace a battery while another battery (or batteries) continues to power the unit, ensuring that the UPS is not temporarily unavailable. Also, you can use multiple UPS units so that you can service one UPS while the remaining units continue to supply power (see Figure 4-5).

Generally, administrators seek about 15 minutes of backup power for servers. Depending upon the business need, administrators might seek up to eight hours of backup power, such as for PBX telecom systems and Internet connections. However, UPS equipment providing eight hours of backup is large and expensive. If you want backup power for an extended period of time, consider a backup generator with a UPS. The primary power service in the event of an outage comes from the generator, not the UPS. However, the generator usually takes several seconds to come fully online (known as **generator kick**, **kick**, or **kickstart**). The UPS in this context provides power during the seconds required for the generator to come online.

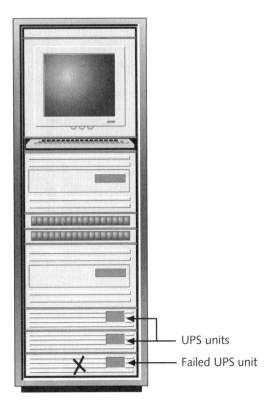

Figure 4-5   N+1 redundancy: if one UPS is unavailable, the remaining units continue to supply power

 A **line conditioner** filters out power inconsistencies, temporarily bridges power in the event of a brief brownout, suppresses high voltage spikes, and provides overall buffering between utility power and the system. This chapter does not separately address line conditioners because most server-level UPS systems already include line conditioning capability.

Determining UPS Requirements

Determining your exact UPS requirements involves several variables, including power requirements of individual servers and networking equipment and/or rack power, one or more monitors, and so forth. The best way to calculate these needs is to add the total power requirements of the rack or server. Some sources recommend looking at the UL (Underwriters' Laboratory) sticker (if present) on the back of the unit to determine its total power requirement, but I do not. The UL sticker is a measure only of what the manufacturer submitted as the default configuration for this server, and servers often include additional equipment. Instead, measure the wattage required by your load equipment. Let's say that on a particular server, you need 600 W (which includes 50% overhead, as recommended earlier). When you visit the web site of a UPS manufacturer, you only see UPS systems rated in volt-amps (VA), and notice that a volt-amp is calculated using the same formula as watts: volts × amps. Since the formula is the same, does that mean watts and VA are the same thing? No, they are not. The difference is "where" the power occurs.

Power coming "in" from the utility company is measured in watts. That's what you pay for on your electric bill, and it is also sometimes called **actual power** or **true power**. However, as the electricity passes through the server's power supply, capacitors, inductors, and other equipment, we must account for a difference between the power that comes "in" to the power supply and power that goes "out" of the power supply. Power going "out" is known as **apparent power**. The difference between actual power and apparent power is known as the **power factor**, which is usually a difference of about 60%.

To boil it all down, it comes to a simple factor in determining UPS power requirements. Take the VA rating of the UPS and multiply that number by .60 to determine the number of watts that this UPS will support. For example, if the UPS is 1000 VA, then the watt rating for the same UPS is 600 W (1000 × .60 = 600 W). In the example stated at the beginning of this discussion, a 1000 VA UPS would exactly meet the 600 W power requirements of the server equipment. However, to plan for future expansion and add a margin of safety, you should increase to the next higher available VA rating from the UPS manufacturer.

Next, determine the amount of time (known as the **run time**) you require to power the server. Realize that VA × high run time = lots of money. Run time is not a calculation you make on your own; you have to contact the UPS manufacturer to make that determination. This is best accomplished by visiting a UPS web site and using online tools to arrive at the best product for your needs. (Try Hands-on Project 4-4 at the end of this chapter.)

> **TIP** Avoid including printers in the total UPS power requirements, because documents can usually be printed any time; risk of data loss is a more immediate concern. Also, printers can be electrically "noisy," drawing varying levels of power; when performing a print operation, they are extremely demanding, electrically speaking. (Inkjet printers require much less power than laser printers and are better to include on a UPS if you absolutely must have a printer during a power outage.)

Site Preparation

In addition to calculating the total power requirements for your servers, you must also consider the physical space that a UPS requires. Batteries can be quite large, and several models allow you to daisy chain multiple external battery packs together to extend UPS run time. This can require a great deal of space. One solution is a rack-mounted UPS. All vendors are moving to rack-mounted models in various formats. You can connect UPS units either in the same rack or in adjacent or back-to-back racks to increase run time or provide UPS fault tolerance (see Figure 4-6a). Also, you can use a rack-mounted

UPS with an external battery pack (see Figure 4-6b). These solutions are not something administrators arbitrarily piece together. Instead, always consult the UPS manufacturer, which will advise you on permissible physical connections, safety, power capacity, and run time.

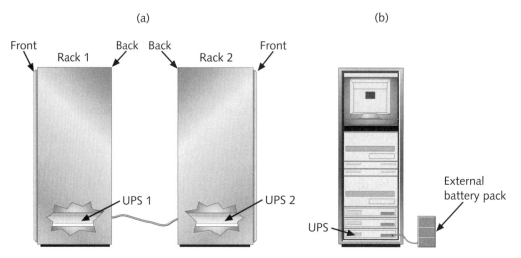

Figure 4-6   To provide extra power, connect two UPS systems back to back (a) or use an external battery pack (b)

It is important to realize that adding batteries to the UPS does not increase its volt-amp rating. For example, adding an extra battery will not upgrade your 1000 VA UPS to 1500 VA. Instead, it only extends run time. If the run time is 15 minutes, adding an extra battery will power the 1000 VA UPS for a few more minutes. The only way to increase VA is to use a more powerful UPS.

Rack-mounted UPS systems, especially larger ones, are extremely heavy and usually require assistance to install and service. Because of the weight, you should place them at or near the bottom of the rack (see more about rack-weight distribution later in this chapter).

The largest UPS systems can be huge. For example, the APC Silicon DP3500E is 70 inches high, 94 inches wide, 31 inches deep, and weighs a staggering 5500 pounds. Regardless of the size, the following checklist will help you to plan site requirements, particularly for larger systems:

- For larger UPS systems, notify building engineers, electricians, and electrical engineers; for extremely heavy systems, also notify structural engineers. Verify that all aspects of the site are safe.

- Do not place monitors or other devices that are highly sensitive to electro-magnetic fields (EMF) near the UPS. A larger UPS might emit an EMF that affects computer monitors, but probably not other equipment.

- UPS systems generate heat. Make sure the HVAC system can accommodate the heat output.

- Plan for any rewiring so that load equipment can reach the UPS. To prevent overloading the circuit, place larger UPS systems on a single, dedicated circuit.

- Verify sufficient clearance for adequate airflow, probably around 12 inches (0.31 m) behind a freestanding UPS array and 48 inches (1.22 m) in front (see Figure 4-7). Ensure adequate space to reach all switches, jacks, outlets, and so forth.

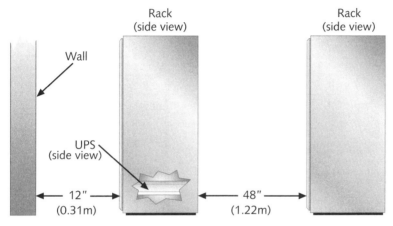

Figure 4-7   Allow enough space for airflow and equipment access

- Many UPS units have an optional earth ground to which you can ground the unit (in addition to existing AC grounding). Locate a suitable ground location reachable from the UPS.

- Get help—even in smaller units, the batteries are surprisingly heavy.

- Some larger freestanding units are on rolling casters to make movement easier. Make sure you lock the wheels when not moving the unit.

The following is a list of major vendors of UPS equipment:

- Tripp-Lite—*www.tripplite.com*

- American Power Conversion (APC)—*www.apc.com*

- Best Power—*www.bestpower.com*

- Liebert—*www.liebert.com*

- MGE—*www.mgeups.com*

- Oneac—*www.oneac.com*

- Sutton Designs—*www.suttondesigns.com*

THE RACK

In addition to configuring the system itself, you must determine the best physical orientation for the server—freestanding or rack mounted. Except for the smallest networks, you should plan to install servers in racks (this is the general assumption of this and following chapters unless stated otherwise). Racks provide an advantage in server rooms where the need for server and network equipment grows but floor space does not. By stacking equipment in a rack, you increase computing assets vertically in the same floor space that would have otherwise consumed precious floor space. This space savings is known as **density**. For example, in Figure 4-8, six servers on a table require about six feet of floor space. Using racks in the same six feet, you can install 18 8-way servers.

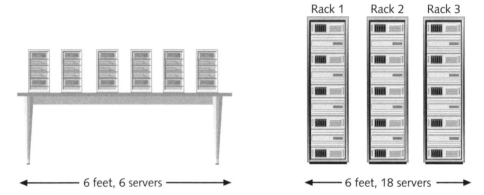

Figure 4-8   Density allows for more equipment in the same horizontal floor space

If you have existing servers in the tower configuration and want to place them in a rack, you can either place them on a vented shelf that mounts inside the rack or obtain a vendor kit that adapts the server to lay on its side and install it in the rack along telescoping rails. Nearly all network equipment (except, perhaps, for small workgroup hubs or switches) is rack-mountable. When you decide to use a rack, you must carefully consider several factors, including heat, ventilation, power, weight, grouping, and accessibility.

Physical Characteristics

Physical rack characteristics vary from one vendor to the next. However, general characteristics are listed here. All aspects of equipment installation revolve around the physical dimensions of the rack as follows (see Figure 4-9):

- *Units*: Rack equipment is measured in **EIA (Electronic Industries Alliance) units**, or **U**. One EIA unit (1U) is equal to 1.75 vertical inches (4.45 cm). For example, Tripp-Lite makes a rack-mounted UPS that is only 1U in size. Server appliances are usually between 1U for network appliances dedicated to a single purpose and up to 7U (12.25 inches, or 31.12 cm) for 8-way servers. Datacenter servers larger than 8-way (such as a 32-way) are usually in their own dedicated enclosure.

- *Height*: Including frame, bezels, and feet or rolling casters, a full-height rack (42U) is about 6 feet (1.8 m). Various manufacturers make smaller racks as well, with common sizes at 22U, 24U, and 36U. Some manufacturers offer rack extensions, which add about 8U to the height. See Table 4–3 as a reference (casters or feet not included).

Table 4-3   Rack Heights in Units, Inches, and Centimeters

Height in Units	Height in Inches	Height in Centimeters
22U	38.5	97.8
24U	42.0	106.7
36U	63.0	160.0
42U	73.5	186.7

- *Depth*: Racks are about 36 inches (.98 m) deep, with usable depth around 28 or 29 inches (between .71 and .73 m). Try not to use space beyond the usable depth, because you will still need room at the back to work, and for PDUs, cables, and other specialized devices that you do not need to see from the front.

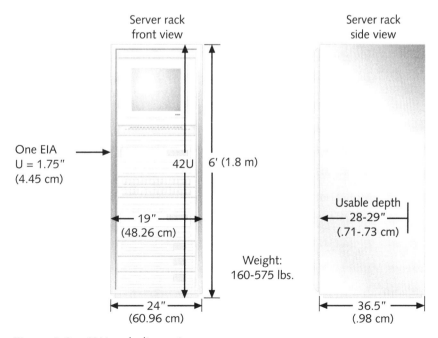

Figure 4-9   42U rack dimensions

- *Width*: Rack-mountable equipment requires a RETMA (Radio Electronics Television Manufacturers Association) industry standard opening of 19 inches (48.26 cm). Exterior width is usually about 23–24 inches (58.5 cm).

- *Weight*: Weight varies depending upon whether the rack includes ballast or doors, which weigh about 30 pounds each. 42U racks can weigh around 160–250 pounds empty, and can accommodate about 2000 pounds of equipment. (IBM has a heavy-duty rack that weighs 575 pounds empty!) 24U racks are about 210 pounds empty, and can accommodate about 1000 pounds of equipment.

Racks can also include several other items:

- *Stabilizing feet*: Moving rack equipment in and out while servicing it presents a physical danger of the rack falling over. Stabilizing feet extend beyond the rack and help prevent it from tipping over when you work on equipment. The HP Rack System/E includes both a front and rear retractable anti-tip foot for added safety.

- *Leveling screws*: Similar to the leveling screws under a washing machine (but capable of much greater weight loads), you turn the screws until the rack is level.

- *Wheels*: Usually made of polyurethane to reduce the effect of bumps, jolts, and uneven floors when moving the rack. The wheels can support a great deal of weight, usually 1000 pounds *each*.

- *Filler panels*: Purely cosmetic, these panels cover up empty slots for a more professional, finished look.

- *Side panels*: Also cosmetic, side panels cover up the exposed sides of the rack. These are unnecessary where you join two racks together.

- *KVM/concentrator/switchbox*: A **keyboard, video, mouse (KVM)**, also called a concentrator or switchbox, enables you to control multiple servers from a single keyboard, video monitor, and mouse.

- *Cable management arm*: It is important that when you service equipment and pull it out of the rack, all the cables do not come loose. Instead of bunching up the cable slack in a tangled mess at the back, you can Velcro cables to a **cable management arm (CMA)** that keeps cables neat while allowing them to extend when you pull out equipment. Cable management brackets also can be used to guide cables vertically within the rack.

- *Ballast*: Dead weight placed vertically, at the sides of the rack or at the bottom of the rack, to add stability when heavy equipment is required higher in the rack. A single ballast usually weighs about 30 pounds.

- *Short rear door*: The rear door has a gap of a few inches at the bottom to facilitate cabling out of the rack while maintaining security.

Cooling

Many racks include an option for front and rear lockable doors. Most doors are perforated safety glass or steel, providing about 60% opening for adequate ventilation, which in most racks is through convection (see Figure 4-10). Some manufacturers (such as Compaq) offer a multi-angled door design that enhances convection cooling. Warm air rises to the top of the rack, which may also be perforated.

4

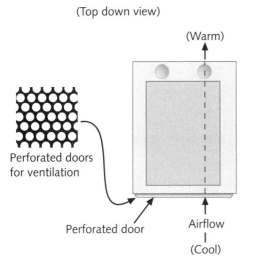

(Top down view)

(Warm)

Perforated doors for ventilation

Perforated door

Airflow

(Cool)

Figure 4-10   Perforated doors assist cooling through convection and fan-propelled airflow through equipment

To ensure adequate cooling in the rack, you can install fans in the top panel to increase availability of cool air inside the rack and draw warm air out (see Figure 4-11). Other temperature-control solutions cool from the front to the back, which is a function of the equipment in the rack. For example, a server might have a fan at the back of the unit that draws air into louvers at the front, and expels warm air out the back. Even in this case, you might still install fans at the top, which will help to more quickly expel naturally rising warm air while also drawing cooler air from the bottom of the rack. (Recall from Chapter 2 that some floors have air-conditioning vents beneath the racks.) This is also a more significant concern when the rack includes items that run hot, such as UPS systems and disk arrays.

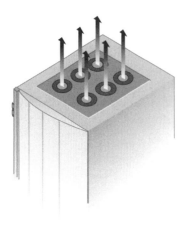

Figure 4-11   Fans in the top of the rack draw warm air out while cool air enters from the bottom

Be careful not to place anything on the top surface of the rack, which would inhibit dissipation of warm air. Be careful not to place racks so that the back of a rack faces the front of another to avoid the intake of warm air. Instead, you should place racks back to back and allow adequate space between rows of racks (see Figure 4-12).

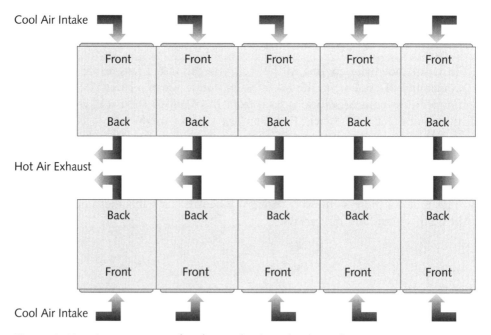

Figure 4-12   Arrange rows of racks in a back-to-back configuration

Although a rack with doors can also be classified as a cabinet, the remainder of this book classifies both types as a rack unless specified otherwise.

Configuration

Configuring the rack well directly affects the level of practical usability and prevents the need to rearrange equipment in the future. Major vendor web sites offer rack configuration utilities as either downloadable programs or web-based applets. These utilities are the most effective way to configure a rack, especially if all rack equipment is from the same vendor. If you make an unwise choice, the utility might alert you and ask if you want to select an alternative. Even if you do not stay with the same vendor for all equipment in your rack, you can use a rack configuration utility to approximate like equipment. For example, the HP Netserver LXR 8500 is very similar in power requirements and dimensions to the Dell PowerEdge 8450. The following is a short list of vendors offering rack configuration utilities:

- Dell—*www.dell.com* (download). A good, basic rack configuration utility.

- Compaq—*www.compaq.com* (web-based). Offers the advantage of not having to install yet another program on your computer. Offers two modes, one for novices and one for those more experienced in rack configuration.

- Hewlett-Packard—*www.hp.com* (download). This one is excellent in terms of usability and has a low learning curve. In Hands-on Project 4-5 at the end of this chapter, you will use the HP Rack Assistant utility to practice configuring a rack.

- IBM—*www.ibm.com* (download). The most detailed tool, but it will take a little longer to learn its usage and options (see Figure 4-13).

While extremely useful and educational, these utilities cannot account for every contingency, and you will have to monitor the results for accuracy and practicality in your own real-world environment. Also, most of these utilities do not fully consider the implications of joining two racks together, especially in terms of sharing cabling between the racks. Therefore, you should be able to wisely configure a rack for weight distribution, device grouping, and cable management as described in the following sections.

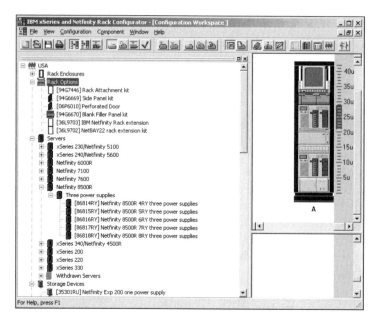

Figure 4-13   The IBM Netfinity Rack Configurator is an excellent tool

Weight Distribution

Larger 8-way rack servers can weigh upward of 175 pounds, and UPS systems like the APC Smart-UPS 5000 RM is 5U and weighs 320 pounds! The general rule of thumb is to *place the heaviest items at the bottom of the rack*, which minimizes the chances of the rack tipping over. Therefore, unless the UPS is small (1U or 2U), you should almost invariably place it at the bottom. If other planning factors such as device grouping prevent you from placing all the heavier items at the bottom, try to avoid placing heavier items any higher than 36 inches (.91 m) up the rack, and consider adding one or more ballasts. Each ballast is 1U and weighs 30 pounds. Other heavy items include mass storage items such as a DLT (Digital Linear Tape, a backup device) and a disk array. (HP recommends placing the DLT just above the UPS.) It should not adversely affect weight distribution if you need to insert a keyboard/mouse between heavy devices.

It is very important that you pull out only one piece of rack equipment at a time to avoid tipping. Even equipment that is only moderately heavy has a greater impact on server balance when it is pulled "out of center." A rack can easily exceed 1000 pounds, and could seriously injure or kill someone if it fell over. When working on a rack, don't forget to extend stabilizing feet if they are available (see Figure 4-14).

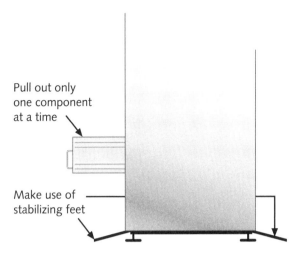

Figure 4-14   Pull out only one device at a time, and use stabilizing feet to prevent tipping

Device Grouping

Grouping devices involves a delicate balance between weight distribution and logically placing components where cables from one component can reach other components. Also, for purposes of usability, some types of equipment should be placed where they are most usable. For example, although the keyboard is lightweight, placing it at the top of the rack would make it inaccessible to administrators. If administrators work on the server in a standing position, you should place the keyboard in the middle of the rack (or a little lower if administrators will be seated). The logic of some devices is also important. For example, certain devices might need to be closer to one another for cables to reach.

Another reason to group equipment in a different way than you would if only considering weight might be clustering. As introduced in Chapter 1, clustering involves two or more servers serving data from the same physical media (hard drives). In the rack, you might have (starting from the bottom) at least one UPS, Cluster Server 1, a disk array that contains data, and then Cluster Server 2 (see Figure 4-15).

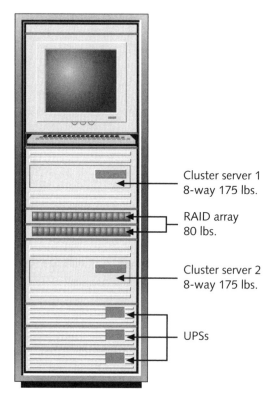

Cluster server 1
8-way 175 lbs.

RAID array
80 lbs.

Cluster server 2
8-way 175 lbs.

UPSs

Figure 4-15   A cluster might change the usual weight distribution order

Cable Management

One of the primary goals in cable management is neatness. While this might sound compulsive, organization is critical in the server room. When equipment fails, administrators must have minimal distraction in finding the proper equipment. When trying to access equipment at the back of the rack (to replace a power supply, for example), you do not want to fight your way through a morass of cable. With cables neatly aligned along a CMA and placed out of the way with cable management brackets, guides, and so forth, you should be able to quickly access the equipment you need. Figure 4-16 is a good example of neatly arranged cable.

Another factor that affects where you place equipment is cable length. The effective cable reach of pieces using a CMA will be shorter because several inches (perhaps 28 or more) will be used by the arm. However, the shorter cable reach is well worth the improved organization and secure connections that a CMA provides (see Figure 4-17).

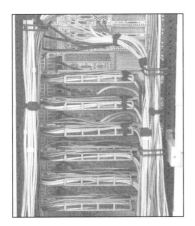

Figure 4-16   An HP rack with neatly arranged cable

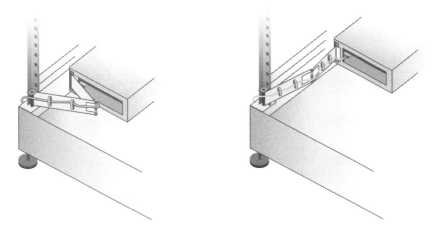

Figure 4-17   The CMA expands and contracts when you move the server

If cable lengths are too short, you might have to place dependent equipment closer to one another. For example, a light, 1U web server near the top of the rack must back up its content to a DLT located at the bottom of the rack. If the cable lengths are not sufficient, you might have to move the heavy DLT higher in the rack, lower the 1U web server, or move the 1U web server to an adjacent rack in a lower position closer to the DLT. Many devices cannot use an extension to make up the shortfall in cable lengths. For example, there is no such thing as a SCSI cable extension.

Cable lengths become a more visible restriction when you consider a monitor, which is usually placed higher in the rack than the server. Typically, the monitor cable can reach the server over a maximum of 29U. If necessary, you can purchase an inexpensive VGA extension cable. I recommend you use as short a length as necessary (hopefully 6 feet or less), because longer lengths are not good for video signal integrity.

In the absence of a CMA, you might consider using a straight point-to-point cabling method with no intermediate cable management. However, this is the least desired method because the rack becomes more difficult to manage when you have cables hanging in the way. Also, unless there is a method to secure the cable ends (such as thumb screws), they are more likely to fall off. Some rack equipment has a cable tray option extending from the back of the equipment. The point of the cable tray is to lessen the pull of gravity on the cable connection and reduce the likelihood of the cable falling out (see Figure 4-18).

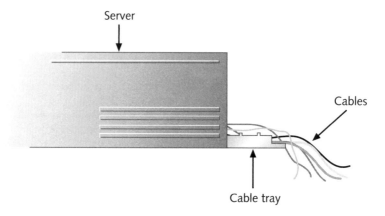

Figure 4-18 A cable tray helps cables to stay plugged in

Sometimes you need to use multiple devices from several racks that connect to a physical and logical center. For example, Figure 4-19 shows a centrally located server that connects to several devices such as DLT backup equipment, a SCSI disk array, and a Fibre Channel disk array. If other planning factors prevent you from placing all the equipment in the same rack, then centrally locate the server between racks containing the equipment.

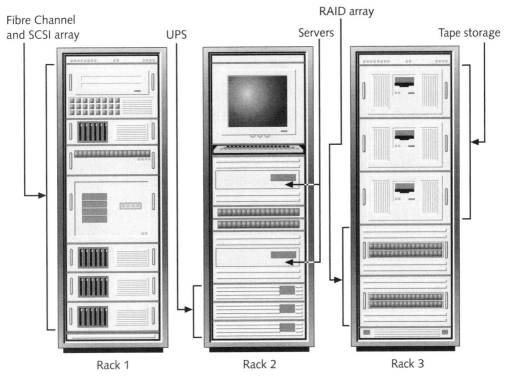

Figure 4-19   Place the server central to the other equipment to which it connects

 Be sure to route cables so that they cannot be stepped on or tripped over, and do not place any equipment on top of the cables.

Power

The need for a UPS was established earlier in this chapter. A UPS is only as good as its availability, so each piece of rack equipment must be able to connect to the UPS. The UPS has a limited number of outlets (perhaps six), and in a fully loaded rack, that's probably not enough. However, by using a rack-mounted PDU, you can create more outlets (see Figure 4-20). Make sure that the devices you attach to it do not exceed 80% of the PDU's power rating. You install the PDU in the rack in any of several configurations. Usually, you try to locate the PDU at the rear of the rack and as close to the bottom as possible.

Figure 4-20   The PDU provides the functionality of a power strip at much higher power capacity

Vertically installed PDUs attach to either the left or right rack post (see Figure 4-21). However, most PDUs use 11U vertically, so you can probably only install three on one rail, left or right. Another factor that limits PDU installation is the type of server. Some servers slide out of the rack at the rear instead of the front (the HP NetServer LXr Pro8, for example). In this case, a horizontal PDU in the same space as the server would interfere with server removal. In a vertical PDU configuration, also be careful not to install the PDU at the location of the locking latch, and face the PDU inward so that rack covers do not block outlets.

Figure 4-21   A vertical PDU installation

A horizontal installation usually allows for cleaner routing of power cables, and can be mounted behind most rack equipment in the same EIA unit except for very deep, large rack components such as some large servers. If installation behind a unit is not acceptable, you can also mount PDUs in the bottom of most racks (see Figure 4-22).

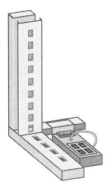

4

Figure 4-22   Mounting in the bottom of the rack does not interfere with other equipment

Many PDUs, especially those with higher voltage, have locking plugs that plug into a locking receptacle to prevent accidental disconnection. The rack utility software from several vendors mentioned earlier calculates the VAs required to service the equipment you propose, and also suggests the quantity and type of PDUs you will need. For an added level of power redundancy, you can use a PDU designed for utility power from two independent circuits. If one of the circuits fails, the other transparently continues to provide service (see Figure 4-23).

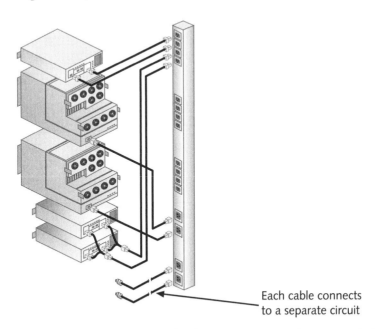

Each cable connects
to a separate circuit

Figure 4-23   For added redundancy, use a PDU that connects to two independent circuits

Turn on components in the rack one at a time to avoid a sudden inrush of power, which might trip the main circuit breaker, UPS fuse or breaker, or PDU fuse or breaker. Usually, you should power up in this order: tape backup, mass storage units, monitor, KVM, and one server at a time.

The KVM

It is impractical to have a separate keyboard, video display, and mouse for each server in the rack. A 42U rack can have 42 separate 1U servers! Instead, it makes more sense to install a single keyboard, video display, and mouse (KVM) that can service all of the connected servers, collectively referred to as a **console** (see Figure 4-24). A KVM console also reduces air-conditioning costs by eliminating multiple heat-generating monitors. You can obtain a basic, inexpensive KVM console for any configuration of workstations or servers, most of which operate between four and eight systems. Some can also be set to continually cycle between servers every few seconds so that you can observe activity on each server.

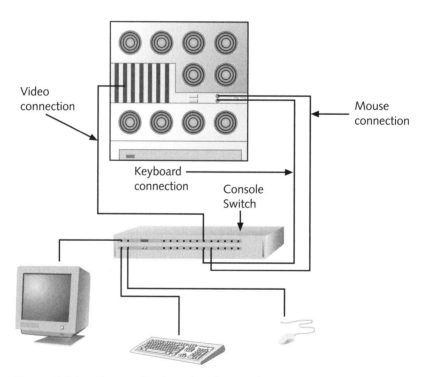

Figure 4-24   Use one keyboard, video, and mouse to control servers through a KVM console

For the rack, you can use several KVM components to arrive at the configuration you want:

- 1U fixed keyboard/mouse tray

- 2U retractable keyboard and mouse tray

- Full-size (about 11U) video display

- 1U or 2U integrated keyboard, trackball, and video display (see Figure 4-25)

Figure 4-25   An integrated keyboard, trackball, and pop-up video display

Whichever configuration you decide on, the clear advantage is that you conserve space by using a single KVM console to manage multiple servers. Also, since each KVM console often manages up to eight servers, vendors usually offer the option to cascade the consoles, which allows you to manage dozens of servers. Some consoles are wireless, and with signal amplification can allow you to control more than 60 servers.

The keyboard, mouse, and video monitor each connect to the KVM console. Then you need one extension cord (male to female) each for the keyboard, video monitor, and mouse for each server. If you have four servers, then you need four sets of extension cords. You can usually purchase the set as a bundled pack from any computer supply source.

KVM switches are available from nearly all major server vendors and most computer stores. APC manufactures an outstanding KVM console that, in addition to standard functions, includes the following features:

- Password security to the KVM console adds an extra level of security.

- An on-screen display with customizable menus allows you to graphically switch between servers.

- Hot-pluggable operation allows you to add servers without having to first power off the KVM or other servers attached to the KVM.

- Mouse reset circumvents a frustration with KVM systems in which the mouse ceases to respond to actions. This feature also allows you to regain control of the mouse without powering down the KVM or the server.

Alternatively, you can usually administer servers from the comfort of your own desktop with a full-screen monitor, keyboard, and mouse, depending on the operating system. For example, you can use the text-based Telnet utility to remotely connect to and administer

UNIX systems and perform router programming. Windows 2000 and NT 4.0 offer administrative tools that you can run from any Windows computer on the network. NetWare offers similar management control.

Rack Installation Tips

The following tips can help you to properly configure the rack:

- Begin building the rack from the bottom up, with heaviest devices at the bottom (as previously discussed).

- If using multiple racks, be consistent in the server numbering scheme in relation to port numbers on the KVM, which helps you to quickly access the right server from one rack to the next instead of using a hit-or-miss method.

- Place servers attached to the same KVM console in close proximity to it so that you can easily view server activity while at the keyboard.

- Group servers that serve a particular purpose in the same physical area. For example, put web servers in one location, file servers in another, application servers in another, and so forth. This helps to minimize trips across the server room when configuring or troubleshooting.

- Remember that at times you must access the rear of the server. Make sure there is adequate space behind the server to open the rear door.

- Place servers that require frequent access (such as those with backup devices) in more easily accessible locations.

- Place servers according to security need. Position high-security servers in highly visible locations where it is more obvious if someone is accessing them.

- For added security, lock the rack doors and install an alarm that trips when the door has been breached.

- Fully loaded racks are extremely heavy, so limit the number of racks that you tie together if you plan to move them, even for routine cleaning. It can be very difficult to roll three attached racks, even with assistance.

- When sliding equipment in and out of a rack, watch your fingers! The slide rails are pinch points.

Hundreds of pages about rack planning and installation can be found at the following sites:
http://netserver.hp.com/netserver/docs/download.asp?file=g_rack_cabling.pdf
http://support.dell.com/docs/systems/smarcon/en/index.htm
ftp://ftp.compaq.com/pub/products/storageworks/techdoc/racksandoptions/14255e2.pdf
www.ibm.com (search for the Netfinity Rack Configurator)

CHAPTER SUMMARY

❏ A server can usually operate acceptably with only a single PSU. A second PSU provides load balancing to reduce demands placed on a single PSU and also provides failover, in case one of the power supplies fails.

❏ Servers offer N+1 expandability for several critical components, particularly the processor and the PSU. The "N" is a variable that refers to the quantity of a given component installed in a system, and "+1" refers to a spare component or opening for a component.

❏ The PSU often uses a variable fan speed, which increases or decreases based upon the amount of heat detected by the PSU thermistor (a type of internal thermostat).

❏ Power Distribution Units (PDUs) often plug into a 208 V outlet and supply power to internal rack components.

❏ Calculating the power needs for a server requires you to know how much power the motherboard, processor, internal adapters, and peripherals require.

❏ Some devices might list volts, watts, amps, or a combination thereof. Use the information you can gather in the following formula: watts = volts $\times$ amps.

❏ Add the total power requirements for all server components, and subtract the total number from the power rating for the power supply. You should have plenty of power to spare if you want the system to be as reliable as possible.

❏ An uninterruptible power supply (UPS) temporarily supplies power using batteries to the load equipment (anything connected to the UPS that draws power, usually servers and possibly other network equipment) in the event of a power outage. The UPS also supplements power in case of a brownout, where utility power continues but is below acceptable operating voltages.

❏ The primary purpose of a UPS is not to continue normal operations for the entire duration of a brownout or power failure. Instead, the UPS provides a few minutes of power to give administrators enough time to send network messages to users (giving them time to save and close files) and gracefully shut down the server using normal procedures in the NOS.

❏ UPS software can assist the administrator by automatically shutting down the server, issuing alerts, and safely storing data that might otherwise be lost.

❏ Backup batteries eventually fail or lose their ability to retain a charge. Server-level UPS systems usually also offer N+1 functionality that allows you to replace a battery while another battery (or batteries) continues to power the unit, ensuring that the UPS is not temporarily unavailable. Also, you can use multiple UPS units so that you can service one UPS while the remaining units continue to supply power.

❏ Generally, administrators seek about 15 minutes of backup power for servers.

❐ Determine the UPS requirements based upon the power supply rating and the amount of time you require to power the server.

❐ The following formula determines VA: volts × amps = VA, and 1000 VA = kVA.

❐ Rack-mounted UPS systems, especially larger ones, are extremely heavy and usually require assistance to install and service. Because of the weight load, you should place them at or near the bottom of the rack.

❐ By stacking equipment in a rack, you increase computing assets vertically in the same floor space.

❐ Rack equipment is measured in EIA (Electronic Industries Alliance) units (U). One U equals 1.75 inches (4.45 cm).

❐ The standard rack is 42U high and has a 19 inch (48.26 cm) opening for equipment.

❐ Stabilizing feet extend beyond the rack and help prevent the rack from tipping over when you work on equipment.

❐ Many racks include an option for front and rear lockable doors. Most doors are perforated safety glass or steel, and provide an opening for adequate ventilation, which in most racks is through convection. You can also install fans in the top.

❐ The general rule of thumb with rack installations is to *place the heaviest items at the bottom of the rack*, which minimizes the chance of the rack tipping over. It is very important that you only pull out one piece of rack equipment at a time to avoid tipping.

❐ Clustering, cable reach, and usability might force exceptions to the rule that the heaviest items always go on the bottom of the rack.

❐ Keep cables neat and within adequate reach of the devices to which they connect. Use a cable management arm (CMA) to prevent equipment from being unplugged when sliding them out of the rack.

❐ Make sure that the devices you attach to a PDV do not exceed 80% of the PDU's power ratings.

❐ Vertical PDU installations allow installation of other equipment in the same EIA units. A horizontal installation usually allows for cleaner routing of power cables and can be mounted behind most rack equipment in the same EIA unit, except for very deep, larger rack components such as some larger servers. You can also mount PDUs in the bottom of most racks.

❐ For an added level of power redundancy, you can use a PDU designed for utility power from two independent circuits. If one of the circuits fails, the other transparently continues to provide service.

❐ Turn on components in the rack one at a time to avoid a sudden inrush of power, which might trip the main circuit breaker, UPS fuse or breaker, or PDU fuse or breaker. Usually, you should power up in this order: tape backup, mass storage units, monitor, KVM, and then one server at a time.

❐ It makes sense to install a single keyboard, video, mouse (KVM) console that can switch back and forth between the connected servers. A KVM console also reduces air-conditioning costs by eliminating multiple heat-generating monitors. Vendors usually offer the option to cascade the consoles, allowing you to manage dozens of servers.

❐ You need one extension cord (male to female) each for the keyboard, video monitor, and mouse for each server.

4

KEY TERMS

actual power (also **true power**) — The power in watts delivered from the utility company.

apparent power — The power delivered to a device after passing through the power supply.

cable management arm (CMA) — Rack equipment that allows orderly arrangement of cables, and expands and contracts so that you can move equipment on the rack without accidentally unplugging it.

console — An inclusive term for the keyboard video mouse (KVM) and all attached servers.

density — A measure of the number of devices or servers within a given area of floor space. Higher density means more servers in a given area, usually accomplished by stacking equipment in racks.

drive logic — The circuitry included in the floppy or hard drive that interfaces with the disk controller.

EIA (Electronic Industries Alliance) unit (U) — A rack unit of measure equaling 1.75 vertical inches (4.45 cm).

generator kick (also **kick** or **kickstart**) — The time required for the generator to come online.

inrush power — Temporary surge of power to the server when it is turned on.

keyboard, video, mouse (KVM) — A console that enables you to control multiple servers from a single keyboard, video monitor, and mouse.

line conditioner — A device that filters out power inconsistencies, temporarily bridges power in the event of a brief brownout, suppresses high voltage spikes, and provides overall buffering between building power and the system.

load equipment — Anything connected to the UPS that draws power, usually servers and possibly other network equipment.

N+1 — A term that describes the expandability of a given server component or components, or space provided for expandable components. "N" is a variable that refers to the quantity of a given component installed in a system, and "+1" refers to a spare component.

power distribution unit (PDU) — A device similar in function to a household power strip that connects multiple devices to a power supply, but it is capable of much higher power capacity.

power factor — The difference between actual power and apparent power.

power supply unit (PSU) — The internal power supply powering a server or servers.

run time — The number of minutes that batteries can power the system.

standby power supply (SPS) — A device or technique that detects an interruption in line power and switches to a large transformer that stores a small amount of power required to bridge the time it takes to switch to battery power.

thermistor — A power supply thermostat that increases or decreases fan speed based on heat generated by the power supply.

REVIEW QUESTIONS

1. Which of the following power supply wattages is likely to be found in a server?

   a. 145 W

   b. 200 W

   c. 250 W

   d. 375 W

2. How is the physical connection of a non-hot-swappable power supply different from a hot-swappable power supply? Choose two.

   a. You must remove individual power connectors.

   b. You must remove the server case cover.

   c. The PSU plugs directly into the chassis without individual cable connections.

   d. The wattage is much higher.

3. What is N+1 redundancy?

   a. It is a measure of the number of functioning hard disks plus one hot spare hard disk.

   b. "N" refers to the quantity of a given component and "+1" refers to a spare.

   c. It is a modem command that dials without waiting for a dial tone.

   d. It refers to the number of processors plus one redundant processor.

4. What might prevent you from turning on an entire rack of equipment at once?

   a. nothing, as long as a UPS is attached

   b. a UPS with not enough capacity

   c. inrush power

   d. a UPS with not enough run time

5. How many amps might a PCI slot use?

   a. 2

   b. 3

   c. 4

   d. 5

6. What is the load equipment?

   a. anything connected to the UPS that draws power

   b. relatively heavy rack equipment

   c. any device requiring more than 1 amp

   d. UPS batteries

7. What is the purpose of a UPS?

   a. to provide extended run time in the event of a power failure

   b. to allow the server to go into a low-power, energy-saving state

   c. to conserve electricity

   d. to provide enough power for a graceful shutdown

8. What is the advantage of the online/double conversion UPS?

   a. no switchover time

   b. reduced energy efficiency

   c. low cost

   d. only converts DC current to AC during a blackout or brownout

9. How does a UPS trigger UPS software to perform actions when power fails?

   a. using a USB or serial port to communicate with the software

   b. Nothing. The software detects dips in power or blackouts by itself.

   c. infrared signals

   d. a directed send through the network

10. What good is N+1 redundancy with a UPS?

    a. It provides additional run time in the event of a power failure.

    b. If a UPS fails, the other continues to provide power redundancy.

    c. It provides additional power capacity.

    d. N+1 is not a UPS function.

11. Where in the rack should you usually place UPS equipment?

    a. at the top

    b. in the middle

    c. anywhere

    d. at the bottom

12. Where are you likely to install additional fans in the rack?

    a. in one of the side panels

    b. in the bottom panel above the floor

    c. in the top panel

    d. in the back of the server

13. What is a primary advantage of a rack?

    a. increased density

    b. less heat buildup

    c. quieter operation because of the doors

    d. better organization of equipment

14. How big is 1U?

    a. depends on the rack manufacturer

    b. 1.75 inches (4.45 cm)

    c. 2.4 inches (6.07 cm)

    d. 1.57 inches (3.99 cm)

15. How much total approximate weight can a full height rack accommodate?

    a. 2000 lbs

    b. 1000 lbs

    c. limited only by floor support

    d. virtually unlimited

16. Where should you generally place the heaviest items in the rack?

    a. top

    b. middle

    c. bottom

    d. anywhere, as long as the overall balance is good

17. What helps to manage cables in the rack?

    a. cable management arms

    b. zip ties

    c. duct tape

    d. the PDU

18. What is the purpose of a KVM?

    a. to use a single console to control multiple computers

    b. to use multiple consoles to control a single computer

    c. to shorten the cable length of I/O devices

    d. to use the multi-monitor capabilities of Windows 2000

19. How does a PDU differ from a standard power strip?
    a. the number of outlets
    b. higher power capacity
    c. lower power capacity
    d. no difference
20. What is the purpose of a ballast?
    a. to add weight near the top of the rack
    b. to add weight to the side of a rack
    c. to fill empty spaces in the front of the rack
    d. to add weight near the bottom of the rack

4

HANDS-ON PROJECTS

Project 4-1

There are several things wrong with the rack depicted in Figure 4-26. Name them, and explain why they are wrong. On a separate piece of paper, diagram a more sensible configuration for this rack.

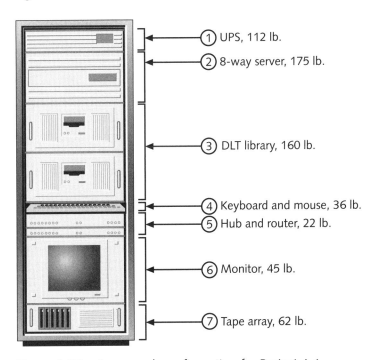

Figure 4-26   Server rack configuration for Project 4-1

Project 4-2

In this project, you will change a redundant power supply.

1. Ensure that server power is on with at least one redundant power supply.

2. Remove one of the power supplies. You might have to first remove the cover.

3. Notice that the power service to the server continues to function.

4. If the power redundancy is 2+1, and the remaining two power supplies provide load balancing (meaning that a single power supply can power the system), then remove another power supply. Power service to the server continues to function.

5. Leave the power supplies out for a few minutes. You might notice the fan on the last remaining power supply speeds up due to higher temperatures as it solely provides power.

6. Reinstall the power supplies you removed earlier, and put the cover back on if you removed it. Shut down the server for the next project.

Project 4-3

In this project, you will connect a UPS to the server.

1. Ensure that the server is powered off.

2. Plug the UPS power cable into utility power. Anything over 200 V might be a locking plug, which prevents accidental removal.

3. Connect the server's power cord to the UPS.

4. Connect the UPS serial or USB cable to the server. Note that the serial cable is usually proprietary to the UPS — you cannot use a standard serial cable.

5. Turn on the server.

6. Verify that the battery is installed (or connected, if external), and then turn on the UPS. Depending on the brand, this might involve simply pushing the power button or pushing and holding it for a few seconds. The battery is probably not fully charged (it usually takes several hours to fully charge a battery).

7. Observe the indicators on the UPS. You can probably see indicators that show the charge percentage, load level, and so forth.

8. When the NOS has loaded, log on and install the UPS management software (such as APC PowerChute).

9. Using the software, access the interface that allows you to configure email or pager alerts when a UPS event (such as power failure) happens. Enter your email address and/or pager number. If connected to the network or phone line, you should receive notification with each configured UPS event.

10. Configure the software to automatically save open documents.

11. Configure the software to automatically shut down after two minutes (you might want more time in the real world).

12. Open a document in a word processor, type in some words, and save the document. Then, type in some more words without saving the document.

13. If the battery has at least a 50% charge, unplug utility power.

14. Watch the system shut down the server.

15. Plug utility power back in, and turn on the server.

16. When the NOS loads and you log on, open the document you created in Step 12. Notice the changes were saved for you automatically.

17. Later, check your email and/or pager for a notification of the failed utility power.

18. Optionally, restart the server but do not let the OS load. You can do this by inserting a blank floppy in the floppy drive assuming the BIOS is set to boot from the floppy. Note the battery level, and then unplug utility power and see how many minutes and seconds the battery is able to power the system.

Project 4-4

In this project, you will choose a UPS system using the APC web site.

1. Using your web browser, go to *www.apc.com*.

2. Navigate to the Selectors section, and choose **Go to the UPS Selector**.

3. Notice that you can select several types of electronic equipment for a UPS. Click on **Server**.

4. You are presented with a list of various servers. Choose a high-end PC server. Suggestions: Compaq 8-way, Dell PowerEdge 8450 rack mount, HP Netserver LXr 8500dc.

5. Enter information about the server such as the chassis type (select **Rack Mount**), monitor, number of processors, and so forth. Enter whatever you like, but be somewhat realistic; otherwise, there won't be a UPS powerful enough. Because the voltages are likely to be high, select a NEMA L6-30P plug type (a locking, 30 amp plug).

6. You are returned to the initial screen to choose more equipment if necessary. You can add more if you like, and when finished, continue on to the Preferences section.

7. You might have to back up and make a change here or there, but eventually you will find one or more solutions from APC.

8. On a separate sheet of paper, answer the following questions:

    a. How long will the server run with this UPS?

    b. What percent of the maximum capacity is used by this UPS?

    c. How many watts?

    d. What type of connections (plugs and receptacles) does it offer?

9. Close the web browser.

Project 4-5

In this project, you will configure a rack using HP Netserver Rack Assistant.

1. Navigate to the Hewlett-Packard web site at *www.hp.com*.

2. Access the **Products and Services** section of the site.

3. Under Server, select **PC Server**.

4. Under Accessories, select **Rack Solutions**.

5. Navigate to the link for the rack assistant. (Try a search if you cannot navigate your way to the link.)

6. Download the software and install it on a Windows computer.

7. Start the software, and open a new rack when prompted.

8. Choose the rack attributes. For the rack voltage, select 200/208. Leave the rules selected. The software offers you suggestions about your configuration and stack equipment according to predefined rules. Use a stand-alone rack.

9. Add items to the rack as you like by double-clicking them. Add at least two servers, two mass storage units, a keyboard/monitor, and at least one UPS. You will notice that as you add items, statistics about the weight, voltage, BTU/hour (heat measurement), and so forth appear on the right.

10. When you print or save the document, the Rack Assistant offers you suggestions that you can accept or deny.

11. Close the Rack Assistant, and then close the web browser.

Project 4-6

In this project, you will install rack equipment in the rack.

1. Access a rack at least 24U in height. Have various pieces of equipment that you can add to the server, such as at least one server, KVM, monitor, PDU, and UPS. If available, also try to have cable management equipment.

2. Arrange the equipment from heaviest to lightest. This is not necessarily the order in which you will install the equipment, but it is a guideline.

3. If the rack has stabilizing feet (highly recommended), extend or attach them.

4. Install the UPS in the bottom of the server. Remember that to install the UPS and all other heavy items, you should get help from another person.

5. Install one or more PDUs. Plug the PDU into the UPS. Do not plug in the UPS. This project is for installation purposes only; you will not be powering up equipment.

6. Install either the server or the mass storage device above the UPS. This can go either way depending upon the weight of the mass storage device. Lighter storage devices can be installed higher in the rack or where it is easier to access the equipment to change tapes.

7. Place the KVM at a comfortable height and the monitor at a viewable height.

8. Route the cables along cable arms and brackets if available.

9. If you have two or more servers to install, use the KVM to make appropriate connections between the two. Remember that for each server, you need one set of extension cords for the keyboard and mouse (both round PS/2 connectors) and a video cable. If you have two servers, then you need two sets of extension cords.

4

CASE PROJECTS

1. Your multimedia organization has recently absorbed a small corporation in Hutchinson, KS. Your supervisor wants you to travel to Hutchinson to ensure that the single server in that office is as close as possible to the same hardware reliability as servers in the main office. You arrive at the new office and find that the "server" is really just a high-end PC workstation with Windows NT 4.0 installed on it. In addition to its role as a server, the graphic artists also access the computer for high-end graphics work. You are concerned about all the modifications to the system. On a 250 W power supply, the server has the following installed hardware running 24/7:

Component	Watts
Motherboard	30 W
Pentium III 750 MHz	25 W
4X AGP	30 W
256 MB RAM	20 W
Four occupied PCI slots	20 W
3.5 inch floppy drive	5 W
3 IDE 7200 internal hard disks	45 W
2 CD-ROMs	50 W
Total wattage	**225 W**

What problem(s) do you see with this server and what solution(s) would you recommend?

2. Your large enterprise has grown very quickly over the past three years. You have experienced difficulty keeping up with rapid expansion, but you are traveling to several offices over the next few months to try to ensure that each site has the necessary power redundancy available. You visit the Livermore, CA site and immediately hear concern from the local administrator that the last time a brownout occurred, the UPS system in one of the racks provided power for only five minutes before losing power. You analyze the rack in which the UPS is installed, and it seems that the UPS carries sufficient VA to power the rack for at least 15 minutes. What could be causing the short power duration?

5

HARD DISK INTERFACES AND RAID

After reading this chapter and completing the exercises, you will be able to:

♦ Identify basic physical hard disk components

♦ Compare physical and logical drives and describe their functionality

♦ Identify major file systems

♦ Identify characteristics of the IDE interface and configure IDE cabling and connectors

♦ Identify characteristics of the SCSI interface and configure SCSI cabling and connectors

♦ Become familiar with Fibre Channel technology and storage area networking

♦ Identify and configure various types of RAID

The physical hard disk is the focal point of the enterprise. The operating system, applications, and data are stored on the hard disk, and without hard disk storage, there is nothing for anyone to "do" on the network. Therefore, it makes sense that server storage be protected against failure and that administrators configure storage so that it is as fast as reasonably possible. This chapter opens with a brief inventory of hard disk physical components, differentiates physical and logical drives, and describes the major file systems commonly in use on servers. To operate the hard disk, an IDE or SCSI controller and attachment interface are necessary. Also, you will need to be aware of rules that govern appropriate connections and compatibilities for a given hard disk configuration, especially for SCSI.

Although desktop users commonly use only a single physical hard disk, server administrators often manage dozens of hard disks—most of which require high performance, redundancy, or both using various RAID implementations. When administrators add or replace a drive, it is vital to do so with minimal disruption (if any) to users, and this chapter shows you various ways to do this. Part of administering server storage is proper maintenance, and you will learn about several such utilities. Finally, you will learn about network storage, including a new technology known as Fibre Channel that provides outstanding performance.

HARD DISK COMPONENTS

Although we use the term "hard drive" or "hard disk," a hard disk is really multiple physical platters inside a sealed, dust-free housing. The manufacturing process is extremely controlled—there is no tolerance for contaminants (such as dust particles)—and manufacturing specifications are extremely tight. Most hard disks include the following major physical components (use Figure 5-1 for reference as you read the rest of this section):

- Disk platters
- Drive heads
- Actuator mechanism

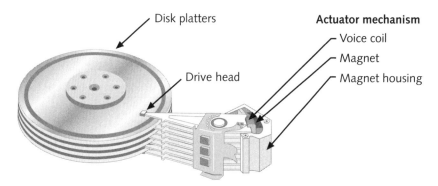

Figure 5-1 Hard disk components

The hard disk also consists of the following components not visible in Figure 5-1:

- Spindle motor
- Logic board
- Connectors
- Jumpers

Though it would be impractical to exhaustively describe each hard disk component, you should be aware of their basic functionality. At the end of this chapter, you will perform an exercise (Hands-on Project 5-1) in which you will visually identify physical hard disk components.

Disk Platters

The **disk platter** is a rigid disk inside the sealed hard disk enclosure. In the past, disk platters have been composed of a metallic aluminum/magnesium alloy, a lightweight and rigid material. On the surface, a syrup containing iron-oxide particles was evenly spread across the disk using centrifugal force. It is this material that stores the magnetic data on the platter. With the cover off the sealed enclosure, you can see that the platter is a brownish or amber color. While you might still have disks in use that were manufactured using this process, it is not implemented in current manufacturing because the oxide medium is soft, making it susceptible to damage if the drive head touches the surface during operation, usually due to a jolt or vibration. (This is known as a **head crash**.) A head crash often (but not always) corrupts the data or compromises the integrity of the recording media.

Current manufacturing procedures have abandoned the metal platter in favor of a glass platter (actually a glass-ceramic composite) because it does not flex as metal can, allowing the platter to be about one-half the thickness of a metallic platter. Thinner platters allow room for more platters in the same drive housing, hence higher-capacity drives. Most current hard disks utilize four platters, but high-capacity drives can use upward of 11. Also, the glass platter is more thermally stable than metal, minimizing the expansion or contraction that occurs with temperature changes.

One way to apply the medium to the platter is to process the platter through a series of chemical baths that leave several layers of metallic film in an electroplating method similar to that used to affix chrome to car bumpers. A better, newer method is to apply a **thin-film** magnetic medium over the glass platter, providing greater density. The thin-film medium is more expensive than electroplating, and it is applied through a process known as "sputtering" in which the material is applied in a continuous, nearly perfect vacuum. Thin-film media are much harder than oxide media. The result is that it is more difficult (nearly impossible) to crash the media. Thin-film media are like a silvery mirror in appearance.

Drive Heads

The **drive head** reads and writes data to the magnetic media on the disk platter. Each platter has two drive heads: one that reads media from the top and another that reads media from the bottom. When stationary, the drive heads are actually parked on the media surface. When the drive is in use and spinning, the air pressure from the movement of the platter separates the drive heads from the surface of the media. Because the drive heads are ganged together in a head rack to a single actuator mechanism (see next paragraph), each head moves across its respective platter in unison with the other heads of the drive.

 The air in the drive is specially filtered in two ways. First, a recirculating filter continuously cleans the air as it rotates from platter movement. Because the drive is assembled in a clean room, it does not clean generic dust particles, but small particles from the media scraped from the disk as the heads skid on the surface during takeoff and landing (spinning up and powering down). Another filter cleans air that enters the drive as a result of barometric equalization with outside air, which is necessary to float the drive heads properly.

The **actuator mechanism** is the mechanical component that physically positions the drive heads at the appropriate location on the disk platter to read or write data. Most actuator mechanisms today use the **voice coil** construction, which derives its name from audio speaker technology using an electrically charged coil. Fluctuations in the electrical charge move the coil to various positions over the platter similar to the way a speaker coil moves to create audible vibrations in a speaker cone. The actuator mechanism has no intelligence of its own in determining the appropriate location; it depends upon the **servo mechanism**, which detects precise cylinder locations on the platter using **gray code**, a special binary code written to the drive by the drive manufacturer that identifies physical locations on the drive. You cannot alter or erase this code, even with the FDISK utility or FORMAT command (these are described in the next section).

Older hard disks required a program to manually park the heads when powered off to avoid having the heads skitter across the surface, causing damage. Today, drives automatically park their heads using a spring and magnetic force. When the drive powers off, the magnetic force of the voice coil actuator dissipates, and a spring drags the head rack to a park-and-lock position.

The physical components described above are relatively durable considering their precise nature. For example, specifications for many drives indicate the MTBF is approximately 1,200,000 hours (that's almost 137 years) and can sustain shock up to 300 Gs (the force of gravity times 300). I once taught a seminar that required me to hot-swap disks on stage. Being highly coordinated and dexterous, I dropped the hard disk from waist height onto a concrete floor. We all gasped, but it turned out fine because the drive suffered no damage and the show went on.

The environment is still extremely important for hard drives, particularly the temperature. We have already discussed adequate ventilation and cooling, but if your office is in a colder environment, also consider condensation. When a drive comes delivered to you from a cold truck in the middle of winter, allow plenty of time for the drive to warm up (acclimate) to room temperature before using the drive to prevent condensation on internal components. If the drive has been in an environment colder than about 50 degrees F (10 degrees C), allow it to sit at room temperature for several hours before opening the package.

PARTITIONS AND LOGICAL DRIVES

Nearly all operating systems use a storage system that begins with basic Microsoft MS-DOS hard disk partitions. During OS installation, many operating systems (NetWare, for example) might modify the partition or create another partition. To further subdivide and organize storage on partitions, you create logical drives. This section briefly discusses partitions and logical drives.

Creating a Partition

5

The operating system—whether it is as simple as MS-DOS or as sophisticated as NetWare—requires a defined boundary on the hard disk on which to place its files. The purpose of the partition is to provide this boundary. A partition can be a primary partition or an extended partition (see the section on logical drives). A **primary partition** is a bootable partition on which you can install operating system files. The MS-DOS **FDISK** utility is usually used to create the partition. You can create up to four primary partitions using Windows NT/2000 disk management, but this will be unusual unless you intend to install multiple operating systems on the same server (as in a classroom or lab environment). Typically, you create one primary partition and an extended partition, which can, in turn, contain logical drives.

After creating the partition(s), you must reboot before using the **FORMAT** command to create the file system. If you try to format without rebooting, you will get an error message.

 Even if you don't use Windows 98 in your environment, I recommend you obtain a Windows 98 startup disk because it has several useful utilities, including FDISK and FORMAT. Booting from the Windows 98 startup disk automatically loads drivers that work with most CD-ROMs, avoiding the need for you to create a customized disk with your specific CD-ROM drivers. I'd also add the **SMARTDRV.EXE** utility and load it prior to installing the NOS because its ability to cache file reads in advance significantly decreases installation time.

Run the FDISK utility by typing FDISK at the MS-DOS command prompt. With more recent versions of FDISK (as in Windows 95B or later), notification that the hard disk is larger than 512 MB appears, and a lengthy prompt asks if large disk support is desired over 2 GB. Nearly always, you want to respond Yes to this option. The series of FDISK menu options is easy to navigate, so I won't detail how to use each one. However, Table 5-1 lists the common options.

Table 5-1   Common FDISK Options

Option	Notes
Create DOS partition or Logical DOS Drive	DOS partition can be a primary or extended partition. Logical DOS drive first requires an extended partition.
Create Extended DOS Partition	Contains logical drives
Set active partition	The BIOS searches for a bootable, active partition, so you must set this to start the operating system. Some operating systems automatically set the partition active at installation.
Delete partition or Logical DOS Drive	Deletes the partition—be careful, you cannot recover data on a deleted partition!
Display partition information	Shows partitions on the drive. Note that any non-FAT file system (described later in this chapter) might appear as a non-DOS partition.

 There are third-party alternatives to FDISK and FORMAT. One alternative is GDISK from Symantec, a command line utility that works much faster and offers more flexibility than FDISK and FORMAT. GDISK accompanies Symantec Ghost, a disk duplication software product. Another alternative is PartitionMagic from PowerQuest, which has a more intuitive graphical interface and is a favorite among administrators for quickly resizing and moving partitions as well as converting them from one file system to another.

Logical Drives

A **logical drive** is a section on the hard disk that appears to the operating system as if it were a separate, distinct hard disk and has its own drive letter. A logical drive requires an extended partition, which can take the place of one of the four primary partitions. You can have a maximum of either four primary partitions or three primary partitions and one extended partition. The sole purpose of the **extended partition** is to store logical drive(s). Logical drives can be lettered up to Z. Within available disk space limitations, you can create as many logical drives in the extended partition as you want. Use FDISK to create the logical drives.

Once the partitions and/or logical drives are created, you must reboot the system and then format the drives. If you do not reboot the system prior to formatting, you are likely to receive an error message. Because the partition is only a storage boundary, you also need to format the partition or logical drive before you can store files on it. It is much like a parcel of land with room for a parking lot. A pavement company can apply asphalt to the entire area available for parking (partitioning), but before people can park, the asphalt must be "formatted" with lines.

Many operating systems include utilities that allow you to create and manage additional logical or primary partitions. For example, Windows 2000 Server includes the Disk Management console with which you can create additional partitions and software RAID configurations (described later in this chapter).

FILE SYSTEMS

A file system is a structure that an operating system uses to name, store, and organize files on a disk. As you administer various operating systems, it is important to understand the basics of each file system. (The following are general descriptions, and are not intended to be exhaustive.)

FAT/FAT32

The Microsoft-based **File Allocation Table (FAT)** file system is compatible with nearly any operating system and uses an invisible table near the top of the partition that points to the physical location of data on the disk. It is the simplest file system, and the network operating systems discussed in this book can all be installed with a FAT file system, though you will often choose to convert to another file system during or after the installation, primarily because of the following FAT limitations:

- *Small volume size*: FAT only supports volumes up to 2 GB in size—tiny even by current home user standards.

- *Large cluster size*: The file system stores data on the drive in 32 KB "chunks" known as clusters or allocation units. If you save a file that is only 2 KB in size, it must use all 32 KB of the cluster, wasting the remaining 30 KB. The space of wasted kilobytes is known as **slack**. Even with hard disk storage at a relatively inexpensive level in recent years, the excessive slack of the FAT file system is undesirable and quickly adds up to several megabytes of wasted space.

- *Limited file size*: The maximum file size is 2 GB. While this seems large, it is woefully insufficient for most corporate databases.

- *Security*: FAT offers no local security. Therefore, any passerby with a boot floppy can fully access the files on the local hard disk. Of course, physical security measures should prevent local access; nevertheless, administrators usually prohibit a strictly FAT file system on the server.

FAT32 is the next (and last) generation of the FAT file system. It overcomes the first two weaknesses of the FAT file system by offering large disk support up to a theoretical 2 TB and using only 4 KB cluster sizes for a significant reduction of slack. However, Windows 2000 only allows up to 32 GB. Also, the maximum file size is 4 GB, but that's still too small for many corporate requirements. Administrators avoid FAT32 because it does not offer security. Microsoft offers a secure file system with the NTFS file system.

NTFS

The **NT File System (NTFS)** is a reference to the Microsoft Windows NT file system. NTFS is compatible only with Windows NT 3.1 or better (including Windows 2000) and is not directly compatible with other operating systems. NTFS volumes offer the following benefits:

- *Large volume size*: NTFS can support extremely large volumes, though the practical limit according to Microsoft is 2 TB.

- *Small cluster size*: NTFS formats clusters at 4 KB each by default on partitions larger than 2 GB, though you can select a cluster size from 512 bytes to 64 KB.

- *Large file size*: File size is limited only by the available drive space.

- *Security*: Unless using hacker's tools, a passerby cannot boot and access files on a local NTFS volume unless they also have a user account that is authorized to access those files. Also, administrators can apply very specific levels of file and folder security that are unavailable on a FAT file system. For example, you could allow a user to save a file or folder but not delete files or folders.

- *Compression*: Though FAT offers compression through Microsoft utilities, these utilities are not considered reliable enough to be practical for server use. NTFS allows you to compress files and folders using a highly reliable compression scheme, conserving disk space.

- *Data integrity*: NTFS includes mechanisms designed to ensure that data is properly and completely written to the drive.

- *Windows 2000 NTFS features*: Under Windows 2000, a variety of new features appear in NTFS 5. You can encrypt files and folders with a nearly unbreakable encryption scheme, and set quotas so that users do not abuse file storage privileges. Besides the file system itself, the operating system offers many useful capabilities for managing partitions and files, including the **Distributed File System (Dfs)** to deploy what appears to be a single directory structure over multiple physical file servers. Windows 2000 also has offline storage to migrate seldomly used files to a slower and less expensive storage medium such as tape.

HPFS

IBM uses the **High Performance File System (HPFS)**, which bears many similarities to NTFS in basic structure. In fact, Windows NT was originally supposed to be named OS/2 Version 3.0 in 1993. However, IBM is not currently pursuing further developments to HPFS, and so NTFS has surpassed HPFS in many respects. HPFS is designed to provide local security similar to NTFS, but also coexists with an MS-DOS partition, allowing you to dual-boot between either MS-DOS or OS/2. OS/2 includes the **Journaled File System (JFS)**, which contains its own backup and recovery capability.

Using an indexing system and log to corroborate file changes, JFS can interoperate with the operating system to repair corrupt files. HPFS supports a maximum partition size of 2 TB and 2 GB file sizes, which was a staggering size when OS/2 was at its peak. HPFS also offered long file name support (up to 254 characters), 512-byte clusters, intelligent link tracking (you can move a file and the "shortcut" automatically points to the new location), and efficient file distribution on the hard drive to minimize fragmentation. Along with OS/2, Windows NT 3.x can also access HPFS partitions.

 Though OS/2 is much less popular than other NOSs, the CompTIA Server+ exam requires knowledge of its basics.

5

Linux/UNIX File Systems

There are dozens of different "flavors" (versions) of UNIX in use. For the most part, this book and the CompTIA Server+ exam gravitate toward Linux as the specific implementation of UNIX. UNIX implementations generally use the **UNIX File System (UFS)**, the **Network File System (NFS)**, or **AFS**, which stems from Carnegie-Mellon's Andrew File System. Linux often uses the **Filesystem Hierarchy Standard (FHS)**, which is more a directory structure than a file system (see *www.pathname.com/fhs* for the complete standard). Finally, you can also create Linux-specific partitions—Linux swap, Linux native, and Linux RAID, each of which is addressed further in Chapter 8.

UNIX file systems have a higher administrative learning curve—you must use an arcane command line interface. However, several interfaces (such as X Windows) now allow you to perform many UNIX administrative functions using a GUI. Also, various flavors of Linux characteristically include a GUI.

NetWare

The traditional **NetWare file system** competes directly with Microsoft's NTFS, and therefore offers similar features: You can use very large volumes and files, and the cluster size is efficient. Using the traditional NetWare file system, you can create a NetWare **volume**, which is a collection of files, directories, subdirectories, and even partitions. You can combine separate partitions that together comprise a volume. File storage is also efficient because NetWare volumes can use suballocation. A NetWare volume can subdivide a block (a Microsoft cluster is a NetWare "block") to minimize slack space. Unfilled blocks are subdivided into 512-byte suballocation blocks, which can then be used to store data from one or more other files.

Like NTFS, NetWare offers file compression. You can manually activate compression by flagging files and directories with the IC (immediate compress) command or by using the SET command at the server console to configure a file inactivity delay, after which compression occurs automatically. NetWare offers a distributed file system and offline file storage similar to Windows 2000 Dfs and offline file storage, respectively.

NetWare 5.x uses two file systems: the "traditional" NetWare file system described above and a new NSS file system described later in this section. Be careful not to use an "NFS" acronym for the traditional NetWare file system because it is easily confused with the NFS of the UNIX Network File System.

NetWare 5.x also includes additional features in its optional **Novell Storage Service (NSS)** file system. The purpose of NSS is to increase performance and total storage capacity. NSS offers several improvements over the traditional NetWare file system:

- *Large files*: Instead of the traditional 2 GB limitation, files can now be up to 8 TB each! Also, you can store *trillions* of files in a single directory, compared to the 16 million entries per volume under traditional limitations.

- *Performance*: Large files typically take a long time to open, but NSS provides rapid access regardless of size. Also, mounting a volume (preparing it for use) is much faster.

- *Flexible storage management*: You can create up to eight NetWare partitions on a single disk and create unlimited volumes per partition.

You can't just install an NSS file system; you have to first have the traditional NetWare file system and then add NSS.

THE IDE INTERFACE

Integrated Drive Electronics (IDE) can refer to any hard disk with an integrated controller. However, it is more technically accurate to apply the term **ATA (AT Attachment)** to what we usually call an IDE drive, because the drive plugs into the 16-bit ISA bus known as the AT bus. In spite of this technicality, this book and most references use the terms IDE and ATA synonymously. Recall that an IDE drive includes the controller in the circuitry attached to the drive. When people colloquially say that they are installing an "IDE controller," what they really mean is that they are installing a **host adapter**, the more accurate term for what is usually referred to as an IDE or SCSI hard disk controller. The host adapter is the physical interface between the hard disk and the computer bus. As you can see, disk interface terminologies are replete with inaccuracies (and we have only gotten started). As we delve into the IDE interface and its variations, you'll learn synonyms for various interfaces.

Although the ATA interface attaches to the 16-bit ISA bus, it is not a performance concern because even two of the fastest IDE drives cannot saturate the ISA bus.

Other devices besides hard disks can plug into the ATA interface, usually CD-ROM drives and tape drives. These devices require a variation on the ATA specification known as the **ATAPI (ATA Packet Interface)** specification. The SCSI interface, discussed later in this chapter, can also accept other devices. For this chapter's purposes, however, we are only concerned with hard disks for both interfaces.

 Many times, an inaccuracy in terminology develops when a hard disk drive manufacturer coins a term to help sell its product. For example, ATA-2 is often referred to by its marketing term EIDE.

5

The next few sections will describe variants of the ATA interface. Early generations of the ATA interface will be discussed in less detail, because you are not likely to find them in servers. However, some information about them is relevant because standards introduced with them carry through to current ATA specifications.

ATA-1

The following major features characterize the **ATA-1** standard:

- Signal timing for DMA and Programmed I/O (PIO), which utilizes the processor to handle disk transfers but is superceded by DMA and Ultra-DMA
- 40/44-pin cable connections (44-pin connections use four more pins to supply power to notebook hard drives)
- Determination of master, slave, or cable select using jumpers (discussed later in this chapter)
- Transfer rate of 3.3 MBps to 8.3 MBps depending on the PIO or DMA mode

ATA-2

The following major features characterize the **ATA-2** standard:

- Large drive support for up to 137.4 GB (previously 8.4 GB)
- Faster PIO and DMA transfer specifications
- Power management support
- Removable device support
- PCMCIA (PC card) support
- Reports drive characteristics to software (useful for Plug and Play)
- Transfer rate of 8.3 MBps to 16.6 MBps depending upon the PIO or DMA mode

Before proceeding, let's sort out some more terms. ATA-2 is synonymous with the unofficial marketing terms Fast-ATA, Fast-ATA-2, and Enhanced IDE (EIDE). EIDE has become one of the most accepted terms, and it applies in a general way to ATA-2 or better. The true published specification is AT Attachment Interface with Extensions, but people seldom use that title.

In order to support drives larger than 8.4 GB, you must also have an operating system that is capable of recognizing larger drives. The following operating systems support drives larger than 8.4 GB:

- *Windows 95B or later*—Using FAT32, you can format drives up to 2 TB.

- *Windows NT 4.0*—This OS supports larger drives out of the box, but not on the bootable drive. For the bootable drive, you must first apply Service Pack 4 to enable large drive support.

- *Windows 2000*—This OS provides native support for larger drives.

- *OS/2 Warp*—With a Device Driver Pack upgrade, a boot partition can be only as large as 8.4 GB. If you use HPFS, OS/2 supports up to 64 GB.

- *NetWare 5.x*—This OS provides native support for larger drives.

ATA-3

The following major features characterize the **ATA-3** standard:

- Includes Self Monitoring and Reporting Technology (S.M.A.R.T.), a predictive technology that enables the operating system to warn of a device's degradation. S.M.A.R.T. has its basis in preceding technologies known as Predictive Failure Analysis (IBM) and IntelliSafe (Compaq). Drives might use one of the three technologies, or a combination. For example, some Compaq systems use both IntelliSafe and S.M.A.R.T. If the hard disk begins to show signs of failure, you will see messages in the server's system log, RAID log, or in a vendor-supplied monitoring and reporting utility.

- Optional security mode that protects access to the drive with a password

- Transfer rate of 11.1 MBps to 16.6 MBps depending on the PIO or DMA mode

 S.M.A.R.T. has made its way into the SCSI world of hard disks as well (see more about SCSI later in this chapter). This significantly adds to the administrator's ability to monitor the health of internal and external SCSI disks and RAID configurations.

ATA-4

The following major features characterize the **ATA-4** standard:

- Addition of the ATAPI standard to attach other types of devices

- Advanced power management

- Specification of an optional 80-conductor, 40-pin cable-select cable to reduce noise

- Improved BIOS support for a theoretical capability of 9.4 trillion gigabytes, though the actual ATA standard is still limited to 137.4 GB

- Ultra-DMA (UDMA) support, increasing the transfer rate to 33 MBps

ATA-4 is probably the most groundbreaking standard in terms of current IDE performance. It introduced a level of performance (which was increased even further with ATA-5 and ATA-6) that had been formerly available only on the SCSI interface. Other terms for ATA-4 include Ultra-DMA and Ultra-ATA. In reference to the transfer rate, you might also see UDMA/33 or Ultra-ATA/33. In previous ATA implementations, data is transferred once each clock cycle. Ultra-ATA differs in that data transfers twice for each clock cycle, once at the rising edge and once at the trailing edge. Ultra-DMA also adds a cyclical redundancy check (CRC) to ensure the integrity of data.

To support Ultra-ATA/33 and later, a compatible drive, BIOS, operating system, and host adapter interface must be in use. In the BIOS, most manufacturers now include an artificial "32-bit" transfer. Recall that IDE operates at 16 bits on the ISA interface, even though the host adapter is usually a PCI card. The BIOS now includes functionality that allows for two 16-bit transfers to occur at once, hence the "32-bit" transfer.

Under ATA-4 and higher, a single drive on the IDE cable must be at the end of the cable (no "stub" allowed). Otherwise, signaling problems can occur. Under earlier ATA versions, a stub was OK but inadvisable.

If you have any older ATA-1 through ATA-3 drives, don't throw them away just because current standards are ATA-4 or better. The ATA specification requires successive ATA iterations to be backward compatible. For example, you could still attach an ATA-1 drive to an ATA-4 or higher host adapter for cheap (but slower) storage. Note that as a general rule, if you mix ATA standards on the same cable, both devices operate at the performance level of the slower standard.

ATA-5

The following major features characterize the **ATA-5** standard:

- 80-conductor cable required (as opposed to optional) in order to achieve the maximum transfer rate. You can use a standard 40-pin cable but only at a maximum transfer rate of 33 MBps.

- Added to the ATA-5 specification is an IEEE-1394 (FireWire) link that allows use of an ATA drive on the FireWire interface. (**FireWire** is an extremely fast bus allowing up to 63 connected devices and up to 3200 Mbps throughput in the latest version.)

- Transfer rate of 66 MBps, achieved by reducing setup times and increasing the clock rate. Later implementations of ATA-5 achieve 100 MBps under the marketing title of Ultra-DMA/100. This came about as a result of manufacturers that could match the 100 MBps transfer rate of the ATA-6 standard but did not want to wait for the completed standard.

Starting with ATA-5 and ATA-6 (see next section), you are most likely to have to add an adapter to achieve the maximum throughput because it takes several months and sometimes over a year for motherboard IDE interfaces to catch up to the latest ATA standard.

ATA-6

At this writing, the **ATA-6** standard was still under development. The current draft of this standard is the 475-page 1410D Revision 1b (*www.t13.org/project/d1410r1b.pdf*). However, this standard should include all features of previous ATA standards plus a formalized 100 MBps specification.

Table 5-2 summarizes the IDE standards covered in the previous sections.

Table 5-2   IDE Standards

IDE Standard	Also Known As	Performance
ATA-1		3.3–8.3 MBps
ATA-2	AT Attachment Interface with Extensions, Fast-ATA, Fast-ATA-2, and Enhanced IDE (EIDE)	8.3–16.6 MBps
ATA-3	EIDE	11.1–16.6 Mbps
ATA-4	Ultra-DMA, Ultra-ATA, UDMA/33, or Ultra-ATA/33	33 MBps
ATA-5	Ultra-DMA/100 for 100 MBps implementations	66–100 MBps
ATA-6		100 MBps

ATA Cable

The standard ATA cable connecting the drive to the host adapter is a 40-pin ribbon cable (see Figure 5-2). To prevent incorrect connections, a cable key (protruding notch) on the cable matches a corresponding gap in the IDE connection on the hard drive. The cable should have one striped wire (usually red, sometimes blue) that indicates Pin 1. Pin 20 is not used, and is usually absent from the drive, and a corresponding block in position 20 appears on the cable, also preventing backward insertion (see Figures 5-2 and 5-3). Orient the connection so that Pin 1 on the cable is adjacent to the power cable connection. Because the cable is not shielded, you are limited to a length of 18 inches (457.2 mm). A longer cable could be more sensitive to timing and electrical noise issues, resulting in data corruption. The host adapter connected to the other end should also have a cable key, stripe, and absent Pin 20, and most manufacturers include a marking on the PCB (printed circuit board) that indicates Pin 1.

The cable length of 18 inches (457.2 mm) is usually plenty for a desktop workstation, but in full-size server tower cases in which the controller is farther away from the drive bays, this might cause a problem. If the ATA host adapter is a card (as opposed to integrated on the motherboard), move it as close as possible to the drive locations. Otherwise, if you need longer lengths, you can obtain a longer, custom-made IDE cable, but at the risk of performance degradation and data loss.

5

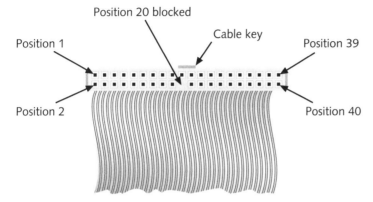

Figure 5-2   Standard 40-pin IDE connector

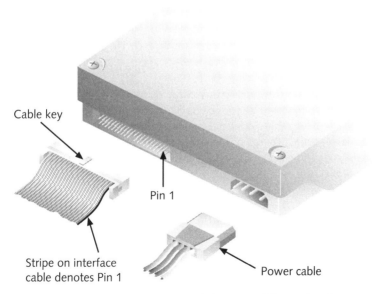

Figure 5-3   Correct orientation of the IDE cable on the drive

You can connect a maximum of two devices to a single ATA connector. The cable and its dimensions appear in Figure 5-4. Also, 80-conductor cables are identical except for an additional 40 grounded conductors. At one end of the cable, an IDE port connector is blue. Two more connectors appear on the cable—the first one is at the opposite end and is black and the middle one is gray. Connect the first hard disk to the black end connector. If you only have one hard drive, also make sure you connect it to this one and not the middle connector. Otherwise, the dangling connector on the end (the "stub") is not well terminated. Although it is not against ATA specifications, attaching a single drive to the middle connector is not recommended. Connect a second hard drive to the middle gray connector.

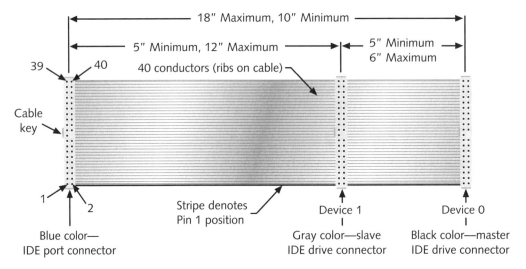

Figure 5-4 ATA 40-pin color-coded cable

 You might find some systems, usually very cheap desktop PCs, which have none of the color-coding that you use to make proper connections. As a result, you have to guess which way to orient the cable. Fortunately, if you attach it in an upside-down orientation, it does not damage the drive or host adapter because the cable is not powered—it only carries data signals. If you plug a non-color-coded cable in and the drive doesn't work, just turn the cable over.

As an option, you can use the 80-conductor 40-pin cable with ATA-4, but it is required with ATA-5 and ATA-6 (see Figure 5-5). An 80-conductor 40-pin cable leads to the question: If there are 80 conductors, why isn't it an 80-pin cable? The additional 40 conductors are connected to ground only, and do not have a corresponding pin on the drive. Remember that an IDE cable is not shielded in any way, and is susceptible to electrical noise, usually crosstalk from adjacent conductors (hence the ground wires between signal wires). The extra grounded conductors absorb much of the electrical noise that would otherwise defeat the added performance of ATA-4 and better drives.

While optional on ATA-4, I recommend the 80-conductor cable for any version of ATA because of better signal quality.

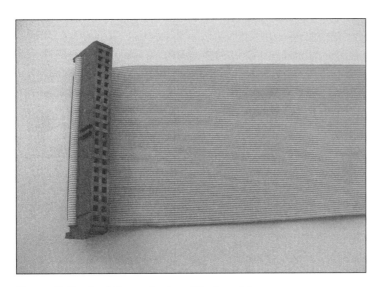

Figure 5-5   An 80-conductor, 40-pin cable

 If you connect a faster device such as a hard disk and a slower device such as a CD-ROM to the same IDE cable, the hard disk performance will suffer while waiting for the CD-ROM to finish its tasks. Because IDE is not capable of simultaneous I/O, one device must wait for the other before performing tasks. In this case, it would be better to obtain another ATA host adapter and keep slower devices (such as CD-ROMs and tape drives) on one IDE connector and hard drives on the other.

Master, Slave, and Cable Select

Because you can place two drives on an IDE host adapter, there must be a determination as to which one is the **master** and which one is the **slave**, especially because the master receives a drive letter assignment from the operating system first, and is also the device on which a boot record must be found. Otherwise, the master and slave drives are equivalent despite the implication of the names. You can use two methods to specify which drive is master and which is slave: First, you can set the jumper on the drive to indicate a master or slave setting. The drive manufacturer specifies these jumper settings in the drive manual or online documents. For example, Figure 5-6 shows the settings downloaded from Maxtor for the Diamondmax 80 Ultra-DMA/100. Most manufacturers also include an indication on the PCB or somewhere on the drive case as to which jumpers to set for master, slave, or cable select. Although you might need to change the jumper setting to specify master or slave for some older IDE drives, newer drives allow **cable select**, which means that the drive's position on the cable indicates whether it is a master or slave. Place the drive on the end of the 80–conductor cable to make it a master, and on the middle connector to make it a slave.

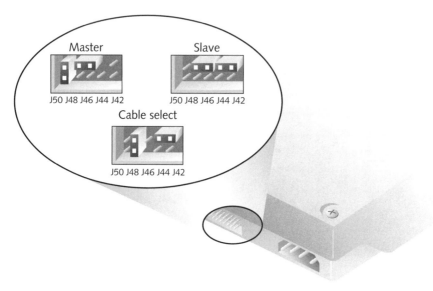

Figure 5-6   Jumper settings for master, slave, or cable select

 Cable select does not work on a standard 40-pin cable unless you use a specially config-ured cable. To make matters more complicated, the master/slave position on a 40-pin standard cable is reversed—the master drive is on the middle connector and the slave drive is on the end connector.

 It's not as much an issue as it used to be, but sometimes if you mix two drives from different vendors on the same IDE channel, you may experience problems. For example, the system might be unable to detect one of the drives, or if the drives are different sizes, report both drives at the smaller size. If you experience problems of this kind and are certain jumpers and locations on the IDE cable are correct, consider placing drives of the same manufacturer (and perhaps the exact same model) on the same cable.

The Pros and Cons of IDE/ATA

Current ATA implementations have some compelling advantages for use in the server world, but also have several disadvantages. If the disadvantages outweigh the advantages, and budgeting is sufficient, you will probably choose the more expensive SCSI interface (discussed later in this chapter).

Pros

- *Inexpensive*—Both the drives and host adapters are very inexpensive; even administrators on the tightest of budgets can probably afford a few new IDE drives.

- *Reasonable performance*—In less demanding situations where the server is not a heavily utilized file server, the reasonably good performance might be acceptable considering the low cost.

- *Simple configuration*—Plug it in and format the drive. That's pretty much it, and you don't usually have configuration complications, which you might experience with SCSI, for example (discussed later in this chapter).

Cons

- *Only two drives*—Two drives might seem like a lot for a workstation, but a server often connects to many more drives for purposes of performance, redundancy, and total available storage.

- *Slower device throttling*—Mixing slower devices with faster ones can drag the performance of the faster one.

- *Cable length*—18 inches (457.2 mm) is very limiting in a full-size server.

- *No simultaneous I/O*—Only one IDE device can operate at a time on a single IDE channel. SCSI, which does permit simultaneous I/O, might be much more attractive in terms of performance.

- *No native redundancy*—You cannot take a standard ATA drive and host adapter and configure hardware RAID. However, software RAID is available on certain operating systems (Windows 2000, for example). Also, some manufacturers such as Promise Technology Inc. (*www.promise.com*) are making ATA adapters that allow you to configure several levels of RAID. (See more about RAID later in this chapter.)

 Although simultaneous I/O is not supported on a single IDE channel, you can place two drives on separate IDE channels. In this configuration, each drive can operate simultaneously.

- Despite advertised transfer rates, most of the time you only get that rate from cached data. Data retrieved fresh from an Ultra-ATA/100 hard disk can usually only be sustained at about 40 MBps.

 More information about ATA/IDE can be found at *www.ata-atapi.com* and especially *www.pcguide.com*.

THE SCSI INTERFACE

SCSI (Small Computer System Interface) technology, like ATA, has seen multiple generations of specifications, and includes an abundance of technical details beyond the scope of this book. However, as a server administrator, you must be aware of the major SCSI standards in order to provide the best available compatibility solution with the best possible performance. Properly configuring your SCSI hard drives also avoids complex troubleshooting.

As with IDE, SCSI drives include the controller circuitry directly on the hard disk assembly (HDA). In fact, some sources claim that hard disk manufacturers nearly mirror their drives in all physical respects and only change the circuitry to distinguish IDE and SCSI, often differentiated by only a single chip. What most people call the SCSI "controller" is actually the SCSI host adapter—similar to the inaccurate reference to an IDE "controller." However, although an IDE device communicates directly on the system bus, a SCSI device first communicates with the CPU through the SCSI host adapter.

At the end of this section, you will see a listing of the various pros and cons of using the SCSI interface. Generally, however, the main "pro" is that it performs exceptionally well in multiple disk configurations. The main "con" is that when you combine the more expensive SCSI hard disks with the more expensive SCSI host adapters, the price tag is significantly higher than an IDE configuration.

SCSI standards range from SCSI-1 to SCSI-3 and encompass several variations in between. You are unlikely to find SCSI-1 in modern server implementations, but you need to know some basics about it according to the stated CompTIA Server+ exam objectives. SCSI-2 (especially the Fast and Wide iterations) and some SCSI-3 variants are more likely to be found in servers today. With most SCSI standards, you will see which cables and/or terminators are required, all of which are explained in more detail later in this chapter.

 Each succeeding version of the SCSI standard is backward compatible with all preceding versions. In theory, you could put a SCSI-1 hard disk on a SCSI-3 host adapter. However, such drastic implementations are not recommended because of complicated cabling adapters, termination incompatibilities, and performance limitations.

A more complete description of the various signaling types, cables, and connectors appears after the sections on individual SCSI versions.

SCSI-1

SCSI-1 started off as just "SCSI" but was later renamed SCSI-1 to avoid confusion with successive SCSI standards. The following major features characterize the SCSI-1 standard:

- 8-bit **parallel bus**, meaning that multiple wires on the cable can transmit data at the same time. This is what allows SCSI to use simultaneous I/O.

- 50-pin Centronics-style external connector and low-density pin header internal connector

- Single-ended (SE) transmission

- Passive termination (the simplest type of termination, but also the least reliable; see later section on SCSI termination)

- Optional bus parity checking

- 5 MHz operation

- Transfer rate of 4 MBps (asynchronous) or 5 MBps (synchronous)

SCSI-1 is now considered obsolete and has been retired by ANSI and replaced with SCSI-2.

SCSI-2

SCSI-2 is essentially SCSI-1, plus the following optional features:

- **Fast SCSI** operating at 10 MHz instead of 5 MHz

- **Wide SCSI** utilizing 16-bit transfer instead of 8-bit (which is "narrow")

- 50-pin high-density connectors

- Active termination (see later section on SCSI termination)

- High Voltage Differential (HVD) is used to extend bus length. HVD is now considered obsolete in favor of Low Voltage Differential (LVD). (HVD and LVD are covered later in the chapter.)

- **Command queuing** allows the host adapter to send as many as 256 commands to the drive. The drive stores and sorts the commands for optimum efficiency and performance internally before responding to the host adapter. Multitasking operating systems such as OS/2, Windows NT, and Windows 2000 can take advantage of command queuing.

- Transfer rate of 10 MBps at 16 bits and 5 MHz (Wide SCSI), 10 MBps at 8 bits and 10 MHz (Fast SCSI), or 20 MBps at both 10 MHz and 16 bits (Fast and Wide)

SCSI-3

SCSI-3 is the most confusing of the SCSI standards, because once again, manufacturers have used misleading marketing language. In addition, the SCSI-3 standard is not a complete standard of its own. Instead, it is more a collection of documents covering new commands, electrical interfaces, and protocols. A manufacturer could comply with only one of the major SCSI-3 additions and still label the product "SCSI-3." Nonetheless, subdividing SCSI-3 into several smaller standards helps SCSI-3 implementations to develop more quickly than waiting for the entire standard to be published and approved.

SPI SCSI-3 Parallel Interface

SPI is the SCSI-3 Parallel Interface, better known by the marketing terms Ultra SCSI or Wide Ultra SCSI. Along with this standard is the separate **SCSI Interlock Protocol (SIP)** defining the parallel command set. This standard was published as three documents offering the following features:

- 10 MHz bus speed, which is really no faster than SCSI-2. This is an example of how a manufacturer could use the 10 MHz bus speed (Fast SCSI) and call it SCSI-3 even though it offered no performance advantage.

- Fast-20 offers transfer rates up to 40 MBps using 20 MHz signaling.

- 68-pin P-cable and connectors for Wide SCSI

SPI-2

Also known as Ultra2 SCSI and Wide Ultra2 SCSI, **SPI-2** is characterized as follows:

- Single Connector Attachment (SCA-2) connectors. A successor to the problematic original SCA connector, this is the connection type that is mostly used in a chassis that contains several hot-swappable SCSI drives.

- Fast-40 40 MBps transfer rate on a narrow (8-bit) channel or 80 MBps on a wide (16-bit) channel. LVD is required for these data rates.

- LVD signaling to replace the previous SE signaling is required to achieve the faster throughput of Ultra2 or Ultra2/Wide speeds (40/80 MBps). You can use an SE device on the LVD SCSI chain, but doing so switches the chain to SE mode, which throttles the performance of the chain to SE-level performance at a maximum of 40 MBps and shortens the total cable length to as little as 5 feet (1.5 meters) in Fast-20 mode.

- 68-pin Very High Density Connector (VHDC) makes the connectors and ribbon cables smaller. This is important in SCSI because the older connectors and ribbon cables could be quite large and cumbersome.

SPI-3

SPI-3 was still in the draft stage at the time of this writing, although SCSI manufacturers have already implemented many of its features, including:

- Improving the earlier parity check, the **cyclical redundancy check (CRC)** is a calculation used by the sending device based on the data in the packet. The data arrives at the destination target and another calculation is performed using the same "formula." If the calculation in the packet matches the calculation performed by the destination device, the data is complete and considered error free.

- Domain validation improves the robustness of data transfer. In the past, the host adapter would send an inquiry to the SCSI device to determine its supported transfer rate. If the interconnection between host and device did not support the full transfer rate, then the device became inaccessible. With **domain validation**, the determined transfer rate is tested, and if errors occur, the rate is incrementally reduced and again tested until no errors occur.

- **Double transition (DT) clocking** transmits data on both the rising and falling edges of the clock. On a 16-bit, 40 MHz bus, this yields a transfer rate of 160 MBps.

- **Packetization** reduces the overall communication method to transfer data. Previously, data was transferred over the SCSI bus using a series of phases to set up and transfer data. Packetization streamlines this process by combining the process into a packet, reducing overhead.

- **Quick Arbitration and Selection (QAS)** eliminates the previously required **arbitration** method in which devices contend for control of the bus. Much of the prioritization is based on the device's priority level based on its **SCSI ID**, a unique number for each SCSI device. Because no data transfer can occur during the time that arbitration takes place, it adds overhead to the bus. QAS reduces overhead by reducing the number of times that arbitration must occur and by allowing a device waiting for bus access to do so more quickly.

SPI-3 is also known as Ultra3 SCSI.

Ultra160 and Ultra160+

The five features listed for SPI-3 sometimes cause a problem in the way a SCSI product is marketed. A manufacturer might include only one of the five items and call its product SCSI-3. Most manufacturers prefer to have more stringent requirements, so for the Ultra160 and Ultra160+ standards, the product must include:

- DT clocking at 160 MBps

- Domain validation

- CRC

QAS and packetization are optional for Ultra160, but required for Ultra160+.

SPI-4

SPI-4 was still in draft form at the time of this writing, but most hard disk and host adapter manufacturers have products using the standard's 320 MBps data rate. This data rate is accomplished by doubling the bus speed from 40 MHz to 80 MHz and using DT clocking. Manufacturers are calling this standard Ultra320. Other special features are not yet confirmed.

For more information on this emerging standard as well as other SCSI standards, see *www.t10.org*.

Table 5-3 summarizes SCSI standards and performance.

Table 5-3   SCSI Standards

SCSI Standard	Also Known As	Performance
SCSI-1 Async	Asynchronous	5 Mhz/8-bit/4 MBps
SCSI-1 Fast-5	Synchronous	5 MHz/8-bit/5 MBps
SCSI-2 Fast-5/Wide	Wide	5 MHz/16-bit/10 MBps
SCSI-2 Fast-10	Fast	10 MHz/8-bit/10 MBps
SCSI-2 Fast-10/Wide	Fast/Wide	10 MHz/16-bit/20 MBps
SPI (SCSI-3) Fast-20	Ultra	20 MHz/8-bit/20 MBps
SPI (SCSI-3) Fast-20/Wide	Ultra/Wide	20 MHz/16-bit/40 MBps
SPI-2 (SCSI-3) Fast-40	Ultra2	40 MHz/8-bit/40 MBps
SPI-2 (SCSI-3) Fast-40/Wide	Ultra2/Wide	40 MHz/16-bit/80 MBps
SPI-3 (SCSI-3) Fast-80DT	Ultra3 (Ultra160)	40 MHz/16-bit/160 MBps
SPI-4 (SCSI-3) Fast-160DT	Ultra320	80 MHz/16-bit/320 MBps

SCSI CONFIGURATION

Configuring SCSI devices requires knowledge of the various types of SCSI, cables, capabilities, and terminators. One of the most common sources of frustration and troubleshooting is an improperly configured SCSI bus. When configuring SCSI from scratch, first consider the budget available to you. SCSI can quickly become cost-prohibitive, especially with several high-performance hard drives. Closely associated with the cost is the level of performance and amount of storage you want. Of course, the more you want, the more you pay.

 Administrators tend to gravitate toward SCSI drives for most purposes, but if you are using only a single disk in your system, it is much more cost-effective to use ATA-4 or better because the performance is reasonably close to SCSI and the cost is a comparative bargain.

SCSI Cables and Connectors

Although you won't see every possible combination of cables and connectors listed here, you should be aware of those that are most commonly used. A narrow bus width (8 bits) is physically and logically smaller than the wider 16-bit bus. The 8-bit, 50-conductor cable is also known as **"A" cable** and the 16-bit, 68-conductor cable as **"P" cable**. (Other cables have been proposed, but have not come to fruition because the standards never caught on with manufacturers.)

The "A" cable is a low-density cable with a Centronics-style connector (see Figure 5-7) and 50 conductors. The "A" cable is used only in 8-bit (narrow) implementations. If you have both narrow and wide cables, you can continue to use both standards with special adapters such as the one in Figure 5-8, which reduces a 68-conductor cable to a 50-pin connector.

5

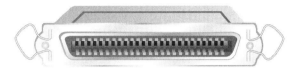

Figure 5-7   50-pin, low-density "A" cable connector

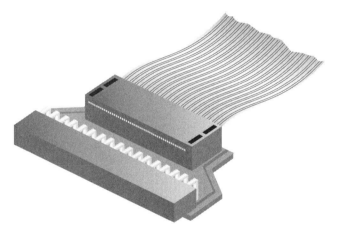

Figure 5-8   50-pin connector on a 68-conductor cable

All this talk about 8-bit and 16-bit widths leads to the question: What about 32-bit widths? While it sounds like a good idea (and probably is), manufacturers have scoffed at a 32-bit cable standard because of exorbitant development and manufacturing costs.

Thankfully, in the SCSI-2 standard, a high-density 50-pin SCSI connector was introduced to save space, because large SCSI connectors such as the Centronics type are cumbersome and can quickly take up space in a cabinet. Also, instead of using the wire latches on either side of the connector to attach and remove the connector, you use squeeze-to-release clip locks.

On the SCA-2 connector, the chassis has the female connector and the drive has the male connector. (Recall that this is the connector that allows hot-pluggable hard drives.) On the outside edges of both connectors are advanced grounding contacts that allow you to pull out or plug in a SCSI drive without negative electrical consequence (see Figure 5-9). Because you can't see the actual connection take place inside the chassis, this is known as **blind connector mating**. The connector provides both signal and power, and is an 80-pin connector offering only wide (not narrow) SCSI.

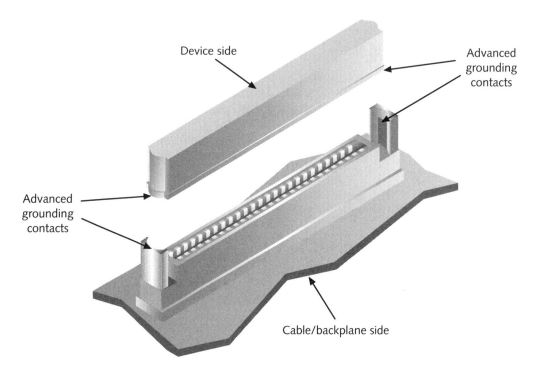

Figure 5-9 SCA-2 SCSI attachment

With SCSI-3, you most often find the wide SCSI cable using a 68-pin connector both internally (inside the case) and externally (outside the case and connected to the server's SCSI host adapter).

Some SCSI connectors, though rare, are 25-pin connectors created for economy of both design and dollars. This connector is streamlined compared to the 50-pin cable, and accomplishes this design mostly by removing grounding—an inadvisable practice. Recall that grounding is a contributor to signal integrity. Because the signal quality is not as good as standard 50-pin or greater SCSI cable, and because the connector is visually identical to the commonly used DB25 parallel cable connector, this style of cable/connector is not recommended. Accidentally plugging printers into the SCSI connector or vice versa can damage equipment.

Connectors are designed for either internal or external use. External cables are usually round with thumbscrews or clip-lock connections on the connector. The round cable is highly shielded and well engineered against signal degradation and interference. As a result, it is also relatively expensive. Internally, you will see ribbon cable in any of several types.

Signaling

In order to obtain the correct accessories for your SCSI chain, you must first know what kind of signaling is in use on the bus. **Signaling** generally describes transmission of data using electrical impulses or variations. These electrical transmissions represent data that the sender originates and the receiver translates based upon a mutually agreed-upon method. There are three types of signaling on the SCSI bus, detailed in the following sections. You must be careful about mixing devices intended for one type of signaling with devices intended for another type of signaling, because one or more devices might stop functioning or become damaged. Also, you must know the signaling before you can properly terminate a SCSI bus.

SE

Single-ended (SE) signaling, the original signaling method used on the SCSI-1 bus, uses a common signaling method in which a positive voltage represents a one and a zero voltage (ground) represents a zero, resulting in binary communication. SE signaling is available for any SCSI-1 or SCSI-2 implementation as well as SCSI-3 SPI-1. With most electronic signaling methods, you have a built-in opposition: the faster the transmission speed, the shorter the maximum cable length. Of the three signal types, SE is most susceptible to this limitation. On a Fast-20 bus, for example, an SE cable can only be 5 feet (1.5 meters) long.

HVD

High Voltage Differential (HVD) signaling is also available for any SCSI implementation up to SCSI-3 SPI-1. If you can use SE for the same SCSI implementations, then why use HVD? HVD, as the name implies, uses comparatively more electrical power than the other two types of signaling, resulting in greater allowable bus lengths. Whereas the SE cable is limited to 5 feet (1.5 meters) over Fast-20, an HVD cable can reach 82 feet (25 meters). The "differential" in HVD represents a kind of signaling in which the signal is comprised of the difference in a pair. A one is represented when one wire in the pair transmits a positive voltage, and the other wire transmits zero voltage. The receiving device detects the "difference" between the voltages, and translates it as a one. To transmit a zero, both wires carry a zero voltage. This signaling method is much less susceptible to interference, signal degradation, signal bounce, and crosstalk, allowing HVD to transmit over such a great distance.

It is rare to find HVD in PC servers. It is more often found in older minicomputers and never gained the popularity of SE, primarily because of a higher cost factor.

Do not mix HVD and SE devices on the same bus. Because of the significantly higher voltage of HVD, SE devices could get smoked—literally.

LVD

Low Voltage Differential (LVD) signaling is the signaling method you are most likely to find today, and it is similar to HVD except, as the name implies, it uses a lower voltage. Advantages of LVD are that you can use both LVD and SE devices on the same bus without electrical hazard, and it allows a longer maximum cable length—up to 39 feet (12 meters). Many SCSI devices are multimode devices; that is, they can operate as either LVD or SE depending on the signaling method of the other devices on the chain. Multimode devices can be indicated in several ways, usually depending on the preference of the company marketing the product. However, it is usually abbreviated as LVD/MSE (where M is multimode) or LVD/SE.

Note the following about using LVD:

- A single SE device among LVD devices on the same chain will drop all devices to SE compatibility. This could have a significant impact if the cable is over 5 feet (1.5 meters) when you add the SE device, because the cable would now be too long.

- Some multimode devices have a jumper setting that forces SE operation. If you want to use LVD, be sure that no devices have enabled this setting.

- Use either LVD or multimode LVD/SE terminators.

- You cannot operate both HVD and LVD on the same bus for reasons of electrical incompatibility, which could damage LVD devices.

- LVD is the only available signaling method for Ultra3, Ultra160, Ultra160+, Ultra320, and probably any other standards that emerge in the near future.

Because the connectors are identical regardless of the signaling method, look for a special symbol on the connector. This will help ensure that you do not mix signaling standards, especially by adding HVD among SE or LVD devices. The signaling symbols appear in Figure 5-10.

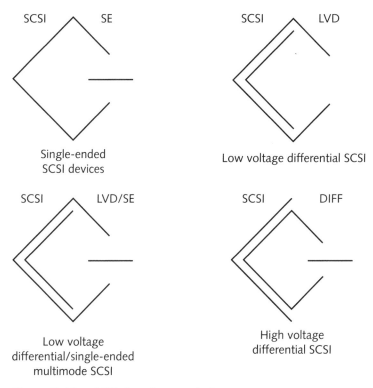

Figure 5-10   SCSI signaling symbols

SCSI Termination

Termination (using terminators at the ends of a SCSI chain) is critical to assure error-free operation on the SCSI chain. A **terminator** absorbs the transmission signal to avoid signal bounce, making it appear to the devices that the cable is of infinite length. Terminators also regulate the electrical load, and are therefore critical in establishing a reliable communications medium. Proper termination requires a terminator at both ends of the SCSI cable. Some devices (and most high-performance host adapters) either automatically terminate or have a setting that allows you to specify termination. Otherwise, obtain a terminator to place over the last connector on the chain. If the last position is in use by a device that does not terminate itself, you can place a terminator over the connection, which allows signal transfer to and from the device while also providing the necessary termination. This is known as **pass-through termination** (see Figure 5-11).

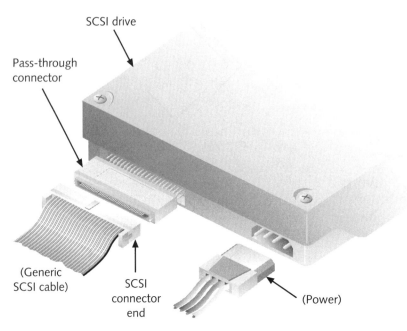

SCSI drive

Pass-through
connector

(Generic
SCSI cable)

SCSI
connector
end

(Power)

Figure 5-11   Pass-through termination connects the chain on one side of the
terminator and the device on the other

 Differential drives do not normally include the ability to terminate, so you will
have to provide a terminator. You can also purchase cables that have terminators built into the end.

The terminators must also have terminator power supplied, or they cannot properly terminate. If the host adapter does not supply power to the terminator, you can configure a
setting on one of the SCSI devices (usually via a jumper) to supply power to a terminator.

 Some administrators configure all SCSI devices to supply power to terminators; that
way it never slips through the cracks.

The following list describes the various types of SCSI terminators:

- **Passive termination**—This is the simplest type of termination, but is
  also the least reliable. Passive terminators use resistors to terminate the
  SCSI chain, similar to terminators on coaxial Ethernet networks. Passive
  terminators usually work best on short, SE SCSI-1 buses. It is unlikely
  you will find many passive terminators in servers.

- **Active termination**—A requirement for faster, single-ended SCSI, active termination adds voltage regulators to provide a more reliable and consistent termination. Another type of active termination is active negation termination, which uses a more complex circuit to stabilize the voltage supply level, further eliminating electrical noise from the signal. Negation terminators are usually only a little more expensive than plain active terminators ($5–10) so I recommend them.

- **Forced perfect termination (FPT)**—In this technology, the termination is forced to a more exact voltage by means of diode clamps added to the terminator circuitry. This advanced form of active termination is very clean, and is the best termination available for an SE bus.

- **HVD termination**—A high voltage bus requires a high voltage terminator. That's pretty much it.

- **LVD termination**—A low voltage terminator for the LVD bus. Many LVD terminators are LVD/SE terminators to accommodate buses with multimode devices. When operating in SE mode, the terminator functions as an active terminator.

Be careful if your server environment mixes narrow SCSI technologies with newer, wider SCSI technologies. First, to place both narrow and wide devices on the bus, you will have to provide an adapter to convert from one width to the other. Converting wide devices to a narrow bus wastes 8 bits of transmission and severely limits the potential of the wide device. On the other hand, converting from 8 bits to 16 bits does nothing to improve the performance of attached 8-bit devices because 8 bits is the highest level of operation anyway. Along with the conversion, you must also consider how termination will affect the two widths. Do you terminate for the 8-bit devices? If so, what about the 16-bit devices? Terminating only for the 8-bits would leave the 16-bit devices with 8 unterminated bits. These dangling bits are called the **high byte** (also known as high 9), and when you have a mix of wide and narrow devices, you can obtain special multimode terminators.

Multimode terminators flash colors indicating which signaling method is in use. For example, if it's running SE, it might blink yellow, and if it's running LVD, it might blink green. This can be useful in troubleshooting the SCSI chain if you wonder why it seems to be running slow or unreliably over 3-meter lengths—it could be running SE, (just check the light to verify) when you want LVD so that you can benefit from faster speed and longer cable.

Drive Configuration (SCSI ID and LUN)

Knowing the various SCSI technologies, cables, connectors, and termination is fine, but of course you have to also plug it all in! The problem is that with SCSI, misconfiguration can cause many hours of baffling troubleshooting. This section shows you how to correctly configure the devices on the SCSI bus.

Topology

Topology, the physical and/or logical layout of equipment, is simple for SCSI: Use a bus topology because that's all that's available (logically similar to a network bus topology). **Daisy chain** your SCSI devices so that they appear one after the other along the cable. In complicated configurations, you might accidentally connect the bus to itself somewhere along the line, creating a loop. Don't do that or the bus won't work! When configuring a chain from scratch, one end usually connects to the terminated host adapter (unless it's between an internal and external chain) and the other end is terminated as well. The order of the drives (and other SCSI devices, if any) doesn't matter in terms of performance or priority. That's one of the advantages of SCSI—a slower device on the bus doesn't bottleneck all the other devices. In a simple configuration using two SCSI hard disks and a SCSI scanner (see Figure 5-12), the layout is a bus and both ends are terminated.

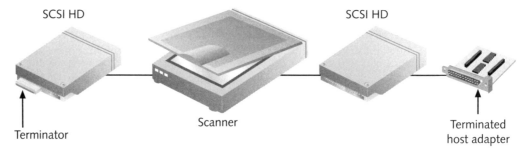

Figure 5-12   A simple SCSI bus topology with terminators at both ends

Realize that although termination takes place at the end of the SCSI bus, the SCSI host adapter is not always at one end of the chain. Because most host adapters have connections for both internal and external devices, a host adapter so connected would appear in the middle of the SCSI chain. In this case, you will have to be sure not to terminate the host adapter (see Figure 5-13).

You are likely to find a SCSI host adapter with multiple channels in many implementations. The primary benefits to multiple channels are twofold: First, having two separate channels allows for twice as many devices. Second, you can configure the two channels to support different signaling technologies. For example, if you have a few SE devices and a few LVD devices, you don't want to mix them or else you'll suffer the performance and length limitations of SE for all the devices. Instead, make one channel SE and the other LVD. That way, the LVD devices can operate at full capacity.

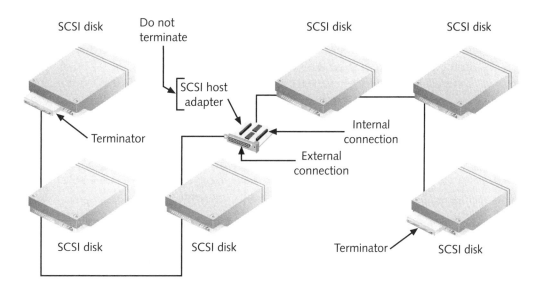

Figure 5-13 Do not terminate a host adapter appearing in the middle of the SCSI chain

 TIP Reduce inrush power required of the power supply when powering on the server by specifying a power-on delay for the internal SCSI drives. This can be performed via the SCSI BIOS. Similarly, you can delay the powering on of IDE drives in some system BIOS settings. External SCSI drives in their own cabinet enclosure usually have an independent power supply in the cabinet, so power-on delay is not an issue.

SCSI ID Assignment

Each device on the SCSI chain must have a unique SCSI ID number. You configure the device SCSI ID using jumpers, a wheel, or a button on the device, and the adapter is usually preset at ID 7, though you can change it (possibly with a jumper but usually through a software utility). Although you can change the host adapter's SCSI ID, it is highly inadvisable. ID 7 is the highest priority of all the SCSI numbers. The range of available IDs depends on whether you are running narrow (8 IDs) or wide (16 IDs). SCSI ID assignment is important not only to uniquely identify each device, but also to establish which devices have priority when arbitrating over the bus. Arbitration occurs when it must be determined which of two or more devices have control over the bus. Usually, you want to assign a higher priority to slower devices such as scanners or tape drives to make sure that faster devices do not dominate the bus.

The priority of SCSI IDs range from the highest to lowest as follows: 7, 6, 5, 4, 3, 2, 1, 0. On a wide bus, the range is 7, 6, 5, 4, 3, 2, 1, 0, 15, 14, 13, 12, 11, 10, 9, 8. When you install an internal hard disk—simply a matter of screwing it into an available drive bay and plugging in the power and SCSI cables—you also need to configure a SCSI ID using jumper settings. External SCA devices, however, usually configure their own SCSI IDs automatically as soon as you swap the drive into its bay. This is needed to reduce the configuration time, as time is usually of the essence in swapping these drives.

 You can divide a single SCSI bus into multiple SCSI **segments** so each device must have a unique ID. However, each segment is electrically independent, and therefore capable of the maximum cable length as if it were truly its own bus. Each SCSI segment requires its own termination.

Along with the unique SCSI ID number is the **logical unit number (LUN)**. The LUN is a subunit of the device, and is used to identify items within the device. For example, a multi-disc CD-ROM changer probably assigns a unique LUN to each disk. If the CD-ROM drive is SCSI ID 5, the first LUN is probably LUN 0, the second is LUN 1, and so forth. Some host adapters do not support LUNs—the absence of LUN support makes the bus scan process during startup faster; so if you need LUN support, make sure the SCSI host adapter supports it. Administrators are not normally concerned with changing LUNs because the device manufacturer defines them.

SCSI Pros and Cons

SCSI has many pros and cons, but as mentioned earlier, the pros far outweigh the cons in most enterprises, and particularly for servers.

Pros

The benefits of SCSI are as follows:

- *Performance*—Aggregating the performance of multiple disks as in a RAID array (covered later in the chapter) generates an appreciable performance gain. The more disks you add, the better the performance (up to the available throughput of the SCSI channel).

- *Expandability*—Several meters of cable length is enough for most SCSI implementations. Most use LVD, which allows for 12 meters. Also, compared to ATA standards that limit you to two disks, the expandability of using up to 15 devices on a SCSI chain is impressive.

- *Redundancy*—Several RAID implementations including RAID-1 and RAID-5 protect your data even if a hard disk fails.

Cons

The drawbacks of SCSI are as follows:

- *Difficult to configure and troubleshoot*—SCSI has so many varying standards, and there are so many opportunities for incompatibility and wrong termination, that it might take a while to get SCSI rolling, especially if you are trying to piece together a SCSI implementation out of existing equipment. If you build from scratch using consistent standards, it's much easier.

- *Expensive*—Smaller organizations or those that have a tight budget might not be able to afford SCSI.

- *Performance*—The performance improvement is not that noticeable if you're only using a single SCSI disk. SCSI shines when using multiple disks for performance and fault tolerance. Otherwise, you're better off saving the money and using ATA-4 or better.

Server administrators usually prefer SCSI because of its advantages in an enterprise environment.

SCSI SUMMARY

In addition to the information in Table 5-3, remember the following about SCSI:

- 8-bit SCSI can connect up to seven devices (actually it's eight devices, but the host adapter counts as one).

- 16-bit SCSI can connect up to 15 devices (actually 16, but the host adapter counts as one).

- Exception to the number of devices: SPI (SCSI-3) Fast-20/Wide can use 15 devices on an HVD cable and seven devices on an SE cable.

- "A" cable is always used for 8-bit SCSI.

- "P" cable is always used for 16-bit SCSI.

- SPI-1 SCSI can use SE at 10 feet (3 meter) lengths, but only 5 feet (1.5 meters) if four or more devices are on the chain.

- Maximum length for all HVD signal cable is 82 feet (25 meters).

- Maximum length for all LVD signal cable is 39 feet (12 meters), but if the chain consists of the host adapter and only one device, you can extend length to 82 feet (25 meters).

SCSI and RAID are troubleshooting studies of their own, and heavily emphasized on the Server+ exam. Properly configuring your SCSI and RAID devices
as instructed in this chapter is an important start; however, to account for the
many other troubleshooting scenarios you might encounter, refer to a special
section, SCSI and RAID Troubleshooting, in Chapter 12.

FIBRE CHANNEL

Fibre Channel (FC) is a storage technology that can use gigabit Ethernet networks,
but is primarily intended for fiber optic cable as the name implies. (Fibre Channel technology has roots in Europe, hence the spelling of "Fibre" instead of "Fiber.") FC is a
form of storage categorized under the **storage area network (SAN)** umbrella. SAN
is a general term that refers to any network-based storage solution that is not server-
based. SAN is becoming huge in the server world. Comprehensive coverage of SAN is
beyond the scope of this book because it encompasses more than just server issues. In
this section, you learn the basics of FC.

First, let's separate out from the discussion another growing storage solution that is
sometimes confused with FC—**network attached storage (NAS)**. NAS is one or
more storage devices attached to a network, most commonly Ethernet. A NAS device
is easy to configure and use, because you just attach it to the rack, plug it into the network, flip its power switch, and voilà! It's ready to use. NAS devices are as accessible as
any other device on the network. For smaller organizations, you can use a freestanding
NAS device, or for the enterprise, rack models are available. Regardless, when you attach
and power up the device, it receives an IP address and identifies the type of network in
use. If you want to configure a static IP address, configure security settings or access privileges, or configure RAID, you can launch a management utility (usually browser-based
so you can launch it from anywhere in the enterprise) and make changes. NAS devices
are very inexpensive compared to FC. NAS devices as well as SAN storage have a significant benefit over traditional file servers in that, well, you don't *have* a file server! This
removes an expensive piece of hardware and greatly reduces administration.

In a SCSI FC implementation, a special SCSI host adapter designed for FC connects to
the FC bus, which can be up to 10 kilometers (more than 6 miles) in length! That's the
benefit of using fiber instead of copper.

FC is run in its own storage "network" of either **Fibre Channel Arbitrated Loop
(FC-AL)** or switched fabric. In FC-AL, you can connect 126 storage devices to a
special fiber hub in a physical star, logical loop topology. However, all devices on the
FC-AL share the available bandwidth, which is OK in many implementations if it
meets the needs of the enterprise (see Figure 5-14).

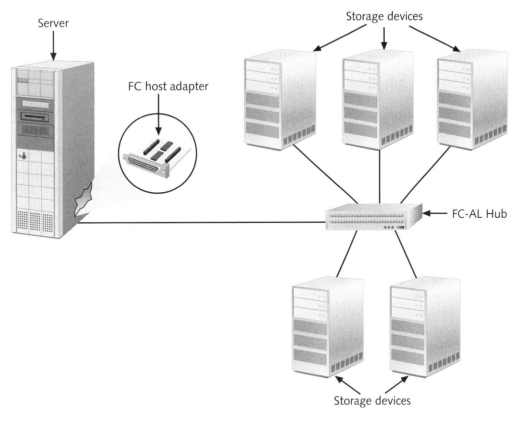

Figure 5-14 An FC-AL configuration connects to a fiber hub and shares available bandwidth

In high-level implementations, you can use a switched fabric to connect to up to 15.5 million storage devices, and the full bandwidth of the channel is available to each device! As you might guess, this implementation is extremely expensive. The term **switched fabric** is somewhat vague in terms of its physical configuration. Simply put, it means that servers storing information on an FC device can reach the device using any number of physical paths. This is analogous to a phone call to a friend in another state. Call her today, and the phone company will route your call using the best path it deems practical. Call her tomorrow, and the phone company might or might not use the same path. However, it doesn't matter to you or to her, so long as the call connects.

Some people have prematurely dismissed FC as too slow at its rated throughput of 100 MBps, especially compared to Ultra160, which can reach up to 160 MBps. In reality, FC is much faster because SCSI cannot sustain speeds of 160 MBps; that's just its burst speed when feeding data from cache. Instead, it will usually dish data out at a sustained rate of around 50 MBps. FC, on the other hand, can sustain data transfer at about 97.5 MBps. The storage media can be whatever file format suits you, and you can use RAID if you like.

It is common to also attach high-speed, high-capacity tape storage to FC.

Typically administrators do not purchase the FC equipment and configure it themselves. Instead, you contract with a SAN storage company specializing in FC to supply the equipment and connect it all together. Maintenance is not usually an issue either, as the storage company also provides maintenance. Larger enterprises often have full-time employees from the storage company on site at all times to maintain and administer the storage and tapes.

The expense of FC is very high, and thus is usually seen in enterprises that need to store terabytes of data, such as in a large data center. The storage devices for a single terabyte of data alone can cost up to $750,000 before installation and costs of other associated equipment, with many implementations totaling millions of dollars.

 When receiving FC equipment, be prepared for units weighing upward of a ton and measuring about 7 feet (2.13 meters) high and 10 feet (3.05 meters) wide.

RAID

RAID stands for either Redundant Array of Inexpensive Disks or Redundant Array of Independent Disks. It doesn't really matter—it's just that the history of RAID has changed over the years and the acronym has changed with it. What matters is how you use RAID in the enterprise, and that you understand the characteristics of several levels of RAID, particularly RAID-0, RAID-1, RAID-5, and RAID-0+1.

The main purpose of RAID is to use multiple disks to improve performance, provide redundancy, or both. You configure a RAID array via host adapter hardware or software, though in most cases hardware RAID is preferred for reasons we will discuss at the end of this section. To the operating system and applications, the drives are logically a single drive.

With a controller that supports it, you can obtain a significant performance benefit using a **RAID cache**. Regardless of the version of RAID you use, the host adapter can have a certain amount of memory, usually a minimum of 32 MB, though better adapters have at least 128 MB. The memory is often supported by a battery backup for data integrity, similar to CMOS. The RAID cache fills with data sequentially beyond the actual requested data in anticipation that the next data will soon be requested. If the data is indeed required, the RAID cache serves data more quickly than if data must be retrieved directly from disk.

RAID-0

RAID-0, also known as **disk striping**, lays down data across two or more physical drives. RAID-0 provides no redundancy—if one of the drives fails, all the data is lost, so you must provide another solution for redundancy such as tape backup or RAID-0+1 (see later section). RAID-0 yields a performance advantage because you can aggregate the performance of multiple drives. The SCSI bus can deliver data in a matter of microseconds, but the data transfer of a single disk takes milliseconds, hence a bottleneck at even the fastest drives. RAID-0 helps to mitigate this bottleneck because multiple disks can simultaneously deliver data at once. For example, a RAID-0 array consisting of four drives provides roughly four times the performance of a single drive serving the same data because all four drives on a SCSI chain can operate at once. In Figure 5-15, the letters on each of the drives represent a portion of data, illustrating how the data appears on the drives. In any of the RAID levels, you can further improve performance by dedicating a single drive to each host adapter. (Using two host adapters and one drive on each is known as **duplexing**.) It is possible to use RAID-0 in an IDE implementation, but because IDE can operate only one drive at a time, there is no performance advantage.

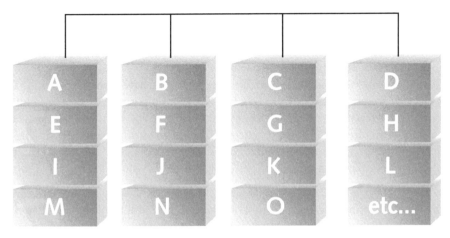

Figure 5-15   This RAID-0 array uses four drives to quadruple hard disk performance

Part of the POST process involves searching for a configurable BIOS from other hardware, particularly SCSI host adapters. To configure a RAID-0 drive once the proper SCSI connections have been made, enter the SCSI adapter's BIOS. Typically, a message appears instructing you to press a keyboard combination to access the BIOS. Then, use the menu system to specify the type of RAID you want to use and save changes.

RAID-1

RAID-1, also known as **disk mirroring**, requires at least two disks to provide redundancy. It can also provide improved performance, but only if using duplexing. In a RAID-1 array, the controller writes the same exact data to two disks at the same time. You can configure multiple adapters, each having two channels with a disk on each channel and capable of simultaneous I/O, to further increase performance (see Figure 5-16).

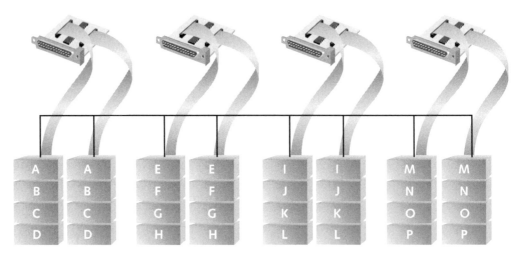

Figure 5-16   RAID-1 using multiple controllers provides both mirroring and high performance

RAID-1 has a higher cost factor or "overhead." If you have two mirrored 40 GB drives, the total raw storage available is 80 GB, but you can only use 40 GB because 40 GB must be available for the mirror. The overhead is 50% because you only use half of the actual disk space. Also, if the drives are not the same size, the mirror is the size of the smaller drive. You can configure RAID-1 through software (using Windows NT/2000, for example), but it requires processor utilization; so in performance terms you're better off using hardware RAID through the controller.

In the event of a failed drive in a RAID-1 array, simply pull out the failed drive and insert a new one. Depending on the method used to configure RAID, you must manually regenerate data from the remaining drive to the new drive through software or BIOS, or the mirror regenerates automatically. With automatic regeneration, the user experience is not disrupted, although performance may suffer temporarily until all data is regenerated to the new drive.

RAID-0+1

As the name implies, **RAID-0+1** offers the best of both worlds: the performance of RAID-0 and the redundancy of RAID-1. In this implementation, two channels and at least four drives are required. Data is striped across two or more disks in the first channel (RAID-0), and the data from the first channel is mirrored to disks in the second channel (RAID-1) in the same striped layout as shown in Figure 5-17. This implementation has a 50% overhead.

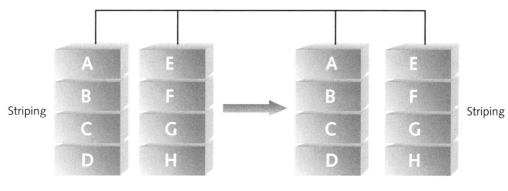

Figure 5-17   A RAID-0+1 array

 Contrary to some sources, this is *not* the same as RAID-10. Although RAID-10 also uses both mirroring and striping, one channel mirrors the data and the other channel stripes the same data (see Figure 5-18). In RAID-10, overhead is higher, although two disks could fail and you would still have enough fault tolerance to rebuild the data.

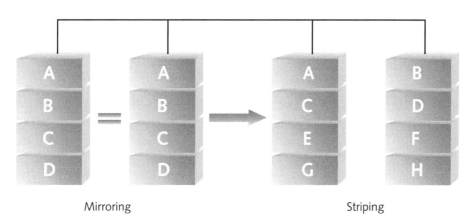

Figure 5-18   A RAID-10 array

RAID-5

RAID-5 offers the performance benefit of RAID-1 striping but also adds redundancy by use of parity. In the case of RAID-5, **parity** is an encoding scheme that represents data appearing on other drives (sometimes called striping with parity). RAID-5 requires at least three hard disks to implement. The host adapter writes data to drives 1 and 2, and on disk 3 writes parity data. At the next write, data writes to drives 2 and 3, and on disk 1 writes parity data, and so on in round-robin fashion (see Figure 5-19). If the first disk fails, replace it. Then, the system regenerates the data that was supposed to be on the first drive using the parity on disk 2 and disk 3. SCSI is the best choice for this RAID implementation because it offers simultaneous I/O; that is, data reads occur from multiple drives at the same time.

RAID-5 has a lighter overhead in terms of disk space than RAID-1. Overhead is $1/X$ where X is the number of disks in the array. For example, a five-disk RAID-5 array would have an overhead of $1/5$, or 20%. The overhead space is utilized by the parity data.

RAID-5 arrays can take quite a while to rebuild data to a new replacement drive. Also, parity calculation requires CPU cycles, and can significantly affect server performance, especially while rebuilding data to a replacement drive.

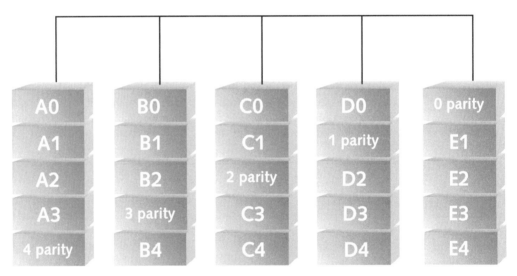

Figure 5-19   RAID-5 writes parity bits across members of the array, and uses the bits to reconstruct data if a drive must be replaced

RAID-1 and RAID-5 reconstruct data with the least amount of disruption if the hard disks are hot-swappable and data is reconstructed on the fly as opposed to rebooting and accessing the BIOS to reconstruct the data.

 Although manufacturers such as Promise Technology offer EIDE host adapters providing RAID-0, 1, 5, and 0+1, performance benefits are best with SCSI because EIDE cannot perform simultaneous I/O.

Regardless of the RAID configuration you choose (if any), be sure to optimize the hard disk so that it performs at its best. One of the most useful utilities for this purpose is defragmentation software, which arranges the data on your hard disk in a sequential fashion so that reads require less back-and-forth action to locate all the data. (See Chapter 11 for more about defragmentation.)

Software RAID vs. Hardware RAID

Network operating systems such as Windows NT/2000 and Novell NetWare offer software RAID. Software RAID has advantages and disadvantages, as seen in Table 5-4.

Table 5-4 Advantages and Disadvantages of Software RAID

Advantages	Disadvantages
Software RAID is built into the NOS, and is less expensive than hardware RAID.	Less robust than hardware RAID. If the operating system becomes corrupt, the array is at risk.
Generally an easy-to-use graphical interface. You can create a RAID array in a matter of minutes, perhaps without rebooting the system.	Limited configuration capabilities. You are usually limited in the types of RAID configurations you can use. In Windows 2000, for example, you can create a RAID-0, RAID-1, or RAID-5 array but not other RAID configurations such as 10 or 0+1.
	Uses the CPU to perform parity calculations.

Hardware RAID offers advantages and disadvantages, as seen in Table 5-5.

Table 5-5 Advantages and Disadvantages of Hardware RAID

Advantages	Disadvantages
More reliable and robust	More expensive
Faster performance because it is dedicated to RAID functions. Also, parity calculations are handled by hardware RAID (not the main CPU), which is faster than software RAID.	If you need to access the SCSI BIOS, a reboot is required.
The array remains regardless of corruption to the operating system.	

All things considered, experienced administrators usually recommend hardware RAID as a better solution because of its dependability and performance.

CHAPTER SUMMARY

- Most hard disks include the following major physical components: disk platters, drive heads, head actuator mechanism, spindle motor, logic board, connectors, and jumpers.

- Most current hard disks use between 4 and 11 glass-ceramic platters coated with magnetic media using a thin-film process.

- Drive heads read and write data on the top and bottom of the platter, and glide on a cushion of air when the drive is in operation. When inactive, the heads automatically park.

❐ An actuator mechanism physically positions the drive heads over locations on the platters determined by the servo mechanism.

❐ Hard disks can, to a degree, sustain hostile conditions such as shock up to 300 Gs, and last nearly 137 years.

❐ A primary partition boots to the operating system, while an extended partition exists for the purpose of storing logical drives. A logical drive is a section on the hard disk that appears to the operating system as if it were a separate hard disk and has its own drive letter.

❐ FDISK is the primary tool for creating and deleting partitions. You can also use third-party tools such as GDISK (from Symantec) or PartitionMagic (from PowerQuest).

❐ The File Allocation Table (FAT) file system is a Microsoft-based file system compatible with nearly any operating system. FAT has a limit of 2 GB partition size and offers no security. FAT32 offers a 2 TB partition size.

❐ NTFS, the native file system for Windows NT and Windows 2000, can support extremely large volumes, but it reaches a practical limit at 2 TB. NTFS supports other features such as encryption, compression, and disk quotas.

❐ HPFS is the operating system of OS/2, and usually coexists with a FAT partition.

❐ Linux and UNIX can use UFS, NFS, or AFS file systems.

❐ NetWare uses a NetWare volume in its file system. A NetWare volume is created during installation, and you can add more as necessary. Recent versions of NetWare also offer the NSS file system, which increases performance and storage capacity.

❐ IDE and ATA are interchangeable terms, though IDE (and EIDE) is actually a marketing term and not a true standard. ATA/IDE operates at a current maximum of 100 MBps and uses no more than two drives per channel. ATA does not support simultaneous I/O.

❐ ATA cable is either 40-conductor/40-pin or 80-conductor/40-pin. The latter is used for current ATA-4 and ATA-5 implementations.

❐ Drives can be configured with jumpers to be master or slave. One is not better than the other, except that the master receives preference when the system looks for a boot drive. Cable select makes this easy by automatically detecting that the middle connector is the slave and the end connector is the master.

❐ ATA drives are inexpensive and easy to configure, but you can only connect two drives to an 18-inch (457.2 mm) cable and the performance is not as good as SCSI.

❐ What most people call the SCSI "controller" is actually the SCSI host adapter—similar to the inaccurate reference to an IDE "controller."

❐ SCSI has several versions, each with different benefits and capabilities. Currently, SCSI-3 Ultra320 is the fastest available standard. SCSI uses 8- or 16-bit implementations, A or P cables, and lengths from 5 feet (1.5 meters) to 82 feet (25 meters).

- SCA-2 is the SCSI connection that allows you to plug a hot-swappable drive into an array.
- The SCSI chain is a bus topology and must be properly terminated at both ends using passive, active, forced perfect, HVD, or LVD terminators.
- Never mix HVD devices with LVD or SE devices, as they can damage other equipment.
- SCSI devices must each have a unique SCSI ID. The host adapter is usually ID 7. Devices can also have a subset of identification numbers known as the LUN.
- The priority of SCSI IDs range from the highest to lowest as follows: 7, 6, 5, 4, 3, 2, 1, 0. On a wide bus, the priority is 7, 6, 5, 4, 3, 2, 1, 0, 15, 14, 13, 12, 11, 10, 9, 8.
- Table 5-3 summarizes SCSI specifications.
- NAS is inexpensive network storage that is very easy to install, and you access it from the network (it has an IP address).
- Fibre Channel (FC) is intended for very large storage needs, often in the terabyte range. FC is very expensive but has extremely fast sustained throughput and room for lots of devices.
- All RAID implementations are best served over a SCSI bus, not IDE.
- RAID-0 is striping across at least two drives and offers high performance but no redundancy.
- RAID-1 is mirroring data onto two or more drives simultaneously. Overhead is high at 50%.
- RAID-5 is striping with parity, and is both fast and redundant.
- RAID-0+1 is both mirroring and striping.
- Hardware RAID is usually better than software RAID because it is faster and more reliable.

5

KEY TERMS

"A" cable — 8-bit, 50-conductor SCSI cable.

active termination — A requirement for faster, single-ended SCSI, active termination adds voltage regulators to provide a more reliable and consistent termination. Another type of active termination is active negation termination, which uses a more complex circuit to stabilize the voltage supply level, further eliminating electrical noise from the signal.

actuator mechanism — A mechanism that physically positions the drive heads to the appropriate location on the disk platter to read or write data.

AFS — Refers to Carnegie-Mellon's Andrew File System, a UNIX file system.

arbitration — Determination of which of two or more devices has control over the bus.

ATA (AT attachment) — Drive technology that attaches to the 16-bit AT bus.

ATA-1 — An ATA standard that supports master, slave, or cable-select determination using jumpers and connecting to a 40-pin cable. The transfer rate is 3.3–8.3 MBps.

ATA-2 — An ATA standard supporting large drive support up to 137 GB. Also known as Fast-ATA-2 and Enhanced IDE (EIDE).

ATA-3 — An ATA standard that supports S.M.A.R.T. and transfer rates up to 16.6 MBps.

ATA-4 — An ATA standard that introduced the optional 80-conductor/40-pin cable and transfer rates up to 33 MBps. Also known as Ultra-DMA and Ultra-ATA. In reference to the transfer rate, you might also see UDMA/33 or Ultra-ATA/33.

ATA-5 — An ATA standard requiring the 80-conductor cable, also adding support for the IEEE-1394 (FireWire) specification and a 66 MBps transfer rate. Later implementations achieve 100 MBps and are also known as Ultra-DMA/100.

ATA-6 — The upcoming official 100 MBps ATA standard.

ATAPI (ATA Packet Interface) — A specification that allows other devices besides hard disks to plug into the ATA interface.

blind connector mating — Refers to the fact that you can't see the SCSI hot-plug connection take place inside the chassis.

cable select — The IDE drive's position on the cable indicates whether it is a master or slave.

command queuing — A method that allows the host adapter to send as many as 256 commands to the drive. The drive stores and sorts the commands for optimum efficiency and performance internally before responding to the host adapter.

cyclical redundancy check (CRC) — A calculation used by the sending device based on the data in the packet. The data arrives at the destination target and another calculation is performed using the same "formula." If the calculation in the packet matches the calculation performed by the destination device, the data is complete and considered error free.

daisy chain — Connecting one device after another on a SCSI bus.

disk mirroring — See RAID-1.

disk platter — A rigid disk inside the sealed hard disk enclosure. Magnetic media on the surface of the platter store the actual hard disk data.

disk striping — See RAID-0.

Distributed File System (Dfs) — A Windows NT/2000 service that deploys what appears to be a single directory structure over multiple physical file servers.

domain validation — The determined SCSI transfer rate is tested, and if errors occur, the rate is incrementally reduced and again tested until no errors occur.

double transition (DT) clocking — Transmitting data on both the rising and falling edges of the clock cycle. On a 16-bit, 40 MHz bus, this yields a transfer rate of 160 MBps.

drive head — A magnetically sensitive device that hovers over the hard disk platter and reads or writes data to the hard disk.

duplexing — Two host adapters with one drive on each adapter.

extended partition — A partition that provides the ability to store logical drives.

Fast SCSI — SCSI operating at 10 MHz instead of 5 MHz.

FAT/FAT32 — A Microsoft-based file system. FAT is capable of 2 GB partitions and FAT32 is capable of 2 TB partitions. Neither file system offers local security features.

FDISK — An MS-DOS utility used to create hard disk partitions.

Fibre Channel (FC)— A storage area network (SAN) SCSI technology that can use gigabit Ethernet networks, but is primarily intended for fiber optic cable as the name implies.

Fibre Channel Arbitrated Loop (FC-AL) — A connection of up to 126 devices on a shared bandwidth fiber hub.

File Allocation Table (FAT) — A Microsoft-based file system compatible with nearly any operating system.

Filesystem Hierarchy Standard (FHS) — A UNIX directory structure to which Linux complies.

FireWire (IEEE 1394) — An extremely fast bus allowing up to 63 connected devices and up to 3200 Mbps throughput in the latest version.

forced perfect termination (FPT) — An advanced form of SCSI termination in which termination is forced to a more exact voltage by means of diode clamps added to the terminator circuitry. FPT is very clean, and it's the best termination available for an SE bus.

FORMAT — A command line utility that creates a Microsoft-based FAT file system.

gray code — A binary code that identifies physical locations on the drive. Gray code is written to the drive by the drive manufacturer.

head crash — When the drive head contacts the disk platter during operation. This can result in corrupt data or damaged hard disk media, especially on older drives.

high byte — The dangling bits resulting from terminating only 8 bits on a 16-bit bus (also known as high 9). Use special terminators that will terminate both the 8 and 16 bits.

High Performance File System (HPFS) — The native file system of IBM OS/2.

high voltage differential (HVD) signaling — SCSI signaling circuitry that uses a comparatively high voltage to extend the length of the SCSI chain to as much as 82 feet (25 meters).

host adapter — The more accurate term for what is usually referred to as an IDE or SCSI hard disk controller. The host adapter is the physical interface between the hard disk and the computer bus.

HVD termination — High voltage termination for HVD signaling.

Integrated Drive Electronics (IDE) — Refers to any hard disk with an integrated controller. Closely associated with the ATA standard.

Journaled File System (JFS) — An OS/2 file system that contains its own backup and recovery capability. Using an indexing system and log to corroborate file changes, JFS can interoperate with the operating system to repair corrupt files.

logical drive — A section on the hard disk that appears to the operating system as if it were a separate hard disk, and that has its own drive letter.

logical unit number (LUN) — A subunit of the SCSI device, used to identify items within the device.

low voltage differential (LVD) signaling — Similar to HVD except for use of lower voltage and shorter cable lengths (39 feet, or 12 meters).

LVD termination — Low voltage termination for LVD signaling.

master (drive) — The drive that receives the first drive letter assignment from the operating system and contains a boot record.

network attached storage (NAS) — One or more storage devices attached to a network, most commonly Ethernet. Simple to configure, you plug in the power, connect it to the network, and turn it on.

NetWare File System — Novell's file system that offers large volume support, efficient cluster size, and local security.

Network File System (NFS) — A UNIX file system that makes files accessible over a network.

Novell Storage Service (NSS) — Operates alongside the traditional NetWare file system to support large files, improve performance, and provide flexible storage management.

NT File System (NTFS) — A Microsoft-based file system designed for Windows NT/2000, offering large volumes and local security.

"P" cable — 16-bit, 68-conductor SCSI cable.

packetization — A data transfer method that reduces the overall communication overhead. Previously, data was transferred over the SCSI bus using a series of phases to set up and transfer data. Packetization streamlines this process by combining the process into a packet, reducing overhead.

parallel bus — A SCSI reference meaning that multiple wires on the cable can transmit data at the same time.

parity — In SCSI, an encoding scheme that represents data appearing on other drives.

passive termination — The simplest type of SCSI termination, but also the least reliable. Passive terminators use resistors to terminate the SCSI chain, similar to the way terminators are used on coaxial Ethernet networks. Passive terminators usually work best on short, SE SCSI-1 buses. It is unlikely you will find many passive terminators in servers.

pass-through termination — If the last position on the SCSI chain is in use by a device that does not terminate itself, you can place a terminator over the connection, which allows signal transfer to and from the device while also providing the necessary termination.

primary partition — A bootable partition on which you can install operating system files.

Quick Arbitration and Selection (QAS) — Reduces overhead by reducing the number of times that arbitration must occur and by allowing a device waiting for bus access to do so more quickly.

RAID-0 — Also known as disk striping, a level of RAID that lays down data across two or more physical drives, benefiting from the combined performance of all drives in the array.

RAID-1 — Also known as disk mirroring, a level of RAID in which the controller writes the exact same data to two disks at the same time (redundancy).

RAID-0+1 — A level of RAID that offers the performance of RAID-0 and the redundancy of RAID-1. In this implementation, two channels and at least four drives are required. Data is striped across two or more disks in the first channel (RAID-0), and the data is mirrored to disks in the second channel (RAID-1).

RAID-5 — A level of RAID that offers the performance benefits of RAID-0 striping but also adds redundancy by use of parity with less overhead.

RAID cache — A high-speed memory cache that fills with data sequentially beyond the actual requested data in anticipation that the next data will soon be requested. If the data is indeed required, the RAID cache serves data more quickly than if data must be retrieved directly from disk.

Redundant Array of Inexpensive (or **Independent**) **Disks (RAID)** — Utilization of multiple disks to improve performance, provide redundancy, or both.

SCSI-1 — The original SCSI implementation.

SCSI-2 — A version of SCSI that introduced Fast and Wide data transmission.

SCSI-3 — A compilation of several different documents, SCSI-3 can be mostly equivalent to SCSI-2 in its features unless several of the various SCSI-3 features are applied. At present, SCSI-3 can be as fast as 320 MBps under Ultra320.

SCSI-3 Parallel Interface (SPI) — See SPI.

SCSI ID — Unique numbering for each SCSI device to ensure proper SCSI operation.

SCSI Interlock Protocol (SIP) — The SCSI-3 parallel command set.

segment — In reference to SCSI, dividing a SCSI bus. Each SCSI segment is electrically independent, and therefore capable of the maximum cable length as if it were truly its own bus. Each segment requires its own termination, and each device must still have a unique SCSI ID across all segments.

servo mechanism — Detects precise cylinder locations on the platter using gray code.

single-ended (SE) signaling — The original signaling method used on the SCSI-1 bus, uses a common signaling method in which a positive voltage represents a one and a zero voltage (ground) represents a zero, resulting in binary communication.

slave (drive) — Equal in every way to the master, except that it does not receive the first drive letter assignment nor contain a boot record.

slack — Space wasted when data does not fill a complete allocation of cluster space.

signaling — Transmission of data using electrical impulses or variations. These electrical transmissions represent data that the sender originates and the receiver translates based upon a mutually agreed-upon method.

SMARTDRV.EXE — An MS-DOS-based caching utility that significantly speeds up file reads and writes.

SPI — SCSI-3 parallel interface, defining SCSI-3 standards in SPI-1 through SPI-3 releases. The original SPI release has been renamed SPI-1 for clarity when comparing against other successive SPI versions. SPI-1 is also known as Ultra SCSI or Wide Ultra SCSI.

SPI-2 — Also known as Ultra2 SCSI and Wide Ultra2 SCSI, a SCSI-3 standard that introduced SCA-2 connectors LVD signaling, and Fast-40 40 MBps transfer rate on a narrow (8-bit) channel or 80 MBps on a wide (16-bit) channel.

SPI-3 — Still in draft stage at the time of this writing, a SCSI-3 standard that introduces CRCs for data integrity, domain validation, DT clocking, packetization, and QAS. Also known as Ultra3 SCSI.

SPI-4 — The latest SCSI-3 specification, still in draft form at the time of this writing. Most hard disk and host adapter manufacturers have products using the standard's 320 MBps data rate. This data rate is accomplished by doubling the bus speed from 40 MHz to 80 MHz and using DT clocking. Manufacturers are calling this standard Ultra320.

storage area network (SAN) — Generally refers to Fibre Channel and any other type of network-based storage solution that is not server-based.

switched fabric — A somewhat inexact reference to the connection to the FC storage. The connection can use any number of connection routes, depending on which one is deemed best at that particular moment.

terminator — A connector placed the end of a SCSI chain that absorbs the transmission signal to avoid signal bounce, making it appear to the devices as if the cable was of infinite length. Terminators also regulate the electrical load, and are therefore critical in establishing a reliable communications medium. Proper termination requires a terminator at both ends of the SCSI cable.

thin-film — A magnetic medium applied to disks in a near perfect, continuous vacuum.

traditional NetWare file system — Offers similar, competitive features to the NTFS file system, and allows you to create NetWare volumes.

Ultra160, Ultra160+ — A collection of SCSI-3 standards that ensure compliance with a minimum level of SCSI-3 standards, offering speeds of 160 MBps.

UNIX File System (UFS) — The UNIX file system, which supports large volumes and local security.

voice coil — A construction used by the hard disk actuator mechanism to move from one location to the next.

volume — In NetWare, a collection of files, directories, subdirectories, and even partitions.

Wide SCSI — Utilizing 16-bit transfer instead of 8-bit (which is "narrow" SCSI).

REVIEW QUESTIONS

1. Which of the following are physical hard disk components? (Choose all that apply.)

   a. disk platters

   b. spindle motor

c. compact disc

d. head actuator mechanism

2. A head crash is:

   a. the drive head colliding with the sprocket

   b. the drive head colliding with the disk platter

   c. the drive head in contact with a stationary platter

   d. the inevitable conclusion to a wild party

3. A primary partition:

   a. is contained in an extended partition

   b. contains logical drives

   c. always represents the entire hard disk

   d. can contain a bootable operating system

4. Which of the following is not a hard disk utility?

   a. GDISK

   b. FDISK

   c. FORMAT

   d. TETRIS

5. What is "slack" on a hard disk?

   a. corrupt data on the physical media

   b. cluster space that is only partially occupied

   c. excessive free space

   d. unterminated SCSI signals

6. The better technical term for IDE is:

   a. EIDE

   b. ATA

   c. SCSI

   d. FC-AL

7. Which two ATA implementations can use 100 MBps?

   a. ATA-3

   b. ATA-4

   c. ATA-5

   d. ATA-6

5

8. What is an advantage of IDE/ATA?

    a. up to 15 devices on a single channel

    b. connects to a very fast switched fabric

    c. inexpensive

    d. up to 82 feet (25 meter) cable length

9. What is a synonym for an IDE or SCSI controller?

    a. host adapter

    b. array control unit

    c. domain controller

    d. SCA connector

10. What does a SCSI parallel bus allow?

    a. arbitrated I/O

    b. simultaneous I/O

    c. LVD

    d. multiple channels on a single controller

11. Which version of SCSI introduced both Fast and Wide implementations?

    a. SCSI-1

    b. SCSI-2

    c. SCSI-3

    d. SCSI Fast and Wide have been formally introduced as a standard.

12. What is command queuing?

    a. a method that allows the host adapter to send up to 256 commands to the drive

    b. ordering of I/O operations on the IDE host adapter

    c. a memory queue that caches sequentially read hard disk data

    d. a management system that reorders unprocessed commands to the host adapter

13. A Wide SCSI implementation would use which of the following items?

    a. 8-bit cable

    b. 50-pin connector

    c. 68-pin connector

    d. 16-bit cable

14. What does an SCA-2 connector allow you to do?

    a. replace disk platters on the fly

    b. hot swap hard disks

c. hot swap terminators

d. convert from a 50-pin device to a 68-pin cable connector

15. How does double transition (DT) clocking improve SCSI performance?

a. transmits data twice per second

b. transmits data on the rising and falling edges of the clock cycle

c. fills the RAID cache during idle periods

d. relieves the main CPU of parity processing burdens

16. Why shouldn't you mix HVD devices with LVD devices?

a. The LVD devices can be damaged by the higher voltage.

b. The HVD devices will block communication on the bus.

c. The HVD devices will shorten the overall cable length.

d. The LVD devices can damage the HVD devices.

17. What is the best form of termination for an SE bus?

a. LVD termination

b. HVD termination

c. passive termination

d. FPT

18. What is the SCSI ID of most host adapters?

a. 0

b. 1

c. 7

d. 15

19. Which of the following is not a benefit of Fibre Channel?

a. simple installation

b. extremely high performance

c. extremely high storage quantity

d. extremely high number of connected devices

20. If you want both high performance and redundancy, which two RAID implementations would be suitable?

a. RAID-0

b. RAID-1

c. RAID-5

d. RAID-0+1

HANDS-ON PROJECTS

Project 5-1

In this project, you will inspect the physical hard disk components.

Your instructor should have an old scrap hard disk for you to examine. If necessary, unscrew the cover (ask for a special torx screwdriver if necessary). Examine the inside of the disk and answer the following questions:

1. What color is the platter? What does this tell you about how it was manufactured?

2. How many platters are there?

3. Observe the heads. Are they in contact with the platter?

4. Optionally, plug the drive into a power connector with the cover off and watch the action of the drive. Don't touch the components while plugged in and running.

Project 5-2

In this project, you will install two IDE hard disks on a channel.

Connect a hard disk to a computer (it can be a desktop PC or a server) as follows:

1. Take the case off the computer.

2. Locate the IDE connectors. They are probably on the motherboard, but might be on an add-in host adapter. On the motherboard, they are usually labeled in the circuit board as IDE 1 and IDE 2 or IDE 0 and IDE 1.

3. Connect the black end of an 80-conductor, 40-pin IDE cable to the IDE connector. Verify correct orientation using the stripe on the cable, a notch, and a missing pin 20 (refer to Figure 5-3). Depending on the manufacturer, not all these features may be available, but there should be enough to orient the cable correctly. The objective is to line up Pin 1 with the highlighted stripe on the cable (usually red or blue). Pin 1 on the motherboard might be labeled with a number "1" or a triangular arrow.

4. On the drive, configure the jumpers for cable select by placing a jumper over the appropriate pins. Usually, there is a CSEL marking on the drive that indicates which pins you need to jumper. If there is insufficient information, ask your instructor for direction.

5. Optionally, install the drive into a drive bay in the computer. This is not strictly necessary because the drives will be grounded through the power connector. However, do not place the drive anywhere such that the circuit board on the hard drive is in contact with any other metallic components in order to avoid electrical damage. Your instructor will advise you.

6. Connect the IDE cable to the drive. The master drive goes on the opposite end from the host adapter IDE connection, and since there is only one drive, connect it to the master position. Again, verify proper alignment using the stripe, notch, and missing Pin 20. As a rule, the stripe on the cable is adjacent to the power supply connector on the hard drive.

7. Plug in power to the hard drive. The power connector is keyed so it will only fit using the proper orientation.

Project 5-3

In this project, you will access the BIOS configuration to view details about a drive.

1. Turn on the power to the computer. Access the BIOS (look for a message telling you how or ask the instructor).

2. Navigate the menu system and locate information about the drive. Who is the manufacturer? How many megabytes are on the drive? (Not all BIOS will allow you to view this information. If so, proceed to Step 3.)

3. Navigate to where you can adjust the boot order. If necessary, adjust the boot order to boot from the floppy disk first, then the hard disk.

4. Exit the BIOS, saving changes.

Project 5-4

In this project, you will boot to a Windows 98 boot floppy, use FDISK to partition the drive, and FORMAT to format the drive. (If you are familiar with FDISK and FORMAT, you can skip this project.)

1. Place a Windows 98 startup disk into the floppy drive.

2. Turn on the computer, and wait for the boot floppy to display a menu. Select the option to **Start computer without CD-ROM support** and press **Enter**. (If the system starts with CD-ROM support, that's OK; it just takes longer to boot and we don't need the CD-ROM right now.)

3. Type **FDISK** at a command prompt and press **Enter**.

4. You are prompted for whether you want to enable large disk support. Select **Y** and press **Enter**. (If an NTFS partition is already on the disks, also answer **Y** to the next prompt to treat NTFS partitions as large.)

5. An FDISK Options menu appears. Select option **4** to view the partition information (there might not be anything). If there are existing partitions, what types are there?

6. Press the **Esc** key to return to the FDISK Options menu.

7. If there are partitions on the disk, select option **3**, Delete partition or Logical DOS Drive. If there are no partitions, proceed to step 10.

8. You must delete logical drives before deleting an extended DOS partition. If you try to delete a partition prematurely, the FDISK messages will tell you what you need to do. Delete all partitions, deleting the primary DOS partition last.

9. Press the **Esc** key to return to the FDISK Options menu.

10. Enter **1** to create an MS-DOS partition or Logical DOS Drive.

11. Enter **1** again to Create a Primary DOS Partition. FDISK checks the drive integrity before proceeding.

12. A prompt asks if you want to use the maximum available space; enter **N** and press **Enter**. You do not want to use the entire space so that you can create extended partitions and logical drives. Your instructor will guide you as to how much space to use.

13. FDISK verifies drive integrity again. Then enter the amount of space to create and press **Enter**. The partition is created.

14. Press **Esc** to return to the main FDISK Options menu.

15. You must set the partition to active, or it will not be bootable. Select option **2** to do this, and enter a **1** to specify the partition you want to make active.

16. Press **Esc** to return to the main FDISK Options menu, and **Esc** again to exit FDISK.

17. Now you must reboot the computer, or else the FORMAT command in the next step will not work. The Windows 98 startup disk should still be in the floppy drive.

18. At the boot menu, again start without CD-ROM support.

19. Type **FORMAT C: /S** (the /S switch makes the drive a system, or bootable disk).

20. A warning informs you that all data on the drive will be lost. Type **Y** and press **Enter**. The FORMAT process might take a few minutes depending on the size of the partition.

21. After the format is complete, you can enter a volume label of up to 11 characters. Type **Master** and press **Enter**. The drive is now available for use.

Project 5-5

In this project, you will configure a SCSI host adapter and two or three SCSI hard drives.

1. We are switching gears from IDE to SCSI—so with the power off, remove the IDE host adapter (if installed as a card) and IDE hard disk.

2. Read any identifying information from a SCSI host adapter provided by your instructor. Who is the manufacturer? What is the model number? Does it specify its capabilities (bit width, signaling method, etc.)? Optionally, you might also browse to the manufacturer's web site to glean more information about this specific adapter.

3. Install the SCSI host adapter into an available PCI slot. (For specifics about PCI card installation, see Chapter 6.)

4. Plug the SCSI drives into any available connector on the provided SCSI cable but not the last connector. If the cable is round, then it's for external use. If it's flat ribbon, then it's for internal use. Plug the other end of the cable into the host adapter connector. (The equipment provided should all match compatible specifications.) Before proceeding, do you think it is appropriate to turn on power and use the hard drive? Why or why not?

5. In answer to the question above, you should not turn on the system yet because nothing has been done about termination. A terminator is supplied by your instructor. Identify the terminator and write down what type it is: HVD, LVD, SE, mixed, passive, etc.

6. Plug the terminator into the last connector on the cable.

7. Ask your instructor about terminating the host adapter, as the method might vary from one adapter to another. Most likely, you can specify termination in the BIOS settings, which we'll look at in the next project.

Project 5-6

In this project, you will access the SCSI host adapter bus and configure a RAID solution.

1. Confirm correct termination and connections on the SCSI drive and host adapter. Then, power on the system.

2. After the system POST, you should see a BIOS screen for the SCSI host adapter. It might not be visible for long, so stay sharp. Look for instructions that indicate how to access the SCSI BIOS (often for Adaptec controllers, press Ctrl+A). If you can't find any, your instructor will inform you as to how to access the SCSI BIOS.

3. Once in the BIOS, use the menu system to verify that the drive appears correctly on the bus.

4. Using the SCSI BIOS system, configure the RAID array. Experiment and create what you like. The BIOS probably offers several choices. Consider creating a RAID-0 or RAID-5 array if you have three drives, or a RAID-1 if you have only two drives. Building the arrays could take quite a while with larger drives.

Note that in an actual implementation, if the boot device will be part of the array, you must create it prior to installing the operating system.

CASE PROJECTS

1. Sal, an ad-hoc administrator from another site, cannot understand why the hard disks on his newly configured IDE controller do not function. He says that the IDE controller is compatible with Ultra-DMA/100, although the two brand-new hard disks he placed on a single channel are both Ultra-DMA/66. Sal is certain that he has the right cable because he counted all 40 conductors and knows that he needs 40 pins to make the connection. When he powers up the computer, a POST message appears stating that he has no operating system. What should you tell Sal?

2. You have again volunteered your services to the nonprofit organization, KidHelp. KidHelp has been growing rapidly and has developed a database that is over a terabyte in size. Currently, KidHelp uses several file servers that collectively store the database, but they want to centralize into a single storage solution. A wealthy donor has told them to procure the best solution regardless of cost. Also, they want fast, regular backups and immediate protection in the event of a hard drive failure. What solution might you suggest to KidHelp?

6

SERVER UPGRADES

After reading this chapter and completing the exercises, you will be able to:

- Prepare for a server upgrade
- Adequately test and pilot the server upgrade
- Verify availability of system resources
- Inventory hardware
- Upgrade the processor, memory, BIOS, power supply, UPS, and adapters

Upgrading a server is a more serious matter than upgrading a desktop PC, because it affects a network of users instead of a single individual. This chapter covers the many steps you should take to prepare for the upgrade, as well as how to perform the upgrade itself. It concludes with a checklist to help ensure that you are well prepared for an upgrade and that it goes smoothly.

Preparing for a Server Upgrade

A familiar looking truck pulls up and out hops an overnight delivery employee with a box containing your server upgrade hardware. He places the package on the counter and utters a quick "sign here and have a nice day." Before you even head back to your cubicle, the truck is rumbling down the street for the next "absolutely, positively has to be there overnight" delivery. What you've just seen is the fastest part of a server upgrade.

As the administrator, you must execute every other part of the upgrade with the utmost care and sensibility. First, you probably have to obtain approval to perform the upgrade, which involves budgeting, planning, and presenting your plan to others. Even if you have autonomous power to make decisions for server upgrades, you still need to plan carefully, because if something goes wrong, you are the responsible party. You must also time the upgrade so that it has a minimal impact on productivity and user experience. Be sure to educate users as to what to expect regarding any upgrades that directly affect them. Finally, before performing the physical upgrade, verify that all the server components are there and in working order. With proper planning and precautions, you are now ready to perform an upgrade.

When to Upgrade the Server

On a simple level, an administrator might perform an upgrade in just minutes without notifying anyone. For example, perhaps a server just needs more memory costing less than $200. In many organizations, administrators have discretionary spending for smaller amounts, and it should only take a few minutes to shut down, install the memory, and restart the server. However, upgrading a server can require a significant investment in time, planning, and, of course, money—especially for larger upgrades that have a significant impact on the operations of the IT department, users, or your business audience.

For example, if an organization primarily employs eight NetWare 3.12 servers and would like to upgrade the servers to Windows 2000 Server, it is likely that the new system will need significantly more powerful hardware, as the minimum system requirements for NetWare 3.12 are much lower than for Windows 2000. (Granted, this is a drastic upgrade, but it makes very clear the effect that an upgrade can have on a network.) The organization will likely have to upgrade all major components, including the processors, memory, hard disks, and possibly even the motherboards. A mass migration and upgrade like this would probably be more cost-effective if the servers were replaced with new ones.

Moreover, this upgrade affects more than just how the IT department administers the servers—network resources for users might be located differently. Logon scripts mapping to NetWare printers won't work anymore, and users that have manually created shortcuts to network resources will no longer be able to access those resources. The impact of an upgrade this drastic would require significant planning, proper timing, a smoothly executed upgrade process, adequate personnel, and plenty of communications with the users notifying them of the upgrade and its impact on their day-to-day functions.

 A migration from NetWare to Windows 2000 servers can be less disruptive if you retain the NetWare server names. That way, shared resources will have the same network path if you also keep the same directory structure. Also, consider gradually upgrading one server at a time using a pilot program (as described later in this chapter), and check the impact as you go. This might help prevent a system-wide network failure or disgruntled users if something goes wrong.

Many times, upgrading the server is a necessary step in response to poor server performance. To fully justify expenditures in time and money, you should create a performance **baseline** so that you can define an acceptable level of performance. (Chapter 11 discusses performance monitoring and optimization, including the establishment of a baseline.) If you see the server begins to perform poorly on a regular basis when compared to the baseline, consider upgrading components that might be a bottleneck. For example, a heavily utilized database server will have higher demands placed on the processor than a simple file server. Upgrading or adding another processor might help the system to perform better.

 Before upgrading a server component, pause to verify identification of the actual bottleneck. For example, a server that shows heavy hard disk utilization might not need a larger or faster hard disk. Instead, first check memory utilization. Most NOSs utilize a swap file mechanism that substitutes hard disk space for memory in a low memory situation. Therefore, heavy hard disk utilization could actually be a memory issue that would be minimized with a memory upgrade.

You might take that same database server and consider upgrading it not only to an acceptable level of performance, but beyond current needs in a proactive approach to extend the server investment. This might prevent the repeated expense of upgrading again in a few months as demand on the server grows. For example, if the database server has one 700 MHz Pentium Xeon processor now, you might consider installing two 1 GHz processors, if the motherboard supports it. A proactive upgrade such as this is sometimes also in anticipation of financial timing. For example, in some organizations, if the department does not use its entire budget in a given time, then the next budget allocation might shrink because of a perception that the department does not need as large a budget since it didn't spend the entire budget last time. Although this kind of budgeting model has obvious weaknesses in logic and wisdom, it is nevertheless a reality in many organizations.

Other reasons for a proactive approach might include the anticipation of an upcoming merger with a new parent company. Perhaps your current intranet is for general information only and does not have a high hit rate. However, the new parent company requires you to post a great deal of company information on the intranet, such as details on employee benefits, company announcements, web-based collaboration software, and so forth. In this case, you might consider several upgrades, including adding another NIC to the server, to increase network throughput in anticipation of a higher hit rate.

Timing the Upgrade

Generally, the IT professional tries to keep as low a profile as possible within his or her organization. Why? Because when the administrator has a high profile, it's usually because something is wrong with a server or the network, and users tend to immediately think of administrators as having caused the problem! When users don't notice your presence in the organization, it usually means you are doing your job well. An ill-timed server upgrade (or scheduled maintenance) can give the administrator a very high profile; therefore, you should make sure that days or weeks before the upgrade, you monitor server utilization to determine periods of peak usage and periods of lowest usage. Of course, you want to perform any upgrades that make the server unavailable only during periods of low usage. If your organization is most active during business hours, you can stay late or arrive early to perform your upgrades while nobody else wants to access server resources. However, many organizations, especially larger ones, operate continuously. In addition, if the organization is global, users on one side of the globe might access resources while users on the other side of the globe are sleeping. This type of continuous access means that some types of upgrades will definitely take place while some users are attempting to gain access to resources. If the server must be taken offline, you can either temporarily transfer the role of server to another server or you can notify users in advance so they don't expect access during the time of the upgrade. Some upgrades (such as adding a disk to an array) might not require any downtime, and users will never notice the difference. On the other hand, upgrades such as adding processors or memory require the server to be turned off, and you should schedule an appropriate time and notify users in advance.

Notifying Users

Notifying users of a server upgrade helps to reduce the administrator's visibility and avoid unnecessary calls to the IT department. Even if you try to upgrade the server during the lowest usage periods, someone will still wonder why the server is unavailable, so the notification should help. Also, a public advance notice such as an email broadcast shows that you made a reasonable effort to notify users.

Broadcast company email is a common notification method, as are notices on the company Internet or intranet. Start notification as far in advance as is practical, which will vary from one organization to the next. (Some well-organized organizations have a written administrative policy for planned downtime notification.) I recommend an initial notification far in advance, and then as the upgrade approaches, notify a few more times with increasing frequency up until the actual upgrade event.

 Notification is not important *only* for when users lose access to the server. If the server is a load-balancing server, users will notice slower response and you should notify them in advance.

Notify the users when the server will be unavailable and for how long. If possible, also state how the planned downtime benefits the user. This helps to psychologically cushion the inconvenience for users when they understand it is ultimately for their benefit. For example, most users would be grateful if you were to add more storage to the email server so they could store more messages.

6

 When a server goes offline unexpectedly and not as a result of upgrades or maintenance, you should attempt to send out a message to all users to stem the certain flood of calls about the inaccessible server.

 Try to maximize the upgrade process so that other tasks can be completed in the same approximate time without increasing the impact on user access. For example, any time you want to work inside the server case, you might as well get a vacuum or a can of compressed air and eliminate the dust. Since that's probably also a regularly scheduled maintenance item, doing it now saves the separate task of doing it later.

Confirm That You Have Necessary Upgrade Components

Avoid unproductive downtime during an upgrade by confirming that all the necessary components for a successful upgrade are accounted for. For example, some hardware might not respond appropriately to the operating system without the proper BIOS upgrade, so you need both the BIOS upgrade and the hardware itself. When you perform an upgrade, be careful about the drivers that come with the hardware. (A **driver** is a software interface that allows the hardware to function with the operating system.)

You do not know how long the device has been on the shelf, and the drivers might be outdated. Save yourself the task of time-consuming troubleshooting after the upgrade that might occur due to an outdated or incompatible driver. After checking to see if the device is compatible with the other hardware and network operating system (NOS), download the most recent driver from the vendor's web site. While you're there, check the FAQ section to address and prepare for any issues you might encounter during the upgrade.

Download and expand the drivers into a permanent network directory from which you install the drivers. You might need to reinstall the drivers from time to time, and many NOSs default to installing drivers from the original installation path. Also, the drivers are immediately available to other servers on which you perform the same upgrade. Make sure you dedicate each directory to only a specific vendor and a specific device, because driver files might have the same name (especially from the same vendor) and you might accidentally overwrite files.

Similarly, check with the NOS vendor to see if there are known problems with the particular device and/or driver you want to install. A Readme.txt file often accompanies drivers and updates. Although this file is usually a statement of obvious information ("this driver upgrades your network card"), it might also contain important information ("this update only applies to Windows 2000"). Many administrators ignore this little file, but at the very least, you should scan it for any red flags or installation tips. The NOS web site often informs you of incompatible devices and provides solutions. Often, the solution is to avoid specific conflicting hardware devices or to install a NOS upgrade, patch, or hot fix. If the NOS vendor's support team does not list any known problems, check with other sources, such as newsgroups focused on the specific hardware and/or NOS vendors.

We administrators tend to be somewhat stubborn about reading directions, preferring to figure things out for ourselves. However, it often pays to read instructions in order to avoid problems later. I recently installed a security camera that attached to the USB port of a server, hoping that the Windows 2000 Server Plug and Play detection process would find the drivers on the camera's CD-ROM, as with most other installations for which Windows does not have a driver. Nothing worked. Had I read the instructions, I would have known that you must install the software and drivers first, and then install the camera. This would have saved me quite some time in trying to troubleshoot something that had a plain solution to begin with.

The level of precaution recommended in these pre-upgrade tasks might seem overly cautious. If you were performing a simple upgrade on a home PC, it might be. However, because of the impact the server has on an organization, every precaution is necessary.

Planning for Failure

Anybody who has administered computers for more than a few weeks knows that even the most meticulous and professional upgrade attempt sometimes encounters unanticipated problems, conflicts, or incompatibilities. In preparing for this possible contingency, administrators should prepare adequate failsafe measures to quickly recover from the problem or continue service to users through redundancy while troubleshooting the failed upgrade.

Always back up the server before performing any hardware or software upgrades. I recommend that you do not depend upon the normally scheduled backup rotation, because if a problem occurs, the backup can be slightly outdated. For example, most backups take place in the middle of the night, but if you perform the upgrade after everyone leaves work but before the backup, then one day's working data is in jeopardy if a problem occurs. Instead, take the server off of the network so that new data cannot be written to it. Next, perform a full backup of at least the data, and possibly also the operating system. Now you have a snapshot of the system before the upgrade, and if necessary, a restore should replace the data intact.

 Consider using imaging software such as PowerQuest DriveImage or Norton Ghost. This exactly duplicates the hard disk to a single image file for restore should a problem occur. You can store the image on a network share or one or more CD-ROMs, and protect it with a password in case the CD-ROM falls into unauthorized hands. Alternatively, many network cards are now bootable, allowing you to access the network and restore the image to the server from the network share. If you have to restore the image, it is much faster than reinstalling the operating system, reinstalling all of the server applications, and then restoring the data from a conventional backup.

In addition to creating a backup, other failsafe methods can also ensure server availability. For example, recall from Chapter 1 that clustering is utilization of two or more servers hosting the same application. If one of the servers is unavailable (as might occur during an upgrade), the remaining servers in the cluster continue to provide service. With a mission-critical server or application, you probably already have clustering enabled.

Absent a cluster, administrators might have a **hot spare**, which is a specific component (usually a hard drive) or a complete server that can immediately be available on the network and transparently perform the exact same functions as the original.

Verifying System Resources

You never seem to have enough PCI slots for the devices you want to install in a server. While you might have a free ISA slot, you probably don't care because fewer devices are ISA compatible. However, PCI slots represent valuable slot real estate that quickly fills up. In a typical server, you probably have five PCI slots. Account for two network cards for better throughput and availability, a SCSI card for tape devices, and another for hard disks, and you're almost out of expansion slots already. If so equipped, you can add a mezzanine or riser board to the motherboard to expand the number of available slots. Whatever the case, in larger environments the administrator probably does not know offhand exactly how many expansion slots remain in each server. Before making plans to add a device, verify that sufficient slots are available.

Even if a slot is available, you might encounter issues with available IRQs, DMAs, or I/O ports. These are each limited resources that most devices require to communicate with the operating system and other devices, and they are defined as follows:

- An **interrupt request (IRQ)** is a request that the device uses to "interrupt" the processor to ask for processor resources. There are 16 IRQs, numbered 0–15. Several IRQs are preassigned. For example, the COM1 serial port usually has IRQ 4. PCI IRQ steering (described in Chapter 3) can allow multiple devices to use the same IRQ if no more unique IRQs are available. However, ISA devices cannot take advantage of this benefit.

- A **Direct Memory Address (DMA)** is a resource that ISA devices use to directly access memory without first having to access the processor, both increasing device performance and reducing processor load. There are eight DMA channels, numbered 0–7.

- An **I/O port** is a location in memory that the processor uses to communicate with a device.

- A **memory address** is a dedicated region in system memory that some devices reserve and that is unavailable for use by any other device, application, or the operating system. This can help device stability by ensuring that nothing else trespasses the memory, which causes system errors.

If you are out of IRQs and IRQ steering is not available, or if you are out of available DMAs, then you must remove (or disable) an existing device that requires those same resources, or you cannot upgrade the server. I/O ports are usually plentiful, and if two devices request the same I/O port, you can usually reassign one of them to an alternate port.

Depending upon the chassis and power supply, you might not have sufficient expansion space to add more hard disks, tape drives, or removable storage such as Zip drives, CD-ROMs, or DVD devices, all of which require a drive bay, either internal or external. Drives installed in an internal drive bay are neither accessible nor visible when the case is attached. Most commonly, you install hard disks internally. It would be impractical to install removable storage or CD-ROM/DVD drives internally, so you want to use an external drive opening, which means that you can access and see the drive. Besides drive bay availability, you need a power supply that can handle the additional power requirements of the devices and has sufficient power connectors for each drive. You can use a Y-cable split that converts a single power connector to two, but if you're using several of these, you might be overloading the power supply. Generally, the more powerful the power supply, the more power connectors it includes.

 TIP   If you want to install a 3-1/2 inch hard disk but only have a 5-1/4 inch drive opening, purchase an inexpensive adapter kit that adds brackets to the outside of the drive, expanding it to fit into the larger 5-1/4 inch opening. Sometimes the adapter kit is included with the new drive.

A standard desktop or entry-level server tower case has space for perhaps four internal drives and two or three external drives. A server has significantly more storage space. For example, the Compaq ProLiant 8000 has internal drive cages for 21 hot-plug hard disks. Regardless, verify available drive bays as necessary.

 If you plan to install a large quantity of internal hard disks, consider adding one or more additional cooling fans to compensate for the additional heat.

Making an Inventory

One of the most frustrating things about installing hardware is finding it! Even relatively small organizations quickly accumulate quite a few loose components, chips, hard disks, and so forth. When a server fails, you must know exactly where to find replacement parts, so you should carefully inventory (and lock up) all parts that have any value. Organize smaller loose parts in appropriately sized storage bins, trays, and cabinets. Having an inventory also helps you to control and be aware of possible theft.

In addition, you should know what equipment is in each server for proper asset tracking, budgetary projections, and warranty service. Especially in large environments, manual inventory of installed hardware is an arduous and seemingly endless task, further complicated when there are multiple sites. I recommend procuring software that can automatically scan your entire network to inventory not only installed hardware in your servers and clients, but also installed software. Some programs can also identify network devices such as hubs, routers, switches, and so forth. One of the most popular programs is Microsoft Systems Management Server, for which you can find detailed inventory instructions at *www.microsoft.com/technet/SMS/c0318341.asp* or perform a search for the title "Administering Inventory Collection." Also check into the following other vendors:

- Hewlett Packard's OpenView at *www.openview.com*
- IBM Tivoli at *www.tivoli.com*
- Computer Associates Unicenter TNG at *www.cai.com*

Note that all these products require hardware that is capable of responding to queries from the software. You can still manually inventory hardware that does not automatically respond to the software, but this is becoming less of an issue as more hardware is designed to be compatible with inventory software.

When receiving new equipment or equipment transferred from another office, always request that an inventory list be included with the shipment. This helps to ensure that equipment arrives as promised and that the server from the home office that has 512 MB RAM doesn't suddenly appear in your office with only 128 MB. Another reason for the inventory list is that it helps you in assembling the equipment. Many servers and their associated equipment involve dozens of parts, including zip ties, cable management systems, fans, screws, keys, books, warranty cards, power cords, and so forth. It is extremely frustrating to unpack and assemble an entire server and rack, only to find that you are missing a vital component that you would have known about had you compared the physical parts to an inventory list.

TEST AND PILOT

The potential impact of some upgrades (both if they succeed and if they fail) might require an isolated **pilot program** in which you thoroughly test the upgrade for reliability and performance prior to deployment throughout the organization. A pilot program isolates a server upgrade in a portion of the network that makes performance easier to determine and lessens negative impact should some part of a major upgrade fail. Some organizations require a pilot program for nearly any hardware, operating system, or software change. However, pilot programs are not usually intended for common upgrade items such as installing a hard disk, network card, or memory. Most implementations might involve something like an upgraded NOS, an entirely new NOS (migrating from UNIX to NetWare 5.x, for example), or a change in hardware architecture (such as a change from UNIX-based Alpha architecture to Windows-based Intel architecture). If the upgrade works well in its initial pilot, you can extend the pilot programs to other segments of the network to see if the results are also successful under different circumstances. Finally, when the upgrade is fully tested and has satisfactorily passed the pilot phase, you can deploy the upgrade throughout the remainder of the organization as necessary. As an example for the current context, which focuses mostly on hardware, consider a pilot program for upgrades of the BIOS, motherboard, processor (especially if changing platforms from, say, AMD to Intel), and anything else you think might significantly impact the network if it fails or requires isolated analysis.

The CompTIA Server+ Exam Blueprint recommends pilot programs when upgrading processors, hard disks, memory, BIOS, adapters, peripherals (both internal and external), service tools, and the UPS. This doesn't leave much out. Though in the real world you might not pilot every item (who implements a pilot program for a new mouse?), approach the exam as if you would.

Sometimes, a test lab environment precedes the pilot phase. The test lab can be a special network segment completely detached from the remainder of the network in which administrators can perform drastic tests on the server without concern for affecting users or other production servers.

Once you successfully implement the upgrade changes, make sure that the improvement is more than just a perception. Start recording the performance of the server and/or network as it applies, and compare it to the previous baseline and performance prior to the upgrade. You should be able to find an improvement in the targeted upgrade area. For example, if you added another processor, you should see overall processor utilization drop to a lower percentage (where lower percentages equal better performance). After recording performance statistics, you should be able to change the baseline's level of acceptable performance. In most organizations, the baseline is a moving target that you periodically reset as server demands increase. If responsible parties (you and management) determine that network or server responsiveness no longer meets an acceptable range of performance, then a decision must be made: Either reset the baseline at the new level of performance or modify network or server equipment to return to the original (or better) level of baseline performance.

Note When confirming a successful upgrade, you can check for the obvious items such as proper functionality of the hardware. Don't forget, however, that most NOSs have logs that might also record errors in a problematic upgrade.

Be sure that after performing the upgrade, you record it to an easily accessible source for troubleshooting and asset-tracking purposes. Some organizations might have a log book next to the rack where changes are hand-written; others might have a computer-based log, such as a database or a spreadsheet, saved to an administrative network share. I prefer the latter method, because the log is accessible from any administrator's desktop. For example, in troubleshooting a server in Denver, an administrator in Phoenix can open the server log on a network share and see if any recent hardware upgrades might have caused a problem.

PERFORMING THE UPGRADE

When you've completed all the steps outlined here to prepare for an upgrade, you should be ready for the hands-on work of upgrading a server or server components. Before you start, though, be sure that you've taken precautions to prevent electrostatic discharge.

Avoiding Electrostatic Discharge

Before touching anything inside the server, it is critical to exercise precautions against **electrostatic discharge (ESD)**. You have probably experienced ESD at no significant harm to yourself many times, particularly if you live in an area where winters are cold and the wind blows (Chicago is a great example!). Once you are in from the cold and touch a door handle (or pet the cat), an ESD occurs. ESD occurs when two objects with differing electrical potential come into contact with one another because the electrical charges seek to equalize. While you are outside in the cold wind, the energy from the wind can build up electrical potential in you. When you touch an object in the house with less electrical potential, static electricity discharges from you to that object.

Although people are hearty enough to sustain a static shock, servers and their components are not. Before you touch a server for any reason, including component installation or inspection, you must be certain that you present no ESD threat.

Although it doesn't seem like much, if you can feel the static discharge, then you probably discharged around 3500 volts. If you also hear the discharge, then you probably discharged around 5000 volts, and if you see the discharge in a lighted room, then you probably discharged around 8000 volts. It is easy to build up this voltage—walking across the floor can generate 15,000 volts, and removing bubble pack from a carton can generate as much as 26,000 volts. It only takes 100–1000 volts to negatively impact server components, and at lower levels you might not feel, hear, or see the discharge.

You might unknowingly damage a component with ESD in two ways. First, an upset failure affects only the reliability and/or performance of a component. This is perhaps the worst of the two types of damage because it is difficult to detect and consistently reproduce. (For example, it takes 200–3000 volts to damage a server's CMOS.) The second way ESD affects a component is a catastrophic failure, which immediately damages the component so that it ceases to function properly.

Semiconductor Reliability News attributes approximately 60% of electronic component failures to ESD.

In seeking to prevent static discharge, take the following precautions:

- *Touch the chassis*—Touching the chassis grounds you and equalizes the voltage levels between you and the server. This is not a sufficient precaution, however, because as time passes, voltage can build up in you again, particularly if you are wearing leather soles on carpet. Touching the chassis is only a temporary, initial precaution. If you cannot utilize a better method, such as using an ESD protection kit (see below), then continue to touch the chassis periodically.

- *Unplug the power*—Many people assume that because the power cord is plugged into a grounded outlet, the case is protected against ESD. While it is true that the plug does lead to earth ground, that is not what is important in preventing ESD. What you are seeking is equalization in electrical potential. Plugged or unplugged, touching the chassis temporarily equalizes electrical potential. Moreover, it is safer to unplug the server. By leaving the server plugged in, you risk accidentally bumping the power switch. Installing or removing a device with the power on is catastrophic to most components (unless they are hot-swappable) and introduces the risk of system-wide electrical damage, not to mention the unpleasant surprise of receiving an electric shock. Also, many power supplies continue to supply low-voltage power to the motherboard, even when switched off. By implementing proper grounding measures and unplugging the server, you can avoid a potential mishap.

- *Use a grounding kit*—These come in several forms. At the lowest end, a portable grounding kit uses a wrist strap with an alligator clip that attaches to the server chassis (see Figure 6-1). (Be sure to attach it to an unpainted surface for best contact.) This has the same effect as touching the chassis to equalize electrical potential, except that it is not temporary because the connection is constant.

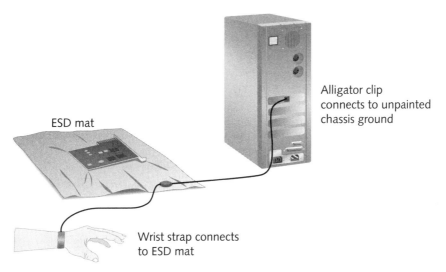

ESD mat

Alligator clip
connects to unpainted
chassis ground

Wrist strap connects
to ESD mat

Figure 6-1   A portable grounding kit and mat

A hardware repair bench normally includes a grounded floor mat (also called a map) that connects to earth ground at a nearby electrical outlet (this does not affect the operation of other devices plugged into that outlet). Another mat on the benchtop is also grounded—either to the floor mat or independently to another electrical outlet. The user wrist strap connects to either mat or the server chassis (see Figure 6-2). Because both mats, the wrist strap, and the chassis are all grounded, they possess the same electrical potential, eliminating the risk of ESD. The wrist strap usually includes a resistor designed to negate a high-voltage electrical charge, in case the technician accidentally touches a high-voltage item such as internal components in the power supply or the monitor. Both items retain high amounts of voltage even when unplugged. Full-time repair facilities normally ground the entire workbench.

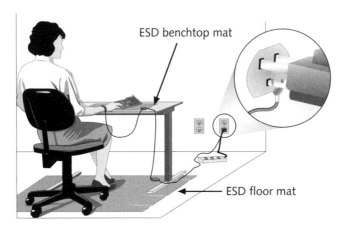

Figure 6-2 A workstation grounding kit

For more information on specific grounding kits, refer to the following web sites (also see *www.3m.com/ehpd/esd_training* for more about ESD in general):

- Specialized Products Company at *www.specialized.net*

- 3M Corporation at *www.3m.com/ehpd/workstation*

- Jensen Tools at *www.jensentools.com*

 If you find that the cord attached to the wrist strap gets in your way as you work, you can instead use a heel strap that attaches to your shoe.

Other tips for avoiding ESD include:

- *Take it to the mat*—As you install and remove components, be sure to place them on the mat. You might be tempted to place the computer itself on the mat, but that is unnecessary, provided you grounded it properly. Leave it off the mat so that you have some workspace.

 Some people recommend placing components on a sheet of aluminum foil. I cannot recommend this because some components contain tiny built-in batteries. If the batteries short out, they can become extremely hot in an instant, and might even explode (think firecracker). Batteries are not always easily identifiable on the board.

- *Handle with care*—If you find yourself without ESD protection, be sure you handle loose adapter cards by the metal bracket that attaches to the chassis. The internal ground circuitry of the card is connected to the bracket, so touching the bracket prevents ESD from damaging the card components. If the device does not have a bracket (a motherboard, for example), handle it by the edges and try to avoid touching any of the items on the surface of the card. Do not touch the metal edge of the adapter that goes inside the expansion slot, because even minor soiling from oils in your hand can contribute to corrosion. Do not stack components.

- *Bag it*—Place loose components into ESD-resistant bags. Remove any other type of packing material, such as Styrofoam, bubble wrap, or cellophane, because they tend to build and hold a static charge.

- *Take off the jewelry*—Metal jewelry can conduct electricity. It is a good idea to remove any jewelry from your hands and wrists (watch, rings, bracelets) before working on the server. Also, jewelry can catch onto components and wiring and hinder your dexterity.

6

Now that you've made all the preparations for a server upgrade and have ensured that you are protected against ESD, you can proceed to upgrade server components.

Upgrading the Processor

Before upgrading the processor, perform a few tasks to prevent serious problems or damage. Primarily, you want to verify that the BIOS and motherboard support the processor, and if using SMP, that the new processor is compatible with the existing processor.

Generally, it's a good idea to keep your BIOS version as up-to-date as possible—this chapter addresses this issue later. Because the BIOS directly affects the communication between the processor and the rest of the system, the importance of BIOS compatibility is obvious. Besides keeping up-to-date, also access the BIOS settings and verify that it supports SMP. A PC server usually allows 4-way SMP unless a mezzanine board or other motherboard modification allows you to expand to 8-way or greater SMP.

Next, check the motherboard to see if the proposed processor is compatible. The form factor of a given processor might physically fit in several different motherboards, but that does not mean it is compatible. Recall that a processor operates at multiples of the bus speed. This is one of the factors that limits the available upgrade path in your server. For example, you cannot replace a 700 MHz Pentium III with a 900 MHz Pentium III. The 700 MHz Pentium III is designed to operate on a 100 MHz bus. However, the 900 MHz processor is designed to operate on a 133 MHz bus, which will not allow the processor to function properly on a 100 MHz bus. Also, a given chipset might not be compatible with the proposed processor. To determine the compatible processor upgrade path for the server, you could research the motherboard manufacturer's web site. However, it is better to verify the upgrade path with the actual server vendor because they might have integrated something else into the system that affects upgrade compatibility.

Adding another processor to an existing processor involves more than simply making sure that both processors are the same speed. The processors should be identical in every way, including cache size, form factor, and stepping. For example, there are at least eight different 700 MHz Pentium III Xeon processors. While they all operate at 100 MHz, they vary in L2 cache size—either 1024 KB or 2048 KB—and the new processor cache must match the existing processor cache size. When adding another processor, verify that the new processor's **stepping** (the processor version) matches that of the existing processor. As Intel manufactures processors, minor problems, incompatibilities, or inaccuracies might be discovered from time to time. While the chances that these flaws will negatively affect server operation or compatibility are minimal, Intel usually corrects them when practical, so two processors of the same speed and cache still might not be exactly the same. You can also look on the processor to find its specification number (or **S-spec**)—an alphanumeric code that uniquely identifies each processor version and is more specific than the processor stepping. Figure 6-3 shows an S-spec (the last item on line 3, SL4MF). Notice also that the first line indicates 1000 MHz, 256 KB L2 cache, 133 MHz bus speed, and 1.7 V power.

Figure 6-3   The S-spec on this processor is SL4MF

Processor Slots and Sockets

The processor and its respective slot or socket appear in two primary formats. Sockets accommodate a processor format known as the **Pin Grid Array (PGA)** processor, which can be a flat, thin ceramic device with hundreds of gold pins on the bottom. These types of processors fit inside a motherboard socket receptacle that accepts each of the pins on the processor. The most recent implementation is the **Staggered Pin Grid Array (SPGA)**, which staggers the pin arrangement to squeeze more pins into the same space (see Figure 6-4). The PGA has two formats: standard PGA and the flipped chip PGA (FCPGA), referring to the fact that the processor die is "flipped" upside down on the die. The PGA format makes no difference in the actual installation except that FCPGA includes a fan in addition to the heat sink (described later in this section).

Figure 6-4   An SPGA processor

The slot format processor can be a larger device that stands upright inside a mother-board slot, similar to adapter or memory slots (see Figure 6-5). This format is referred to as the **Single Edge Contact Cartridge (SECC)**. The **Single Edge Contact Cartridge2 (SECC2)** format is a similar form factor, except it exposes the contacts at the bottom. The slot format processor includes a specially constructed plastic and metal housing that often includes an on-board cooling fan. Processor manufacturers have flip-flopped over the years regarding which format they use. Most processors use the socket format; however, Intel seems to favor the SECC slot format for the Xeon at this point. Whichever format is used, we will consider the housing and CPU collectively to be the processor.

Figure 6-5   A Pentium III Xeon processor in the SECC format

Table 6-1 lists the types of sockets and slots in current use.

Table 6-1   Sockets and Slots Used by Various Processors

Socket or Slot	Processor
Socket 370 (or PGA370)	Socket versions of the Intel Pentium III and Celeron
Socket 7 (or Super 7 when faster than 66 MHz)	Intel Pentium, Pentium MMX, AMD K5, K6, K6-2, K6-3
Socket 8	Pentium Pro
Socket A	AMD Duron and PGA format Athlon
Slot 1 (or SC-242)	Slot versions of the Intel Pentium III, Celeron, and Pentium II
Slot 2 (or SC-330)	Intel Pentium II and III Xeon
Slot A	AMD Athlon

Inserting the processor, either AMD or Intel, into a socket is an easy matter. Look carefully at the pins on the processor and match them to the socket on the motherboard. You will usually see a bevel that prevents you from accidentally inserting the processor in the wrong orientation. Simply match the bevel on the processor to the bevel on the socket. Before you insert the processor, lift up a lever next to the socket. The lever is the lock that holds the processor in place, and the feature is known as **zero insertion force (ZIF)** because when you insert the processor, gravity alone should be enough to seat the processor into the socket (see Figure 6-6). Sometimes you might have to help gravity a little bit, but very little pressure is required. If the processor does not seem to drop easily into the socket, do not force it. If you do, you may be buying another new processor.

Slots are keyed so that, again, you can only insert the processor in one orientation. However, be aware that it requires significantly more force to insert the processor into a slot, and the retention mechanism has guiding slots that facilitate this (see Figure 6-7). Use the retention mechanisms on either end of the processor to release it from the slot if you need to remove it later, but sometimes that can be a challenge as well. Most current processors require a slot.

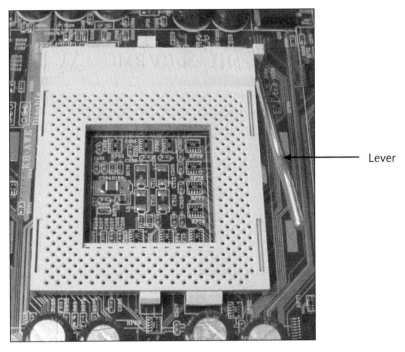

Lever

6

Figure 6-6   A ZIF socket uses a lever to lock the processor in place

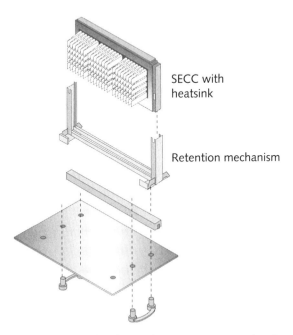

SECC with
heatsink

Retention mechanism

Figure 6-7   The slot and its retention mechanism

Removing the slotted processor properly is a matter of experience and getting a feel for removing the processor, which is usually seated very firmly in the slot. You have to balance the objective of removing the processor with a prudent degree of restraint, and this might require some experience. A safer method is to procure a processor extraction tool. Flotron (*www.flotron.com*) makes such a tool (see Figure 6-8).

Figure 6-8   A processor extraction tool

Processor Cooling

Processors can get very hot, and you must exercise care in cooling them properly using a **heat sink**—an attachment to the processor that either dissipates heat passively, through aluminum cooling fins, or actively, using a small cooling fan, usually in addition to cooling fins. When you purchase a "boxed" processor, it includes a cooling solution from the manufacturer. If it is "bare," then it has no cooling solution and you must determine a way to cool it yourself. Processors with only passive cooling depend upon airflow from the power supply and/or other cooling fans in the system. I usually recommend using active cooling even when only passive is required and even if the boxed processor only includes passive cooling.

 Other server components, particularly ribbon cables for hard drives, can block airflow. Be sure to route cables so as not to impede airflow.

Socket processors usually have a fan mounted on top of the cooling fins. The short fan power cable is usually sufficient to reach the motherboard power connection for the CPU, and is often marked on the motherboard as "CPU FAN." Attaching this type of heat sink to the CPU (see Figure 6-9) typically uses a clip that you hook to a notch on one side of the socket. On the other side, you press down on the clip until it hooks onto the notch on the other side of the socket. Figure 6-9 shows the aluminum cooling fins, clip, fan, and thermal tape.

Figure 6-9   A heat sink

Figure 6-10 shows the installed heat sink, fan, and fan power connection to the motherboard. Inserting the heat sink might take considerable force; take care that the heat sink is oriented and aligned properly.

Figure 6-10   The installed heat sink, fan, and fan power connection

If you want to provide maximum cooling, you can buy third-party heat sinks and fans that are usually much larger than those that come from the manufacturer and provide even better cooling. Normally, these are no more than $50.

Be careful that other cables do not contact the active heat sink cooling fan, because the resistance from the contact slows down the RPMs (and hence the cooling) and shortens the life of the fan.

Processors that go into slots, such as the SECC for the Pentium II/III or the SECC2 for the Pentium III Xeon processor, use a similar cooling method to the socketed processors, except that the form factor is rectangular and larger to accommodate the larger slotted processors.

Most heat sinks include a small amount of thermal tape located at the contact point between the bottom of the heat sink and the surface of the processor. The purpose of the thermal tape is to act as a conductor through which heat is transferred from the processor to the heat sink. Otherwise, there would be a narrow gap of air between the processor and heat sink, and air by itself is not a good conductor. Many technicians prefer to apply inexpensive thermal grease instead. A small amount of grease fills the gap and draws away heat better than thermal tape.

Notifying the Operating System

In Windows NT and Windows 2000, you must notify the operating system of a change from one processor to multiple processors; otherwise, the operating system does not recognize or use the additional processor(s). The steps to make this change in Windows 2000 are as follows:

1. Right–click My Computer and choose Manage.

2. Select Device Manager in the left tree pane.

3. Expand the Computer node in the right tree pane. The type of computer appears under Computer, and is probably Standard PC or Advanced Configuration and Power Interface (ACPI) PC.

4. Whichever type of computer appears, right-click it and choose Properties.

5. Click the Driver tab of the Properties sheet.

6. Click the Update Driver button.

7. Click Next to skip the introduction of the Upgrade Device Driver Wizard.

8. Select Display a list of the known drivers for this device so that I can choose a specific driver, and then click Next.

9. Select the Show all hardware of this device class option. The screen shown in Figure 6-11 appears.

10. Select the multiprocessor option that matches your computer, and proceed to the end of the wizard.

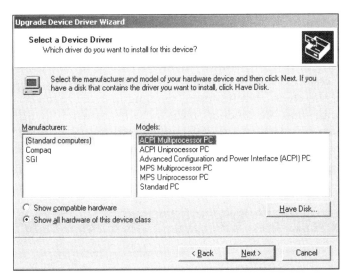

Figure 6-11   Choose ACPI Multiprocessor PC or MPS Multiprocessor PC as it applies

Microsoft offers a series of utilities with the Windows NT 4.0 Resource Kit. Run the UPTOMP utility from the command prompt, or reinstall the operating system to use multiple processors.

In current servers, it is uncommon to have to set a jumper to the correct voltage, CPU multiplier, and bus speed, but check documentation first, especially for Socket 7 or Super 7. If the voltage is set improperly, the processor might not function correctly or excessive voltage might damage the processor. Socket 370, Slot 1, Slot 2, and Slot A each adjust the voltage automatically. However, BIOS settings might be available to overclock the performance (not recommended for servers).

Upgrading Memory

Memory module upgrades will usually be DIMMs. (SIMMs are rarely found on current servers, though older workstations might still use them.) Fortunately, you cannot accidentally install the incorrect memory technology because the memory units have different installation notches, pin count, or length. For example, you cannot install a DIMM in an RDRAM slot. However, you will still need to verify that the memory you are upgrading is of the proper speed and matches other memory already installed in the system.

Technically, you can mix different speeds of memory, although it is not a good practice. For example, you can install 133 MHz SDRAM modules on a 100 MHz bus with existing 100 MHz modules. However, performance of all modules will be limited to 100 MHz. You cannot mix memory speed within a single SIMM memory bank.

Identifying Memory

Identifying existing memory and the memory the motherboard supports is more time-consuming than actually placing the memory modules. Absent the documentation that came with the server, you can identify memory modules by reading the actual chips on the module, counting the chips, and measuring the length. As discussed in Chapter 3, you can read the numbers on the module's memory chips to determine the speed in nanoseconds (ns), which correlates to a manufactured speed. (For your reference, a portion of Table 3-4 appears here as Table 6-2.) For example, if the number ends in –10, then you have 10 ns speed designed for a 66 MHz bus.

Table 6-2 SDRAM speed

Speed in ns	Rated Speed in MHz
15	PC66
10	PC66
8	PC100
7.5	PC133

Not every manufacturer includes these speed markings on their memory chips.

Determine if an error correcting function such as parity or ECC is present in the module. There are several ways to verify this, but the simplest and most foolproof method is to count the number of chips on the module. If the number is evenly divisible by three, then you have either ECC or parity memory. For example, nine chips on the module is evenly divisible by three ($9/3 = 3$), identifying the module as ECC or parity. If the part number on each chip is the same, then you have ECC, which includes the error correcting function in each chip. If one of the chips has a different part number, then you have parity memory, because the chip that is different is solely responsible for the parity function on behalf of all the memory chips on the module.

Identify a SIMM as a 72-pin module with a single notch in the bottom center, measuring 4.26 inches, or 108.2 mm (see Figure 6-12), and identify a 168-pin DIMM with two notches at the bottom, measuring 5.26 inches, or 133.8 mm (see Figure 6-13). The notches in the bottom are spaced slightly differently. The left notch spacing defines the module as registered, buffered, or unbuffered, and the right notch spacing defines the module voltage at 5.0 V or 3.3 V. Again, the notching makes it impossible to make a mistake with buffering or voltages when installing the modules.

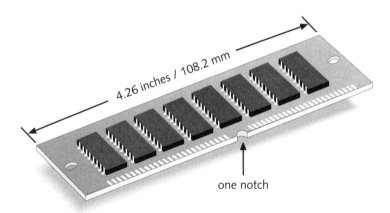

one notch

Figure 6-12 A 72-pin SIMM

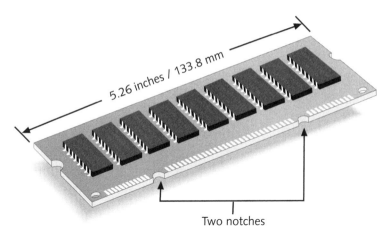

Two notches

Figure 6-13 A 168-pin DIMM

The next generation of SDRAM, the 184-pin DDR DIMM, is an important memory module with which you should be familiar. High-end workstations and servers are increasingly requiring DDR SDRAM because of its extremely high throughput (up to 2656 MBps). You physically insert this module into the slot in the same way as the 168-pin DIMM; however, you can identify it with a single key notch at the bottom indicating its voltage (2.5 V) and with two notches on either end. The module is the same length as a standard SDRAM DIMM, measuring 5.256 inches, or 133.5 mm (see Figure 6-14).

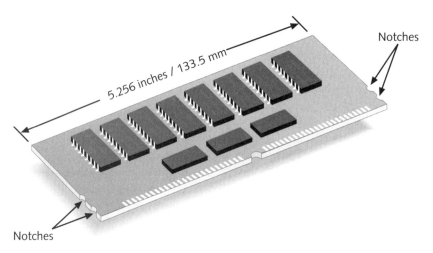

Figure 6-14   A 184-pin DDR SDRAM DIMM

Also look at the physical characteristics of the module. Recall that RDRAM RIMMs have immediately identifiable metal heat spreaders covering the memory chips (see Figure 6-15). Another verification of RDRAM is if empty memory slots on the motherboard have a C-RIMM that completes the continuity, permitting memory data to pass through each slot.

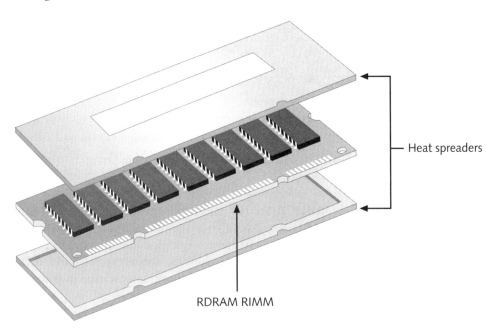

Figure 6-15   An RDRAM RIMM with heat spreaders pulled away

Installing Memory

Installing memory is a straightforward matter. Both SIMMs and DIMMs have notching that prevents you from installing them in the wrong slots. The trick is to make sure that you have fully seated the memory into the slot.

 Memory modules are particularly sensitive to ESD, so be sure to exercise appropriate precautions.

For a SIMM, insert the module at a 45-degree angle to the SIMM slot by pressing down firmly. A notch on one end of the module matches a protrusion on the slot to prevent backward insertion. Tilt the module toward the locking clips until they snap into place. Tabs on the locking clips should fit precisely into holes on the SIMM (see Figure 6-16). If the holes do not appear to match up, you probably have not pressed the module down far enough into the slot. To remove the SIMM, use your fingers to separate the locking clips from the holes in the module while simultaneously tilting the module up and out.

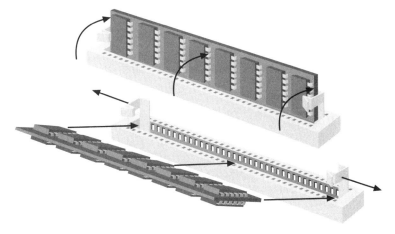

Figure 6-16   Inserting a SIMM into the slot

You are more likely to be installing a DIMM, which requires 90-degree, straight downward insertion into the DIMM slot. However, you will not tilt the module forward like the older SIMM. Instead, locking ejector tabs automatically clamp onto the module when the DIMM is fully seated, though you might also press them into place to verify proper locking (see Figure 6-17). To remove the DIMM, press down on top of both ejector tabs simultaneously, and the module should come out.

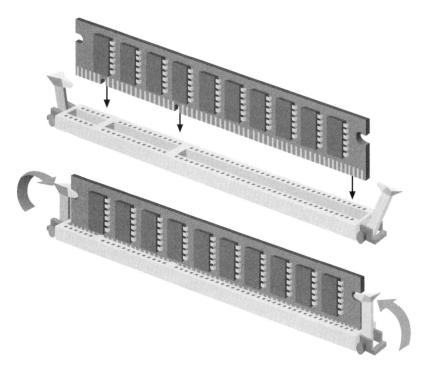

Figure 6-17   The DIMM is inserted with locking ejector tabs

 I've installed DIMMs into extremely tight slots that required considerable pressure to seat them in the slot. When inserting DIMMs, you should feel a confirming "sink" into the slot. Sometimes the ejector tab will flip into place and give the illusion that the module is fully seated when it is not. If you turn on the computer and see memory errors or the system does not execute its POST, check the seating of the modules—they are probably not making contact with the slot.

Remember the following guidelines when installing memory:

- Match the manufacturer of existing memory when possible. Production variances are probably slight, but might produce an unacceptable risk in mission-critical servers. On desktop PCs, mixing manufacturers is a more acceptable risk.

- Try to plan server purchases with as few modules as possible to maximize future upgrade possibilities. For example, instead of two 64 MB DIMMs, install a single 128 MB DIMM.

- If the memory modules vary in size, install the largest modules (in megabytes) in the lowest numbered slot for best performance.

- Verify that the operating system is capable of recognizing the memory you install. For example, Windows NT 4.0 can utilize only 4 GB of memory regardless of motherboard capacity.

- Installing large quantities of memory (2–4 GB or more) might require special configuration of the NOS. Check with the vendor to verify. For example, Windows 2000 Advanced Server allows you to access large amounts of memory by adding the "/PAE" switch (enabling Physical Address Extension) to the Boot.ini bootup file.

- Large quantities of memory might also require specific hardware compatibility. For example, Windows 2000 Advanced Server can utilize PAE only with a Pentium Pro processor or later, 4 GB or more of RAM, and an Intel 450 NX or compatible chipset or later.

- Although the current motherboard and BIOS will automatically detect new memory, verify this in the BIOS to confirm proper seating of the memory.

- Most NOSs include a virtual memory feature that corresponds to the amount of physical memory installed in the system. When you increase the amount of physical memory, also increase the amount of virtual memory, which might be referred to as a swap file. However, in large memory implementations, it might be impractical to create a 4 GB swap file that matches 4 GB of physical memory. In this case, about 2 GB is usually acceptable.

Memory modules and sockets designed for low-cost appeal might use tin contacts. Many sources tell you to avoid mixing gold modules with tin sockets (and vice versa) because contact between the two creates an oxidization known as "fretting corrosion," affecting good electrical contact and possibly creating all kinds of instability and memory error problems. However, this issue is less of a problem than it used to be because tin contacts are rarely produced, especially for server platforms. All industry-standard DIMMs use gold contacts.

Updating the BIOS

In years past, it was impossible to update the BIOS without first removing the BIOS, which might involve soldering tools. Current PCs and servers offer **flash BIOS**, which means you can download the most recent update from the vendor's web site and apply it to the server without replacing the BIOS.

To keep on top of the most recent updates, consider checking with the server vendor to see if they offer a notification service that sends you an email when a BIOS update (or other updates such as a driver) is available. Dell, for example, offers such a service.

Before updating the BIOS, read all available documentation about the update (a Readme.txt file usually accompanies the BIOS update). This is important to determine the purpose of the update and if it solves any problems you might be experiencing.

Update the BIOS as follows:

1. Download the BIOS update from the system vendor. Although major BIOS manufacturers such as Phoenix Software, Award Software, and American Megatrends Inc. (AMI) make most BIOS found in servers, you should not seek or use updates from the BIOS manufacturer. Server vendors work extensively to tailor a specific BIOS exactly for the server vendor's motherboard.

2. Execute the downloaded file. Typically, this will copy all necessary flash BIOS files to a blank floppy disk.

The boot disk should be as clean as possible. It should be a system disk containing only basic boot files (IOS.SYS, MSDOS.SYS, COMMAND.COM) but no memory management drivers such as HIMEM.SYS.

3. Record current CMOS settings. Most BIOS updates either automatically reset the CMOS for you or recommend that you manually reset the CMOS to default settings. You can use the recorded CMOS settings to reconfigure the CMOS to your preferences after the update is complete.

Instead of writing down each setting, consider using the Shift+PrtScn (Print Screen) keys to send the CMOS configuration screen to a locally attached printer. You will have to perform a manual form feed on laser printers to print the page.

4. Boot from the flash BIOS disk. If the extracted files do not create a bootable system disk, use any DOS or Windows 9x system to first format the disk as a system disk.

5. The flash BIOS usually presents a list of options for what you want to do. Select the option to update the BIOS.

6. After the BIOS update is finished, manually reboot the computer if the updated BIOS does not do so automatically.

7. Upon reboot, access the CMOS settings and reset the values back to default. Otherwise, the system might not function correctly.

8. Reboot the server and again access the CMOS settings, entering in your preferred settings recorded in Step 3.

Recovering the BIOS

If the BIOS is corrupt, you cannot boot the system at all—not even with a valid flash BIOS disk. In fact, the display adapter is probably unavailable, further complicating matters. A corrupt BIOS can be caused by a number of things, including ESD to the BIOS EPROM, an interrupted flash BIOS update, or a virus. Regardless of what causes the corruption, the system cannot function until you repair the BIOS. While some systems might vary (specific instructions are probably in the documentation), the following are the usual steps to take in recovering the BIOS:

1. Turn off the system power.

2. Having removed the server cover, look for a motherboard jumper that allows you to enter recovery mode. Check motherboard documentation to find the jumper if it is not printed obviously on the motherboard.

3. Insert the latest flash BIOS update into the floppy drive.

4. Turn on the system power. A corrupt BIOS usually means that even the video display is not functioning, so you will have to listen to beep(s) to track what is taking place in the BIOS recovery:

   ■ The BIOS sounds a single beep when it passes control to DOS on the bootable flash BIOS floppy. DOS executes the Autoexec.bat file on the floppy, which in turn runs the flash BIOS update executable.

   ■ A single beep indicates commencement of the flash operation.

   ■ Two beeps indicate a recovered system BIOS.

   ■ Two more beeps indicate successful completion of the recovery.

   ■ A constant series of beeps indicates a failed recovery attempt.

   The recovery process usually takes between three to five minutes.

5. Remove the recovery diskette, and turn off server power.

6. Restore the motherboard jumper to its original position.

 The server might have a read-only jumper position that prevents viruses from writing to the BIOS.

7. Turn on the system power, and access the BIOS settings to enter your preferences.

 After rebooting, a CMOS checksum error or some other problem might appear. Try to reboot again (by powering off and on) to see if that resolves the problem. If not, enter the CMOS setup utility to check and save settings. You can often resolve CMOS checksum errors by accessing CMOS settings, saving the settings, and then rebooting.

Upgrading a Power Supply

If you suspect a power supply is not performing reliably or to specifications, you can first verify this using a **digital multimeter (DMM)**. The DMM measures AC voltage, DC voltage, continuity, or electrical resistance (see Figure 6-18). In this section, we are mostly concerned with the DC voltage readings.

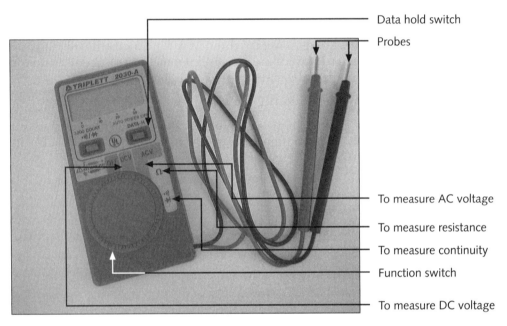

Data hold switch

Probes

To measure AC voltage

To measure resistance

To measure continuity

Function switch

To measure DC voltage

Figure 6-18   A digital multimeter

 TIP   Memory parity check error messages are often an indicator of a problematic power supply. Recall that memory must be continually charged to retain its data. If the power to memory fluctuates, you are likely to lose data. If parity check messages consistently identify the same location in memory, then the problem is probably with a bad memory module. If the parity check messages are in different locations, then the problem is probably power-related.

Using a Multimeter

A multimeter should help you clarify whether a power supply is operating within specifications. Although a multimeter can be analog (using a needle to show measurements), you should use a digital multimeter for best accuracy.

To check the operating voltage of a power supply using a DMM, use the following procedure:

1. Take the server cover off and power up the system.

2. The DMM has two probes: red and black. Find the power supply connector that connects to the motherboard, and locate the Power_Good pin (pin 8; third pin from the left on the unnotched side). Insert the red probe into the connector at pin 8 (see Figure 6-19). Inserting the probe alongside a live connection like this is known as **backprobing**.

Backprobe inserted in pin 8

Figure 6-19   Backprobing the ATX power supply connector

3. Touch the black probe to a ground, such as the chassis.

4. The DMM should read between +3 V and +6 V. If not, then the system cannot see the Power_Good signal and does not start or run correctly.

5. Repeat this process for other connectors (use Tables 6-3 and 6-4 as a reference). Connectors are in the +/-3.3 V, +/-5.0 V, and +/-12.0 V range. You should not see more than 10% variance from this range, and only 5% variance is acceptable for high-quality power supplies.

If the voltage readings are outside an acceptable range, replace the power supply.

Table 6-3   Pin Assignments for the ATX Power Connection

Pin Number*	Color	Voltage
1	Orange	+3.3 V
2	Orange	+3.3 V
3	Black	Ground
4	Red	+5 V
5	Black	Ground
6	Red	+5 V
7	Black	Ground
8	Gray	Power_Good
9	Purple	+5 VSB (Standby)
10	Yellow	+12 V
11	Orange (or Brown)	+3.3 V
12	Blue	−12 V
13	Black	Ground
14	Green	PS_On (power supply on)
15	Black	Ground
16	Black	Ground
17	Black	Ground
18	White	−5 V
19	Red	+5 V
20	Red	+5 V

*Pins 1–10 appear on the non-keyed side, and 11–20 on the keyed side.

Table 6-4   Drive Connections

Pin Number	Color	Voltage
1	Yellow	+12 V
2	Black	Ground
3	Black	Ground
4	Red	+5 V

If the DMM requires you to specify a maximum voltage range before testing equipment, set it at 20 V, because servers use +5 V or +12 V. Setting it too low might "peg the meter," overloading the DMM and possibly damaging it. Many higher-quality DMMs have autoranging capability to automatically determine the best setting.

Replacing the Power Supply

Wise server choices include redundant power supplies, so hopefully replacing a power supply, while urgent, does not involve downing the server. Many redundant power supplies include lights, beeps, or both to alert you of an impending failure as well as total failure. Naturally, you want to replace the power supply when warning of impending failure occurs, instead of waiting for total failure. Check with the vendor documentation for specific instructions on replacing the power supply (PSU). Generally, replacing a hot-swappable redundant power supply is quick and easy:

1. Verify that the replacement PSU is compatible. For hot-swappable server PSUs, I recommend using the server vendor PSU instead of a third-party PSU for best reliability.

2. If necessary, unscrew the power supply from the chassis. Normally, redundant power supplies use a lever or handle instead of screws to attach to the chassis. Flip the lever/handle or unscrew, and then pull the PSU out of the server (see Figure 6-20). You will probably perform this action from the back of the server in most cases, so make sure you have enough space to either slide the server out of the rack far enough to reach behind the server from the front of the rack or that sufficient space exists behind the server to both open a door (if present) and remove the power supply from the back of the rack. Be sure to use both hands when removing the PSU; it might surprise you how heavy it can be.

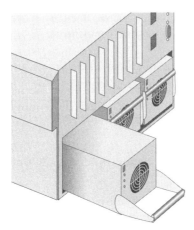

Figure 6-20   Pull down the handle and pull out the hot-swappable PSU

Verify that the remaining power supply or power supplies are capable of powering the server and all components prior to removing a PSU from the server. Otherwise, the server may go down hard and possibly damage the operating system, applications, or data.

3. Replace the power supply by reversing the steps above. Hot-swappable PSUs plug directly into connections on the server without requiring you to remove the cover and attach power cables individually.

If the replacement power supply is an upgrade, not a matter of replacing a failed PSU, then you can perform the above steps one PSU at a time until all are up to the new level. Be sure to verify vendor documentation to see if the server supports the new power level.

For power supplies that are not hot-swappable, continued operation of the server is not possible when the power supply fails, and replacing the PSU is an immediate concern. Do *not* attempt to repair the PSU; even unplugged it retains a high level of dangerous electricity. It is more prudent to spend the money on a new PSU. Also, if it suits you, there is more flexibility in choosing a different vendor with non–hot-swappable power supplies. Make sure that the new power supply will fit the chassis. Some server vendors use specially designed PSU form factors that prevent you from choosing a generic replacement.

Replace the non–hot-swappable PSU as follows:

1. Power down the system if it is running.

2. Unplug the power cable.

3. Remove the server cover.

 At your discretion, consider *not* grounding yourself in this rare case. If there is a chance that the PSU might ground to you, extremely high voltage could be discharged, resulting in serious injury. Just keep touching the chassis and be extra careful about not touching other ESD-sensitive components.

4. Unplug all PSU cable connections to the motherboard, fans, drives, and so on.

5. Unscrew the PSU from the chassis. Non–hot-swappable PSUs do not have handles or levers to release them from the chassis. Some servers might require that you first remove other components such as adapters or hard disks in order to reach the PSU.

6. Remove the PSU. (If you have time, this is a good time to blow out or vacuum out dust.)

7. Replace with a new PSU by reversing the steps above.

 I don't think you'll see this configuration, but older AT power supply connections use two connectors to connect to the power supply. If you see this, make note of the connector orientation, because mixing them up can burn up the motherboard or components. Also, it's easy to accidentally make the "off by one" connection where you skew the connector to the board by one pin. Remember that the two black ground wires in each connector should be adjacent to avoid a mix-up (see Figure 6-21). ATX-style motherboards, on the other hand, use a single connector that is keyed to prevent backward installation.

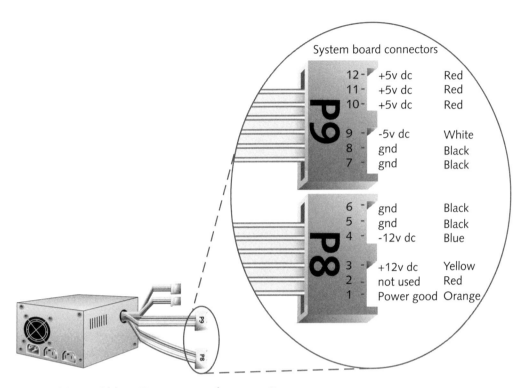

Figure 6-21   Older AT power supply connections

Upgrading Adapters

Upgrading adapters is a fairly straightforward process. Actually, you cannot normally upgrade adapters—any features or characteristics of the adapter are static except for driver updates, BIOS updates (as is the case with SCSI adapters), video adapters with upgradeable memory, or LAN adapters to which you can add a "wake on" LAN chip for network booting. To install new features, simply replace the adapter. When installing the adapter into a slot, the following guidelines define what you can do:

- An 8-bit ISA card can fit into a 16-bit ISA or EISA slot.
- A 16-bit ISA card can fit into a 16-bit ISA or EISA slot.
- A 32-bit PCI card can fit into a 32-bit or 64-bit PCI slot.
- A 64-bit PCI card only fits into a 64-bit PCI slot.

When installing the adapter, apply firm, even pressure when guiding the adapter into the slot. Be sure to orient the server so that you apply downward pressure (toward the tabletop) instead of sideways to avoid tipping the server over. Try to visually line up the card with the slot to ensure success. Often, you will have to remove adjacent cards first for better visibility and more working room. As you press down on the adapter, you should feel the card "sink" into the slot (see Figure 6-22). If the retaining bracket is not flush against the chassis, then the card is probably not fully seated. Once seated, screw in the retaining screw. Be sure to cover empty slot openings on the back of the chassis to help provide good airflow.

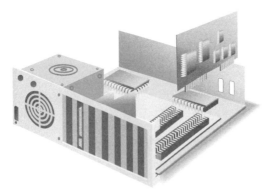

Figure 6-22 Inserting an adapter into its slot

 Though unusual with quality components, I have sometimes found cards that could not be fully seated because the retaining bracket was flush against the chassis, preventing further downward motion. If this is the case, you should choose a different adapter. I have also seen cards that, when fully seated, still had clearance between the retaining bracket and chassis. Again, choose a different adapter if possible. Otherwise, you might have to use a pair of needle-nose pliers and carefully bend the adapter to make it fit.

 The AGP graphics slot is further away from the fastening point on the chassis than other bus interfaces, such as PCI. As a result, AGP cards are a little more susceptible to "walking" out of the slot during shipment. When you receive a new server, I recommend pressing down on all removable components, including the AGP adapter, to ensure proper seating of cards. New motherboards often include an AGP card retention mechanism that snaps over the slot and locks the card into place via a retention notch.

Upgrading adapter drivers is normally a matter of connecting to the vendor web site, downloading the drivers, extracting them to a temporary location on the hard drive, and installing them. Hands-on Project 6-7 guides you through this process step-by-step.

Upgrading the UPS

When upgrading the UPS, realize that the upgrade requires you to power down all systems connected to the UPS, because an "upgrade" is really a replacement. For example, if a rack has three 8-way servers in it and a large UPS for redundant power, and the administrator knows that the UPS will not supply adequate power after adding another 8-way server, he or she might proceed as follows:

1. Power off all load equipment attached to the UPS.

2. Replace the UPS with a model having sufficient power capacity and runtime.

3. Plug in all equipment and again power up the systems on the new UPS.

Of course, because the servers must be offline while the UPS is being replaced, redundant servers must perform the same services. If this redundancy is not available, notify the users of the planned downtime and perform the upgrade during low usage periods. Also, perform a backup prior to the upgrade. The batteries on a new UPS probably do not hold enough charge to provide adequate runtime if utility power were to fail soon after the upgrade, and a recent backup will assist the recovery.

Alternatively, if the rack has N+1 UPS redundancy (as discussed in Chapter 4), then the administrator can upgrade one UPS while another continues to provide redundancy. If utility power is interrupted during the upgrade, the redundant UPS will continue to supply power.

6

SERVER UPGRADE CHECKLIST

The following checklist should help you to perform carefully planned upgrades:

- ❏ Set a baseline of acceptable performance.
- ❏ Confirm NOS compatibility.
- ❏ Notify users if the upgrade affects them.
- ❏ Record settings if applicable (e.g., CMOS settings prior to BIOS upgrade).
- ❏ Verify available resources for the device (IRQ, DMA, I/O).
- ❏ Download the most recent driver(s) and BIOS upgrade.
- ❏ Read instructions, FAQs, and newsgroups.
- ❏ Inventory delivered parts.
- ❏ Perform a tape backup.
- ❏ Upgrade to the latest BIOS version.
- ❏ Perform the physical installation using sound ESD practices.
- ❏ Test and pilot the implementation.
- ❏ Reset the baseline.

CHAPTER SUMMARY

❏ Upgrading a server can require a significant investment in time, planning, and, of course, money—especially for larger upgrades that have a significant impact on the operations of the IT department, users, or your business audience.

❏ Many times, upgrading the server is a necessary step in response to poor server performance. To fully justify expenditures in time and money, you should create a performance baseline so that you can define an acceptable level of performance.

❏ You might take that same database server and consider not only upgrading it to an acceptable level of performance, but also upgrading it beyond current needs in a proactive approach to extend the server investment.

❏ Upgrade the server only during periods of lowest utilization to minimize the impact on users.

❏ Notifying users helps to reduce the administrator's visibility and avoid unnecessary calls to the IT department. Public advance notice such as an email broadcast documents that you made a reasonable effort to notify users, and tells them how the upgrade will benefit them.

❏ Before performing the upgrade, apply the latest flash BIOS upgrade and the most recent available drivers.

❏ Read all documentation and available FAQs or newsgroups relevant to the upgrade and NOS installation.

❏ The potential impact of some upgrades (both if they succeed and if they fail) might require an isolated pilot program where you can thoroughly test the upgrade for reliability and performance prior to full deployment throughout the organization.

❏ Perform baseline performance tests before and after the upgrade to measure any changes in performance.

❏ Log upgrades to an easily accessible location to assist in troubleshooting and asset tracking.

❏ Always back up the server before performing any hardware or software upgrades.

❏ You can use clustering or a hot spare to continue providing service during the upgrade process.

❏ Before upgrading, verify the availability of slots and resources.

❏ Verify inventory of parts on hand and delivered parts for accounting purposes and to ensure that the upgrade proceeds smoothly.

❏ ESD poses a threat to electronic devices, and administrators should implement antistatic measures such as an antistatic wrist bracelet and mat.

❐ When upgrading a processor, verify that the motherboard and BIOS can accept the new processor. If adding a processor for SMP, match the new processor's stepping, cache, form factor, and speed exactly to the existing processor.

❐ Processors fit in either a socket or slot. Sockets have a ZIF lever to lock the processor into place, and slots have a retention mechanism on the side. Both formats are keyed so that the processor can only be inserted in the correct orientation.

❐ For Windows NT or Windows 2000, you must take measures to notify the operating system of an additional processor.

❐ When adding SIMM or DIMM modules, match the speed of existing modules.

❐ If the number of SIMM/DIMM modules is evenly divisible by three, then you have either ECC or parity memory. If the part number on each chip is the same, then you have ECC, which includes the error correcting function in each chip. If one of the chips has a different part number, then you have parity memory.

❐ RDRAM RIMMs have metal heat spreaders covering the memory chips.

❐ For a SIMM, insert the module at a 45-degree angle to the SIMM slot by pressing down firmly. Tilt the module toward the locking clips until they snap into place.

❐ Installing a DIMM requires 90-degree, straight downward insertion into the DIMM slot. Locking ejector tabs automatically clamp onto the module when the DIMM is fully seated, though you might also press them into place to verify proper locking.

❐ Match the memory module manufacturer when possible. Try to plan server purchases with as few modules as possible to maximize future upgrade possibilities. If the memory modules vary in size, install the largest modules (in megabytes) in the lowest numbered slot for best performance.

❐ Verify that the operating system is capable of recognizing the memory you install. For example, Windows NT 4.0 can utilize only about 4 GB regardless of motherboard capacity. Installing large quantities of memory (2–4 GB or more) might require special configuration of the NOS. Large quantities of memory might also require specific hardware compatibility.

❐ Although current motherboards and BIOS will automatically detect new memory, verify this in the BIOS to confirm proper seating of the memory.

❐ When you increase the amount of physical memory, also increase the amount of virtual memory and adjust the size of the swap file.

❐ Current PCs and servers offer flash BIOS, which means that you can download the most recent update from the vendor's web site and apply it to the server without replacing the BIOS. Before you perform a flash BIOS upgrade, be sure to record existing CMOS settings because you must reenter them after the upgrade.

❐ You can recover a corrupt BIOS using a flash BIOS floppy, but only by using beeping sounds to track the progress because the display is not available.

6

❐ If you suspect a power supply is not performing reliably or to specifications, verify PSU performance by using a digital multimeter (DMM).

❐ Do *not* attempt to repair a PSU; even unplugged it retains a high level of dangerous electricity.

❐ An 8-bit ISA card can fit into a 16-bit ISA or EISA slot, a 16-bit ISA card can fit into a 16-bit ISA or EISA slot, a 32-bit PCI card can fit into a 32-bit or 64-bit PCI slot, and a 64-bit PCI card only fits into a 64-bit PCI slot.

❐ Upgrading the UPS is really a replacement, and unless you have redundant UPS systems powering the rack, you must plan for downtime.

KEY TERMS

backprobing — Inserting the probe alongside the live connection.

baseline — Performance data that reflects an acceptable level of system performance.

digital multimeter (DMM) — A device that measures AC voltage, DC voltage, continuity, or electrical resistance.

Direct Memory Address (DMA) — A resource that ISA devices use to directly access memory without first having to access the processor, both increasing device performance and reducing processor load. There are eight DMA channels, numbered 0–7.

driver — A software interface that allows the hardware to function with the operating system.

electrostatic discharge (ESD) — A discharge of electrical energy that occurs when two objects with differing electrical potential come into contact with one another because the electrical charges seek to equalize.

flash BIOS — BIOS that can be updated via software instead of physical removal of the EPROM.

heat sink — An attachment to the processor that either dissipates heat through cooling fins or a small cooling fan in addition to cooling fins.

hot spare — A specific component (usually a hard drive) or a complete server that can immediately perform on the network and transparently perform the exact same function as the original.

interrupt request (IRQ) — Request that a device uses to "interrupt" the processor to ask for processor resources. There are 16 IRQs, numbered 0–15.

I/O port — A location in memory that the processor uses to communicate with the device.

memory address — Some devices reserve a dedicated region in system memory that is unavailable for use by any other device, application, or the operating system. This can help device stability by ensuring that nothing else trespasses the memory, which causes system errors.

pilot program — Isolating an upgraded server in a portion of the network that makes performance determination easier to determine and lessens negative impact should some part of a major upgrade fail.

Pin Grid Array (PGA) — An arrangement of pins on the underside of a processor. The pins fit inside a corresponding PGA socket.

S-spec — An alphanumeric code printed on the processor that uniquely identifies the processor version and is more specific than processor stepping.

Single Edge Contact Cartridge (SECC) — A slot format processor that stands upright inside a motherboard slot, similar to adapter or memory slots.

Single Edge Contact Cartridge2 (SECC2) — A longer form of the SECC slot that accommodates Pentium Xeon processors.

Staggered Pin Grid Array (SPGA) — Same as a PGA processor or socket format, except in a staggered arrangement to squeeze more pins in the same space (as opposed to straight rows).

stepping — The version of a processor.

zero insertion force (ZIF) — A socket format that allows gravity alone to seat the processor. The processor is then locked into place with a locking lever.

6

REVIEW QUESTIONS

1. Which of the following might be cause to upgrade the server? (Choose all that apply.)

   a. You want the latest technology.

   b. Server performance is insufficient.

   c. timing in relation to the budget

   d. planning for future events

2. When should you upgrade the server?

   a. during peak utilization

   b. during lowest utilization

   c. between 12:00 AM and 3:00 AM

   d. during the weekend

3. Why should you notify users of a planned upgrade? (Choose two.)

   a. to inform users as to how the upgrade benefits them

   b. to increase visibility of the administrator so that people know you're actually working

   c. to reduce support calls during server downtime

   d. to let users know who to call if the upgrade seems to be taking too long

4. Which of the following is an important factor in ensuring that the hardware operates correctly with the operating system?

   a. BIOS

   b. parity memory

   c. error correcting code (ECC)

   d. bus speed

5. If the cover is off the server during the upgrade, you might as well:

   a. leave it off for optimum cooling

   b. clean the dust from the inside

   c. test each electrical lead

   d. upgrade the memory

6. Where can you check to see if an upgrade might cause a problem? (Choose all that apply.)

   a. vendor's web site

   b. FAQs

   c. newsgroups

   d. all of the above

7. A pilot program ensures which of the following? (Choose two.)

   a. safety for passengers

   b. that the upgrade is reliable

   c. that an upgrade failure affects a smaller scope

   d. that the upgrade is successfully deployed across the organization simultaneously

8. In a real production enterprise, you should use a pilot program for which of the following? (Choose two.)

   a. changing any hardware, no matter how small

   b. upgrading to a different NOS

   c. changing the processor platform

   d. upgrading the monitor to a larger size

9. The purpose of the log book is to:

   a. blame someone else if a problem occurs

   b. assist in troubleshooting upgrades

   c. record system errors

   d. record when tape backups are performed

10. Before an upgrade, why would you perform a full backup instead of depending upon the normal tape rotation?

   a. The normal tape rotation might not be as current.

   b. The tape in the rotation might not have sufficient remaining space.

   c. The normal tape rotation might not backup all the data.

   d. You want the backup to reflect the most recent changes to the data.

11. Which of the following is a resource you should verify is available prior to a hardware upgrade?

   a. IRQ

   b. serial port

   c. parallel port

   d. electrical load

12. If you touch a server component and discharge static, it is only a problem if you can:

   a. see the spark

   b. feel the electrical discharge

   c. hear the electrical discharge

   d. always damage components with static discharge

13. Absent any grounding equipment, what can you do to protect against ESD?

   a. touch the server power cable

   b. touch the server chassis

   c. discharge ESD against something else first

   d. leave the server plugged in

14. What is the purpose of taking inventory? (Choose two.)

   a. to fairly distribute server equipment among all sites in the enterprise

   b. to assist in budgetary projections

   c. to avoid having to halt the upgrade because of missing parts

   d. none of the above

15. Which of the following is not important in upgrading the processor?

   a. verifying stepping, cache size, and speed

   b. verifying that the new processor is compatible with the motherboard

   c. verifying that the new processor is compatible with the BIOS

   d. verifying that the processor is at least 400 MHz

16. Into which of the following socket or slot can you install a Pentium III Xeon 700 MHz processor?

    a. Socket 370

    b. Socket 490

    c. Slot 2

    d. Socket A

17. What can you identify about a memory module with nine chips, one having a different part number on it than the others?

    a. The memory is a RIMM.

    b. The memory is EDO memory.

    c. The memory is ECC.

    d. There is insufficient data to make a determination.

18. What should you do prior to a flash BIOS upgrade?

    a. record all BIOS settings

    b. reset BIOS to default settings

    c. remove the CMOS from the motherboard

    d. remove the CMOS battery

19. Which of the following does a multimeter not test?

    a. resistance

    b. voltage

    c. continuity

    d. MHz

20. Which of the following applies to a hot-swappable power supply? (Choose all that apply.)

    a. It is removable with a handle or lever.

    b. It screws onto the chassis.

    c. It is not technically hot-swappable; you must first plug/unplug all power cables.

    d. It does not supply redundancy unless you have an N+1 configuration.

HANDS-ON PROJECTS

Project 6-1

In this project, you will update the flash BIOS. It does not matter if the system already has the current version of the BIOS; you can still flash it.

1. Turn on the server and check to see what version of the BIOS is on the system. If the screen flashes by too quickly, you can usually freeze it by pressing the **Pause** button on the keyboard, and then resume by pressing the **Spacebar**. Make a note of the BIOS version.

2. Access the BIOS settings, and record whatever settings you see that look like settings you might want to restore later. For purposes of this course, it is probably OK to bypass restoring the settings later because the server is not an in-use production server and it is not important that preferences and configuration be restored.

3. Connect to the server vendor's web site (not the web site of the BIOS manufacturer).

4. Navigate to the support pages, and locate the downloads for the server. Download the most recent BIOS update.

5. Format a floppy and leave it in the drive.

6. Execute the BIOS download by double-clicking it from the vendor's web site. Follow the on-screen instructions. When finished, the flash BIOS should be on the floppy.

7. Reboot the server with the flash BIOS floppy in the floppy drive. If the system boots to the NOS, then properly shut down the system, reboot again, and adjust the BIOS so that it boots from the floppy before the hard disk. If the system cannot boot from the floppy, you must make the floppy bootable. Do this by accessing a Windows 9x computer and from an MS-DOS prompt, type **SYS A:**. The necessary system files then transfer to the floppy.

8. The flash BIOS offers you an option to perform the flash BIOS update; go ahead and do so.

9. If the system does not reboot at the end of the flash BIOS update, reboot it.

10. View the BIOS version upon reboot. Is it a newer version?

11. Access the CMOS settings. Have any customized settings been reset to default settings?

12. Reset the CMOS to defaults, save the settings, and reboot.

13. Confirm a successful boot to the operating system.

Project 6-2

In this project, you will determine available system resources on a Windows 2000 server.

1. Start up and log on to a Windows 2000 server using the Administrator account.

2. Right-click the **My Computer** icon on the desktop and click **Manage**. The Computer Management screen appears.

3. Click **Device Manager** in the left tree pane.

4. Browse various devices in the right pane by expanding the device category and double-clicking specific devices. For example, double-click the **Network adapters** category, and then double-click a specific network adapter.

5. Select the **Resources** tab of a device.

6. What Input/Output Range (that is, the I/O port), Memory Range, DMA, and Interrupt Request does the device use? (Be careful *not* to make changes.) Click cancel to close the network adapter's properties.

7. Simplify the view so that you don't see devices as much as you see the resources in use. Click the **View** menu and then select **Resources by type**. Now, you should see all four categories of resources. Browse through the resources. In the Interrupt Request category, you might see several devices using the same IRQ (probably IRQ 9). Recall from Chapter 3 that this is because of IRQ steering, which allows the sharing of an IRQ among PCI devices.

8. If a printer is available, print out a summary by clicking the **View** menu, and then **Print**.

9. Close the Computer Management window.

Project 6-3

In this project, you will connect an ESD grounding kit to the server chassis in preparation for the other projects to follow.

1. Unplug the power cord from the server.

2. Remove the cover from the server.

3. Attach the wrist strap to your wrist. If necessary, adjust the wrist strap first.

4. Snap the cord to the wrist strap if not already connected.

5. Snap the other end of the cord to the grounding mat.

6. Connect the cord from the grounding mat to the server chassis using the alligator clip.

7. If the mat has another cord that connects to the ground prong of a power cord plugged into an electrical outlet, go ahead and connect it.

8. You are now at equal electrical potential to the server, and should not discharge any static when touching server components.

Project 6-4

In this project, you will use a multimeter to check the power supply power using backprobing.

1. Using a digital multimeter, set the controls to read 20 V DC.

2. Plug in the server and turn on the power. Leave the cover off.

3. It might be best to tip the server on its side if it's a tower, so that the motherboard is parallel with the tabletop.

4. Find the power supply connector that attaches to the motherboard, and locate pin 8 (use Table 6-3 as a guide).

5. Insert the red probe into the connector along pin 8 so that it touches the metal connection inside the connector.

6. Touch the black probe to the chassis for grounding.

7. Read the multimeter. It should read between +3 V and +6 V. What is the voltage reading?

8. Repeat this process for the remainder of the motherboard connector pins, again using Table 6-3 as a guide. Approximately what percentage variance do you typically see?

9. Backprobe the +5 V and +12 V pins on a hard disk connector (use Table 6-4 as a guide).

10. Leave the server cover off.

Project 6-5

In this project, you will add a processor to a motherboard with an existing processor.

1. Shut down and power off the server if it is still on. The server should have Windows 2000 Server or Advanced Server installed using a single processor.

2. Verify that your grounding kit and wrist strap are connected, and unplug the power cord from the server.

3. Identify the type of socket or slot the motherboard accepts, and the kind of processor that is installed in the server. If you cannot easily identify this information, power up the system and access the BIOS, where you should be able to find the information. Write down the information on a separate piece of paper.

4. With the power off, install a matching processor into the other slot or socket.

5. Power up the system again. Although Windows 2000 Server runs fine, it is not using the second processor until you change the Computer driver to ACPI Multiprocessor PC or MPS Multiprocessor PC as follows:

   a. Right-click **My Computer** and choose **Manage**.

   b. Select **Device Manager** in the left tree pane.

   c. Expand the Computer node in the right tree pane. The type of computer appears under Computer, and is probably Standard PC or Advanced Configuration and Power Interface (ACPI) PC.

   d. Whichever type of computer appears, right-click it and choose **Properties**.

   e. Click the **Driver** tab of the Properties sheet.

   f. Click the **Update Driver** button.

   g. Click **Next** to skip the introduction of the Upgrade Device Driver Wizard.

   h. Select **Display a list of the known drivers for this device so that I can choose a specific driver**, and then click **Next**.

    i. Select the **Show all hardware of this device class** option. The screen shown earlier in Figure 6-11 appears.

    j. Select the multiprocessor option that matches your computer, and proceed to the end of the wizard.

6. Follow the prompt that appears requesting you to reboot the server.

7. After the reboot, click **Start**, point to Programs, point to Administrative Tools, and click **Performance**. On the toolbar, click the **Add** button to display the Add Counters dialog box. By default, it opens to the Processor performance object. In the right side of the interface under *Select instances from the list*, you should see _Total (aggregate of all installed processors), 0 (the first processor), and 1 (the second processor). This verifies that Windows 2000 Server properly detected both processors.

8. Click the **All instances** radio button and close the Add Counters dialog box.

9. Perform a number of activities (open a program, play a sound clip, and so on). In the Performance window, you should see activity from both processors.

10. Close all open windows and shut down the server.

Project 6-6

In this project, you will add memory to the motherboard.

1. With the case still open from the previous project, look at the memory module(s) installed on the motherboard. Using the information presented in this chapter, identify what kind of memory it is—SIMM, DIMM, or RIMM; include information on parity, ECC, and speed where relevant.

2. Remove the memory module and reinstall it.

3. Start the server. If the system does not POST, the module is not fully seated in the socket. Turn off the power and try again.

Project 6-7

In this project, you will install a PCI network card using available drivers, and then download the latest drivers from the vendor web site and update the drivers.

1. Remain properly grounded and unplug the server. Install a PCI network card in any available PCI slot on the Windows 2000 server.

2. Start the server. Windows 2000 Server includes many drivers for various NICs and might automatically install drivers. If not, supply drivers from a floppy that accompanies the NIC as prompted by the operating system.

3. Access the network card in Device Manager to verify that it is working properly.

    a. Right-click **My Computer**.

    b. Select **Manage**.

c. Select **Device Manager** in the left pane.

d. In the right pane, expand the Network adapters item by clicking the "+" sign.

e. Right-click the network card and select **Properties**.

4. The vendor might have provided an updated driver for the network card. Download the newest driver from the Internet (if necessary, use a different computer).

5. Read the vendor instructions that might specify the purpose of the driver update and installation information. In most cases, the driver files are in a self-extracting executable file. Extract the files.

6. Open the NIC property sheet in Device Manager (if it is not already open), and select the **Driver** tab.

7. Click the **Update Driver** button, and click **Next** to start the Upgrade Device Driver Wizard.

8. Select the item **Display a list of the known drivers for this device so that I can choose a specific driver** and click **Next**.

9. Click the **Have Disk** button and navigate to the location of the extracted drivers. Then, finish the wizard.

10. Close all open windows and shut down the server.

CASE PROJECTS

1. Your organization of 80 users requires a memory upgrade of the only logon server. The organization keeps typical business hours, but some people start work early or stay late. You have a regular backup that takes place every night at 11:00 PM. What strategy should you use to upgrade this server?

2. Utility power to your server rack of three servers fails. You have a single UPS, but as soon as it starts to supply power, it issues a message that the UPS is overloaded and fails to supply power. Utility power comes back on in a few minutes, and the servers start to boot. What should you do?

NETWORKING

After reading this chapter and completing the exercises, you will be able to:

♦ Identify bus, ring, and star network topologies

♦ Discuss NetBEUI, IPX/SPX, and TCP/IP protocols

♦ Describe Token Ring and Ethernet media access methods

♦ Specify the purpose of bridges, switches, hubs, and routers

♦ List thinnet, shielded twisted-pair, unshielded twisted-pair, and fiber optic cable characteristics

♦ Make your own straight-through and crossover cables

♦ Describe network adapter teaming techniques

♦ Understand networking with a modem pool

Administrators encounter a myriad of network technologies and must be able to identify each one in order to take the best course of action in planning, extending, or troubleshooting the network. At the logistical center of every enterprise network is one or more servers; the goal of this chapter is to familiarize you with various ways to connect to that server.

As you analyze a network context, it is important to identify the network topology, protocol, and media access method in use, as each has advantages and disadvantages that affect network performance. Equally important is the choice of intermediate network equipment that directs data from one location on the network to another. Choosing the proper equipment in a given network context helps to ensure that servers have high availability.

NETWORK TOPOLOGIES

A network **topology** is the geometric configuration of devices, nodes, and cable links on a network. Topologies define how nodes connect to one another. A **node** is an active device connected to the network, such as a computer or a printer, or networking equipment such as a hub, switch, or router. (A host, defined in Chapter 1, is generally used interchangeably with node, but it is specific to devices using the TCP/IP protocol.) Nodes can be arranged in a bus, star, or ring configuration.

When discussing network topology, make sure you understand the difference between the physical topology and the logical topology. The physical topology is the layout of the actual connections between devices, while the logical topology is a representation of how data travels on the network. This distinction is observed throughout the chapter.

Before delving into the world of network topologies, let's look at bandwidth, which highlights several networking issues including topology, media access method, and physical media (cable).

Bandwidth

Recall that bandwidth is the transmission capacity of the network within a fixed amount of time. This is one of the fundamental factors that affect your choice of topology, media, and media access methods. Bandwidth has a direct correlation to the **data rate**, which is the actual quantity of data transferred within the limitations of the bandwidth. Bandwidth is usually expressed in bits per second (bps), kilobits per second (Kbps), kilobytes per second (KBps), megabits per second (Mbps), megabytes per second (MBps), gigabits per second (Gbps), gigabytes per second (GBps), terabits per second (Tbps), or terabytes per second (TBps). Note that the word "bits" is represented by a lowercase "b" and "bytes" (which is eight bits) by an uppercase "B."

For reference purposes, Table 7-1 shows most of the connection types with their associated data rates, bandwidths, and the time it takes to transfer 100 KB of data.

Bus

A **bus topology** consists of nodes linked together in a series where each node is connected to a common backbone cable or bus (see Figure 7-1). (A **backbone** is a larger, common avenue through which data transfers take place from smaller lines connected to it.) The signal is sent in both directions and has two endpoints (terminators) to prevent the signal from endlessly cycling through the cable. A major disadvantage of the bus topology is that it is more difficult to troubleshoot and locate a break in the cable or a faulty machine on a bus. A break anywhere in the cable will cause the entire segment to be inoperable until the break is repaired. Examples of bus topology include 10Base2 and 10Base5 Ethernet systems (addressed later in this chapter).

Table 7-1   Network Connection Types

Connection	Data Rate*	Bandwidth	Time per 100 KB
14.4 modem	1.8 KB	14.4 Kb	55 sec
28.8 modem	3.6 KB	28.8 Kb	27 sec
33.6 modem	4.2 KB	33.6 Kb	23 sec
56K modem	7 KB	56 Kb	14 sec
ISDN	7–16 KB	56–128 Kb	14–6 sec
Frame Relay	7–64 KB	56–512 Kb	14–1.5 sec
T-1	32–193 KB	256–1544 Kb	3.1–.5 sec
DSL	188 KB	1.5 Mb	.53 sec
Cable modem	188 KB	1.5 Mb	.53 sec
Fast Ethernet	1.25 MB	100 Mb	.08 sec
T-3	5.5 MB	44 Mb	.01 sec

* The actual data rate is slightly less than these figures because of overhead that occurs with framing the bits of data.

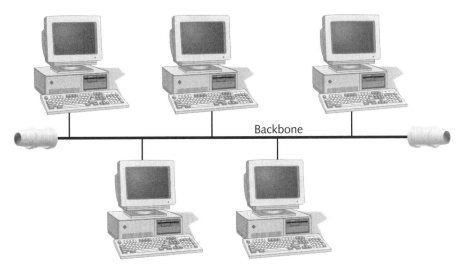

Figure 7-1   A backbone utilizes a bus topology to connect nodes

Ring

A **ring topology** network is a local area network (LAN) where all of the nodes are connected in a closed, single, logical communication loop (see Figure 7-2). Each device is connected directly to two other devices, one on either side. Information passes from station to station around the ring, each node reading the messages that are addressed to it and forwarding messages that are not. As with the bus network, each node must be able to identify its own address to successfully receive a message. A technique called

token passing manages line access so that two messages are not transmitted at the same time. A token is a frame of bits (the token may be "empty" or contain a message) that is passed from one station to the next. When a node needs to transmit data and receives an empty token, it holds on to the token and records its own address, the destination address, and the message into the token before passing it on to the next station. Stations only transmit messages when the token is empty.

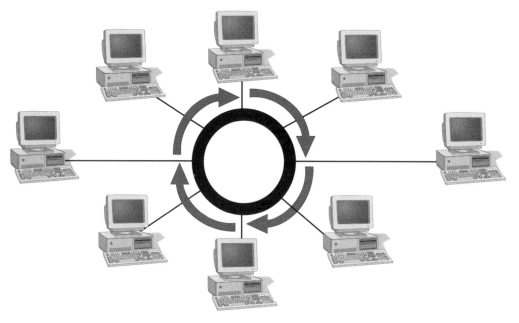

Figure 7-2   The ring topology

The destination station reads the message and consequently marks the token as having been read. The token passes from one node to the next until it completes a full circuit and reaches the originating station, where the message is discarded and the token is again marked as empty. Each node has a **transceiver**, which repeats the signal to move it around the ring.

Following are advantages of the ring topology:

- They can span greater distances than other network types—bus networks, for example.

- The level of signal deterioration is low because each station repeats the signal, and collisions are low because only the station that holds the token can transmit.

- It is very good for a small network of computers that entail high transmission speeds compared to 10BaseT Ethernet (addressed later in this chapter) or for larger networks where each station has a comparable workload.

Following are disadvantages of the ring topology:

- It can be tricky to trace a problem on the cable segment if the LAN is large.

- Each station's attached network interface must be continually active and the failure of a single station will halt a unidirectional ring network.

- It is complex to configure and requires relatively expensive hardware for each computer to interface with the network.

- Transmission delays tend to be long, even with moderate traffic levels.

 Although a network design might utilize a logical ring topology as described here, the layout of the cables, nodes, and network equipment might physically be a star topology. (See the next section.)

7

Star

A **star topology** is a network configuration in which all of the nodes connect to a central network device such as a hub or switch (see Figure 7-3). All nodes receive the same signal, reducing effective bandwidth, and the central network device can become a bottleneck because all data must pass through it. Standard twisted-pair Ethernet networks using 10BaseT or 100BaseTX technology (addressed later in this chapter) commonly use the star topology.

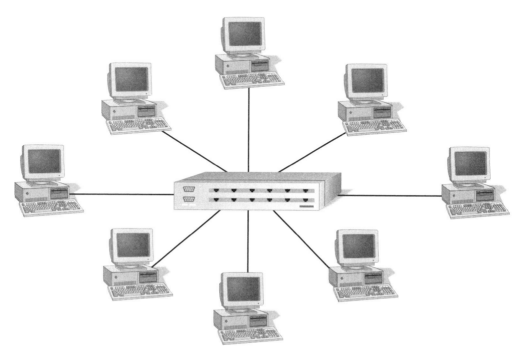

Figure 7-3   The star topology

Following are advantages of the star topology:

- A single failed node does not adversely affect the rest of the network.
- It is relatively straightforward to install and manage.
- Isolating and repairing bad segments is easier.
- It offers good capacity for network growth.

Following are disadvantages of the star topology:

- It requires a lot more cabling than bus or ring networks.
- The entire network becomes ineffectual if the central network device fails.

Hybrid Topologies

Network topologies are seldom of only one type. Except in the smallest environments where you could connect every user to a hub, topologies are usually a mixture. For example, a hybrid Ethernet network often uses a combination of the bus topology using either coaxial cable or fiber optic cable to connect multiple star-wired hubs. This creates a bus connection between the two hubs, while the hubs themselves are star-wired (see Figure 7-4). In the case of a Token Ring network, the network is a physical star and a logical ring, and various Token Ring networks can be connected together in a physical bus topology.

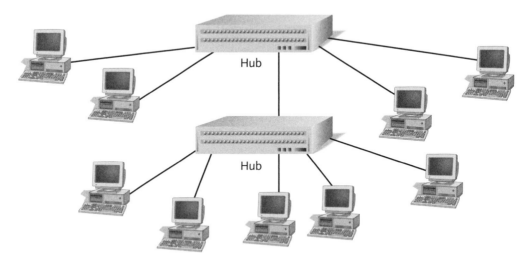

Figure 7-4   Ethernet networks commonly combine the bus and star topologies

 There are several other hybrid network topologies, which are well covered in Chapter 5 of *Network+ Guide to Networks* by Tamara Dean (Course Technology, 2000).

PROTOCOLS

Recall from Chapter 1 that a protocol is a set of governing standards that determines how network devices communicate with one another. Also, a protocol defines how computers identify each other on a network, the form that the data should take in transition, and how this information is processed once it reaches its final destination. Protocols also define procedures for handling a lost or damaged packet—the electronic package that contains the network data. A protocol determines the type of error checking to implement, the data compression method (if any), how the sending device indicates that it is finished sending, and how the receiving device indicates that it is finished receiving.

There are several standardized protocols from which administrators can choose, each having its own particular advantages and disadvantages. Common protocols include NetBEUI, IPX/SPX, and TCP/IP. This chapter addresses TCP/IP more thoroughly than the other protocols because TCP/IP is more common and includes several utilities that you will certainly use to troubleshoot network connectivity and configuration.

Ultimately, all protocols are only a means to transport the network message to the node's physical address, known as the **MAC (Media Access Control) address**, which globally and uniquely identifies a network device. To find the MAC address of a network interface card (NIC), look at the MAC address printed on the NIC, or you can type IPCONFIG /all from a command prompt, which shows the MAC address as shown in the following example: Physical Address. . . . . : 00-03-47-12-39-FF. (See more about IPCONFIG later in this chapter.)

NetBEUI

NetBEUI is the **NetBIOS Enhanced User Interface**. Recall from Chapter 1 that NetBEUI is a fast protocol designed for small networks and requires no configuration. However, it is not a routable protocol and is not efficient in larger networks because it frequently rebroadcasts to locate other nodes on the network. It does not cache previously located nodes, and it does not use name resolution services such as DNS or WINS. (See more about DNS and WINS in Chapter 9.)

IPX/SPX

IPX/SPX (Internetwork Packet Exchange/Sequence Packet Exchange) is the default Novell protocol implementation for all versions of NetWare until 5.0, which can also use TCP/IP. IPX/SPX might require some configuration to identify the network on which the node exists, and like NetBEUI, it does not have name resolution services. However, IPX/SPX includes a caching mechanism so that it is not necessary to rebroadcast to locate recently accessed nodes. IPX/SPX was most popular when Novell NetWare networks required it, but current versions of NetWare can use TCP/IP instead, and many organizations are phasing out IPX/SPX.

TCP/IP

TCP/IP (Transmission Control Protocol/Internet Protocol) is actually a suite of protocols commonly in use on most networks and the Internet. However, administrators consider TCP/IP to be a single protocol. TCP/IP is more difficult to plan and configure, although it is also scaleable and routable, which is why it is the protocol of the Internet and most enterprise networks.

 Covering all aspects of the TCP/IP protocol—including theory, configuration, and planning—is beyond the scope of this book. However, if you want to know more about TCP/IP, read any of dozens of comprehensive TCP/IP books.

The Internet (IP) Address

All protocols require a way to uniquely identify nodes. TCP/IP uses a unique IP address, similar to the way the U.S. Postal Service uses a combination of zip code, state, city, and street name to find its "nodes." An IP address appears as four sets of digits, each separated by a dot—215.161.122.231, for example. A host with this IP address must be unique on the LAN to avoid conflicts with other hosts, and it must be globally unique if the host IP address is exposed to the Internet. Each IP address also requires a **subnet mask**—another series of numbers which, when compared against the IP address, identifies the specific network to which the host belongs. As an example, Figure 7-5 shows a screen shot of an IP address and subnet mask for a Windows 2000 server.

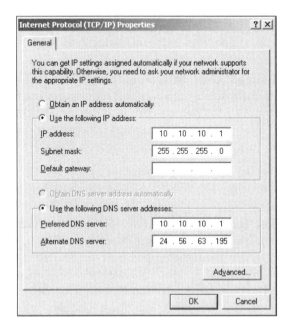

Figure 7-5   The TCP/IP configuration of a Windows 2000 server

Subnetting the Network

Administrators also use a subnet mask to divide a range of IP addresses into multiple smaller networks. The reason for doing this is twofold. First, you might not need all the IP addresses available on a single network. Instead, you can split the IP address range among several separate networks. Second, administrators subnet their networks to split up a collision domain, characteristic of Ethernet networks. (A **collision domain** refers to a network boundary in which multiple nodes could potentially attempt to access the network at the same time.) This chapter addresses Ethernet in more detail later, but for current purposes, understand that hosts on Ethernet networks have no arbiter to negotiate when network access is available (unlike the token of a ring network). As a result, network traffic grows exponentially as the number of nodes on a single network increases. Subnetting a larger network into smaller networks reduces the number of data collisions (and subsequent retransmissions) that take place when two hosts attempt to communicate at the same time. (A **collision** results when two devices or hosts transmit packets to the network at the same time.)

> You can increase effective throughput to and from servers by installing network adapters with multiple ports, or multiple NICs in a single server. This makes the server **multihomed**. Similarly, you can use **port aggregation** software to combine multiple ports from the server into what is perceived as a single connection to the network but with bandwidth that is multiplied times the number of ports. Note that both multihoming and port aggregation only increase throughput of available bandwidth. The effectiveness of both methods diminishes with overutilized bandwidth.

Verifying TCP/IP Configuration and Connectivity

Connectivity or configuration problems with TCP/IP networks can involve lengthy and baffling troubleshooting. Fortunately, most network operating systems include a suite of TCP/IP configuration and troubleshooting tools to help diagnose problems.

Ping

Ping (packet internet groper) is an all-purpose utility for verifying that a remote host is accessible by sending small packets of data to which an accessible host responds. Ping tests connectivity at different stages between the host and destination to determine the point of failure at which a packet is dropped, and also tests basic networking connectivity. For example, an unplugged network cable would prevent Ping from reaching its destination, alerting you to a physical network problem (provided all TCP/IP configuration is correct).

In an IP network, Ping sends a single short data burst packet and then listens for a single packet in reply. Ping places a unique sequence number on each packet it transmits, and reports on the sequence numbers that come back to it. This is how Ping determines if packets have been dropped, duplicated, or reordered. Ping checksums (checks for errors) in each packet it exchanges. Ping places a time stamp in each packet, which echoes back and computes the length of time for packet exchange. This is called the **round-trip time (RTT)**. Some routers silently discard undeliverable packets. Others mistake that a packet transmits successfully when it has not. Therefore, Ping may not always provide reasons why packets go unanswered. Ping does not perform analysis and cannot tell you why a packet was damaged, delayed, or duplicated. Ping also will not offer a play-by-play account of every host that handled the packet and everything that happened at every step of the way. Dropped packets are an unfortunate fact of networking life. There are common situations, typically involving crowded wide area networks (WANs), in which even modern TCP implementations cannot operate without dropping packets. Since TCP will retransmit missing data, there is no reason for alarm unless a large number of retransmissions noticeably affects network performance.

IPCONFIG

IPCONFIG is a Microsoft utility that displays a wide variety of IP configuration data for a Windows 98/ME/NT/2000 system including the IP address, subnet mask, default gateway, and other information (see Figure 7-6).

 TIP   You can use the similar *netconfig* command for Linux/UNIX machines.

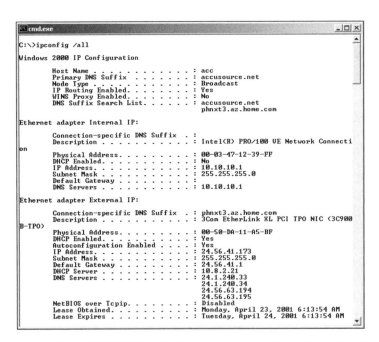

Figure 7-6   IPCONFIG /all displays complete IP configuration information

The most commonly used IPCONFIG switches are:

- /all—displays all available IP configuration information

- /release—releases IP configuration for DHCP clients

- /renew—renews the DHCP-assigned client IP address; useful when the DHCP configuration changes and you want to apply the changes to the DHCP client

ARP

ARP (Address Resolution Protocol) displays the resolution between the IP address and the physical (MAC) address on the NIC by building a table as IP addresses resolve to MAC addresses. You can also modify the ARP cache and table entries. For example, you can use the —s switch to add a static host-to-MAC address entry to the ARP table. The advantage of this would be to improve IP-address-to-MAC-address resolution time. To view the ARP table, type ARP —a, and to add an ARP entry, type ARP —s <IPAddress> <MAC address> (see Figure 7-7).

7

```
cmd.exe                                                          _ |□| x|

C:\>arp -a

Interface: 10.10.10.1 on Interface 0x1000004
  Internet Address      Physical Address     Type
  10.10.10.5            00-e0-29-62-0d-de     dynamic
  10.10.10.11           00-50-04-29-5b-33     dynamic
  10.10.10.13           00-80-c8-fd-97-fa     dynamic

C:\>arp -s 10.10.10.1 00-03-47-12-39-FF

C:\>arp -a

Interface: 10.10.10.1 on Interface 0x1000004
  Internet Address      Physical Address     Type
  10.10.10.1            00-03-47-12-39-ff     static
  10.10.10.5            00-e0-29-62-0d-de     dynamic
  10.10.10.11           00-50-04-29-5b-33     dynamic
  10.10.10.13           00-80-c8-fd-97-fa     dynamic

C:\>
```

Figure 7-7   Use ARP for IP-address-to-MAC-address issues

TRACERT

TRACERT is the trace routing utility that works like Ping but shows the actual router hops taken to reach the remote host. This is handy if you want to find at which point a packet is being dropped or where a bottleneck may exist on the network (see Figure 7-8).

```
cmd.exe                                                               _|□|x|
C:\>tracert www.accusource.net

Tracing route to accusource.net [199.227.124.246]
over a maximum of 30 hops:

  1    60 ms    60 ms    60 ms  10.8.2.12
  2    60 ms    60 ms    70 ms  10.8.2.2
  3    70 ms    60 ms    70 ms  bb1-atm6-2.1-ceflayer.rdc1.az.home.net [24.7.70.
49]
  4   100 ms    70 ms    71 ms  c1-pos4-0.phnxaz1.home.net [24.7.74.165]
  5    71 ms    80 ms    80 ms  c1-pos2-0.sndgca1.home.net [24.7.65.134]
  6    80 ms    70 ms    80 ms  c1-pos1-0.anhmca1.home.net [24.7.64.69]
  7    70 ms    80 ms    80 ms  c1-pos1-0.lsanca1.home.net [24.7.65.169]
  8    70 ms    70 ms    80 ms  home-gw.la2ca.ip.att.net [192.205.32.245]
  9    80 ms    90 ms    81 ms  gbr3-p50.la2ca.ip.att.net [12.123.28.130]
 10   101 ms   100 ms   100 ms  gbr3-p30.dlstx.ip.att.net [12.122.3.69]
 11   110 ms   120 ms   110 ms  gbr2-p11.dtrmi.ip.att.net [12.122.3.38]
 12   120 ms   121 ms   100 ms  gbr3-p60.attga.ip.att.net [12.122.1.141]
 13   120 ms   130 ms   120 ms  gbr4-p40.ormfl.ip.att.net [12.122.2.182]
 14   120 ms   120 ms   121 ms  gbr2-p100.ormfl.ip.att.net [12.122.5.134]
 15   120 ms   140 ms   130 ms  ar5-p3110.ormfl.ip.att.net [12.123.32.94]
 16   140 ms   130 ms   131 ms  12.126.145.42
 17   140 ms   140 ms   140 ms  ft1-core1b-v5.valueweb.com [216.219.251.2]
 18   140 ms   151 ms   140 ms  chara.valueweb.net [199.227.124.246]

Trace complete.
```

Figure 7-8   TRACERT identifies each router hop

NETSTAT

NETSTAT shows TCP/IP protocol statistics using any of several options. One of the most useful options is –r, which shows the routing table (see Figure 7-9). This is useful in verifying the efficiency of the routing tables.

```
cmd.exe                                                               _|□|x|
C:\>netstat -r

Route Table
===========================================================================
Interface List
0x1 ...........................  MS TCP Loopback interface
0x1000003 ...00 50 da 11 a5 bf ...... 3Com EtherLink PCI
0x1000004 ...00 03 47 12 39 ff ...... Intel(R) PRO Adapter
===========================================================================
===========================================================================
Active Routes:
Network Destination        Netmask          Gateway       Interface  Metric
        0.0.0.0          0.0.0.0       24.56.41.1    24.56.41.173       1
     10.10.10.0    255.255.255.0     10.10.10.1      10.10.10.1       1
     10.10.10.1  255.255.255.255      127.0.0.1       127.0.0.1       1
 10.255.255.255  255.255.255.255     10.10.10.1      10.10.10.1       1
     24.56.41.0    255.255.255.0    24.56.41.173    24.56.41.173       1
   24.56.41.173  255.255.255.255      127.0.0.1       127.0.0.1       1
 24.255.255.255  255.255.255.255    24.56.41.173    24.56.41.173       1
      127.0.0.0        255.0.0.0      127.0.0.1       127.0.0.1       1
      224.0.0.0        224.0.0.0     10.10.10.1      10.10.10.1       1
      224.0.0.0        224.0.0.0    24.56.41.173    24.56.41.173       1
255.255.255.255  255.255.255.255    24.56.41.173    24.56.41.173       1
Default Gateway:       24.56.41.1
===========================================================================
Persistent Routes:
  None
C:\>
```

Figure 7-9   NETSTAT -r shows the routing table

NETWORK MEDIA ACCESS METHODS

Network communication requires a **media access method**, a way to place the data packets transmitted from the NOS to the physical network device (such as a NIC) and then to the wire. Several media access methods fulfill this role, each having its own characteristics.

Token Ring

Token Ring is a type of network where all of the computers are arranged in a circle. A special bit pattern, called a token, moves around the circle. To send a message, a station grabs the token, affixes a message to it, and then allows it to continue around the ring network. As a network protocol like Ethernet, Token Ring refers to the PC network protocol developed by IBM that has been standardized with the IEEE 802.5 standard. Token Ring is different from Ethernet in that all messages are transferred in one direction along the ring at all times. Numerous PC vendors have been proponents of Token Ring networks at different times; therefore, these types of networks can be found in many organizations.

Token Ring networks run at 4 or 16 Mbps. If a 16 Mbps adapter exists on a network where 4 Mbps adapters exist, you must configure the 16 Mbps adapter to run at the slower 4 Mbps speed. If you mix the two speeds on the same network, serious communication problems occur.

As the name implies, the Token Ring media access method utilizes a logical ring topology. However, the physical layout is usually a star topology with each host connecting to a **multistation access unit (MAU)**, which looks much like a hub except that it includes an RI (ring in) and RO (ring out) port. Tokens still pass from one host to the next in a logical ring (see Figure 7-10).

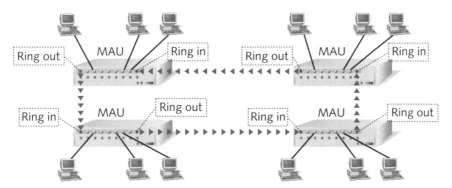

Figure 7-10   Tokens pass from one host to another in a unidirectional logical ring topology

Ethernet

Ethernet is by far the most widely used media access method today because it offers a nice balance between cost, speed, and ease of installation. Since Ethernet utilizes shared media between nodes, there are rules for sending packets of data to avoid collisions and protect the data. Though Ethernet collisions are unavoidable, you want to minimize their occurrence as much as possible to optimize available bandwidth, not waste it with excessive collisions. A large number of collisions can occur because there are too many users on the network contending for bandwidth. Segmenting (subnetting) the network into separate, smaller networks joined together with a switch or router is one way of reducing traffic on an overcrowded network. The Institute for Electrical and Electronic Engineers (IEEE) has defined standards for Ethernet known as the **802.3 Standard**, which defines how to configure an Ethernet network as well as how elements in an Ethernet network interact with one another. By following the 802.3 standard, network equipment and network protocols can communicate properly.

 Carrier Sense Multiple Access with Collision Detection (CSMA/CD) describes the method Ethernet devices use to negotiate access to the wire and retransmit in case of collisions. The sending host monitors the voltage level of the wire, and if no transmission is occurring, the host sends data. If two or more hosts determine that the network is clear and begin sending data at the same time, Collision Detection (CD) handles timely attempts to retransmit data for each host.

Although electrical signals on Ethernet travel at speeds nearing the speed of light, it still takes a finite amount of time for the signal to travel from one end of a large Ethernet network to another. In larger network designs, the signal quality begins to depreciate as segments exceed their maximum length. Ethernet hubs repeat the signal, extending the maximum length, and connect two or more Ethernet segments of any media type. A **hub** provides a universal link for devices in a network and sends all incoming data out to all ports (hence, to each node). There are several types of hubs, including:

- A **passive hub**, which provides a channel for the data, enabling it to go from one device (or segment) to another.

- An **intelligent hub** (or **managed hub**), which includes additional components that enable administrators to monitor the traffic passing through the hub and to configure each port in the hub.

- A **switching hub**, which reads the destination address of each packet and then forwards the packet to the correct port.

If the hub is attached to a backbone, then all computers can communicate with all the hosts on the backbone. A very important fact to note about hubs is that they only allow users to share Ethernet bandwidth. A network of hubs/repeaters is called a "shared Ethernet," meaning that all member hubs contend for data transmission on a single network (collision domain). The number of hubs in any one collision domain is restricted by the 802.3 rules. This means that individual members of a shared network will only get a percentage of the available network bandwidth.

Ethernet is governed by the "5-4-3 rule" of repeater placement. This rule means that the network can only have five segments connected; it can only use four repeaters; and of the five segments, only three can have users attached to them—the other two must be inter-repeater links. If the design of the network breaks these rules, then the timing guidelines will not be met and the sending node will resend that packet, resulting in lost packets and excessive resent packets. This can adversely affect network performance by slowing down the network and creating problems for applications.

Fast Ethernet

Fast Ethernet (IEEE 802.3u) offers higher transmission speeds than 802.3 Ethernet. (Fast Ethernet is also known as 100BaseT.) Fast Ethernet allows for fewer repeaters because the data travels so quickly that host NICs cannot always compensate for collision detection and consequent retransmissions in a timely manner. In Fast Ethernet networks, there are two classes of repeaters. Class I repeaters have a latency of 0.7 microseconds or less and are limited to one repeater per network. Class II repeaters have a latency of 0.46 microseconds or less and are limited to two repeaters per network. Fast Ethernet can be deployed to desktops and servers by installing Fast Ethernet NICs and using Fast Ethernet switches and repeaters. This standard raises the Ethernet speed limit from 10 Mbps to 100 Mbps with no changes to the existing cable structure or connectors. Most of today's networks have a mixture of standard Ethernet networks (10 Mbps) and Fast Ethernet (100 Mbps).

Full-duplex Ethernet

There is another variation of Ethernet called **full-duplex Ethernet**. By simply adding another pair of wires (total of six wires) and removing collision detection, you can double the connection speed. Hosts can simultaneously send and receive data similar to a telephone conversation in which both parties can speak at once. (Half-duplex would be more like a CB radio conversation.) In terms of Fast Ethernet, 200 Mbps of throughput is the theoretical maximum for a full-duplex Fast Ethernet connection. This type of connection is limited to a node-to-node connection and often links two Ethernet switches. Full duplex is just another method used to increase bandwidth to dedicated workstations or servers by doubling the bandwidth on a link, providing 20 Mbps for Ethernet and 200 Mbps for Fast Ethernet. To use full duplex, special NICs are installed in the computers and a switch is programmed to support full-duplex operation.

 You can't use full duplex with a hub, because the nature of full duplex requires a dedicated connection. Therefore, you would have to use a switch (which provides full bandwidth to each port) instead of a hub (which shares bandwidth with other ports).

Gigabit Ethernet

Gigabit Ethernet is a newer version of Ethernet that supports data-transfer rates of 1 Gigabit (1000 megabits) per second. The first Gigabit Ethernet standard (802.3z) was ratified by the IEEE 802.3 Committee in 1998 and is defined by the frame format, the use of CSMA/CD, the use of full duplex, the use of flow control, and the management objects defined by the committee. Gigabit Ethernet is basically Ethernet, only faster. Most organizations use Gigabit Ethernet as a backbone technology and for server connections. Gigabit Ethernet is a future technology that promises a migration path beyond Fast Ethernet; the next generation of networks will support even higher data-transfer speeds. The first installations will require fiber optic media for long connections between buildings, and short copper links for connections between servers and hubs. Over time, as the market for workgroup and desktop Gigabit Ethernet services develops, customers will demand Gigabit links that are compliant with the installed base of Category 5 UTP wiring that is used for standard Ethernet. (Wiring specifics appear later in this chapter.)

NETWORK EQUIPMENT

Repeaters allow networks to broaden the distance limitations of the cabling; however, repeaters support only a limited number of stations. As we saw earlier, with shared Ethernet, the likelihood of collision is higher as nodes are added to the shared collision domain. Using a bridge or switch to segment the traffic is a good way to resolve this problem. A switch can replace a hub or repeater and improve network performance. Bridges and switches allow LANs to expand considerably because they can maintain full Ethernet segments on each port. Bridges and switches can also filter network traffic so that traffic destined for the same network does not pass through the switch to another network. Traffic destined for another network is forwarded to the other network.

Bridges

Though there are several types of bridges, the basic function of a **bridge** is to connect separate networks. Bridges connect similar or different network types, like Ethernet and Token Ring. In this scenario, bridges map the Ethernet addresses of the nodes residing on each network segment and let only certain traffic pass through. When the bridge receives a packet, it determines both the destination host and the source host location. The bridge drops (filters) the packet if the source and destination are on the same segment. If the source and destination are on different segments, the bridge passes the packet on to the correct segment. This is why bridges are called "store-and-forward" devices; they analyze the Ethernet packet before making the decision to filter or forward. By using bridges to filter packets and regenerate forwarded packets, one can split a network into separate collision domains, allowing for more repeaters to be used in the total network design and achieving greater distances. In Figure 7-11, a message from a host on Segment 2 passes through the bridge to Segment 1 only when the message is addressed to a host on Segment 1. This differs from a single segment connected to a repeater, which would repeat the message to all hosts.

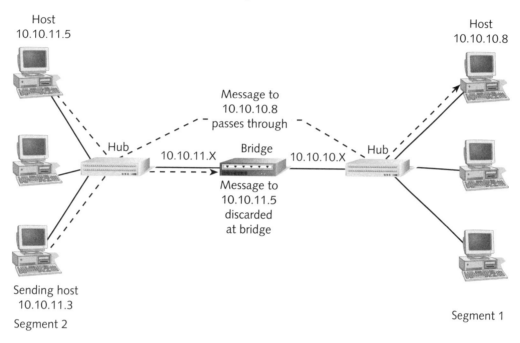

Figure 7-11 Only traffic destined for 10.10.10.8 passes through the bridge

Switches

Like bridges, there are several types of Ethernet switches, the details of which are beyond the scope of this book. Ethernet switches are an expansion of the concept in Ethernet bridging. **Switches** separate a network into collision domains so that network rules can be extended. Each of the segments attached to an Ethernet switch has a full 10 or 100 Mbps of bandwidth shared by fewer users, resulting in better performance (see Figure 7-12).

In addition to determining when to forward or filter a packet, Ethernet switches totally regenerate the packet, allowing each port on a switch to be treated as a complete Ethernet segment able to support the full length of cable as well as all of the repeater restrictions. Ethernet switches also recognize bad packets and instantly drop them from the network. This action keeps problems restricted to a single segment and prevents them from disrupting the rest of the network. Newer switches offer even higher bandwidth through Fast Ethernet, fiber, or ATM. These technologies link switches together or give added bandwidth to high-traffic servers.

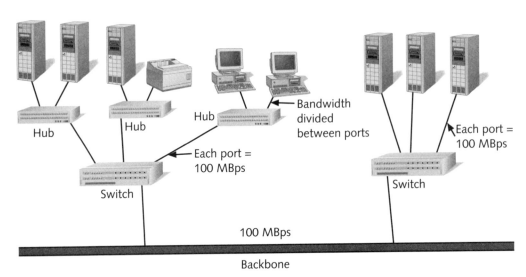

Figure 7-12 Switches offer full bandwidth to each port and forward or filter traffic similarly to a bridge

There is also another device that interconnects WAN links or the Internet to your network. This device is a CSU/DSU (Channel Service Unit/Digital (or Data) Service Unit). This device is necessary to connect the network to an external digital line such as a T-1 Internet line. (Sometimes the acronym is reversed and appears as DSU/CSU, but the meaning is the same.)

Routers

A **router** connects multiple networks using routing tables and routable protocols. Routers use headers and a forwarding table to determine where packets go, and communicate with other routers to calculate the best route between any two hosts. Routers determine whether to forward or filter a packet based on the IP address and subnet mask, which identifies the network to which a host belongs. The router filters a message destined for a host on the same network, and forwards messages destined for a host on a different network. While this functionality sounds similar to a bridge or switch, it differs in that a bridge or switch is not designed to enable networking over a large geographical area (such as a WAN), and routers are typically more capable of handling extremely high throughput. Also, because of the route calculations, routers can intelligently determine the best path from source to host over multiple routers. Switches and bridges do not include this kind of intelligence.

For example, in Figure 7-13, a user in Workgroup C sends a print job to a network printer located in Workgroup A. The message goes through Hub C to Router C. Router C analyzes the packet and determines that the message should go to Router A based on the message destination. Router C determines the best path to Router A, which might be to send the message directly to Router A instead of first passing it to Router B.

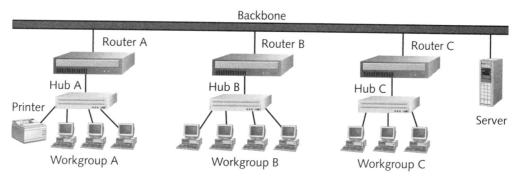

Figure 7-13   Routers determine the best route for sending messages

7

NETWORK CABLING

An important part of designing and deploying a network is selecting the appropriate cable medium. The cable provides the conduit for all network communications. The network media access method standard of the NIC and the physical topology affect the cable choice and implementation. The most common types of LAN cabling in use today are coaxial (thinnet and thicknet), shielded twisted pair, unshielded twisted pair, and fiber optic.

 Although this chapter primarily addresses physical cable media, there are wireless options that comply with the new Ethernet 802.11b standard to allow transmission at rates up to 11 Mbps using radio frequency within a specific radius.

Thicknet

Thicknet is based on the 10Base5 standard, which transmits data at 10 Mbps over a maximum distance of 500 meters (1640.4 feet). Thicknet is about 1 cm thick and has been used for network backbones because of its durability and maximum length. Many current thicknet implementations are being replaced by fiber optic media (addressed later in this chapter).

Thinnet

Thinnet is based on the 10Base2 standard (10 Mbps/Baseband transmission) that utilizes RG-58 A/U or RG-58 C/U 50 ohm coaxial cable with maximum segment lengths of 185 meters (606.9 feet). The RG-58 cable is less expensive and easier to install than the thicknet cable used for the 10Base5 standard, mostly because it is thinner (approximately 0.5 cm or .2 inch) and more flexible. While thinnet is gradually fading into networking history, you will still find it in several existing (but not new) network implementations. Cables in both the 10Base5 and 10Base2 systems interconnect with BNCs (British Naval Connectors) (see Figure 7-14). The network interface card in a computer requires a T-connector to attach two cables to a NIC. A BNC barrel connector connects two cables. Any unused connection must have a 50 ohm terminator to prevent signal bounce.

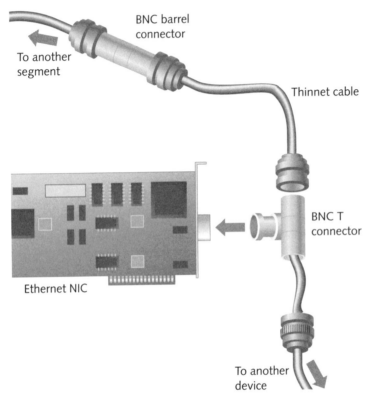

Figure 7-14   Thinnet uses several types of BNCs

 Though RG-58 thinnet looks like TV cable, it is not, and the two cable types are not interchangeable because of differences in ohm impedance. Both thicknet and thinnet are 50 ohms, and TV cable is 75 ohms.

Shielded Twisted Pair (STP)

Shielded twisted-pair (STP) cable includes screened twisted-pair cable and foil twisted-pair cable and provides reliable connectivity. STP involves two copper wires, each encased in its own color-coded insulation, and then twisted together to form a "twisted pair." Multiple twisted-pairs are then packaged in an outer sheath to form the twisted pair cable (see Figure 7-15). The cable minimizes the possibility of **crosstalk** (intruding signals from an adjacent twisted pair or cable) by increasing the number of twists per inch. Early telephone signals were actually sent over a form of twisted-pair cable, and almost every building today still uses twisted-pair cable to carry telephone and other signals. Although coaxial and fiber optic cable were developed to handle higher-bandwidth applications and support emerging technologies, twisted-pair cable has evolved so that it can now carry high-data-rate signals.

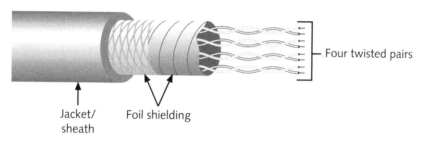

Four twisted pairs

Jacket/   Foil shielding
sheath

Figure 7-15   STP cable

7

STP cable encases the wires in a conducting metal shield to reduce the potential for EMI (as discussed in Chapter 2). Recall that electric motors, power lines, fluorescent lighting, and a variety of other devices cause EMI and, as a result, disruptions in network communications. STP cable effectively prevents radiation and blocks interference as long as the entire end-to-end link is shielded and properly grounded. The maximum length of STP is 100 meters (328.08 feet) with a speed of up to 500 Mbps. Although length becomes a problem with STP, it is inexpensive and easy to install.

STP cable can use several types of connectors, but only RJ-45 connectors are used in current networking contexts. **RJ-45 (registered jack–45)** is an eight-wire connector that connects Ethernet network devices. RJ-45 connectors look similar to the RJ-11 connectors that are used for connecting telephone equipment, but they are wider because they connect eight wires instead of four (see Figure 7-16).

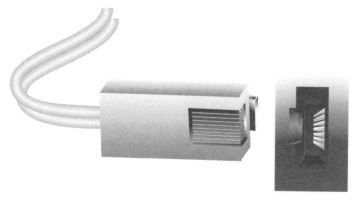

Figure 7-16   RJ-45 male and female connectors

Unshielded Twisted Pair (UTP)

Unshielded twisted-pair (UTP) cable, on the other hand, does not rely on physical shielding to block interference, but uses balancing and filtering techniques to reduce signal interference. Noise is induced equally on two conductors, which cancel out at the receiver. With correctly designed and manufactured UTP cable, this technique is easier to maintain than the shielding permanence and grounding of an STP cable. UTP cabling does not offer the high bandwidth or the protection from interference that coaxial or fiber optic cables do; however, millions of nodes are wired with UTP cable due to its lightweight, thin, and flexible nature. UTP cabling is a low-cost, manageable solution that is widely used for LANs and telephone connections. It is also quite adaptable and dependable, even for higher-data-rate applications. Like STP, UTP uses RJ-45 connectors. UTP has a maximum length of 100 meters (328.08 feet) and can support speeds of up to 100 Mbps.

Table 7-2 summarizes the various network cable types discussed so far.

Table 7-2   Network Cable Summary

Cable Type	Maximum Length	Maximum Speed
Thicknet (10Base5)	500 meters (1640.4 feet)	10 Mbps
Thinnet (10Base2)	185 meters (606.9 feet)	10 Mbps
Shielded twisted pair (STP)	100 meters (328.08 feet)	10, 100, 1000 Mbps depending on the category of cabling
Unshielded twisted pair (UTP)	100 meters (328.08 feet)	10, 100, 1000 Mbps depending on the category of cabling

UTP cable has evolved over the years, and different varieties are available for different needs. Improvements such as variations in the twists, individual wire sheaths, or overall cable jackets have led to the development of several standards for STP/UTP cabling. Here are some of the most popular specifications, each using four wire pairs:

- *Category 3 (Cat 3)*—Provides signal throughput up to 10 Mbps. Cat 3 is permissible for 10 Mbps Ethernet; however, the slightly more expensive Cat 5 is more common and reliable. You can also find Cat 3 cable in older 4 Mbps Token Ring network implementations.

- *Category 4 (Cat 4)*—Provides signal throughput up to 16 Mbps. Cat 4 is common in 16 Mbps Token Ring network implementations. Cat 5 is preferred over Cat 4 in most cases.

- *Category 5 (Cat 5)*—Provides signal throughput up to 100 Mbps. Cat 5 is the most common network cable in use today, and is used for Ethernet as well as other fast networking technologies. Cat 5 can be used for 10BaseT, 100BaseT, 1000BaseT, and Token Ring networking. Note that Enhanced Cat 5 (Cat 5e) is available for optimum reliability and performance. Cat 5e is only marginally more expensive yet reduces crosstalk by using a twisted string or plastic rib to separates the pairs and keeps the wires in proper position along the whole length of the cable. Cat 5e also uses better insulation and a thicker jacket.

- *Category 6 (Cat 6)*—A heavily shielded implementation of twisted-pair cabling. Each of four pairs is wrapped in foil insulation, and even more foil wraps around the bundle of pairs. A fire-resistant sheath covers the outer foil layer. Cat 6 cabling provides excellent resistance to crosstalk and can support up to six times the throughput of Cat 5.

RJ-45 Pin Assignments

Cables normally connect to RJ-45 connectors in what is known as a "straight-through" configuration. This means that whatever color insulated wire is on the first pin on one end is the same color insulated wire on the first pin of the connector on the other end, and so on through all eight wires. Straight-through cabling is the most commonly used configuration and connects servers and workstations to wall connectors, hubs, and other network equipment.

While there are a few standards for determining the wiring order within the jack, it really doesn't matter as long as the wires on one end correspond exactly to the wires on the other end and the scheme is consistent throughout your organization. For reference sake, Figure 7-17 shows the Electronic Industries Association/Telecommunications Industry Association (EIA/TIA) 568A and 568B cable end standards. Generally speaking, 568B is more common in business and industry, and 568A is required in certain government installations. For straight-through cable, just make sure that both ends use the same configuration.

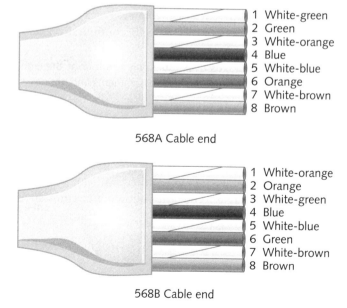

568A Cable end

568B Cable end

Figure 7-17   The EIA/TIA RJ-45 wiring standard

Crossover Cables

Crossover cables are useful in connecting two computers directly to one another. This is handy for quick connectivity without intermediate hubs or other network equipment as well as diagnostic contexts in which you want to isolate a host from the network and connect to it directly. Crossover cables are also required to daisy chain network devices. For example, crossover cables would interconnect a series of stackable hubs or switches (see Figure 7-18).

Figure 7-18 Crossover cables daisy chain network devices such as hubs

In a crossover configuration, you simply reverse the green and orange pairs. A simpler way to view this is to look at Figure 7-17 again. Recall that a straight-through cable uses the exact same pin configuration on both sides of the cable. For a crossover cable, simply use the 568A configuration on one end and the 568B configuration on the other.

 Both a straight-through cable and crossover cable only use four of the eight pins: 1, 2, 3, and 6! You could goof the other wire assignments and not notice the difference.

How to Cut and Crimp RJ-45 Connectors

Although you can buy premade cables up to 25 feet (7.62 m) in length with guaranteed connectivity from manufacturers such as Belkin (*www.belkin.com*), you might find it worth your while to make your own cable under the following circumstances:

- You require lengths of cable longer than 25 feet (7.62 m).

- It is more economically feasible to purchase cable-making materials in bulk than premade cables.

- You want to create both standard and crossover cables.

- You want to choose your own color cable, useful for identifying cable runs to various parts of the building.

TIP   Many organizations choose orange cable to uniquely identify crossover cables.

To make your own cable, you will need the following materials:

- *Modular plug crimp tool*—These pliers allow you to crimp the connector onto the cable (see Figure 7-19) and often include sharp blades for stripping the jacket and insulation from cable. (Be careful of the blades!)

7

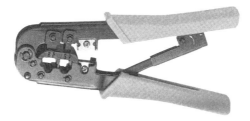

Figure 7-19   Most crimp tools include strippers and are able to crimp four to eight wires

- *Universal UTP stripping tool*—This optional tool is useful if you strip a lot of cable; it strips both round and flat cable (see Figure 7-20).

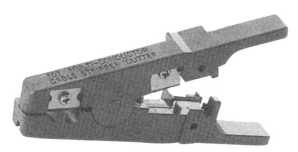

Figure 7-20   A universal UTP stripping tool

- *Diagonal cutters*—Use "diags" to cut cable off of the reel and to evenly trim pair ends during cable assembly (see Figure 7-21).

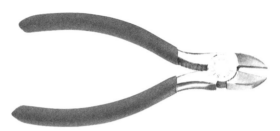

Figure 7-21   Diagonal cutters neatly cut and trim cable

- *Spooled cable*—UTP bulk cable is wound onto a spool inside a box (see Figure 7-22), and many manufacturers include an outlet from which to pull cable. There may also be a metering device so that you can measure the amount of cable pulled.

Figure 7-22   Spooled cable feeds through an outlet

- *Snagless boots*—Optionally, add a snagless boot (see Figure 7-23) to prevent the clip on RJ-45 cable from overextending and snapping off, which is a common problem when handling Cat 5 cable.

Figure 7-23   A snagless boot protects the RJ-45 clip

Cut and crimp your network cable as follows:

1. Pull the amount of cable you require. Cable is relatively inexpensive, so consider overestimating—too little cable requires you to start over, but seldom do you have too much.

2. Use the diags to cleanly cut the cable.

3. If you want to use snagless boots, thread two (one for each end) onto the cable. Make sure they are a few inches away from where you will crimp the ends to keep them out of the way.

4. Using the stripper or crimper, strip about an inch of the outer jacket off the end of the cable. Be careful not to cut into the insulation of the pairs inside. Although you can use the diags or some other tool to do the same task, I think you'll like the neatness of a stripper/crimper. Insert the end under the blade, lightly squeeze the crimper, and twist. This action cuts the outer jacket, which should then easily pull off.

5. Separate each of the four wire pairs and straighten them into the wiring order you choose (refer to Figure 7-17).

6. Evenly snip the end of the wires using the diags to expose a half inch of the wire pairs. (Originally, we cut one inch off of the jacket, but that was just to make handling the small wire pairs easier.) This should allow you to insert the wire pairs all the way into the end of the RJ-45 connector without leaving too much untwisted wire, which would cause crosstalk signaling problems. Also, half-inch exposure positions the jacketed portion of the cable under a plastic plug or wedge that clamps down onto the jacket.

 Some sources recommend stripping the end of each individual wire, which is completely unnecessary and extremely time-consuming, as the crimper forces connection pins to pierce the insulation, making a solid connection.

7. Insert the wire ends all the way into the RJ-45 jack—be careful not to get the wires crossed or bent. Once you get the wires into their respective grooves in the jack, the rest is easy.

8. Confirm that the wiring order is correct.

9. Hold the cable (not the plug) and insert the plug into the crimper tool. If the crimper tool has plugs for multiple connectors, look for the one marked "8P."

10. Squeeze the crimper around the connector. Most crimpers are ratcheted so that the crimpers hold their place if you lose or need to readjust your grip partway through. The crimper includes two plungers that attach the connector (see Figure 7-24). The leftmost plunger depresses a plug or wedge onto the jacket to prevent strain from dislodging the connector. The second plunger depresses a two-pronged metal pin into each wire, creating the actual connection.

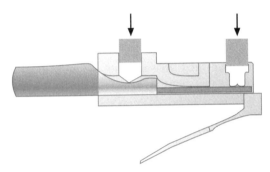

Figure 7-24   Two plungers attach the connector to the cable

11. Inspect the cable with the RJ-45 clip facing away from you. You should be able to see the wiring order through the clear plastic, as seen in Figure 7-25. If it's wrong, just use the diags to snip off the connector and start over again. (And don't feel bad—everybody goofs a plug sooner or later.) Also, give it a gentle tug; the connector shouldn't budge.

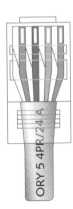

Figure 7-25   Inspect the wiring order

12. Repeat all steps for the other end of the cable.

13. Finally, if you included snagless boots, push them over the connectors.

Get more practice in making cables in Hands-on Project 7-1 at the end of the chapter.

10BaseT

The 10BaseT standard (also called twisted-pair Ethernet) uses a twisted-pair cable (such as Cat 5) with maximum lengths of 100 meters (328.08 feet). The cable is thinner and more flexible than the coaxial cable used for the 10Base5 or 10Base2 standards. If you were cabling for a 10BaseT network, the use of two pairs of Cat 3 wires would be sufficient; however, Cat 5 is a better choice in new implementations for purposes of signal quality and future upgrades.

100BaseT

The committee responsible for 100BaseT kept the 100 Mbps Ethernet standard as close to the original Ethernet definition as possible. Therefore, 100BaseT utilizes the Carrier Sense Multiple Access with Collision Detection (CSMA/CD) shared-media access method supported in earlier versions of Ethernet. The simplicity of this media access method might make it attractive to companies using traditional Ethernet. Because it is 10 times faster than Ethernet, it is often referred to as Fast Ethernet. Officially, the 100BaseT standard is called IEEE 802.3u. There are several different cabling schemes that can be used with 100BaseT, including the following:

- *100BaseT4* uses an extra two wires (four pairs) of normal-quality twisted-pair wires for use with Cat 3 UTP cable.

- *100BaseTX* Fast Ethernet uses two pairs of high-quality twisted-pair wires for use with Cat 5 UTP cable. The 100BaseTX standard has become the most popular due to its close compatibility with the 10BaseT Ethernet standard.

- *100BaseFX* is used with fiber optic cable that, for the most part, connects hubs and switches either between wiring closets or between buildings. 100BaseFX uses multimode fiber optic cable to transport Fast Ethernet traffic.

Fiber Optic Cabling

Fiber optic cable employs a technology that uses glass (or plastic) threads (fibers) to transmit data using light pulses from one end of the cable to the other. A fiber optic cable consists of a core of glass threads, each of which is capable of transmitting light pulses. A cladding surrounds the fibers, mirroring light back into the core. Plastic and braided Kevlar form the protective jacket (see Figure 7-26). The receiving end of the message converts the light signal to binary values. The maximum length is 25 km (15.5 miles) with speeds up to 2 Gbps. Fiber optics is not a particularly popular technology for workstations because it is so expensive. However, it is often used for a network backbone. Fiber cabling has been deployed as the primary media for campus and building backbones, offering high-speed connections between diverse LAN segments. Today, with progressively more complicated applications such as high-speed ISPs and e-commerce, optical fiber may soon become the primary media providing data to the desktop. Fiber has the largest bandwidth of any media available. It can transmit signals over the longest distance at the lowest cost, with the fewest repeaters and the least amount of repairs.

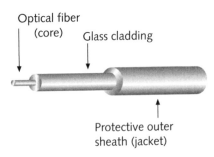

Figure 7-26   Fiber optic cable

Following are advantages of fiber optics:

- Fiber optic cables have a much greater bandwidth than metal cables to carry more data.
- Fiber optic cables are less susceptible to interference than metal cables.
- Fiber optic cables are much thinner and lighter than metal wires.
- Data can be transmitted digitally rather than in analog format.
- Fiber is immune to EMI and radio frequency interference (RFI). Because it does not conduct electricity, fiber optic cable can also be useful in areas where large amounts of EMI are present, such as on a factory floor.
- There are no crosstalk issues.
- Fiber is impervious to lightning strikes and does not conduct electricity or support ground loops.
- Fiber-based network segments can be extended 20 times farther than copper segments.
- Fiber cable cannot be tapped, so it's very secure.
- Fiber transmission systems are highly reliable.

Despite the numerous advantages of fiber, the cables are expensive to install, are more fragile than wire, and are difficult to split.

NETWORK ADAPTERS

Many NIC adapters comply with Plug and Play specifications so that they can be automatically configured without user intervention. On a non-Plug and Play system, the configuration must be done manually through a software program and/or DIP switches or jumpers, especially on older NICs. Network adapter cards are available to maintain practically every networking specification, including Fast Ethernet. Fast Ethernet NICs are often 10/100 Mbps capable and will automatically adapt to the proper speed. For network operating systems, adapter-teaming techniques can be used to offer additional bandwidth and improved performance. **Adapter teaming** is the process of installing two or more network adapters in a server and then logically grouping them so that they appear to the operating system as a single network interface. There are several different types of teaming techniques, including Adaptive Fault Tolerance (AFT), Adaptive Load Balancing (ALB), and link aggregation.

> Increase network performance to and from the server and the client by installing only 32-bit PCI network cards instead of 8- or 16-bit ISA network cards. The PCI cards can provide several times the network throughput because of the wider data path and more efficient use of the faster PCI bus.

Adaptive Fault Tolerance (AFT)

Adaptive Fault Tolerance (AFT) can provide an easy and effective method for increasing the availability of network server connections. By simply installing two or more server network adapters and configuring AFT, you have an emergency backup connection between the server and the network. If there is any problem with a cable, NIC, switch port, or hub port on the primary adapter, the secondary adapter can kick in within seconds to provide transparent recovery for applications and users. AFT can be configured with just two server adapters. Certain vendors and manufacturers provide automatic AFT support when multiple server adapters are configured.

A critical point of vulnerability on your network is corporate or departmental servers, where a failure or bottleneck can be disastrous to productivity. AFT technology usually supports up to four adapter teams with two to four adapters on each team. Depending on the vendor, AFT solutions can be made up of various adapter types and speeds as long as there is at least one primary server adapter in the team. The primary server adapter will generally pass its MAC and Layer 3 address to the failover adapter(s). This type of AFT requires the NIC vendor to provide a driver model that can take advantage of this technology.

Adaptive Load Balancing (ALB)

Adaptive Load Balancing (ALB) is a technique of guaranteeing a consistent level of high server throughput and transparent backup links by implementing multiple NICs and balancing the data transmission load across them. ALB is also known as asymmetric port aggregation. With Intel components, for example, you can use as many as four server adapters, connect them to a switch, and configure them to work as a team for an aggregate throughput of up to 400 Mbps with Fast Ethernet adapters or 8 Gbps with Gigabit Ethernet adapters. All of the adapters in a team must be connected to a switch, and the team is assigned a single network address. (ALB is designed to work with a switch, whereas AFT works with either a hub or a switch.) With ALB, all of the traffic moving from the network server is automatically balanced between up to four links. This can assure fast throughput with no need to restructure or reconfigure the network. An illustration of ALB can be seen in Figure 7-27.

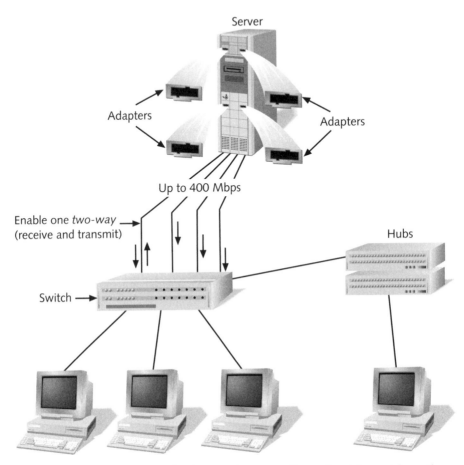

Figure 7-27   Adaptive Load Balancing increases throughput to and from the server

ALB offers a simpler and better way to move more data faster through the server by enabling each adapter to essentially add another 100 Mbps link, or channel. ALB also delivers the same fault-tolerance benefits as AFT technology, because if one link fails, the others will continue to provide network connectivity. Therefore, with ALB technology, it is no longer necessary to segment the network if the server link becomes a bottleneck. Instead, you can eliminate the bottleneck quickly and easily by installing two adapters in your server and configuring ALB with the driver software. This requires no client configuration, and clients do not have to be routed to communicate with each other. In addition, traffic is balanced along all of the server adapters. As with AFT, an intelligent, adaptive agent is included with the software driver. This driver dynamically manages the server adapter team and evenly distributes the load among them by constantly analyzing the traffic flow from the server. One channel within an ALB team carries traffic to and from the server while the others carry traffic from the server only. This load balancing of server traffic assures that all users enjoy the same network response from the server. By taking advantage of ALB, a four-link configuration can yield an aggregate throughput of approximately 400 Mbps.

An intelligent adaptive agent in the driver will also continuously analyze the traffic flow from the server and distribute the packets based on destination addresses. Load balancing can occur only on routed protocols (IP and NCP IPX). Multicast/broadcast and nonrouted protocols such as NetBEUI and Microsoft IPX are transmitted only over the primary adapter.

For AFT and ALB technologies, you can usually choose a primary and secondary role for selected adapters. The primary adapter will carry the majority of the traffic. With AFT, it will be the only adapter used until that link fails. With ALB and nonroutable protocols, it will be the only adapter used. It will also be the only adapter used for broadcast and multicast traffic.

Link Aggregation

Link aggregation is the process of combining multiple adapters into a single channel to provide bandwidth greater than the base speed of the adapter (10, 100, or 1000 Mbps). Link aggregation works only across multiple source address/destination address pairs. ALB mode provides aggregation in both directions with aggregation-capable switches. Intel's version of link aggregation, for example, must be used with an Intel Express switch capable of link aggregation and must match the capability of the switches. All adapters share a single MAC address. Link aggregation can be implemented in Windows 2000 and Windows NT 4.0, NetWare 4.1 and above, SCO UnixWare (10/100), and Linux.

NETWORKING WITH A MODEM POOL

Although networking is mostly LAN/WAN communication between hosts, remote access (the ability to connect to a particular server or the LAN over a phone line or Internet connection) is increasingly a concern for networked organizations as well. Most users have Internet access at home, and there are methods with which users can securely connect directly to the LAN through their ISP. However, there will likely be a need for users to directly dial into the LAN using conventional voice telephone lines, or POTS (Plain Old Telephone Service, also known as PSTN, Public Switched Telephone Network). Some network policies require dialing in directly because dedicated phone lines have less chance of exposure to mischievous Internet users. However, dialing in requires a modem on both ends. On the user end, this is an inexpensive device that's possibly already integrated into the motherboard of the computer. On the server end, you must provide a receiving modem to receive dozens or hundreds of callers at once (even thousands of callers at once if you run an ISP).

Servicing so many users quickly presents a problem. Because you typically install a modem in a free expansion slot on the computer, you probably only have room for one to three modems on a server. If you service dozens or hundreds of dial-up users, this type of modem installation is not feasible. Instead, you can install a **modem pool**, which uses one or more external physical devices that represent several modems (see Figure 7-28).

Figure 7-28   An analog modem pool

Starting from the user's remote dial-up attempt, Figure 7-29 illustrates the various equipment to which the user transparently connects as well as the function of each component. Here's how a modem pool works:

1. The user dials in, usually using a standard analog modem.

2. The dial-in attempt passes through normal Telco channels.

3. The dial-in attempt rings into the network modem pool, usually over a T-1 connection (a high-bandwidth phone connection capable of voice and data transmission).

4. A modem in the modem pool accepts the call. Note that although each modem in the pool operates independently, multiple users dial in using the same telephone number. Modem pool intelligence logically separates each call.

5. The call is useless until it reaches the LAN or server. Depending on the vendor, the modem pool device connects to an adapter card (which performs the serial processing on behalf of the server), or connects directly to a port on a network device such as hub, switch, or router.

6. The server either restricts the call to itself (somewhat unusual but sometimes implemented as a security measure to protect the LAN) or, more commonly, connects the call to the LAN. Once connected to the LAN, the user experiences the same connectivity as when locally connected to the LAN (except at slow modem speed).

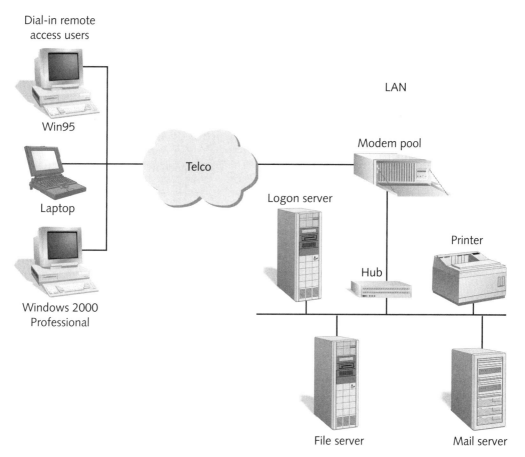

Figure 7-29   Connecting remote users to the LAN

The modem pool can be a desktop device, but larger implementations usually implement one or more rack-mounted devices. A modem pool is either analog or digital.

- *An analog modem pool* has a very basic chassis construction that provides expansion slots for multiple modems (usually 16). The chassis, in turn, connects to an adapter card in the server. This implementation is fading away because a digital implementation offers much higher density and more sophisticated configuration.

- *A digital modem pool* is a device with circuitry and intelligence to comprise the modems. Some vendors' modem pools (for example, Equinox/Avocent) accept SIMM modules (not to be confused with memory modules) that represent multiple modems. For example, a digital modem pool with four installed SIMM modules, each representing six modems, has a total of 24 modems. Digital modem pools can accept standard analog modem calls or digital ISDN calls. You can daisy chain multiple devices attached to the adapter card to increase density.

Besides accepting dial-in modem and ISDN calls, many modem pools also dial out. This is a common implementation to increase security to verify that only connections to a specific phone number are accepted. A fax pool uses a very similar construction.

Many modem pool implementations (such as the Cisco AS5800 Universal Access Server) are capable of modem pool partitioning. This is useful when you want to use separate phone numbers to connect various modem protocols such as V.90, V.34, and K56flex (see Figure 7-30).

Modems		Modems in pool	Assigned number
56K modems	◄--------------	24	555-1111
V.34 modems	◄--------------	24	555-2222
V.90 modems	◄--------------	24	555-3333

Figure 7-30 Separate phone numbers connect various modem protocols

Vendor software allows you to configure connections. For example, you can limit bandwidth, the number of simultaneous connections, the length of time a user can connect, and so forth.

Connecting the modem pool device is usually very simple. You install the device in a standard 19-inch wide rack opening (see Chapter 4), connect the incoming communication line, and then connect the modem pool device to the network equipment (see Figure 7-31).

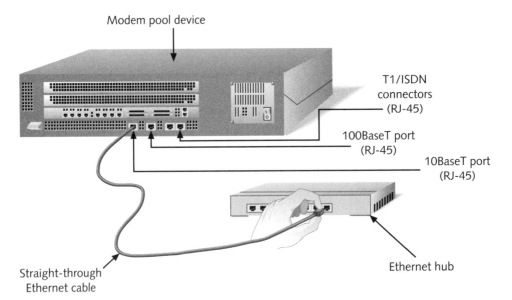

Figure 7-31 A common modem pool connection scenario

CHAPTER SUMMARY

❑ Bus networks are comparatively inexpensive and easy to install for small networks. However, it is more difficult to troubleshoot and locate a break in the cable or a faulty machine on a bus.

❑ When a node on a Token Ring network needs to transmit data and receives an empty token, it holds on to the token and records its own address, the destination address, and the message into the token before passing it on to the next station. As long as the token is not marked as empty, all of the other stations will not transmit messages. The token passes from one node to the next until it completes a full circuit and reaches the originating station, where the message is discarded and the token is again marked as empty.

❑ Ring topology has the following advantages: It can span greater distances than other network types; it offers low signal deterioration; collisions are low because only the station that holds the token can transmit; and it is good for a small network requiring high transmission speeds or for larger networks where each station has a comparable workload.

❑ Ring topology has the following disadvantages: It can be tricky to trace a problem on the cable segment if the LAN is large; each station's attached network interface must be continually active and the failure of a single station will halt a unidirectional ring network; it is complex to configure and requires relatively expensive hardware for each computer to interface with the network; and transmission delays tend to be long, even with moderate traffic levels.

❑ In the star topology, all nodes receive the same signal, reducing effective bandwidth, and the network device can become a bottleneck because all data must pass through it. Standard twisted-pair Ethernet networks using 10Base5, 10BaseT, or 100BaseTX technology commonly use the star topology.

❑ Star topology has the following advantages: A single failed node does not adversely affect the rest of the network; it is relatively straightforward to install and manage; isolating and repairing bad segments is easier; and it offers good capacity for network growth.

❑ Star topology has the following disadvantages: It needs a lot more cabling than bus or ring networks; and the entire network becomes ineffectual if the central network device fails.

❑ Ultimately, network protocols are only a means to transport the network message to the node's physical address, known as the MAC (Media Access Control) address, which globally and uniquely identifies a network device.

❑ NetBEUI is not a routable protocol. It is not efficient in larger networks because it frequently rebroadcasts to locate other nodes on the network since it does not cache previously located nodes and does not use name resolution services such as DNS or WINS.

❏ IPX/SPX includes a caching mechanism so that it is not necessary to rebroadcast to locate recently accessed nodes, but it does not utilize name resolution services such as DNS or WINS.

❏ Administrators consider TCP/IP a single protocol, though it is actually a suite of protocols. TCP/IP is more difficult than other protocols to plan and configure, although it is also scaleable and routable, which is why it is the protocol of the Internet and most enterprise networks.

❏ TCP/IP uses a unique IP address to identify each node. An IP address appears as four sets of digits, each separated by a dot. An IP address must be globally unique if the host is on the Internet. Each IP address also requires a subnet mask that, when compared against the IP address, identifies the specific network to which the host belongs.

❏ Administrators use a subnet mask to divide a range of IP addresses into multiple smaller networks because they might not need all the available IP addresses on a single network. Instead, you might split the IP address range among several separate networks. Administrators also subnet their networks to split up a collision domain.

❏ Improve network throughput to and from the server using multihoming—multiple network connections to a single server. You can also use port aggregation to combine multiple server network connections into a single, logical network connection with bandwidth that is multiplied times the number of ports.

❏ Ping tests connectivity at different stages between the host and destination to determine the point of failure at which a packet is dropped, and also tests basic networking connectivity.

❏ IPCONFIG is a Microsoft utility that displays a wide variety of IP configuration data for a Windows 98/ME/NT/2000 system, including the IP address, subnet mask, and default gateway.

❏ ARP displays the resolution between the IP address and physical (MAC) address on the network interface card by building a table as IP addresses resolve to MAC addresses.

❏ TRACERT is a trace routing utility that works like Ping but shows the actual router hops taken to reach the remote host.

❏ NETSTAT with the −r option shows routing tables.

❏ Token Ring networks, which operate at 4 or 16 Mbps, use the ring topology.

❏ Ethernet is the most widely used access method because it offers a nice balance between cost, speed, and ease of installation. Since Ethernet utilizes a shared medium between nodes, there are rules for sending packets of data to avoid conflicts and protect the data.

❏ With Carrier Sense Multiple Access with Collision Detection (CSMA/CD), the sending host monitors the voltage level of the wire, and if no transmission is occurring, the host sends data. If two or more hosts determine that the network is clear and begin sending data at the same time, Collision Detection (CD) handles timely attempts at retransmitting data for each host.

❑ A hub provides a universal link for devices in a network and sends all incoming data out to all ports and, hence, to each node.

❑ A network of hubs/repeaters is called a "shared Ethernet," meaning that all members of the network are contending for data transmission on a single network (collision domain).

❑ The Ethernet network can only have five segments connected; it can only use four repeaters; and of the five segments, only three can have users attached to them—the other two must be inter-repeater links. This is called the "5-4-3 rule."

❑ Fast Ethernet (100BaseT) offers transmission speeds up to 100 Mbps over Cat 5 cable and RJ-45 connectors.

❑ By simply adding another pair of wires (total of six wires) and removing collision detection, you can double the connection speed, creating full-duplex Ethernet, which must use switches.

❑ Gigabit Ethernet is a full-duplex media access method supporting transfer rates up to 1 Gbps.

❑ A bridge connects similar or different network types, such as Ethernet and Token Ring. Bridges drop (filter) the packet if the source and destination are on the same segment. If the source and destination host are on different segments, bridges pass the packet on to the correct segment.

❑ Switches separate a network into collision domains so that network rules can be extended. Each of the segments attached to an Ethernet switch has a full 10 or 100 Mbps of bandwidth shared by fewer users, resulting in better performance.

❑ A router connects multiple networks using routing tables and routable protocols. Routers use headers and a forwarding table to determine where packets go, and communicate with other routers to calculate the best route between any two hosts.

❑ Thinnet is based on the 10Base2 standard (10 Mbps/Baseband transmission) that utilizes RG-58 A/U or RG-58 C/U 50 ohm coaxial cable with maximum segment lengths of 185 meters (606.9 feet).

❑ Shielded twisted-pair (STP) cable involves two copper wires, each encased in its own color-coded insulation, which are twisted together to form a "twisted pair." Multiple twisted pairs are then packaged in an outer sheath to form the cable. The cable minimizes the possibility of crosstalk by increasing the number of twists per inch. STP uses RJ-45 connectors.

❑ Unshielded twisted-pair (UTP) cable uses RJ-45 connectors. UTP has a maximum length of 100 meters (328.08 feet) and can support speeds up to 100Mps. UTP uses balancing and filtering techniques through media filters to reduce signal interference. Noise is induced equally on two conductors, which cancel out at the receiver.

❑ Category 3 (Cat 3) cable provides signal throughput up to 10 Mbps and is common in older 4 Mbps Token Ring network implementations. Category 4 (Cat 4) cable

7

provides signal throughput up to 16 Mbps and is common in 16 Mbps Token Ring network implementations. Category 5 (Cat 5) cable provides signal throughput up to 100 Mbps and is used for Ethernet as well as other fast networking technologies. Cat 5 can be used for 10BaseT, 100BaseT, 1000BaseT, and Token Ring networking.

❐ Cat 5 cables normally connect to RJ-45 connectors in what is known as a "straight through" configuration, in which the color insulated wire on the first pin on one end is the same color insulated wire on the first pin of the connector on the other end, and so on through all eight wires.

❐ Crossover cables connect two computers directly to one another and also daisy chain network devices. A crossover cable uses the 568A configuration on one end and the 568B configuration on the other.

❐ You probably want to make your own cable if you require lengths of cable longer than 25 feet (7.62 m), if it is more economically feasible to purchase cable-making materials in bulk than premade cables, if you want to create both standard and crossover cables, or if you want to choose your own color cable (useful for identifying cable runs to various parts of the building).

❐ The 10BaseT standard (also called "twisted-pair Ethernet") uses a twisted-pair cable (such as Cat 5) with maximum lengths of 100 meters (328.08 feet).

❐ 100BaseT utilizes the CSMA/CD shared-media access method supported in earlier versions of Ethernet. The simplicity of this media access method might make it attractive to companies using traditional Ethernet. Because it is 10 times faster than Ethernet, it is often referred to as Fast Ethernet.

❐ 100BaseT networking uses 100BaseT4, 100BaseTX (the most common implementation), or 100BaseFX cabling schemes.

❐ Fiber optic cable uses glass (or plastic) threads (fibers) to transmit data using light pulses from one end of the cable to the other, and consists of a core of glass threads, each of which is capable of transmitting light pulses. A cladding surrounds the fibers, mirroring light back into the core. Plastic and braided Kevlar form the protective jacket. The maximum length is 25 km (15.5 miles) with speeds up to 2 Gbps.

❐ The following are characteristics of fiber optic cable: much greater bandwidth than metal cable to carry more data; less susceptible to interference than metal cable; much thinner and lighter than metal cable; data can be transmitted digitally rather than in analog format; it is immune to EMI and RFI; it can be useful in areas where large amounts of EMI are present; there is no crosstalk; it is impervious to lightning strikes and does not conduct electricity or support ground loops; network segments can be extended 20 times farther than copper segments; and it cannot be tapped, so it's very secure.

❐ A modem pool can be a desktop device, but larger implementations usually have one or more rack-mounted devices. A modem pool falls under one of two categories: analog (a chassis for multiple physical modem adapters) or digital (a device with circuitry and intelligence to comprise the modems).

KEY TERMS

802.3 Standard — An Institute for Electrical and Electronic Engineers (IEEE) networking standard that defines the rules for configuring an Ethernet network as well as determining how elements in an Ethernet network interact with one another. By following 802.3, network equipment and network protocols can communicate properly.

adapter teaming — Installing two or more network adapters in a server and then logically grouping them so that they appear to the operating system as a single network interface.

Adaptive Fault Tolerance (AFT) — Installing two or more server network adapters to provide an emergency backup connection between the server and the network. If there is any problem with a cable, NIC, switch port, or hub port on the primary adapter, the secondary adapter can kick in within seconds to provide transparent recovery for applications and users.

Adaptive Load Balancing (ALB) — A technique of guaranteeing a consistent level of high server throughput and transparent backup links by implementing multiple NICs and balancing the data transmission load across them. ALB is also known as "asymmetric port aggregation."

ARP (Address Resolution Protocol) — Displays the resolution between the IP address and physical (MAC) address on the NIC by building a table as IP addresses resolve to MAC addresses. You can also modify the ARP cache and table entries.

backbone — A larger, common avenue through which data transfers take place from smaller lines connected to it.

bridge — A network device that connects separate networks together. Bridges connect similar or different network types, such as Ethernet and Token Ring.

bus topology — A network topology in which nodes link together in series where each node is connected to a common backbone cable.

collision—An event that results when two nodes transmit packets to the network at the same time.

collision domain — A network boundary in which multiple nodes could potentially attempt to access the network at the same time.

crosstalk — Intruding signals from an adjacent twisted pair or cable.

data rate — The actual quantity of data transferred within the limitations of the bandwidth.

Fast Ethernet — A 100 Mbps Ethernet implementation, also known as 100BaseT.

fiber optic cable — Technology that uses glass (or plastic) threads (fibers) to transmit data using light pulses. The receiving end of the message converts the light signal to binary values. The maximum length is 25 km (15.5 miles) with speeds up to 2 Gbps.

full-duplex Ethernet — The addition of another pair of wires (total of six wires) to Ethernet cable and removing collision detection to double the connection speed. Hosts can simultaneously send and receive data similar to a telephone conversation in which both parties can speak at once. (Half-duplex would be more like a CB radio conversation.)

7

Gigabit Ethernet — Supports data transfer rates of 1 Gigabit (1000 megabits) per second.

hub — A networking device that provides a universal link for devices in a network and sends all incoming data out to all ports (hence, to each node).

intelligent hub (or **managed hub**)—A hub that allows administrators to monitor the traffic passing through the hub and configure each port in the hub.

IPCONFIG — A Microsoft utility that displays a wide variety of IP configuration data for a Windows 98/ME/NT/2000 system, including the IP address, subnet mask, and default gateway and other information.

IPX/SPX (Internetwork Packet Exchange/Sequence Packet Exchange) — The default Novell protocol implementation for all versions of NetWare until 5.x, which can also use TCP/IP.

link aggregation — Combining multiple adapters into a single channel to provide bandwidth greater than the base speed of the adapter (10, 100, or 1000 Mbps). Link aggregation works only across multiple source address/destination address pairs.

MAC (Media Access Control) address — A globally unique identifier found on each NIC.

media access method — A method to place the data packets transmitted from the NOS software to the physical network device (such as a NIC) and then to the wire.

modem pool — One or more external physical devices that represent several modems.

multihomed — Computers using NICs with multiple ports or multiple NICs to increase effective network throughput.

multistation access unit (MAU) — A networking device that looks much like a hub except that it includes an RI (ring in) and RO (ring out) port. Tokens still pass from one host to the next in a logical ring.

NetBEUI (NetBIOS Enhanced User Interface) — A small, fast protocol optimized for small networks.

NETSTAT — A command-line networking utility that shows TCP/IP protocol statistics using any of several options. One of the most useful options is –r, which shows the routing table. This is useful in verifying the efficiency of the routing tables.

node — An active device connected to a network, such as a computer or printer, or networking equipment such as a hub, switch, or router.

passive hub — A standard hub that simply receives signals and repeats them out to all ports.

Ping (packet internet groper) — An all-purpose utility for verifying that a remote host is accessible by sending small packets of data to which an accessible host responds.

port aggregation — Similar to multihomed computers, port aggregation uses software to combine multiple ports from the server into a single logical connection to the network but with bandwidth that is multiplied times the number of ports.

ring topology — A network topology in which all of the nodes are connected in a closed, single, logical communication loop.

round-trip time (RTT) — The time it takes for a Ping packet to reach its destination and return to the source.

RJ-45 (registered jack-45) — An eight-wire connector that connects Ethernet network devices.

router — A network device that connects multiple networks using routing tables and routable protocols. Routers use headers and a forwarding table to determine where packets go, and communicate with other routers to calculate the best route between any two hosts. Routers determine whether to forward or filter a packet based on the IP address and subnet mask, which identifies the network to which a host belongs. The router filters a message destined for a host on the same network, and forwards messages destined for a host on a different network.

shielded twisted pair (STP) — Network cable that consists of two copper wires, each encased in its own color-coded insulation, which are twisted together to form a "twisted pair." Multiple twisted pairs are then packaged in an outer sheath to form the twisted-pair cable.

star topology — A network configuration in which all of the nodes connect to a central network device such as a hub or switch. All nodes receive the same signal, reducing effective bandwidth, and the central network device can become a bottleneck because all data must pass through it.

7

switch — A networking device that separates a network into collision domains so that network rules can be extended. Each of the segments attached to an Ethernet switch has a full 10 or 100 Mbps of bandwidth shared by fewer users, resulting in better performance.

switching hub — A hub that reads the destination address of each packet and then forwards the packet to the correct port.

subnet mask — A series of network identification numbers which, when compared against the IP address, identifies the specific network to which the host belongs.

TCP/IP (Transmission Control Protocol/Internet Protocol) — A suite of protocols in common use on most networks and the Internet.

thinnet — Based on the 10Base2 standard (10 Mbps/Baseband transmission), networking cable that utilizes RG-58 A/U or RG-58 C/U 50 ohm coaxial cable with maximum segment lengths of 185 meters (606.9 feet).

thicknet — Based on the 10Base5 standard, which transmits data at 10 Mbps over a maximum distance of 500 meters (1640.4 feet). Thicknet is about 1 cm thick and has been used for backbone media because of its durability and maximum length.

topology — The geometric configuration of devices, nodes, and cable links on a network. Topologies define how nodes connect to one another.

TRACERT — A command-line trace routing utility that works like Ping but shows the actual router hops taken to reach the remote host.

transceiver — A device in a Token Ring node that repeats the network signal to move it around the ring.

token passing — A method of collision avoidance that prevents two nodes from transmitting messages at the same time.

unshielded twisted pair (UTP) — Network cabling that does not rely on physical shielding to block interference (as does STP), but uses balancing and filtering techniques to reduce signal interference. Noise is induced equally on two conductors, which cancel out at the receiver.

REVIEW QUESTIONS

1. Which network topology does a network backbone use?

   a. star

   b. bus

   c. hub

   d. ring

2. When can a node in the ring topology transmit a message?

   a. when the node receives an empty token

   b. when the node receives a token with the parity bit set to 1

   c. when the node receives a token with the parity bit set to 0

   d. any time it receives a token

3. What do you call a node on a TCP/IP network?

   a. Ping

   b. plug

   c. host

   d. gateway

4. What is the unit of measurement that corresponds to 1000 bits per second?

   a. Mbps

   b. Kbps

   c. Tbps

   d. Gbps

5. Which of the following network topologies best describes a network configuration where all of the nodes are connected to a centrally located hub or switch and is commonly used for standard twisted-pair Ethernet networks using 10BaseT or 100BaseTX?

   a. ring

   b. bus

   c. star

   d. mesh

6. Which of the following is characteristic of NetBEUI?

   a. routable

   b. caches location of other nodes

   c. no configuration

   d. complex configuration

7. IPX/SPX is the default protocol of which NOS?

   a. Windows NT 4.0

   b. NetWare versions before 5.0

   c. OS/2

   d. Linux

8. What is the purpose of a subnet mask?

   a. identifies the host's IP network

   b. uniquely identifies the host

   c. filters packets destined for the same network

   d. forwards packets destined for a different network

9. Which of the following are valid network diagnostic tools that are common to most operating systems? (Choose all that apply.)

   a. Ping

   b. TraceIP

   c. ARP

   d. NETSTAT

10. Why might you want to subnet the network?

   a. to break up the collision domain

   b. to give each department its own network

   c. to increase collisions

   d. to reduce traffic on the Token Ring network

11. Which one of the following is *not* a recognized version of the Ethernet standard?

   a. Fast Ethernet

   b. Gigabit Ethernet

   c. Token Ethernet

   d. Full-duplex Ethernet

   e. Switched Ethernet

12. Which one of the following cable types consists of four twisted pairs of copper wire terminated by RJ-45 connectors, supports frequencies up to 100 MHz and network speeds up to 100 Mbps, and can be used for 10BaseT, 100BaseT, and Token Ring networking?

   a. Category 3

   b. Category 4

   c. Category 5

   d. Category 2

7

13. Which one of the following is *not* a valid version of the 100BaseX specifications?

  a. 100BaseT4

  b. 100BaseTX

  c. 100BaseFX

  d. 100BaseF4

14. What is the purpose of IPCONFIG?

  a. to display name resolution results

  b. to display routing tables

  c. to display host IP configuration data

  d. to display router hops to a destination node

15. What is the difference between a MAU and an Ethernet hub?

  a. An Ethernet hub has an RI and RO port, and a MAU does not.

  b. An Ethernet hub is only found on a ring network, and a MAU only on a bus network.

  c. An Ethernet hub sends data in both directions in the ring, and a MAU sends data in only one direction.

  d. A MAU has an RI and RO port, and an Ethernet hub does not.

16. Which of the following is characteristic of a collision domain?

  a. Token Ring media access method

  b. Ethernet media access method

  c. A MAU arbitrates collisions.

  d. Any network with more than two nodes qualifies as a collision domain.

17. 10BaseT Ethernet networks use which of the following rules?

  a. 5 (segments) 4 (hubs) 3 (three of five segments can have users)

  b. 7 (segments) 6 (hubs) 5 (five of five segments can have users)

  c. 6 (segments) 5 (hubs) 4 (four of six segments can have users)

  d. use as many segments, hubs, and users as necessary within acceptable performance standards

18. A crossover cable:

  a. uses the same wiring order on both ends

  b. uses exactly the opposite wiring order on both ends

  c. connects a computer to a hub

  d. reverses orange and green pairs

19. How does a hub address a message destined for another network?

    a. It forwards the message directly to the other network.

    b. It repeats the signal indiscriminately through all ports.

    c. It directs the message only to the port of the specific destination host.

    d. It forwards the packet to other members of the ring.

20. What is the most common type of network cable in use today?

    a. thinnet

    b. Cat 3

    c. Cat 4

    d. Cat 5

7

HANDS-ON PROJECTS

Project 7-1

In this project, you will construct a straight-through cable and a crossover cable. You will need two or more RJ-45 jacks, about three feet of Cat 5 cable, diagonal cutters, and a crimper. You will use the cables you make in Project 7-2.

1. Measure about three feet (one meter) of cable from the spool.

2. Use the diags to cleanly cut the cable.

3. Using the crimper, strip about an inch of the outer jacket off the end of the cable. (If the crimper does not have blades for this purpose, you will need a stripper.) Be careful not to cut into the insulation of the pairs inside. Insert the end under the blade, lightly squeeze the crimper, and twist. This action cuts the outer jacket, which should then easily pull off.

4. Separate each of the four wire pairs and straighten them into the 568B wiring order (refer to Figure 7-17).

Evenly snip the end of the wires using the diags to expose a half inch of the wire pairs. This should allow you to insert the wire pairs all the way into the end of the RJ-45 connector.

5. Insert the wire ends all the way into the RJ-45 connector, being careful not to get the wires crossed or bent. Grooves in the connector help to guide the wires.

6. Confirm that the wiring order is correct.

7. Hold the cable (not the plug) and insert the plug into the crimper tool. If the crimper tool has plugs for multiple connectors, look for the one marked "8P."

8. Tightly squeeze the crimper around the connector.

9. Inspect the cable with the RJ-45 clip facing away from you. You should be able to see the wiring order through the clear plastic (as shown in Figure 7-25). If it's wrong, just use the diags to snip off the connector and start over again. When finished, give it a gentle tug—the connector shouldn't budge.

10. Repeat all steps for the other end of the cable.

11. Create a crossover cable using all the same steps, except that this time in Step 4 you will use the 568B connection on one side and the 568A connection on the other.

Project 7-2

In this project, you will construct a star topology network using a hub, the cables you made in Project 7-1, and at least two nodes.

1. Plug the power supply into one hub and make sure the power comes on (you should see one or more LED lights). Plug a straight-through network cable into one of the ports. Try to avoid using the last port, as some hubs link that port to the uplink so that you can only use either the last port or the uplink but not both.

2. Connect any Windows 2000 node to the hub with the other end of the straight-through cable.

3. Turn on the Windows 2000 computer.

4. Plug the power supply into a second hub and make sure the power comes on.

5. Plug a straight-through network cable into one of the ports, again avoiding the last port.

6. Connect another Windows 2000 node to the second hub with the other end of the straight-through cable. Coordinate with another student if using their computer.

7. Turn on the second Windows computer.

8. Using your crossover cable, connect the uplink ports between the two hubs.

Project 7-3

In this project, you will configure the IP address on the two Windows 2000 computers from Project 7-2 and verify their connectivity with Ping. This project requires you to log on as a local Administrator. Ask your instructor for the appropriate user name and password.

1. After the Windows computers have booted, verify that a link light appears on the network card, signifying connectivity.

2. Click **Start**, point to **Settings**, and click **Network and Dial-up Connections**. The Network and Dial-up Connections dialog box appears.

3. Right-click **Local Area Connection**, and click **Properties**.

4. In the Properties dialog box, click **Internet Protocol (TCP/IP)** and then click **Properties**. (Be careful not to uncheck Internet Protocol (TCP/IP).)

5. Configure the IP address to **10.10.10.X** where X is any number between 1 and 254 of your choosing. Configure the subnet address to 255.255.255.0.

6. Verify connectivity using the Ping utility. Ping the IP address of another connected node from a command prompt by typing **ping 10.10.10.X** where X is the address of the other node. You should see four replies if the nodes are properly configured and connected.

7. Close the Command Prompt window.

Project 7-4

In this project, you and a teammate will create a share and transfer a large quantity of files, and then observe the collisions on the hub(s). Perform the actions below on both computers.

1. On one of the Windows computers using Windows Explorer, create a folder from the C drive, **C:\Transfer**.

2. On the other computer, share the CD-ROM drive by right-clicking it and choosing **Sharing** from the context menu. Share the folder with default permissions.

> ⚠ **Caution** In actual practice, sharing the CD-ROM on a server is not advisable because it opens security vulnerabilities.

3. Insert a CD-ROM with several files or the CD-ROM that came with this book.

4. On the first computer, use Windows Explorer to type **IPAddress** into the address bar at the top, where **IPAddress** is the IP address of the other computer. A list of shares appears in the details (right) pane of Windows Explorer.

5. Double-click the shared CD-ROM. You should see several files and/or folders. Select them all and copy them to your own C:\Transfer folder created in Step 1. Try to time the transfer so that both computers download contents of the CD-ROM from one another at the same time.

6. Observe the hub. The lights should blink constantly during the transfer, indicating collisions during the transfer. This is normal for an Ethernet network, even with only two hosts.

7. When the transfers are complete, delete the C:\Transfer folder and close Windows Explorer.

Project 7-5

In this project, you will reconfigure the computer's TCP/IP settings and connect to the Internet. Then, you will use the TRACERT command to trace the route to a few web sites.

1. Connect one of the Windows computers used in the other projects in this chapter to a line that has access to the Internet (your instructor will guide you).

2. Access the TCP/IP settings and configure them to receive an IP address automatically (from a DHCP server). If necessary, reboot the computer.

3. Browse to *www.ox.ac.uk*. This is the home page for Oxford University in London, England.

4. Open a command prompt. In the command prompt window, type **tracert** ***www.ox.ac.uk***.

5. Observe the number of hops required to access the site, which vary depending upon your physical location and Internet service provider. TRACERT counts up to 30 hops. The page you viewed in Step 3 came to you across all the routers you now observe in the TRACERT results.

6. Close the Command Prompt and browser windows.

Project 7-6

In this project, you will draw a network diagram that involves all three major topologies: bus, ring, and star.

1. On a separate sheet of paper, draw all three major network topologies, and interconnect them using any series of hubs, MAUs, bridges, and routers. There are scores of possible configurations that you can devise.

2. Share your network diagram with a classmate. At any point in the two diagrams, draw in a connecting device that might connect your two networks. For example, you could use a router or bridge to attach two bus topologies, or you could use a bridge to attach a Token Ring topology to an (Ethernet) star topology.

CASE PROJECTS

1. As a network consultant, you have been asked to analyze the network at Edna's Home Made Pies factory. The company has grown considerably since its inception six years ago, and users regularly complain about poor network performance, particularly in terms of logon response in the morning (all users report to work at 8:00 AM) and database performance. The owner, Edna, asks you to analyze the network and server placement within the network, and then to make recommendations.

   Upon arriving at the factory, you locate the server room, which has a wiring closet in the same room, and view all network equipment. Here are your findings:

   ❏ A Novell NetWare server processes the user logons. It has a single 4 Mbps Token Ring network adapter.

   ❏ A Windows NT 4.0 server runs the SQL database. Edna hires a database administrator to regularly optimize the database, and you cannot find any problems with the database itself. This server is on a 16 Mbps Token Ring network adapter on the same ring as the NetWare server.

   ❏ A bridge appears to attach the server room servers on a Token Ring network to the user's Ethernet star topology. Last year, Edna had another consultant install the user workstations with Ethernet network adapters capable of up to 100 Mbps, but slow demand for pies restricted the budget to perform any more improvements.

   Given these findings, what would you recommend?

2. You are at a conference a few miles away from your workplace when your pager indicates a network emergency. Apparently, a network intern has done something to the physical network that has cut off several workstations from an Ethernet segment, and has taken a Linux server offline. When you arrive back at work, you inspect the physical connections and find the following:

   ❏ Network cables daisy chain a series of stackable hubs. None of the cables are loose, and the power is on to each hub. Nevertheless, all hosts attached to hub C can only communicate with one another, and no hosts on any of the other hubs.

   ❏ The Linux server seems to be operating properly, and the physical network connection to a switch is not loose. Nevertheless, you do not see a link light on the switch for this Linux server connection. Other connections to the switch show a green link light.

   Given these findings, what could be causing the problems?

8

CONFIGURING A NETWORK OPERATING SYSTEM

After reading this chapter and completing the exercises, you will be able to:

♦ Identify network operating system (NOS) characteristics and versions

♦ List NOS hardware requirements

♦ Perform NOS installations and upgrades

♦ Properly shut down the NetWare, Linux, OS/2, Windows NT, and Windows 2000 network operating systems

---

Most enterprises do not run a single network operating system (NOS). Instead, there is often a mix of NOSs that you must be prepared to administer. Although it is beyond the scope of this chapter (and book) to detail each operating system's features and functions, it will be important for you to know the general capabilities and minimum hardware requirements of the major NOSs, and how to ensure compatibility with installed devices. This chapter covers general installation procedures, how to configure virtual memory swap files, how to perform upgrades, and how to properly shut down the Novell NetWare, Linux, OS/2, Windows NT 4.0 Server, and Windows 2000 Server NOSs.

Several operating systems include automated setup installations that require little or no interaction. This book addresses only the interactive installation you would normally see in a manual, step-by-step installation.

GENERAL NOS CONFIGURATION CONCEPTS

Although each network operating system covered in this chapter has its own configuration process, all NOS configurations involve some general elements and concepts that I briefly describe before detailing how those elements are implemented in individual NOSs.

Hardware Requirements

This chapter is organized by network operating system, and each respective section will list the minimum system hardware requirements for that NOS, including requirements for processor, RAM, and hard disk space. Each NOS also requires a keyboard, mouse, CD-ROM, network card, and VGA or better video display, but for this chapter I assume that these items are always present.

Vendors list the minimum requirements as a standard practice and also to qualify for various types of contracts for which a bid is required (government contracts, for example). However, these requirements are usually only sufficient to install the operating system — how well it runs is another matter. A production server will languish in attempting to provide service to the network with only the vendor's recommended minimum requirements.

Preparing server hardware for NOS installation involves the right perspective. Instead of trying to get away with as little as possible, the administrator's perspective should be nearly the opposite: obtain hardware that is powerful enough for current and future requirements. Administrators must remember to anticipate what kinds of demands will be placed on the server. Is it a file server? Better have a lot more hard disk space than the manufacturer recommends. Is it going to run applications such as a database? Better also add a lot of memory and much more processing power. Will the server provide intranet or Internet web content? Add another network card or two for load balancing or adaptive fault tolerance.

NOS Installation

A common task in server administration is installation of the NOS. Before you start the installation, be certain that the installed hardware meets at least the minimum system requirements as recommended by the vendor, and also be certain that installed devices are compatible.

Before you begin any NOS installation, write down the following information for which the installation may prompt you: an IP address for the server, an IP address of a DNS server, the name of your domain, the name of your computer, and so forth.

Virtual Memory/Swap Files

In addition to giving hardware requirements for various NOSs, this chapter also explains how each NOS deals with virtual memory, an important area of configuration for a network operating system. **Virtual memory** uses a portion of hard disk space to extend RAM. It is a logical (as opposed to physical) memory area that is supported in conjunction with physical RAM. Think of virtual memory as an alternate set of memory addresses. Programs use these virtual addresses rather than real addresses to store instructions and data. These virtual addresses are then converted into real memory addresses when the program or data is actually required. The main goal of virtual memory is to enlarge the address space that a program can use. To facilitate the copying of virtual memory into real memory, the operating system divides virtual memory into pages, each of which contains a fixed number of addresses. Each page is stored on a disk until it is needed. When the page is needed, the operating system copies it from disk to main memory, and translates the virtual addresses into real addresses.

The process of translating virtual addresses into real addresses is called **mapping**. Copying virtual pages from disk to main memory is known as **paging** or **swapping**. Swapping is a useful technique that enables a computer to execute programs and manipulate data files larger than main memory. The operating system copies as much data as possible into main memory, and leaves the rest on the disk. When the operating system needs data from the disk, it exchanges a portion of data in main memory with a portion of data on the disk. Each time a page is needed that is not currently in memory, a **page fault** occurs. An invalid page fault occurs when the address of the page being requested is invalid. In this case, the application is usually aborted. All major NOSs require virtual memory. This chapter explains how to create swap-file space for each respective NOS. (Chapter 11 addresses how to optimize and size the swap file.)

8

Performing Upgrades

Sometimes it is not necessary to "flatten" the system (use FDISK to repartition and format the disk). Although a clean install has advantages, sometimes it can be disruptive, time-consuming, and unnecessary. When upgrading a system from one released version to the next (Windows NT 4.0 to Windows 2000, for example), it might be best to take 15 minutes or half an hour to perform an upgrade, which will retain all the existing applications and many configuration settings. Compare this to perhaps a day for a clean install depending on the number of applications and configurations that you need to make. When Microsoft initially began the daunting task of upgrading its data center of more than 350 servers, administrators flattened NT 4.0 systems and performed clean installs of Windows 2000. Microsoft decided to perform upgrades instead on some servers, and noticed that there was no appreciable difference in stability or function. Thereafter, Microsoft upgraded the rest of its systems.

While upgrades don't work smoothly for everyone under all circumstances, you should consider the time savings involved. Although NOS upgrades are not specifically a CompTIA Server+ exam item, they are an important part of administration. Administrators considering a mass upgrade will want to test and pilot first (see Chapter 6), and if successful, perform the remaining upgrades.

Proper Shutdown

Although servers will ideally run indefinitely without a need for maintenance, whether planned or unplanned, you will eventually have to shut down or reboot a server. Often, this is necessary to return a server to healthy status when its performance is poor or it seems unstable. Most network operating systems also require a reboot any time you make a significant change such as adding hardware, a service, or an application. A shutdown might also be required for the mundane but regular task of blowing dust out of the case. For whatever reason, you should know how to properly shut down various operating systems, because an improper shutdown can corrupt data files, applications, and the operating system itself.

When performing a planned server shutdown, it is critical for system administrators to have a good grasp of how the servers and clients are being used and actively involve users in scheduling downtime. The concepts behind performing a proper shutdown are fundamental to all network operating systems. For example, on most systems, a server shutdown will cause all user processes to be killed. If users on a system are running tasks that take a long time to complete, then shutting the system down and killing all of the processes will severely impact the productivity of users—possibly resulting in data loss. Also, user workstations might lock up or hang while waiting for some kind of response from the server. Therefore, whenever possible, administrators should give users as much lead time as possible when scheduling a shutdown. Server operating systems discussed in this book are generally stable enough to seldom, if ever, need a shutdown (except for regular maintenance).

NOVELL NETWARE

Novell NetWare is a widely accepted local area network (LAN) operating system that was developed by Novell Corporation. NetWare runs on a variety of different LANs, including Ethernet and IBM Token Ring networks, and was arguably the NOS market leader until the mid '90s when Windows NT 4.0 came on the scene. NetWare offers users and programmers a reliable interface that is independent of the underlying hardware that transmits data. Depending on the version, NetWare uses either a bindery or directory service design to manage the majority of the resources.

A **directory service** is a network service that identifies all of the resources on a network and makes them available to applications and users. These resources can include email addresses; user, group, and computer accounts; and devices such as printers. A main goal of a directory service is to make the physical network topology and protocols invisible so that a network user can access any resource without knowing where it is or how it is physically linked. Three of the most important directory services are **Lightweight Directory Access Protocol (LDAP)**, a standard that defines a method of creating searchable network resources and is used primarily for accessing information directories such as Windows 2000 Active Directory and NetWare Directory Service (NDS), which is used on Novell NetWare networks. Virtually all directory services are based on the **X.500 ITU** standard, originally a standard for searching email directories. However, the standard is so large and complex that no vendor complies with it completely.

The NetWare operating system has the following characteristics:

- NetWare 3.x uses a bindery to provide network clients with the information that is stored on the NetWare server's local directory partitions. A **bindery** is restricted to the server on which it resides, and users can only use resources managed in the same bindery to which they log on. If users want to access resources located in another part of the network, they must log on to another server's bindery.

- NetWare 4.x and 5.x use the more advanced **Novell Directory Services (NDS)**. NDS uses a scalable tree structure that extends throughout the enterprise. The administrator can plan and configure the NDS tree so that users from anywhere in the organization can access resources throughout the organization with a single logon.

- NetWare 5.1 incorporates new web and application server technologies that extend an organization's contact to the realm of e-business and web-based network management. NetWare 5.1 includes tools to make the once-complicated process of web application development, deployment, and management much simpler. Novell NetWare works well with most client operating systems, ranging from MS-DOS to OS/2 and any version of Microsoft Windows.

- NetWare 5.1 offers a GUI interface known as **ConsoleOne**, which is a central management point for performing NetWare administration. This console remedied complaints about the text-only administration of previous versions of NetWare (see Figure 8-1).

- **Zero Effort Networks** (**Z.E.N.** or **ZENworks)** is a NetWare suite of software management tools that administrators use to manage the user or server operating system environment by automatically distributing applications and controlling the user desktop using ZENworks for Servers and ZENworks for Desktops.

- Using NetWare 5.1, your network can run in a pure IP environment without retaining older IPX-based functionality. (Older versions of NetWare used IPX/SPX as the default network protocol.)

8

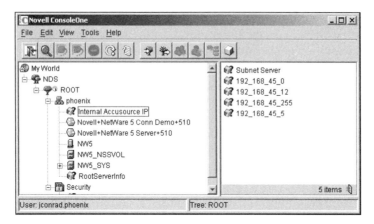

Figure 8-1 The NetWare 5.1 GUI interface, ConsoleOne

Prior to the Internet's rapid growth, using IPX/SPX was not a significant administrative concern. However, administrators trying to merge existing IPX/SPX networks with other IP-based servers and the Internet will appreciate the simplification of using a single protocol. By using only IP traffic, your organization can:

- *Reduce the routing burdens associated with forwarding multiple protocols.* This benefit is twofold: First, the administrator does not have to program and maintain routers with both IPX and IP forwarding information; second, reducing the routing load to a single protocol extends the effectiveness of the router. For example, you might have to replace a saturated router in the IPX/SPX and TCP/IP environment. However, scaling down to only TCP/IP might reduce router traffic to the point that you can save a great deal of money by keeping the existing router.

- *Conserve valuable network bandwidth.* Instead of transmitting two protocols over the wire, each host transmits only one.

- *Eliminate the need to support other client protocols* on desktop computers.

- *Optimize remote connectivity.* Transmitting multiple protocols makes an already slow dial-up modem connection even slower.

Versions

There are several versions of NetWare in use today. The most recent version, and the subject of the rest of this section, is NetWare 5.1. Here are the different versions of NetWare:

- NetWare 2.12

- NetWare 386 (became NetWare 3.11)

- NetWare 3.12

- NetWare 4.0 – 4.1

- IntraNetware 4.11

- NetWare 5.0

- NetWare 5.1

You are most likely to find NetWare 3.12 or later in production environments.

NetWare 5.1 Minimum Requirements

The minimum hardware requirements for a NetWare 5.1 server are as follows:

- A server-class PC with any Pentium II or higher processor.

- A DOS partition that will start the server and load the NetWare operating system. While the partition can be as small as 30–35 MB, Novell recommends 100 MB, which is very little considering the size of modern hard disks.

- At least 1.3 GB of disk space on the SYS volume beyond the DOS partition is needed for the standard NetWare components and WebSphere Application Server for NetWare. (**WebSphere** is an IBM application for building and managing web-based applications.)

- 128 MB of RAM is required for the standard NetWare components. Installing the WebSphere Application Server for NetWare requires 256 MB. Novell recommends 512 MB for higher-end servers.

The base software requirement to start the installation is DOS 3.3 or later. You can use a non-Microsoft version of DOS; Caldera DR-DOS 7 is included on the NetWare 5.1 License/Cryptography disk. The other software components that you will need are the NetWare 5.1 Operating System CD, the NetWare 5.1 License disk, and the Novell Client for DOS and Windows 3.1x. This client is useful for installing NetWare from an IPX NetWare server over the network. You will need the proper DOS CD-ROM drivers for your CD-ROM as well, unless the CD-ROM is bootable.

 If this is the first NetWare 5.1 server on your network, you must make sure that this server will be a reliable, accessible, and continuous part of the network, because it lays groundwork for the remainder of the enterprise installation and must be available.

You must have Supervisor rights (which allow you to perform administrative tasks) at the root of the NDS tree. If this is not the first NetWare 5.1 server on the network, you must have Supervisor rights to the container where the server will be installed. (A **container** is a general term for an Organization or Organizational Unit, which are hierarchical components of the NDS tree. All network objects must reside in a container in the tree.) You will need to have read rights to the Security container object for the NDS tree as well.

You may also need some optional client connection utilities for installing from a network such as the Novell Client for DOS and Windows 3.1x. This allows you to boot a computer from DOS or Windows 3.x, connect to an IPX network share on a NetWare server running IPX, and install NetWare. If connecting to an IP server, use the IP Server Connection Utility instead.

Creating a floppy that both loads the appropriate network card drivers and connects to an IP host over the network can be quite time-consuming, frustrating, and filled with trial and error. Fortunately, Novell includes specific instructions for creating such a floppy in the file named Products\serverinst\ipconn.txt on the Novell client CD. Although these instructions don't work for every network card and every IP network connection, at least they provide a good groundwork for creating your own IP network boot floppy.

This book makes no attempt to detail each individual step in performing an operating system installation. Instead, the purpose of each respective operating system's installation section is to provide an overview of the installation process.

Installing NetWare 5.1

To install NetWare 5.1 on a server:

1. Create an MS-DOS primary partition and set it to active using FDISK. This will be your boot partition that boots to DOS and loads NetWare as well as any drivers for your CD-ROM, SCSI drives, and so forth. The installation will suggest a partition size for you. If you want to record **memory core dump** data (a representation of the contents of memory in the event of a problem, also known as simply a "memory dump"), size the partition to the recommended size plus the amount of RAM in your system. For example, if the installation recommends 100 MB and you have 512 MB of RAM, the optimum partition size would be 612 MB. Most server operating systems offer some facility to store memory dump data, but it is extremely complex and is usually meaningful only to programmers adept at its interpretation.

2. If you boot from the CD-ROM, the installation automatically seeks a suitable boot partition and, if none is found, offers to create one for you. This partition will contain the necessary files to start NetWare.

 Creating a bootable partition during installation will delete all data on the hard disk, even data on other partitions.

3. Booting from the NetWare 5.1 installation CD starts the installation for you. If using a boot floppy to access the CD-ROM, insert the NetWare 5.1 CD. At the CD drive or network drive prompt, enter Install. The initial screens of the installation program will display in text-based mode. You can accept the detected and default settings, or you can modify the settings to meet the needs of your networking environment. You can also start the installation by booting with the network floppy mentioned earlier to access the installation files from a server.

Booting from a floppy requires you to create a bootable MS-DOS system disk with drivers for your CD-ROM drive. Also, you must create an Autoexec.bat and Config.sys file and make sure that the logical filename of your CD drive (specified in the Config.sys and Autoexec.bat files) is not CDROM or CDINST. The Config.sys file must contain a FILES=40 and BUFFERS=30 statement.

4. As you go through the installation, you will see prompts to confirm or select various hardware in the system. For example, Figure 8-2 shows that NetWare detected several drivers that would work for the installed NIC, so I had to choose the correct one.

```
NetWare Installation

Multiple drivers were found that support the following ADAPTER:
  PRODID: PCI.1022.2000.0000.0000.10  BUS: PCI  CLASS: LAN
  HINNAME: PCI.SLOT_2  HINNUMBER: 2  SUBCLASS: ETHER
Select the driver (LAN) that best matches your system, or press F10.

  CNEAMD.LAN  | Novell Ethernet PCnetPCI, PCnetPCI_II, PCnet-Fast
  PCNTNW.LAN  | AMD Ethernet PCnet-FAST, PCnet-FAST+
  PCNTNW.LAN  | AMD Ethernet PCnet-PCI, PCnet-PCI_II

        "Supported Hardware" PCNTNW.LAN
        AMD PCnet-PCI, PCnet-PCI II Ethernet card
        "Help" PCNTNW.LAN
        This driver (PCNTNW.LAN) supports the network
        board installed in an PCI system.
              (To scroll, <F7>-up <F8>-down)

Enter=Select a driver
Alt+F10=Exit  F10=Continue-no selection  F3=Display full list        F1=Help
```

Figure 8-2   Verify or select the correct hardware during NetWare installation

I recommend using a NIC that is known to be automatically detected by the installation. Otherwise, you must specify the make and model of the network card from a list or provide the drivers from a floppy. Unfortunately, some NIC manufacturers no longer make a NetWare driver, so this might be limiting. After specifying the NIC, specify its resources such as IRQ, I/O port, and so forth. This can involve a great deal of trial and error as you determine which resources are available and which resources work with that particular network card. Automatically detected cards usually do not require you to manually specify resources.

5. Choose how you want to partition the hard disk space (see Figure 8-3).

The first volume NetWare creates is called the SYS volume, and Novell recommends you make it at least 200 MB (a complete install with all documentation requires about 600 MB). This volume should be used for only NetWare system files and **NetWare Loadable Modules (NLMs)** (NetWare programs and applications)—not user data. This makes recovering a problematic system easier and faster, especially for backup and restore, and if you need to reinstall the SYS volume, doing so does not destroy user data.

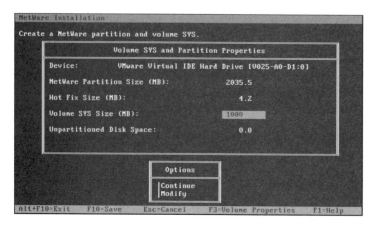

Figure 8-3 Choose how you want to partition the hard disk space

6. Continue with the installation and into the GUI mode, answering the questions based on your organizational requirements.

 During the text-based installation, much of your hardware is automatically detected, but do not expect this detection to be as thorough as Windows Plug and Play. Be familiar with the exact hardware in the server, because you might have to inform the installation of several items such as storage adapters (IDE or SCSI), PCI hot plug capability, or network boards. For example, if installation does not properly detect your network card, you will have to manually select it from a list of network boards or have the NetWare drivers for the card available on disk, and you might also have to enter the hardware resources that the board requires (IRQ, I/O address, and so forth).

Most of the NetWare 5.1 installation steps are self-explanatory; however, there are some key issues that you will need to address during the installation process, as follows:

- Decide which version of NDS you will use. NetWare 5.1 allows you to use either NDS 8 (default) or NDS 7. NDS 8 provides the enhanced NDS functionality needed by many new web networking products, such as WebSphere. If your NDS tree has not already been updated for NDS 8, you must have Supervisor rights at the root of the NDS tree to install NDS.

- You can create two types of volumes during the installation process: traditional NetWare volumes or Novell Storage Services (NSS) volumes, as discussed in Chapter 5. If you want an NSS volume, you must leave unallocated space on the hard disk and create the NSS volume after you have installed NetWare and booted the server.

- Specify the amount of space for a **hot fix** redirection area on the hard disk. NetWare verifies the integrity of all disk writes, and if a write fails this verification, the data is redirected to the hot fix area and the original destination is marked as unusable. The default size of the hot fix area is a small percentage of a partition's total size.

- As mentioned earlier, NetWare 5.1 can process IP network packets and traditional IPX packets. You can install networking protocols to support IP, IPX, or both. In the GUI installation stages, you can specify protocols. Novell's IPX allows you to continue using IPX-based applications. If IPX is the only protocol installed on your server, it will actively process IPX packets and ignore packets using other protocols, such as IP. If you have network clients or applications that require IPX and IP, you can install both protocols at the expense of more network traffic from clients as both protocols broadcast and communicate.

 You can also install IP with IPX Compatibility. This binds both protocols to a network card, with preference for communicating over IP. IPX is in passive mode, dormant until an IPX request arrives. Then, NetWare communicates using IPX. This is a graceful way to transfer to IP and support both protocols at a low cost to network bandwidth.

8

- Don't forget to enter a **host name record** (otherwise known as an **"A" record**) for the server prior to installation on your DNS server. During installation, you will enter one or more DNS name servers, and the NetWare server must be able to locate the name server and verify the host record. This is required in order to allow clients to find the server using its host name. (Chapter 9 further explains DNS.)

- You will either join the server to an existing tree or create a new one. A NetWare tree defines the structure of the organization, its subdivisions, and the objects contained therein. Objects (a resource such as servers, printers, users, and groups) reside in a context within the tree. Think of a context as a subdivided portion of the tree. For example, you install a file server for the graphics department of a company named KidHelp in Phoenix. The tree might be named KidHelp, and within that tree is the context. The context of the file server might appear something like O=Phoenix,OU=Graphics. (The root name is implied; you don't need to specify it when naming objects.)

- Finally, NetWare 5.1 must have a valid license in order to function as a server. You can install the license from the NetWare 5.1 License/Cryptography disk or browse to a directory that contains NetWare 5.1 licenses. Although the server can be installed without a license, the unlicensed server will allow only two user connections. After installation, you can use the NetWare Administrator utility to install additional licenses.

NetWare servers by default start from the MS-DOS partition when you turn on the server. If you like, you can start the server manually as follows:

1. Turn on the power, and the system will boot to an MS-DOS prompt on the boot partition (usually C:\).

2. Start the server by accessing the nwserver directory—type *CD \nwserver* and press Enter.

3. Type *server* and press Enter. The server starts and launches into the GUI. Many experienced NetWare administrators prefer to do a lot of the administration at the command line. You can close the GUI if you like and perform administration from the command console.

 TIP   You can also place these actions in Autoexec.bat to automatically start the server.

Creating NetWare Swap-File Space

Except for the SYS volume, NetWare volumes do not have default swap-file space. It is not advisable to use only the SYS volume for swap files, because this volume is typically already very busy. Instead, you should place one or more swap files on other high-performance volumes with plenty of free space. To add a swap file to a volume, execute the SWAP ADD command from a server console prompt. It does not matter if the volume is **mounted** (that is, ready for use). If not mounted, the swap file is created once you mount the volume. Swap files are deleted when the volume is dismounted, requiring you to re-create the swap file when it is mounted again. To avoid this inconvenience, you can add the SWAP ADD command to the startup file, Autoexec.ncf. NetWare swap files are dynamic, becoming larger or smaller as necessary. You can learn more about the SWAP command by typing *swap add* at a server console prompt.

Performing an Upgrade to NetWare 5.1

If you are upgrading an existing server from a previous version of NetWare, the installation will detect the previous version and prompt you to either upgrade or start a new installation. Upgrading will retain all your server data such as files, directory structures, partitions, and volumes. During an upgrade, the upgrade program may skip entire sections otherwise seen in a new installation, as the upgrade program automatically detects and configures several of the setup tasks. You can upgrade an existing server running NetWare 3.x, NetWare 4.x, or NetWare 5 to NetWare 5.1.

Before introducing a NetWare 5.1 server into an existing network that contains NetWare 4.x servers, run the NetWare Deployment Manager to prepare the NetWare 4.x version of NDS for an upgrade to NetWare 5.1 NDS.

To update an existing NetWare 4.x network to NetWare 5.1, you must log on from a Windows 95/98 or NT workstation as a Supervisor. Next, run NetWare Deployment Manager (Nwdeploy.exe) from the NetWare 5.1 Operating System CD and complete the network preparation tasks.

After you have completed the Network Preparation section of NetWare Deployment Manager, you should prepare the computer to be a NetWare server. NetWare 5.1 simplifies the NDS upgrade process by verifying that your NDS tree is ready for the version that you choose to implement.

TIP Access more in-depth information on installation and upgrading to Novell NetWare 5.1 at *www.novell.com/documentation/*.

Performing a Proper NetWare Shutdown

To properly shut down a NetWare server:

1. Close the GUI by clicking the red Novell item in the lower left corner of the screen.

2. Select the Close GUI item, and answer "Yes" to the confirmation prompt. When the GUI closes, you are left at the "Servername:" prompt, where servername is the name of the NetWare server.

3. Type *down* and press Enter to close all services and files. A handy feature of NetWare is that in this process, a notification of the downed server is delivered to all attached workstations. If you would rather just reboot the server, type *restart server* and press Enter.

 For NetWare 4.11, you must also type *exit* and press Enter.

4. At the C:\NWSERVER prompt, turn off the power.

UNIX/LINUX

I don't typically like to give history lessons on computing, but for UNIX, it is relevant and explains why there are dozens of different versions. UNIX is an interactive time-sharing operating system invented in 1969 by Ken Thompson. Brian Kernighan and Dennis Ritchie, the inventors of C, are also considered coauthors of the operating system. UNIX is a popular multiuser, multitasking operating system designed to be small and flexible and used mostly by programmers. Although it has developed significantly over the years, UNIX still uses its original cryptic command names along with its general lack of user friendliness. This is changing, however, with graphical user interfaces such as **X Windows** and **GNOME**.

UNIX has been a popular choice among universities and corporations because of its low cost and the fact that programmers familiar with the C high-level programming language can modify the code to specific requirements. UNIX has split into two main dialects: AT&T's System V and the University of California, Berkeley version known as BSD 4.1, 4.2, or 4.3. Within the two main versions, there are dozens of other modified versions ("flavors").

Most UNIX flavors are designed for CISC-based computing. For our purposes, we will focus on Linux, because it is a PC-compatible flavor of UNIX, the Server+ exam is PC-centric, and most anything that would be true of Linux for our purposes also applies sufficiently to UNIX.

Linux is a version of UNIX that, like other flavors, is open source code. Linus Torvalds authored early versions of Linux with the objective of creating a relatively small UNIX source code that would run on Intel-compatible computers (as opposed to the CISC-based processors of other UNIX versions). Boxed versions of Linux available from the vendors listed in the next section of this chapter are preferable in many cases, because although you have to pay for the boxed version, the coding has already been tested, associated tools are included, and technical support is available. Linux has become one of the hottest operating systems in the past few years, and has unexpectedly begun to compete strongly against Microsoft Windows NT/2000.

One potential challenge to the new Linux user is the plethora of new commands, features, applications, and other components. As you familiarize yourself with Linux, realize that much of its administration, especially with early versions of Linux, involves the command line. If you are accustomed to MS-DOS commands, you will have to make a point of *not* using MS-DOS commands in Linux: They don't work. You can tap into more about Linux commands by looking on the hard disk at the /usr/doc files after installation is complete. On all Linux distributions, there is a huge amount of miscellaneous documentation stored in this /usr/doc/ directory. Each version of Linux makes its own directories under /usr/doc where it places files like FAQs and installation guides. There are many sources of information on Linux on the Internet as well. One central clearinghouse is the Linux documentation project located at *www.linuxdoc.org*.

Linux offers all the services and features you would expect to see on a server, including:

- IP services like DHCP, DNS, web hosting, and firewall support
- Application support for a wide range of applications such as IBM's mainstream database product, DB2, Sun Microsystem's office suite, StarOffice 5.2, and Computer Associates' ArcServIT backup software
- Mail server services
- File and printer services
- SMP support
- E-commerce support
- Clustering and load balancing

Versions

There are several versions of Linux because of its open source code, and there are many vendors from whom you can obtain boxed sets of Linux. The major Linux vendors are listed here:

- *SuSE Linux.* You can find an installation guide in several different formats for SuSE on an FTP server at *ftp://ftp.suse.com/pub/suse/i386/current/docu/*.

- *Caldera Linux.* This company also offers Caldera Volution, which is a Linux management solution designed for network management. You can get more information on this flavor at *www.caldera.com*.

- *Mandrake Linux.* The install guide for this Pentium-optimized Linux version can be found at *www.linux-mandrake.com*.

- *Debian Linux.* You will find the "Guide to Installing the Free Software Foundations Debian Linux on Intel-Based Machines" at *www.debian.org*.

- *Red Hat Linux 7.x.* This is probably the most popular build of Linux. The Red Hat "Getting Started Guide," installation FAQs, and other important documentation can be downloaded from *www.redhat.com/support/*. The FAQs list minimum system requirements in addition to more technical issues. Unless stated otherwise, Linux references in this book are to Red Hat.

Linux Minimum Hardware Requirements

Unlike some other versions of UNIX for the PC, Linux is very small. You could actually download one of the smaller, free releases and run an entire system from a single high-density 5.25-inch floppy! To run a complete Linux system on today's computers, there are obviously other hardware requirements. Linux, because of its open source nature, is continuously expanding, with more features being added every day. Hardware compatibility is very broad, especially compared to the earliest releases of Linux. Check with the Linux vendor, but most commonly available video cards, SCSI drivers, NICs, and so forth should be supported.

Linux hardware requirements are humble, but particular. You do not need to have the most advanced or most recent server to run Linux. As with all operating systems discussed in this chapter, there are two primary options for obtaining a computer to run Linux. The first option is to buy a computer with Linux preinstalled. In my view, this is the best alternative if you need a business server or high-performance workstation, and it applies to all NOSs. You can choose from brand-name machines like Dell, VA Research, Compaq, HP, and many other top PC manufacturers. Red Hat posts a list of certified systems by manufacturer on its web site (*www.redhat.com*). Also look for upcoming systems that will use the 64-bit processing power of the AMD Sledgehammer.

A second viable option is to use an existing PC or assemble one and then perform a custom Linux installation. This is somewhat more common in the Linux community because of a "do-it-yourself" attitude prevalent among Linux fans. A disadvantage to rolling out your own Linux implementation is that there is no support except for what is freely available through newsgroups and web sites. If a critical Linux server experiences a failure, you are unlikely to have the patience required to post a newsgroup message and then wait a couple of days for an answer (if any). With major server vendors, you usually have 24/7 emergency software and operating system support as well as overnight delivery for failed hardware.

Hardware compatibility is most important if you are installing on an older system or building a new system from scratch. Red Hat Linux 7.x should be compatible with most hardware in systems that were factory built within the last couple of years. With hardware specifications changing almost daily, however, there is never any guarantee that your hardware will be 100% compatible. Therefore, you should collect all of the system hardware information that you can. *The Official Red Hat Linux Reference Guide* on the Documentation CD has instructions in the Installation-Related Reference area (including instructions for Windows users) that will assist you. You can also use Red Hat's online resources to make sure that your hardware is compatible. The easily navigable hardware compatibility list is located at: *hardware.redhat.com.*

Linux hardware requirements are somewhat inexact since multiple vendors have different requirements. However, for a basic installation, most any server should suffice. This is because Linux code is exceptionally trim compared to larger operating systems such as Windows 2000 Server with its 40 million lines of code. However, as with other NOSs, remember that more is better when it comes to running a production server. General minimum hardware requirements for Linux are as follows:

- *Intel 80386 processor or higher.* Intel-compatible processors such as AMD and Cyrix also work with Linux.

- *32 MB of RAM.* Although you can locate and download very thin Linux versions requiring as little as 2 MB, feature-complete Linux versions such as Red Hat Linux usually recommend 64 MB.

- *500 MB of hard disk space.* Although if you install absolutely all features in a Red Hat installation, you'll need nearly 2 GB. (So much for the trim Linux OS.)

Installing Linux

Linux is very flexible about coexisting with other operating systems, and the **Linux Loader (LILO)** allows you to select which operating system you want to boot when you start the server. As a general rule, configuring the system to boot to more than one operating system is usually a smoother process if you install the other operating system(s) first, and Linux last.

When you read Red Hat Linux documentation, you might see mention of a partitionless installation. Do not mistake this to mean that the installation does not use a partition at all. A **partitionless** installation is a reference to using an existing DOS or Windows partition instead of creating a partition manually during installation using FDISK or Red Hat's **Disk Druid** partitioning tool.

Although you can choose from several methods to install Red Hat Linux, this chapter assumes installation from the CD-ROM. Absent the CD-ROM, you can make an installation floppy disk to initiate an installation, for example, because you downloaded Red Hat Linux rather than purchasing an official boxed set. You need to use the Linux boot floppy to launch the installation as opposed to booting an MS-DOS floppy and running Setup.exe. To begin the process, you will need a blank, formatted, high-density (1.44 MB) 3.5-inch floppy disk. The images directory in the Red Hat Linux source files contains the boot images for various contexts such as a standard boot to the Linux installation program, activating a PCMCIA socket, or booting to a Linux network share location. Extract the image file to a floppy using the *rawrite* utility found in the dosutils directory.

8

If your system doesn't support a CD-ROM (**El Torito**) boot, Red Hat Linux offers another choice that still allows you to start the installation directly from a CD-ROM. Use a boot floppy that loads your CD-ROM drivers (such as the Windows 98 boot floppy) and run the Autoboot.bat file from the \dosutils directory on the Linux CD-ROM to start the installation. (You cannot just boot to the floppy and then run a Setup.exe or Install.exe file from the CD-ROM.)

Although you can use a text-based Linux installation, we will assume use of a GUI installation. You can select the same options during both installations, except that the GUI version also offers explanations of your options to the left of the screen and is more intuitive. At the opening installation screen, press Enter or wait 60 seconds for the GUI installation to automatically begin. (If you insist, you can type *text* and press Enter at the Welcome screen to enter text-based setup.) As with the other NOS installations addressed in this chapter, not every installation step and option is listed. However, the basic Red Hat Linux 7.0 steps are as follows:

1. Select the installation type: Workstation, Server System, or Custom System. One of the primary differences in these installations is how the partitions are handled (see Figure 8-4).

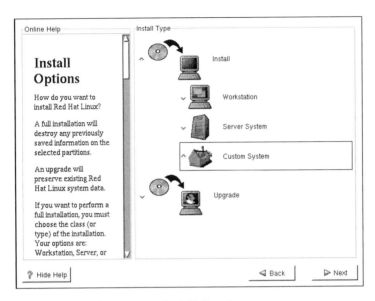

Figure 8-4   Select a Linux installation type

- *Workstation*: Removes all existing Linux partitions on all disks, and then uses all available unpartitioned space for the installation. Non–Linux partitions are left alone, and you can still boot to them after the Linux installation.

- *Server System*: Removes all partitions on all drives!

- *Custom System*: Provides an opportunity for you to manipulate free space and existing partitions to your liking.

We will proceed under the assumption of installing a Custom System.

2. Configure partitions using either the Red Hat Linux Disk Druid utility or FDISK. As a minimum, you will need:

- Root partition ("/"), which is the main repository for files (except boot files).

- Swap partition equal to the amount of RAM in the system or 16 MB, whichever is larger.

- Boot partition ("/boot"), which contains the OS kernel, and as the name implies, boots to Linux. This partition does not need to be large and is usually no larger than 16 MB.

- Using the Disk Druid utility, you can also create a RAID 0, 1, or 5 array, and other partitions as it suits your needs. Figure 8-5 shows the Disk Druid utility being used to create partitions.

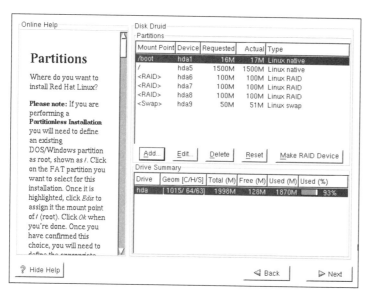

Figure 8-5   Creating partitions with Disk Druid

3. Enter the server's network configuration, including IP configuration, host name, gateway, and DNS server(s) (see Figure 8-6).

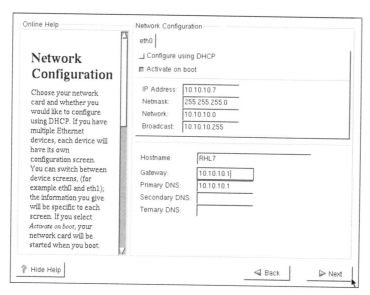

Figure 8-6   Configuring Linux IP settings

4. Select a root password, which allows you to completely administer the server. Also add one or more user accounts.

5. If you want to use security mechanisms such as MD5 passwords or Kerberos, configure the appropriate information.

6. Select the various features you want to install and proceed through the installation. Setup creates partitions as specified and copies installation files to the hard drive.

As addressed in Step 2 in the Installing Linux section, you create Linux swap-file space during installation using the Disk Druid utility.

Performing a Proper Linux Shutdown

There are three possible states you can end up in when you shut down a Linux server. You can place the server in one of these states either from a GUI interface or an **X Term** session, which is a text-based terminal interface within your GUI. The first state, while not technically a shutdown, is single-user mode. System administrators will often bring a UNIX system down to **single-user mode**, which closes user connections, to perform full backups of the file system, ensuring that there are no locks on open files. This is not a complete shutdown because the operating system is still running and the processor is still active, but from a network user perspective it is. To enter single-user mode, access a boot prompt and enter *Linux single*. When finished, you can restart the computer by pressing Ctrl+Alt+Del or entering the shutdown –r command (see below).

A second state is to completely shut down the system so that it is ready to be powered off. A complete shutdown is often done when hardware maintenance is planned for the machine or any other time the machine is to be powered off. A shutdown of this type uses the shutdown –h command (-h meaning "halt") to specify that the system should be completely shut down and the processor halted. When you halt the system, all processes are killed, and the sync command is called to write the memory-resident disk buffers to disk, after which the CPU is halted.

If you truly want the power to be turned off with the shutdown command, press the power switch on the server. The shutdown –h command only kills processes and halts the CPU — but the power remains on.

The third state is when the system is being rebooted. The shutdown –r command (-r meaning "reboot") accomplishes a reboot. If you are in text mode instead of a GUI (not a virtual console), press Ctrl+Alt+Del. On an MS-DOS computer, this would reboot with any running applications still active and files still open, possibly damaging the system or data. A Linux computer will close files and kill services and applications before rebooting.

You can log out, reboot, or halt from any of the GUI interfaces such as GNOME using the Start style button in the lower left of the screen — select Logout and make your choice (see Figure 8-7).

Figure 8-7   Choose to logout, halt, or reboot the Linux server

Once a system is brought up to **multi-user mode** (meaning the server and its resources are available to network clients), it is common for the system to run for many days, possibly even months, without being shut down or rebooted.

8

OS/2

OS/2 is an operating system for personal computers developed originally by Microsoft and IBM, but sold and managed exclusively by IBM. OS/2 is compatible with DOS and Windows; therefore, it can run most DOS and Windows programs in addition to native OS/2 applications. OS/2 is known for rock-solid performance and reliability on high-end server platforms, which is one reason why it is favored in many banking and financial institutions. In fact, it is likely that when you use an ATM bank card, an OS/2 server actually performs the transaction. Also, OS/2 is the preferred platform for IBM's Lotus Notes email application.

Despite its strengths, OS/2's Presentation Manager interface is showing its age when compared to the Windows NT/2000 desktop, and IBM's marketing department doesn't appear to be addressing the issue as Windows 2000 outsells all other NOSs today. As a result, existing OS/2 markets are starting to slip and IBM is having difficulty breaking into new markets. Many speculate about IBM's support of OS/2 although IBM asserts that it stands firmly behind the product now and for the future.

OS/2 is available as a workstation product (OS/2 Warp 4), a server product (Warp Server 4), and an e-commerce server product (OS/2 Warp Server for E-business). Unless otherwise specified, the remainder of this book refers only to the server products collectively as "OS/2."

OS/2 has many outstanding characteristics as follows:

- It is very flexible. You can connect to most any type of server, including all of IBM's other servers (AS/400, for example), NetWare, and Windows NT/2000. Moreover, you can connect an OS/2 domain to an NT domain transparently — users can access resources across both platforms without additional logons.

- The **Journaled File System (JFS)** of OS/2 Warp Server for E-business provides astonishing file system stability. JFS keeps a journal of file writes and, in the event of corruption, can restore data in a matter of minutes or seconds, usually transparently to users. If the system must be rebooted, OS/2 plays back the journal, immediately recovering all the data. Also, JFS increases the maximum file size from 2 GB to 2 TB.

- The **Logical Volume Manager (LVM)** feature allows you to span a single partition across multiple physical disks, and partitions can increase in size without reformatting. You can also add or move hard drives without altering the drive letter.

- The OS/2 TCP/IP stack is very robust and capable (supporting up to 64,000 concurrent sockets), offers improved buffer management, is optimized for HTTP connections, and the FTP and TFTP utilities are now multithreaded applications.

- OS/2 supports up to 64 processors out of the box—server vendors do not need to develop specialized drivers to enable this support.

- OS/2 supports **Dynamic DNS**, the ability to accept name registrations from DHCP clients automatically. (Otherwise, somebody has to manually enter all the records and remove or change outdated records.)

- Its advanced printing capability allows printing PostScript files to non-PostScript printers.

- Built-in alerts warn administrators in advance of hardware problems such as low disk space or exceeding a CPU threshold.

Versions

OS/2 versions are OS/2 LAN Server 1.0, 1.2, 1.3, 2.0, 3.0, 4.0, Warp Server 4, and Warp Server 4 for E-business. You are likely to see only a version of Warp 4 in today's servers.

OS/2 Minimum Hardware Requirements

The hardware requirements for OS/2 vary depending on the specific version of OS/2 Warp Server installed and the applications you wish to run on the machine. Here are the minimum requirements for OS/2 Warp Server for E-business:

- Intel-compatible 133 MHz processor or better

- 64 MB of RAM

- 120 MB of hard disk space for base operating system, or 200 MB for the operating system plus all default components

To ensure that your hardware is compatible with OS/2, search for IBM's Device Driver Pack at *www.software.IBM.com/os/warp/support*.

Installing OS/2

To install OS/2 Warp Server for E-business:

1. Insert the bootable CD-ROM and boot the server. If the server is not compatible with El Torito, create a set of three boot floppy disks using the CDINST utility located on the included Server Pak CD-ROM. Booting from these disks will allow access to most CD-ROMs.

2. The OS/2 CD scans the system, looking for the number of processors installed in the system. Also, a conversion utility automatically marks any existing volumes for conversion to the new LVM partitioning scheme.

 OS/2 no longer uses FDISK to manage partitions; instead, the LVM utility performs partitioning functions.

3. Upon reboot, use LVM to specify the partition on which you want to install OS/2. Set the partition as installable and press F3 to exit the LVM utility, saving changes when you exit.

4. Formatting options appear. For a clean install, choose to format using a long format (similar to an MS-DOS unconditional format). This formatting process can take several minutes depending on the size of the volume. However, it marks bad blocks on the disk so that data is not saved there.

5. Upon reboot into a GUI, a panel appears from which you can confirm detected hardware or make changes as necessary. From this GUI, you will select locale, keyboard, mouse, CD-ROM, printers, SCSI adapters, power management, and so forth (see Figure 8-8).

6. Select the services you want to install (see Figure 8-9) and proceed through the interface to select the file system options you want (HPFS and/or JFS).

7. After a reboot, you must select the LAN server components, again using a GUI. These components include the TCP/IP configuration, file and print sharing services, remote access capabilities, and so forth.

8. Finish the installation, and OS/2 is ready to boot into production.

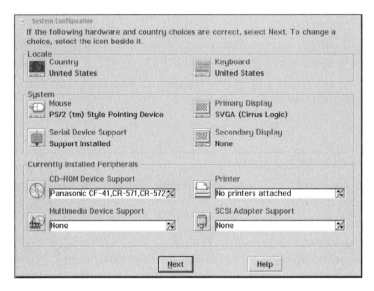

Figure 8-8   Change the OS/2 system configuration as necessary

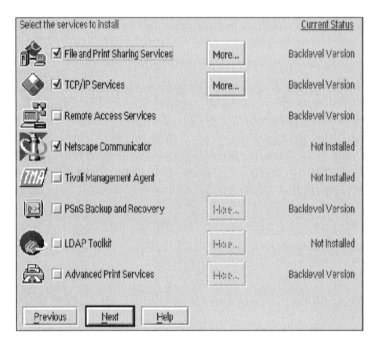

Figure 8-9   Choose from a list of available OS/2 server services

Performing an Upgrade to OS/2 Warp

Upgrading OS/2 is a process much like the installation described, except that previous settings from the OS/2 installation are preserved. During the upgrade, you can choose to migrate existing configuration files to the Config.sys and Autoexec.bat files. Because these files are much more complex under OS/2 than in most Microsoft MS-DOS/Windows installations, you might want to keep these settings to avoid reconfiguring the files from scratch. Near the end of the upgrade (which IBM refers to as a "migration"), a comparison panel appears that allows you to compare the previous configuration file to the new configuration file. You can edit the new configuration as necessary.

 For existing servers, run the CHKINST utility that comes with OS/2 Warp Server to check your installation and generate a log file report of steps you should take before performing setup.

 Run the PREPMNT utility to upgrade disk drivers (if necessary) prior to upgrading to OS/2 Warp Server.

Creating OS/2 Swap-File Space

A swap file is used in OS/2 as in most other operating systems. Configure the swap file by adding a line to the startup file, Config.sys, as follows:

SWAPPATH=<DriveLetter and Path> *InitialSize MaximumSize*

For example, to configure a swap file on drive C with an initial size of 8 MB and a maximum size of 20 MB, you would enter:

SWAPPATH=C: \OS2\SYSTEM 8192 2048

The swap file is stored by default in the \OS2\SYSTEM directory and is named Swapper.dat.

Performing a Proper OS/2 Shutdown

To shut down OS/2, right-click anywhere on the Warp 4 desktop, and select Shut down from the menu. You can also lock the computer (which requires user credentials to unlock), or log off the network.

 IBM's *www.redbooks.ibm.com* site is a very well-documented source of OS/2 information.

WINDOWS NT SERVER

Organizations currently using Windows NT Server primarily use Windows NT 4.0. Though you might occasionally find version 3.51, this book focuses on NT 4.0 to be current with most environments and because what is true of NT 4.0 is also true of NT 3.51 for our purposes.

The original version of Windows NT was scheduled as a cooperative effort with IBM and was supposed to be another version of OS/2.

Windows NT 4.0 offers the following operating system characteristics:

- A Windows 95-based interface makes it easy to locate administrative tools and applications, and makes it easier to operate compared to command-line-based operating systems (such as the earlier versions of NetWare and Linux).

- The interface and architecture make Windows NT capable of running local user applications—word processors, spreadsheets, even a game of Solitaire if nobody's looking. Other network operating systems, such as earlier versions of NetWare, are not designed for local application support.

Even though you can install user applications on a server, it is better to avoid this. Fewer applications mean less overhead in terms of memory, processor, and hard disk utilization, freeing those resources for true server functions. Also, using an application on a local server requires you to log on, and this is not prudent for most production servers because of the security risk involved if a passerby accesses your logged-on server while you are away from the server.

- Windows NT supports all the major TCP/IP services necessary for an IP network, including DNS, DHCP, and even a basic routing facility, though software routing cannot usually compare to a true hardware router.

- The architecture of Windows is such that it allows a simple user interface while simultaneously limiting what the user can do. Even Windows NT 4.0 Workstation does not allow users to make major changes to the system (such as installing applications). This significantly reduces the administrators support burden, because user-installed applications often adversely affect the stability of the operating system.

- Windows NT introduces domains to the network. A Windows NT **domain** is different than an Internet domain (which is the hierarchical naming facility of the Internet) and is mostly implemented as a security boundary. For example, users in Domain A can access resources in Domain A. If the organization also has a Domain B, users in Domain A cannot cross domains to access resources unless administrators specifically create a trust relationship between the two domains.

- The NTFS file system is Microsoft's first effort at securing hard disk resources, and especially for a first effort, they did a great job. Only persons to whom permission is granted can access a given file or folder. (See more on NTFS in Chapter 5.)

- Windows NT supports multiple protocols, including NetBEUI, IPX/SPX, and TCP/IP.

Windows NT Server 4.0 Minimum Hardware Requirements

Windows NT Server 4.0 has fairly high hardware requirements compared to NetWare 3.x and 4.x, Windows NT 4.0's primary competition at its introduction in 1996. However, at current levels of commonly available hardware, the requirements should not be difficult to match or exceed. The minimum system hardware requirements are as follows:

- Intel-compatible 486/25 MHz processor

- 16 MB of RAM

- 124 MB of hard disk space

 Each NOS lists minimum hardware requirements that are well below what you would actually want in a production environment, but the NT minimums are probably the least realistic.

Access the Hardware Compatibility List (HCL) from the Microsoft web site at *www.microsoft.com/hcl.*

Installing Windows NT 4.0 Server

Installing Windows NT 4.0 Server is a fairly straightforward process. First, you must find a way to access the CD-ROM. The easiest way is to configure the BIOS settings in an El Torito-compatible system that can automatically access and boot from the CD-ROM. If your system is not El Torito-compatible, you can use the three floppy disks in the Windows NT boxed set. Boot from the first floppy and change disks when prompted. These disks also load CD-ROM drivers so that you can access the source files on CD-ROM. Finally and as a last resort, use any MS-DOS system boot floppy (such as a Windows 98 startup disk) that also loads your CD-ROM drivers.

Though you can launch setup after booting from a Windows 98 startup disk, it has several drawbacks. Windows NT does not recognize FAT32 partitions, so if you use a Windows 98 startup disk to create partitions, be sure to answer "N" (no) at the FDISK prompt to enable large disk support, which causes partitions to be formatted for FAT32. Otherwise, Windows NT will not be able to locate a suitable partition in which to copy installation files. Also, booting from a Windows 98 startup disk "locks" the hard drive, which means that the Windows NT installation will not be able to copy files to it. If you use a Windows 98 startup disk, type "lock c:" at a command prompt to remedy this situation. Also, there must be an existing FAT partition of at least 123 MB to store setup files. These drawbacks make booting from the Windows 98 floppy the least attractive choice, but it will do if necessary.

1. After booting from the CD-ROM or NT boot floppies, setup begins automatically, and you can skip to Step 4. If booting from a boot floppy with CD-ROM drivers, change to the CD-ROM drive (we'll assume it's drive D).

 TIP Installation proceeds much faster with both Windows NT and Windows 2000 if you first copy the Smart Drive executable to the boot floppy. Smart Drive caches read from the CD-ROM. At the MS-DOS prompt, simply type SMARTDRV to load Smart Drive. This only applies to installations that use a manually configured MS-DOS or Windows 98 boot floppy because the Windows NT boot floppy and bootable CD-ROM automatically load caching.

2. Go to the \i386 directory. This is the directory used for installing NT to an Intel-based PC server. However, you can also install Windows NT on a PowerPC, MIPS, or Alpha-processor-based server.

3. Type *winnt /b* and press Enter. This initiates the text mode portion of setup, which starts by copying setup files to the local hard disk (see Figure 8-10).

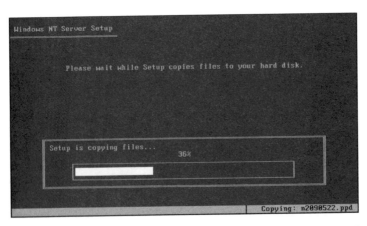

Figure 8-10 The Windows NT 4.0 file copy stage of text mode setup

 Note The "/b" prevents manual creation of the three boot floppy disks, which can also be created after installation by typing *winnt /ox* from a command line in Windows NT. These disks are duplicates of the floppies included in the NT box and are useful for accessing the CD-ROM to start setup and for repairing an ailing NT installation.

4. Proceed through the setup process, following the prompts. You are prompted to specify any additional storage devices such as SCSI cards that might not have been detected by setup (see Figure 8-11). If so, supply the drivers from a floppy disk. (If you booted from a generic floppy, a reboot occurs between Step 3 and 4).

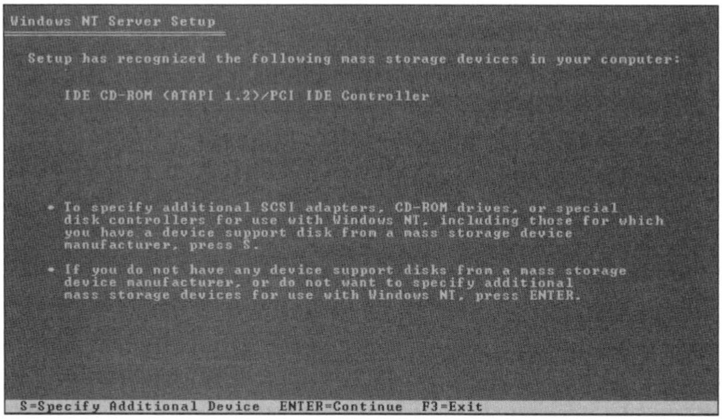

Figure 8-11   Add additional drivers for devices not detected by setup

5. Basic hardware detection finds hardware such as keyboard, mouse, and display adapters. This level of device detection is very basic; a more in-depth and accurate detection occurs closer to the end of the setup process (see Figure 8-12).

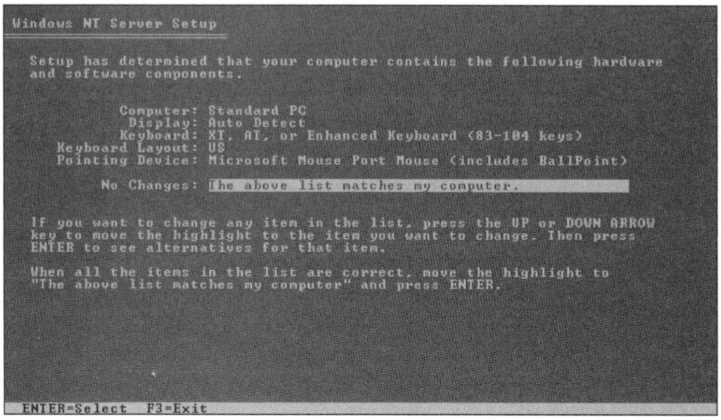

Figure 8-12   Basic device detection as determined by Windows NT 4.0

6. Select a partition in which to install the operating system. If none of the existing partitions suit you, you can delete or create other partitions. Assuming that you started with a FAT partition, setup offers you the chance to convert to an NTFS partition. For sake of performance and security, it is normally best to choose the NTFS conversion at this point (see Figure 8-13).

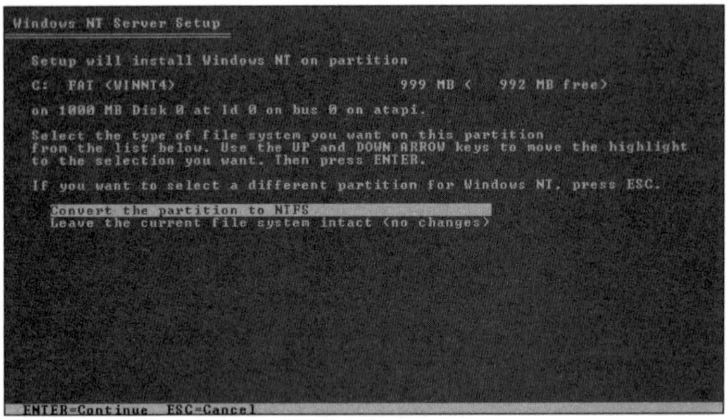

Figure 8-13 Convert partitions to NTFS

You can also convert from FAT to NTFS after NT is installed, except that this conversion does not apply security permissions to certain sensitive system directories for Windows NT. Use the C2 Configuration utility included in the Windows NT 4.0 Resource Kit to automatically reset default permissions. If you convert to NTFS during setup, however, default security permissions are applied.

7. Setup copies more files to the hard disk. When prompted, press Enter to reboot the system. If you opted to convert from FAT to NTFS, the conversion takes place. This concludes the text portion of the setup process. The graphical portion begins after the reboot.

8. Enter your name and organization.

The name you enter here is the name of the person legally liable for properly licensing the product. So if at all possible, enter your boss's name.

9. Enter the CD Key that accompanied the product.

10. Select a licensing mode (see Figure 8-14):

   ■ **Per server**: Enter the number of concurrent connections allowed under the licensing scheme you purchased. Choose this method if clients will usually connect to only one server. If you have 100 users connecting to four servers, then each server would require 100 licenses—a total of 400. This would not be cost-effective.

   ■ **Per seat**: Each client that connects to this server must be properly licensed. This is much more cost-effective than the per-server licensing scheme if clients connect to multiple servers. Continuing the earlier example, a per-seat licensing solution would require only 100 client licenses, one for each user workstation regardless of the number of servers to which the client connects. You can convert from per server to per seat, and money spent on per-server licensing can be directly applied to the new per-seat licensing scheme. Conversion is a one-time, one-way event. You cannot convert from per seat back to per server.

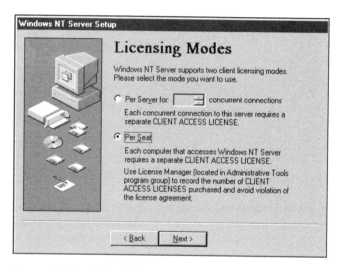

Figure 8-14   Select the per-server or per-seat licensing mode

11. Enter a computer name. This name is how the server is identified and must be unique within the network.

12. Choose the role of this NT server (see Figure 8-15):

- **Primary Domain Controller (PDC)** — Stores the only read/write copy of the directory database. This database is a record of user and computer accounts, and is used for logging on users.

- **Backup Domain Controller (BDC)** — Stores a read-only copy of the directory database, and is useful as an extension to the PDC for logging on users and computers. You must have a PDC before you can have a BDC.

- **Stand-alone Server** — Does not store the directory database and is not a member of the domain. This type of server does not share users or groups from the domain controller, but is useful for other resources and services for which users do not require direct access (for example, a web server allowing anonymous access or a DNS server).

- **Member Server** — Is a member of the domain but does not contain a copy of the directory database. Because it is a member of the domain, administrators can configure access permissions to its resources using domain user and group accounts. To configure a member server, you install it as a Stand-alone server, and later join it to the domain. A member server can be useful as a file, print, or application server, or provide one or more services (see Chapter 9).

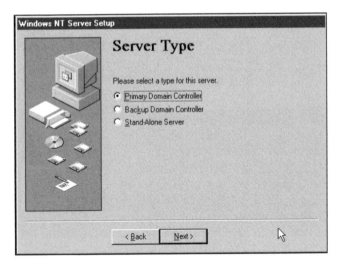

Figure 8-15   Select a role for the server

13. Continue through the installation, answering prompts and choosing installation options. You will enter a password for the local Administrator account (don't forget it) and install a network adapter if one is not detected automatically.

 If you experience difficulty installing the network card at this point but want to proceed with the installation, choose the MS Loopback Adapter, which is a software trick allowing you to install networking components without an actual physical network adapter.

14. When finished with all the setup prompts, the system boots to the standard Windows NT 4.0 desktop.

Upgrading to Windows NT 4.0 Server

To initiate the upgrade, just insert the Windows NT 4.0 Server CD into the CD-ROM drive. A prompt appears to automatically begin installation or you can run Winnt32.exe from the \i386 directory. Despite Microsoft's own success in upgrades, I still recommend a clean install whenever possible, because an upgraded system can inherit remnant bugs or files that are not used in Windows NT 4.0.

 Winnt.exe executes the Windows NT/2000 setup process from MS-DOS. From within existing Windows operating systems that you want to upgrade, use Winnt32.exe.

Creating Windows NT 4.0 Swap-File Space

Windows automatically creates its own swap file as part of installation. Typically, the swap-file defaults are of acceptable size, though you might want to change the drive on which the paging file appears for performance reasons (see Chapter 11).

To modify **paging file** configuration (as it is called in NT 4.0/Windows 2000):

1. Right-click My Computer on the desktop (or double-click the System icon in Control Panel).

2. Select Properties from the menu.

3. Click the Performance tab, and then click the Change button in the middle of the dialog box (see Figure 8-16).

4. Specify the drive, initial size, and maximum size. Remember to click the Set button after configuring the paging file.

5. Click OK twice.

6. Reboot the system.

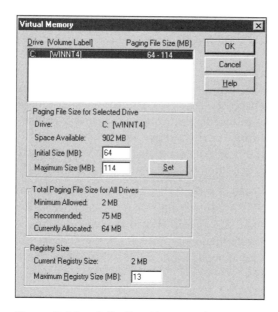

Figure 8-16   Adjusting the virtual memory paging file

Performing a Proper Windows NT 4.0 Shutdown

Shutting down any Windows operating system is very easy. Simply click Start, click Shut Down, and select from a list of options to shut down the computer, restart the computer, or close all programs and log on as a different user (see Figure 8-17). When the computer is "shut down," you must still turn off the power, or you can click a Restart button if you change your mind and want to reboot the operating system.

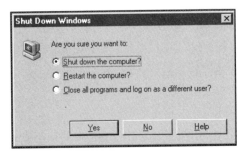

Figure 8-17   Choose to shut down, restart, or log off

WINDOWS 2000

The Windows 2000 operating system family from Microsoft provides a significant advancement in features, stability, and increased runtime over its venerable NT predecessor. Although we will continue to see Windows NT 4.0 on servers everywhere for a few more years, Windows 2000 looks poised to eclipse NT 4.0 in many organizations.

The characteristics of Windows 2000 are as follows:

- The primary characteristic of Windows 2000 is arguably its new directory service, known as Active Directory. **Active Directory** is a comprehensive database capable of storing millions of objects such as users, groups, computers, and more. In terms of functionality, Active Directory users can log on and access resources anywhere in the enterprise regardless of geographic location or where the user account was originally created.

- Active Directory domains evolved from the original Windows NT 4.0 domains. Whereas under Windows NT an organization might have multiple domains in a flat namespace such as Domain A, Domain B, and Domain C, Active Directory uses a DNS hierarchy such as DomainA.DomainB.DomainC. Also, Active Directory provides a structure allowing administrators to consolidate all NT 4.0 domains into a single domain.

NetWare administrators will notice some similarities between the tree structure of NetWare 4.x and later and Windows 2000 Active Directory. This is because both operating systems use the LDAP standard.

- In the past, Microsoft environments have relied heavily on WINS as the name resolution service for Microsoft network NetBIOS hosts. Windows 2000 allows the administrator to shed the need for WINS because DHCP clients can automatically register themselves in the DNS database using Dynamic DNS. In the past, someone would have to manually enter DNS registrations. However, Windows 2000 still offers the WINS service to support NetBIOS clients.

- Windows 2000 offers strong **scalability** (the ability to grow in terms of the number of processors) in that you can use 4, 8, or even 32 or more processors in a single SMP system. To be fair, I should emphasize that all NOSs in this chapter support SMP. Microsoft claims to have an extremely efficient architecture that allows SMP systems to obtain a high level of performance.

- Up to 8 GB of memory support allows Windows 2000 Advanced Server to handle large and demanding files and applications.

- No other operating system offers as much broad hardware compatibility support, thanks to true Plug and Play capabilities.

- Built-in clustering support in Windows 2000 Advanced Server and Windows 2000 Datacenter Server allows a server in a cluster to fail or be removed for routine maintenance while remaining members of the cluster continue to provide service.

- Windows file protection prevents new software installations from replacing critical Windows 2000 system files. This makes Windows 2000 more stable than past Windows versions. Also, Microsoft has instituted a thorough testing process for hardware manufacturers, in which their drivers must be proven safe and stable under Windows 2000. If a driver passes Microsoft's tests, a validating certificate is attached to the drivers.

- Administrators were frequently aggravated when a seemingly minor change to Windows NT 4.0 required a reboot before the change could take effect. Microsoft greatly reduced the number of events for which you have to reboot the system in Windows 2000. For example, you can change the IP address on a running system, and the change takes place after a few seconds without a reboot.

Versions

Windows 2000 comes in the following versions:

- *Windows 2000 Professional.* Though not a server operating system, this is the ideal client for Windows 2000 servers, especially for purposes of centralized administration and automated software distribution. Windows 2000 Professional supports up to 4 GB of RAM and 2-way SMP.

- *Windows 2000 Server.* The core server product capable of 4 GB of RAM and 4-way SMP.

- *Windows 2000 Advanced Server.* Windows 2000 Server plus support for clustering, up to 8 GB of RAM, and 8-way SMP.

- *Windows 2000 Datacenter Server.* Windows 2000 Advanced Server plus support for up to 64 GB of RAM and 32-way SMP.

Windows XP is the desktop successor to Windows 2000 Professional but has mostly the same platform and architecture, and is designed to finally replace the Windows 9.x architecture. Windows .NET is the upgrade to Windows 2000 Server.

Windows 2000 Minimum Hardware Requirements

Windows 2000 Server lists somewhat more realistic minimum hardware requirements than Windows NT 4.0 Server; however, you should still obtain server equipment that is as capable as prudently possible. Minimum system hardware requirements are as follows for Windows 2000 Server and Windows 2000 Advanced Server:

- Intel-compatible 133 MHz processor or higher. (Windows 2000 Datacenter Server requires the same minimum hardware, except that the processors must be Pentium III Xeon or higher)

- 128 MB of RAM, though Microsoft strongly recommends at least 256 MB

- 2 GB hard disk with 1 GB of free space

You can verify the compatibility of specific hardware by visiting the Microsoft web site at *www.microsoft.com/hcl*.

You cannot purchase Windows 2000 Datacenter Server off the shelf and install it wherever you like. Instead, only system integrators can purchase the product and sell it preinstalled with the server.

Installing Windows 2000 Server

The general steps for installing Windows 2000 are very similar to Windows NT 4.0:

1. After booting from the CD-ROM, setup begins automatically, and you can skip to Step 4. If booting from a boot floppy with CD-ROM drivers, change to the CD-ROM drive (we'll assume it's drive D).

2. Go to the \i386 directory. This is the directory used for installing NT to an Intel-based PC server. Windows 2000 only installs on Intel-based processors.

3. Type *winnt* and press Enter. This initiates the text mode portion of setup. Windows 2000 does not create the boot floppies by default; so the /b option is not necessary, as it was for NT 4.0.

4. Proceed through the setup process, following the prompts such as license agreement, partitioning, and additional storage devices (for example, SCSI adapters) that might not have been detected by setup. If so, supply the drivers from a floppy disk. (If you booted from a generic DOS floppy, a reboot occurs between Step 3 and 4.)

5. Basic hardware detection finds hardware such as keyboard, mouse, and display adapters. This level of device detection is very basic; a more in-depth and accurate detection occurs closer to the end of the setup process.

6. Select a partition in which to install the operating system. If none of the existing partitions suit you, you can delete or create other partitions. Assuming that you started with a FAT partition, setup offers you the chance to convert to an NTFS partition. For sake of performance and security, it is normally best to choose the NTFS conversion at this point.

 You can also convert from FAT to NTFS after installation. A Windows 2000 server automatically applies security permissions appropriately when converted to NTFS.

7. Setup copies more files to the hard disk. When prompted, press Enter to reboot the system. If you opted to convert from FAT to NTFS, the conversion takes place. This concludes the text portion of the setup process. The graphical portion begins after the reboot.

8. Confirm the locale and keyboard settings, and then enter your name and organization.

9. Select a licensing mode under the same guidelines discussed in the Windows NT 4.0 section.

10. Enter a computer name. This name is how the server is identified and must be unique within the network. Then enter the password for the Administrator account.

11. Continue through the installation, answering prompts and choosing installation options.

12. Select typical or custom network settings. Choosing Typical really means that the computer will be configured as a DHCP client. Choosing custom settings exposes the network property sheet so that you can manually configure IP settings (see Figure 8-18).

13. Choose to make the computer a member of a workgroup or a domain.

8

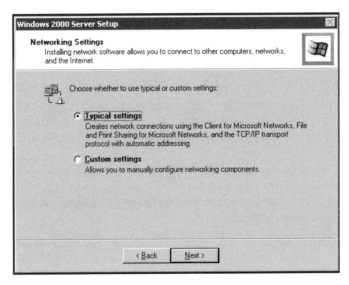

Figure 8-18   Choose Typical for DHCP clients, and Custom for manual IP configuration

In Windows NT 4.0, you would choose the server role during installation. But Windows 2000 servers always install as member servers (member of a domain but not a domain controller) or a stand-alone server (not a member of a domain). After installation, you can make the Windows 2000 server a peer domain controller by running DCPROMO from a command line, which launches a domain controller installation utility. All Windows 2000 domain controllers are peer domain controllers. This means that each domain controller has both a read and write copy of the directory database.

14. When finished with all the setup prompts, more files copy to the hard disk and a prompt requests that you reboot.

15. After the reboot and logon, you see the standard Windows 2000 desktop.

Upgrading to Windows 2000 Server

You can upgrade a Windows NT 3.51 server or Windows NT 4.0 server to Windows 2000 Server. You cannot upgrade any desktop client operating system to Windows 2000 Server. The easiest way to upgrade to Windows 2000 is to simply insert the CD and allow Autoplay to start setup. If Autoplay is disabled, you can run Winnt32.exe from the \i386 directory. A prompt asks whether you want to perform an upgrade or clean install (see Figure 8-19).

Figure 8-19   Select an upgrade or clean install

Creating Windows 2000 Swap-File Space

As with most Windows installations, Windows 2000 automatically configures a swap file for virtual memory use. You can adjust the size, move, or split the paging file among available drives using the System Properties as follows:

1. Right-click My Computer and click Properties (or select System from the Control Panel). The System Properties dialog box opens.

2. Click the Advanced tab and select the Performance Options button.

3. In the Performance Options dialog box, click the Change button.

4. The dialog box that appears next is nearly identical to the Windows NT 4.0 Virtual Memory dialog box (refer to Figure 8-16). Enter the size of the swap file, click Set, and then click OK. Adjusting the swap file is one of the few reboot events in Windows 2000.

Performing a Proper Windows 2000 Shutdown

Shut down a Windows 2000 server similarly to a Windows NT 4.0 server. Click Start, click Shut Down, and select your shutdown option (see Figure 8-20). Windows 2000 has better power management than Windows NT 4.0, and it is more likely to turn off the power through the operating system. On some systems, you will still press the power button to turn off power to the server—just wait for the message that says it is safe to turn off the server.

Windows 2000 also allows you to place the system in a low-power standby state, or hibernation, which saves the complete contents of RAM to disk. When you turn on the power again, the contents on disk are reloaded into RAM; this is faster than a standard startup of the operating system.

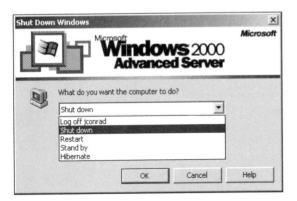

Figure 8-20   Windows 2000 allows log off, shut down, restart, stand by, and hibernate

UPDATING A NETWORK OPERATING SYSTEM

There is a slight difference between a patch, fix, and update. However, the differences do not matter for our purposes—I'll collectively call these updates. Inevitably, an operating system requires an update. There are many possible reasons for this, including:

- *Security vulnerability.* These updates usually come out as quickly as possible from the vendor. Unless there exists a compelling reason to avoid it, you should nearly always apply security updates for obvious reasons.

- *Incompatibility.* Even after rigorous testing, an operating system is likely to encounter compatibility problems with some number of applications. How quickly an update is released depends on the severity of the problem.

- *Poor functionality.* An operating system simply doesn't function as promised, and requires an update to fix the problem.

- *Added features.* Prior to the release of the next major version of an operating system, a vendor might release additional features for free. For example, Microsoft released the Option Pack for Windows NT 4.0, which improved NT 4.0's Internet server features.

Regardless of the reason for an update, you should regularly check with the manufacturer of your operating system to see if there are any updates available that might be useful to you. In the server context, I discourage applying updates just because one exists. While an update might be designed to fix one problem, it might accidentally create some other problem or incompatibility. At the least, you should thoroughly test updates before placing them into production.

To help you keep abreast of important updates, some vendors send you email when one is released. With Windows 2000, Windows Critical Update Notification periodically checks the Microsoft web site to see if a new update is available and notifies you of the update with a visual indicator. The Windows Update site scans your system and offers updates available for your system. You check off the upgrade items you want and apply the updates over the Internet (see Figure 8-21), simplifying the more cumbersome process in Windows NT 4.0 in which you have to download an update, extract the files to a temporary location, and run the update.

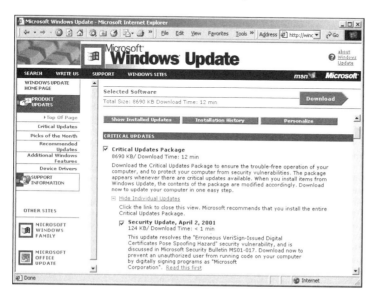

Figure 8-21   The Windows Update site automatically scans your system and notifies you of updates available for your system

Not all updates install with the same procedures—the best practice is to read the web site documentation that describes the update to find out how to apply it. For example, Red Hat site updates have an encrypted authentication that you decrypt to verify that the update is truly a Red Hat update and not from a malicious source.

CHAPTER SUMMARY

❑ A production server will quickly languish in attempting to provide service to the network with only the vendor's recommended minimum hardware. Preparing server hardware for NOS installation involves the right perspective. Instead of trying to get away with as little as possible, the administrator's perspective should be nearly the opposite: obtain hardware that is reasonably powerful enough for current and future requirements.

❏ The process of translating virtual addresses into real addresses is called mapping. Copying virtual pages from disk to main memory is known as paging or swapping. Swapping is a useful technique that enables a computer to execute programs and manipulate data files larger than main memory.

❏ Novell NetWare is a widely accepted LAN operating system developed by Novell Corporation. NetWare runs on a variety of different LANs, including Ethernet and IBM Token Ring. NetWare offers users and programmers a reliable interface that is independent of the underlying hardware that transmits data. Depending on the version, NetWare uses either a bindery or directory service design to manage the majority of network resources. NetWare 3.x uses a bindery, but NetWare 4.11 and later versions use NDS.

❏ NetWare offers very capable web and application server technologies, a GUI known as ConsoleOne, the ZENworks network management tool, and flexible TCP/IP IPX/SPX options.

❏ Install NetWare on at least a server-class PC with a Pentium II or higher processor, a DOS partition between 30 and 100 MB, and at least 1.3 GB disk space on the SYS volume beyond the DOS partition for the standard NetWare products and WebSphere Application Server for NetWare. Also include at least 128 MB of RAM for the standard NetWare components.

❏ Use a network card that is automatically detected by the NetWare installation. Otherwise, you must specify the make and model of the network card from a list or provide the drivers from a floppy. Automatically detected NICs usually do not require you to manually specify resources.

❏ Decide which version of NDS you will use. NetWare 5.1 allows you to use either NDS 8 (default) or NDS 7. NDS 8 provides the enhanced NDS functionality needed by many new web networking products, such as WebSphere.

❏ The first volume NetWare creates is called the SYS volume, and Novell recommends you make it at least 200 MB (a complete install with all documentation requires about 600 MB). The SYS volume should be used for only NetWare system files and NetWare Loadable Modules (NLMs; NetWare programs and applications)—not user data.

❏ It is not advisable to use only the SYS volume for swap files, because this volume is typically already very busy. Instead, you should place one or more swap files on other high-performance volumes with plenty of free space. Create or manage swap-file space with the SWAP ADD command.

❏ To shut down a NetWare server, enter *down* at a command prompt to close all services and files. A handy feature of NetWare is that in this process, a notification of the downed server is delivered to all attached workstations. If you would rather just reboot the server, enter *restart server*.

❑ UNIX has been a popular choice among universities and corporations because of its low cost and the fact that programmers familiar with the C high-level programming language can modify the code to specific requirements. UNIX has split into two main dialects: AT&T's System V and the University of California, Berkeley version known as BSD 4.1, 4.2, or 4.3. Within the two main versions, there are dozens of other modified versions ("flavors").

❑ Linux is a version of UNIX that, like other flavors, is open source code. Linus Torvalds authored early versions of Linux with the objective of creating a relatively small UNIX source code that would run on Intel-compatible computers (as opposed to the CISC-based processors of other UNIX versions). Several vendors offer Linux in boxed sets.

❑ A Linux installation requires at least an Intel-compatible 80386 processor or higher, 32 MB of RAM, and 500 MB of hard disk space.

❑ The Linux installation is best launched from CD-ROM. You can use the Disk Druid utility to manage the hard disk partitions. You will need at least a root partition, swap partition, and boot partition.

❑ You can shut Linux down to single user mode (where all users are disconnected and files are closed), a halt state, or you can reboot the server.

❑ Linux offers GUI interfaces that make administration much simpler than the text-only command line interface of UNIX/Linux.

❑ OS/2 is known for rock-solid performance and reliability on high-end server platforms, which is one reason why it is favored in many banking and financial institutions, and also offers support for up to 64 processors. OS/2 offers the Journaled File System (JFS) for data integrity and Logical Volume Manager (LVM) for very flexible partition and disk management.

❑ The OS/2 installation requires at least an Intel-compatible 133 MHz processor, 64 MB of RAM, and 120 MB of hard disk space for the base operating system, or 200 MB for the operating system plus all default additional components.

❑ When upgrading to OS/2 Warp Server, it is usually best to migrate existing configuration files (Autoexec.bat and Config.sys) to avoid reconfiguring the files from scratch.

❑ Create an OS/2 swap file by using the SWAPPATH syntax: SWAPPATH=<DriveLetter and Path> *InitialSize MaximumSize*.

❑ You can shut down the OS/2 operating system by right-clicking anywhere on the Warp 4 desktop and choosing Shut Down from the menu. You can also lock the computer (which requires user credentials to unlock) or log off the network.

❑ The Windows NT operating system has a Windows 95-based interface and allows you to run local user applications, and introduces a security boundary known as an NT domain, which is not the same as a DNS domain.

8

❑ Windows NT requires at least an Intel-compatible 486/25 MHz processor, 16 MB of RAM, and 160 MB of hard disk space. You can verify compatibility of hardware devices at *www.microsoft.com/hcl*.

❑ You can boot to a Windows 98 floppy to start a Windows NT installation, but it can cause compatibility problems with FAT32 partitions and lock the hard drive. You can convert the FAT file system to NTFS either during or after the installation.

❑ Windows NT licensing modes can be either per server or per seat. You can install the server as a Primary Domain Controller (PDC), Backup Domain Controller (BDC), member server, or stand-alone server.

❑ Create the Windows NT or Windows 2000 paging file using the System properties of the server. To shut down Windows NT or Windows 2000, click Start, and then click Shut Down.

❑ Windows 2000 introduces its LDAP directory service, Active Directory, which can store several types of objects and uses the DNS hierarchical namespace. Dynamic DNS services allow clients to self-register their host names.

❑ The Windows 2000 installation requires an Intel-compatible 133 MHz or higher processor (Xeon III or better for Datacenter Server), 128 MB of RAM, and 2 GB of hard disk space with 1 GB of free disk space.

❑ You will periodically have to update the operating system for reasons of security, incompatibility, poor functionality, or added features. Each NOS specifies a different method for installing updates, but the vendor download sites should provide specific instructions.

Key Terms

Active Directory — Microsoft's LDAP directory service for Windows 2000 that is a comprehensive database capable of storing millions of objects such as users, groups, computers, and more. In terms of functionality, Active Directory users can log on and access resources anywhere in the enterprise regardless of geographic location and where the user account was originally created.

Backup Domain Controller (BDC) — A Windows NT server that stores a read-only copy of the Primary Domain Controller's (PDC's) directory database, and is useful as an extension to the PDC for logging on users and computers. You must have a PDC before you can have a BDC.

bindery — A NetWare directory of users, groups, and network resources that provides network clients with the information that is stored on the NetWare server's local directory partitions. A bindery is restricted to the computer on which it resides, and users can only use resources managed in the same bindery to which they log on.

ConsoleOne — A central management point for performing NetWare 5.1 administration.

container — In Novell NetWare, a general term for an Organization or Organizational Unit, which are hierarchical components of the NDS tree. All network objects must reside in a container in the tree.

directory service — A network service that identifies all of the resources on a network and makes them available to applications and users. Resources can include things like email addresses; user, group, and computer accounts; and peripheral devices such as printers.

Disk Druid — A Linux disk partitioning utility.

domain — In Windows NT or 2000, a security boundary. Not the same as a DNS domain.

Dynamic DNS — The ability to accept name registrations from DHCP clients automatically.

El Torito — A CD from which you can boot the computer, provided the BIOS supports this feature.

GNOME — A GUI for UNIX administration.

host name ("A") record — A DNS entry that resolves a host's IP address to its host name, allowing users to access a server using the name instead of the IP address.

hot fix — A NetWare feature that verifies the integrity of all disk writes, and if a write fails this verification, the data is redirected to a hot fix area and the original destination is marked as unusable. The default size of the hot fix area is a small percentage of a partition's total size.

Journaled File System (JFS) — An OS/2 file system that keeps a journal of file writes and, in the event of a corruption, can restore the data in a matter of minutes or seconds, usually transparently to users.

Lightweight Directory Access Protocol (LDAP) — A directory service standard for enabling searches and queries to locate, identify, and utilize resources among networks.

Linux Loader (LILO) — A Linux boot management utility that allows you to select from two or more operating systems at boot time.

Logical Volume Manager (LVM) — An OS/2 utility that allows you to span a single partition across multiple physical disks, and partitions can increase in size without reformatting. You can also add or move hard drives without altering the drive letter.

mapping — In virtual memory, copying virtual pages from disk to main memory.

member server — A Windows NT server that is similar to a stand-alone server, but is a member of the domain.

memory core dump — Representation of the contents of memory in the event of a problem, also known as simply a "memory dump."

mount — A reference to preparing a Novell NetWare volume for use. You mount or dismount volumes.

multi-user mode — The mode in which a Linux/UNIX server and its resources are available to network clients.

NetWare Loadable Module (NLM) — Programs that run on a NetWare server. An NLM might include a management utility or server-based applications such as a database engine.

8

Novell Directory Services (NDS) — A scalable Novell NetWare tree structure representing resource information that extends throughout the enterprise. The administrator can plan and configure the NDS tree so that users from anywhere in the organization can log on and access resources anywhere in the organization without a second logon.

page fault — When the operating system requests a needed page of data or instructions that is not currently in memory.

paging (or **swapping)** — Copying virtual pages from disk to main memory.

paging file — Microsoft term for a Windows NT 4.0 or Windows 2000 swap file.

partitionless — Using an existing DOS or Windows partition instead of creating a partition manually during installation using FDISK or Red Hat's Disk Druid partitioning tool.

per seat — A licensing scheme that requires each client that connects to the server to have proper licensing.

per server — A licensing scheme that represents the number of concurrent connections allowed under the licensing scheme you purchased.

Primary Domain Controller (PDC) — A Windows NT server that stores the only read/write copy of the directory database. This database is a record of user and computer accounts, and is used for logging on users.

scalability — A server's ability to grow in terms of the number of processors.

single-user mode — In UNIX/Linux, a mode in which user connections are closed, ensuring that there are no locks on open files. This is not a complete shutdown because the operating system is still running.

stand-alone server — A Windows NT server that is not a member of the domain and does not store the directory database, but is useful as a file, print, or application server, or provides one or more services.

virtual console — A separate Linux context to which you can log on and perform various tasks while other virtual consoles or a GUI also run.

virtual memory — A portion of hard disk space that extends RAM memory.

WebSphere — An IBM application for building and managing web-based applications.

X.500 ITU — Originally a standard for searching email directories but has much broader application. The standard is so large and complex that no vendor complies with it completely.

X Term — A text-based terminal interface within the Linux GUI.

X Windows — A GUI for the UNIX administration.

Zero Effort Networks (Z.E.N.) or **ZENworks** — A NetWare tool that administrators use to manage the user or server operating system environment by automatically distributing applications and controlling the user desktop.

REVIEW QUESTIONS

1. What is the purpose of a swap file?

   a. to boost the effectiveness of the processor

   b. to allow processes to alternate between processors in an SMP server

   c. to transfer data from slower pages in RAM to faster pages in RAM

   d. to extend the range of physical RAM to virtual memory on the hard disk

2. Which of the following is a widely accepted local area network (LAN) operating system that was developed by Novell Corporation and runs on a variety of different types of LANs, including Ethernet and IBM Token Ring networks?

   a. NetWorks

   b. GateWare

   c. Warp

   d. NetWare

3. What GUI interface makes managing NetWare more intuitive for the administrator?

   a. Crayon Manager

   b. Program Manager

   c. InterfaceOne

   d. ConsoleOne

4. How can you simultaneously support both IPX/SPX and TCP/IP on a NetWare network with minimal additional network traffic?

   a. segment the network into a separate IPX/SPX and TCP/IP network

   b. install IP with IPX compatibility

   c. use switches instead of routers

   d. remove all IPX/SPX applications

5. How can you automatically create swap-file space on one or more NetWare volumes when the operating system boots?

   a. create a visual basic script

   b. add the SWAP ADD command to the Autoexec.ncf file

   c. access the System properties in Control Panel and select the Advanced tab

   d. You cannot. NetWare does not support swap files.

6. How should you prepare NetWare version 4 for an upgrade to version 5.1?

   a. No actions are necessary; just insert the 5.1 CD and setup automatically begins.

   b. Run the NetWare Deployment Manager.

   c. Uninstall NetWare 4 first, and then install NetWare 5.1.

   d. First upgrade to NetWare 5.0, then upgrade from 5.0 to 5.1.

7. Which of the following is a network component that identifies resources like email addresses, computers, and peripheral devices on a network and makes them available to applications and users?

   a. network operating system

   b. local area network

   c. redirector

   d. directory service

8. Which of the following is an interactive time-sharing operating system invented in 1969 by Brian Kernighan and Dennis Ritchie, the inventors of C?

   a. Linux

   b. NetWare

   c. OS/2

   d. UNIX

9. Which utility do you use in Red Hat Linux 7 to make a boot diskette under MS-DOS?

   a. rawrite

   b. dosutils

   c. dd

   d. makedisk

10. Linux is free over the Internet and PCs are inexpensive. Why not build your own Linux server?

    a. A server from a major vendor with Linux preinstalled offers better support and reliability.

    b. You cannot obtain Linux off the shelf; it must come preinstalled on a server.

    c. There is no way to do it without violating the Linux licensing agreement.

    d. Linux does not work with PC servers, only CISC-based processors such as Alpha.

11. Which of the following offers you the chance to boot from multiple operating systems?

    a. NWLoader.nlm

    b. LELA

    c. MultiBoot

    d. LILO

12. You want to create a partition for swap-file space during the Linux installation. Which partitioning utility should you use?

   a. FDISK

   b. JFS

   c. Disk Druid

   d. LVM

13. Why would you proceed with caution before installing a Linux server system?

   a. It requires significantly more system resources than the workstation installation.

   b. It removes all partitions on all drives.

   c. It flushes the cache, possibly discarding important data.

   d. It automatically creates a root volume but no boot volume.

14. To properly shut down Linux:

   a. hit the power button, and all services and files automatically close

   b. enter *shutdown −r* and then turn off the power

   c. enter *shutdown −h* and then turn off the power

   d. enter *die die die* and turn off the power

15. Why does OS/2 have a loyal following among banks and financial institutions?

   a. It is completely void of floating point calculation errors.

   b. It is extremely stable and reliable.

   c. It is necessary because only OS/2 can load extremely large databases.

   d. It is free.

16. The Journaled File System (JFS) is:

   a. a detailed record of bad file writes

   b. an extremely powerful and flexible tape backup system

   c. an OS/2 facility that enables nearly immediate recovery of files when a bad write occurs

   d. an auditing tool that keeps accurate record of which persons accessed any given file at any given time

17. How can you check for preinstallation steps that might be necessary before upgrading to OS/2?

   a. run the PREINST utility

   b. run the PREPMNT utility

   c. check the existing CHKPNT log file in the System directory

   d. run the CHKINST utility

8

18. What program can you run that will help Windows NT 4.0 or Windows 2000 installations to proceed much faster?

   a. SMARTDRV

   b. QUICKTIME

   c. POGOSTCK

   d. SPEEDISK

19. Windows 2000 offers what new directory service?

   a. NDS

   b. DDNS

   c. WINS

   d. Active Directory

20. Why aren't there PDCs and BDCs in a Windows 2000 domain?

   a. Windows 2000 has finally discarded the outdated domain model.

   b. All domain controllers in Windows 2000 are peer domain controllers.

   c. All Windows 2000 servers are member servers only.

   d. All Windows 2000 servers are stand-alone servers only.

HANDS-ON PROJECTS

Project 8-1

In this project, you will analyze the hardware on three systems (see Table 8-1) and determine which one is least acceptable as a NetWare 5.1 server installation candidate. The server will run the WebSphere Application Server for NetWare.

Table 8-1   Choices for Project 8-1

Server1	Server2	Server3
Pentium III Xeon 733 MHz	Pentium II Xeon 400 MHz	Pentium II 233 MHz
1 GB of free disk space	4 GB of free disk space	2 GB of free disk space
1 GB of RAM	128 MB of RAM	512 MB of RAM

Which of the servers in Table 8-1 is the best candidate? Explain why the other two servers would not be the best choice.

Project 8-2

In this project, you will install the Windows 2000 Server operating system on a server. Before installation, verify that the hard disk has at least 2 GB of FAT- or FAT32-formatted disk space available, a 133 MHz Pentium or compatible processor, and 128 MB of RAM.

1. Insert a boot floppy with CD-ROM drivers for the server CD-ROM or a Windows 98 startup disk, and boot the computer. If the server is El Torito-capable, then boot from the CD-ROM (you might have to specify this boot option in the CMOS). If booting from the CD-ROM, skip to Step 5.

2. If you booted from a floppy, be sure to type **SMARTDRV** and press **Enter** at a command prompt. This loads the Smart Drive caching utility. If you booted from the CD, then caching loads automatically. If necessary, be sure to manually add the SMARTDRV.EXE file to the boot floppy.

3. If prompted, specify the location where the Windows 2000 files are located. In most cases, this will be D:\i386, where D is the CD-ROM drive, and the entry probably already appears by default. Press **Enter** to start the file copy process.

4. Remove the bootable media, whether it's the floppy or the CD-ROM, and press **Enter** to reboot. If you do not remove the media, the installation might start over again.

5. If you have a SCSI host adapter, press **F6** when prompted. Otherwise, skip to Step 7.

6. Press **S** to direct Windows 2000 to look for the SCSI drivers. You will need a floppy diskette containing the drivers.

7. A prompt appears asking whether you want to repair an existing installation or proceed with a Windows 2000 installation. Press **Enter** to set up Windows 2000.

8. The license agreement appears. Press the **F8** key to indicate that you agree.

9. You are prompted to select a destination for the installation. In this screen, you can create or delete partitions as necessary. You probably have a C: partition already formatted. Make sure to select it and press **Enter**.

10. Choose the option to **Convert the partition to NTFS** and press **Enter**.

11. Press **C** to confirm that you want to convert the partition to NTFS.

12. Setup examines your hard disk, and then begins to copy more files to the local drive. Afterward, the system reboots itself (or you can hasten this by 15 seconds by pressing **Enter** at the prompt).

13. The file system conversion to NTFS takes place, and a reboot occurs. No steps are required on your part.

14. Setup boots into the GUI mode of setup, and your first prompt is for regional settings. Adjust these if necessary, and click **Next** through the GUI screens as you complete Steps 15 through 23.

Unless necessary, don't change these settings, because it will be much more difficult to read the screens later on when they're in a foreign language and the keyboard layout has changed.

15. Enter a Name and Organization.

16. When prompted, enter the CD-KEY.

17. Leave the licensing mode at per server, and enter a number at least equal to the number of computers in the classroom.

18. A randomly generated computer name appears. Change it if you like or as directed by your instructor.

19. Enter and confirm a password. Record the password so you don't forget it.

20. A list of Windows components appears. You can click around and view the various options if you like, but for now, leave the options as selected.

21. Enter the correct date, time, and time zone as necessary.

22. Leave the Network Settings at the default Typical settings.

23. Leave the computer in a workgroup with the default name "workgroup."

24. When setup is complete, click **Finish** to reboot the system. The server will now boot into Windows 2000, ready for use.

Project 8-3

In this project, you will configure the paging file for Windows 2000 Server.

1. Right-click **My Computer** on the Windows 2000 desktop.

2. Click **Properties**.

3. Click the **Advanced** tab.

4. Click the **Performance Options** button.

5. Click the **Change** button in the Virtual memory frame.

6. You probably have a drive C with a specific paging file size already set. Change the initial size to **300** and the maximum size to **600**. (These are somewhat arbitrary numbers; in a later chapter, we discuss sizing the paging file.)

7. Click the **Set** button.

8. Click **OK** on all open dialog boxes.

9. A prompt notifies you that you must reboot. Click **Yes** to allow the reboot to occur.

10. When the system reboots, the paging file will be reset to the new sizes. Repeat Steps 1–5 to confirm this, and then cancel all open dialog boxes.

Project 8-4

In this project, you will apply one or more updates to the newly installed Windows 2000 installation completed in Project 8-2.

1. In Windows 2000, click the **Start** button and select **Windows Update**.

2. Click the link that says **Product Updates**. An ActiveX utility scans your system to see what updates have been applied and what updates might be useful for you.

3. What updates are available for your installation of Windows 2000? Select some updates. Look carefully at the size of the downloads; if your Internet connection is slow, be conservative in the interest of time.

4. When you have selected the updates you want, click the **Download** button. A summary screen shows you what is about to be downloaded.

5. Click **Start Download**, and then click the **Yes** button in the license agreement screen.

6. The update takes place. If you see a prompt to reboot, go ahead and do so.

7. Your system has now been updated with the components you selected.

8. Return to the Windows Update site, and click the link that shows you which updates have been applied to your system. Notice that you can uninstall updates, which is sometimes necessary if the update has an unexpected and detrimental effect.

8

Project 8-5

In this project, you will identify features of the Red Hat Linux operating system.

1. Browse to *www.redhat.com*.

2. Browse to the Products and Services section.

3. Select the **High Availability Server**. What support is included with this product?

4. Access product information for the Red Hat Professional Server. It is important to choose a NOS that has applications available for it. What are a few of the software packages included with this product?

5. Close the browser.

Project 8-6

In this project, you will find more detailed information about OS/2 from the Redbooks IBM site.

1. Open your web browser to *www.redbooks.ibm.com*.

2. Select the link for **Redbooks online**.

3. In the Redbook Site Search, enter the words "OS/2 warp server" and click **Search**.

4. Select the search result **OS/2 Warp Server for e-business**. If this item does not appear, enter a new search for **SG24-5393**, which is the corresponding document number.

5. Select the link that allows you to view this redbook document online. Choose to view using the PDF link. Adobe Acrobat Reader must be installed. If necessary, you can detour to *www.acrobat.com* to download and install the software and then return to this site.

6. Using the navigation bar at the bottom of the PDF file, access page 35 of 472. How much virtual memory address space can applications address?

7. Access page 118 of 472. Under Section 4.1.4, what limitation does JFS have?

8. Browse through other chapters and write down four more features about OS/2 that you think would be of significance to server administrators. Chapters 1 and 2 will probably provide the best information.

CASE PROJECTS

1. Mario, a new administrator in your Hopewell, VA remote site, has recently purchased an inexpensive server with no operating system. Mario installed NetWare 5.1 on the server and successfully joined it to the existing NetWare tree in your organization. Unfortunately, even though the demands on Mario's server are moderate, it seems to respond very slowly to client requests. Mario says that the hard disk is constantly active. User files take a long time to load, and the email application on the NetWare server does not perform acceptably. What do you think is the problem, and what could Mario have done to avoid this situation?

2. Tammy's supervisor tells her to procure a dual-processor Pentium III Xeon server as a logon server/print server with 1 GB of memory and an 80 GB array of SCSI disks. Tammy just learned that the graphics division is moving to her floor, and she must provide print support for PostScript print jobs, but she does not have a PostScript printer. Also, because the server is a file server, Tammy decides she wants the best possible reliability she can find for the file system in case files become corrupt during a write action. Tammy thinks that her shiny new server will provide plenty of power, but she is unsure of which operating system would work best for her needs. What would you tell Tammy to do?

9

NETWORK OPERATING SYSTEM SERVICES AND APPLICATIONS

After reading this chapter and completing the exercises, you will be able to:

♦ Identify and understand major network operating system services

♦ Discuss the different ways that servers run network applications

♦ Describe the function of monitoring agents

♦ Specify the functions of the server as a network device

This chapter is about the purpose of having a server. So far, you have been exposed to extensive information about servers, from their environment to identifying and upgrading their hardware, and more. However, none of these things has any meaning except to support the main purpose of having a server (implied in its name): to serve the networking and information-processing needs of an organization. In this chapter, you see how a server uses its various services to make the network run properly and ensure that information gets from one location to the next. An important part of transferring this information is the server's role as a network device, moving data in a fast, efficient manner. Servers also run applications for the network that are too demanding to run on client machines, and they can greatly reduce the processing and storage burden on individual client machines. Because servers are critical to the mission of an organization, administrators must have a way to track server activity and receive immediate notice should something not function properly.

SERVICES

Recall from Chapter 1 that a service provides features to the network. NOS manufacturers include several services with their operating systems, and software packages also often add one or more services. For example, many UPS units include software utilities that install a service to manage the UPS. Many services, including all those discussed in this chapter, include a software interface so that the administrator can configure how the service works. Other services are necessary simply as a function of the operating system. For example, Windows 2000 includes the Plug and Play service as part of the operating system, but you don't administer or configure the service itself. The remainder of this section addresses configurable services.

 The services on Linux and UNIX systems are known as **daemons**, but for our purposes we will use only the term "services" unless otherwise necessary.

DHCP

Each host on a TCP/IP network must have a unique IP address. If two hosts on the network have the same IP address, communication problems occur. In Windows NT, the first host that enters the network with a given IP address retains it when a second Windows NT host with the same IP address enters the network. The second host, however, cannot communicate. Both hosts enter a record of the duplicate IP address problem in the System log. Duplicate IP addresses are one of the most common problems in IP networks with **static IP addresses**—that is, where someone manually enters a permanent IP address for a host, which includes IP configuration such as the subnet mask, name servers, and routers. Human error and a lack of good records can lead either to wrongly configured IP addresses that do not communicate properly on the network or to duplicate records (as just mentioned). Furthermore, it requires a significant investment in time for technicians to manually enter static IP addresses on hundreds or thousands of individual clients.

This kind of problem can be avoided by the use of a **Dynamic Host Configuration Protocol (DHCP)** server. A **DHCP server** automatically allocates IP addresses to hosts on the network. Recipients of DHCP-allocated IP addresses are known as DHCP clients, and in order to receive the IP address, you must specify this in the client's network properties. For example, Figure 9-1 shows the NETCONFIG utility on a Red Hat Linux server, which you use to enter IP configuration information. The setting "Use dynamic IP configuration (BOOTP/DHCP)" instructs the client to seek a DHCP server on the network from which to obtain an address. (**BOOTP** is the Bootstrap Protocol and, similar to DHCP, uses a BOOTP server that can distribute IP addresses to clients.)

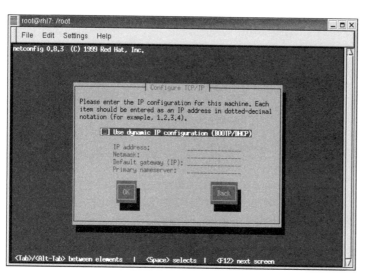

Figure 9-1   "Use dynamic IP configuration (BOOTP/DHCP)" means to use a DHCP server

The Lease Process

When a client receives an IP address from the server, it has obtained a **lease**. Similar to the lease of property or a car, this lease is for a limited duration. Administrators can adjust the lease from a few hours to several days, depending on the nature of client access. For example, in a typical office building where the network hosts are mostly desktop computers and very few changes occur on the network, you might configure leases that last for days. However, if you run an ISP (Internet service provider), the lease duration is probably an hour or less, because you do not want users who have disconnected to retain the address lease while it would otherwise be available to the next user.

The client initiates the lease process with a **discovery broadcast** seeking a DHCP server. A broadcast to all hosts is necessary, because the host does not yet have an IP address with which to communicate, nor does it know the IP address of the DHCP server. All available DHCP servers respond to the client with an **offer** of a specific IP address and configuration. The client responds with a **request**, which is an acceptance of the offer from one of the randomly selected DHCP servers while rejecting offers from the rest. Finally, the server issues the IP configuration, which it confirms with an **acknowledgment**. Using the first letter of each of the four steps, you can easily remember the process with the mnemonic "DORA." Figure 9-2 illustrates this process.

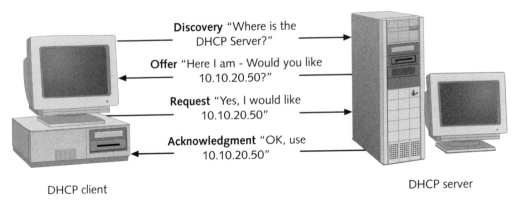

Discovery "Where is the
DHCP Server?"

Offer "Here I am - Would you like
10.10.20.50?"

Request "Yes, I would like
10.10.20.50"

Acknowledgment "OK, use
10.10.20.50"

DHCP client

DHCP server

Figure 9-2   The DORA lease process

TIP

Although using DHCP for client IP address configuration helps ensure accurate IP addressing and reduces the administrative burden of manual configuration, it is best not to use DHCP for servers, printers, and network equipment so that those addresses are always consistent. You do not want a printer, for example, to lease a changing IP address because it becomes unavailable to clients attempting to access the printer's original address.

A DHCP server usually distributes not only the IP address and subnet mask to the client, but also many other configuration items such as the IP address of the gateway (router) and DNS (Domain Name System) and WINS (Windows Internet Naming Service) name servers. In Windows 2000 or NT, you can configure DHCP by opening the DHCP item (Start, Programs, Administrative Tools, DHCP). NetWare also has a GUI console that you can use to configure both DHCP and DNS. Figure 9-3 shows the NetWare DNS/DHCP Management Console interface. Linux, because of its UNIX origins, still requires configuration of the DHCP service through the text-based dhcpd.conf file.

When configuring DHCP, you must know the range of IP addresses you want to use on the network (known as a **scope**). You can use private IP addresses, which are practically limitless and for which there is no direct access from Internet hosts, or you can use public IP addresses. As a security precaution, most administrators prefer private IP addresses for their network hosts. Once you determine the scope you want to use, you enter a starting IP address and an ending IP address on the DHCP server. Hosts then lease the IP addresses one at a time in sequential order. The administrator ensures that enough IP addresses are available in the scope to service all hosts on the network, and usually add a margin for growth.

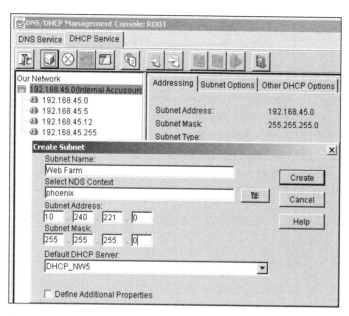

Figure 9-3   Use the NetWare 5.1 DNS/DHCP Management Console to configure DHCP

Be careful about testing IP scopes on the network. If someone introduces a DHCP server with incompatible or duplicate addresses on the network and the organization is large, then the new DHCP server will start to answer DHCP client requests. Those clients will then be incorrectly configured in the network, and it could be very difficult to find out exactly where the rogue DHCP server is and shut it down. Windows 2000 requires administrators to perform an additional step of authorizing a DHCP server before it functions on the network. This helps to ensure that a rogue DHCP server does not enter the network.

For sake of network availability and redundancy, implement more than one DHCP server. If one server fails, another DHCP server can continue to provide service. The redundant DHCP server(s) will have a compatible range of IP addresses usable on the network, but none of the IP addresses overlap from one DHCP server to the next. If it is not practical to use two DHCP servers in the same network segment, you can program routers to forward BOOTP or DHCP broadcasts to another DHCP server on a different segment. Also, the operating system might include a mechanism by which a host listens to DHCP discovery broadcasts and forwards the discovery inside a packet that is sent directly to the IP address of a DHCP server. For example, in Windows NT and Windows 2000, the DHCP relay agent performs this function.

Some organizations consider use of a DHCP server a security threat. The concern is that a stranger could enter the building as a visitor and locate an available network jack. Then, by turning on a laptop and leasing an address, the stranger's laptop becomes a part of the network and can begin to explore the network to provide information that would allow unauthorized access to resources.

DNS

People tend to remember names better than numbers. However, network hosts are identified using numbers. Though administrators are likely to have memorized the IP addresses of several key network resources such as printers, routers, web servers, mail servers, and logon servers, nobody memorizes the IP addresses of an entire enterprise. When users want to access a network resource or web site, they do not type in an IP address such as *www.199.227.124.246.net*. Instead, users would type the name, *www.accusource.net*.

It is the DNS server that transparently allows users to operate this way, because the **Domain Name System (DNS)** server stores a record of both the IP address and host name, and uses these records to service name resolution requests. DNS is actually a replacement for the HOSTS plain text file used in all major NOSs. The **HOSTS file** contains static, manual entries of host-to-IP address mappings, much like this entry for a computer named websrv6:

109.54.94.197 websrv6.accusource.net

With the growth of the Internet, using a HOSTS file to resolve web sites became impractical years ago. DNS also requires manual configuration but is much more flexible in its administration. However, many organizations still use the HOSTS file because at boot time, the file is loaded into memory for quick resolution of a network host without a DNS server.

DNS Name Resolution

Although the length of time you wait for most host name resolution requests to resolve is perceptibly short, the resolution process might actually take place through several DNS servers across a wide geographic area. For example, when you type *www.accusource.net* into a web browser, the computer issues a query to its configured DNS server, which then resolves the name to an IP address. As the Internet is large and even the most capable DNS server does not have all DNS records, the DNS server often references other DNS servers to answer a request. Forwarding the request like this is known as a **recursive query**. While waiting for another DNS server to resolve the request, the original DNS server becomes the resolver while the client simply waits for an answer. In a recursive query, the resolution burden rests with the DNS server to either resolve the name itself or resolve it using other DNS servers (compare this to an iterative query, following). This process is illustrated in Figure 9-4.

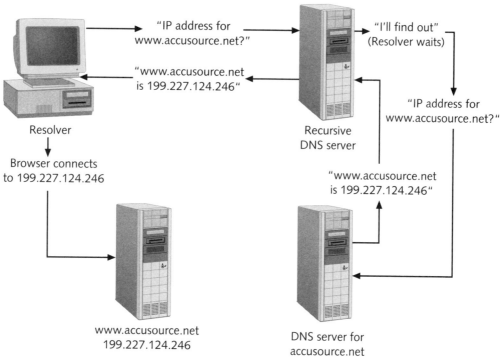

Figure 9-4 A recursive query

 Internic is the governing body responsible for naming and managing the DNS domain namespace. The domain space is a hierarchical tree of names created to manage DNS requests using separate authoritative DNS servers to manage each domain space such as .com, .gov, .edu, .net, .org, and so on. See more about Internic at *www.internic.org*.

The DNS server can also be configured to work in an **iterative query** mode. When the DNS server receives a request for which it does not have an answer, it refers the resolver to more authoritative DNS servers further up the hierarchical DNS namespace tree. The iterative DNS server is then relieved of the resolution burden, because it is the client resolver that references other DNS servers. In turn, the next DNS server to which the resolver passes the request might forward the request to yet another DNS server.

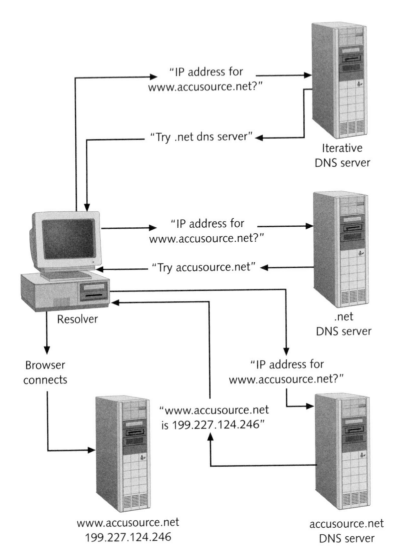

"IP address for www.accusource.net?"

"Try .net dns server"

Iterative
DNS server

"IP address for www.accusource.net?"

"Try accusource.net"

Resolver

.net
DNS server

Browser
connects

"IP address for www.accusource.net?"

"www.accusource.net is 199.227.124.246"

www.accusource.net
199.227.124.246

accusource.net
DNS server

Figure 9-5   An iterative query

TIP

For infrequently accessed Internet sites or sites that have only recently become registered, a client web browser might time-out on the first attempt while waiting for various DNS servers to resolve the request. Often, if you try a couple more times, DNS servers through which the request passed the first time will have cached some results, helping to speed up the resolution.

DNS Zones

Many large organizations have one or more full-time employees whose main function is to create and maintain DNS database records. Except for Dynamic DNS records, which this chapter discusses later, most DNS records require someone to make a manual entry on the DNS server. Each NOS has a different interface for creating such records, but if you know DNS, then you can create the DNS records on almost any GUI once you get used to its interface. For example, the DNS/DHCP Management Console for NetWare 5.1 has a handy toolbar for configuring DNS (see Figure 9-6).

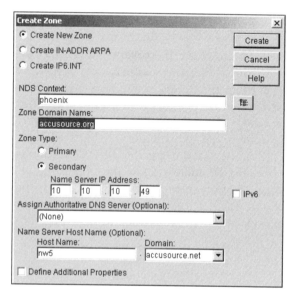

Figure 9-6   Use the DNS/DHCP Management Console to create DNS servers and zones

This section provides some basics and helps you learn some of the most commonly used types of records; the rest is a matter of learning the interface.

Before you go about creating DNS records, you need a DNS zone. The **DNS zone** is a naming boundary that you probably see every day when using the Internet. For example, in *www.course.com*, "course.com" is a zone and "www" is the name of the web server in that zone. The zone "contains" the records. When you create a zone, you also add a record for the DNS server that is the **Start of Authority (SOA) server**. The SOA server is the authoritative source for information about the domain, and the domain cannot function without it. In the configuration screen for a new zone, the NOS might include fields for you to provide the name SOA record as in Figure 9-6 (referenced above) where the NetWare console labels it "Assign Authoritative DNS Server." Windows 2000 automatically assumes that the SOA server is the DNS server on which you create the zone, and creates it for you. If this is not correct, you can manually change this. An SOA record is also required for the reverse lookup zone (discussed later in this chapter).

If you use UNIX/Linux, then you need to learn the text-based format in which you add zones to the named.conf file, and then create separate database files (*.db) that store the individual records for each zone. One of the major flavors of UNIX is BIND (Berkeley Internet Name Domain), and it has a very reliable, time-tested facility for DNS. In fact, Internet DNS servers are typically UNIX servers. You can use BIND DNS on a Linux server; however, although the service is very reliable, the interface is text-based and not as intuitive as other NOSs. For example, here is an excerpt from a named.conf file for accusource.net:

```
zone "accusource.net" {
type master;
file "accusource.db";
```

After you create the zone, you should also create the **reverse lookup zone**, otherwise known as the IN-ADDR.ARPA zone. This zone performs the reverse of a normal query: Instead of resolving a name to an IP address, you're resolving an IP address to a name. A reverse lookup is not as frequently used as a forward lookup, but it is useful if you know the IP address of a host and want to determine its name. Recently, I suspected that a server with a particular IP address was returning errors, but I couldn't remember which server had that specific IP address. By using the *PING* -a command, which returns the host name of the associated IP address, I saw the host name of the server. The host name implied its physical location and role, making it easier to find the specific server. Reverse lookups are also useful for verifying the claimed identity of a connecting host as a security precaution. Another reverse lookup tool is the NSLOOKUP tool available with Windows NT/2000.

DNS Records

Creating records is a straightforward process that again is mostly a matter of using the operating system interface or manually entering records in UNIX/Linux.

The following list is not exhaustive, but it itemizes the main DNS records of which you should be aware:

- **SOA record**. As discussed earlier, an SOA record identifies the authoritative name server for a given domain.
- **Name Server (NS) record**. Specifies what DNS servers are delegated servers for the domain, meaning that the server specified in the record can resolve queries authoritatively.
- **PTR (pointer) record**. The actual record used in reverse lookups.
- **Address (A) record**. Also known as a host record, this is the actual record that resolves the host name to the IP address.
- **Mail Exchanger (MX) record**. Routes mail to the appropriate server(s) for members of the domain. If you have multiple MX records for the same domain, you can prioritize the mail servers with numbers between 0 and

65,535, with lower numbers having the highest priority. In Figure 9-7, this mail server with a priority of 10 would have a higher priority than a mail server with a priority of 20.

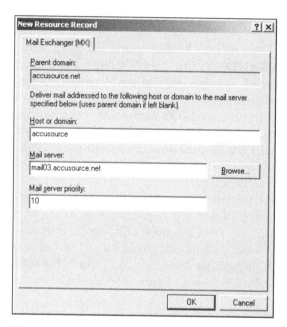

Figure 9-7   A Windows 2000 MX record with a priority of 10

- **CNAME record**. Stands for canonical name record, and is an alias that points to another host. You use CNAME records every time you browse the Internet. When you type *www.xyz.com* into a web browser, "www" represents a server located in the xyz.com domain. However, very few companies actually name their web servers "www." Let's say that the xyz.com domain's web server is actually named websrv13. That would make its true Internet address websrv13.xyz.com. However, most organizations prefer not to expose the true name of their web server on the Internet for security reasons. The xyz.com DNS administrator would then create a CNAME record that directs inbound requests for www.xyz.com to websrv13.xyz.com in a completely transparent way to the users. CNAME records are also useful in directing inbound requests to any of multiple servers. For example, if xyz.com has 13 web servers, a CNAME for each server can be used to direct inbound requests to any one of the 13 web servers.

A common way of directing inbound requests to any of multiple web servers is to use the round-robin method, which you configure using the DNS server properties. DNS directs the inbound request to a host, and then sends the host to the bottom of the list. DNS directs the next request to the next host, and in turn sends that host to the bottom of the list and so on, until the original host returns to the top of the list.

Be meticulous about DNS administration. DNS is a critical service because it points to other services. For example, it might direct network clients to mail servers, logon servers, web/intranet servers, and so on. DNS problems can bring down an entire network. In fact, some major web sites have become unavailable for hours or days because of an incorrect DNS record.

Before closing the discussion on DNS records, I should point out an exciting new technology known as **Dynamic DNS (DDNS)** that greatly reduces the burden of manually creating DNS records. In network environments where Microsoft operating systems exist, NetBIOS names, instead of host names, identify network nodes. Introducing the mechanisms necessary to use and resolve NetBIOS names adds overhead and administration to the network. Beginning with NetWare 5.1 and Windows 2000, you can now rid the network of reliance on NetBIOS because you can instead use DDNS. Using traditional DNS, this would have required the administrative nightmare of manually creating, updating, and deleting DNS records, which usually makes registering hundreds or thousands of desktop clients completely impractical. Now, because of an interaction with the DHCP service, DDNS can accept automatic registrations from clients when they receive their IP configuration from the DHCP server. This capability is not limited to NetWare 5.1 and Windows 2000—any environment including UNIX that implements RFC 2136 can use DDNS. (RFC is "request for comments" and is the titling method used by the Internet Engineering Task Force to identify documents.)

Types of DNS Servers

There are three primary types of DNS servers: primary domain servers, secondary domain servers, and caching-only servers.

- **Primary domain server** is the starting point of all DNS records, containing a read/write-capable zone database: you can add, remove, or modify DNS records from a primary domain server.

- **Secondary domain servers** receive a read-only copy of the zone database from a primary domain server. Secondary domain servers are useful for providing redundancy and load balancing.

- **Caching-only servers** have no zone database, either of their own or copied through a zone transfer from a primary domain server. Caching-only servers mostly function only to improve performance by reducing the number of forwarded queries. When a caching-only server retrieves a resolved query, it stores the result in memory for a period of time known as the **time to live (TTL)**.

When a DNS zone is created, there is a master-slave relationship between the primary master server, master servers, and slave servers as follows:

- **Primary master servers** are the first and final authority for all hosts in their domain. There is only one primary master server per zone, and they are the source for records that are copied to master or slave DNS servers.

- **Master servers** are authoritative DNS servers that transfer zone data to one or more slave servers. ("Authoritative" means that the server is configured to host the zone and return query results.)

- **Slave servers** are authoritative servers that receive the **zone transfer** (a copy of the zone DNS database) from the master server and are named in the zone by NS records.

WINS

The **Windows Internet Naming Service (WINS)**, as the name implies, is a Microsoft invention. In a Microsoft network, there are two types of names, and a client might possess one or both of them: a host name, as discussed in the previous section on DNS, and a NetBIOS name. WINS is a service that performs a similar function to DNS, except that it resolves NetBIOS names instead of host names. (Recall that **NetBIOS** is a broadcast-based name resolution scheme where a client simply broadcasts the NetBIOS name of the computer it wishes to reach to all of the computers on a subnet.) The broadcast message identifies a computer that acknowledges the broadcast and establishes a communication link. The limitations of this are clear from the fact that it is a broadcast message and therefore cannot be routed to another subnet. This resolution method also creates more traffic on the subnet due to the nature of broadcast messages. WINS mitigates both of these problems by registering the NetBIOS names and resolving them to IP addresses that are routable and destination-specific. WINS is only a necessary evil to overcome the inherent limitations of NetBIOS names. Some network applications use WINS to locate network hosts. Also, mapping drives using the *NET USE* command use WINS.

Windows 2000 changes this reliance on WINS for name resolution by registering Windows 2000 computers, servers, and domain controllers via DDNS (as discussed earlier in this chapter). In a strictly Windows 2000 networking environment, DNS is the only name resolution service that is necessary. However, if you have pre-Windows 2000 Microsoft clients, or if you have network applications that require a NetBIOS interface to resolve host names, you will likely need to run the Windows NT or Windows 2000 WINS service.

WINS is a method by which user-friendly NetBIOS computer names can be resolved to IP addresses for the purpose of allowing such communication between hosts on different subnets. In order for this resolution to occur, network hosts must have a way to dynamically add, remove, or update their names in the WINS database. The WINS database is only as good as the accuracy of the records that are contained in it. The database must reflect any changes made to a client's configuration with as little delay as possible. The administrative overhead required to make these changes manually would be prohibitive, so the need for a dynamically updated database is clear.

Name registration occurs when a WINS client requests the use of a NetBIOS name from the WINS server. The WINS server can either accept or reject the request for a NetBIOS name made by the WINS client. The response that is given depends on several factors. If the requested name does not already exist in the WINS database, the WINS server accepts the request and creates a record containing the name of the NetBIOS client and its IP address, among other things. The WINS server also sends an acceptance message containing the TTL parameter to the requesting client.

Resolving NetBIOS Names

Windows 2000 client name resolution follows a very specific order. WINS is one step in that order and is used only after exhausting the first two options. When a Windows 2000 client attempts to reach another host by name, the client determines whether or not to use DNS. DNS resolves the name for the client if there are more than 15 characters or if there are periods in the name. NetBIOS names must be 15 characters or less and cannot contain periods, making DNS the only service that could properly resolve the name.

If the name is 15 characters or less and does not contain periods, the second step is for the client to check its remote name cache stored in RAM for resolution to the IP address. (This is the first step for non-Windows 2000 clients.) The remote name cache is a location in memory that stores recent NetBIOS names to IP address resolutions. This is the most efficient method of name resolution because all the client reads is its own memory.

If the name is not in the cache, the client will contact the configured (either statically or through DHCP) WINS servers to see if there is a record in the database for the requested computer name. If there is a record for the NetBIOS name, the WINS server returns the IP address to the requesting client. The client then uses the address to connect to the desired server.

If the name is not in the WINS database, the client will broadcast the name to the subnet in hope that the desired server will respond. The main limitation of broadcasts is that routers cannot forward broadcast messages to another subnet—so a client that is on another subnet will not be able to respond.

If the broadcast fails, the client will check its LMHOSTS file to see if there is a static entry for the NetBIOS name. The **LMHOSTS file** is a static text file that lists NetBIOS-name-to-IP-address mapping and is the NetBIOS equivalent of the HOSTS file. You can configure entries in the LMHOSTS file to load individual records into the remote name cache at system startup. Therefore, Windows 2000 queries those LMHOSTS records at the very beginning of this process.

If the LMHOSTS file fails to provide resolution, the client queries the DNS resources. First, it queries for HOSTS files. For example, if you know that a client will need to access a specific logon server, adding the name of the host separated by the host's IP address automatically loads the name mapping into memory. If this fails, the client queries the configured (static or DHCP) DNS servers. Figure 9-8 illustrates the process of NetBIOS name resolution.

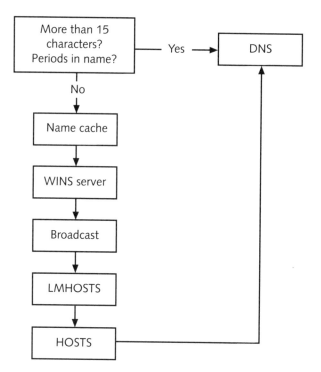

Figure 9-8 NetBIOS name resolution order

 As a memory aid, you can take the first letter of each step in the order and correlate it to the first letter of the following sentence: "Can We Buy Large Hard Drives" (Can = Cache, We = WINS, Buy = Broadcast, and so on).

WINS Replication

As a network becomes larger than just one subnet, and for the sake of redundancy, you should use more than one WINS server. No matter how many WINS servers you have in your network, you will still only have a single WINS database. With multiple servers and one database, **replication** (copying the database from one server to another) is extremely important to ensure that all of the WINS servers have a consistent copy of the database.

You configure each WINS server with one or more replication partners in such a way that all of the WINS servers will eventually receive each change that occurs on a single WINS server. When a WINS client registers its name and IP address with a WINS server, that server is the owner of the record and the record propagates to all of the other WINS servers through a series of replication partners. WINS replication is incremental, meaning that only the changes in the database replicate, not the entire database. The entire database replicates only when you install a new WINS server on the network.

All WINS servers maintain an owner-version mapping table that it builds dynamically and stores in memory. WINS servers use this table in the replication process to identify the server's replication partners and the version of the information that is contained on that server. The field in the table that is important for replication is the Highest ID field, which stores the highest known version ID that is contained on the replication partner. Remember that all records have a Version ID field, which records the highest value contained in all of the version IDs received from a particular replication partner.

Pull Replication Partners

A **pull replication partner** is a WINS replication partner that requests and then accepts changes from its push replication partners. At specified intervals, and when a WINS server starts, the pull replication partner requests all records from the push partner that have a higher version number than the last entry received from that particular pull partner. The amount of time between pull requests is called the **replication interval**, which can be set globally for all WINS servers or can be set at each WINS server that is configured as a pull partner.

The pull replication partner initiates the replication by sending a **replication trigger** message to a push replication partner. When the push replication partner receives the trigger, it scans for the highest version ID contained in the database for all WINS servers on the network. This highest ID for each owner is compared to the highest ID records that the pull replication partner currently has. All of the records that have version ID numbers that fall between the two replicate to the pull partner initiating the replication.

Push Replication Partners

A **push replication partner** is a WINS replication partner that responds to requests for changes from its pull replication partners. Push replication occurs when the WINS server starts or when a set number of name-to-address changes have occurred in the replica contained in the push partner. You can set this value in the properties of the push replication partner WINS server. By default, the number of changes that are required to initiate a push replication is 20. If you enable persistent connections, which is not the default, the number of changes that are required to initiate a push replication is set to zero and any changes are replicated as soon as they are made. You can configure a push replication partner in this situation to initiate changes less frequently. The push/pull replication process is illustrated in Figure 9-9.

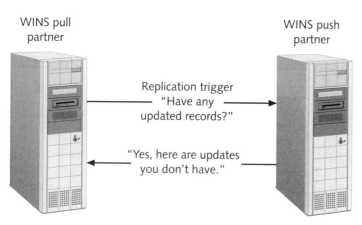

WINS pull
partner

WINS push
partner

Replication trigger
"Have any
updated records?"

"Yes, here are updates
you don't have."

Figure 9-9   The WINS replication process

Push/Pull Replication Partner

A push/pull replication partner acts as both a push and a pull replication partner. This is the default replication functionality for Windows 2000 WINS servers. In general, setting up WINS servers to be push/pull replication partners is the simplest and most effective way to ensure full replication between replication partners.

> Avoid the use of unidirectional replication partners. There are some cases in large networks where the use of unidirectional partners can limit the amount of traffic created over slow WAN links. When configuring unidirectional partners, you should be careful that each server has at least one replication partner. Also, balance unidirectional partners configured over a WAN link with another link in the opposite direction to some other location in the network. Finally, configure primary and secondary WINS servers as direct replication partners of each other.

WINS Proxy Agent

Non-WINS clients use broadcast messages to locate other nodes on the network by default. Broadcast messages are not routed, so that if the client attempts to contact another computer located on another subnet, the non-WINS client must use a statically configured LMHOSTS file to resolve the IP address so that the client can be contacted.

A **WINS proxy agent** is a WINS-enabled computer that you configure to listen on the subnet for WINS broadcast messages, such as query, refresh, release, and registration. The WINS proxy then communicates with the WINS server to resolve or register NetBIOS names.

When a non-WINS client sends a broadcast query for a node on the network using a NetBIOS name, the node with that name responds if it is on the same subnet as the broadcasting node. The WINS proxy agent does not respond to a query message if the non-WINS client is on the same subnet. The WINS proxy agent determines that it is on the same subnet as the requesting client by comparing its address with the address of the requesting client using the subnet mask.

If the node is not on the same subnet, the WINS proxy agent intercepts the broadcast and checks its own cache to see if it has a record of the NetBIOS name and its associated IP address. If it is in the cache, the WINS proxy agent sends the IP address to the non-WINS client so that it may now send routable, directed packets to the desired node.

If the name is not in the cache, the WINS proxy agent queries the WINS server using directed packets. The WINS server then responds with the IP address that is associated with the NetBIOS name. The WINS proxy agent then forwards the information to the non-WINS client and stores the information in its cache for future use.

To configure a WINS-enabled Windows 2000 computer, you must edit its Registry by adding the value EnableProxy to the HKEY_LOCAL_MACHINE Registry subkey as follows:

HKEY_LOCAL_MACHINE\SYSTEM\CurrentControlSet\Services\Netbt\Parameters.

You must set the value to 1 to enable the WINS proxy agent. The type of data is REG_DWORD, and is shown in Figure 9-10.

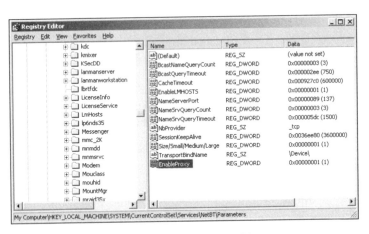

Figure 9-10   The EnableProxy registry subkey

Mail Services

Email used to be available only for internal communications within the office. However, with the ever-expanding Internet, email has become a global medium for both internal and external communications. Email is now possibly the most heavily utilized service in most organizations, and is also the most visible to users. If the web site goes down, users might not notice for a while and can probably continue most of their job functions. If email services fail, users start calling immediately. Running email services involves knowing the main components, adequately preparing the hardware, and planning for disaster, which is discussed in Chapter 10.

Email Protocols

Email requires a transport protocol to get it from one place to another. Each email protocol has its own unique purpose, as listed below:

- **Simple Mail Transport Protocol (SMTP)**. As the name implies, this protocol is very simple. In fact, by itself it only transports basic text—you could not use SMTP alone to send a binary email attachment such as a multimedia file. MIME (see next) adds this functionality. SMTP is the protocol that transfers or forwards mail to an email server. However, when clients retrieve email, they typically use IMAP or POP3.

- **Multipurpose Internet Mail Extensions (MIME)**. This protocol adds the mail capability of attaching and transferring multimedia file attachments. To use MIME, you must also have an email client capable of decoding the MIME format.

- **Post Office Protocol 3 (POP3)**. Both POP and IMAP (see next) use the SMTP protocol for the actual transfer of information, and both allow messages to be stored on the mail server for incoming email. Then when you log on, you download all the email using POP3 with no selectivity.

- **Internet Message Access Protocol (IMAP)**. In its current version (IMAP4), IMAP allows the email client to leave messages on the mail server even after logging on instead of downloading each one. This is useful for keeping email in a central location where it can be organized, archived, and made available to remote locations. You can also search through mail for certain keywords while it is still on the mail server, and selectively download messages that match the search. IMAP integrates with MIME so that users can read the mail header information and then decide whether to separately download the attached files. Compare this to having to download the files with the email before you can read the header, which can take considerably longer with large files.

Notice that some of the email protocols depend upon or interact with others. The protocols are not mutually exclusive, and one email transaction might require several protocols. For example, a friend might send you an email with an attached JPEG picture from his vacation. The message is sent to the server using SMTP, and MIME allows the JPEG picture as an attachment. You dial up to an ISP with IMAP capability and see the header that reads: "A great picture from my vacation." Because you are on a very slow dial-up line and expect the JPEG to be large, you decide not to download it. However, you are expecting an important JPEG file from a co-worker that you want to use in a presentation the next day—so you search for it, again because of IMAP capability. IMAP allows you to find the message, which can then be downloaded.

All email applications include a message store that stores mail until the client downloads it.

Email Server Applications and Requirements

Email has in many ways reduced paper communications, such as the ubiquitous interoffice memo. Software products such as Novell GroupWise and Microsoft Exchange extend the basic communication features of email, offering a host of features such as online collaboration, calendars, newsgroups, contact information, chat functions, and more. Mail servers must also be able to store the messages until the client requests and downloads them. These functions significantly contribute to the hardware requirements of a mail server, which vary broadly depending on the product and utilization. For example, Linux can use the BIND Sendmail program, which requires light hardware resources, because it offers primarily plain email functionality and does not include many of the shiny new features found in some other email server products. Nevertheless, Sendmail is a long-standing favorite among email administrators as it is highly reliable. Find out more about Sendmail at *www.sendmail.org*.

Because a mail server is highly visible, it must be protected with regular backups and additional servers for purposes of redundancy and failover. Also make sure that additional DNS servers are available. Outgoing mail from your organization could go to any of countless other domains, and if you are suddenly without a DNS server to instruct the mail server as to the location of these other mail servers, the mail will not go.

Consider creating an alliance with another organization so that you can act as fault-tolerant partners. If one organization's site goes down and is unavailable to receive mail, the other organization will receive and temporarily store mail until the other's site is back up. Otherwise, the email is likely to bounce back to the sender.

Prepare other servers and network functions in the organization to send and receive mail. The following list should be a minimum starting point:

- Most organizations have firewalls to protect the network from the Internet. Be sure to open the firewall to the protocols mentioned in the previous section so that messages can pass into and out of your organization.

- Add the appropriate MX records to identify and prioritize the email servers. If you also have a backup remote site with mail servers, be sure to configure the MX priority number to be higher than the local mail servers.

- Provide plenty of hardware. If there's any server that you can't underestimate, it's the mail server. Mail taxes every main hardware component, including memory, processors, and hard disk storage. For example, Microsoft Exchange 2000 Server requires 128 MB of RAM (256 MB recommended), 500 MB on the hard disk where you install Exchange 2000, and 200 MB of additional space on the system drive. Note that this is on top of the Windows 2000 operating system, which has minimum requirements of its own, and that a server configured with these minimums will only be able to handle very light mail traffic. A production mail server is likely to have upward of 1 GB of RAM and several gigabytes of disk space to store all the messages.

 TIP Mail programs allow the administrator to set quotas on the user mailbox size. I strongly recommend mail quotas to conserve disk space and improve backup and restore time. A large credit card company in my area made the mistake of not implementing quotas, and many users have mailboxes over 1 GB in size. The strain is so heavy on the mail system that about every week a hard disk fails. Figure 9-11 shows the interface for configuring mail quotas for Exchange 2000.

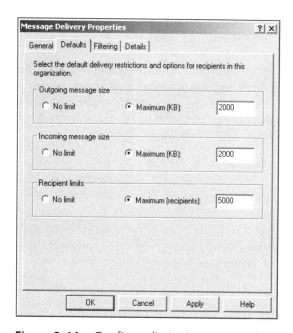

Figure 9-11   Configure limits (quotas) on the size of messages and the permitted number of recipients

- Mail server hard disk performance quickly degrades because of the constant write activity. Be sure to defragment the hard disk regularly.

- Mail is also very taxing to network bandwidth. Make sure that you have plenty of available bandwidth, and also consider using a multihomed NIC configuration (such as adapter teaming).

- Because mail service is so active and demanding, mail servers should generally be dedicated to mail instead of serving multiple purposes. If necessary, you might include a relatively light additional service such as DHCP, but also using the mail server as a heavily utilized database application server would be out of the question.

■ Email is often the primary vehicle by which viruses invade a network. It would be foolish not to implement a comprehensive and reliable antivirus solution to check email.

Choose your mail server product very carefully. If you later decide to change to a different product, it can be very disruptive, even though most products include a means by which a competitor's mail service can be converted. Also, the mail product can alter the operating system. For example, Exchange 2000 adds modifications to the Windows 2000 Active Directory schema that are permanent. Even if you uninstall Exchange 2000, the schema changes remain. On the plus side, the mail product can greatly simplify administration. For example, you might be able to create a user account and simultaneously create a mail account instead of creating them separately. Likewise, carefully select the email client to reduce licensing expenses and support burdens.

■ Prepare for legal issues. Most companies consider employee email to be company property when delivered to a company address using company equipment. Many employees disagree. When users are hired, be sure to notify them in writing that email is neither the property of the employee nor private, if that is the company position.

Web and FTP Servers

Even small and medium-sized organizations usually have a web presence—a web site seems to be as necessary as company stationery. A few years ago, some segments of the IT talent pool knew how to set up a web site, usually on a UNIX server. Now, it is a given that administrators know at least the basics of web site configuration and administration. This section addresses the server's role as a web and FTP server.

Web Server Requirements

As with mail servers, web and FTP servers (which we will collectively refer to as only "web servers") are normally dedicated solely to those respective functions. The specific type of web server you run depends largely on the needs of the organization, the number of hits (visitors) on the site, and the type of access. For light-duty web service, virtually any server might be able to run the site. An administrator might configure Internet Information Server (IIS) on a Windows NT server, create some basic content, and probably have the site running and available in less than an hour. However, a web site of this scale will not suit most active business concerns. A medium-sized or large organization usually requires web service with:

■ Dedicated bandwidth to Internet traffic that is separate from the LAN connection to the Internet. Although you could share the bandwidth, LAN traffic might adversely affect the responsiveness of the web site and vice versa.

- A large, fast, and redundant disk storage solution such as Fibre Channel RAID for multimedia or file downloads. Consider placing download files on an FTP server because it is a more efficient file transfer protocol than HTTP. You can configure the link on the web page to point to an FTP site to initiate the download—the user does not have to type in an FTP address. Plain web page content by itself does not usually require a great deal of hard disk space.

- Adequate processing power. Processing power requirements vary greatly. For example, a web server can answer thousands of hits per day, yet have relatively little processor utilization if the web content is simple. However, more complex functions such as online transaction processing (OLTP), as required for Internet credit card purchases, can require significantly more processing power. The transaction itself will take place in a back-end database on a different server; however, the encryption required to validate the server and clients requires processing power. That's why if you visit your bank's web site, the home page probably loads quickly (little processing involved). But logging in using 128-bit Secure Sockets Layer (SSL) encryption to access your bank account requires a lot more processing power, and it may take several seconds to access your information.

- A digital certificate that validates the organization to the public. The digital certificate is an authentication mechanism using a form of digital identification, which enables SSL encryption between clients and hosts. For example, VeriSign (*www.verisign.com*) is a leading source of digital certificates. When visitors access a site, they want to know that the site is reputable and trustworthy, especially for online SSL transactions. A certificate is like a recommendation from the Better Business Bureau, only better.

- Adequate memory. As much of the entire web page content as possible (except for download files and streaming media) should fit into main memory. As visitors access the site, the pages load into cache, where they are available at a much faster rate than by using disk retrieval.

- Redundant servers. If the web site is simply "Here's some info about our company," then it might not be worthwhile to invest in one or more redundant servers. However, if the site contributes directly to your business's revenues, redundancy is critical so that if a web server fails, another can continue to provide service (usually through clustering). In a large web site with frequent traffic, a web server farm probably has several clusters, each comprised of several servers.

- A secure firewall if the site is connected to your LAN. However, it is a better practice to protect normal traffic to and from the LAN and to place web content on a physically separate and independent Internet connection. This is a security precaution ensuring that even if a malicious Internet user breaches your web security, the LAN is still unreachable.

9

■ One or more webmasters to create and manage the content. In a smaller organization, the network administrator might fulfill this function, but larger organizations have full-time employees or contractors.

 Most webmasters are experts at creating web content only! They are not web server administrators, and should not be given access to web administration tools.

In the past few years, all major server manufacturers have brought 1U or 2U servers to market. These are dedicated network appliances that serve only one purpose and are not intended for multiple services or applications. High-density, low-cost web servers are increasingly popular for serving web content. The local hard disk only stores the NOS and web server software, while the web content is usually on a separate array, so only a single local hard disk is required. You can also consider using caching-only servers that only cache web content for increased responsiveness. These servers can cache inbound Internet traffic (known as forward proxy) to improve performance for your users or for your web site. Reverse proxy caches your site's content for Internet clients accessing your web servers. This offloads incoming requests for static content, increasing the number of concurrent users or connections the web server is able to maintain, while at the same time improving the browsing experience for those users pointing their browsers to the web server.

After configuring the web servers with adequate hardware, you have another issue to consider: Where do you put the server? You can place the server in your local organization, except that if the site is large and busy, the physical plant might not be sufficient, and building another server room might not be practical. Many organizations co-locate their web servers at a company whose primary business is to provide a highly available physical site for your web. This provides many advantages:

■ Co-locators provide the physical plant, including power and environmental controls. Using co-location is generally very cost effective compared to building from scratch.

■ Site traffic has no impact on your local network utilization, and because the site is physically disconnected from your LAN, a breach in web security does not directly affect local operations.

■ Bandwidth availability is excellent, as most co-locators are directly tapped into the Internet backbone and usually offer extremely high throughput and redundancy through a **SONET** ring, which is a fiber optic transmission medium that is self-healing. If a line is cut, traffic redirects to another ring.

■ Co-locators offer guaranteed uptime. While policies vary from one co-locator to the next, redundant power (including UPS systems and backup generators), redundant Internet connections, fire detection and extinguishing, and a high level of security help make sure your site stays available. In addition, co-locators provide on-site personnel 24/7.

- Stringent security requires administrators visiting their servers to have a passkey of some kind to open the door and access the site. Security cameras are everywhere.

- Administrators can still remotely monitor and manage the site over the Internet.

Colloquially speaking, administrators refer to a co-location arrangement as "ping power pipe." You can "ping" the server from anywhere on the Internet to see if it responds, "power" is always available, and the "pipe" is the line to the Internet.

In Hands-on Project 9-4 at the end of this chapter, you will visit the web site of a co-locator.

Configuring a Web Server

Each major NOS offers a different product for web management, as listed below:

- OS/2 and NetWare 5.1—WebSphere: an IBM product that provides excellent management tools with a relatively intuitive graphical user interface. OS/2 can also use a combination of WebSphere, HTTP Server, Lotus Notes Domino, and Apache.

- UNIX/Linux—Apache: a text-based tool that (as usual for UNIX products), is open source code, highly reliable, and not at all intuitive. However, a newer version of Apache for Windows NT is in development and should be more intuitive.

Perhaps the reliability of UNIX and Apache is best attested to by Microsoft itself. For years, Microsoft ran a version of UNIX known as FreeBSD and Apache web services for the Microsoft Hotmail web site. In 2000, Microsoft finally switched to their own products: Windows 2000 and IIS 5.0.

- Windows NT/2000—Internet Information Server (IIS): the best testament to IIS is that Microsoft's own web site, one of the largest and busiest in the world, runs IIS 5.0. The GUI is simple to operate, yet is rich in features.

Each of these products is a study in itself; however, Hands-on Project 9-4 at the end of the chapter will step you through the basics using IIS 5.0 on Windows 2000 Server. In addition, there are scores of third-party web server software products vying for position within the ever-expanding web server market.

Remote Access Service

Remote access service (RAS) is the ability of a server to accept a connection from a client even when physically disconnected from the LAN. Users establish the connection on their end through dial-up modem connections or existing Internet connections using a **virtual private network (VPN)**. Once the connection is established, the user experience is the same as if directly connected to the local LAN, except that over a dial-up connection, network responsiveness is much slower. A VPN connection can be much better because although it usually takes place over the public, unsecured Internet, the session is protected inside an encrypted virtual "tunnel" that is extremely difficult for intruders to breach. The VPN can be just as slow (or slower because of the encryption overhead) if the Internet connection is dial-up, but with the availability of high-speed Internet access, a user might experience significantly better performance.

Regardless of the method, RAS represents another arena of responsibility for the administrator. You provision the server to accept RAS connections, and you also ensure that the connections are secure. The physical preparations for a modem pool were discussed at the end of Chapter 7. In Hands-on Project 9-7, you will use Windows 2000 as an example of configuring a server so that it is ready to accept the connections.

 You can also create VPNs inside your LAN to further guard against intruders. For example, if you wanted to protect a server that contained sensitive information, you could open it up only to users permitted to connect through a VPN (in addition to setting appropriate file and logon permissions as usual). Anyone intercepting the VPN session between user and server is very unlikely to retrieve any useful information.

 Although a persistent hacker could obtain the phone numbers for dial-up connections, you should make it as difficult as possible. Instruct users not to share the phone numbers with persons outside your organization. If you suspect a compromised number, change it as soon as possible.

Protocol Support

You are already aware of the basic protocols such as TCP/IP, IPX/SPX, and NetBEUI. You can usually use each of these protocols to communicate with a RAS server. However, there are additional protocols that are used to establish and secure the connection.

The first type of protocol is a line protocol. Network protocols are designed for network media such as 10BaseT Ethernet over CAT5 cable. When RAS clients dial in to the server over a phone line, TCP/IP alone won't work, because it is incompatible with conventional phone lines. Instead, when clients dial up the modem and establish a connection, a line protocol encapsulates the network protocol. Encapsulated packets are then sent across the connection where the server unwraps the line protocol packet. The packet then transmits over the network like an ordinary network packet. This process is illustrated in Figure 9-12, in which the PPP packet encapsulates a TCP/IP packet.

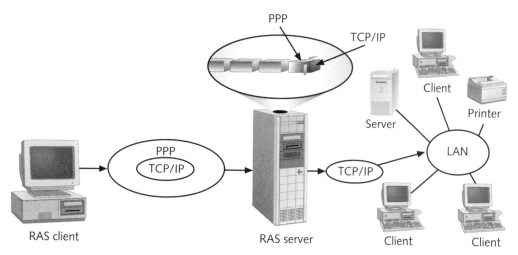

Figure 9-12   Line protocol encapsulation

The following are the two most common line protocols:

- **Point-to-Point Protocol (PPP).** A very flexible line protocol, PPP interoperates with a variety of RAS software packages. PPP supports the NetBEUI, IPX/SPX, and TCP/IP protocols, data compression and encryption, and authentication protocols (addressed later in this chapter). The NetWare implementation of PPP is PPPRNS (Point-to-Point Protocol Remote Node Service) and is very similar, though it does not support NetBEUI.

- **Serial Line Internet Protocol (SLIP).** A more common line protocol in the past than it is today, SLIP uses only the TCP/IP protocol and is useful for UNIX connections. In Windows, when you connect with SLIP, a Windows Terminal dialog box opens allowing you to perform an interactive logon with the UNIX server. SLIP is very basic and does not support authentication protocols, encryption, or compression.

In addition to a line protocol, you need a tunneling protocol in order to establish a VPN connection. There are two primary tunneling protocols:

- **Point-to-Point Tunneling Protocol (PPTP).** A popular and easy-to-configure tunneling protocol. Configure both the server and the client to establish the VPN connection using PPTP and make the connection.

- **Level 2 Tunneling Protocol (L2TP).** A newer VPN protocol that requires an established certificate authority. Clients establishing a connection must download a certificate from the certificate authority. The certificate then validates the connection attempt over the VPN connection attempt.

Security Protocols

Logging on remotely exposes the connection to eavesdroppers who could tap the connection and retrieve user name/password combinations. To avoid this vulnerability, you need to select an encryption method. The most common ones are listed below and are supported in varying degrees by all the major NOSs.

- **Password Authentication Protocol (PAP)**. PAP sends logon information in clear text—using a packet sniffer, an eavesdropper can analyze the packet and retrieve the logon data. PAP is the last resort—use it only when the server you dial into does not support any of the other authentication protocols.

- **Shiva Password Authentication Protocol (SPAP)**. Shiva products (acquired by Intel) are a popular alternative to Microsoft RAS solutions. Shiva encrypts authentication credentials for Shiva LAN Rover software.

- **Challenge Handshake Authentication Protocol (CHAP)**. CHAP is a flexible and common authentication protocol that supports encryption for a variety of operating systems. Microsoft has two specific implementations: MS-CHAP for all Windows clients and MS-CHAP v2 for Windows 2000 clients.

Configuring RAS on a Server

Each network operating system has unique methods for configuring a RAS server. The important thing is to know about all the protocols discussed so far in this chapter, because a critical matter in configuring client/server RAS communication is ensuring that settings on both sides match. Mismatched settings do not cause a poor connection; they usually prevent connection altogether. You must then determine what caused the problem. Most of the time, connection problems relate to mismatched security protocols. For example, if you are trying to connect using PAP but the RAS server accepts only MS-CHAP v2, the client logon attempt will be denied.

Figure 9-13 shows a Windows 2000 dial-up client with authentication settings for PAP, SPAP, and CHAP. As a rule, connection attempts first try the most secure available method and, failing that, move to the next most secure method until all available authentication methods are exhausted. Figure 9-14 shows the default Windows 2000 Server dial-in settings. The client shown in Figure 9-13 will not succeed in the connection attempt to this server, because only MS-CHAP and MS-CHAP v2 are permitted.

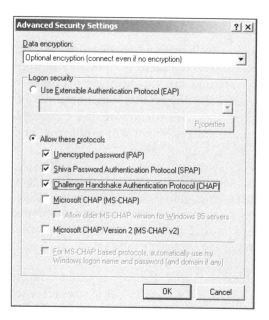

Figure 9-13   Windows 2000 dial-up client authentication

9

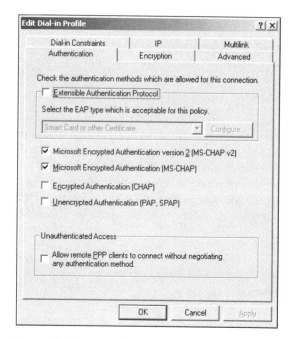

Figure 9-14   Windows 2000 Server dial-in settings

Fax Services

Faxing has become a vital business activity. While some organizations use fax machines and only require light usage, others might send hundreds or thousands of pages each day. For organizations that require high-volume fax capability, it becomes completely impractical to stand in line at the fax machine hoping that someone ahead of you is not faxing *War and Peace*. Fortunately, a combination of hardware and software technology makes sending and receiving faxes much more efficient and productive, and users can perform fax functions from their desks.

Even with the best fax server systems, most organizations will still keep some fax machines around, as it is still practical for sending copies of physical documents. Also, if you want to send a quick fax to someone and do not expect to do so again, it's probably easier to just punch in the number and hit "send" than to enter all the contact information in the fax software.

A fax server comes in two basic hardware formats: turnkey and computer-based. **Turnkey fax servers** are self-contained, freestanding devices in which fax software and hardware are already installed, and except for some company-specific configurations, they are ready to use right out of the box. Our attention will focus on the alternative, computer-based fax servers, which require separate hardware and software.

Fax hardware can consist of a simple fax modem that is shared from a single PC. While this might be acceptable for a small workgroup requiring only light-duty fax service, our focus will be on higher-volume solutions for which you will need one or more fax boards. Besides the fact that a single fax board can send or receive many times more faxes than a conventional fax machine, a fax board offers several other characteristics and advantages:

- Fax boards are specially tuned for fast **handshakes** (that soothing squawking noise that faxes and modems make when establishing a connection) and fax compression. This only saves a few seconds, but when multiplied by the number of users and the long distance rate of faxes (especially overseas), it makes a big difference. In addition, fax boards have a higher throughput than conventional faxes, so even at 14.4 Kbps, it can send a page in about 15 seconds instead of 60 seconds.

The most common fax speed remains 14.4 Kbps even though there is also a 28.8 Kbps standard available.

- Resolution is usually better on a fax server than most conventional fax machines. Also, the fax software often includes the ability to "clean up" unclear faxes.

- Security-sensitive documents are vulnerable to the curious on a conventional fax machine. Once at a company where I worked, a manager faxed a spreadsheet of all the salaries for employees in my department and left it on the machine. A co-worker found and read the spreadsheet. (No matter what I did, I couldn't get him to tell me other people's salaries; perhaps he knew it would make me mad.) On a fax server, you fax from the desktop and nobody else sees it.

- A fax server saves users the frustration of clearing jams, replacing toner and paper, waiting in line, and beating the machine with other office equipment.

- Most fax machines collect data on inbound and outbound faxes, but you print it out and that's that. A fax server allows you to organize the data and use software products specially designed for reporting (such as Crystal Reports). Reports are useful for determining which users or departmentrs send and receive the most faxes, finding out when fax traffic is heaviest, and so on. Reports are also as permanent a record as you like, whereas fax machine logs must be periodically cleared.

- Inbound faxes can go to a departmental printer, or remain electronic and go to fax software or, better yet, an email inbox on the user's computer.

- The fax software automatically fills in cover sheet information, such as who is sending the document and the number of pages. Broadcast fax cover sheets can name individuals instead of all parties.

- Mobile users might be unavailable to receive a physical fax at the office. Using client fax software, they can have the fax forwarded to their email inbox or to a printer at their current location.

Fax boards are PCI, and therefore can be installed in most computers—PC or otherwise. However, fax server software is usually a UNIX, NetWare, or NT/2000 product. Many vendors also include software that integrates with Lotus Notes, Microsoft Exchange, Novell GroupWise, SMTP/POP3, and more.

You can combine other services or functions with a fax server, but be aware of the kinds of resources it requires. First, faxing requires processing power for compression, error correction, data packet creation, and other fax-related processes; so you should not share any processor-intensive functions with the fax server. An exception for this can be made if the fax board itself offloads these duties from the processor. Second, if faxes are stored on the server, plan for plenty of hard disk space. Calculate for the average size of inbound faxes and the length of time they are likely to be stored. In many cases though, you will offload the faxes to another server such as a Novell GroupWise or Microsoft Exchange Server. Memory requirements are not high; you usually only need enough to run the fax software, probably 32 MB.

For more about fax servers, consult:

- *www.faxserverfaq.com*

- *www.dialogic.com*

- *www.facsys.com*

SNA Server

Systems Network Architecture (SNA) Server harkens back to 1974 and IBM's networking standards for mainframes. In those days, users sat at dumb terminals that accessed a mainframe server through a text-based terminal session. The reason why this history is important is that the basic mainframe architecture still exists today, and access to many midrange systems is similar—IBM's AS/400 and AS/390 servers, for example. Users must connect to these servers, but usually do not sit at dumb terminals anymore. Now, users usually sit at Microsoft Windows clients and connect to the mainframe using a terminal emulator that appears to the server as if it were a dumb terminal. However, making a straight connection like this from Windows and maintaining all the features of Windows and the mainframe at the same time is not always practical or possible. SNA Server is a Microsoft product that acts as a gateway between the client and the mainframe.

Microsoft has a successor to SNA Server: Host Integration Server, which is compatible with Windows NT 4.0 and integrates with Windows 2000. For the sake of our discussion, we will collectively refer to these products as SNA Server.

The following list briefly describes several main features of SNA Server:

- Windows users connect to the mainframe (known in this context as a "host," not to be confused with simply a TCP/IP host) through client software. From a web browser, a user can click on a link that automatically downloads the necessary client software to their local computer. The client software allows users to be a "client" to the host and run whichever terminal emulation software or application suits their needs.

- Users have difficulty remembering passwords, and experience even more difficulty if they must log on more than once—first to a Windows 2000 server and then to a host. Often, the accounts are not synchronized (the user name and/or password is different), further complicating matters. Using SNA Server, administrators can synchronize user accounts so that they are consistent between the host and the Windows NT or Windows 2000 domain, and changing the password on one system automatically synchronizes with the other.

- Database availability is improved because SNA allows users to access mainframe-based databases such as DB2 (an IBM database).

- Uniform performance monitoring allows the administrator to use Windows NT/2000 Performance Monitor to analyze server performance on hosts.

- Administrators streamline the burden of file resource access. SNA applies Windows NT/2000 file security on shared folders as if the resource was on a local Windows NT/2000 server. This allows you to apply the same security permissions and access rights as with any other file.

- Print compatibility is improved because users can send mainframe print jobs to LAN printers without changing host applications.

- SNA server failure has less impact on user productivity because you can use multiple SNA servers for failover and load-balancing purposes.

- By itself, a logon using a 3270 terminal, for example, is sent in clear text, making it easy for someone intercepting the sign-on to read the user name and password. SNA Server encrypts the data streams between the server and client.

APPLICATION SERVERS

You can run applications in one of three basic implementations: dedicated, distributed, or peer-to-peer.

- **Dedicated application**—As discussed with some of the services earlier in this chapter (email services, for example), servers sometimes run only a single application or service and nothing else. This helps to assure that application performance is unhindered by interference from other applications or services and also contributes to the stability of the server. The application software does not run on the workstation, though a client piece might, such as using Outlook Express to retrieve email from a UNIX Sendmail dedicated server.

- **Distributed application**—The application runs on the server. The client can send requests to the server but does not run the application or perform processing. Probably the most common example of this type of application is a database. The client sends a query to the database server, which returns the results of the query to the client.

- **Peer-to-peer (P2P) application**—A good example of a peer-to-peer application is the controversial Napster music-sharing service. A P2P application server primarily exists to run software that allows peer computers to communicate with one another. In the case of Napster, the peers search for and download music from one another. The server functions mostly as a gateway for the clients. An important issue with P2P servers is that they provide appropriate security measures so that users can search for and download files from other users without being able to access unauthorized materials.

MONITORING PROTOCOLS

Most networks are much larger than the administrator can practically administer if he or she had to physically visit each server and network device. Therefore, a means by which administrators can access remote servers is necessary. Each network operating system allows general administration from afar using various administrative tools. For example, you can manage a NetWare 5.1 server using the NWAdmn32.exe program from any Windows client regardless of geographic distance. However, administrators also require a way to proactively monitor servers and network equipment like routers, hubs, and switches. How does the administrator know when a router becomes saturated beyond its ability to function? Is there a way that administrators can see an increasing trend in network traffic and prepare a proactive solution? The answer to both questions is found in the monitoring protocol.

There are two primary monitoring protocols: Simple Network Management Protocol (SNMP) and Desktop Management Interface (DMI), with SNMP being the most prevalent.

SNMP

Simple Network Management Protocol (SNMP) is really of no use by itself. Its usefulness is comprised of several elements that work together with the ultimate purpose of informing the administrator of a changing trend in the use of an object or alerting the administrator of an error, failure, or condition. For example, an administrator might want to know well in advance when the 100 GB disk array is down to 10 GB so that he or she can make sure that more storage is available. This prevents the reactive response in which users complain about out-of-disk-space errors and the administrator must scramble at the last minute to find additional storage. With third-party SNMP software, the administrator can be notified in a number of ways about the low-storage problem. The administrator can configure a response in any of several forms, such as an email message, pager alert, or network message to a workstation at which the administrator is logged on.

A useful SNMP solution consists of several individual components:

- **SNMP management system**—Also known as a management console, this is the computer that runs SNMP management software. The software can run on any compatible computer; it does not have to be a server, though it often is. The SNMP management system sends requests for information from the monitored system, known as the SNMP agent. Except for an alarm-triggering event, the SNMP agent does not normally initiate messages.

- **SNMP agent**—A service that runs on the actual object you want to manage or monitor. For example, if you have a web server and want to receive an alert when the number of concurrent connections exceeds a certain threshold, you would configure the web server as an SNMP agent.

- **Management Information Base (MIB)**—A database of definitions for the specific device being monitored. For example, one of the MIB values associated with a particular device could be "sysUpTime," which specifies the elapsed time since the managed device was booted. Similar to host-name-to-IP-address mapping, a MIB value has an official name and a dot notation. For example, the dot notation for sysUpTime is 1.3.6.1.2.1.1.3.0, though it's obviously easier to use the official name.

- **Communities**—A group of hosts that use the same community name. You can name the community whatever makes sense for your organization. The community name is not so much a grouping as it is a small measure of security. When SNMP queries are issued to a community, only members of that community respond, and the community name functions as a rudimentary password.

 SNMP has no security of its own, and a malicious user with a packet sniffer could retrieve SNMP traffic, and then through impersonation, return false information to the SNMP management system. Newer implementations of SNMP are introducing public key/private key verification techniques to prevent this situation.

- **Traps**—When the SNMP agent issues a message to the SNMP management system, it is known as a trap.

As an example of configuring an SNMP agent, look at the Windows 2000 SNMP Service Properties dialog box in Figure 9-15. The check boxes in the Service frame specify what type of device is involved. For example, if the device is a router, you would select the Internet item. For explanation of the other devices, use the online Help function.

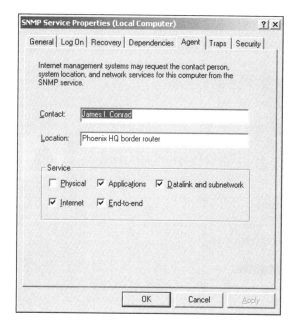

Figure 9-15   Configuring the SNMP agent properties on a Windows 2000 server

Continuing the Windows 2000 example, notice the Traps tab shown in Figure 9-16. Here, you specify the community name and the trap destination. The agent can only send messages to hosts that know the community name.

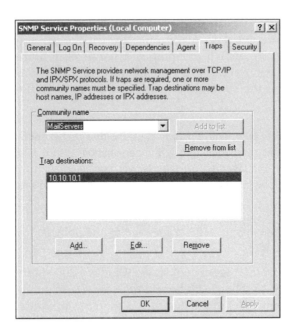

Figure 9-16   Specify the community name and the trap destination's IP or IPX address

Finally, specify rudimentary security on the Security tab, where you select accepted management systems with which the agent is allowed to communicate (Figure 9-17).

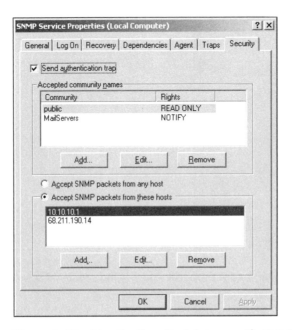

Figure 9-17   Use the Security tab to specify SNMP management systems with which this host can communicate

You might also find RMON on certain network devices. **Remote monitoring (RMON)** is an extension of the SNMP protocol and provides more comprehensive network monitoring capabilities. Instead of devices answering queries from the SNMP management system, RMON proactively sets off alarms for a variety of traffic conditions. As the full RMON protocol is quite comprehensive, only portions of it are usually placed into network devices such as routers.

There are several utilities and applications that use SNMP; however, the three most significant vendors are:

- Computer Associates' Unicenter TNG (*www.ca.com*)

- IBM's Tivoli (*www.tivoli.com*)

- Hewlett-Packard's OpenView (*www.hp.com*)

DMI

The **Desktop Management Interface (DMI)** is similar to SNMP, except that it contains specific information about an actual device. Instead of using a MIB, DMI uses a **Management Information File (MIF)** database that can contain information such as model ID, serial number, memory, and port addresses. DMI often runs in conjunction with SNMP. For example, when an SNMP query arrives at the agent, DMI can enter MIF information in the SNMP MIB.

9

THE SERVER AS A NETWORK DEVICE

Network operating systems can enable a server to fulfill roles traditionally reserved only for hardware network devices such as routers, bridges, and firewalls. I recommend that you stick with the faster and more reliable hardware solutions for the most part, because servers must simultaneously cope with countless other activities and variables. For example, how often does a router crash because of a software bug? Never. But a server functioning as a router must not only perform routing functions, but also simultaneously load millions of lines of operating system code into memory, run a few services just to stay alive (if not perform additional functions), share processor utilization with other functions, depend upon many other physical devices in the server (each one representing another possible point of failure), and so on.

Nevertheless, for the smaller, value-conscious organization or a smaller department within an organization, a server network device might suit your needs. For example, even if you work for a gigantic organization, if it has a small satellite office in Nome, AK, with only five workstations and one server, it's probably not cost effective to install a Cisco router costing thousands of dollars to connect the office to a WAN. Instead, you would use the existing server. Because there is likely to be very little network traffic going through the server anyway, the risk is reduced to the point of being acceptable.

The Server as a Router

Configuring the server as a network device such as a router (also known as a gateway for our purposes) requires at least two network cards. In the case of a server configured as a router, one NIC connects to one network or subnet, and the other NIC connects to another network or subnet. The static IP address you assign to each respective NIC is in the same network range as the subnet to which it connects, as illustrated in the NetWare 5.1 example Figure 9-18. You will also configure the NICs the same way if the server functions as a firewall or bridge.

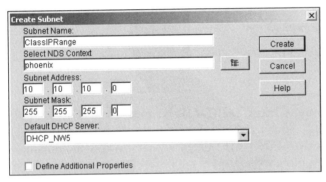

Figure 9-18   The NIC for each respective network matches the network address of the subnet to which it connects

 A server router connecting two different types of networks (for example, Ethernet and Token Ring) also acts as a bridge. There is not a specific configuration in most NOSs to make the server a bridge only.

After configuring the NICs, it's only a matter of configuring the respective operating system to perform the function you want. For example, to configure Windows 2000 as a router, you would use the Routing and Remote Access (RRAS) tool (Start, Programs, Administrative Tools, Routing and Remote Access). If this is the first RRAS function you have configured, a wizard guides you through the process. Otherwise, you will have to manually add a routing protocol such as RIP or OSPF and then specify the NICs participating in the routing function. (A brief explanation of these routing protocols follows.)

RIP

Router Information Protocol (RIP) is a distance vector-based protocol, which identifies the best route for a destination based on the number of hops (number of routers that the message passes through). RIP has the following advantages:

- *Configuration*—You enable RIP on the router interface; no further configuration is necessary.

- *Simplicity*—Routing table advertisements are very simple (compared to OSPF) and easier to read.

- *Compatibility*—Most routers are compatible with RIP.

RIP is a fine protocol for simple purposes, but it can run into problems in more complex routing scenarios. Its disadvantages include:

- *Delayed convergence*—**Convergence** is the state in which all routers connected to a network have the same updated information. RIP exchanges routing tables in an unsynchronized and unacknowledged manner. Consequently, internetwork convergence might take several minutes, a costly lapse in a production network.

- *Larger routing table size*—Multiple routes to a network destination can appear as multiple entries in the routing table. Though this might not affect smaller networks, large networks with multiple paths can generate hundreds or thousands of entries in the RIP routing table.

- *Greater network traffic overhead*—Because of the larger routing tables generated by RIP, route advertising requires more network overhead. Route advertising continues to update routing information every 30 to 90 seconds, even after convergence. This means that the router's entire routing table is passed to all other known routers.

- *Poor scalability*—RIP broadcasts its entire routing table, making them much larger than OSPF tables. This generates an unreasonable degree of network traffic on larger networks. Also, RIP only accepts up to 15 hops.

- *Routing loops*—When a router learns of a downed link, it notifies a neighbor, which in turn notifies its neighbors. However, if an upstream neighbor issues its 30–90 second update table before it learns of the downed link, then all its downstream neighbors view the downed link as available again. This routing loop is difficult to troubleshoot and usually requires manual intervention to fix.

Note The routing loop description here is only one type of routing loop and is known as "counting to infinity." Several other types of routing loops could occur within a RIP network.

- *Less efficient*—Because RIP builds best path determination based only upon the number of hops to a destination, the path can sometimes be less efficient. For example, it might take only three hops to get from Network A to Network F. However, one of the hops must take place over a 56 Kbps demand-dial link. A faster route might exist over a four-hop T1 link, but a RIP-based router will not use it.

9

OSPF

The **Open Shortest Path First (OSPF)** routing protocol builds its routing tables using a link-state algorithm, which calculates the shortest path to each host based on the network topology, not just the fewest number of hops (as with RIP). The algorithm uses not only hop count, but also other factors, such as available bandwidth and network congestion, to determine the best path to a destination. Routing tables are smaller and update more often, but they are more efficient and converge more quickly than RIP. OSPF is quickly replacing RIP in most implementations. OSPF has the following advantages:

- *More rapid convergence*—OSPF routers converge much more quickly than RIP routers and are not susceptible to routing loops.

- *Smaller routing table size*—Instead of storing every possible path to a destination, the SPF algorithm calculates the best path and stores only that path in the routing table.

- *Less network traffic overhead*—Because of smaller routing tables, and because routing tables are not broadcast redundantly, OSPF requires less network traffic.

- *Hop count*—There's virtually no limit on hop count.

- *Scalability*—All of the above features make OSPF more scalable and suitable for large networks.

- *Compatibility*—Most current network devices can accept and use the OSPF protocol.

The OSPF routing protocol also has some disadvantages, but they are largely outweighed by the advantages:

- *Greater use of resources*—The database of link-state advertisements and the SPF calculations required for path determination require more memory and processor use than RIP.

- *More complex configuration and use*—Link-state protocol implementation requires careful planning, and the configuration options are more extensive than for RIP. Link-state protocols are also more complex and difficult to understand than RIP; however, this might not be a direct concern unless you need to perform detailed network analysis.

As a rule, most network administrators prefer the scalability, flexibility, and accuracy of the OSPF protocol over RIP.

The Server as a Firewall

Recall from earlier discussions that a firewall protects your LAN from other networks (usually the Internet). A proxy server serves the same function by impersonating the internal client, and is a term we will use interchangeably with firewall. The proxy accepts

Internet requests from the LAN client, represents the client on the Internet, and issues the request to the Internet destination host. When the Internet host returns an answer (usually a web page), the proxy forwards the content to the original LAN client. The proxy server performs this function for all its internal clients and, to the Internet at large, appears to be a single, very busy Internet client. The proxy also prevents LAN users from accessing sites forbidden by the organization.

A firewall server can be a hardware or software solution, and is in itself a form of routing. However, server firewalls can offer very sophisticated and advanced features, making potential weaknesses in operating stability a more acceptable risk, especially when there are redundant proxy servers.

Besides protecting the LAN, a proxy server improves Internet performance for the clients by using caching. When the proxy server delivers a web page to a client, it also caches the page in memory and on a hard disk cache. The proxy server delivers the same content to the next client that wants to view the same page. This saves Internet network bandwidth and greatly improves responsiveness for frequently accessed pages.

Although you can configure the basic NOS to perform some firewall functions, such as allowing access only to certain IP addresses, you configure a proxy server using additional server software in most cases. For example, Novell NetWare uses an add-on product called BorderManager, and Windows NT/2000 use Microsoft Proxy Server 2.0 or Internet Security and Acceleration (ISA) Server.

9

CHAPTER SUMMARY

- ❐ DHCP automatically distributes IP addresses to DHCP clients, avoiding the error-prone and time-consuming process of manually entering IP configuration on hosts. The DHCP lease process uses a discovery, offer, request, and acknowledgment process.

- ❐ DNS resolves IP addresses to names and vice versa, replacing the need for a HOSTS file. The resolver is the client waiting for a name resolution answer. If a DNS server does not have the answer to a request, it can use other DNS servers in a recursive query or use an iterative query, which simply refers the original resolver to another DNS server.

- ❐ DNS servers are useful for forward lookups, in which a resolver submits the host name and requests an IP address, or reverse lookups, in which the client submits the IP address and requests the host name. There are several types of DNS records, including A records, MX records, and CNAME records.

- ❐ There are several types of DNS servers, including primary master, master, slave, secondary domain, and caching-only.

- ❐ Beginning with NetWare 5.1 and Windows 2000, you can rid the network of reliance on NetBIOS because you can instead use Dynamic DNS (DDNS). Because of an interaction with the DHCP service, DDNS can accept automatic registrations from clients when they receive their IP configuration from the DHCP server. Any environment including UNIX that implements RFC 2136 can use DDNS.

❏ WINS is a method by which user-friendly NetBIOS computer names can be resolved to IP addresses for the purpose of allowing such communication between hosts on different subnets. Name registration occurs when a WINS client requests the use of a NetBIOS name from the WINS server. The WINS server can either accept or reject the request for a NetBIOS name made by the WINS client. The response that is given depends on several factors.

❏ Name resolution on a WINS network attempts name resolution in the following order: DNS (if the name is more than 15 characters or contains periods), name cache, WINS server, broadcast, LMHOSTS file, HOSTS file, and DNS. As a memory aid, you can take the first letter of each step in the order and correlate it to the first letter of the following sentence: "Can We Buy Large Hard Drives" (Can = Cache, We = WINS, Buy = Broadcast, and so on).

❏ No matter how many WINS servers you have in your network, you will still only have a single WINS database. With multiple servers and one database, replication is extremely important to ensure that all of the WINS servers have a consistent copy of the database.

❏ WINS replication occurs through pull replication partners, which request WINS updates from their configured push replication partners. Only the changed or new WINS records replicate, not the entire WINS database. If a client is not WINS-compatible, a WINS proxy agent can register on behalf of the non-WINS client.

❏ Mail services are a critical part of most organizations. Email requires one or more of several protocols, including SMTP, MIME, POP3, and IMAP. Main email server applications include Lotus Notes, Novell GroupWise, Microsoft Exchange, and UNIX/Linux Sendmail. Whatever your choice, you should carefully protect your email with redundant mail servers for failover purposes. Also make sure additional DNS servers are available to direct mail to the appropriate domains.

❏ When configuring your mail server, be sure to open the firewall to mail-related traffic, add appropriate MX records in DNS, and supply plenty of RAM and hard disk space. Be sure to defragment the mail server hard disk frequently. For best performance and reliability, dedicate the server to only mail. Have a comprehensive anti-virus solution to protect the network, which includes the servers and especially all workstations with email clients because mail is a common carrier of viruses.

❏ Your web servers should have plenty of Internet bandwidth, which is best accomplished by separating it from LAN bandwidth using a dedicated Internet connection. Plan for plenty of fast hard disk space for file downloads and streaming multimedia. Users will trust your content more (especially online transactions) if you have a digital certificate.

❏ Install enough memory so that much of the web content can be cached, and install redundant web servers for failover. Protect your LAN from attacks on the web servers by separating it with a firewall. Do not allow webmasters to administer the web site itself.

❏ A co-location site can provide "ping power pipe" availability for your web with excellent bandwidth availability and redundancy, redundant power, security, and regulated environmental controls.

❏ Common web server software includes Apache, WebSphere, Lotus Notes Domino, and Microsoft IIS.

❏ Remote access service (RAS) is the ability of a server to accept a connection from a client even when physically disconnected from the LAN. Users establish the connection on their end through dial-up modem connections or existing Internet connections using a virtual private network (VPN). Once the connection is established, the user experience is the same as if directly connected to the local LAN, except that over a dial-up connection, network responsiveness is much slower.

❏ RAS uses basic network protocols, but also requires a line protocol such as PPP or SLIP; security protocols such as PAP, SPAP, CHAP, MS-CHAP, or MS-CHAP v2; and tunneling protocols such as PPTP or L2TP. One of the most important things to remember about RAS server configuration is that the RAS client settings must match or else the connection will fail.

❏ Fax servers offer advantages over fax machines such as greater speed, improved resolution, better security, better reporting, routing, and forwarding to another fax machine or email inbox. Fax servers consist of a fax board and fax software.

❏ SNA Server acts as a gateway between network clients and mainframe or midrange hosts. Clients then connect using terminal emulation. Users can gain access to large mainframe databases such as DB2, administrators can monitor performance on hosts, host print jobs can go to LAN printers, and logon security is improved.

❏ SNMP is a management protocol. Its usefulness is comprised of several elements that work together with the ultimate purpose of informing the administrator of a changing trend in the use of an object or alerting the administrator of an error, failure, or condition. SNMP functionality relies on an SNMP management system, an SNMP agent, a MIB, traps, and communities.

❏ Desktop Management Interface (DMI) is similar to SNMP, except that it contains specific information about an actual device. Instead of using a Management Information Base (MIB), DMI uses a Management Information File (MIF) database that can contain information such as model ID, serial number, memory, and port addresses. DMI often runs in conjunction with SNMP.

❏ A server can function as a network device such as a router (using RIP or OSPF) or a firewall/proxy. Routing functions are best performed by hardware routers unless it is not necessary or cost effective.

❏ RIP is simple but limited to 15 hops and susceptible to routing loops. OSPF is practically unlimited in the number of hops and uses a routing algorithm for creating routing tables. OSPF is much more efficient than RIP.

9

❐ The server can also act as a firewall/proxy server to protect the LAN from malicious Internet users and prevent LAN users from accessing forbidden web content. Besides this protection, a proxy can cache web content for faster delivery of web content and reduced burden on Internet lines.

KEY TERMS

acknowledgment — In DHCP, a confirmation from the server to the client that the DHCP lease process completed successfully.

address (A) record — Also known as a host record, this is the actual record that resolves the host name to the IP address.

BOOTP — The Bootstrap Protocol; uses a BOOTP server that can distribute IP addresses to clients (similar to DHCP).

caching-only server — A DNS server that has no zone database, either of its own or copied through a zone transfer from a primary domain server. Caching-only servers mostly function to improve performance by reducing the number of forwarded queries.

Challenge Handshake Authentication Protocol (CHAP) — A flexible and common authentication protocol that supports encryption for a variety of operating systems. Microsoft also has two specific implementations: MS-CHAP for all Windows clients and MS-CHAP v2 for Windows 2000 clients.

CNAME record — Stands for a canonical name record and is an alias that points to another host.

communities — A group of hosts that each use the same community name. You can name the community whatever makes sense for your organization. The community name is not so much a grouping as it is a small measure of security. When SNMP queries are issued to a community, only members of that community respond, and the community name functions as a rudimentary password.

convergence — A state in which all routers connected to a network have the same updated information.

daemon — The Linux and UNIX name for a service.

dedicated application — A server running a single application or service and nothing else. This helps to assure that application performance is unhindered by interference from other applications or services and also contributes to the stability of the server.

Desktop Management Interface (DMI) — Similar to SNMP, except that it contains specific information about an actual device.

DHCP server — A server that automatically allocates IP address configuration to DHCP clients.

discovery broadcast — A broadcast initiated by a DHCP client that seeks a DHCP server.

distributed application — The application runs on the server. The client can send requests to the server but does not run the application or perform processing.

DNS zone — A naming boundary for which a DNS server is responsible.

Domain Name System (DNS) — A service that stores a record of both the node's IP address and host name, and uses these records to service name resolution requests.

Dynamic DNS (DDNS) — Automatic registrations from clients at the time they receive their IP configuration from the DHCP server.

Dynamic Host Configuration Protocol (DHCP) — A protocol that allows its clients to lease IP address configuration automatically from a DHCP server.

handshake — The squawking noise that faxes and modems make when establishing a connection.

HOSTS file — A plain text file that contains static, manual entries of host-to-IP-address mappings.

Internet Message Access Protocol (IMAP) — In its current version (IMAP4), IMAP allows the email client to leave messages on the mail server even after logging on instead of downloading each one.

iterative query — When a DNS server refers the resolver to another DNS server that might be able to resolve the request.

lease — The length of time for which a client receives IP configuration from a DHCP server.

Level 2 Tunneling Protocol (L2TP) — A relatively new VPN protocol that requires an established certificate authority. Clients establishing a connection must download a digital certificate from the certificate authority. The certificate then validates the connection attempt over the VPN connection attempt.

LMHOSTS file — A plain text file that contains static, manual entries of NetBIOS name records.

Mail Exchanger (MX) record — Routes mail to the appropriate server(s) for members of the domain.

Management Information Base (MIB) — A database of definitions for the specific SNMP device being monitored.

Management Information File (MIF) — A DMI database of information such as model ID, serial number, memory, and port addresses.

master server — An authoritative DNS server that transfers zone data to one or more slave servers. ("Authoritative" means that the server is configured to host the zone and return query results.)

Multipurpose Internet Mail Extensions (MIME) — A protocol that adds the mail capability of attaching and transferring multimedia file attachments. To use MIME, you must also have an email client capable of decoding the MIME format.

Name Server (NS) record — Specifies what DNS servers are delegated servers for the domain, meaning that the server specified in the record can resolve queries authoritatively.

NetBIOS — Broadcast-based name resolution scheme where a client simply broadcasts the NetBIOS name of the computer it wishes to reach to all of the computers on a subnet. The broadcast message identifies a computer that acknowledges the broadcast and establishes a communication link.

9

offer — The DHCP server's proposed IP address and configuration to the DHCP client.

Open Shortest Path First (OSPF) — A routing protocol that builds its routing tables using a link-state algorithm, which calculates the shortest path to each host based on the network topology, not just the fewest number of hops (as with RIP).

Password Authentication Protocol (PAP) — A security protocol that sends logon information in clear text. Using a packet sniffer, an eavesdropper can analyze the packet and retrieve the logon data.

peer-to-peer (P2P) application — The server primarily exists to run software that allows peer computers to communicate with one another.

Point-to-Point Protocol (PPP) — A very flexible line protocol that interoperates with a variety of RAS software packages. PPP supports the NetBEUI, IPX/SPX, and TCP/IP protocols, data compression and encryption, and authentication protocols.

Point-to-Point Tunneling Protocol (PPTP) — A popular and easy-to-configure VPN tunneling protocol.

Post Office Protocol 3 (POP3) — A line protocol that allows messages to be stored on the mail server for incoming email.

primary domain server — The starting point of all DNS records. The zone database is readable and writeable on the primary domain server: You can add, remove, or modify DNS records.

primary master server — There is only one primary master server per DNS zone, and it is the first and final authority for all hosts in their domain. Primary masters are the source for records that are copied to master or slave DNS servers.

PTR record — The actual record used in reverse lookups.

pull replication partner — In WINS, a replication partner that requests and then accepts changes from its push replication partners.

push replication partner — In WINS, a replication partner that responds to requests for changes from its pull replication partners.

recursive query — A query forwarded from one DNS server to another.

remote access service (RAS) — The ability of a server to accept a connection from a client even when physically disconnected from the LAN.

remote monitoring (RMON) — An extension of the SNMP protocol, providing more comprehensive network monitoring capabilities. Instead of devices answering queries from the SNMP management system, RMON proactively sets off alarms for a variety of traffic conditions.

replication — Copying the database from one server to another, as in the case of a WINS server.

replication interval — The amount of time between WINS pull replication requests.

replication trigger — The WINS pull partner's message that initiates replication with the push partner.

request — The DHCP client's acceptance of the DHCP offer.

resolver — A host that requests DNS name resolution.

reverse lookup zone (IN-ADDR.ARPA) — Useful for performing the reverse of a normal query: Instead of resolving a name to an IP address, it resolves an IP address to a name.

Router Information Protocol (RIP) — A distance vector-based protocol that identifies the best route for a destination based on the number of hops.

scope — A range of IP addresses that the DHCP server distributes to DHCP clients.

secondary domain servers — A DNS server that can receive a read-only copy of the zone database from a primary domain server. Secondary domain servers are useful for providing redundancy and load balancing.

Serial Line Internet Protocol (SLIP) — SLIP uses only the TCP/IP protocol and is useful for UNIX connections. SLIP is very basic and does not support authentication protocols, encryption, or compression.

Shiva Password Authentication Protocol (SPAP) — Shiva products (acquired by Intel) are a popular alternative to Microsoft RAS solutions. Shiva encrypts authentication credentials for Shiva LAN Rover software.

Simple Mail Transport Protocol (SMTP) — A mail protocol that transports only basic text. SMTP is the protocol that transfers or forwards mail to an email server.

Simple Network Management Protocol (SNMP) — A network monitoring and management protocol. Its usefulness is comprised of several elements that work together with the ultimate purpose of informing the administrator of a changing trend in the use of an object or alerting the administrator of an error, failure, or condition.

slave server — An authoritative DNS server that receives the zone transfer from the master and is named in the zone by an NS record.

SNMP agent — A service that runs on the actual object you want to monitor using an SNMP management system.

SNMP management system — Sends requests for information from the monitored system, known as the SNMP agent.

SONET — A fiber optic transmission medium that is self-healing. If a line is cut, traffic redirects to another ring.

Start of Authority (SOA) server — The authoritative server for information about the domain; the domain cannot function without it.

static IP address — An IP address that is manually and permanently assigned to a network host.

Systems Network Architecture (SNA) Server — A Microsoft product that acts as a gateway between the client and the mainframe.

time to live (TTL) — In DNS and WINS, the length of time a record is stored.

trap — A message issued from the SNMP agent to the SNMP management system.

turnkey fax servers — Self-contained, freestanding devices in which the software and hardware are already installed. Except for some company-specific configurations, they are ready to fax right out of the box.

virtual private network (VPN) — A communications session protected inside an encrypted virtual "tunnel" that is extremely difficult for intruders to breach. VPN is most commonly used over an Internet connection.

9

Windows Internet Naming Service (WINS) — A Microsoft NetBIOS name resolution service.

WINS proxy agent — A WINS-enabled computer that listens on the subnet for WINS broadcast messages, such as: query, refresh, release, and registration. The WINS proxy then communicates with the WINS server to resolve or register NetBIOS names.

zone transfer — A copy of the zone DNS database that is copied to another DNS server.

REVIEW QUESTIONS

1. Which service automatically distributes IP configuration to clients?

   a. DHCP

   b. DNS

   c. SNA

   d. DISTIP

2. Which of the following is the correct order in the lease process?

   a. Offer, discovery, acknowledgment, request

   b. Discovery, acknowledgment, offer, request

   c. Discovery, acknowledgment, request, offer

   d. Discovery, offer, request, acknowledgment

3. DNS is an alternative to which text file?

   a. LMHOSTS

   b. HOSTS

   c. Readme.txt

   d. HOST

4. A resolver is:

   a. an authoritative server that solves conflicting IP address issues

   b. a service that removes outdated WINS records

   c. a server that returns iterative queries

   d. a client that requests DNS name resolution

5. A DNS zone is:

   a. a physical boundary where a host must reside in order to become a resolver

   b. a naming boundary

   c. another term for a Windows NT/2000 security domain

   d. the authoritative server for all name resolution within a domain

6. Which of the following DNS records resolves the host name to an IP address?

   a. PTR records

   b. SOA records

   c. MX records

   d. A records

7. Which of the following DNS servers does not have any permanent DNS records?

   a. caching-only

   b. slave

   c. secondary

   d. primary

8. Which operating system primarily uses NetBIOS names?

   a. Linux

   b. OS/2

   c. Windows

   d. NetWare

9. What does DDNS do?

   a. automatically registers NetBIOS names

   b. automatically registers DNS names

   c. recognizes when DNS server records are out of date and automatically replicates a more up-to-date zone

   d. dynamically configures a host's IP configuration

10. What does a push partner do?

    a. responds to pull partners' replication triggers and sends WINS updates

    b. responds to other push partners' replication triggers and sends WINS updates

    c. automatically replicates WINS data to DNS servers

    d. forces an update on pull partners

11. You have an OS/2 server that does not use WINS. The network is Windows NT 4.0. How can you make the OS/2 server available in WINS?

    a. use the WINS update agent

    b. use the WINS proxy agent

    c. use the SNMP agent

    d. You cannot do anything to resolve this.

9

12. Which of the following mail protocols allows you to search for specific mail on the server and download only select items?

    a. POP3

    b. SMTP

    c. MIME

    d. IMAP

13. What special hardware factors might you consider for an email server?

    a. additional hard disk space

    b. powerful processing capability

    c. additional RAM

    d. all of the above

14. Why might you want to have a dedicated, separate Internet connection to the web server? (Choose two.)

    a. So LAN traffic does not affect web server responsiveness.

    b. So Web traffic does not affect LAN responsiveness.

    c. This is a requirement for an effective firewall.

    d. A separate connection offers no practical benefit.

15. How might RAM improve web server performance?

    a. Web server software is particularly memory-hungry.

    b. RAM is not particularly an issue with web content.

    c. More web content can be cached into RAM and served faster than from the hard disk.

    d. FTP and streaming media can be stored wholly in memory.

16. What is one of the disadvantages of most UNIX services?

    a. The graphic-based interface is not consistent from one version of UNIX to another.

    b. The text-based administration is not intuitive.

    c. UNIX services are historically less stable than other operating systems' services.

    d. The UNIX services are completely incompatible with any other operating system.

17. What is the difference between PPP and SLIP?

    a. PPP offers a GUI, and SLIP does not.

    b. PPP supports more protocols than SLIP.

    c. PPP is available only on Windows systems, and SLIP is only available on UNIX clients.

    d. There is no perceptible difference besides the spelling.

18. How are fax servers better than fax machines? (Choose all that apply.)

    a. Fax boards transmit faxes much faster.

    b. Fax servers can better protect sensitive documents from prying eyes.

    c. Fax servers automatically fill in some information.

    d. Fax servers do not jam.

19. What is the purpose of an SNA server?

    a. connect Macintosh clients to the same network as Windows clients

    b. connect clients to mini and mainframe hosts over a terminal session

    c. separate the public Internet from the private LAN

    d. allow dial-up clients to access the LAN as if connected locally

20. You receive a message on your pager that a particular router is flooded. Which service made this notification possible?

    a. PAGER

    b. SNMP

    c. RAS

    d. PPTP

9

HANDS-ON PROJECTS

Project 9-1

In this project, you will configure a NetWare 5.1 server with the DNS and DHCP Management Console. This requires an existing NetWare 5.1 server and a Windows 2000 Professional or Server or greater client. If the Windows computer does not have Novell Client for Windows 2000, download and install it from *www.novell.com*. The NetWare 5.1 server should have a static IP address of 10.10.10.5 and a subnet mask of 255.255.255.0. The Windows 2000 client should have a static IP address of 10.10.10.1 and a subnet mask of 255.255.255.0.

1. Log on to the NetWare 5.1 server with Admin rights. Your instructor will tell you which account and password to use.

2. From the Windows 2000 client, ping the NetWare 5.1 server to verify connectivity. Enter **PING 10.10.10.5** at a command prompt. You should see replies come back.

3. Install the DNS-DHCP Management Console. Double-click **My Network Places**, and browse through **Entire Network**, **NetWare Services**, and **NetWare Servers**.

4. The name of the NetWare server should appear in a window. Double-click the NetWare server. If more than one appears, ask your instructor which one to double-click.

5. Double-click through the path **SYS:PUBLIC\DNSDHCP**.

6. Double-click the **Setup.exe** file to begin setup, and proceed through the setup prompts. At the end, you will be prompted to copy the snap-in files. Select this option and click **Next**.

7. You are prompted for the location of the NetWare Administrator utility. This is the location of NWAdmn32.exe. Use the Browse button to access the SYS:Public\win32 directory. Click **Next** to complete the steps in the wizard.

8. Browse to SYS:Public\Win32 and double-click the **NWAdmn32.exe** file. If a Tip appears, close it. (Consider making a shortcut to the desktop to make this more accessible.)

9. From the NetWare Administrator, click the **Tools** menu, then **DNS–DHCP Management Console**.

10. Leave the console open for the next project. Feel free to look around in the console, but do not change anything.

Project 9-2

In this project, you will access the DNS-DHCP Management Console and enter a DHCP scope. Then you will boot the Windows 2000 client to receive IP configuration from the DHCP server.

1. The DNS-DHCP Management Console is still open from Project 9-1. If it is not, refer to Steps 8 and 9 to open it.

2. At the top of the interface are two tabs: DNS Service (default) and DHCP Service. Click **DHCP Service**.

3. A single Our Network item appears on the left; there are no scopes created yet. On the toolbar, click the second icon from the left (it looks like a box).

4. The Create New DHCP Record appears. Select the **DHCP Server** item and click **OK**.

5. The Create DHCP Server text box appears. Type in the name of the NetWare 5.1 server in its context. Your instructor will tell you how to enter the context. You can also browse for it if you like. Then, click **Create**.

6. The server object appears at the bottom of the console. Click the "box" toolbar button again, and in the Create New DHCP Record dialog box, click **Subnet** and then **OK**.

7. The following information should be entered for servers that are not on the same network. If your class has multiple servers on the same network for this project, your instructor will provide different configuration information. For the Subnet Name, enter **ClassIPRange**, use the current NDS context, or enter a context specified by your instructor.

8. Enter a subnet address of **10.10.10.0** and a subnet mask of **255.255.255.0**. The dialog box should look similar to the one shown in Figure 9-19. When finished, click **Create**.

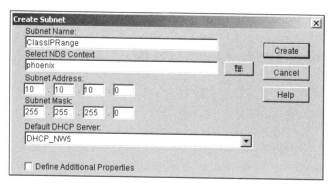

Figure 9-19   Creating a new DHCP record

9. The current DHCP configuration could cause a problem in a production environment. The NetWare 5.1 server IP address is 10.10.10.5, and yet this address is in the range you just created. You don't want a client to attempt to lease this address. (Even though there are mechanisms that prevent this, you don't want to take chances.) In the left pane, click the **10.10.10.0** (ClassIPRange) item and select the "Box" icon again. The Create New DHCP Record dialog box appears.

10. Click the **IP Address** item and click **OK**. Enter IP address **10.10.10.5**, verify that the Assignment Type is Exclusion, and click **Create**. Now, the DHCP server will not lease that IP address.

11. With the 10.10.10.0 (ClassIPRange) item still selected, click the **Other DHCP Options** tab. Then click the **Modify** button.

12. Configure the DHCP client's DNS server. Select the Domain Name Server (Code 6) and click Add.

13. At the bottom of the dialog box, click the **Add** button. Enter the IP address for an available DNS server as told by your instructor. Click **OK** to close all dialog boxes.

14. Boot the Windows 2000 computer and log on as a Domain Admin. Configure the IP address of the local Windows 2000 computer to use the newly configured NetWare DHCP server. Click **Start**, point to Settings, and click **Network and Dial-up Connections**. The Network and Dial-up Connections screen opens.

15. Your local area connection appears in the window. Right-click it and choose **Properties**.

16. Scroll down to Internet Protocol (TCP/IP), click it, and click the **Properties** button.

17. Click the **Obtain an IP address automatically** item and the **Obtain DNS server address automatically** item. Click **OK** to close all dialog boxes and reboot.

Windows 2000 should automatically request and receive a new DHCP-assigned IP address once you close the Local Area Connection dialog boxes. However, rebooting is a good way to ensure that a lease occurs.

18. After logging back on as a Domain Admin, click **Start**, click **Run**, type **CMD**, and press **Enter**.

19. In the Command Prompt window, type **IPCONFIG /ALL** and press **Enter**. You should see a 10.10.10.x address and a DNS server address as specified in Step 17. The DHCP server successfully leased an IP address to the Windows 2000 DHCP client.

Project 9-3

In this project, you will configure a Windows 2000 web server.

1. Log on to a Windows 2000 server using an account with Domain Admin membership. Your instructor will tell you what user name and password to use.

2. Using Windows Explorer, create a new folder named **My Web** on the C: drive.

3. Using Microsoft Word or any other word processor capable of saving a file as a web page, create a new document and type in a few words (careful, other people might see this later).

4. From the File menu, click **Save As** and navigate to the C:\My Web folder. Then from the Save as type drop-down list at the bottom, choose **Web Page** and name the document **Default**.

5. Click **Start**, point to Programs, point to Administrative Tools, and click **Internet Services Manager**.

Despite the fact that you are in a console called Internet Services Manager, you are using Internet Information Server 5.0.

6. In the left pane, you see the name of your server. Expand it and locate Default Web Site. Right-click it and click **Browse** to verify that IIS and the browser are operating correctly. Two browser windows open to an excellent online help resource about configuring a Windows 2000 web. Close the browsers.

7. In the left pane, right-click the server, then point to **New** and click **Web Site**.

8. The Web Site Creation wizard begins. Click **Next** to start configuration and after each step where it applies.

9. Enter a description of the site (Class Web, for example). This is for your reference only; the Internet public does not see it.

10. In the IP Address and Port Settings page, select the IP address of the local computer from the drop-down list. Click **Next**.

11. In the Path text box, enter **C:\My Web**. Be sure to leave the Allow anonymous access to this Web site checked.

12. Leave the default Web Site Access Permissions, and finish the wizard.

13. Right-click the new web site in the left pane and click **Browse**. Your web site now appears in the browser.

14. If connected to other web sites on the same network, you can ask another student for their IP address (use the IPCONFIG command to determine this) and type **http://IPAddress** where IPAddress is the other student's IP address. The other student's web site appears in your browser.

15. Close all open browsers and the Internet Information Services console.

Project 9-4

In this project, you will visit *www.inflow.com* to see an excellent example of not only a co-location facility, but also an enterprise server environment.

1. Using your web browser, access the *www.inflow.com* web site.

2. On the home page, there should be a link to Take a video tour. Click this item.

3. A RealPlayer streaming media presentation begins. If you do not have RealPlayer installed, follow the link to install RealPlayer and return to this site.

4. What kind of physical security does Inflow have?

5. When can you expect Inflow personnel to be available to monitor your applications and equipment?

6. What facility controls does the staff monitor?

7. How does Inflow ensure uninterrupted power?

Project 9-5

In this project, you will create a DNS zone in Windows 2000.

1. Click **Start**, point to Programs, point to Administrative Tools, and then click **DNS**. If this item does not appear, install it using the Add Remove Programs item in Control Panel. DNS is a subset of Networking Services.

2. Right-click the name of the server in the left pane, and choose **New Zone**. A wizard begins. Click **Next** to start it and after each step.

3. Select a standard primary zone.

4. Select a forward lookup zone.

5. Type a name for the zone. This would be the name of the zone only, not the name of existing or planned hosts. If you had a server named Mail1 and a domain named accusource.net, you would enter only accusource.net here, not Mail1.accusource.net.

6. A file stores the DNS database. Leave the default value and finish the wizard.

Project 9-6

In this project, you will create an A record in the zone created in Project 9-5.

1. In the left pane, select the zone you created in Project 9-5.

2. Right-click the zone and choose **New Host** from the menu. (You might have to refresh the zone by right-clicking on it, and then selecting "Refresh" from the menu.)

3. Enter any name here; this is a fictitious record.

4. Enter the IP address; any address will do.

5. Notice that Windows 2000 will also automatically create an associated PTR record if you so configure it. We haven't created a reverse lookup zone, so it doesn't apply here.

6. Click **Add Host**, and a confirmation screen appears. Click **OK** and then click **Done** on the New Host dialog box.

7. Open a command prompt, and ping the new record by its full name in the form: *host.domain*. For example, if you created student.class.com, type **ping student.class.com**. The request will time-out, but you will see that it is indeed attempting to ping the name and IP address you entered.

8. Delete the zone by right-clicking it and selecting **Delete**.

Project 9-7

In this project, you will create a RAS VPN server and a dial-up connection on a Windows 2000 server. Then you will connect to the VPN server.

1. Click **Start**, point to **Programs**, point to **Administrative Tools**, and click **Routing and Remote Access**.

2. Click on the name of the local server. Notice the red arrow indicating that the service is neither configured nor running. Right-click it and select **Configure and Enable Routing and Remote Access**.

3. Another handy wizard begins. Click **Next** to start it and again after each step.

4. Click on the **Virtual private network (VPN) server** option.

5. TCP/IP should be listed as a protocol. Click **Next**.

6. Specify the **<No internet connection>** option. Normally, you would use an Internet connection, but for our purposes, this should suffice.

7. Leave the Automatically setting for clients to receive IP addresses from a DHCP server.

8. Click **No, I don't want to set up this server to use RADIUS now**, and finish the wizard. After a few moments, the RRAS service starts.

9. Click the **Ports** item in the left pane. Notice that you have both PPTP and L2TP ports through which clients can connect. Because we have not configured a certificate structure, we will use PPTP.

10. Minimize the RRAS console.

11. Click **Start**, point to **Settings**, and click **Network and Dial-up Connections**. Double-click the **Make New Connection** item. Guess what, another wizard! Click **Next** here and after each step. (If you have not previously specified the area code in which the computer resides, you might be prompted to enter this information first.)

12. Click **Connect to a private network through the Internet**.

13. If the Windows 2000 computer has an existing dial-up connection, click **Do not dial the initial connection**. If we had a dial-up Internet connection, this screen would configure it to dial automatically when we initiated a VPN connection.

14. Enter the IP address of the local server. Again, you can use IPCONFIG from a command prompt to find this information.

15. It doesn't matter if you select For all users or Only for myself.

16. Leave the Enable Internet Connection Sharing for this connection unchecked, and finish the wizard.

17. The Connect Virtual Private Connection dialog box appears immediately. Type in your user name and password, and click **Connect**.

18. If the connection is denied, you will need to access your user account in Active Directory Users and Computers located in Administrative Tools (Start, Programs, Administrative Tools). In your user account properties, click the Dial-In tab and grant yourself access (see Figure 9-20 for reference). The default is to deny access as a security precaution.

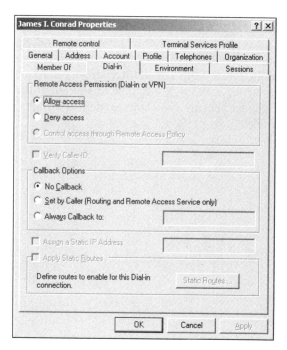

Figure 9-20   Grant yourself remote access permission if necessary

19. Besides practice for configuring RRAS and dial up connections, using a VPN to connect to the same local computer is an excellent way to troubleshoot other dial-in conditions and rules (compared to waiting a minute for a real modem to handshake and connect). Windows 2000 has complex but effective conditions under which users can dial up.

CASE PROJECTS

1. You have been hired to design a technology update for a medium-sized organization. The organization currently uses UNIX servers, Windows 2000 Professional clients, and a single Windows NT 4.0 server running SNA Server so that clients can run a terminal session to an AS/400 DB2 database. There are only about 200 users, but it is quite cumbersome for the administrator to manually enter the host records for each client and server into the DNS database file. Also, each desktop has statically configured IP information. The organization has made a significant investment in the AS/400 server and database, and you are required to keep it in the new plan, but you are authorized to purchase two or three new PC servers as needed. What should you propose to improve the administration of this network?

2. A local charity, KidHelp, asks you to contribute your knowledge and expertise. KidHelp is new to the Internet. KidHelp has been using a shared Internet connection through a cable modem for desktop client Internet access. Management is concerned that a malicious Internet user might attempt to somehow damage the KidHelp network servers or clients because the cable modem is always on. What can you recommend to KidHelp?

10

DISASTER PLANNING

> **After reading this chapter and completing the exercises, you will be able to:**
>
> ♦ Describe the primary methods and devices used to back up critical data
>
> ♦ Identify methods for creating a high-availability network
>
> ♦ Explain the contents of a spare-parts kit for efficient hardware repair
>
> ♦ Identify key areas for SNMP monitoring
>
> ♦ Determine key server management and disaster recovery strategies for preserving system uptime

No matter how diligent you are at purchasing the best hardware possible and configuring it correctly, network failures are going to occur, either on a small scale when network equipment fails or on a large scale as in a natural disaster. Returning users to a state of productivity as quickly as possible after one of these failures is, of course, the goal. Being able to do so, however, requires a great deal of planning. If you rely upon sudden genius in the hour of need, you are likely to be disappointed.

One of the most important elements of a disaster recovery plan is a tape backup system. The administrator must not only know how to implement various types of backup strategies, but also physically store the tapes in the most appropriate locations. Besides the risk of losing data, the administrator must ensure that network resources are available, not only for normal productivity but also in case a server fails. This is where redundancy solutions such as clustering are critical for servers. Hopefully, you will be able to monitor the servers and predict when an impending failure is near. Recall from Chapter 9 that SNMP can alert you of such problems. Be sure to set SNMP thresholds so that you are notified well in advance of potential problems. Should problems occur that require only hardware replacement, be sure to keep compatible replacement hardware on hand in a spare-parts cabinet. In Chapter 2, you learned about the hazards that dust and heat pose to the server, and you should be certain to continue regular maintenance to guard against such problems.

In the worst-case scenario, a disaster occurs that physically obliterates the site. In this case, you must have a disaster recovery plan that reestablishes operations as quickly as possible, and probably involves one or more alternate sites.

BACKUPS

Although fault-tolerant hardware and devices can reduce total system downtime, the greatest potential loss in the event of a system failure of any kind is the loss of data. Even during normal day-to-day operations, data can become corrupt or lost. For example, users sometimes accidentally overwrite their own files with blank data or perhaps an application crashes while a file is open, resulting in a corrupt file. Having that data available for restoration is the highest-priority item in the preparation for disaster recovery.

TIP   The basic theory behind backing up data is simple: Never put yourself in a position where critical data for the survival of your network or business is permanently unavailable.

There are many backup devices from which to choose, and several backup methods that can be employed, but the goal is to never be without your mission-critical data. You will also have to decide who is going to be responsible for accomplishing the backups, and to what level these backups need to be secured. Which devices and methods you choose are not as important as the choice to develop and deploy a backup strategy.

Hewlett-Packard cites industry experts who estimate that the quantity of data increases 50% annually. If these figures hold true for your organization, then the need for accurate backup and restore operations is obvious, as is the need to select the appropriate backup hardware and strategies.

Types of Backup Hardware

Factors to consider when you purchase a backup unit include:

- The amount of data you need to back up
- Whether your backup software supports the unit
- The amount of money you want to spend
- The amount of time it takes to back up and restore data

You also need to consider the value of your data: Put a price tag on your data and on the time you'd need to rebuild the data if you lost it. Be willing to spend as much money on a device as some ratio of what you calculate your data to be worth.

There are many different types of backup media and devices, from removable media cartridges to CD-ROMs and magnetic tape. You need to determine the best balance between speed of backing up the data, speed of restoration, the quality and function of supported backup programs, and storage media requirements. Then, choose a unit that provides the technology you need to back up and restore data efficiently and effectively within the parameters of your situation.

For example, some products use optical disks, which is a great solution for **Hierarchical Storage Management (HSM)** in which infrequently used data is moved from fast, expensive hardware (hard disks) to slower, less expensive media such as optical disks or magnetic tape. (An **optical disk** is any disk written and read by laser, including CD-R, CD-RW, DVD, and so forth.) However, optical disks are a poor solution if you want to back up large amounts of data quickly. In that case, you will usually turn to the ubiquitous and cost-effective tape drive. Tape drives offer the lowest cost per megabyte of storage, the greatest degree of flexibility compared to comparable-capacity devices, and are very portable.

The choices available in backup devices have greatly expanded over the last few years due to advances in technology. Table 10-1 introduces the most common backup solutions in the server realm: tape and CD laser devices.

Table 10-1   Common Server Backup Devices and Media Types

Device (Category)	Media Type	Pros	Cons
Tape drives (magnetic)	DAT, DDS, DLT	Inexpensive media, faster transfer	Expensive drives
CD (laser)	CD-ROM, CD-R, CD-RW	Inexpensive media	Limited software support for drive interface, not as flexible in terms of recording data as other solutions, slower than tape

Tape devices are generally the most popular server backup devices. Some devices support multiple tape formats, and others support only one. Some are very expensive, and some are not. The faster units are more expensive, as are units that have larger media capacities and/or automated handling of multiple media. One factor that often forces you to choose the large, more expensive drives is the backup window. The **backup window** is the optimal period of time in which you can perform a backup, and is usually when most files are closed. If your organization has a very small backup window, you need a very fast and expensive tape backup solution.

Tape devices are known for their long-lasting performance between hardware failures, which is partly attributable to the reliable tape drive mechanics and robotics that some systems include. Despite this reliability, you should research a vendor's service contract to ensure that the contract includes same-day on-site or overnight cross-shipping service if the unit fails.

Competition in the tape backup arena has created an abundance of dubious performance claims. You need to determine the type of files the vendor used to test the drive and the type of test the vendor ran, because many claims are a result of using totally compressible files. These tests don't take into account that many file types can't be compressed—so the tests don't simulate real-world scenarios.

Whichever type of tape drive you install, consider the importance of the tape drive driver. Plug and Play operating systems such as Windows 2000 and Linux might automatically detect hardware and install drivers of their own for the tape device. However, there might be features of the device that do not become available until you install the driver directly from the manufacturer. For example, many tape drives include hardware compression in which tape drive electronics compress data as it writes to tape, relieving the compression burden from the processor. However, unless you use the vendor drivers, the feature might not be available and you would then have to fall back to software compression utilizing the processor.

Be sure to upgrade tape drivers when upgrading from one drive to another. For example, upgrading from a stand-alone tape device to an autoloader without also upgrading the driver will likely result in a unit that will not back up at all or might only back up to a single tape.

No matter what type of drive you choose, versions of most backup products are available with a choice of SCSI, EIDE, or parallel port interfaces, except for the very high-end products, which all have SCSI interfaces. Additionally, some older, low-end products, particularly tape drives, also come in versions that connect to the floppy disk controller. Parallel port and floppy disk interfaces will not be considered further in this discussion of server backup solutions.

Departmental servers that might not require extremely high-capacity backup solutions might only require a single stand-alone EIDE tape device. These devices provide reasonably good performance at up to about 20 GB of compressed data. For the best backup performance, especially for use on higher-end workstations and certainly for all servers, the interface option of choice is SCSI. When assessing the cost of your backup solution, you'll need to add the price of a good-quality SCSI interface card for your server if you don't have one already, though most high-end workstation PCs and servers are already based on SCSI disk subsystems and therefore won't require an additional interface. In either case, check the type of physical SCSI connector fitted to a drive before buying to make sure you won't need additional cables or adapters. An additional benefit of SCSI is system responsiveness. With EIDE tape drives, some tape operations, such as cataloging the contents of the tape or re-tensioning, will temporarily dominate the system and affect responsiveness. Because of the nature of SCSI, you can perform nearly any tape function with minimal impact on overall system responsiveness.

If it is not cost prohibitive, take performance a step further and choose a tape solution that is Fibre Channel compatible.

Automated Tape Solutions

For a large-scale enterprise, none of the backup solutions outlined so far would be sufficient. Instead, you should probably investigate a backup technology that can automatically change tapes in a largely unattended fashion. Often large and extremely expensive, these automated tape devices are typically tape libraries that use autoloaders (see Figure 10-1). A **tape library** is a self-contained tape backup solution that is preloaded with several tapes. Most tape libraries include **autoloaders** to automatically load and swap tapes. In addition to automatic tape rotation, these devices can automatically clean tape heads.

Figure 10-1   A tape library using an autoloader

Automated backup solutions also mitigate potential human error. What if someone backed up Server_A and accidentally marked the tape Server_B? Restoring Server_A data might never occur unless someone manually goes through all the tapes searching for the data. Automated backup solutions won't write a label for you, but once you place the first set of tapes in the drives and properly configure the software, you can remove the human error factor from the tape backup. Plus, backups can be a tedious chore fraught with misplaced tapes, unmarked or mismarked tapes, incompatible tapes, and so on.

 Many of the problems listed above relate to multiple persons performing backups. Make sure that only designated individuals perform the regular backups and that a written, logical procedure is defined.

Also, a properly configured tape library takes only a fraction of the time otherwise required with a manual backup. This becomes more of an issue as more data centers operate around the clock instead of during business hours, because the available backup window grows smaller.

Another big advantage of automated backup libraries is the extensive **online retention period (OLRP)**, the period for which data can be restored from tape without manual intervention. Because a library can store several generations of backups at once, if you want to restore a file from, say, five weeks ago, you don't have to rummage through the storage cabinet to find the right tape. Instead, you can use the tape library software to locate and restore from the correct tape for you.

 You might not have an automated backup device available, but at the very least, use a single tape drive to schedule nightly backups. Once you configure the scheduling software, all you have to do is replace tapes as necessary. I know somebody at a fast-growing organization who apparently got frustrated with the daily manual backup chore and stopped making tapes altogether. This became a big problem when a catastrophic server crash necessitated recovery using a recent tape backup—*which didn't exist.*

At the highest level, you'll see tape libraries that can support dozens of drives and hold several hundred cartridges (see Figure 10-2). At that level, you will probably not configure the tape solution yourself; you'll tell vendor representatives what your objectives are and they will configure the library for you or provide guidance.

Figure 10-2   The StorageTek L700 can store up to 678 tapes and has up to 20 drives

Types of Backup Tape Media

Tape media fall under a number of standards. The most common for smaller tape devices is probably the **Quarter Inch Cartridge (QIC)**, which as the name implies is a quarter inch in width. QIC cartridges have evolved over the years, starting at about 20 MB and progressing to 80 MB. The QIC Wide (8 mm) tape was developed to squeeze more data into tape cartridges, but you probably won't see QIC or QIC Wide in use on servers anymore. However, you should keep some drives on hand that can at least read this format, as there are about 200 million QIC cartridges worldwide and it might be necessary to restore an older archive. In 1994, a 3M spinoff (Imation) created a new QIC standard known as **Travan**. A Travan drive can reach compressed capacity of about 20 GB and is useful for home, small office/home office (SOHO), or small departmental backups. Because Travan drives accept the QIC format, they are usually backward read compatible with preceding QIC standards.

Travan NS (network series) (see Figure 10-3) is the most recent implementation of the Travan standard and addresses two main issues: compression and verification.

Figure 10-3   The Travan NS tape cartridge

10

Before Travan NS, data compression was always software based, taxing the processor and severely limiting other server functions. I recall when using early QIC and Travan technology that I often could not perform the simplest tasks while a backup was taking place. If I tried to do too much, the system would usually hang. Travan NS tapes and drives offer hardware compression instead, relieving the compression burden from the CPU.

> **TIP** Any tape backup job still affects system responsiveness regardless of the tape format and drive technology. Whenever possible, perform backups during off-peak times. This helps to assure that fewer files are open, which might prevent them from being backed up and cause inconsistency when comparing them against a backup verification. Also consider performing backups remotely from servers or workstations that do not carry a significant role on the network.

Table 10-2 provides a summary of Travan cartridge information.

Table 10-2   Travan Standards*

Cartridge Name and Alias	Native Capacity Compressed Capacity	Read/Write Compatibility	Read Compatibility
Travan-1 (TR-1)	400 MB 800 MB	QIC-80, QW-5122	QIC-40
Travan-2 (TR-2)**	800 MB 1.6 GB		
Travan-3 (TR-3)	1.6 GB 3.2 GB	TR-2, QIC-3020, QIC-3010, QW-3020XLW, QW-3020XLW	QIC-80, QW-5122, TR-1
Travan-8 GB (Travan 4, TR-4)	4 GB 8 GB	QIC-3095	QIC-3020, QIC-3010, QIC-80, QW-5122, TR-3, TR-1
Travan NS-8	4 GB 8 GB		QIC-3020, QIC-3010, QIC-80
Travan NS-20 (TR-5)	10 GB 20 GB	QIC-3220	Travan-8 GB, QIC-3095, TR-4

* Not every Travan standard is described in this book, but this chart will be useful when you need to determine backward compatibilities. Compatibilities may vary from one drive manufacturer to another.

** Travan-2 never really got off the ground.

Another type of tape drive found on backup systems is a **digital audio tape (DAT)** drive. DAT was originally designed as a high-fidelity digital replacement for standard analog audio cassettes and, as happened with CD audio disks, the format was quickly picked up by the computer industry. While the mechanics of reading and writing to Travan, QIC, and similar format tapes are analogous to the way audio signals are written to a standard audio cassette, writing data to a DAT is similar to the way video signals are written to a video cassette. Rather than the tape being moved linearly across a static head, it is moved across an angled, rotating head (see Figure 10-4). The result of this **helical scanning** is that a DAT can hold a higher density of data in a given area than other tape technologies. However, it is mechanically much more complex and potentially more expensive to repair should something go wrong. Such devices are usually significantly faster than more conventional linear drives both in the time taken to read or write data and in how quickly an individual file can be located.

 Tape drives reading DAT pull the tape inside the drive to thread it. Be sure that you do not attempt to pull out a tape while it is active or you could have a real mess on your hands.

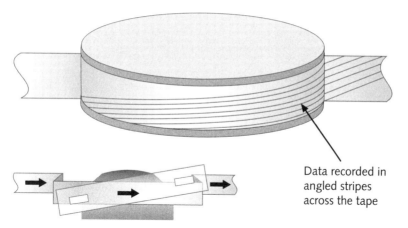

Data recorded in
angled stripes
across the tape

Figure 10-4   An angled DAT drive head stores more data on the tape

 Only QIC tapes and drives read or write to QIC tapes and drives. In other words, you cannot use a digital tape in a QIC drive or a QIC tape in a digital drive. In the digital arena, larger tape drives of each category are backward compatible with smaller drives of the same type.

When Sony released its 8 mm video cassette technology, which is mechanically and conceptually similar to 4 mm DAT technology but with an 8 mm rather than a 4 mm tape width, its potential as a backup medium was once again seized upon by the computer industry. But unlike the case for 4 mm data drives, where a large number of makes and models are available, only a very few manufacturers took up the 8 mm helical scan challenge.

A variation of the 8 mm helical scan technology called **Advanced Intelligent Tape (AIT)** has recently become available (see Figure 10-5). AIT is a Sony invention that makes backup and restore operations faster because of an optional Memory in Cassette (MIC) chip that is able to quickly locate which of the 256 tape partitions contain the data. Compare this to traditional methods in which you must scan the tape to locate data. Larger amounts of compressed data can fit onto one tape, making it the highest-capacity helical scan format available and allowing it to compare more favorably in terms of capacity with another commonly found tape format, **digital linear tape (DLT)** (Figure 10-6).

Figure 10-5   The AIT tape has a memory chip to quickly locate data

Figure 10-6   A DLT cartridge

Depending on the drive and media used, the DLT format allows up to 70 GB of compressed data to be stored on one rather large tape, which, unlike 8 mm or 4 mm helical scan technology, passes linearly over a fixed head.

Like Travan NS technology, DLT drives can simultaneously read and write, allowing them to perform extremely well, and in some cases even better than an 8 mm helical scan tape. Because they are in general significantly faster and more capacious than any other technologies, AIT, conventional 8 mm helical scan, and DLT drives are also more expensive.

One of the latest tape formats is the ultra-high-capacity **Ultrium** format. The Ultrium format is actually a subset of the **Linear Tape Open (LTO)** technology—a collaborative effort headed up by HP, IBM, and Seagate. Ultrium features include:

- *Single reel*—Internal cartridge mechanics maintain the tape, and because it is pre-threaded inside the cartridge (as opposed to threading tape through the tape drive), Ultrium-compatible drives will potentially be less complicated. Figure 10-7 shows a cutaway of the Ultrium tape cartridge.

- *High storage capacity*—Ultrium tapes offer a native capacity of up to 200 GB and data transfer of 20–40 MBps. The Ultrium LTO format is expected to be available in four different generations as advances in the technology develop, culminating in up to 1.6 TB per cartridge and up to 320 MBps (see Table 10-3).

- *Cartridge memory*—Ultrium cartridges can contain **LTO-CM (Linear Tape Open - Cartridge Memory)** right on the cartridge that stores a redundant file log and user-defined information. If you want to know what is on a given tape, you can use an external reader to access the memory. The LTO-CM uses an RF (radio frequency) interface. Compare this to the lengthy process required of other tape types for which you insert the tape into the drive and then use the backup software to build a catalog. This process can take several minutes, whereas Ultrium memory allows immediate access.

- *Error correction*—LTO technology provides two levels of error correction that can recover data even when longitudinal scratches appear on the media. Simultaneous read/write capability allows for real-time verification of data.

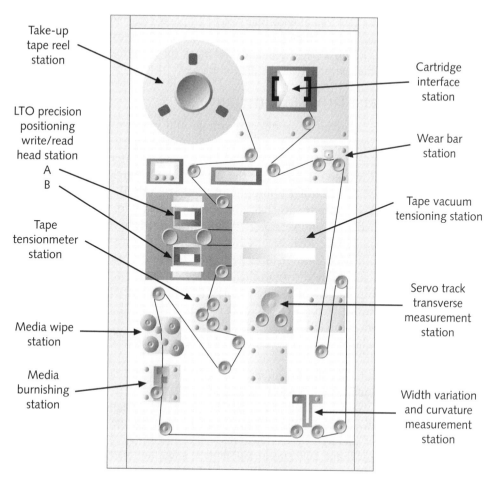

Figure 10-7   The Ultrium tape cartridge uses a single spool and is pre-threaded inside the cartridge

Table 10-3 summarizes information about the Ultrium format.

Table 10-3   Ultrium Format

Feature	Generation One	Generation Two	Generation Three	Generation Four
Capacity: Native Compressed	100 GB 200 GB	200 GB 400 GB	400 GB 800 GB	800 GB 1.6 TB
Transfer Rate: Native Compressed	10–20 MBps 20–40 MBps	20–40 MBps 40–80 MBps	40–80 MBps 80–160 MBps	80–160 MBps 160–320 MBps

Another LTO format known as Accelis proposes extremely fast data retrieval from anywhere on the tape in between 6.3 and 9.6 seconds. At this writing, Accelis is only a paper standard, and many speculate that Accelis drives and tapes may never actually be produced.

Tape and Tape Drive Maintenance

Tape media are relatively delicate, and you should exercise care when handling them. The magnetic metal oxide that coats the film on the tape is susceptible to wearing off slightly over time. For the most part, this won't have an effect on the ability of the tape to store data. However, it does affect the drive itself as literally miles of tape stream over the heads, capstans, and roller components. Just like a VCR, a tape drive requires regular cleaning of the components that come into contact with the media. Without proper cleaning, tape backups can lose integrity when the heads have difficulty reading or writing through the "gunk" that forms over the heads. Some newer media such as AIT include a built-in head cleaner; however, even in the cleanest environments tape drives will eventually accumulate contaminants. Dirty capstans and rollers can cause media to stick to the components and create a horrible mess when you have to untangle yards of loose tape from inside the drive. Good luck preserving the integrity of the tape after that! Some devices include automatic cleaning capability; otherwise, you will have to either procure cleaning tapes or use the old cotton swab and cleaning solution method.

Be careful about how you repurpose a previously recorded tape. In the past, when administrators had an old tape that they wanted to recycle to store new data, they would **bulk erase** the tape using a big magnet. Obviously, since tape is a magnetic medium, bulk erasing wipes out the existing data. With current tape technology, do *not* erase tapes in this way. Tapes now come pre-formatted, and bulk erasure will remove important markings from the tape. Once this occurs, there is no way for the tape drive to orient the tape to a known starting position or locate boundaries to logically store the data. If you want to erase a tape, use tape backup software, which can usually perform a quick erasure by removing the table of contents, or a secure erasure, which overwrites the tape with zeros and ones.

A tape written under one software vendor's program usually cannot be read by another vendor's program. This makes a corporate-wide policy that uses the same backup software critically important.

If you've performed even a single tape backup, then you know by listening that the drive fast-forwards and rewinds the tape quite a lot. This is okay, and is the nature of the backup. However, over time and especially if the tape does not go all the way from one end of the tape to the other, varying levels of tension will occur at various locations on the spool, and could affect read/write reliability. Temperature changes, which cause the tape to expand and contract, and dropping a tape can also affect its tension level. Tape software offers utilities to **re-tension** the tape (see Figure 10-8), which fast-forwards to the end without reading or writing data, and then rewinds all the way to the beginning again. This process makes tension even throughout the tape.

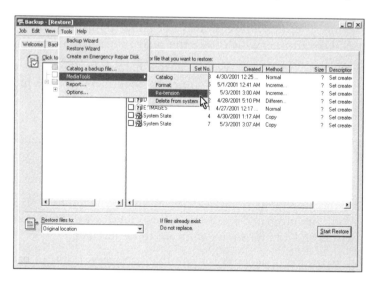

Figure 10-8 For even tension throughout the tape, the Windows 2000 Backup utility re-tensions the tape

If you need to retrieve data from a tape that has been erased or partially over-written with other data, contact a data recovery specialist. Their services are very expensive, but they can retrieve data from tapes as well as failed hard drives, often with a high success rate.

Backup Software

On the whole, lower-cost tape drives, and some disk-based devices intended for use with stand-alone PCs, come bundled with backup software. The software tends to be quite basic, but it usually does the job it is intended to do. Such software is not capable of servicing more sophisticated backup solutions such as automatic tape changers, remote backup, or backing up open files. On the other hand, most high-end tape drives and most disk-based products do not come bundled with software, and this should be taken into consideration when comparing costs, because the software is an additional several hundred dollars per server. Software for high-end tape drives includes many more features, and at a reduced cost per remote station.

If you need software as part of your backup setup, there are a number of packages available, ranging from replacements for bundled software to high-end products capable of backing up a whole room full of servers onto several tape drives, in some cases simultaneously. Depending on your needs, features to look for in backup software include the following:

- The ability to restore your hard disk in its entirety without requiring you to reinstall the operating system manually. This software feature creates an image of the disk and stores it on tape. This is not unlike Symantec Ghost or PowerQuest DriveImage, which store the image on a hard drive.

- The ability to treat a backup tape as a virtual hard disk, albeit a very slow one. This capability sometimes uses the right-click menu from Windows Explorer, allowing you to perform the backup in a similar way to using the Send To item when copying a file to a floppy disk.

- A built-in data compression capability should your drive not include its own hardware data compression facilities.

- The ability to scan for viruses during backup or restore operations.

- Built-in tape management facilities that can tell you when to replace or swap tapes. Robotic or automated media-switching devices will often require proprietary drivers and administrative software to be installed.

- The ability to create an account for you that has access rights to back up all data regardless of ownership. In a Windows NT/2000 environment, this account would belong to the Backup Operators group. The account is usually able to log on as a service and, therefore, perform backup without an administrator performing an actual logon.

- The ability to perform unattended backups. The software often creates a special account that can log on by itself at scheduled times to start the backup.

- The ability to run commands before and after the backup. This is useful for stopping services or applications that would interfere with the backup utility and restarting them afterward.

Storing and Securing Backups

There are several steps that you can take to enhance the security and operation of your backup and restore operations. You should also take steps to secure your backup cartridges.

When you develop a backup plan, consider the following recommendations:

- Secure both the storage device and the backup cartridges. Data can be retrieved from stolen cartridges and restored to another computer.

- If the software supports it, add security measures to the tape. You might be able to protect the media with a password or allow restore operations only by the Administrator or Owner accounts as shown in the Windows 2000 backup in Figure 10-9.

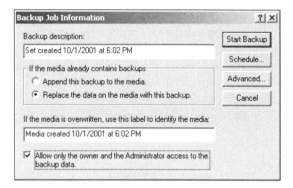

Figure 10-9   You can specify that only the Owner or Administrator accounts are allowed to restore backups

- Back up an entire volume by using the normal backup procedure. In case of a disk failure, it is more efficient to restore the entire volume in one operation than to also include differential or incremental backups.

- Keep at least three current copies of backup cartridges. Store one copy at an off-site location in an environmentally controlled, secure environment. Check for a service bureau in your area that can provide this storage. Most service bureaus also have tape drives that can read and restore the tapes for you if necessary. In preparation for disaster recovery, know how long it takes to physically retrieve the tapes from off-site locations. Store another copy near a server that can restore from the tape in a secure, locked, fireproof cabinet. The last tape can be stored wherever it suits you; its main purpose is redundancy in case one of the other tapes becomes damaged or defective. Some organizations with a WAN infrastructure send a copy of the normal backup to another office across the WAN. That way, if the local off-site location and the local office become unavailable (as in a natural disaster), you still have the copy that was sent to the other office.

Backup Types

A **normal backup** copies all selected files and clears the archive bit on each one. This identifies the file as having been backed up. The next time the file is modified, the archive bit is automatically set (added). Files or directories that have been moved to new locations are not marked for backup. Most backup software allows you to back up only files with this marker set and to choose whether or not to mark files when they are backed up. The archive bit is significant in relation to the incremental and differential backups. Normal backups are the easiest to use for restoring files because you need only the most recent backup file or tape to restore all of the backed-up files. Normal backups take the most time because every file that is selected is backed up, regardless of whether it has changed since the last backup.

An **incremental backup** backs up only those files that have been created or changed since the last normal or incremental backup, which can reduce the amount of time that is required to complete the backup process. It marks files as having been backed up by clearing the archive bit. You should create a complete normal backup of your system before you run incremental backups. If you use a combination of normal and incremental backups, you must have the last normal backup set as well as every incremental backup set that has been made since the last normal backup—in chronological order—to restore your data.

 The archive bit is easily observable by viewing the properties of a file. For example, in Windows Explorer, you would right-click a file and view its properties.

The advantage of an incremental backup is that the backup process is typically faster than both a normal or differential backup. The disadvantage is that it takes longer to restore the backup because you might have to supply multiple incremental tapes created since the last normal backup.

A **differential backup** copies files that have been created or changed since the last normal or incremental backup, which can reduce the amount of time that is required to complete the backup process. It does not mark files as having been backed up. You should create a complete normal backup of your system before you run differential backups. If you are doing normal and differential backups, you must have the last normal backup set and the last differential backup sets to restore your data.

The advantage of the differential backup is that it is faster than the normal backup and only requires two backup sets to restore data: the original normal backup and the corresponding differential backup. The disadvantage is that differential backups take longer to back up data.

A **copy backup** copies all selected files, but it does not mark each file as having been backed up. Copying is useful to back up files between normal and incremental backups because it does not affect other backup operations. A **daily backup** copies all selected files that have been modified on the day that the daily backup is performed. The backed-up files are not marked as having been backed up.

 Backups protect against data loss caused by a virus. Because some viruses take weeks to appear, keep normal backup tapes for at least a month to make sure that you can restore a system to its uninfected status.

Using Incremental Backups

Let's assume that you implement a normal backup, and that you do not want to do a normal backup every day. Performing an incremental backup will make the most sense in order to keep track of what files are backed up (unlike a differential backup). For example, suppose you're doing an incremental backup of 850 MB of data. If you did the normal backup on Monday, all 850 MB would be placed on the tape on that day. On Tuesday, the incremental backup day, only the files that you've created or changed since Monday would be backed up—so you may back up only a few megabytes at that time. On Wednesday, you'd back up only the files that you've created or changed since Tuesday, and so on. Because each incremental backup only backs up data since the last normal or incremental backup, the backup is relatively fast.

Unfortunately, incremental backups have their disadvantages. Although they are quicker than normal backups, it takes longer to restore a file when incremental backups are involved in the process. For example, suppose you needed to restore a file you backed up on Monday. This file would be included in the first backup of the set, since you performed a normal backup on Monday. However, to ensure that you were restoring the most recent version of the file, you'd have to search all remaining backups in the set to see if the file had changed since then. Another disadvantage to this type of backup is the fact that you must have all backups in the set available in order to restore only one file.

If you're planning to use an incremental backup, you might consider starting a new backup set every Monday that would include the backups for Monday through Friday of that week. Of course, if your servers are heavily utilized on weekends, you can schedule Saturday and Sunday backups as well. You can also make the length of time between creating new backup sets as long or as short as your needs dictate.

Develop a Backup Strategy

Regular backups of local hard disks prevent data loss resulting from disk drive failures, disk controller errors, power outages, virus infection, and other possible problems. Backup operations that are based on careful planning and reliable equipment make file recovery easier and less time consuming. There are several backup strategies, though the most common strategy is known as the Grandfather-Father-Son (GFS) strategy (described below). Your backup strategy will usually use some combination of normal, incremental, or differential backups.

Developing a backup strategy involves not only determining when to perform backups, but also testing the data with random and scheduled verification to make sure that tape devices and media are functioning properly. Also, make sure that throughout the organization, the persons or departments responsible for handling backup and restore operations are well informed as to what exactly they should back up. You would not want to be caught in the awkward situation where someone asks you to restore a file that you didn't even know you were supposed to back up.

The Grandfather-Father-Son Backup Strategy

There are several generally accepted backup strategies; however, many of them are based on the popular **Grandfather-Father-Son (GFS)** backup strategy (otherwise known as the Child-Parent-Grandparent method). This backup strategy uses three sets of tapes for daily, weekly, and monthly backup sets, and you implement it as follows:

1. *Back up the "Son"*—Label four tapes as "Monday" through "Thursday." These Son tapes are used for daily incremental backups during the week. For subsequent weeks, reuse these same tapes.

2. *Back up the "Father"*—Label five tapes as "Week 1" through "Week 5." These Father tapes are used for weekly normal backups on Friday, the day you do not perform a Son backup. Once you make the tape, store it locally. Reuse the tapes when each tape's respective week arrives. Depending on your backup policy, periodically duplicate a Father tape for off-site storage. You can use another drive to perform a simultaneous backup, or some backup software might offer a tape copy feature.

3. *Back up the "Grandfather"*—Grandfather tapes are used for a normal backup performed on the last business day of the month. No standard labeling scheme is stated, but consider labeling three tapes as "Month 1" through "Month 3." The tapes are valid for three months and are reused every quarter.

At a minimum, the GFS strategy requires 12 tapes if you add them all together, assuming that no one backup exceeds the capacity of a single cartridge.

Of course, you can modify this scheme as it suits your backup policy, but the GFS strategy is a logical, reliable place to start. For example, if you want to keep a year's data archived at all times (instead of only a quarter's), then for the Grandfather tapes you would label 12 tapes "Month 1" through "Month 12" and reuse the tapes every year. An illustration of the GFS rotation scheme appears in Figure 10-10.

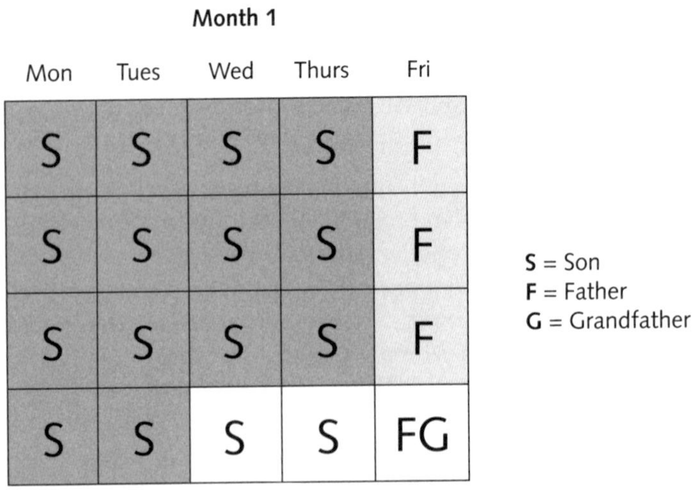

Month 1

Mon	Tues	Wed	Thurs	Fri
S	S	S	S	F
S	S	S	S	F
S	S	S	S	F
S	S	S	S	FG

S = Son
F = Father
G = Grandfather

Figure 10-10   The GFS tape rotation strategy

The Six-Cartridge Backup

If you want to use fewer tapes, consider the **six-cartridge backup** strategy. This might be a better choice for smaller business or sites that do not generate large quantities of data. The disadvantage of the six-cartridge strategy is that you have a shorter archive history—only two weeks, whereas the GFS strategy is a quarter.

To perform a six-cartridge backup:

1. Label six cartridges "Friday 1," "Friday 2," "Monday," "Tuesday," "Wednesday," and "Thursday."

2. Perform the first normal backup onto the "Friday 1" tape. Store the tape off-site.

3. On Monday, perform an incremental backup onto the "Monday" tape. Store the tape on-site.

4. Repeat the incremental backup onto tapes "Tuesday," "Wednesday," and "Thursday" on the corresponding days.

5. Perform the second normal backup onto the "Friday 2" tape. This completes the backup cycle. Store the cartridge off-site. On each successive Friday, alternate between the "Friday 1" tape and the "Friday 2" tape.

Note that the Friday tapes are always stored off-site, as illustrated in Figure 10-11. This can cause a problem when it is necessary to restore data, because you will have to physically retrieve the tape, and this might not suit the time frame necessary to restore the data. As with the GFS method, you can modify the six-cartridge method to suit your needs.

10

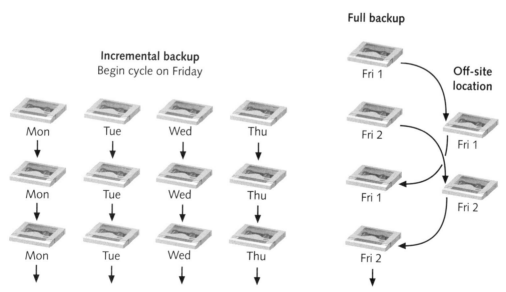

Figure 10-11   The six-cartridge backup strategy stores Friday tapes off-site

To avoid the need to retrieve a Friday tape from off-site storage when you need to restore data, make the Monday backup a normal backup and the Tuesday, Wednesday, and Thursday backups incremental to the Monday backup.

The Tower of Hanoi

Finally, there is the **Tower of Hanoi backup** method, borrowing from a mathematical logic game of the same name. Use five sets of media for this rotation, labeling each "A" through "E" and proceed as follows:

1. On day one, back up to "A." Reuse the "A" tape every other day.

2. On day two, back up to "B." Reuse the "B" tape every four days.

3. On day four, back up to "C." Reuse the "C" tape every eight days.

4. On day eight, back up to "D." Reuse the "D" tape every 16 days.

5. On day 16, back up to "E." Reuse the "E" tape every 32 days.

 As a memory aid to the Tower of Hanoi rotation, just notice that each tape is reused in a pattern similar to binary notation. Look at the "reuse" schedule at the end of every step above. Notice that you reuse tapes every 2, 4, 8, 16, and 32 days.

An advantage of the Tower of Hanoi rotation is that you always have a daily history of data extending back 32 days. This is a flexible backup strategy requiring only five tapes (assuming each backup only requires one tape). If you want long-term archiving, you can remove a tape and store it off-site. Label the tape with the date and replace it with another. For example, if you want to archive the "E" tape, place a date on it, send it to storage, and label a new cartridge "E" that will continue the rotation. Also, you can extend the history if you like. By adding an "F" backup every 64 days, you now have a 64-day history. Keep adding letters until you reach the history you want.

The rotation scheme is best understood by viewing Figure 10-12.

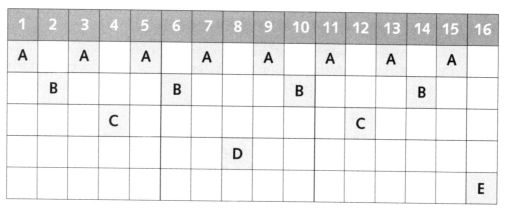

1	2	3	4	5	6	7	8	9	10	11	12	13	14	15	16
A		A		A		A		A		A		A		A	
	B				B				B				B		
			C								C				
							D								
															E

return to day 1

Figure 10-12 Tower of Hanoi media rotation schedule

Document the Process

Keeping accurate backup records is essential for locating backed-up data quickly, particularly if you have accumulated a large number of backup cartridges. Thorough records include cartridge labels, catalogs, and online log files and log books.

- *Cartridge labels*—Cartridge labels for write-once cartridges should contain the backup date, the type of backup (normal, incremental, or differential), and a list of contents. If you are restoring from differential or incremental backups, you need to be able to locate the last normal backup and either the last differential backup or all incremental backups that have been created since the last normal backup. Label reusable media, such as tapes or removable disks, sequentially, and keep a log book in which you note the content of cartridges, the backup date, the type of backup, and the date the medium was placed in service. If you have to replace a defective cartridge, label it with the next unused sequential ID, and record it in the log book.

- *Catalogs*—Most backup software includes a mechanism for cataloging backup files. Backup software typically stores backup catalogs on the cartridge and temporarily loads them into memory. Catalogs are created for each backup set or for each collection of backed-up files from one drive.

- *Log files*—Log files include the names of all backed-up and restored files and directories. A log file is useful when you are restoring data because you can print or read this file from any text editor. Keeping printed logs in a notebook makes it easier to locate specific files. For example, if the tape that contains the catalog of the backup set is corrupted, you can use the printed logs to locate a file.

10

HIGH SERVER AVAILABILITY AND REDUNDANCY

File services, print services, and client–server applications rely not only on the availability of the computers running the services, but also on the availability of network services. In an environment where there is only one computer providing a particular service (file, print, or application), an outage involving that server eliminates the availability of the provided service. To provide both load balancing and redundancy for these services, a group of computers (a cluster), can cooperate in providing these services. This cooperation is managed by clustering software that provides a service to clients in a client–server environment. For example, a public file share, a web server, or a database application can all be managed as resources.

A cluster improves the availability of client–server applications by increasing the availability of server resources. Using a cluster, you can set up applications on two or more servers (nodes) in a cluster. Each node connects to a shared storage media. Clusters present a single, virtual image of the cluster to clients (see Figure 10-13). If one node fails, the applications on the failed node are available on the other node. Throughout this process, client communications with applications usually continue with little or no interruption. In most cases, the interruption in service is detected in about five seconds, and services can be available again in as few as 30 seconds (depending on how long it takes to restart the application).

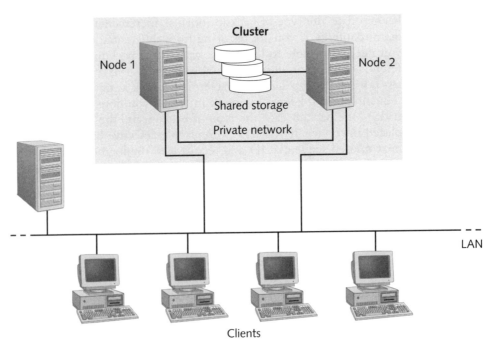

Figure 10-13   Cluster technology connects two or more servers to common shared storage

Clustering provides high availability and fault tolerance by keeping a backup of the primary system available. **Static load balancing** remains idle and unused until a failure occurs, which makes this an expensive solution. An **active cluster** is a clustering method in which all nodes perform normal, active functions and then perform additional functions for a failed cluster member. For example, redundant systems might have one node in the cluster servicing web clients while the other node provides access to a database. If either node fails, the resource (either the web server or database server) fails over to the other node. The node that is still functioning responds to both web and SQL requests from clients (see Figure 10-14). In a **passive cluster**, a server with identical services as its failover partner would remain in an idle node state until such a time as the primary node fails.

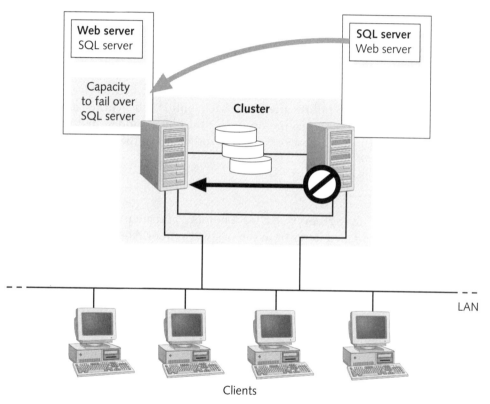

Figure 10-14   Active cluster redundancy

CPU, I/O, storage, and application resources can be added incrementally to efficiently expand capacity, making the solution highly scalable. This creates reliable access to system resources and data, as well as investment protection of both hardware and software resources. Clusters are relatively affordable because they can be built with commodity hardware (high-volume components that are relatively inexpensive).

By clustering existing hardware with new computers, you protect your investment in both hardware and software: Instead of replacing an existing computer with a new one of twice the capacity, you can simply add another computer of equal capacity. For example, if performance degrades because of an increase in the number of clients using an application on a server, you can add a second server to a cluster, which improves performance and also increases availability.

 Clients typically access network applications and resources through network names and IP addresses. When these network applications and resources are hosted within a Microsoft Cluster Server (MSCS), clients can continue to find and access the resources, even though they may move between nodes. MSCS enables this by failing over both the IP address and network name for a given resource.

Failover

Failover is the process of having cluster resources migrate from an unavailable node to an available node. A related process, **failback**, occurs when service transfers back to the node that has been offline after it is back online. The cluster automatically initiates failover when it detects a failure on one of the cluster nodes. Because each cluster node monitors both its own processes and the other node, the need for failover is detected without delay.

Spare Parts

For hardware failure recovery, having a number of spare parts available will save the time needed to order failed items from the original vendor. Also, as equipment ages, the availability of the parts needed to continue operation may diminish as well. All parts to be considered available as replacements for a given computer system must be compatible with both the operating system in use and other components within the system. The best strategy for mission-critical systems is to have a set of matching parts available. Some vendors, such as Intel, sell spare-parts kits comprised of the most critical system components, including:

- 12 V VRM (a voltage regulator module that helps ensure clean power to the motherboard)
- Fans
- Hot-swap bay assembly with SCSI backplane
- Power supply
- CD-ROM drive
- Floppy drive
- Cables

Using the spare-parts kit, you use parts as necessary and immediately call the vendor to replace the parts you use. That way, the spare-parts kit is always ready for service. Be sure to also have additional spare parts, which might not be included in a spare-parts kit, such as:

- Network card
- Memory modules
- Processor
- Hard disk
- Hard disk host adapter (EIDE or SCSI)
- Motherboard
- Video card
- Sound card (optional)
- Other miscellaneous I/O boards

Recall from earlier discussions that hot swapping will allow you to replace many of these devices without an interruption in service. This is particularly true of hard disks. Many systems also include a **hot spare** that is connected to the hard disk host adapter along with the other hard disks, but is dormant until another device in the drive array fails. At that time, the hot spare is usually placed into service automatically. For example, if one member of a mirrored (RAID-1) array fails, the hot spare can automatically come online and the remaining member will begin to duplicate to it. The main difference between a hot-swappable disk and a hot spare is that a hot spare is not a Plug and Play item. It must be on the bus at the time of the failure. If it is not, then you must shut down the system and add it to the bus, which would not be necessary with a hot-swappable drive.

 Be sure that you secure the spare parts in a locked cabinet. Most of the parts are small and easily stolen.

SNMP SETTINGS

In Chapter 9, you learned the basics of SNMP. SNMP is a critical element for disaster avoidance, detection, and recovery. The following is a short list of common SNMP items for which you will want to configure your SNMP management system to assist in disaster prevention and recovery:

- Network protocol identification and statistics
- Dynamic identification of devices attached to the network (discovery)
- Hardware and software configuration data

- Device performance and usage statistics
- Device error and event messages
- Program and application usage statistics

The items in the list can help to detect impending problems and verify that a proposed solution worked effectively. For example, if you suspect network traffic to be excessive on an Ethernet network, you could configure the SNMP agent to issue a trap when it detects over 30% network utilization on a given segment. After replacing a hub with a switch to increase throughput and reduce collisions, the same SNMP agent can confirm (by absence of a trap) that the solution worked.

In general, agents do not originate messages—they only respond to messages. The exception is an SNMP trap triggered by a specific event such as a system reboot or illegal access. Traps and trap messages provide a rudimentary form of security by notifying the management system any time such an event occurs. Typically, you configure the management system to issue an email, fax, network message, or pager alert. For pager alerts, some systems require an external modem, but I usually circumvent that by using email instead to send text messages to a cell phone or email-capable pager.

 TIP If your cabinet and SNMP management software support it, you can add a layer of physical security to the server cabinet by configuring SNMP to issue a trap any time the cabinet door opens. If you're the only one who is supposed to access the cabinet and your pager receives an SNMP message while you're away at lunch, then you know somebody is illegitimately accessing the cabinet.

SERVER MANAGEMENT AND MAINTENANCE

Server management and disaster recovery are really two balancing components in the same overall server health management scheme. You use server management software and faithful physical management of the server to prevent disaster. Then, you use disaster recovery techniques to fix the inevitable problems that occur.

Server Management Software

There is a broad selection of server management software. In earlier chapters, we have mentioned third-party management products such as IBM Tivoli or Computer Associates' Unicenter TNG. In this section, third-party products can still play a role, but servers also usually include less comprehensive software that provides basic system monitoring functions. These utilities often integrate with the system BIOS or CMOS settings, and display or issue an alert when a problem appears. For example, Figure 10-15 shows a very simple server monitoring utility that monitors temperature, fan speed, voltages, and more.

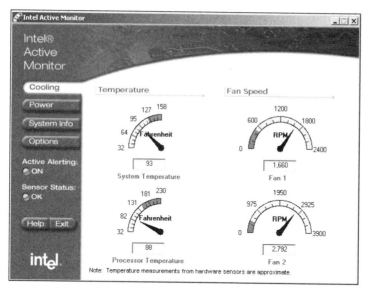

Figure 10-15   A monitoring utility displays basic server health issues

Server motherboards and management software usually offer features such as:

- *Failure detection.* Detects changes in temperature, voltage, fan speed or failure, disk drive problems or failure, power supply failure, processor status, and ECC memory errors.

- *Software monitoring.* Detects hung applications. For serious problems, you can use management software to perform a graceful shutdown or reboot.

- *Event logging.* Events are stored in NVRAM (nonvolatile RAM) so that if power is lost, the records remain.

- *Emergency Management Port* (Intel boards). A feature that allows you to remotely turn on, off, or reset the server and view the event log. These features require an external modem and are very useful for remotely monitoring servers over a wide geographic area from a single location.

- *Security monitoring.* A jumper setting enables chassis intrusion detection. Some systems will automatically blank the video when the chassis or cabinet is open, and a password is required to resume normal video.

 TIP   Most server boards include a server management utility, but if yours does not, I recommend downloading at least a monitoring utility such as the Motherboard Monitor (freeware) from nearly any popular download site, or *www.tweakfiles.com/diagnostic/ motherboardmonitor.html*.

Larger organizations need more than a local server management utility, and opt instead for enterprise management software such as HP's Openview or CA's Unicenter TNG.

A very significant advantage of this type of software is that you can manage the entire network from a single seat, regardless of the physical location of any one server. For example, in Figure 10-16, I used CA's Unicenter TNG to access the California network and, in Figure 10-17, the North American network. The figures are shown using a map feature of Unicenter in 2D, but you can also use 3D graphics. Using the map view, you click on any of your networks to access information and administer it.

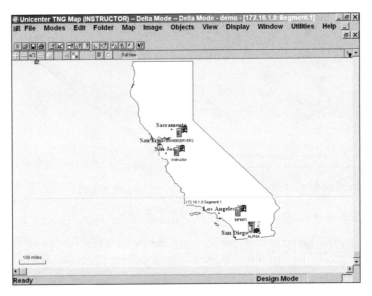

Figure 10-16   Unicenter TNG allows you to visually access your server

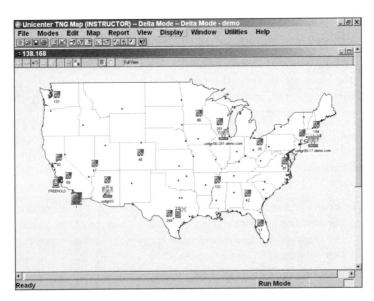

Figure 10-17   A demonstration of the Unicenter TNG map feature

Physical Care and Maintenance

Recall from Chapter 2 that two primary factors contribute to hardware device and computer peripheral failure: dirt and heat. Regular cleaning of computer equipment and adequate ventilation are necessary in order to maximize the lifetime of the equipment.

Hard disk drives, for example, are prone to failure in high-heat environments. Their mechanical nature causes a great deal of friction, as the platters can spin in excess of 15,000 revolutions per minute (rpm). Stack several disks inside of a single computer without proper ventilation, and the combined heat of several drives can damage the electrical components, leading to drive failure. If a drive fails and data is lost prior to a timely backup, an expensive data recovery service bureau will need to be employed to open the disks and attempt to extract the data from the failed device.

Note

Consider checking into a server chassis that includes airflow guides. These guides are paddles near the cooling fans that allow you to direct the airflow as desired. This is very handy when the drives or other hot components are located some distance from the actual fans or are not in the path of the normal airflow. For example, Supermicro offers airflow guides on some of its popular models (see Figure 10-18).

10

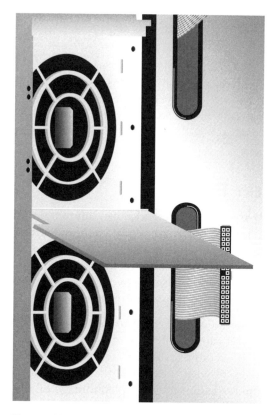

Figure 10-18   You can direct the airflow using adjustable airflow guides

Related to the heat and dust that accumulate during the normal use and function of your equipment is the age of the equipment and/or the time that this equipment has been in service. Regular monitoring of your system's performance is necessary to note changes in I/O and other performance measures unrelated to changes in network access or activity.

If a device is performing slowly or is experiencing an increase of random or unexplained errors, it may be in an early stage of failure and should be replaced as soon as possible. Some devices, such as a power supply, cannot be easily monitored without server management software, but can lead to systemwide failures if performance begins to deteriorate. A power supply whose voltage is beginning to drop significantly or fluctuate can affect many components in the system both in terms of quality and length of service. If you suspect a power supply failure, replace it immediately to avoid further damage to other system components.

Probably the most common maintenance issue for servers is planned downtime to blow out dust. The frequency of this task varies greatly depending on the environmental conditions at the site. Until you can determine the rate at which dust accumulates in the case, check accumulation weekly. Once you determine an optimum frequency for this planned downtime, be sure to schedule it regularly. When dusting, remember to remove the server from the server room if you are blowing out dust in order to avoid contaminating the environment. Remove dust from every place you can, though the chassis fans and power supply fans accumulate dust most quickly.

 Don't forget to blow out CD-ROM and floppy drives. The floppy drive in particular is relatively open, even with the protective flap that covers the opening. I recently threw away about three floppies that the drive wouldn't read. I realized that it was too much of a coincidence for all of the disks to be bad. So I removed the floppy, blew out the dust, and almost choked on the cloud.

DEVELOPING A DISASTER RECOVERY PLAN

A **disaster recovery plan (DRP)** for a large enterprise can amount to hundreds of pages with thousands of contingencies. These complicated details and scenarios, if left unplanned, can go unaccomplished, leading to an unacceptable extension of system outage. When putting together a DRP, there are many items that need to be considered and included. Practical implementations will vary from one network to another, but the most important matter is to develop a disaster recovery plan in the first place.

The DRP is critical because in a disaster, the tendency is to hastily assemble a short list of recovery steps that come to mind. This can actually extend the time it takes to recover from disaster, because it is difficult to account for every recovery procedure. A DRP specifies what actions need to be taken, in what order, after the destructive event. Each scenario, from a single desktop computer failure to a complete outage of an entire site, should have a plan of action for those responsible. Depending on the severity of the event, these actions can include:

- Evacuation of facility and notification to emergency services
- Notification sequence for team leaders and backups
- Establishing a temporary business recovery command center
- Preliminary and detailed damage assessment
- Recall of vital records from off-site storage

In the event of a site-wide or catastrophic failure, longer-term issues must be addressed:

- Handling legal, financial, and insurance issues
- Dealing with the news media to mitigate misinformation
- Locating interim facilities to restart your business
- Recovery of PCs, LANs and midrange systems
- Establishing voice and data communication
- Addressing human resource and accounts payable/receivable issues
- Replacement of equipment, furniture, and supplies
- Notification to clients, customers, suppliers, and stockholders

10

A disaster recovery plan is only a possibility when there is actually a team to develop it. Assemble members from each major branch or function of your organization, because disasters affect all aspects of the organization, not just the IT department. The disaster recovery team needs to work well together in order to minimize downtime and loss of productivity. Preparing a disaster recovery plan can take months and, depending on the size of the organization, perhaps over a year.

 TIP For an example of comprehensive disaster recovery services, see BMS Catastrophes (*www.bmscat.com*). For help in planning a disaster recovery solution, see Davis Logic (*www.davislogic.com*).

Using Alternate Sites

In larger computing environments, it is not practical to have enough computers in store and configured to replace most of the equipment all at once. Larger companies, universities, and institutions cannot afford to carry more that 1% or 2% of the total hardware collection in recovery-based inventory. Also, in the event of facility-, site-, or campus-wide failure, there may be more than computers that need to be replaced: Facilities may also have to be recovered as in the case of a flood, tornado, or other natural disaster.

In preparation for large-scale recovery, consider alternate sites. They can range from simple data collection and warehousing services designed to return data as needed to continue business operations, to full-scale facility duplication (**hot sites**) designed to replicate all of the hardware, software, and data infrastructure necessary to assume all business functions in the event of a primary facility failure. These hot sites are very expensive to maintain, as they have nearly a complete replica of all computers in the central facility, but if a large-scale outage will cost the company its existence, the price is worth it.

Hot Sites

Usually, a hot site is a shared facility with a number of subscribers from different geographic locations, each of which share in the cost of maintaining the fully operational center. Each subscriber usually occupies the hot site for up to six weeks after a disaster. These facilities are also available for subscribers to exercise their recovery plan in test mode.

Hot site recovery is appropriate for a computer operation that has more than a 24-hour outage tolerance. Data centers requiring faster service restoration must invest in redundant (spare) equipment that is immediately available to satisfy this need. Conversely, facilities that can afford to wait several weeks before restoring service need not engage a hot site, for they will have time to order and install new equipment.

Cold Sites

Many service bureaus augment their hot site service with a **cold site** feature. This is a facility designed to receive computer equipment. All power, water, air conditioning, raised floor, and other items requiring a long lead-time to acquire, install, and make ready to house a computer center are in place.

Should a company be unable to return to its home-computing center within a tolerable time frame, it would make arrangements to occupy this cold site. Computers, peripheral equipment, and related services would be ordered (purchased, leased, or rented) and made ready to assume the company's processing workload. Cold sites would be used until the home site was repaired or rebuilt.

Site Management

The business processes can be quite complex as remote sites, either hot or cold, are implemented. Bad planning in these areas leads to confusion and delay. Several important steps are necessary to determine the activities and timeframes surrounding service and equipment movement and delegation between the central (or original) site, hot sites, cold sites, and their return to the repaired or newly constructed site.

- Determine the extent of the damage and if additional equipment, services, and supplies are needed.

- Take care to adequately cover telecommunications issues. Most medium-sized and large organizations usually have a number of telecommunications services (such as leased lines and fiber) connecting campuses and other facilities. This means that, in the event of a disaster, such connections to other facilities may have to be abandoned, re-routed, or installed to the hot and/or cold sites in order to establish connectivity to such other operational facilities. Detailed records of current operations must be carefully reviewed to be certain that your disaster recovery plan covers every conceivable technical aspect of recovering all critical services and data in the least amount of time.

- Obtain approval for expenditure of funds to bring in any needed equipment and supplies. I recently read of a corporation that set up an agreement with their bank so that in the event of a catastrophic disaster, the bank would supply a mobile branch staffed with at least two tellers who would dispense the finances and keep all necessary records.

- Notify local vendor marketing and/or service representatives if there is a need for immediate delivery of components to bring the computer systems to an operational level, even in a degraded mode.

If an alternate site is necessary, the following additional major tasks must be undertaken:

- Obtain governmental permissions and assistance as necessary. For example, you are likely to need building permits to construct even a temporary site.

- Coordinate moving of equipment and support personnel into the alternate site. Be sure to hire the services of a dependable security firm to protect company assets, because looting is to be expected.

- Bring the tape backups from off-site storage to the alternate site.

- As soon as the hardware is up to specifications to run the operating system, load software and run necessary tests. One of the best solutions is to record recent images of server hard drives for a fast restore.

- Prepare backup materials and return these to the off-site storage area.

- Coordinate client activities to ensure that the most critical jobs are being supported as needed.

- Be sensitive to the employees involved in the relocation. For example, in a natural disaster, employees might be suffering from the death of friends or loved ones, or they might be without a home.

- As production begins, ensure that periodic backup procedures are being followed and materials are being placed in off-site storage periodically.

- Keep administration and clients informed of the status, progress, and problems.

10

CHAPTER SUMMARY

- Even in normal day-to-day operations, data can become corrupted or lost. Being able to restore data and applications quickly is essential.

- Factors to consider when you purchase a backup unit include the amount of data you need to back up, whether your backup software supports the unit, and the amount of money you want to spend.

- Optical disks are a good backup solution for moving infrequently used data from fast, expensive hardware (hard disks) to slower, less expensive media. However, optical disks are a poor solution if you want to back up large amounts of data quickly.

- In determining the capacity of a backup medium, you must determine the type of files the vendor used to test the drive and the type of test the vendor ran, because many capacity claims are based on using totally compressible files. These tests don't take into account that many file types can't be compressed—so the tests don't simulate real-world scenarios.

- For a large-scale enterprise, you should probably investigate an automated backup technology such as tape libraries that use autoloaders to change tapes in a largely unattended fashion. Automated tape libraries have an extensive online retention period (OLRP). At the highest level, tape libraries can support dozens of drives and hold several hundred cartridges. At that level, you will probably not configure the tape solution yourself; you tell vendor representatives what your objectives are and they will configure the library for you or provide guidance.

- There are a number of tape media standards. The most common for smaller tape devices is probably the Quarter Inch Cartridge (QIC), which as the name implies is a quarter inch in width. For server use, you probably won't see QIC and QIC Wide, which is actually .315 inches (8 mm) wide, in common use anymore.

- A Travan drive can reach compressed capacity of about 20 GB and may be useful for home, SOHO, or small departmental backups. Because Travan drives accept the QIC format, they are usually read compatible with preceding QIC standards.

- Travan NS (network series) is the most recent implementation of the Travan standard and addresses two main issues: hardware compression and fast verification.

- The mechanics of reading and writing to Travan, QIC, and similar format tapes are analogous to the way audio signals are written to a standard audio cassette. The mechanics of writing data to a DAT, in contrast, are similar to the way video signals are written to a video cassette. Rather than the tape being moved linearly across a static head, with DAT the tape is moved across an angled, rotating head.

- AIT is a Sony invention that makes backup and restore operations faster because of an optional Memory in Cassette (MIC) chip that is able to quickly locate which of the 256 tape partitions contain the data.

◻ Depending on the drive and media used, the DLT format allows up to 70 GB of compressed data to be stored on one rather large tape, which, unlike 8 mm or 4 mm helical scan technology, passes linearly over a fixed head. Like Travan NS technology, DLT drives can simultaneously read and write, allowing them to perform extremely well, and in some cases even better than 8 mm helical scan tape.

◻ The Ultrium tape format uses a single reel that stores more tape for large capacity—up to 1.6 TB per cartridge at a transfer speed up to 320 MBps. Ultrium tapes also have a memory chip that transmits its characteristics over an RF signal.

◻ Just like a VCR, a tape drive requires regular cleaning of the components that come into contact with the media. Without proper cleaning, tape backups can lose integrity when the heads have difficulty reading or writing through the "gunk" that forms over the heads. Some devices include automatic cleaning capability; otherwise, you will have to either procure cleaning tapes or use the manual cotton swab and cleaning solution method.

◻ Because tape is a magnetic medium, bulk erasing wipes out the existing data. With current tape technology, do not bulk erase. Tapes now come preformatted, and bulk erasure will remove important markings from the tape.

◻ Tape software offers utilities to re-tension the tape, which fast-forwards to the end without reading or writing data, and then rewinds all the way to the beginning again. This process makes tension even throughout the tape. Uneven tape tension can affect read/write reliability.

◻ On the whole, lower-cost tape drives, and some disk-based devices intended for use with stand-alone PCs, come bundled with backup software that provides only basic functionality. More sophisticated backup software is considerably more expensive.

◻ Secure backups in a locked, fireproof cabinet. You can also apply password protection to the backups and require that only the Administrator or Owner accounts can access it. You can also keep backups off-site at a service bureau.

◻ A normal backup copies all selected files and clears their archive bit.

◻ An incremental backup backs up only those files that have been created or changed since the last normal or incremental backup, which can reduce the amount of time that is required to complete the backup process. It marks files as having been backed up.

◻ A differential backup copies files that have been created or changed since the last normal or incremental backup, which can reduce the amount of time that is required to complete the backup process. It does not mark files as having been backed up.

◻ A copy backup copies all selected files, but it does not mark each file as having been backed up. Copying is useful to back up files between normal and incremental backups because it does not affect other backup operations.

10

- A daily backup copies all selected files that have been modified on the day that the daily backup is performed. The backed-up files are not marked as having been backed up.

- The Grandfather-Father-Son (GFS) backup strategy backs up incrementally Monday through Thursday, with a normal backup on Friday. Once a month, another normal backup is made.

- The six-cartridge backup strategy is similar to the GFS strategy, except that you do not use monthly backups and you have a two-week tape history.

- The Tower of Hanoi backup strategy requires only five tapes and creates a history that extends at least 32 days.

- Keeping accurate backup records is essential for locating backed-up data quickly, particularly if you have accumulated a large number of backup cartridges. Thorough records include cartridge labels, catalogs, online log files, and log books.

- To provide both load balancing and redundancy, a group of computers (a cluster) can cooperate in providing services. This cooperation is managed by clustering software that provides a service to clients in a client-server environment. If one node fails, the applications on the failed node are available on the other node. Throughout this process, client communications with applications usually continue with little or no interruption.

- For hardware failure recovery, having a number of spare parts available will save the time needed to order failed items from the original vendor. Some vendors, such as Intel, sell spare-parts kits comprised of the most critical system components.

- Many systems also include a hot spare that is connected to the hard disk host adapter along with the other hard disks, but is dormant until another device in the drive array fails.

- System monitoring software can detect problems such as failing hard drives, fans, power supplies, and high temperature.

- Heat is destructive to electrical components, and dust magnifies heat problems. Therefore, schedule a regular maintenance program to dust out servers.

- The combined heat of several drives in a single server can damage electrical components leading to drive failure. Be sure to provide ventilation to the drives.

- It is essential to assemble a disaster recovery team and develop a disaster recovery plan. Practical implementations will vary from one organization to another.

- In preparation for large-scale recovery, consider alternate sites. They can range from simple data collection and warehousing services designed to return data as needed to continue business operations, to full-scale facility duplication (hot site) designed to replicate all of the hardware, software, and data infrastructure necessary to assume all business functions in the event of a primary facility failure. Hot sites are very expensive to maintain, as they have nearly a complete replica of all computers in the central facility.

❏ Hot site recovery is appropriate for a computer operation that has more than a 24-hour outage tolerance.

❏ Many service bureaus augment their hot site service offering with a cold site feature. This is a facility designed to receive computer equipment. All power, water, air conditioning, raised floor, and other items requiring a long lead-time to acquire, install, and house a computer center are in place.

❏ Carefully consider alternate site plans, whether hot sites or cold sites. Without alternate site plans, the tendency is to make up a plan as you go, which leads to confusion and delays.

KEY TERMS

active cluster — A clustering method in which all nodes perform normal, active functions and then perform additional functions for a failed cluster member.

Advanced Intelligent Tape (AIT) — A Sony invention that uses an optional Memory in Cassette (MIC) chip on 8 mm tape that is able to quickly locate which of the 256 tape partitions contain the backed-up data.

autoloaders — Robotics inside a tape library that automatically swap tapes in and out of drives.

backup window — The optimal period of time in which you can perform a backup, usually when most files are closed.

bulk erase — Removal of data from magnetic tape using a large magnet. This is not a standard practice anymore, because most tapes require special markings that bulk erasure removes.

cold site — A disaster recovery facility designed to receive computer equipment. All power, water, air conditioning, raised floor, and other items requiring a long lead-time to acquire, install, and house a computer center are in place.

copy backup — A backup that copies all selected files, but does not mark each file as having been backed up. Copying is useful to back up files between normal and incremental backups because it does not affect other backup operations.

daily backup — A backup that copies all selected files that have been modified on the day that the daily backup is performed. The backed-up files are not marked as having been backed up.

differential backup — A backup that copies files that have been created or changed since the last normal or incremental backup, which can reduce the amount of time that is required to complete the backup process. It does not mark files as having been backed up.

digital audio tape (DAT) — Originally a high-fidelity digital recording format, now used on 4 mm and 8 mm tape backups. Uses helical scanning to record data.

digital linear tape (DLT) — A digital tape recording format that allows up to 70 GB of compressed data to be stored on one rather large tape, which, unlike 8 mm or 4 mm helical scan technology, passes linearly over a fixed head.

10

disaster recovery plan (DRP) — A comprehensive plan designed to recover an organization to productivity after a disaster.

failback — A clustering term referring to restoring resources to a node that has been offline when it comes back online.

Grandfather-Father-Son (GFS) — A backup strategy that uses three sets of tapes for daily, weekly, and monthly backups, retaining three months of data.

helical scanning — A tape recording method that uses a rotating tilted head to record at an angle, allowing a higher-density recording format on the tape.

Hierarchical Storage Management (HSM) — A storage management strategy in which infrequently used data is moved from expensive hardware (hard disks) to less expensive media such as optical disks or magnetic tape.

hot site — A location containing computers and necessary peripheral equipment that may be occupied or utilized by a subscriber immediately after a disaster declaration to restore its own systems, applications, and data.

hot spare — A hard disk connected to the host adapter along with the other hard disks. It is dormant until another device in the drive array fails. At that time, the hot spare is usually placed into service automatically.

incremental backup — A backup of only those files that have been created or changed since the last normal or incremental backup, which can reduce the amount of time that is required to complete the backup process. It marks files as having been backed up by setting the archive bit.

Linear Tape Open (LTO) — A collaborative technology effort headed up by HP, IBM, and Seagate to provide extremely high tape capacity and restore capability.

Linear Tape Open - Cartridge Memory (LTO-CM) — Memory in Ultrium tapes that transmits tape characteristics using radio frequency (RF) signals.

normal backup — A backup that copies all selected files and clears the archive bit for each one.

online retention period (OLRP) — References how far back in time a tape library can restore from tape without manual intervention.

optical disk — Any disk written and read by laser, including CD-R, CD-RW, DVD, and so forth.

passive cluster — A clustered server with identical services as its failover partner. A passive cluster partner remains in an idle node state until such a time as the primary node fails.

Quarter Inch Cartridge (QIC) — A common tape format that is a quarter inch wide. A variant of QIC is the QIC Wide format, which is .315 inches (8 mm) wide. QIC cartridges are generally not sufficient for server purposes.

re-tension — Fast-forwards tape to the end without reading or writing data, and then rewinds all the way to the beginning again. This process makes tension even throughout the tape.

six-cartridge backup — Similar to a GFS backup strategy, but with a two-week history.

static load balancing — A clustering technology in which a cluster member remains idle until a failure occurs.

tape library — A self-contained tape backup solution that is preloaded with several tapes. Most tape libraries include autoloaders to swap tapes.

Tower of Hanoi backup — A tape strategy that requires relatively few tapes and backs up a daily history of 32 or more days.

Travan — Created by Imation, a QIC-based standard capable of up to 20 GB compressed capacity.

Travan NS — A Travan format that can use hardware compression and fast data verification.

Ultrium — A tape format that offers a native capacity of up to 800 GB and data transfer of 80–160 MBps. Ultrium tapes use a single reel cartridge that makes room for more tape and less mechanics. Ultrium cartridges can contain memory right on the cartridge that stores a redundant file log and user-defined information.

REVIEW QUESTIONS

1. What is the minimum number of tapes required in a GFS tape backup strategy?

   a. 12

   b. 24

   c. 48

   d. 60

2. You wish to back up all of the files on a hard disk in your computer. You have just replaced your old, single-media tape device with a new, 12-tape automated tape library system. When you attempt to initiate the backup, the process fails. What should you do?

   a. Install the driver for the new device.

   b. Restore the catalog from the old device, and then try the backup again.

   c. Make sure that you use only new blank tapes for the backup.

   d. Reboot the computer.

3. Your company's Internet servers are becoming overloaded due to an increase in commerce traffic to your web site. You decide to implement a clustering solution. What kind of clustering model should you implement in order to provide the desired load balancing?

   a. active cluster

   b. passive cluster

   c. disruptive cluster

   d. peanut cluster

10

4. Which of the following are necessary for disaster recovery?

   a. hot site

   b. hot-swap implementation

   c. data backup

   d. fire drills

5. Which backup media will provide the greatest storage capacity?

   a. DAT

   b. DLT

   c. Travan

   d. Ultrium

6. You want to have a separate location prepared to transfer all data management services immediately upon the failure of your network operations center. What type of site do you set up?

   a. alternate site

   b. backup storage site

   c. hot site

   d. cold site

7. Why should one or more backups be stored off-site?

   a. for security reasons

   b. because backup data is not usually needed quickly

   c. so it is available to a remote site

   d. so that primary site disasters will not affect the data

8. Which of the following are not part of a disaster recovery plan?

   a. handling legal, financial, and insurance issues

   b. performing a tape backup immediately after disaster strikes

   c. locating interim facilities to restart your business

   d. recovering PCs, LANs, and midrange systems

9. Which backup method provides the fastest backup time?

   a. Grandfather, Father, Son

   b. six cartridge

   c. Tower of Hanoi

   d. incremental backup

10. Which of the following utilizes a form of memory inside the tape? (Choose all that apply.)

    a. AIT

    b. DAT

   c. Ultrium

   d. QIC

11. Which of the following backs up data and clears the archive bit?

   a. normal backup

   b. differential backup

   c. copy backup

   d. daily backup

12. Which of the following Travan tape formats offers the highest compressed capacity?

   a. Travan-8

   b. Travan NS-8

   c. Travan TR-4

   d. Travan NS-20

13. Which backup strategy provides the least expensive media allocation?

   a. Grandfather, Father, Son

   b. Tower of Hanoi

   c. normal daily backup

   d. RAID-1

14. Which SNMP component should be configured in order to report errors, security breaches, or other event notification?

   a. SNMP trap

   b. SNMP Management Information Base

   c. SNMP community name

   d. SNMP host name

15. Why should spare network components be kept on-site?

   a. to configure new computers on the network quickly

   b. to provide for efficient replacement of equipment as part of a maintenance cycle

   c. to allow for efficient replacement of failed components of similar types

   d. to allow for efficient replacement of failed components of dissimilar types

16. For large-scale recovery of failed components, what site strategy is most appropriate?

   a. hot site

   b. cold site

   c. no alternate site; keep required spare components at primary site

   d. no alternate site; implement an active clustering solution

10

17. A _____ is a facility that has no equipment of its own, but has all the necessary facilities and environmental controls to accept server equipment.

   a. hot site

   b. cold site

   c. data center

   d. service bureau

18. For recovery from a primary facility failure with less than 24-hour downtime tolerance, what alternate site strategy is most appropriate?

   a. hot site

   b. cold site

   c. no alternate site; implement an active clustering solution

   d. no alternate site; implement a passive clustering solution

19. You want administrators to be notified of system failures as soon as possible, regardless of the time of day the failure occurs. You should implement a(n):

   a. SNMP management system

   b. tape backup strategy

   c. Management Information Base

   d. remote notification system

20. You have purchased hard disks for replacement of existing units if and when the existing units fail. You wish to be able to replace these hard disks without losing any system availability. Which elements are required to achieve this?

   a. hot-swap device capability

   b. active clustering

   c. passive clustering

   d. hot site

   e. cold site

HANDS-ON PROJECTS

Project 10-1

In this project, you will create a list of spare server components that could be found in a locked storage cabinet.

Compile a parts list for quick restoration of a server in the event of a non-system-wide failure.

Project 10-2

In this project, you will fill out a planning chart to implement a Grandfather-Father-Son (GFS) backup strategy.

You are implementing a GFS backup strategy. You desire to have one unique backup tape for each week in a month, with one unique tape for each quarter of the year. Daily and monthly tapes can be reused. Fill in the "First Quarter" chart below with the tape used. Tapes are marked with the number of the tape preceded by the day (Monday, Tuesday, etc.), month (m), or quarter (Q). Assume four weeks per month. The third week is filled in for you.

Monday 1	Tuesday 1	Wednesday 1	Thursday 1	Friday 3

10

Project 10-3

In this project, you will create a Tower of Hanoi backup strategy chart.

You wish to implement a Tower of Hanoi backup strategy using only four media sets. You want to maintain the greatest amount of historical backups possible. Fill in the first 14 days in the chart below with the proper allocation of backup sets for each day's backup. Label the sets A, B, C, and D.

Day	1	2	3	4	5	6	7	8	9	10	11	12	13	14
Set														

Project 10-4

In this project, you will learn more about how a tape library works.

1. Using your Internet browser, access *www.storagetek.com*. StorageTek is a leading manufacturer of enterprise backup solutions.

2. Click the **products** link, and access information about the StorageTek L20 Tape library. This is one of StorageTek's smallest tape libraries, but it includes an informative video presentation.

3. Click a link that allows you to view the product video. If you do not have the QuickTime plug-in, follow the directions to download QuickTime, or download it from *www.quicktime.com* and then view the video.

4. Close the browser window that displayed the video, but leave the main browser open.

5. In the browser, click again on the **products** link.

6. Browse to find information on a high-end tape library such as the L700.

7. On a separate sheet of paper, write down the product name, how many drives it has, and how many tapes it can store.

8. Leave the browser open for the next project.

Project 10-5

In this project, you will learn more about disaster recovery.

1. In your web browser, access *www.davislogic.com*. Davis Logic specializes in contingency planning and disaster recovery.

2. On the left side of the Davis Logic web page, click the **Disaster Recovery** link. Notice several publications that would be excellent research guides in planning for disaster recovery.

3. On the Disaster Recovery page, scroll down the page and look for a bulleted list of possible disaster events. In this book, we have specified only a few types of disasters (such as natural disasters) that could make your site unavailable. Write down some other types of events that could constitute a disaster.

4. Close the web browser.

Project 10-6

In this project, you will perform a tape backup.

1. Verify that you have the following:

   - A server with Windows 2000

   - A tape drive

   - Tape media compatible with the tape drive

2. Log on as Administrator or some other user account that has membership in the Backup Operators group. Ask your instructor for assistance if necessary.

3. If you have not already inserted the tape into the drive, do so now. It may take a minute or more for the tape to orient itself in the drive.

4. Using Windows Explorer, create a folder at the root of the drive. Name the folder with your initials, such as "JIC."

5. Open the folder and create a Notepad text file by right-clicking in an empty space in the new folder window, clicking **New**, and then clicking **Text Document**. Name the file **MyText**.

6. Double-click the **MyText** file to open it, and type **This is the original text**. Save and exit the file.

7. Click **Start**, point to **Programs**, point to **Accessories**, point to **System Tools**, and then click **Backup**.

8. The Backup application starts. You can use one of the wizards at another time to see what they do. In this project, however, we will manually back up the file you created in steps 5 and 6. In the Backup application, click the **Backup** tab.

9. Expand the drive on which the folder you created is located by clicking the "+" sign next to the drive. Locate the folder and place a check in the box next to the folder.

10. At the bottom of the interface, verify that the backup destination is the appropriate tape drive. In most cases, it will be Travan.

11. In the Backup media or file name drop-down list, select **New Media**.

12. Click **Start Backup**, and a Backup Job Information dialog box opens. The backup interface should resemble Figure 10-19.

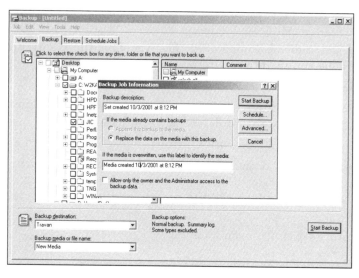

Figure 10-19   Preparing the backup job

13. Optionally, click the checkbox **Allow only the owner and the Administrator access to the backup data**.

14. Click the **Advanced** button. The Advanced Backup Options dialog box opens. Click the options **Verify data after backup** and **If possible, compress the backup data to save space**.

15. Under Backup Type, leave the setting at Normal, but click the drop-down list to look at the other backup options that are available.

16. Click **OK**. Then click the **Start Backup** button in the Backup Job Information dialog box.

17. You might see a message asking if you want to use the media detected in the tape drive. If so, click **Yes**. This does not overwrite the data; it is only a precaution to verify that you know a tape is in the drive.

18. Allow the backup to proceed. If you are prompted to overwrite the tape data, answer **Yes**. The backup may take a minute or two depending on the drive and media type.

19. When the backup is finished, do *not* click the Close button. Click the **Report** button. (Don't worry, you can look at the report later if you accidentally clicked Close.)

20. Observe the type of data that was logged.

21. Close the report, and then close the Backup utility and Windows Explorer.

Project 10-7

In this project, you will change the file you created earlier, and then restore it from tape.

1. Using Windows Explorer, access the folder and file you created in Project 10-6.

2. Open the file, and at the beginning of the file, type **This file is corrupt** as a simulation of a file you might need to restore.

3. Save and close the file.

4. Open the tape backup software (click **Start**, point to **Programs**, point to **Accessories**, point to **System Tools**, and then click **Backup**).

5. Click the **Tools** menu, and then click **Options**.

6. Click the **Restore** tab. By default, the restore process will not overwrite the file on your hard disk. In this case, the file on the hard disk is not missing; it is corrupt. Select the **Always replace the file on my computer** option, and then click **OK**.

7. Click the **Restore** tab in the main interface.

8. In the right pane, you should see the name for the media you created in Project 10-6. In the left pane, expand the "+" signs until you locate the folder that contains your file. Select that folder, and notice that the file appears in the right pane as well, similar to Figure 10-20.

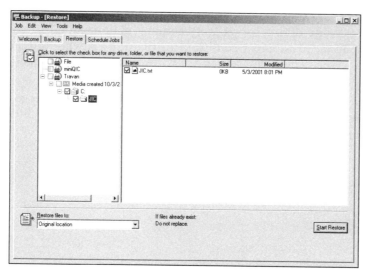

Figure 10-20   Locate the file you want to restore

9. Place a check in the box next to the folder in the left pane, and you will see that the file is automatically selected.

10. Click the **Start Restore** button.

11. A Confirm Restore dialog box appears. Click **OK** to proceed.

12. The file is restored from tape.

13. The Restore Progress dialog box should indicate that one file was processed.

14. Click the **Report** button to review what took place.

15. View the report, and when finished, close the report and then close the Backup utility.

16. Using Windows Explorer, browse to your folder and open the file. The text "This is the original text" should appear instead of "This file is corrupt." This indicates that you successfully overwrote the "corrupt" file with a known good file from backup.

17. Close Windows Explorer.

10

CASE PROJECTS

1. You have been asked to implement a backup strategy for your company. You currently have four administrative personnel responsible for all network support and configuration, including yourself. There is a strong desire to keep any backup processes as simple as possible. The budget for this project is less a concern than is the proper availability of data for recovery and the minimizing of the complexity of the process. Your environment consists primarily of users who store financial data on three servers. The total amount of data to be backed up is slightly over 2 GB. Describe the backup strategy that you will propose.

2. You work for a web services company, providing site hosting services to several hundred clients. What disaster recovery solutions will help you to maintain the high availability that your customers expect?

11

PERFORMANCE MONITORING AND OPTIMIZATION

> **After reading this chapter and completing the exercises, you will be able to:**
>
> ♦ Effectively use performance monitoring tools
> ♦ Establish a baseline
> ♦ Recognize acceptable and unacceptable performance thresholds
> ♦ Provide solutions to performance bottlenecks

Monitoring server performance is a critical function in the enterprise network. Effectively monitoring a server is a scientific process that separates perceived server "slowdowns" from true performance degradation based on empirical data. The data you collect is also useful when proposing major changes to the enterprise network architecture or new equipment. Using the proper tools will help you to obtain accurate data. Each respective network operating system (NOS) discussed in this book has its own set of monitoring and performance tools, and you should know what those tools are and how to use them.

Whichever tool applies to your operating system, it is critical to establish a baseline. The baseline is the fulcrum that balances subjective perceptions of network performance against objective data, and establishes what is to be considered acceptable performance. For systems that do not perform within acceptable parameters, you must accurately determine which server or network components are causing the bottleneck, and take appropriate action.

MONITORING THE SERVER

It's Monday morning. You sit down at your desk and the telephone rings with a complaint that logon is slow. You attempt to log on to your own computer but before you can type a password, another call comes. Same problem. The moment you hang up, the telephone rings again and two co-workers are at your cube wanting to know why they can't log on. Your best response at this point is, "I'm working on it."

So where do you start? Luckily, you have established performance baselines for the logon server. Therefore, you begin by checking the current performance of the server against the baseline. Your Windows 2000 Performance Monitor tells you that the amount of memory in use is extremely high compared with the baseline. You identify the process consuming the memory and discover that the new monitoring agents installed on this server are using more resources than predicted. You terminate the processes temporarily until more memory can be added to the server. Within 10 minutes, the problem is solved and users are logging on quickly.

Performance monitoring—observing, measuring, and recording the performance of critical server and network resources—is essential for troubleshooting and maintaining a network. There are several reasons to monitor servers:

- To become familiar with your server's "normal" performance so you know when there is a problem
- To notice impending problems and prevent them before they occur
- To pinpoint existing problems and identify solutions
- To aid in resource and capacity planning

Performance monitoring is the best tool for systematic troubleshooting, capacity planning, and checking on the "health" of servers. It can mean the difference between being unprepared when a problem comes up, or anticipating a problem and correcting it before users even notice.

Table 11-1 shows some typical server areas that can be monitored.

Table 11-1   Server Monitoring Activities

Monitor ...	To Determine
CPU	CPU utilization and performance
RAM	Memory shortage or damaged memory
Hard disk	Disk performance, capacity, and errors
Paging	Page file size and performance
Caching	Cache allocation and performance
Process	Hung or stopped service or process using high CPU resources
Users	Number of users logged on and types of resources they are accessing

The operating systems discussed in this book use different tools to monitor the performance of server components listed in Table 11-1, but they are used in similar ways: to establish performance baselines, to measure current performance (and perhaps compare it to a baseline), and to keep logs of performance over time.

There are many, many possible performance measures and results, and performance monitoring can, at first glance, be a little overwhelming. The key is to focus on the most significant resources. With performance monitoring, "less is more." Focusing your attention on the most critical resources will help to achieve the most effective results.

USING MONITORING TOOLS

The performance monitoring concepts presented in the previous section are consistent across all platforms. The specific tools and functions vary according to operating system. We will discuss tools for:

- IBM OS/2

- Linux

- NetWare

- Windows NT 4.0

- Windows 2000

The main focus of performance monitoring should be the accurate gathering and interpretation of performance data regardless of which operating system or tool you use. This chapter provides more in-depth coverage of the monitoring tools for Windows NT 4.0 and Windows 2000 as examples, rather than detailing all monitoring functions for all of the operating systems.

Among all the NOSs, there are literally hundreds of different measures of performance. Although it is not practical to define each performance measure, you should be aware of the main tools and resource categories for each operating system. After a brief tour of the primary performance monitoring tools in several operating systems, you'll learn about establishing a baseline and how to use monitoring results for troubleshooting and planning. This chapter also helps you to identify major performance bottlenecks and propose solutions for each area.

IBM OS/2

System Performance Monitor/2 (SPM/2) is designed to analyze hardware and software in the OS/2 environment. SPM/2's primary features for monitoring critical resources are:

- *SPM/2 Monitor*—A Presentation Manager application that displays performance data in graph form. Data is summarized from real-time input.

- *Data Collection Facility*—A tool that gathers data for system resources in use. The information can be displayed with SPM/2 Monitor in the Presentation Manager window as graphic or real-time output. The data can also be logged to a file using the Logging Facility.

- *Report Facility*—A program that generates reports from collected data and is far more detailed than SPM/2 Monitor. Data collected into the Report Facility can be displayed or exported in three formats: summary, tabular, or dump.

- *Logging Facility*—A tool that accesses data from the Data Collection Facility and saves it to log files. Log files are available to the Report Facility.

SPM/2 uses a distributed management approach to performance monitoring. The SPM/2 application is installed on a monitoring station. Servers designated for monitoring collect data and distribute it back to the monitoring station for analysis as shown in Figure 11-1. The advantage of this approach, not only for OS/2 but for any NOS that supports it, is that the overhead required to run the monitoring software does not skew the monitoring results.

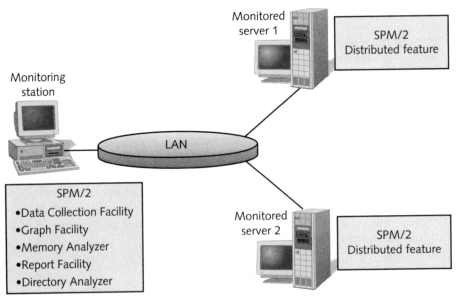

Figure 11-1   SPM/2 uses a distributed feature to remotely monitor servers

Linux

UNIX tools are used to monitor performance on Linux systems. These tools are command-line utilities that provide statistics on CPU usage, memory, disk I/O, and network connections. Although there are multiple UNIX/Linux utilities available for specific monitoring purposes, some of the most commonly used are shown in Table 11-2.

Table 11-2   Common Linux/UNIX Performance Tools

Command	Function
vmstat	Provides information on memory usage, CPU, and interrupts
ps	Lists all processes current running on the system
df	Lists disk space used and available
top	Shows top several processes running and amount of resources they consume

Figure 11-2 shows the output from the *vmstat*, *ps*, and *df* commands.

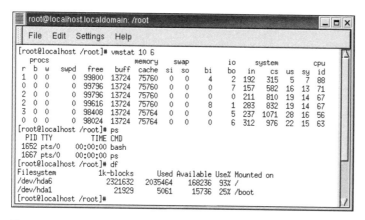

Figure 11-2   UNIX utilities *vmstat, ps,* and *df* provide a snapshot of current system activity

The *vmstat* tool provides real-time performance statistics for several resources. For example, when system performance slows, you can use *vmstat* to provide a quick snapshot of CPU load average to determine what process is causing a bottleneck. The syntax for the utility looks like this:

vmstat *seconds #OfReports*

If you wanted to take a snapshot every 10 seconds and create a total of six reports, you would type *vmstat 10 6*, which is what Figure 11-2 shows. If you do not specify the number of reports, the utility runs continuously until you issue the Ctrl+C command.

11

In addition to displaying the top consuming resources, the *top* command also provides other information such as the number of users logged on, the amount of memory consumed, and how much is swapped out to the swap file. Figure 11-3 shows sample output of the *top* command.

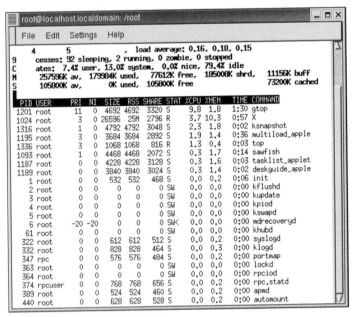

Figure 11-3   The UNIX *top* command provides a comprehensive snapshot of ongoing system activity

 TIP   The *top* command automatically refreshes. This can be advantageous when you are troubleshooting, but keep in mind that the refresh itself consumes resources. Remember the additional load when using the *top* command in heavily loaded systems.

If you also use graphical UNIX/Linux utilities, several other performance monitoring tools might be available to you, including the GNOME System Monitor (Figure 11-4) and the Stripchart Plotter (Figure 11-5), which provides a quick graphical snapshot of processor, swap file, network, and PPP activity.

Third-party tools that provide a graphical interface for monitoring are also useful. For example, Computer Associates' Unicenter TNG, an enterprise management software package, provides a graphical interface to monitor performance on Linux as well as most flavors of UNIX.

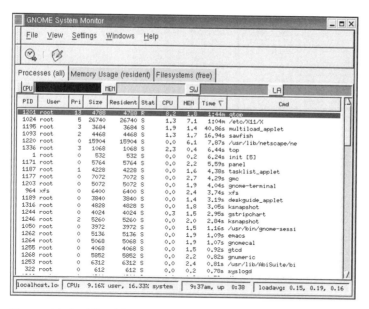

Figure 11-4   The GNOME System Monitor tool

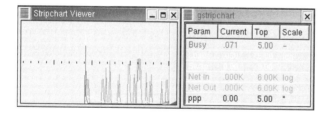

Figure 11-5   The Stripchart Plotter

NetWare

Novell NetWare uses a service known as Traffic Manager to monitor network traffic. Traffic Manager runs on Windows NT computers and uses Windows NT's Performance Monitoring tool to display its data (see next topic).

The Monitor utility is included with NetWare to track server performance (Figure 11-6). Many Novell system administrators will leave this screen on instead of a conventional screen saver! When Monitor is running, four performance indicators are shown:

- *Utilization*: This shows the CPU utilization rate for servicing network requests. If this number is consistently greater than 50–65%, your CPU is a bottleneck. (Specific thresholds are discussed later in this chapter.)

- *Total Cache Buffers*: If this number is quite low, your system will suffer from slow file performance.

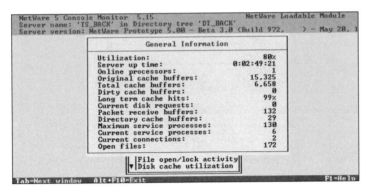

Figure 11-6   The Monitor utility monitors performance under NetWare

- *Current Service Processes:* This indicates outstanding read requests. If a read request is buffered, it means that resources were not available. This may indicate that you need to upgrade your disk controller.

- *Packet Receive Buffers:* This is an indicator that shows packets that are being buffered from workstations.

For a GUI, use the Java-based ConsoleOne.

Administrators running web or FTP services on NetWare servers will probably rely on the Novell Internet Caching System (ICS) utility to track and optimize performance using the ICS caching facility, but it can also be useful for monitoring general server performance and network activity (see Figure 11-7).

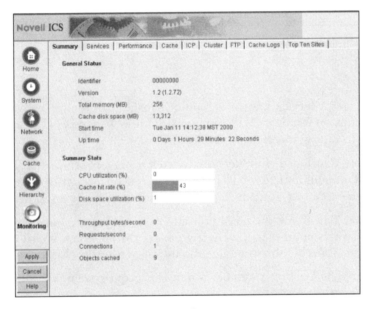

Figure 11-7   The Novell ICS utility

Windows NT 4.0

Performance monitoring on the Windows NT 4.0 operating system uses the Performance Monitor GUI tool. This tool uses objects, instances, and counters to measure performance on local servers or remote systems. Open Performance Monitor on a Windows NT system by clicking Start, pointing to Programs, pointing to Administrative Tools, and then clicking the Performance Monitor icon.

 TIP For best results, monitor an NT server from an NT workstation. Running Performance Monitor locally on the server creates an artificial load that can skew performance data. (Remotely monitoring a server can also add to the network load, although the impact is generally minimal.)

Chart View is the default view for Performance Monitor and provides real-time dynamic snapshots of server activity (see Figure 11-8). Snapshots are taken in one-second intervals by default.

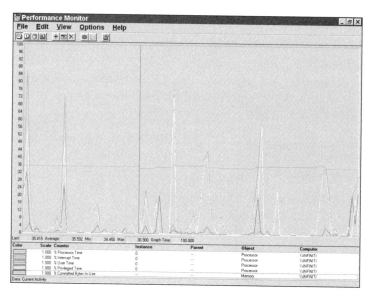

Figure 11-8   Chart View is the default for Windows NT 4.0 Performance Monitor

Performance is measured by choosing objects to monitor. In Performance Monitor, **objects** are resources such as Processor, Memory, PhysicalDisk, and Network Segment. After selecting an object to monitor, you choose specific **counters**, which are measures pertaining to Performance Monitor objects. For example, when monitoring the Processor object, you must specify exactly what it is about the processor you want to monitor by selecting a counter. Some examples of Processor counters are:

■ *% Processor Time*—A primary indicator of overall processor activity.

- *Interrupts/Sec*—The average number of hardware interrupts the processor receives and services per second. During an interrupt, normal processes owned by applications, services, and so forth are unable to perform actions, so you want to be sure to watch this counter.

- *% User Time*—The percentage of processor time spent in user mode, which includes applications, environment subsystems, and integral subsystems. Despite the use of the word "user," this counter is not always tied to user activities per se.

- *% Privileged Time*—The percentage of processor time spent in privileged mode, which is designed for hardware driver activity and operating system components. A high percentage might indicate a failing hardware device or driver that sends out excessive interrupts.

If there is more than one processor on the system, the Processor object will also have multiple **instances** to distinguish one processor from the other. Instances also apply to other resources such as multiple hard disks or multiple NICs. Using instances provides the capability to monitor processors or other components collectively or individually.

You can add objects and counters to the chart that are relevant to the tasks performed by the server. (Information concerning how to determine these objects is presented later in this chapter.)

You can also save settings for objects and counters so that you can return to monitor the same objects and counters at a later date. The simplest way is to save a Performance Monitor file. Once your chart is set, press the F12 key. Enter a name for the file in the Save As dialog box (see Figure 11-9).

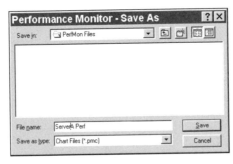

Figure 11-9 Windows NT Performance Monitor settings are saved with a .pmc extension by default

Windows NT 4.0 also uses performance logs to measure historical performance data and to set alerts to call attention to specific threshold breaches. Performance logs are discussed more specifically in the Windows 2000 section.

Windows 2000

Performance monitoring in Windows 2000 uses the Microsoft Management Console (MMC) graphical interface. The Windows 2000 monitoring tool uses objects, instances, and counters in a manner similar to Windows NT 4.0. The steps to open and use the Windows 2000 Performance console, like all management tools in Windows 2000, has changed from NT 4.0. The Performance console can be opened from Administrative Tools or added as a snap-in to an MMC containing other management tools.

 TIP A very handy feature of both Windows NT 4.0 and Windows 2000 is the Explain button that appears when you want to add a counter. By clicking it, an explanation appears for the otherwise cryptic counters in the list (see Figure 11-10).

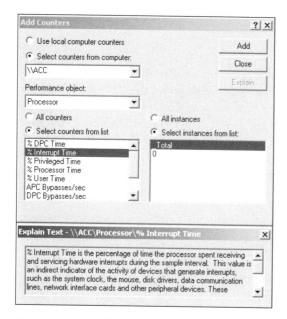

Figure 11-10   The Explain button describes each counter

The Performance console contains two snap-ins: System Monitor, and Performance Logs and Alerts. System Monitor provides real-time snapshots of system resources on local or remote servers (Figure 11-11). The Performance Logs and Alerts snap-in offers two functions:

- Performance logs gather historical performance data over a period of time.

- Performance alerts send messages when designated thresholds are exceeded based on dynamic data.

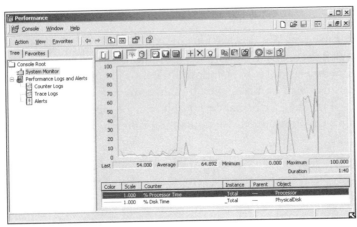

Figure 11-11   The Windows 2000 System Monitor gathering real-time performance data

System Monitor

The Windows 2000 System Monitor relies on objects and counters to display data in the chart. Click the plus sign (+) button in the toolbar above the chart to add objects and counters. From the Add Counters dialog box, you can choose to monitor the local server or a remote server. Figure 11-12 shows the Performance object PhysicalDisk selected from the drop-down list. The counter, % Disk Time, has also been chosen. By reading the information in the Instances list, we can see that the server named "infiniti" has two physical disks. The disks are labeled 0 and 1. The Instances box provides the capability to monitor the disks individually or collectively. Selecting "_Total" monitors both/all physical disks.

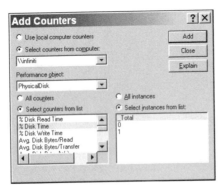

Figure 11-12   The System Monitor Add Counters dialog box

Performance Logs and Alerts

Performance logs monitor resources over a specific period of time. This is termed "historical performance monitoring." The time can be hours, days, or weeks depending on the situation. The log records the data. When logging is completed, the data can be displayed in a static format in the System Monitor screen.

To begin recording performance logs, you must create a log file:

1. Click the plus sign (+) button to the left of Performance Logs and Alerts.

2. Right-click Counter Logs. Select New Log Settings.

3. Give an intuitive name to the new log. Click OK.

Objects and counters must be added to the log for historical data just as you add objects and counters to System Monitor for real-time data.

The objects and counters are the same in Performance Logs and Alerts as in System Monitor, except that they can be configured to record over a specific period of time and can issue alerts upon reaching a specified threshold.

After choosing the objects and counters and returning to the Counter Log dialog box, there are multiple options for the time and frequency to gather data. Notice that the counter samples data every 15 seconds by default, because it is expected that performance logs will record over a longer duration. You can adjust the data-sampling interval as you like, but if you make it too short, the log files can get quite large and unmanageable. Figure 11-13 displays the General tab of the Counter Log dialog box.

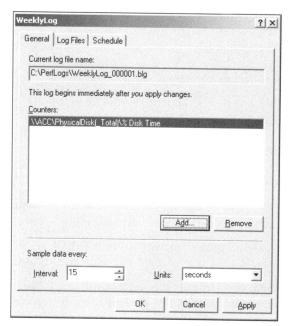

Figure 11-13   The General tab of the Counter Log dialog box

Besides adding counters from the General tab of the interface, you can also select the Log Files tab to specify characteristics of the log file itself, such as maximum size, location, and naming preferences (see Figure 11-14). The Schedule tab shows the total time frame for the log to record data, as compared to the data-sampling interval shown on the General tab, which determines the frequency of system snapshots.

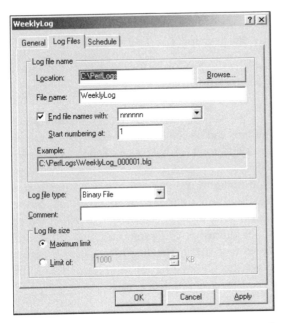

Figure 11-14 The options for the Log Files tab

From the Log Files tab, specify the following items:

- A file location, preferably not on the same disk or system you are monitoring, so as not to skew the results.

- An intuitive file name, so that you and others easily identify the file.

- "End file names with" allows log files to be tagged with sequential numbers or dates.

- The default log file type is binary. Log files can also be saved in formats such as .CSV to enable simple import to databases or spreadsheets.

- Log file size, by default, allows growth potential limited only by the space on the hard disk. This can be limited to a specific size with this option.

Once all parameters are determined, you can start the log manually or schedule it to run automatically in the future. Initiate a manual start from the Performance console as follows:

1. Click the plus sign (+) button on Performance Logs and Alerts.

2. Click Counter Logs. This displays all eligible logs.

3. Right-click the log and select Start.

4. To stop the log manually, right-click the log and select Stop.

The options to schedule the log are displayed in Figure 11-15. Start the log according to time and date. The log is stopped after a specific period of time has elapsed or at an exact time and date. There are also two options to indicate when the log completes. First, you can specify that when a log file reaches a scheduled termination, another log file begins. This is useful for breaking the log files into smaller, more manageable chunks of data. Second, you could run an executable or batch file. For example, you might want to run a .bat file that includes the *net send* command to alert the administrator that the log is complete.

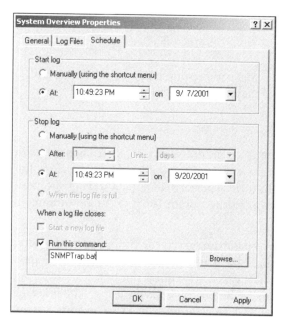

Figure 11-15   Use the Schedule tab to start and stop the log

ESTABLISHING A BASELINE

One of the most important aspects of monitoring performance is establishing a baseline. A **baseline** is established by recording performance data when a server is healthy, or running normally. When problems occur (like the slow logons in the opening scenario), use performance monitoring tools to observe dynamic real-time values. Compare the real-time output with historic performance data to determine the bottleneck in the system. This methodical approach to problem solving will consistently yield faster results than a shotgun approach of random fixes based on experience and luck.

What Is a Bottleneck?

A **bottleneck** refers to the delay in transmission of data through the circuits of a computer's system. When you monitor performance to detect a bottleneck, you are looking for the resource (processor, memory, etc.) that is causing the delay in transmission of data.

Most of us experience bottlenecks every day outside of information technology. Think of a freeway with four lanes heading in the same direction. If traffic is moving at 65 mph on average and a driver moves into the fast (far left) lane and proceeds at 50 mph, this creates a bottleneck. The analogy of a four-lane freeway also relates to servers because there are four basic resources to monitor to create a baseline:

- Processor
- Memory
- Disk subsystem
- Network segment

It is important to note that these are the basic resources, not a comprehensive, detailed picture of a server. We discuss each of these resources in more detail later in this chapter.

When to Create a Baseline

The best time to create a baseline is while the server is experiencing maximum activity. Referencing the logon scenario again, you would create a baseline for the logon server in this network. Record historical performance data during the period of time when the most users are logging on to the system (such as 30–60 minutes after people arrive at work in the morning).

If you were creating a baseline for a database server, the timing might be completely different. Perhaps your company runs the majority of reports on a database server after business hours, between 7 P.M. and 9 P.M. This will be the best time to create the baseline for that database server. You can begin to see why using scheduled performance monitoring (as opposed to manually started monitoring) can be advantageous. In many instances, the optimal monitoring time is not within normal business hours.

What if you are not familiar enough with a server to know the optimal monitoring time? In such instances, use historical performance monitoring to discover the busiest periods of activity. Then create the baseline for that interval.

What to Monitor in a Baseline

Now that you've determined when to monitor performance, the next decision is what resources to monitor. As previously stated, the basics of Processor, Memory, PhysicalDisk and Network Segment are a good place to start. There are exceptions, however, and there is often the need for greater detail.

Returning again to the logon scenario, monitoring the basic resources can provide important information for troubleshooting the slow logon problem. But, based on the specified problem, we can add more objects and create more relevant data. Table 11-3 illustrates possible objects and counters for creating a baseline in the logon scenario for Windows NT or Windows 2000.

Table 11-3   Objects and Counters to Create a Baseline on a Logon Server

Object	Counter
Processor	% Privileged Time
Processor	% User Time
Memory	% Committed Bytes in Use
Server	Logon Total
Server	Logons/sec
Network Segment	% Network Utilization

Note that in addition to the "basic four" resources, we've chosen to monitor the Server object, with counters for logon statistics. These additional resources, when included in the baseline, provide specific data about the number of users who normally log on in the recorded time. Even more useful is the number of logons per second. This statistic gives an objective number to use for gauging logon speed. The nature of "fast" or "slow" is very subjective. Note also that the PhysicalDisk object is excluded from this baseline. Disk activity is not a major factor in the logon process.

PUTTING THE TOOLS TO WORK

Let's continue with the logon scenario to walk through how baseline data and monitoring tools can be used to solve a performance problem. Table 11-4 shows the baseline measurements for the logon server, and Table 11-5 shows the comparative real-time data for the same objects during the Monday morning slowdown.

Table 11-4   Baseline Data for the Logon Server

Object	Counter	Averages (over 30 minutes)
Processor	% Privileged Time	9%
Processor	% User Time	14%
Memory	% Committed Bytes in Use	37%
Server	Logon Total	510 (total over 30 minutes)
Server	Logons/sec	5
Network Segment	% Network Utilization	36%

Table 11-5   Real-Time Data for the Logon Server

Object	Counter	Real-Time Statistics
Processor	% Privileged Time	15%
Processor	% User Time	14%
Memory	% Committed Bytes in Use	39%
Server	Logon Total	1 (one-second snapshot)
Server	Logons/sec	1
Network Segment	% Network Utilization	76%

The first step in interpreting this data is to look for significant changes. In this case, you note the following:

- Processor: % Privileged Time increased by 6%.

- Processor: % User Time is unchanged.

- Memory: % Committed Bytes in Use increased by 2%.

- Server: Logons/sec decreased to 1.

- Network Segment: % Network Utilization increased by 40%.

The most significant changes occurred in the number of logons and network utilization. From this data you can safely say that logons definitely are slow and the bottleneck is the flow of data on the network interface. Solving the problem will require "drilling down" deeper into specifics of network utilization. The value of the baseline is that you have eliminated processor time and memory as possible bottlenecks.

 More specifics and possible resolutions of this scenario are addressed later in the chapter.

CAPACITY PLANNING

The baseline measurements for a server can also be used for capacity planning. This is the practice of monitoring resources for the purpose of projecting the effect of increasing or decreasing workload on a server. By measuring the performance of a server under current conditions, we can project how it will perform under another set of conditions. In the current business environment of mergers and acquisitions, capacity planning makes for a smoother IT transition.

Using our logon scenario, the current network has 750 users. Of these, 510 logged on during the performance monitoring that created the baseline in Table 11-4. You learn in a meeting that your company has acquired another company of equal size. Your IT staff has the task of merging IT departments and will be responsible for user logons and security. You will need to accommodate twice the current number of users on the network. That means 1500 users logging on. Can your server handle the load? Creating baselines for capacity planning will help answer these questions not only for logon servers but also for many network resources.

The sections that follow outline acceptable levels of performance for basic resources (processor, memory, disks, and network utilization) and give solutions to improve performance for each resource. Each of these resources works with the others hand in hand and is capable of influencing the behavior of other resources.

PROCESSOR

Processor time is measured as a percentage of time that the processor is active, executing threads submitted by **processes** (running programs) on the system. (A **thread** is a main component of an application and is the means by which the application accesses memory and processor time). One hundred percent represents constant activity.

Acceptable Processor Performance

A processor running constantly at 100% is overworked and server performance will deteriorate rapidly. Acceptable levels of processor activity extend up to 60–65% on a consistent basis. Levels exceeding 65% during performance monitoring usually indicate that the processor is the bottleneck in the system. However, the specific processor utilization percentage that is acceptable within an organization can vary. For example, perhaps you consider 65% processor utilization to be acceptable for the intranet web server that company employees use. However, for the Internet web transaction server, 65% is way too high, because online purchases will take too long and impatient buyers might cancel transactions.

 It is not unusual for the processor to peak or spike higher than 65% for a brief period of time. When new processes are started or when services are starting after rebooting a server, processor levels spiking to 100% are totally acceptable.

A bottleneck is indicated when known applications, processes and/or services push processor levels beyond 65% for an extended period of time and the processor does not return to lower levels until the applications, processes, or services are terminated.

Processor Solutions

The following sections present different approaches to improving processor performance.

Implement SMP

If the processor is the bottleneck, additional CPUs can be added to a server to improve performance and handle increased loads. All major NOSs under discussion in this book support symmetric multiprocessing (SMP). Many 32-bit applications can benefit from

11

SMP if the code allows **multithreading**, which is the ability to run two or more program threads at once. For example, if a program runs two threads on an SMP system with two processors, each processor can handle a thread simultaneously. With a single processor, the program can still run multiple threads but the processor can only execute a single thread at one time.

Only the simplest programs run a single thread. Most applications (not only on the server but also on most client workstations) run several threads at once.

Add Servers

Sometimes the best solution to a processor bottleneck is to simply add another server, especially when a server is performing multiple tasks that may conflict with each other. For example, a company may be using a single database server to perform sales transactions and provide reports based on those transactions. Transactions and queries for reports may require multiple reads from tables simultaneously. While adding another processor (SMP) may improve performance, a better solution would be to add another server dedicated to running queries to create reports.

Remove Compression

Compression is storing data in a format that requires less space than usual. Simply storing data does not place a greater load on the processor. However, when data is written to the compressed partition or folder, the processor must work harder to calculate the compression algorithms. Removing compression from partitions or folders where data is written frequently can free the processor to perform more critical tasks. The type of data that you choose to compress, if any, is also a factor. Some file types do not compress well, and processor utilization will be wasted on these files. For example, multimedia files such as movie files and JPEG files do not compress well.

Remove Unnecessary Encryption

Encryption uses any of several methods to protect sensitive data from prying eyes. However useful, encryption is processor intensive, and places a greater load on the processor. Just as with compression, the processor performs calculations to encrypt and decrypt data. The operative word in this solution is *unnecessary*. Security is important and when encryption is warranted, the better solution is upgrading or adding additional processors.

Although administrators are usually adept at understanding encryption, you should be careful about users implementing encryption. There are several encryption schemes and utilities available. You do not want users to place encrypted data on network resources where server processors must perform the encryption. In addition, some encryption schemes can make data permanently inaccessible.

Implement Clustering

Clustering is a solution to performance issues that benefit from load balancing. Clustering is connecting two or more computers together in such a way that they behave like a single computer. As a solution to slow processor performance, clustering is essentially adding another computer to aggregate performance in addition to providing fault tolerance.

Remove Software RAID (Especially RAID-5)

RAID (as defined in Chapter 5) provides fault tolerance and in some cases can actually improve performance. Software RAID-5, however, can significantly diminish processor performance. As data is written to the hard disk, the processor must calculate the algorithms for the parity bit that creates fault tolerance. This requires considerable processor time and, consequently, other processes may suffer. If the RAID-5 array is primarily for reading data, this is not an issue because parity calculations are not performed during reads. Hardware RAID-5 does not burden the server CPU because the parity calculation occurs on a separate processor designed for RAID functionality.

Move Processor-Intensive Applications or Services

Moving applications or services that overwork the processor is called load balancing. It includes installing an application or service on a second server, and deleting the application or service from the server that is overworked. For example, if one server is functioning as both the DHCP and WINS server, install WINS on another server and delete WINS from the server with DHCP.

You can also keep the application or service on the original server and then install it on a second server to balance the load between the two servers. This is a common practice in web servers. Instead of overloading a single web server, administrators place the same web content on two or more other web servers, and the web servers take turns in servicing client requests.

Verify Proper Operation of Applications and Drivers

When not running normally, applications or bad drivers can cause excessive processor utilization. To detect problems with applications, monitor the individual process of the application. It will also be useful to monitor the number of threads utilized by the application by using the following object/counter combination:

- Object: Process
- Counter: Thread Count

As an example, in Figure 11-16, Windows 2000 Performance Monitor is monitoring the Diskeeper defragmentation utility running over four threads (numbered 0–4) and utilizing over 60% processor time. In this case, it was acceptable because I deliberately set Diskeeper to run at a high priority and there were no other pressing tasks to run at the time.

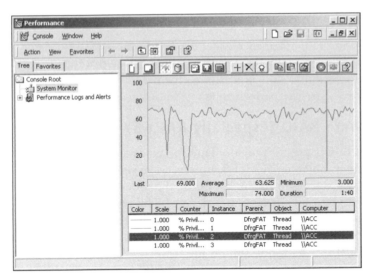

Figure 11-16 Monitor the number of threads in use and the processor utilization they require

A significant change in the number of threads used by an application, compared to a baseline, indicates problems in the application code. Some applications may run multiple instances, which can also increase the load on the processor.

Corrupted device drivers can also demand excessive processor time. An effective measurement for this problem is to monitor the following object/counter combinations:

- Object: Processor

- Counters: % Interrupt Time or Interrupts/sec

Compare the results to a baseline. Significant increases in the number of interrupts indicate problems with hardware devices and/or the drivers. For example, a few years ago, I had a new file server with the best equipment my company could afford at the time. Initially, it performed fine and I largely ignored it except for normal maintenance. One day after clearing dust from inside the server and starting it up, it seemed to take quite a long time to boot. Then, it took a long time to retrieve even the smallest files from the file server. I ran Windows NT Performance Monitor from a different server (so as not to skew the results) to record Interrupts/sec. The interrupts were far above the baseline for this system, and it turned out that the file server's NIC was failing. A failing NIC (and several other types of hardware) will often issue constant interrupts because it is not able to determine that the processor has responded to the interrupt requests. After replacing the NIC, the server returned to its normal level of performance.

 Do not be too concerned if Interrupts/sec is over 100 when idle—the system clock accounts for this by sending regular interrupts every 10 milliseconds.

Set Process Priority

In Windows NT and Windows 2000, you can manually set a process or application to run at a specific priority to ensure that it does not dominate processor utilization at the expense of other applications. You can also adjust the process priority to force the processor to favor the process or application over others. Some applications allow you to adjust settings within the application, or you can use Task Manager to configure the application priority:

1. Press Ctrl+Shift+Esc to access Task Manager.

2. On the Process tab, select the application's process.

3. Right-click the process, click Set Priority, and choose a priority from Low to Realtime (see Figure 11-17).

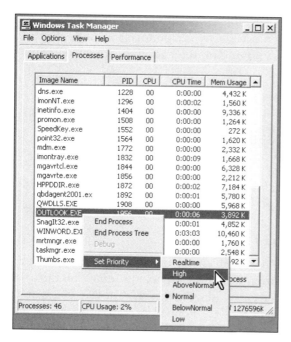

Figure 11-17   Changing the priority level of a process

 Use Realtime priority sparingly, if at all, because if the process runs indefinitely, then the operating system, other server functions, or applications can lock or hang due to a lack of processor time.

MEMORY

The following sections present different approaches to improving memory performance. Memory is indirectly one of the most critical performance factors. A low memory condition causes higher disk utilization due to disk swapping. Low memory also affects stability. Some operating system information can never be swapped to hard disk (such as passwords or other security-sensitive data). However, if you are out of memory, there is no place else for it to go, and the server might fail. It is critical to determine what acceptable memory performance is and how to remedy low memory conditions.

Acceptable Memory Performance

Defining acceptable memory performance is extremely subjective. What is tolerable to one organization may be completely unacceptable to another. Most of the time, memory "performance" (that is, speed) is not an issue because it performs in nanoseconds. However, not having enough memory clearly *is* a performance issue, because the NOS must then turn to virtual memory paging on the hard disk—the most common bottleneck component in the system.

The most important counters for memory are:

- Object: Memory
- Counter: % Committed Bytes in Use
- Counter: Page Faults/sec
- Counter: Available Bytes
- Counter: Pages/sec
- Counter: Pool Non-Paged Bytes

Committed Bytes in Use represents a percentage of the total system memory (physical memory plus virtual memory) currently used by processes running on the computer. The first rule of thumb is that this percentage should remain relatively constant. Only slight variations are acceptable. When processes are stopped or started or the number of connected users changes, variation is normal. However, a steady increase of committed bytes, in the absence of additional processes or user load, frequently indicates a **memory leak**. A memory leak occurs when an application opens a thread but does not close it when the application is finished with it. At first, a memory leak will start more paging, which in itself deteriorates performance. Later, as both memory and available swap file space become more scarce, the memory leak can eventually cause a system crash.

Available Bytes is the amount of physical memory available to processes running on the computer. It reflects the last observed value rather than an average.

Pages/sec is a good indicator of excessive paging in a virtual memory system. Paging is a technique to help ensure that the data needed is available as quickly as possible. Recall from Chapter 8 that the page file is designated space on the hard disk used as memory. Each time a page is needed that is not currently in memory, a page fault occurs. When this value exceeds 20 per second on a consistent basis, performance will deteriorate. Excessive page faults are normally due to insufficient memory or memory leaks.

Pool Non-Paged Bytes is the number of bytes in the nonpaged pool, an area of system memory for objects that cannot be written to disk but must remain in physical memory as long as they are allocated. The Registry, for example, cannot be paged to disk.

Memory Solutions

All solutions to memory problems fall under one general category: add more memory. However, it's important to remember that all resources work hand-in-hand; no resource is independent. Increasing or decreasing one resource will *always* have some impact on others. In the case of excessive paging, adding more memory reduces the need for paging and helps to reduce the hard disk bottleneck.

Add Memory

Adding memory can never harm anything except the budget. There are many instances in which adding memory is the best and easiest solution. The best method to determine when additional memory is justified is through performance monitoring. Without performance analysis, simply adding more memory can mask a more serious underlying problem.

Upgrade the Motherboard to Accept More Memory

All motherboards have a limit on the amount and type of memory that can be installed. When this limit is reached, one solution is to upgrade to a motherboard that accommodates more and/or faster memory. Frequently, this is an expensive solution and in some instances not cost effective based on advances in technology. For example, a motherboard that has an older Pentium processor may be limited to 512 MB of RAM. Even if an upgraded motherboard accommodated 2 GB of RAM, significant performance improvements may not be achieved until the processor is also upgraded. Generally, upgrading the motherboard really means replacing the server. The original server becomes spare parts or is used in a less demanding role.

Increase or Optimize Swap File Size

Swap file space goes by different names but is essentially space designated on a hard disk to act as memory. If all physical memory is used and there is not enough swap space, the system will report out-of-memory errors. One solution is to increase the swap file space, but you should realize that this doesn't really improve performance, since the system is still making slower disk accesses instead of rapid memory accesses. Increasing swap file space only prevents more out-of-memory errors.

Depending on the current space dedicated to the swap file, increasing its size may be only a temporary solution. If the swap space or paging file is increased to meet memory needs, performance monitoring will also reveal a corresponding increase in the number of page faults.

Windows-based servers build a page file equal to the amount of RAM by default during installation. NT 4.0 Workstation and Windows 2000 Professional default to 1.5 times physical memory because it is assumed that there is less physical memory in client workstations. The swap space or paging file functions best at a size of 300–500 MB. A previous rule of thumb was 1.5 to 2 times the size of physical RAM, but with physical memory reaching into gigabytes on servers, this number is no longer reasonable. Too much space allotted to a swap file leads to fragmentation. (Fragmentation is discussed later in the chapter.)

You can improve overall system performance regarding swapping to the hard disk by placing the swap file in an optimum location. By default, most NOSs place the swap file on the same hard disk as the operating system itself (often referred to as the system disk). Because the system disk is often quite active running normal operating system services, the swap file must compete for disk access. If available, it is better to place the swap file on a separate physical disk that is less active (another partition on the same disk provides no benefit). Better yet, you can split the swap file between multiple disks (for example, in RAID-0 striping), so that multiple disks can service swap-file activity at once.

 If you are trying to determine which of two disks would be best to store the swap file, and all other factors are equal, consider the number of heads the hard disks have. The drive with more heads will perform better.

If the swap file has the ability to grow, as is the case for Windows operating systems, it is better to set a fixed size for the swap file that is large enough to service present and future needs. This helps to prevent fragmentation as the swap file adjusts in size.

 As a security precaution, you might consider clearing the swap file when the system reboots. If sensitive information is paged to the swap file and someone is able to gain physical access to it, they might be able to retrieve information from it. This possibility is extremely remote for a number of reasons; however, some highly secure organizations require it. Note that clearing the swap file will cause slower shutdown and startup times while the system clears and re-creates the swap file.

Use Faster Memory

As discussed in Chapter 6, there are different kinds of RAM, some faster than others. SDRAM has almost entirely replaced EDO DRAM and is about twice as fast. SDRAM is capable of synchronizing with the CPU bus and reaching clock speeds of 133 MHz. RDRAM and DDR SDRAM (discussed in Chapter 3) appear to be the next generation of high-performance memory, each capable of more than 1 GBps of data throughput.

Choosing faster memory usually requires a faster motherboard unless, for example, you have 100 MHz SDRAM installed on a 133 MHz bus. In that case, upgrading to 133 MHz SDRAM will take advantage of the faster bus speed.

Distribute Memory-Intensive Applications or Services

As discussed in respect to processors, the best solution to memory problems can be load balancing, because you utilize the hardware resources of another server to alleviate the server load. Thorough performance monitoring and analysis will tell you whether this is the best approach. When monitoring applications and services, pay close attention to which ones are processor intensive and which are memory intensive. A server providing basic file/print services will be memory intensive and probably not place significant demand on the processor. In contrast, a database server providing report functions and servicing multiple queries will be very processor intensive. Familiarity with the relative needs of applications and services in your network will assist you in making the most efficient distribution of resources.

Check for Memory Leaks

Memory leaks were discussed earlier in this chapter in relation to the % Committed Bytes in Use counter. This is perhaps the best indicator of a memory leak. Committed bytes should remain relatively constant. If they continue to increase gradually over time, yet no additional processes are introduced to the server, this is a strong indicator of a memory leak.

The best long-term solution to a memory leak is to contact the vendor so that it can make alterations to the code to stop the leak. Usually, the fix is an update that you can download. The short-term solution is to terminate the application, reboot the server, and restart the application. This forces the application to free memory no longer being used.

11

HARD DISK

As always, the hard disk seems to be the slowest performing of all the server components. Even with SCSI-3, Fibre Channel, and rotation speeds upward of 15,000 rpm, hard disks cannot begin to compete with the speed of the processor and memory. However, you can still arrive at an acceptable level of performance given the physical limitations of hard disks.

Acceptable Hard Disk Performance

Exact thresholds for determining an acceptable speed for the transfer of data from hard disks or any storage devices are even more subjective than memory or processor performance. The key is to obtain baseline numbers on current performance regardless of whether it is perceived to be slow or fast. To determine whether the hard disk is able to reasonably keep up with I/O requests, use the following object and counters:

- Object: PhysicalDisk
- Counter: % Disk Time
- Counter: Current Disk Queue Length
- Counter: Avg. Disk Bytes/Transfer

The % Disk Time counter represents the amount of time that the disk services read or write requests. You generally want to see less than 50% for this counter. Current Disk Queue Length represents the number of outstanding I/O requests waiting for the hard disk to become available. If the hard disk is overly taxed, then there will be several outstanding requests. You generally want to see no more than two requests queued. This counter is an instantaneous view; if you want to check an average over time, PhysicalDisk counters such as Avg. Disk Bytes/Transfer are also available.

Hard Disk Solutions

If the time comes when hard disk performance is deemed to be unacceptable, you can implement solutions such as the ones offered below.

Add or Replace Hard Disks

Hardware or software RAID arrays can significantly increase disk performance and provide fault tolerance. Hardware RAID is superior to software RAID, but it is also more expensive. While arguments abound concerning whether software RAID provides true fault tolerance, this is not the forum for that discussion: We're concerned with performance.

Both hardware and software RAID arrays increase performance by striping data across multiple disks. Because multiple drive heads are working simultaneously to write and/or read data, transfer speeds will be faster than non-RAID disks. For example, you have a software RAID-5 array consisting of three hard disks, and performance is unacceptably slow. By adding another disk, you aggregate total performance across four hard disks instead of three (assuming you are using SCSI, not IDE). The only potential problem might be processor utilization for the parity calculation, in which case you might also need to add a processor, upgrade the existing one, or switch to hardware RAID.

 Software RAID-5 will increase performance on disk reads. Performance suffers on disk writes, however, due to processor-intensive parity calculations.

Defragment Disks

Fragmentation on hard disks occurs through the normal processes of creating, moving, copying, and deleting files. The result, over time, is that single files are spread out in pieces across the disk. If the condition persists, disk transfer rates deteriorate because the drive head must search around and across multiple sectors to read a single file. Comparing real-time and baseline disk activity can provide evidence of fragmentation.

On a Windows NT/2000 server, use the following object and counter to find evidence of fragmentation:

- Object: PhysicalDisk

- Counter: Disk Read Time

Defragmentation relocates fragmented files back into a contiguous layout. Running a defragmentation utility such as Executive Software's Diskeeper (see Figure 11-18) on a regular schedule will yield an appreciable increase in performance. Obviously, defragmentation is highly disk intensive, so you should run it only when disk utilization is at its lowest. You can set defragmentation to start on a schedule, or configure defragmentation to start automatically when the hard disk reaches a certain point of fragmentation. In the enterprise, you will want to use Diskeeper's capability to remotely defragment other servers and workstations.

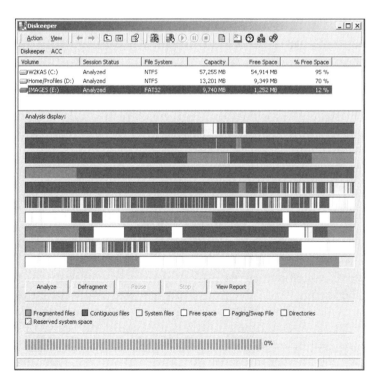

Figure 11-18   Diskeeper defragments the hard disk

There are not many defragmentation utilities for servers. The most common are Diskeeper (www.executivesoftware.com) and Raxco's PerfectDisk 2000 (www.raxco.com).

Add Faster or Additional Controllers

Adding controllers can solve performance problems. It is very similar to adding another lane to a highway. More controllers accommodate more disks. More disks can balance the workload from multiple users. More controllers and/or disks also increase options for deploying RAID arrays.

The most dramatic and fundamental improvement to the disk subsystem is to upgrade from IDE disks to SCSI disks. Traditionally SCSI controllers or interfaces have supported faster data transfer rates than IDE. The gap has narrowed with the introduction of EIDE, ATA-5, and the upcoming ATA-6. (Recall from Chapter 5 that SCSI-3 supports data transfer rates up to 320 MBps, while ATA-5 and ATA-6 support data transfer rates up to 100 MBps.)

Distribute Files

Distributing files works to solve disk performance problems in a way similar to load balancing. Frequently accessed files are distributed over multiple servers instead of residing on a single server. All network operating systems have some form of distributed files. In the Microsoft environment, it is called the Distributed File System (Dfs). Distributing files has the following advantages:

- There is a single access point for users. In Microsoft Dfs, for example, user computers map to a single file share point and still access files on multiple servers. The share point is the Dfs server, which redirects the requests to the appropriate servers. The process is transparent to users and security is maintained no differently than files accessed normally.

- Distributed files can be a cost-effective performance alternative to adding more servers or upgrading processor, memory, and/or disk resources.

Archive Files to Long-Term Backup Media

As hard disks exceed 75–80% of capacity, performance starts to deteriorate. When large portions of data on a disk must be maintained but not frequently accessed, archiving files to long-term storage can both reduce the risk of running out of disk space and improve performance. Offline storage is available from many hardware and software vendors, but the main idea is that when a given file has not been accessed for specific period of time, the file is automatically moved to offline storage, such as an optical drive or tape. Users can still access the data, but it arrives more slowly as it is retrieved from the offline storage media. Windows 2000 Server integrates this capability into the operating system.

Check for Disk Errors

S.M.A.R.T. is an acronym for Self-Monitoring, Analysis and Reporting Technology. It is an open standard for developing disk drives and software systems that automatically monitor the health of the drive and report potential problems. Potentially, this enables proactive solutions to disk errors before actual disk failure. To use S.M.A.R.T., you load software that is able to query and accept messages from the S.M.A.R.T. hard disk. The software is often provided by the disk manufacturer and included with the hard disk or host adapter. Figure 11-19 shows a hard disk monitoring utility included with Promise Technologies' FastTrak 100 IDE host adapter.

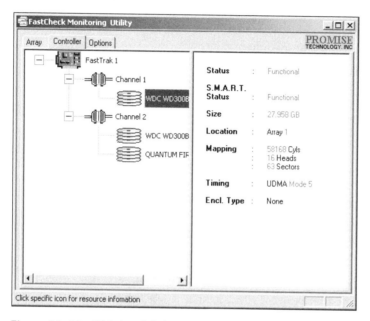

Figure 11-19   This hard disk monitoring utility monitors the health of a hard drive using S.M.A.R.T. reporting

NETWORK

Network performance on a server is contingent on the actual network interface card(s) installed and the components connecting the server to the network, such as cabling switches and/or hubs. Performance Monitor can only measure the traffic on the NICs local to the server.

Acceptable Network Performance

Network utilization is one of the most important network statistics. Most monitoring and reporting tools provide network utilization values as their primary reporting variable. Percentages of up to about 30% network utilization are acceptable. Collision networks (Ethernet) that exceed 30–50% utilization need to be monitored closely to prevent a larger increase of traffic that may cause network delays or low throughput. Server network utilization measures traffic on a specific NIC, and segment utilization measures all traffic on a given segment. Network and server traffic are monitored and analyzed separately, but the acceptable values are the same. Overall network utilization and server network utilization usually affect each other.

To measure the server's ability to send/receive data and handle network requests, monitor the following objects and counters:

- Object: Network Segment
- Counter: % Network Utilization
- Object: Network Interface
- Counter: Output Queue Length

The % Network Utilization counter represents a percentage of network bandwidth in use on the network segment. Each NIC will be an instance of the segment. Output Queue Length measures the number of packets waiting to put out on the network. Values of 1 or 2 are acceptable, but anything higher means your NIC cannot keep up with requests. Multihoming (discussed in the next section) can be a workable solution in this instance.

 TIP The Network Monitor Agent service must be installed on Windows NT 4.0/2000 for the Network Segment object to be available in Performance Monitor.

Network Solutions

If you find that network utilization is too high, consider the following solutions.

Multihoming

A multihomed server has two or more NICs installed. Each NIC has a unique IP address. These addresses can be on the same subnet or segmented in two or more subnets. Multiple network cards can notably improve throughput to the server provided network bandwidth is not oversubscribed. More throughput can provide users faster access to data.

There are disadvantages to multihoming some servers because of name resolution issues. A server with two or more NICs will have multiple IP addresses but only one name. In the Microsoft environment, multihomed servers must be manually designated in the WINS server to guarantee accurate name resolution. DNS names already require manual entry unless you are using dynamic DNS (DDNS), available with Windows 2000 or NetWare. In that case, hosts can automatically register host names to both IP addresses.

Port or Link Aggregation

Introduced in Chapter 7, port aggregation is a software solution to server bandwidth bottlenecks. Port aggregation can double bandwidth to a single segment by combining throughput of two network cards on a single segment. For example, two 10/100 Mbps NICs can be pooled by the software to provide 200 Mbps throughput. Aggregation software also allows a server with multiple NICs to be recognized by a single IP and MAC address. Single IP and MAC addresses overcome the naming resolution problems that can be encountered by standard multihomed servers.

Link aggregation is a hardware and software solution similar to port aggregation. With link aggregation, there is one NIC with multiple ports to provide the additional bandwidth. Link aggregation also requires that only one driver be installed for the network card. This is still a relatively proprietary solution (Intel) and must have compatible switches to deliver maximum performance.

 Multihoming, port, and link aggregation only increase the bandwidth to and from the server, but do nothing to increase the overall bandwidth of the network segment.

Improve Network Equipment

Over the past decade, the lower cost and availability of networking equipment has created enormous growth in IT for small and medium-sized companies. One of the key pieces of equipment is the hub (introduced in Chapter 7). Recall that the hub enables multiple nodes to be linked together on a single bus and communicate data to a common destination. Switches can replace hubs to improve network throughput and performance.

A hub with 16 ports accommodates 16 nodes. Using the analogy of highway traffic, think of each of those ports as a lane of traffic. The exit to the bus from the hub is a single lane. Consequently, a hub forces multiple lanes of traffic (in this example, 16) to a single lane. This results in multiple collisions while contesting for the single lane.

A switch with 16 ports also accommodates 16 nodes. However, a switch maintains each lane of traffic to the exit point on the bus. There are no collisions as the lanes are merged. In Ethernet topology, reduced collisions dramatically improve throughput.

 Some networks combine switch and hub technology. Hubs, rather than individual nodes, are connected to ports on a switch. While there is no absolute right or wrong to network design, without careful analysis of traffic patterns, arbitrarily connecting hubs to switches can erode the additional throughput provided by the switch.

11

Upgrade NICs

Ethernet technology as originally developed was capable of transferring data at speeds up to 10 Mbps. Accordingly, the components (NICs, hubs, bridges, routers) developed for networks provided the same throughput speed. In the mid-1990s, Fast Ethernet (100 Mbps) became more affordable and more prevalent in networks.

Upgrading a network card from 10 Mbps to 100 Mbps can boost server throughput and performance. Also consider utilizing full-duplex NICs instead of half-duplex NICs if you are using hubs instead of switches. Recall that full-duplex uses an additional pair of wires and removes collision detection to double potential throughput. As with any other network equipment upgrade, it is only effective if the network bandwidth is not oversubscribed.

Place the Server on the Other Side of a Network Bottleneck

Simple server placement can sometimes eliminate network bottlenecks. You should perform network traffic analysis to identify a bottleneck, but some solutions are simple and logical.

For example, 12 engineers are working on a project and need to share data. Each engineer has a workstation that connects to the network through a hub to the backbone. The engineers have access to a dedicated server named ENGSRV1. This server is located and maintained in a server room, one among many in racks of servers. The engineers complain about slow response time when they save and access data on the server. System administrators analyze server performance and determine the server is handling requests at an acceptable rate—so the problem does not appear to be in the hardware performance on ENGSRV1. The likely conclusion is a network bottleneck between the engineers and the server.

A possible solution to this bottleneck is to swap the hub where the engineers are connected for a 16-port switch. You can connect the server (ENGSRV1) to the same switch with the engineer workstations and bypass the network bottleneck. This is a very simplified solution but introduces the logic to apply when monitoring and analyzing network performance.

CHAPTER SUMMARY

- ❑ Performance monitoring concepts are consistent across all platforms. The specific tools and functions vary according to operating system.

- ❑ System Performance Monitor/2 (SPM/2) is designed to analyze hardware and software in the OS/2 environment.

- ❑ UNIX/Linux text-based tools such as *vmstat*, *ps*, *df*, and *top* are used to monitor performance on Linux systems. You can also use any of several GUI tools, including the GNOME System Monitor, the Stripchart Plotter, and third-party tools such as Unicenter TNG from Computer Associates.

- ❑ NetWare uses the Traffic Manager tool to monitor network traffic. Traffic Manager works with a Windows NT computer within the Performance Monitor tool. To monitor main system resources such as memory, CPU, and hard disk activity, use the text-based NetWare Monitor utility from the command console. The Java-based ConsoleOne interface also includes a NetWare monitoring utility. To monitor web and FTP servers, use the Novell Internet Caching System (ICS).

❑ Performance monitoring on the Windows NT operating system uses a GUI tool named Performance Monitor, and the default view is Chart View.

❑ Performance monitoring in Windows 2000 uses the Microsoft Management Console (MMC) graphical interface to the System Monitor, but the objects, counters, and instances are nearly identical to those in the Windows NT 4.0 Performance Monitor tool.

❑ The Windows NT/2000 Performance Monitor uses objects, instances, and counters to measure performance on local servers or remote systems. Performance monitoring tools provide both real-time monitoring capability and logging facilities.

❑ A baseline is established by recording performance data when a server is healthy, or running normally. The best time to create a baseline is while the server is experiencing maximum activity.

❑ When you monitor performance to detect a bottleneck, you are looking for the resource (processor, memory, etc.) that is causing the delay in the transmission of data.

❑ Baseline information for a server can also be used for capacity planning.

❑ Within a server there are limited resources that can affect the performance of a given system. Each of the resources work hand-in-hand and are capable of influencing the behavior of one another.

❑ Processor, Memory, PhysicalDisk, and Network Segment are the basic resources to track in performance monitoring.

❑ Processor utilization levels exceeding 65% on a consistent basis during performance monitoring usually indicate that the processor is the bottleneck in the system.

❑ SMP can provide improved performance by making multiple CPUs available to complete individual processes simultaneously.

❑ Writing data to compressed folders and using unnecessary encryption places an extra load on the CPU.

❑ Software RAID-5 can significantly diminish processor performance because the processor must spend resources to calculate the parity bit when writing data.

❑ Monitoring swap space is an important aspect of memory management to avoid out-of-memory errors. You can optimize the swap space by spreading it across multiple disks or a RAID array. Avoid placing the swap space on the system disk.

❑ Page Faults/sec is a good indicator of excessive paging on a Microsoft server.

❑ The best method to determine when additional memory is justified is thorough performance monitoring. The ability to upgrade to more or faster RAM is dependent on the motherboard.

11

❐ An undetected memory leak can not only cause performance deterioration, but a system crash as well.

❐ Hardware or software RAID arrays can significantly increase disk performance and provide fault tolerance. Software RAID-5 will increase performance on disk reads. Performance suffers on disk writes, however, due to processor-intensive parity calculations.

❐ The most dramatic and fundamental improvement to the disk subsystem is to upgrade from IDE disks to SCSI disks.

❐ Distributed file systems enable users to map file resources to a single file share point and transparently access resources from many physical locations.

❐ Overall network utilization and server network utilization usually affect each other.

❐ Multiple network cards can notably improve throughput to the server.

❐ Port or link aggregation can double bandwidth to a single segment by combining throughput of two or more network cards on a single segment.

❐ Upgrading a network card from 10 Mbps to 100 Mbps can boost server throughput and performance.

❐ Switches can replace hubs to improve network throughput and performance.

❐ In Ethernet networks, reducing collisions dramatically improves throughput.

Key Terms

baseline — A collection of data that establishes acceptable performance. You compare variances in performance against the baseline to determine if perceived performance issues are real.

bottleneck — One or more system components that hinder the performance of the rest of the system. Other system components must wait for the bottleneck item to complete its task before resuming activity.

compression — Data formatted to use less storage space than unformatted data.

counter — In Windows NT and 2000 Performance Monitor, a subset of an object that measures a particular aspect of that object.

drivers — One or more files loaded into the operating system to control a hardware device.

instances — In Windows NT and 2000 Performance Monitor, a subset of object counters that distinguishes like objects from one another. For example, instances would apply to multiple processors, hard disks, or NICs.

memory leak — A program that uses system memory but does not release it when finished. A memory leak consumes memory over time, and causes performance problems because more hard disk virtual memory is required. Eventually, memory leaks can cause a system to return out-of-memory messages or crash.

multithreading — Two or more simultaneously running program threads. Multithreading is useful for improving performance. Multithreading requires an operating system that can support this, and programmers must be careful to write applications so that threads do not interfere with one another.

objects — In Windows NT/2000 Performance Monitor, resources such as Processor, Memory, PhysicalDisk, and Network Segment.

process — A running program.

System Performance Monitor/2 (SPM/2) — Tool used to measure performance statistics in the OS/2 operating system environment.

threads — Program units of execution that can run separately from other threads. A thread is also the means by which an application accesses memory and processor time.

REVIEW QUESTIONS

1. Which of the following are components of OS/2 performance monitoring?

   a. Data Collection Facility

   b. System Monitor

   c. OS/390

   d. SPM/2 Monitor

2. The _____ UNIX tool shows resources currently running that consume the most memory.

   a. *vmstat*

   b. Logging Facility

   c. *top*

   d. Committed Bytes

3. The Windows NT Performance Monitor relies on which two elements to measure performance?

   a. objects

   b. cache

   c. services

   d. counters

4. The counter Interrupts/sec is associated with which object in NT Performance Monitor?

   a. Memory

   b. PhysicalDisk

   c. Processor

   d. LogicalDisk

11

5. Windows 2000 real-time performance is observed with the:

   a. vmstat utility

   b. System Monitor

   c. MMC

   d. performance logs

6. A test used to compare performance of hardware/software on servers is called a
   _____.

   a. bottleneck

   b. network segment

   c. baseline

   d. page fault

7. One or more system components that hinder the performance of the rest of the
   system is known as a:

   a. bottleneck

   b. baseline

   c. multihoming

   d. port aggregation

8. To get the most effective comparisons, the best time to create a baseline is:

   a. between 12:00 A.M. and 6:00 A.M.

   b. during times of minimal activity

   c. immediately after rebooting

   d. during periods of maximum activity

9. Predicting server performance using a current baseline and future conditions is called:

   a. network planning

   b. capacity planning

   c. server planning

   d. performance planning

10. When data is written to a compressed partition or folder, the processor must:

   a. remove compression before writing to the disk

   b. hold the data permanently in memory

   c. use multiple controllers

   d. work harder to compress the data before it is written

11. Data encryption affects performance because:

    a. more memory is required to hold the private key

    b. more hard disk space is required to store the encryption bits

    c. additional protocols are necessary to transmit encrypted data over the network

    d. the processor must perform calculations to encrypt and decrypt the data

12. PC133 SDRAM is capable of synchronizing with the _____ and reaching clock speeds of _____.

    a. CPU bus/600 MHz

    b. page file/133 MHz

    c. CPU bus/133 MHz

    d. serial port/600 MHz

13. A _____ is a bug in an application or program that prevents it from freeing up memory that it no longer needs.

    a. memory leak

    b. page fault

    c. SCSI

    d. cluster

14. Software RAID-5 improves performance for _____ operations.

    a. write

    b. delete

    c. read

    d. copy

15. When files exist in noncontiguous pieces on a hard disk, the condition is known as _____.

    a. disk performance

    b. defrag

    c. disk fragmentation

    d. IDE fault tolerance

16. SCSI-3 supports data transfer rates up to _____.

    a. 320 MBps

    b. 40 Mbps

    c. 133 MHz

    d. 600 MHz

11

17. The server named Infinity is approaching 80% disk capacity. There is no budget to increase disk space at this time. Four other servers are available and can reasonably increase file capacity 10–15%. What is a possible solution?

    a. add more memory

    b. upgrade to SCSI

    c. implement a distributed file system

    d. rename the server Finite

18. After monitoring a heavily used file server for two hours, the network analysis shows the Output Queue Length averaged a value of 5 and never fell below 3. What is a possible solution?

    a. add more memory

    b. upgrade the processor

    c. upgrade the motherboard

    d. multihoming

19. Five illustrators work in a remote office across the city from the main office. They each use Windows 2000 Professional workstations. Currently, each illustrator needs to access storyboards on a server in the main office. Only one person accesses the storyboard files from the main office. The illustrators consistently complain about slow access to the server. After monitoring the server, you find it is performing within acceptable parameters. What is a possible solution?

    a. SCSI controller for the server

    b. upgrade to faster memory

    c. move the server to the remote location

    d. print all files and hire a courier

20. _____ can replace _____ to improve network through-put and performance.

    a. IDE/SCSI

    b. hubs/routers

    c. switches/controllers

    d. switches/hubs

Hands-on Projects

 All projects in this chapter are designed for Windows 2000 Server or Professional.

Project 11-1

In this project, you will monitor the Processor object on a Windows 2000 server.

1. Click **Start**, point to **Programs**, point to **Administrative Tools**, and then click **Performance**. The MMC opens.

2. Click **System Monitor** in the left pane, if necessary.

3. Click the plus sign **(+)** in the row of buttons above the chart in the right pane. The Add Counters dialog box opens.

4. Click **Use local computer counters**.

5. From the drop-down list under the Performance object, click **Processor**, if it is not already selected.

6. Click **% Processor Time**, if it is not already selected. Click **Add**.

7. Click **% User Time**. Click **Add**.

8. Click **% Privileged Time**. Click **Add**.

9. Click **% Interrupt Time**. Click **Add**. Click **Close**.

10. Start several applications on the server, such as Paint, Word, and Pinball if available. If possible, start a utility that constantly accesses the processor (for example, a 3D screen saver) and preview it. Notice that the counters increase when the screen saver is running. (This is a very good reason not to run fancy screen savers on a server.)

11. Click the first counter, **% Processor Time**. Press **Ctrl+H**. Notice that the processor line in the chart turns white, making it easier to identify when multiple counters are running at once.

12. Click each of the other counters. Note that each chart line turns white as the counter is highlighted.

13. Click **% User Time**. Press the **Del** key to remove the counter. Repeat for % Privileged Time and % Interrupt Time. The % Processor Time counter should remain.

14. Leave System Monitor open for the next project.

Project 11-2

In this project, you will monitor the basic resource objects as defined in this chapter.

The Network Monitor Agent service must be installed to initiate the Network Segment object (Step 7). If necessary, add this using the Add/Remove Programs Control Panel item. Your instructor can help you add this.

1. In System Monitor, click the **(+)** plus sign in the row of buttons above the chart in the right pane. The Add Counters dialog box opens.
2. Click **Use local computer counters**.
3. Click the **Performance object** list box and then click **Memory**.
4. From the counters list, select **% Committed Bytes In Use**. Click **Add**.
5. Click the **Performance object** list box and select **PhysicalDisk**.
6. From the counter list, click **% Disk Time**, if necessary. Click **_Total** from the instance list, if necessary, and then click **Add**.
7. Click the **Performance object** list box and select **Network Segment**.
8. From the counter list, click **% Network Utilization**. Click on the NIC for your subnet in the Instance list. Click **Add**.
9. Click **Close**.
10. Start several applications on the server, such as Paint, Word, and Pinball if available. If possible, start a utility that constantly accesses the processor (for example, a 3D screen saver) and preview it. Notice that the counters increase when the screen saver is running.
11. Click the first counter, **% Processor Time**. Press **Ctrl+H**. Notice that the processor line in the chart turns white, making it easier to identify when multiple counters are running at once.
12. Click each of the other counters. Note that each chart line turns white as the counter is highlighted.
13. Delete all counters and leave the MMC open for Project 11-3.

Project 11-3

In this project, you will configure a performance log using the basic resource objects.

1. Start in the Performance MMC window that is still open from Project 11-2.
2. Click **Performance Logs and Alerts**.
3. In the right pane, right-click **Counter Logs** and click **New Log Settings**.
4. Type **Test Log** in the Name text box, and click OK. The Test Log dialog box opens.
5. Click **Add**. The Select Counters dialog box opens.

6. Click **Use local computer counters**.

7. Click **Processor** from the Performance Object list box. Click **% Processor Time**, and then click **Add**.

8. Click **Memory** from the Performance Object list box. Click **% Committed Bytes In Use**, and then click **Add**.

9. Select **PhysicalDisk** from the Performance Object list box. Click **% Disk Time** from the Counters list. Click **_Total** from the Instances list. Click **Add**.

10. Click **Network Segment** from the Performance Object list box. Click **% Network Utilization** from the Counters list, and click on the NIC for your subnet from the Instance list. Click **Add**, and then click **Close**.

11. Set the Sample Data Interval to 5 seconds.

12. Click the **Log Files** tab. Change the End file names with option to **yyyymmdd**.

13. Click the **Schedule** tab. In the Start log frame, click **Manually**.

14. In the Stop log frame, click the After option and enter **5 minutes**. Click **OK**.

15. Double-click **Counter Logs** in the right pane. Right-click **Test Log**, and click **Start**.

16. Start several applications on the server, such as Paint, Word, and Pinball if available. If possible, start a utility that constantly accesses the processor (for example, a 3D screen saver) and preview it. Notice that the counters increase when the screen saver is running. (This is a very good reason not to run fancy screen savers on a server.)

17. Wait a minimum of five minutes before starting the next exercise. The Test Log icon will turn red when logging is complete. (It may be necessary to refresh the screen by clicking the **Refresh** button or pressing **F5**.)

18. Leave System Monitor open for the next project.

Project 11-4

In this project, you will view the performance log data from the previous project in the Chart Format.

1. Click **System Monitor** in the left pane. Click the **View Log File Data** button (fourth button from the left).

2. Click **Test_Log** and click **Open**.

3. Click the **(+)** plus sign to Add Counters. The Add Counters dialog box opens.

4. Add all objects and counters available. (Note that only the objects and counters selected for logging are available.) Click **Close**. By default, the data appears in the Chart format, which is useful for graphically viewing performance trends from one point in time to the next.

5. Leave Performance Monitor open for the next project.

Project 11-5

In this project, you will view data in the Histogram and Report formats.

1. With the data from Project 11-4 still displayed in Chart format, click the **View Histogram** button (sixth button from the left). This format is useful for viewing log data at a specific point in time.

2. Click the **View Report** button (seventh button from the left). This format is useful for displaying exact numbers for the specified data.

3. Leave the Performance Monitor open for the next project.

Project 11-6

In this project, you will create a performance alert, send a system message, and observe the results in Event Viewer.

1. In the left-hand pane of the Performance window, click **Performance Logs and Alerts**. Right-click **Alerts**, and then click **New Alert settings**.

2. Name the alert **Processor**. Click **OK**. The Processor dialog box opens.

3. Click **Add**. The Select Counters box opens. Select the **Processor** object.

4. Click the **% Processor Time** counter. Click **Add**. Click **Close**.

5. In the "Alert when the value is:" list box, choose **Over**. Enter **5** in the Limit box.

6. Choose to sample data every 20 seconds.

7. Click the **Action** tab. Accept the default to Log an entry in the application event log.

8. Check the box to send a network message. Enter your computer name.

9. Click the **Schedule** tab. Click the **Start scan Manually** radio button.

10. Choose **Stop scan After 1 minute**. Click **OK**.

11. Right-click the **Processor** alert. Select **Start**. Open several applications to increase processor time. You will begin receiving system messages. Click **OK** to acknowledge the messages. Wait one minute.

12. Click **Start**, point to **Programs**, point to **Administrative Tools**, and click **Event Viewer**.

13. Click the **Application Log**. Note the messages indicating that the processor exceeded the limit set in the alert.

14. Close all open windows.

CASE PROJECTS

1. It's your first week on the job as the administrator. Complaints roll in that logon is slow. When you ask for performance logs on logons, you get blank looks except for one guy who tried once but couldn't remember where the data was saved. You decide to monitor some performance elements yourself, in order to identify what the bottleneck might be.

   Based on the data in Table 11-6, what is the likely bottleneck and a possible solution?

Table 11-6   Sample Data for Case Project 11-1 (Values Are Averages Based on One-Minute Monitor Times)

Object	Counter	Value
Processor	% Privileged Time	84%
Processor	% User Time	52%
Memory	% Committed Bytes in Use	44%
Server	Logon Total	63
Server	Logon/sec	1
Network Segment	% Network Utilization	37%

2. Day 2 on the new job and you are downloading files from the primary file/print server. While no one has complained about the slow downloads, the performance is not acceptable to you. You use Performance Monitor to establish a baseline. Based on the data in Table 11-7, identify the most likely bottleneck and suggest a solution.

11

Table 11-7   Sample Data for Case Project 11-2 (Values Are Averages Based on 30-Minute Performance Log)

Object	Counter	Value
Processor	% Privileged Time	37%
Processor	% User Time	26%
Memory	Page Faults/sec	56
PhysicalDisk	% Disk Time	77%
Network Segment	% Network Utilization	37%

3. The salesman for a new integrated contact management software package is touting the virtues of his wares to your marketing manager. The salesman leaves behind an evaluation copy of the server software. The marketing manager wants to try it out immediately, of course. Like a smart administrator, you install the software on a test system. The next morning, you record a performance log to track the impact of the software. Based on the data in Table 11-8, is there a bottleneck? Is there any evidence of potential problems?

Table 11-8   Sample Data for Case Project 11-3 (Values Are Averages Based on 240-Minute Performance Log)

Object	Counter	Value
Processor	% Privileged Time	12%
Processor	% User Time	9%
Memory	% Committed Bytes in Use	22–53%
PhysicalDisk	% Disk Time	17%
Network Segment	% Network Utilization	8%

12

TROUBLESHOOTING AND PROBLEM DETERMINATION

After reading this chapter and completing the exercises, you will be able to:

♦ Utilize sound troubleshooting logic to determine and solve problems

♦ Document problems and solutions

♦ Check for common causes of server failure

♦ Utilize network, connectivity, NOS, and hardware diagnostic tools

♦ Troubleshoot from a remote location

♦ Recognize and solve boot, virus, and hardware problems

♦ Locate help from vendors and peers

Even top-quality, optimally configured servers eventually develop problems, perhaps even serious enough to debilitate the server. In such events, it is critical that you implement sound troubleshooting logic to determine the exact problem and develop an appropriate solution. Sometimes the administrator becomes aware of server problems through user response to server performance or availability, and the wise administrator will lend some degree of credence even to nontechnical user comments. The administrator should also remain alert to direct and obvious causes of server problems or failure, and this chapter will remind you of some of the areas you should monitor.

Solving server and network problems goes much faster if you use the best tool for a given situation. Otherwise, you have to guess at the possible cause of a problem. Though there are dozens of server tools available that assist the administrator in troubleshooting, you will probably focus on a few favorites as well as the troubleshooting utilities that are included with the operating system. Sometimes you need to troubleshoot a server that is physically out of reach. In this case, some form of remote administration can be very useful in diagnosing and correcting server problems.

Most troubleshooting tools are available from within a functioning operating system. However, if you cannot boot the system, the possibility of recovering a failed server greatly diminishes. Recovering an unbootable system is critical in maintaining server health. For the most serious problems, many administrators restore a known good installation of the operating system using imaging software. Finally, when you cannot diagnose or recover a failed server, you should know where to turn to obtain the help you need, including help from the vendor or peers.

TROUBLESHOOTING AND PROBLEM DETERMINATION

Most of this book has already addressed one aspect of troubleshooting: prevention of problems by properly configuring server hardware and software. However, even with the best of servers, something will eventually go wrong for any number of reasons, including hardware failure, bad drivers, power problems, human error, and software conflicts, among other things. Sometimes there is no way to predict what a combination of hardware and software interactions will produce, and that's when trouble can arise.

Troubleshooting is one of the most frustrating parts of an administrator's job, but when successfully resolved, it is also one of the most rewarding. If you are used to troubleshooting home or workstation PCs, you'll find that the troubleshooting climate in the server room is much different than you are accustomed to. With a PC, troubleshooting success or failure affects only one person, and the pressure to successfully correct a problem is not as heavy. When a server fails, you might have hundreds of corporate users or online customers waiting on you. A single unavailable service or application can cost an organization thousands of dollars (or more) per minute. Hopefully, there is a level of redundancy that will continue to provide at least limited service while a server is down, but the seriousness of correcting server problems remains. During these times of intense pressure, it is critical to approach the troubleshooting puzzle with a logical, ordered perspective as shown in the remainder of this section.

Stay Calm

When catastrophe strikes and the pressure is on to fix a server, your pulse races, the phone rings, the pager sounds, and in the panic, it is easy to randomly stab at possible solutions before you've even confirmed the exact cause of the problem. However, it remains important to remain calm (as much as possible) and to follow a logical, step-by-step approach. The steps and guidelines offered here are not exhaustive, and you can insert steps or principles of your own according to your particular methods of troubleshooting. The important thing is that the administrator *has* a troubleshooting logic and methodology, and calmly pursues it.

Investigate the Problem

Investigation is usually the most significant step in troubleshooting, and it can also be the most frustrating. However, all problems give you at least a starting point. For example, if the server won't turn on, at least initially you would suspect a power problem. Unless the cause of the problem is immediately apparent, the investigation process involves several possible stages, and your primary resource (besides the obvious symptoms of the server problem) begins with the log records. Investigation includes at least checking and keeping accurate log records, checking server messages, and asking analytical questions.

Document the Process

Documentation is a critical part of server administration. Otherwise, you are likely to unnecessarily repeat the same configuration errors or troubleshoot using the same failed methods as before. Good documentation starts with keeping good log records prior to the occurrence of a problem. When configuring server equipment and software, record exactly what you do and the success or failure of each step. Then, the log records have useful meaning when it comes time to troubleshoot.

The server also has records of its own, in the system logs and RAID logs, for example. There is a limit to how large these logs can get. Many RAID cards, for example, have a limited amount of memory to store the data. Be sure that you print out existing logs before clearing them to make room for new events. Server logs are stored on the hard disk but can become quite large. You can usually print these out too, or archive them to tape backup or offline media so that they don't occupy too much space.

With proper documentation, you are ready to use log records to quickly and efficiently troubleshoot the server.

Check Log Records

12

In other chapters, we discussed creating logs of any changes to the server or network electronically or on paper. I prefer electronic logs—that way you can access the log from anywhere on the network. The method you choose is not as important as the fact that you have a history of events that can affect the functionality of the server. Unfortunately, I know many administrators who do not keep logs because they are confident in their ability to remember their actions. However, this does not account for times when the administrator is unavailable, or in medium-sized or large networks where there are multiple administrators who might also need to know the history of a server. Documentation accounts for hardware assets and provides a progressive history that might reveal a series of actions that leads to a problem. Document every action performed on the server that could affect its functionality, including events such as:

- *Adding new peripherals.* Though external peripherals, especially a keyboard, mouse, and printer, might seem inconsequential, they can have a significant effect. For example, if a PS/2 mouse becomes unusable and an administrator replaces it temporarily with an old serial port mouse, a different set of resources will be used, and an IRQ assigned to the serial port will now be utilized, possibly conflicting with another device that previously accessed those resources. Also, these types of peripherals might include software that enables special features such as a printer's double-sided printing capability. Any time you add software, you add hundreds or thousands of lines of code that could potentially interfere with other NOS functions. Peripherals such as new devices added to a SCSI chain become even more significant because of proper termination issues and ID assignments.

- *Installing software.* Although software packages interact with other packages and the NOS much better now than in the past, software bugs and interactions will always be potentially problematic. That's another reason why it is so important to test and pilot software deployments. I recently installed a file server with a CD burner and ATAPI stand-alone tape backup. Everything was fine until I installed the CD burner and tape backup software, which produced a wicked blue screen of death (BSOD) in Windows 2000. When I moved the devices to another server and installed the same software, there was no problem. These types of situations are somewhat out of your control, and you might not know that a problem could occur until testing it for yourself. Having documented that the CD burner and tape backup software produce a BSOD on that particular server will prevent me from making that mistake again.

- *Installing updates or upgrades.* One of the primary purposes of an update is to improve software and hardware compatibility. Nevertheless, some updates could cause more problems than they solve due to unforeseen incompatibilities. (In defense of programmers, it is nearly impossible for them to account for every possible software interaction that could present itself on a server.) In the example above regarding incompatible tape and CD burner software, I hope that the NOS or application vendors write a bug fix for the problem. If I apply such a patch, I'll enter it into the log records so that other administrators will know it is safe to install both applications.

 Documentation of upgrades might also be important for proper license tracking.

- *Installing hardware and drivers.* In a Plug and Play NOS such as Windows 2000, allocating resources to various devices is much more flexible than in the past. Nevertheless, hardware devices will sometimes still conflict with one another. For example, the COM1 serial port typically uses IRQ 4, and many UPS systems connect to COM1. If you add a device that requires IRQ 4 and a power outage occurs, the UPS system might not be able to communicate with the UPS software through COM1. An equally common problem is hardware device drivers, which can cause any number of undesirable interactions such as incompatibility with the NOS, applications, or other devices. Note that while new drivers sometimes cause problems, updated drivers can also resolve problems.

Recall from Chapter 4 that there is a difference between UPS capacity (the volt-amps that the UPS supplies) and the UPS runtime (the amount of time the UPS can supply the volt-amps). People often confuse these two items. In many circles, you will still hear people mistakenly refer to extending the runtime as "increasing UPS capacity." Understanding what people really mean is a matter of understanding the context of the discussion.

 Windows 2000 administrators will help to ensure device and driver compatibility by installing only drivers that are "signed" by Microsoft. Vendors send their devices drivers to Microsoft, where they are tested. If they are deemed stable and compatible, then a digital signature is included with the drivers. If the device is not signed by Microsoft, then Windows 2000 issues a warning like the one that appears in Figure 12-1, and you can deny the installation.

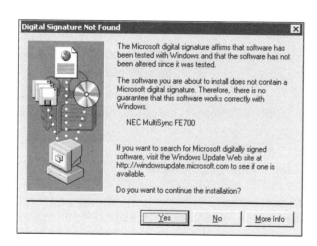

Figure 12-1 Windows 2000 notifies you of unsigned drivers

- *Interacting directly with other servers.* Many types of servers directly interact with other servers. A problem with one server can affect the functionality of any of the other servers. For example, some servers synchronize some type of information with other servers: mail, database, DNS, and WINS to name a few. If an authoritative DNS server were to have a connectivity problem, then you know that none of the other DNS servers to which it replicates will receive DNS updates until the connectivity problem is resolved, meaning that a problem with a single server can have widespread effects on other servers.

- *Stating server purpose.* Without documenting server purpose, various administrators can accidentally change a server's purpose beyond its original capabilities. Documenting a server's purpose can help to ensure that over time, the server is not re-purposed beyond its capabilities unless a compelling and deliberate reason dictates otherwise. For example, you might want a mail server with more resources than it really needs to be used exclusively for mail so that it is as responsive as possible to mail functionality and, more importantly, future growth. If another administrator comes along and sees your shiny mail server with plenty of power to spare, he or she might be tempted to also use it to run another service or application. As the company grows with more new employees using email, you might be shocked to find that your more-than-capable mail server can't keep up because of its additional roles. Specially marking the server as dedicated to mail purposes might help to avoid this type of situation.

- *Identifying people performing work on the server.* If you run into a problem with the server and the documentation doesn't seem to help, the person who last performed the work might have additional insight into the cause of the problem. Similarly, it is important to identify persons to contact should a problem occur. For example, you are the administrator installing a new application on the server. Everything seems to work just fine, but you should document your name as the administrator who performed the installation. Better yet, enter the contact information of the vendor representative and/or technical support person.

- *Stating the purpose of the work on the server.* This allows other administrators to better understand the overall context of the server and the reasons for work that is performed on it.

- *Stating when the work started and finished.* This can help to develop a plan in performing similar tasks on other servers in the network, and can help pinpoint problems that might be attributed to the actions performed on the server.

- *Labeling cables.* Although it's not documentation in a log record, it is still prudent to label cables on both ends for easy identification. If you realize that the network cable to Server1 has a break in it, it's easy to find on the server end, but without labels on the other end, you might have to make random guesses as to which exact cable in the patch panel belongs to the server connection. Labeling is not always possible or practical, particularly in very large installations. Trying to locate the correct unmarked cable requires a Fox and Hound tool (discussed later in this chapter).

 TIP Another reason to keep records is for billing purposes. For example, if you visit a site as a consultant, I recommend that before you leave the site, you write down all actions performed and have someone initial or preferably sign the log to verify it.

Check for Server Messages

Fortunately, all major NOSs include at least rudimentary (though often cryptic) server messages to indicate the successful start or stop of services, various functions, server or software errors, system conditions, and more. For example, in Figure 12-2, this Windows .NET server returned an error that it was unable to find a domain controller to service logon requests. (In this case, the domain controller was down for maintenance.)

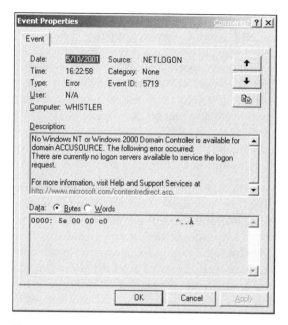

Figure 12-2   Windows 2000/.NET provides troubleshooting tips

Often, a Windows 2000 or Windows .NET event also provides tips on how to remedy the problem you encountered. For example, in Figure 12-3, you can see the beginning of one of four detailed recovery steps.

12

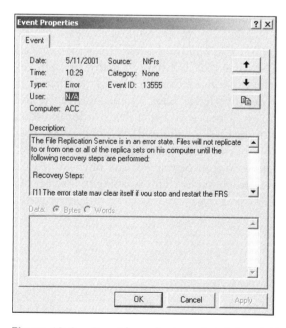

Figure 12-3   Event logs display a brief description of a problem

While writing this chapter, Microsoft revealed that the name of its new server product is Windows .NET, which is why we introduce it here. With Windows .NET, you can click a web page link in the Event Properties dialog box that, with your permission, sends system information to Microsoft that can be used to improve the Windows .NET product (the link is visible in Figure 12-2). Clicking the link takes you to a web page where you can perform research about the specific problem you encountered.

Often, event logs and error messages are cryptic and difficult to interpret. When stumped about what a message means, you can attempt to interpret its meaning by:

- *Referring to events that precede it.* Previous messages might indicate other services or functions that affect the message you are studying. For example, I recently saw a message on a Windows .NET server that indicated it was unable to retrieve a "backup list" after several attempts and that the backup browser was stopping. (The browser role in Windows networks enables you to view computers in My Network Places.) I read the preceding message and saw that the computer from which the server was attempting to retrieve the backup list was unavailable. Then I knew that the real problem was with another server and that if I could get the other server running, this problem would resolve itself.

- *Accessing the vendor's web site.* The NOS and some applications report error events in the NOS error messaging facility. Many error events are numbered—so if you visit the vendor's support web pages and perform a search for the event number, you might find a white paper or some other solution.

Although all error messages should be investigated, some may be innocuous, and as long as they do not affect performance, reliability, or availability, you can ignore them. For example, I regularly see the warning on a Windows 2000 server that appears in Figure 12-4. This occurred on several servers that I installed, many of them even before installing any applications or making configuration changes. I performed a search on "Event ID 3019" on the Microsoft Knowledge Base support site and found an article that explained the event. It's harmless. When you map a drive to local resources (as was the case with some user profile settings I had configured), Windows 2000 may be unable to determine a physical connection speed because it uses a software loopback adapter to locate resources on the same machine instead of using a true physical NIC; this is what generated the warning message. The article states: "This warning message is informational only and can be safely ignored."

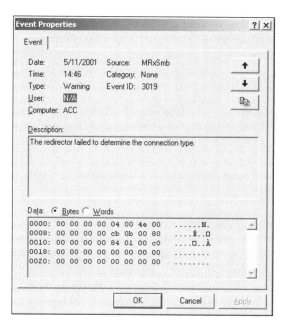

Figure 12-4   Some events are harmless and can be ignored

 TIP   Aelita software offers several excellent administrative utilities, one of which is Aelita Event Management. This utility collects events generated from across the network into an SQL database, which can then be analyzed so that the administrator can see trends in Microsoft operating systems and applications as well as Novell NDS. For example, every time a user sends a print job to a Windows NT 4.0 or Windows 2000 printer, the print job is recorded in the event log. Using this software, you could collect print job information from several departmental print servers and analyze trends to see which departments have the fastest-growing print needs.

Exactly What Happens?

The important thing here is to track the root of the problem. Perhaps the problem initially presents itself through a few user calls saying that they are having trouble with email. Now, you have to ask a series of questions that narrows down the scope of the problem. Otherwise, you are likely to chase problems that don't exist. In determining exactly what happens in the email example, you might ask things such as:

- Are users having trouble sending, receiving, or both? If the user can only send, then SMTP over port 25 is probably working OK. If they can't receive, then perhaps another administrator accidentally blocked POP port 110 over the router, or the server's mail application has wrongly configured ports.

- What are the settings in the user's mail program? Though unlikely that each caller has identically configured the wrong mail settings, perhaps a deployment application that automatically configures the settings is incorrectly configuring each client. Or perhaps a new administrator spelled the name of the mail server incorrectly in the user's POP3 settings.

- Is the problem really with the server? Problems with users' email are a common occurrence and will often keep you pretty busy. However, user complaints about email are not always server related, and that's why you should ask specific questions about exactly what is happening. Most user issues revolve around incorrectly configured client email settings or network connectivity to their computer.

 Do not neglect user input into emerging server problems. Though users are not typically server savvy, their descriptions can help you to narrow down potential server problems, either as they occur or prior to an emerging problem. For example, if a user states that Internet access is too slow, do not dismiss the complaint because you have a high-speed T-1 Internet connection. Perhaps there is a problem with the Internet proxy software, hardware, or both. If the proxy software usually caches Internet content to a particular hard disk that is currently failing, that would explain the slowdown in Internet performance.

How Does It Happen?

Much of the time, a problem occurs as a result of a sequence of events. When troubleshooting user clients, technicians ask the user what the user did to alter the system. (The answer is almost always "Nothing, I didn't change a thing.") With a server, there is usually nobody to ask if the event occurs during operations. That's when the log record comes in handy—so you can see if a previous change contributed to the problem. Also, look at logs generated by the application or NOS. They are often cryptic, but you might be able to distill enough useful information to determine a basic cause.

When Does It Happen?

Narrowing down the problem to a specific time or sequence of events helps you to determine what might be causing the problem. There are often scheduled events on the network that might contribute to the problem, or perhaps it's the result of peak traffic. Continuing the example of users with email problems, you might also ask questions such as:

- Does the problem happen when the users dial up to the network? If so, perhaps the problem is actually related to a RAS server and not email.

- Does it happen during a certain time of the day? Older backup programs cannot back up open mail storage unless it is first closed, which makes it unavailable to users.

- Does the problem predictably repeat itself, or is it intermittent? Problems that repeat predictably are much easier to troubleshoot because you can run performance monitoring applications or view logs to pinpoint when the problem occurs. You might also notice that predictable problems occur at the same time as another event. Intermittent problems are often baffling and difficult to diagnose because the problem might happen when you are not prepared to analyze its cause.

> **TIP** Intermittent hardware problems are often the result of ESD-damaged components, power problems such as power spikes or failing power supplies, or loose connections.

> **Note** You must be sure that the amount of time you spend investigating the cause of a server problem is reasonable. Some organizations have a written administrator's guide that specifies the amount of time in which the administrator must resolve an issue before consulting other avenues, perhaps calling a vendor or referring the problem to another administrator. Do not allow your professional pride to prevent you from asking for help if you need it. Help might resolve the problem sooner and you can add to your own knowledge by learning from others.

CHECK THE OBVIOUS

It happens to every administrator eventually: You spend hours diagnosing the possible cause of a failed server using a full battery of tests, diagnostic software, technical support calls, and perhaps even a call to dial-a-psychic. Finally, you discover the only reason the server won't function correctly is because of an obvious problem that would have taken only a few seconds to remedy.

For example, a few years ago I had a friend (whom I'll call Keith) who worked as a Microsoft Exchange mail administrator for an organization of a few hundred users. The Exchange servers were well-tuned; however, users would periodically call complaining that they could not send or receive email. By the time Keith began to diagnose the problem, it seemed to fix itself and the user could again send and receive. This baffled Keith—he seemed to have done everything right in diagnosing the server but could not find any problems. Finally, he figured out what was causing the problem.

A few weeks earlier, the organization had hired a summer intern to work in the server room. Apparently, he had disconnected the mail server's RJ-45 jack from the patch panel and, in performing his duties, accidentally snagged the clip on the jack and it broke off. Nevertheless, he inserted it back into the patch panel, and apparently there was enough contact to allow normal communications most of the time. The server room was running too hot, and it became necessary to bring in an oscillating fan to temporarily assist the cooling. It so happened that when the fan would oscillate to the patch panel, it

12

would disturb the network cable enough to disrupt connectivity at times, and this accounted for the intermittent problems.

Although this scenario is not something you are likely to encounter, it does emphasize that you cannot forget troubleshooting measures that might at first seem too simple, such as *always check the physical connections*.

Physical Connections

It's easy to assume that because a troubleshooting problem is severe, the solution must be equally severe. There is no logical reason for this; it's just the way people sometimes react to problems in life and in technology. However, you can often save yourself hours (even days) of troubleshooting time if you check the obvious network cabling and physical connections first when troubleshooting hardware or connectivity problems.

Network Cabling

As the network grows, it becomes even more important to remember the importance of a network diagram, which is only as useful as it is accurate. For example, a growing network starts with five segments (three of which have connected nodes and two of which only connect the hubs) and four hubs. Adding another hub and segment to the network results in breaking the 5-4-3 rule discussed in Chapter 7, and you are likely to have very poor connectivity with high collisions. A network diagram helps you to keep track of network growth and avoid overextending its limitations.

With coax and twisted-pair cable, you might also run into a **bend radius** limitation, which impairs signal transmission when the cable is bent at too tight an angle. Typically, the cable should not bend more than four times its diameter to avoid signal loss. You are most likely to see exceeded bend radius where there is too much slack cable and it is all bunched up, or where the path of the cable run takes odd twists and turns.

Also remember not to exceed the maximum cable length for each respective cable type as discussed in Chapter 7.

Connections

Similar to Keith's loose RJ-45 connector mentioned at the beginning of this section, all kinds of connectors can come loose unless they include some kind of retention such as thumbscrews, latches, or locks. RJ-45 connectors are particularly problematic due to a clip that easily snaps off or becomes overextended and weakened. Don't forget to add a boot to the ends of patch cables to protect the clip. Also check component connections. USB connectors are usually tight enough to stay by themselves, but moving other cables and equipment around the connector might accidentally wiggle a USB cord as well, causing it to loosen. The same applies to FireWire connections and serial, parallel, and video connectors—though with the latter items you can use thumbscrews to securely attach the cables.

Inside the case, I have often encountered loose connections, usually with hard disk ribbon cables. Because of the 18-inch limitation of IDE cables, sometimes the cables really stretch to go from host adapter to the actual drive in full-size cases. I recently found an IDE CD-ROM that stopped working. Because of continuous tension on the cable, the connector had come partially loose. Changing the position of the CD-ROM drive in the drive cage so that it was closer to the IDE host adapter solved that problem.

Similarly, I also recently found a file server that only provided intermittent access to the ATAPI tape drive. The connections were tight and correctly oriented, but when the computer would POST, the drive only showed up about half the time. Since no operating system or applications were involved in the POST phase of the boot, the problem was more likely physical. Finally, I realized that the drive seemed rather far away from the IDE connector on the motherboard, yet the cable reached it just fine. After pulling out the cable and measuring it, I immediately realized the problem: Somebody got the bright idea to use a special 24-inch IDE cable because the drive bay was too far away for an 18-inch IDE cable. This meant that the signal strength was compromised and was the reason for this problem. Again, I rearranged components, used an 18-inch cable, and corrected the problem.

 The width of SCSI and IDE ribbon cables often impedes good airflow inside the case. You can try to "flatten" the cables as best you can, but inevitably you'll still have airflow problems. I recently found SCSI and IDE cables from *www.coolerguys.com* that are round instead of ribbon (see Figure 12-5). Replacing ribbon cable with round cable can significantly improve airflow. Also, it is easier to daisy-chain round cable. Sometimes you have to twist ribbon cable because the number 1 pin is on the right on one device and on the left on the next device; this makes the distance between connectors in ribbon cable shorter and sometimes strains the connectors.

12

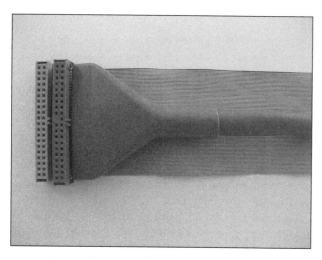

Figure 12-5   Round cables are narrower than ribbon cables, and allow much better airflow inside the case

Come to Your Senses

Your senses can often alert you to problems, hopefully in a proactive way to avoid trouble instead of as a reaction to disaster. You won't have to use all your senses to troubleshoot every situation. (After all, who "tastes" a server?) However, it is important not to ignore sight, sound, smell, and touch when troubleshooting.

People tend to depend on sight as the primary sense, and hopefully you can observe when something is wrong. With sight, just remember not to take anything for granted and to stay alert. Assuming all server hardware is correctly installed and configured, you would particularly want to observe any changes. For example, after sliding a server to the front of the rack, do any of the cables in the back come loose? Even with cable arms, cables sometimes loosen. Consider it a good practice to press in each connection when you reinsert the server.

Listen for unusual noises too, which usually come from the hard disk or a fan. When the hard disk starts to make unusual noises, failure is imminent and you should utilize redundancy measures such as RAID-1 or tape backup and immediately replace the drive. The noise is the result of mechanical failure, and it is normally not worthwhile to attempt to open the case and repair the drive. IDE drives are very cheap to replace, and expensive SCSI disks normally have a warranty program promising overnight delivery of replacements.

When you hear noise in the power supply or case cooling fans, it is usually a result of failing bearings (which under normal conditions provide an extremely smooth, low-friction action). Failure to replace the fan could cause the system to overheat (plus, the noise is really annoying). Replace case cooling fans from your stock of spare parts. With the power supply, replace the entire power supply, as its design is not intended for serviceability. Failure to replace a PSU can result in an overheated power supply, causing it to fail. Though the risk is slight, a fire hazard is also present.

 TIP Fans accumulate dust more quickly than any other single component of the system. Unusual noises might be the result of excessive dust impeding normal operation; see if blowing out the dust eliminates the sound.

Properly designed server rooms have very clean air and are probably one of the healthiest places for people to work. There will probably never be cigarette smoke in the room, and even food and drink are usually against company policy. If you smell anything unusual in the server room, it could be an administrator working long shifts without a shower. The other most likely smell will probably be the plastic-like smell of overheated components or the unmistakable smell of electrical smoke. The human sense of smell is likely to be able to detect these odors prior to a smoke alarm—so go into bloodhound mode and try to locate the source, and then immediately power down the problem equipment. You may be able to catch an electrical fire in the early stages and prevent a halon dump and the resulting mess.

Finally, the sense of touch will help you to detect problems such as an unusual amount of heat for potentially overheating components such as the power supply.

DIAGNOSTIC TOOLS

When troubleshooting server problems, several potential points of failure might be to blame. In order to properly diagnose the problem, the administrator must be aware of various diagnostic tools and their capabilities. The health of the network, while not the main focus of this book, is directly related to the effectiveness of the server, so the basic network concepts discussed in Chapter 7 are very important to remember. Each respective server NOS has accompanying network tools, and third-party vendors also offer a rich assortment from which to choose. Although it's not practical to detail each tool, this chapter addresses several examples of such tools for diagnosing problems with the physical network and network traffic.

Likewise, the administrator might suspect a problem with a physical device but find it difficult to confirm. For example, the administrator suspects a defective memory chip because of recurring blue screens. How can the administrator be certain that the problem is with physical memory and not with a bad driver or application that crashes into other processes in memory? For these types of problems, you need a thorough analysis utility in addition to following the troubleshooting principles in this chapter.

Network Cable Diagnostic Devices

When the network stops, so does your business. The common misconception is that most network issues are difficult to properly diagnose. The truth is that with proper training, finding a network problem is usually a matter of using proper diagnostic equipment discussed here and the troubleshooting methods discussed in the first section of this chapter.

As discussed in Chapter 6, a multimeter combines the functions of a voltmeter (which measures the potential difference, or voltage, between two points) and an ohmmeter (which measures resistance) as well as a few additional functions.

One common application of using a multimeter is to diagnose and troubleshoot network errors on a typical thinnet or 10Base2 network. Recall from Chapter 7 that this cabling requires 50 ohm resistors placed on either end of the bus to properly reflect the signals down the wire. Should a resistor or a T-connector fail, or an individual segment fail, the entire cable segment will fail as well. By using a multimeter, you can effectively troubleshoot by tracking each segment's resistance.

Also, you can use a **time domain reflectometer (TDR)**, a tool that not only detects cable breaks but also provides the approximate distance to the break by measuring the time it takes for a signal to return. A TDR does not tell you exactly what the problem is, but it will tell you where the problem is located on the physical cable.

12

If it interests you, there is a formula to calculate the distance to the problem section of a cable. A signal is sent down the cable, and the TDR measures the time it takes for the signal to return, converting time to distance, which is then divided by the speed of light and multiplied by the proper velocity of propagation (VOP). (VOP is a measure of the speed of light multiplied by mitigating factors that affect this speed, such as the physical cable media. Twisted-pair cable has a VOP of about .65.) Finally, the result is divided by two. The resulting number is the distance to the problem location on the cable.

In addition to checking for cable breaks, also check cable lengths. If you exceed cable lengths only slightly, connectivity problems might appear periodically, but not necessarily on a consistent basis. Similarly, inconsistency in network signaling could occur if you are within maximum cable lengths, but other factors such as radio signals or EMI compromise signal integrity.

Another device in your network diagnosis arsenal is a **Fox and Hound**, or **tone generator and locator**, used to identify cable. Imagine pulling several hundred cables through walls, raised floors, and conduit from the patch panel. Identifying each individual cable ahead of time would be fruitless, as the labeling might not survive the trip. By sending a tone, or a signal, down a cable segment, the Fox and Hound can easily identify each cable, and then you can appropriately label the cable. A Fox and Hound is actually a pair of network tools—a tone generator that applies a tone signal to a wire pair or single conductor (the "fox") and an inductive amplifier locator probe (the "hound") on the other end. At a cross-connect point such as a patch panel, or even at the remote end, you can use the amplifier probe to identify the conductor within a bundle to which the tone has been applied.

The Fox and Hound can also be utilized to troubleshoot physical problems with the cables. For example, some tone generators will also allow you to test resistance levels and provide audible tones to indicate the line condition.

Connectivity Utilities

To test for network connectivity on TCP/IP-based networks, the first tool most seasoned administrators will turn to is the Ping utility, which verifies N etwork layer connectivity. (The Network "layer" is a reference to the third layer of the OSI network model. If you are not familiar with this model, refer to *Network+ Guide to Networks* by Tamara Dean, from Course Technology, ISBN 0-7600-1145-1). Recall from Chapter 7 that the Ping utility verifies remote host accessibility by sending small packets of data to which an accessible host responds. This functionality takes place by sending an "echo request" to a remote host such as another computer or router. If the destination host does not respond, the interface will display some form of an error message, such as "destination host unreachable."

To determine if a host is properly configured on a TCP/IP network, execute the following sequence of steps:

1. Ping the IP address (or host name) of a network device that lies outside of your local router's interface (commonly referred to as your "default gateway").

If the destination host replies, the system is properly configured. If the destination host is unreachable, it is time to locate the issue: Is it a local configuration issue, or is it on an intermediate system?

2. Ping the IP address of the local router's interface to your subnet (default gateway). If this IP address replies, the issue lies outside of the local subnet. Perhaps the destination host is offline, or there is a network issue somewhere in between. If the default gateway is unreachable, determine if the problem lies with the router or in the local system.

3. Ping a local host on the local subnet. If this host replies, the problem most likely resides with the router. Perhaps the router's interface into the LAN is down due to an administrative error, temporary maintenance, an error condition, or because the router itself is in the process of rebooting. Also check the IP address of the default gateway in the system's configuration, as it may be wrong. If the local host does not reply, you probably have an issue with the local system.

4. Ping the local host's IP address. A reply indicates you may have misconfigured your subnet mask. If you do not get a reply, ping the loopback address of 127.0.0.1. If you get a reply, you probably mistyped your IP address when configuring TCP/IP properties. If you do not get a reply, it is time to check the TCP/IP stack, which is often remedied with a simple reinstallation of the protocol. Finally, remember to check physical connectors and drivers:

   - Is the network cable connected to your NIC?

   - Is the network cable plugged into the hub or switch?

   - Are the proper drivers loaded and running?

12

Note

The loopback address is commonly known as 127.0.0.1, but the entire 127.x.x.x range is set aside as loopback addresses. For example, you could also enter 127.255.255.254 to Ping the loopback address.

You can also use several command switches to extend the functionality of the Ping command, as shown in Table 12-1.

Table 12-1 Useful Ping Command Switches

Switch	Purpose	Use it when . . .
-t	Ping the specified host until interrupted.	The standard four packets do not return data for an acceptable length of time. For example, you could run it continuously to identify when a router starts "flapping," which is becoming intermittently available/unavailable. (Linux Pings indefinitely by default.)
-a	Resolve addresses to host names.	You want to verify the presence of DNS reverse lookup records.

Table 12-1   Useful Ping Command Switches (continued)

Switch	Purpose	Use it when . . .
-n *count*	*count* represents the number of echo requests to send.	You want more Ping packets than in a typical Ping, but do not want to Ping indefinitely.
-l *size*	*size* represents the size of the buffer.	You want to test how network equipment handles packets of various sizes.

In past years, malicious users were able to disable servers by sending what is known as the "ping of death," which is a ping –l packet with a very large buffer. NOSs such as Windows NT 4.0 could not handle the large packet and would become disabled. Microsoft and most other NOS vendors have resolved this issue with patches, though many other similar denial-of-service attacks continue to be a serious issue.

With NetWare 5.1, you can also use the TPing command, which is very similar to Ping.

The Ping command is not case sensitive in most operating systems, but remember that UNIX/Linux is case sensitive, so you will need to type "ping" in all lowercase to use the utility. Also, Ping is not a separately loaded program—it is an integral part of the TCP/IP protocol stack. In other words, if you have TCP/IP loaded and functioning correctly, you also have Ping. There is no such thing as a "ping service" or "ping daemon." If you can otherwise access the server (logging in, for example) but cannot successfully ping the server, this indicates that there is probably a problem with the TCP/IP stack on the server, and you will need to reload TCP/IP by rebooting. If the TCP/IP stack is corrupt, you will need to reinstall it.

Another commonly used network diagnostic utility is TRACERT (or TRACEROUTE). Depending upon the operating system or hardware platform, this utility traces the route your packets take to reach the destination host on a TCP/IP network (as discussed in Chapter 7). You may use this utility to determine if there is a network issue between your host and the destination host. The resulting output will show the path of the packet from one hop to another. This may diagnose a slow router, a dead router, or a misconfigured access list.

To speed up TRACERT, you can use the "–d" switch to stop resolving IP addresses to their associated host names. You may also wish to set a maximum trace length by minimizing the maximum number of hops to the target host by using the "-h *maximum_hops*" switch.

Operating System Utilities

Many operating system utilities have already been addressed in Chapter 11, "Performance Monitoring," because performance monitoring is a big part of troubleshooting the server. For example, Chapter 11 mentioned that a very high frequency of unaccounted-for interrupts usually indicates that a hardware device has failed. Performance monitoring tools detect such events. However, there are also utilities that you can use specifically for troubleshooting, many of which are listed in the sections that follow.

OS/2 Utilities

Table 12-2 shows OS/2 utilities that you can use to monitor system health and performance.

Table 12-2   OS/2 Utilities

Utility	Purpose
PSTAT	Displays specific status information about individual processes. For example, it can show threads and DLLs involved in a process as well as memory being shared by other threads.
RMVIEW	Locates and manages hardware resources (IRQ, DMA, I/O, and so forth).
RESERVE.SYS	Allocates resources for devices that are not Resource Manager aware. Resource Manager is an OS/2 function that automatically allocates hardware resources similar to, but not as comprehensive as, Plug and Play.
SystemView	Remotely manages servers and automatically upgrades software.
SMBTool	Captures and displays network traces.

12

 TIP If OS/2 loads a driver that causes problems, you can easily identify which specific driver is to blame by pressing Alt+F2 during the boot when you see a "??? OS/2" message in the upper left of the screen. OS/2 will then display the name of each device driver as it loads, but be aware that the problem driver is often the second-to-last driver (not the very last) displayed on the screen.

 TIP System hangs under any operating system are difficult to handle, because many times you can only guess if the entire operating system has hung or if it is just the operating system interface that has hung (while the operating system continues to run beneath it). With OS/2, you can use the system clock to determine the true state in most cases. Open the system clock and look at the second hand. If it is running, then only the desktop has hung, and you should consider waiting a while longer to see if a task finishes. If the second hand has stopped, the entire OS has stopped.

Novell NetWare Utilities

Table 12–3 lists NetWare utilities that you can use to monitor system health and performance.

Table 12-3   Novell NetWare Utilities

Utility	Purpose
VREPAIR	Repairs a volume.
CONLOG	Captures console messages to a text file for later viewing.
NWCONFIG	Modifies the server configuration, performs management operations, and installs additional products.
WAN Traffic Manager	Manages how and when WAN traffic is sent.
TPCON	Monitors TCP/IP activity.
NCMCON	Controls and monitors hot-plug PCI devices.
DSREPAIR	Repairs NDS database problems.

Besides these utilities, you can continue to use NetWare Administrator (NWADMIN or NWADMN32) or ConsoleOne to perform general administration.

Linux Utilities

Table 12-4 shows graphical (KDE or GNOME) Linux utilities that you can use to monitor system health and performance.

Table 12-4   Linux Utilities

Utility	Purpose
Tripwire	Detects changed files and directories.
KDE Control Center	Provides detailed system information about the system's applications, devices, and GUI interface.
Sysctlconfig	Configures specific settings for networking, file systems, virtual memory, and the kernel.
KDE Task Manager	Similar to Windows NT/2000 Task Manager, you can view each running process and adjust its priority level ("re-nice") or kill it.
tksysv and SysV Init Editor	A system process editor that allows you to add and delete services as well as adjust priority (see Figure 12-6)

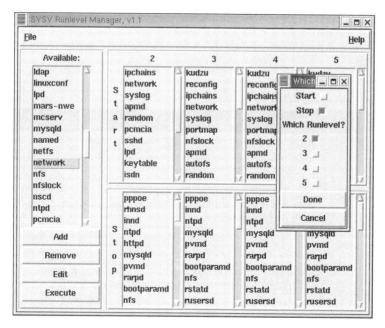

Figure 12-6   The Linux tksysv utility allows you to manipulate various processes

Windows NT 4.0 Utilities

Table 12-5 shows Windows NT 4.0 utilities that you can use to monitor system health and performance.

12

Table 12-5   Windows NT 4.0 Utilities

Utility	Purpose
Disk Administrator	Manages disks and partitions; creates software RAID configurations.
Task Manager	Shows running applications and processes, and allows you to adjust their priority or terminate. Displays real-time processor and memory utilization statistics.
System Properties	Adjusts how applications use memory, copies/deletes user profiles, configures virtual memory, and manages the boot menu.
Windows NT 4.0 Resource Kit	A collection of dozens of various utilities designed to make administration, troubleshooting, and performance monitoring more effective.
Windows NT Diagnostics	Accesses data regarding the system bus, BIOS, CPU(s), display adapter, memory usage, paging file usage, running services, system resources, and more.
Dr. Watson	Debugger for win32 applications. Might not make much sense to you unless you're a developer. Software vendors might ask for a copy of a Dr. Watson output to analyze their programs.
Network Monitor	A basic network sniffer useful for packet analysis.
The /SOS switch	Add this switch to the end of the Boot.ini file to view each driver as it loads, similar to the OS/2 Alt + F2 boot method.

Windows 2000 Utilities

Table 12-6 shows Windows 2000 utilities that you can use to monitor system health and performance.

Table 12-6   Windows 2000 Utilities

Utility	Purpose
Computer Management	Broad management capability that includes event viewer, system information, device management, hard disk management, various services, and other functions.
Task Manager	Shows running applications and processes, and allows you to adjust their priority or terminate. Displays real-time processor and memory utilization statistics.
Windows 2000 Resource Kit	A collection of dozens of various utilities designed to make administration, troubleshooting, and performance monitoring more effective.
Dr. Watson	Debugger for win32 applications. Might not make much sense to you unless you're a developer. Software vendors might ask for a copy of a Dr. Watson output to analyze their programs.
Network Monitor	A basic network sniffer useful for packet analysis.
The /SOS switch	Add this switch to the end of the Boot.ini file to view each driver as it loads, similar to the OS/2 Alt + F2 boot method.
Active Directory Domains and Trusts	Establishes trust relationships between domains.
Active Directory Sites and Services	Manages Active Directory replication between sites.
Active Directory Users and Computers	Creates and manages Active Directory user, group, and computer accounts.
System Information	Comprehensive information about system hardware, components, and software.

System and Hardware Diagnostic Utilities

Because much of troubleshooting is actually a matter of ensuring proper configuration in the first place (and correcting misconfigurations), using the right administration tool is important. Administrative tools for the various operating systems were discussed briefly in Chapter 8.

Besides the administrative utilities included in the NOS, performance monitoring utilities, as discussed in Chapter 11, are also critical because troubleshooting often involves improving the performance of a server. Sometimes a diagnostic utility is included with an installation package for a device as seen in the screenshot for the Intel NIC (see Figure 12-7).

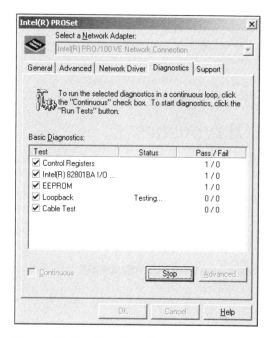

Figure 12-7   Running diagnostics on an Intel NIC

Most server vendors include utilities that perform low-level diagnosis of the server hardware. You can usually place these utilities in a directory and run them from there, or copy the utility to a floppy disk. Floppies are useful for systems that cannot boot properly, or for file systems such as Windows NT NTFS that do not allow direct disk access from a conventional MS-DOS boot disk.

Third-party manufacturers have also made utilities that diagnose hardware. There are several such products, many of which are designed for individual workstation use. One such product that I have found useful on servers is American Megatrends' AMIDiag, which performs extensive diagnostics for workstations or servers. Most utilities of this type can run only from MS-DOS, but AMIDiag offers a convenient and intuitive Windows interface as well. The latest version includes loopback plugs for serial and parallel port testing, and reports detailed information about components, including the motherboard, chipset, memory, and processor. For server components you suspect might be faulty, you can run extensive diagnostics as shown in Figure 12-8.

12

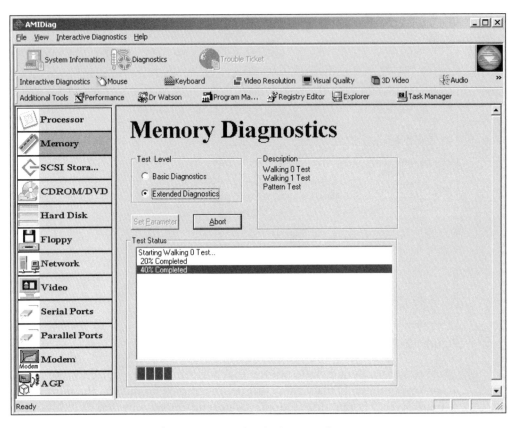

Figure 12-8   AMIDiag performing extensive tests on system memory

In some situations, you might also consider creating a small FAT partition on the hard disk that can be used for several purposes, especially when you need to perform administration on a system without loading the NOS. Typically, loading the NOS causes a problem because the file systems of most NOSs are inaccessible from MS-DOS. You might store common MS-DOS utilities in the partition that are useful for disk management, moving or editing plain text files, and so forth. For example, I would start with:

- ATTRIB—Without ATTRIB to reset attributes on some files, you might not be able to view or change certain files.

- FDISK—For repairing the master boot record using the /MBR switch or adding additional partitions. In the worst case, you will use FDISK to delete partitions.

- FORMAT—To format partitions after using FDISK.

- CHKDSK or SCANDISK—To check the health of FAT partitions.

- MSCDEX—To load CD-ROM capability, also include the CD-ROM drivers.

The partition can also be useful for storing diagnostic software. For example, if the system won't boot, you can't access NOS diagnostics, and the CD-ROM is inaccessible as well, meaning that third-party diagnostics are also unavailable. By storing an MS-DOS diagnostic utility in advance on a separate partition of the hard disk, you save yourself the headache of trying to work around the inaccessible NOS file system.

WORKING REMOTELY

Unless you enjoy working in the tight confines of a server or telecom closet at all hours of the day or night, you will quickly learn to embrace working remotely. Wake-on LAN network adapters, remote management features on the NOS, and third-party remote management software allow the administrator to work from nearly anywhere to administer and troubleshoot the server.

Wake-on LAN

Although most servers run 24/7, organizations that run mostly during business hours might choose to conserve power by putting servers and workstations into a low-power state during off hours, with only certain servers (such as web or RAS servers) running constantly. If the administrator wants to perform administration or troubleshoot during off hours, he or she must typically wait until server utilization is low, which translates into a long day in the server room for the administrator. However, with various remote features such as wake-on LAN, you can administer servers from nearly anywhere (such as the comfort of your own home.)

Wake-on LAN (WOL) is a technology that allows the administrator to remotely wake a computer from its low-power state. WOL allows administrators to "wake up" the server and perform tasks during times of reduced activity. You can use WOL on both Token Ring and Ethernet networks.

WOL works when a **magic packet** (or **wake-up packet**) consisting of 16 copies of the MAC address is sent to the host system from a server system, which has a remote network management application installed. When the WOL NIC receives the magic packet, the server turns on. To enable WOL, you must have the following:

- A WOL network interface card. This card is always awake, listening for the magic packet. In order to do this, the adapter card draws continuous, low power from the motherboard.

- A WOL motherboard BIOS

- WOL remote management software

12

WOL functionality has several advantages, even for client workstations. For example, every workstation in your organization can be started up just before your employees arrive, saving the time and revenue lost while they boot, and avoiding unnecessary energy costs associated with employees leaving systems on all night.

Remote Administration Tools

There are many utilities and tools available that allow you to remotely administer the systems in your network, whether they are across the room or in another state. One of the most widely used is Symantec's pcAnywhere (*www.symantec.com*), which allows you to remotely connect to your server to copy files, run remote applications, or perform any other actions that you would normally do if seated locally at the server.

Another free method of remotely administering servers is Windows NT 4.0 or Windows 2000 Terminal Services. In Windows 2000, use Add/Remove Programs to add Terminal Services. A wizard asks you to specify the mode in which you want the server to run:

- *Application server mode* allows users to run the Windows 2000 desktop and applications from any Windows workstation, even Windows 3.x. The benefit is that you can use older hardware incapable of running Windows 2000 or more demanding applications on its own. Using an older version of Windows, clients can derive all the benefits of a Windows 2000 desktop. Application server mode requires purchase of proper client licenses.

- *Remote administration mode* allows up to two administrators to connect as if local to the server at no additional licensing expense (see Figure 12-9). Of course, this is the mode we are interested in for purposes of remotely administering a server.

Either mode allows an administrator to "shadow" an ongoing session. You can see what applications the connected terminal services user is using and, if you like, operate their keyboard and mouse. For user sessions, this can be an excellent support tool. As a server administration tool, Terminal Services allows you to perform complete administration over a LAN, the Internet, or a dial-up connection. For example, if you are out of town and your pager receives an alert that a service has unexpectedly shut down, you could dial up from your hotel room, establish a terminal session, and restart the service. If the situation is drastic, you could even remotely reboot the server.

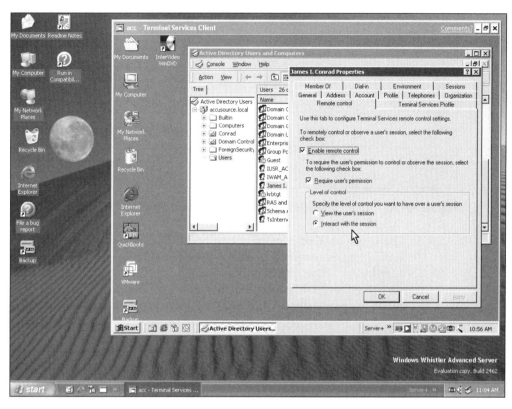

Figure 12-9   Remotely connecting to a Windows 2000 Advanced Server computer from Windows .NET Server

OS/2 has a similar remote administration tool OS known as SystemView Remote Control.

Another way that administrators can connect to and troubleshoot remote desktops and servers with a simple right-click is through the Computer Management console, as follows:

1. From any Windows 2000 desktop, right-click the My Computer icon.

2. Choose Manage. The Computer Management console appears, and by default connects to the local computer.

3. Right-click the Computer Management node at the top of the left pane, and select *Connect to another computer*.

4. Select the computer of your choice from the interface shown in Figure 12-10, and click OK.

12

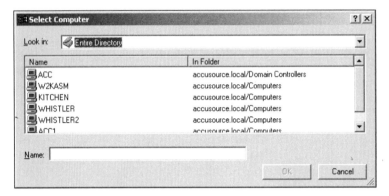

Figure 12-10   Select the computer that you want to remotely administer

5. The Computer Management console displays management nodes for the remote computer (see Figure 12-11) and functions for the most part as if you were locally seated at the server. Some features are disabled; for example, you can view Device Manager hardware settings, but you cannot change them unless seated locally or running over a Terminal Services session.

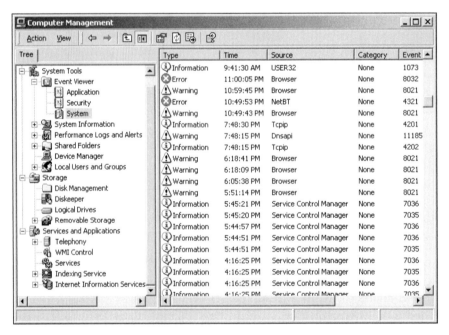

Figure 12-11   Remotely administering a Windows 2000 computer

The above steps apply to Windows 2000 and Windows .NET, but most NOSs offer a similar remote management facility. For example, Windows NT 4.0 has a similar capability, and NetWare has ConsoleOne and Remote Management Facility for general administration and ZENworks for remote control capability. You can also use the RConsole or RConsoleJ. With OS/2, use the SystemView utility (also known as NetFinity).

In addition to software products, there are hardware solutions that provide a great deal of remote administration flexibility. These are usually PCI or ISA cards that occupy an available slot in the server and are connected via a network cable, internal or external modem, or both. One of the best products I have seen is MegaRAC (Remote Access Companion) from American Megatrends. Because of an onboard battery and WOL support, you can administer the server remotely even in the event of a power failure. Some other remote administration tools require the server to be up and running, but this is of little use if you need to remotely change BIOS settings or observe startup error messages, text sequences, and so forth. With MegaRAC, you can still perform all of these actions from a remote station. Some of the features of MegaRAC are as follows:

- Captures the screen when the server crashes so that you can see error messages or what might have caused the problem. This is especially handy for error messages that might appear briefly before an unplanned reboot such as some instances of a BSOD. In addition, it logs the probable cause of the crash.

- Monitors system health including temperatures, fan RPMs, voltages, and alerts for chassis intrusion.

- Allows you to view the graphics display of a remote server to see current activity.

- Allows you to reboot a server and watch the boot process (including POST).

- Provides a special boot to a separate partition that loads diagnostic utilities. You can also insert a floppy in your local computer, and use it to boot the remote server! Very handy for booting an unbootable server, or running utilities or diagnostics that would otherwise require you to visit that server.

- Provides dead server management. When the server fails, MegaRAC can issue an alert to the supervisor and put itself in a special server mode to receive commands from the supervisor, such as performing a reboot or running special diagnostics. This is probably the single most powerful benefit of the product.

12

BOOTING AN UNBOOTABLE SERVER

At some point the inevitable will happen—the server will refuse to boot. Numerous recovery options are available in each NOS, but here we primarily address basic boot functionality to provide you with a starting point for troubleshooting.

Typically, the first option is to uninstall any new hardware devices, device drivers, or software. Windows NT/2000/.NET allows you to boot to the "last known good" state, which bypasses changes made by devices/drivers/software in the last session. If the system still refuses to boot, try using a boot disk. Most operating systems come with one or more bootable floppies or CDs to use during setup. It is always wise to guard these diskettes closely and make backup copies. Instructions for returning to a basic bootable operating system for each respective NOS appear below.

To create boot floppies for a Red Hat Linux system from MS-DOS or Windows:

1. Change directories to the CD disk drive where the installation files are located.

2. Change to the dosutils directory.

3. Execute the *rawrite* command, which then prompts you for the file name of a disk image. Consult your Linux documentation for a suitable boot image. In Red Hat Linux, for example, use the \images\boot.img file on the Red Hat CD-ROM.

 Recall from Chapter 8 that there are several boot images, each with various purposes, such as a conventional Linux boot or booting to a network.

4. Specify the destination letter for the floppy disk (usually "A"). The contents of the image file copies to the floppy.

To create boot floppies for a Red Hat Linux system from Linux:

1. Mount the CD with the installation files.

2. Change directory to the desired image.

3. Execute the following command: *# dd if=boot.img of=/dev/fd0 bs=1440k*.

Create boot floppies for an OS/2 system in any of the following ways:

- Use the Create Utility Diskette utility in the System Setup folder.

- From the command prompt, use the *makedisk* command.

- From the installation files OS2\INSTALL directory, run the Bootdisk.exe program. The disks allow basic access to the hard disk and include simple functions such as a text editor, FDISK, format, and so forth.

To create the boot floppies for a Windows NT-based system:

1. Have three labeled floppy disks ready.

2. Enter *rdisk* from the command prompt, and follow the onscreen directions that automatically appear, swapping disks as prompted.

3. Please note that the disks will be inserted in reverse order; that is, disk 3 will be inserted first, and disk 1 last.

The floppies that the RDISK utility creates are not directly bootable, but contain information that will allow you to run setup in "repair" mode to restore critical boot and system information.

To create the boot floppies for a Windows 2000 system:

1. Have four floppy disks ready.

2. On any Windows or MS-DOS computer, insert the Windows 2000 CD into the CD-ROM drive.

3. Execute the *makeboot a:* command from the *\bootdisk* directory of the CD, and follow the screen prompts to switch disks.

Booting to Windows NT or 2000 with the boot floppy disks does not provide full access to the operating system; it only allows you to use other recovery tools to repair the Registry or add/remove files. Prior to a server boot failure, however, you can create a special (unsupported) boot floppy to access the NOS desktop as follows:

1. Format a floppy disk from within the running Windows NT/2000 NOS. This is important, as it creates a boot sector that would not appear if formatted under MS-DOS or Windows 9.x.

2. Copy the following files to the floppy:
   - BOOT.INI
   - NTLDR
   - NTDETECT.COM
   - [NTBOOTDD.SYS] (if a SCSI adapter is present)
   - [BOOTSECT.DOS] (if the computer dual-boots)

3. Now, provided there are no other NOS problems, the system should boot as usual to the desktop.

 TIP   Boot disks for many operating systems may be found at *www.bootdisk.com*.

Recall that NetWare actually uses a conventional DOS partition to boot. If the boot files are corrupt, you can boot with any bootable MS-DOS floppy and manually create or edit Autoexec.bat and Config.sys files, which service the basic MS-DOS boot. Server boot files include Autoexec.ncf, Startup.ncf, and Config.ncf. As a reference for the correct commands to include, you can copy known good files from another properly functioning NetWare server.

 TIP   NetWare requires at least 10–20% free disk space on the SYS volume to boot reliably. If you suspect disk space is an issue, run "NDIR /VOL," which will show total volume space that is in use and is free. If space is an issue, run "PURGE /ALL" for each volume, which permanently deletes previously erased files (similar to emptying the Recycle Bin on Windows operating systems). If you still haven't opened enough space, you may want to run FILER or NWAdmin to manually remove files.

12

MORE DRASTIC MEASURES

Finally, if server problems are so severe that you cannot recover within a reasonable length of time, you might have to:

- Reinstall over an existing operating system. This is probably a better method than formatting the hard disk and starting over, because reinstallation usually replaces files that might have become corrupt, and applications usually remain intact. I recommend this method in situations where you are certain that there are missing or corrupt NOS files but cannot identify each one and manually replace it within a reasonable length of time. This method is a bit more of a gamble if you are less certain that NOS files are missing or corrupt. If the problem was a virus, for example, reinstallation will probably not prevent the virus from again damaging the NOS. Some NOSs such as Linux also offer special routines that are designed to run a setup program specifically to repair an installation.

- Use cloning software. Alluded to earlier in this book, you can use imaging software to store the entire contents of a partition into a single file that you can later reapply to the same or a different computer. Create an image of a known good NOS installation, so that if problems occur at a later time, you can reapply the known good NOS image and effectively roll back time. I prefer this method when possible, because it restores the server in minutes and you do not have to install applications or spend time configuring services and NOS settings.

- Format the hard disk and reinstall the NOS and all applications, and then configure all services. While this is not too disruptive for a workstation and might take between one and four hours, on a highly utilized server, this could take at least a day and be highly disruptive. If this is the method you use, server logs are again crucial: You would not want to duplicate a series of events that led to the server corruption in the first place. Also, by looking at the recorded purpose of the server, you avoid running services and applications that are unnecessary.

TROUBLESHOOTING VIRUSES

I'll assume we all know that viruses are programs that are sometimes harmless pranks, but more often are self-propagating programs that perform damaging and wide-ranging actions on server and client computers. The most effective way of troubleshooting viruses is to use a preventive, constantly running virus-detection utility that recognizes the presence of a virus and cleans infected files if possible. Unfortunately, if a virus gets loose on a system, there is little that virus utilities can do to undo the damage. A few virus symptoms include:

- Unbootable or intermittently bootable systems. Many viruses, especially early viruses, attack the boot sector.

- Display problems. Some make screens unreadable—although they may or may not damage actual data.

- File destruction. Obviously this is the most comprehensive damage, though some viruses might also slightly alter data and, therefore, are more difficult to notice.

- Unexplained poor performance (for example, slow program load times or disk access times)

- Unexpected low-memory situations

- Strange (even rude!) noises and/or graphics

- Unexplained reduction in available disk space

- Random drive letter reassignment

- Odd error messages

- A growing number of bad hard disk sectors

- Mail servers handling an extremely high number of emails. Some particularly destructive viruses send copies of themselves to all persons in the client mail program's address book.

 If a system becomes infected by a virus, you might be tempted to delete and re-create all partitions. If you then boot from a floppy and reinstall the OS from a CD, you might unwittingly reintroduce the virus if the floppy is also infected. Be sure to scan the boot floppy for infection prior to using it.

12

All major virus detection/protection software should work fine for you; the key is to make sure that the virus definition files that identify signs of a virus are up to date. I prefer to use McAfee's web-based VirusScan Online, which checks for updates automatically on a daily basis, though all these antivirus programs are excellent:

- McAfee VirusScan (*www.mcafee.com*)

- Norton Antivirus (*www.symantec.com*)

- Innoculan (*www.ca.com*)

 For more about viruses and their effects, refer to Jean Andrews' book, *Enhanced A+ Guide to Managing and Maintaining Your PC* (Course Technology, 2000).

TROUBLESHOOTING SPECIFIC FRUS

Recall from earlier chapters that an FRU is a Field Replaceable Unit. Depending on the context, an FRU can refer to the server as a whole or to the components themselves; for example, the power supply is a common FRU.

This section addresses some of the most common symptoms of FRU failure, while Chapters 3, 4, 5, and 6 addressed identification of specific parts and how to replace them.

Power Supply

Unless the system utilizes N+1 power supply redundancy, loss of a power supply means total loss of server function. Signs of a failing power supply include:

- Intermittent memory problems. Because clean, consistent power to the memory ensures its integrity, power problems can cause memory loss or corruption. If you regularly see errors that report a problem in the same memory address, the problem is more likely the actual memory.

- Systems that lock, hang, or reboot. While I was writing Chapter 8 of this book, one of my servers suddenly hung without any apparent reason. A few hours later, it hung again. I realized that juggling five internal hard disks, two CD-ROMs, and a tape drive all at once for the past couple of years was finally too much. And yes, I should have sized the power supply better. Anyway, systems with overtaxed or failing power supplies sometimes exhibit these problems, especially when they get busy.

- Damaged or intermittently failing motherboards. Power irregularities are bad for all electrical components; the motherboard is no exception. Continuing the lesson learned in the previous bullet, I'd like to announce that I am the proud owner of a new motherboard.

- Unusually hot case and power supply. Minutes and seconds without adequate cooling can damage the power supply, and failing fans are often the cause.

Use the backprobing techniques discussed in Chapter 6 to verify proper power supply voltages.

Memory

Memory problems can often be difficult to diagnose. Operating systems and applications are so complex that when a crash occurs, it might be difficult to say for certain whether it was due to a software bug or memory problems. However, the following might help you to diagnose memory problems:

- *Varying part numbers.* Some cheaper memory is really made from manufacturer spare parts. In fact, some memory modules are actually a collection of chips from different manufacturers. In this case, the markings on the chips will all be different. However, recall that it is normal for one chip to have different markings if it is the parity chip. Memory timing is so tight that little if any variation can be tolerated. For server use, do not use modules with varying part numbers.

- *No POST.* There may be no POST if memory is not properly seated, the memory is of poor quality, it uses mixed parts (as described above), or incompatible modules are installed (ECC and non-ECC in the same server, for example).

- *Memory errors in the same location each time.* Most servers include a reporting facility within the CMOS that will show the memory error. If not, and you have the opportunity to otherwise record the memory location, make a note of it. Later, if a memory error appears again in the same location, you know it is because of the memory module, not because of the NOS or applications. However, some device drivers might require the same location in memory, and a bad driver might be disguised as bad memory.

- *Memory-testing utilities.* I again recommend AMIDiag, though there are several utilities that can do this for you. The utility might run from within the NOS, but I suggest running it from a bare boot floppy with no memory management in effect (such as Himem.sys or loadhigh statements).

- *Physical symptoms.* Bad memory chips will often run comparatively hotter than the others. Also inspect the system board slot contacts. If a contact is bent or misaligned, you might have to replace the motherboard.

- *Suspect modules.* When replacing suspect modules, replace them one at a time and test them each time to confirm which modules are bad.

- *Handle with care.* Exercise special care in handling memory modules, which are particularly susceptible to ESD problems.

Hard Disks

Some hard disk problems are obvious—especially when they make that grinding noise that sounds like there's gravel in the drive. If the master boot record is damaged or corrupt (often due to virus infection), the system may not boot. Try booting from a floppy to verify that the system is boot capable, and to rule out other possible problems. Other hard disk problems include data loss or corruption, and unusually high or growing numbers of bad sectors as reported by disk analysis utilities.

 Use the FDISK /MBR switch to reconstruct the master boot record for Windows, MS-DOS, or any other NOS that starts from a DOS-compatible boot partition. Similarly, Windows 2000 allows you to boot to a special recovery console, which allows you direct disk access with the right password. Then, you can use additional boot utilities such as FIXMBR and FIXBOOT.

If you experience hard disk problems, consider the following solutions:

- Perform a thorough disk analysis of the hard disk. All major NOSs have such a utility included, such as Windows CHKDSK command. Also consider third-party utilities, but remember that the more thorough the utility, the longer it will take to analyze the hard disk (perhaps hours). Most NOSs also have hot-fix capability to automatically save data away from detected bad sectors onto healthy disk space.

- Verify proper cabling. For IDE, make sure that the marked Pin1 on the cable is adjacent to the power connector. Also make sure that the power connector is inserted all the way. SCSI connections are a study of their own (refer to Chapter 5 for proper configuration information and the next section for specific troubleshooting issues). Verify proper termination, signaling (HVD, LVD, or SE), and device ID settings.

- Check the POST. ATAPI drives will display their presence during POST, and SCSI adapters such as Adaptec's will show the specific drives in the setup BIOS of the adapter.

SCSI and RAID Troubleshooting

As alluded to in Chapter 5, troubleshooting SCSI is a study of its own. This section addresses these issues specifically, and though some information might overlap Chapter 5, it warrants a solid review. Recall from earlier in this chapter that troubleshooting is mostly configuring devices properly in the first place, and it could never be more true of any device than it is of SCSI drives. Adding to the obvious importance of properly configuring SCSI as an administrator, note that SCSI is heavily emphasized on the Server+ exam!

The following subjects resolve the most common SCSI issues.

Termination, Termination, Termination!

If someone tells you that the new SCSI drive is not working, you can almost assume that it's a termination problem. Even experienced administrators occasionally forget to properly terminate the SCSI chain. Consider the following SCSI termination issues:

- Remember that both ends of a SCSI chain need to be terminated.

- If the drive does not support self-termination, then you must add a terminator to the end of the chain. (The cable might already have a built-in terminator.)

- Most newer drives such as Ultra160 drives do not self-terminate. Some older 50-pin drives offer self-termination.

- If there is no room for a terminator, use a pass-through terminator that both connects the drive to the chain and provides termination. Even better, use a cable that has a terminator already crimped to the end.

- Passive termination is generally considered the worst type of termination because its resistance (132 ohms) varies too greatly from the standard cable resistance of 105 to 108 ohms. Make sure you use active termination instead of passive termination. Even better, use forced perfect termination whenever possible.

- Recall that when adding 50-pin devices to a 68-pin bus, you must specially terminate for the additional pins that the 50-pin device does not use. Although there are 18 additional pins, nine are only for grounding and do not require special treatment. The remaining nine, known as the "high nine," are hot and require you to properly terminate.

Cabling

- Recall from Chapter 5 that 8-bit ("narrow") SCSI always uses 50-pin cables and connectors, and 16-bit ("wide") SCSI always uses 68-pin cables and connectors. Therefore, if you are combining various generations of SCSI technology on the same bus, make sure the cabling remains compatible. For example, Ultra2 SCSI devices (which are usually "wide" devices) use a 68-pin connector and so does Ultra3. In this case, you could mix the technologies.

- If the Ultra2 SCSI device is the more rare "narrow" version requiring a 50-pin connector, then you cannot use it on an Ultra3 68-pin bus without an adapter.

- You can use special adapters to place 50-pin devices on a 68-pin cable.

- Likewise, you can use special adapters to place 68-pin devices on a 50-pin cable.

- This is important: If you mix 50-pin narrow devices with 68-pin wide devices, the net effect is that the 68-pin devices are effectively reduced to 50-pin narrow performance. There are all kinds of converters, custom cables, and so forth that allow you to physically mix and match devices and buses in countless ways, but conversion usually comes at the cost of performance.

- If you have 50-pin and 68-pin devices on a 68-pin bus, place the 68-pin devices nearest the host adapter. Then add and terminate the 50-pin devices.

 TIP If you need to buy SCSI cables, terminators, or adapters, I strongly recommend *www.cselex.com*. Not only is there equipment for most every feasible SCSI combination, but the technical support persons are well-informed and responsive.

12

Device ID

Recall that each device has a method to set the device ID, usually through jumpers as is often the case with hard disks or with a dial.

- Especially on older SCSI, set the booting hard disk to ID 0 or else it might not be recognized as the boot drive.

- If you also have IDE drives in the system but want to boot from SCSI, then configure the system BIOS to boot from the SCSI host adapter as the first bootable device. Some systems may require you to connect the IDE drive to the secondary IDE interface instead of the primary IDE interface.

- Each SCSI device must have a unique ID number. Recall that in order from highest to lowest, the priority order is 0, 7, 6, 5, 4, 3, 2, 1, and then if the bus is also wide, 15, 14, 13, 12, 11, 10, 9, 8.

- The SCSI host adapter is usually set at 7; it is best to leave it at this setting.

RAID

Keep the following RAID tips in mind:

- A RAID log records the state of the RAID array. This log can be in the host adapter BIOS, the system log of the NOS, or separate software.

- With RAID-5, you must keep the drives in the same order in which they were originally configured. For example, if a remote office sends you a pre-configured RAID-5 external array case but takes out the drives and ships them separately, you must place the drives back into the original locations on the SCSI chain. If the drives are placed in a different order, the RAID controller will return a message that the array configuration has changed and that you should reconfigure it.

- Do not move drives configured with one RAID adapter to another RAID adapter. RAID host adapters actually write data to track zero or the last track on the drive, and this information is often largely proprietary. Moving the drives could cause the RAID array to not recognize the drives or worse, destroy data.

- As a rule, any time you "touch" equipment that contains data, back up first. For example, if you are asked to add an additional drive to the RAID array, back it up first! No exceptions.

- The host adapter BIOS automatically implements the hot spare when a RAID drive fails. The interim time between when the original drive fails and the hot spare is fully implemented is known as "degraded mode." For example, if a RAID-5 member fails, it takes time for the array to integrate the hot spare while it reconstructs data from the parity stripe of the other array members.

- If you want fast performance without redundancy, use RAID-0.

- If you want fast read performance and low overhead in terms of usable storage space in the array, use RAID-5. RAID-5 lags behind other RAID methods for write performance because of the parity calculation.

- If you want fast read and write performance at the expense of high disk overhead, use RAID-1.

Adapter Cards

Although it may seem obvious (if the device stops working, it's defective!), there are still a series of questions and solutions you should look into for NIC problems.

- Move the card to another computer. If the problem repeats itself in a known good system, then you have isolated the card as problematic.

- Closely associated with the physical hardware is the device driver. Upgrade the driver to verify that the driver is not corrupt and that it is the most compatible.

Usually, the most recent version will include bug fixes for problems of which the vendor is aware. (You updated a NIC driver in Hands-on Project 6-7.)

- Move the device to a different slot. Some devices perform better when in a different slot, and high-performance devices work nominally better when closer to the processor.

- Check to see if the device is fully seated into the slot.

Processor

The processor might fail, but this is somewhat rare and is usually brought on by overheating. Usually when a processor fails, the system won't even POST. Motherboard failure is also rare but not unheard of, and it is usually brought on by power problems or overheating. If you suspect a motherboard problem, use an extensive diagnostic utility to analyze the board.

TROUBLESHOOTING TIPS

Finally, here are some general troubleshooting tips based on my own experience.

- *It usually takes longer than you think.* When you know what is causing a problem, it is easy to quickly review the steps that it will take to resolve it in your head. However, it is easy to sometimes leave out steps that you don't realize until you're in the thick of a repair. Also, in resolving one problem, other parts of the system are often affected.

- *Start with the simplest solution.* I alluded to this earlier in the chapter, but it is so true. Save time and headaches by starting with the simple causes and solutions. Also, more complex troubleshooting steps tend to affect the rest of the system more significantly. For example, it is much less disruptive to uninstall the most recent application or hardware device than to reinstall the operating system.

- *Move hardware to see if the problem follows.* If you suspect a specific hardware device is problematic, move it from the original system to a known good system and see if the problem repeats itself. If so, you have confirmed the hardware problem. If not, you know that the problem is something else. It might also be possible that the hardware device interacts poorly with other hardware or software in the original system.

- *Always check for updates.* I recently installed a new software package on a Windows 2000 server, and upon reboot, the system returned a BSOD. About ten days later, the vendor came out with a patch for the exact problem I experienced.

12

- *Troubleshoot one issue at a time, and apply one solution at a time.* The tendency is to attempt too many solutions at once. If you think a problem has three possible solutions, do not perform all three at once. Execute each solution individually to see if it is the proper solution. That way, you can enter the exact solution in the server log.

- *Fix or change one thing at a time.* Similar to the above issue, it is not wise to try the "kill two birds with one stone" method of troubleshooting and maintenance. For example, if you install a new hardware device and driver, add new software, and apply an operating system patch all for the same session, how will you know which one caused a problem if the system does not properly function afterward?

- *Progressively document troubleshooting steps.* I like to keep a legal pad nearby, and write down the history of steps I take to troubleshoot an item. This record is unofficial, and once a successful solution appears, I'll enter it into the actual server log. Of course, any of the steps that change the system permanently must also be entered in the server log. The purpose of the history is if the troubleshooting session gets lengthy and tiresome, it is easy to forget whether or not a particular solution was already attempted. In addition, it is easier to backtrack a specific sequence of steps if they make the problem worse or add new problems. I also make a note each time the system successfully reboots. If the server does not reboot successfully, then I can look at the series of steps that led up to that point.

For example, I recently installed a brand new server with all applications. I made a hasty mistake of installing too many apps at once, and upon reboot, the system returned an unrecoverable error. Because I had installed several applications and put off the requisite reboot for each one until I was done with all the applications, I had no idea which application caused the error, or if it was a combination of the applications. Fortunately, prior to the applications, I had used disk imaging software—so I was able to return to a known good state. Then, I performed each installation separately and rebooted after each application. In case you're wondering, the problematic software was a CD-burning software application, which did not seem to operate well with other applications.

Getting Help

Administrators have a tendency to be somewhat independent and determined to single-handedly solve server ills. If the administrator is solving a problem on a workstation or even a home PC, that approach might be OK. But when the network is at the mercy of a failed server, you can't take too long to resolve the issue. One of the best ways to quickly resolve these problems is to get outside help. You will also want to get help if determining the cause of the problem and its solution requires more knowledge than you currently have. It is not good timing to learn a new technology in the midst of a server disaster; therefore, you should consult a source with more information. Somebody has probably already solved the problem you're dealing with; there is no need for you to "reinvent the wheel" on your own. Help is available from a number of sources such as:

- *Web support.* This is usually the first place to go, because most vendors that really want to support the customer will keep searchable white papers and other technical support documents. Using web support also avoids those annoying automated phone menus and repeating messages about your value as a customer. The web is also the main source for product updates, a grateful change from the days when administrators had to order and pay for updates to be mailed on a floppy disk.

- *FAQs.* A listing of frequently asked questions (FAQs) can appear on the application, NOS, or hardware installation disk. While you might not read the entire thing, it might be worthwhile to at least scan it to see if any of the issues it raises will apply to your situation. An FAQ list might also appear on the vendor web site.

- *Phone help.* Contact telephone technical support from the vendor of the product with which you are experiencing a problem. Although it seems that phone technical support persons can sometimes be much less knowledgeable than you are overall, they probably have enough specific knowledge about their product to at least offer some suggestions.

- *Newsgroups.* There are two main types of newsgroups. The first is vendor moderated, which keeps the comments civil and apropos. The second is public and unmoderated, which might be less reverent about the vendor but might also be more truthful. In both cases, you use the newsgroup reader to track a problem to see what the vendor suggests as well as what other administrators might be able to contribute. These can be excellent sources of peer help—chances are, somebody else has experienced a troubleshooting problem similar to yours and can offer a solution. The disadvantage of newsgroups is that they are often not instant solutions. You might post a message today and have to wait several days for an answer, if one returns at all. Similar to the newsgroup is the chat room in which others contribute their knowledge to solving your troubleshooting problem.

- *Email.* Many vendors offer email support. Typically, you go to the support section of the vendor's web site, and if your problem is not solved there, a link might appear for you to contact technical support via email. Sometimes you will receive a response the same day, and sometimes never. I recently received a response to a query I sent six weeks earlier.

- *Newsletters.* Various email newsletters are an excellent source of late-breaking product news and optimization and troubleshooting tips. Newsletters are distributed on a periodic basis—usually daily, weekly, or monthly. For example, Red Hat has several newsletter mailing lists available at *www.redhat.com/mailing-lists*, and an excellent Windows 2000 newsletter can be found at *www.trainability.com*.

12

CHAPTER SUMMARY

❑ By properly configuring server hardware and software, you largely avoid server problems. However, sometimes there is no way to predict what a combination of hardware and software interactions will produce, and problems arise. That's when troubleshooting begins.

❑ It is easy to randomly stab at possible solutions before you've even confirmed the exact cause of the problem. However, it's important to remain calm (as much as possible) and logically approach the problem.

❑ Whether you keep paper or electronic logs, it is crucial that you keep accurate log records so that others can learn the history of the server, avoid past problems, and retain the server's original purpose (unless a compelling and deliberate reason dictates otherwise). The log also records server interaction with other servers, changes relating to applications, updates, and drivers, and the persons performing work on the server.

❑ All major NOSs include at least rudimentary (though often cryptic) server messages to indicate the successful start or stop of services, various functions, server or software errors, system conditions, and more. Go about interpreting cryptic error messages by referring to events that precede it or accessing the vendor's web site.

❑ In analyzing server problems, ask yourself "Exactly what happens?" "How does it happen?" and "When does it happen?"

❑ Server problems often occur as a result of obvious, easily overlooked problems such as physical connections (network cable, network connections) as well as signs that your sense of sight, smell, sound, or touch can detect.

❑ When troubleshooting server problems, several potential points of failure might be to blame. In order to properly diagnose the problem, the administrator must be aware of various diagnostic tools and their capabilities. Each respective server NOS has accompanying network tools, and third-party vendors also offer a rich assortment from which to choose.

❑ Important network diagnostic devices include a multimeter, Fox and Hound (tone generator and locator), and a time domain reflectometer (TDR). Besides the hardware tools, you still have the ever-handy TCP/IP utilities such as Ping and TRACERT. With Ping, you generally ping a device outside the local router's interface, ping the IP address of the local router on your subnet, ping another local host on your local subnet, ping the local IP address, and finally, ping the loopback address (127.x.x.x).

❑ Useful OS/2 utilities include PSTAT, RMVIEW, RESERVE.SYS, SystemView, and SMBTool.

❑ Useful NetWare utilities include VREPAIR, CONLOG, NWCONFIG, WAN Traffic Manager, TPCON, NCMCON, and DSREPAIR.

❑ Useful Linux utilities include Tripwire, KDE Control Center, Sysctlconfig, KDE Task Manager, tksysv, and SysV Init Editor.

❑ Useful Windows NT 4.0 utilities include Disk Administrator, System Properties, Windows NT Diagnostics, and the /SOS switch.

❑ Useful Windows 2000 utilities also include Computer Management, Active Directory Domains and Trusts, Active Directory Sites and Services, Active Directory Users and Computers, and System Information.

❑ Both Windows NT 4.0 and Windows 2000 include Task Manager, respective resource kits, Dr. Watson, and Network Monitor.

❑ The performance monitoring utilities discussed in Chapter 11 are also critical, because troubleshooting often involves improving an underperforming server. Some devices include diagnostic utilities. Most server vendors offer some type of diagnostic utilities that you can use to perform low-level diagnosis of the server. You can also use third-party diagnostics to perform thorough hardware analysis.

❑ Remote administration allows you to administer servers regardless of physical location. Several technologies allow this functionality, including Wake-on LAN network cards, third-party remote administration software, and remote administration hardware.

❑ When a system won't boot, start by uninstalling any new hardware devices, device drivers, or software. Windows NT, 2000, and .NET allow you to boot to the "last known good" state, which bypasses changes made by devices, drivers, or software in the last session. Also, try using NOS utilities to create a bootable floppy disk.

❑ If you cannot recover a server in a reasonable amount of time, you might have to take one or more of the following more drastic measures: Reinstall over an existing operating system, use cloning software to restore a known good instance of the system, format the hard disk and reinstall the NOS and all applications, and then configure all services.

❑ Viruses are a common cause of server failure, and you should use antivirus software to detect and clean infected files. There are many symptoms of virus infection, including rapid and comprehensive file deletion.

❑ This chapter includes tips for troubleshooting and replacing an FRU such as power supply, memory, hard disk, and adapter cards. It also includes the following troubleshooting principles: Troubleshooting usually takes longer than you think; start with the simplest solution; move the hardware to see if the problem follows; always check for updates; troubleshoot one issue at a time and apply one solution at a time; fix or change one thing at a time; and progressively document troubleshooting steps.

❑ Obtain help from other sources when it is taking too long to resolve the problem or you need more information about a technology. Helpful sources include web support, FAQs, phone help, newsgroups, email, and newsletters.

12

KEY TERMS

bend radius — A limitation with network cable that impairs signal transmission when the cable is bent at too tight an angle. Typically, the cable should not bend more than four times its diameter to avoid signal loss.

Fox and Hound (or tone generator and locator) — A pair of network tools. The tone generator applies a tone signal to a wire pair or single conductor and, using an inductive amplifier probe (locator) on the other end, will permit you to identify that conductor within a bundle at a cross-connect point such as a patch panel, or even at the remote end.

magic packet (or wake-up packet) — A packet consisting of 16 copies of the MAC address sent to the host system from a server system, which has a remote network management application installed. When the WOL NIC receives the magic packet, the server turns on.

time domain reflectometer (TDR) — A network troubleshooting device that measures the approximate distance to cable breaks.

wake-on LAN (WOL) — A technology that allows you to remotely wake a computer from its sleep mode. WOL works by sending a "magic packet" from a remote station to the WOL host. The "magic packet" contains 16 copies of the WOL host's MAC address.

REVIEW QUESTIONS

1. Which of the following is not a valid reason to keep a server log record?

    a. to identify and contact persons who have previously worked on the server

    b. to keep a history of actions performed on the server

    c. to increase the administrator's already heavy workload

    d. to track software, updates, hardware, and drivers installed on the server

2. Why might it be important to record servers' interaction with one another?

    a. to see which other servers might be affected if this server stops functioning correctly

    b. to redirect all network traffic to the other servers

    c. so that you can move the RAID array to the most appropriate alternate

    d. to find an alternate for failover purposes

3. Why should you document the person performing the work?

    a. to properly assess blame for failed server administration

    b. to consult that person for more information about the work they performed on the server

    c. to verify that employees are being productive

    d. to make sure only that person works on the server in the future

4. When you see a server message that is difficult to interpret, you should do which of the following? (Choose two.)

   a. Ignore the message and tackle only the easier messages.

   b. Refer to preceding events.

   c. Access the vendor web site.

   d. Clear the error log to get rid of the message.

5. Error messages are:

   a. always critical—interpret every message

   b. seldom critical—only interpret if the server fails

   c. usually critical—some are innocuous as long as they do not affect performance or server availability

   d. worthy of attention only if other people notice server problems

6. When analyzing server problems, you should ask which of the following? (Choose all that apply.)

   a. Exactly what happened?

   b. Who does it affect?

   c. How does it happen?

   d. When does it happen?

7. Troubleshooting solutions are often as simple as:

   a. reprogramming the operating system

   b. an unplugged or loose cable

   c. a failed motherboard

   d. the human genome

8. One of the first things you should check when troubleshooting failed hardware is:

   a. the logs of the last few administrators who also worked on the server

   b. the BIOS version of the system

   c. the warranty

   d. the physical connection

9. Bend radius is:

   a. a reference to the degree to which a cable can be bent before losing signal integrity

   b. a yoga position

   c. a reference to the number of Token Ring hosts permitted in any given ring

   d. accidentally overwriting a recent driver version with an older one

12

10. What is likely to happen if you break the 5-4-3 rule?

    a. host name resolution problems

    b. excessive collisions and poor connectivity

    c. counting to infinity router loops

    d. SCSI ID conflicts

11. After replacing a server in the rack, it might be a good practice to:

    a. dust the case

    b. retract any anti-tipping mechanisms

    c. press in each connection

    d. run CHKDSK

12. An unusual noise in the power supply:

    a. could indicate imminent power supply failure

    b. can be ignored until you smell smoke

    c. indicates a fan problem only—you can continue using the power supply

    d. is not a problem provided the power supply is not also hot to the touch

13. If you suspect a problem with the NIC, how can you diagnose it?

    a. Use a packet sniffer to analyze each packet to see if the problem is consistent across all communications.

    b. Copy a large file to a network share, and see if a CRC check indicates that the file is corrupt.

    c. Use the NIC vendor's diagnosis utility.

    d. From a command prompt, type Ping 127.0.0.1.

14. Besides checking for proper voltages, how else can you use a multimeter?

    a. to check network cable amperages

    b. to check the speed of a cooling fan

    c. to check the resistance on thinnet cable

    d. to detect the location of a break in the cable

15. Which tool checks for breaks in the network cable?

    a. TDR

    b. PDQ

    c. DMZ

    d. PDC

16. Which of the following are valid loopback IP addresses? (Choose two.)

   a. 127.0.1.1

   b. 172.168.0.1

   c. 127.98.67.256

   d. 127.254.254.254

17. What can be sent to a WOL host to wake it up?

   a. a shock packet

   b. a magic packet

   c. a sleep packet

   d. any Ping packet

18. What do you use to create boot floppies for an OS/2 system?

   a. the MAKEBOOT utility

   b. the FORMAT A: /SYS command

   c. the INITIAL utility

   d. the Create Utility Diskette utility

19. The system periodically hangs without explanation. What might be a cause of this?

   a. failing power supply

   b. failing hard disk

   c. improper SCSI termination

   d. insufficient memory

12

20. One of the troubleshooting principles discussed in this chapter is:

   a. Troubleshoot as many problems at once as possible to save time.

   b. Troubleshoot only one issue at a time.

   c. Apply as many solutions at once as possible.

   d. When you finish troubleshooting, try to remember everything you did and write it down.

HANDS-ON PROJECTS

Project 12-1

In this project, you will observe individual drivers loading on a Windows NT 4.0, Windows 2000, or Windows .NET system.

   1. Log on as Administrator.

   2. Right-click **My Computer** and click **Explore**.

3. Double-click **C:\boot.ini**.

The Boot.ini file will not be visible unless you have deselected the option to hide protected operating system files. Select this option from Windows Explorer by selecting Tools, clicking Folder Options, and then deselect the option that appears on the View tab.

4. The Boot.ini file opens in Notepad.
5. Near the end of the file, you will see an entry that looks similar to this:[operating systems]multi(0)disk(0)rdisk(0)partition(1)\WINNT="Microsoft Windows 2000 Server" /fastdetect
6. After the /fastdetect item, add the **/SOS** switch.
7. Save the Boot.ini file and reboot the system.
8. Upon reboot, notice that you can see each driver as it loads. The drivers probably scroll by too fast to actually read each one, but if one of the drivers is problematic, the system will usually pause while trying to load it.
9. Allow the operating system to load normally.

Project 12-2

In this project, you will install Terminal Services on a Windows 2000 server.

1. Log on to a Windows 2000 Server computer as Administrator.
2. Add Terminal Services to the server: Click **Start**, point to **Settings**, and then click **Control Panel**.
3. From Control Panel, double-click the **Add/Remove Programs** item. The Add/Remove Programs dialog box opens. Double-click the net share, and then double-click the Win32 folder.
4. Click the **Add/Remove Windows Components** icon on the left of the interface.
5. Scroll down the list of Windows components. Click the **Terminal Services** checkbox and click **Next**.

Windows .NET servers are automatically configured for remote administration. You only add Terminal Server to run it in Application Server Mode.

6. Select to run the server in remote administration mode, and click **Next**.
7. Finish the wizard and, when prompted, reboot.

Be prepared to supply the Windows 2000 CD-ROM or enter a path to the Windows 2000 source files from which the operating system was installed.

8. Using Windows Explorer, locate C:\WINNT\system32\clients\tsclient\net and share the net folder with default permissions.

9. Close Windows Explorer.

Project 12-3

In this project, you will run a Terminal Services session to connect any Windows client to the Windows 2000 server you used in Project 12-2.

1. Log on to the domain from any Windows 9.x or later client.

If another computer is not available, you can perform all these actions on the Project 12-2 server. You will just connect the computer to itself in a Terminal Services session.

2. Browse Network Neighborhood or My Network Places (as it applies) and locate the server where the \net share exists.

3. Double-click the **\net** share.

4. Locate and double-click the **Setup.exe** file. Click continue to proceed through the wizard.

5. Enter your name and organization, and click OK twice. Then, proceed to install the Terminal Services client with all default settings.

6. If so prompted, reboot the computer.

7. Log on again if necessary, and click **Start**, point to **Programs**, point to **Terminal Services Client**, and click **Terminal Services Client**. A dialog box like Figure 12-12 opens.

12

Figure 12-12   The Terminal Services Client dialog box

8. In the Server section, enter the IP address or host name of the Windows 2000 Terminal Services server.

9. Select a screen area resolution. Make sure that it is no larger than the actual resolution on the client where you are seated.

10. Click **Connect**. At the Windows 2000 logon screen, enter a user name and password and log on to the terminal server. Your desktop environment is virtually the same as if you were locally seated at the server. Browse around the interface—Start menu, Control Panel, and so on. The only difference you should see is perhaps a slightly diminished responsiveness to the mouse and keyboard (more obvious over a dial-up connection) and a limit of 256 colors. Open any window and leave it open.

11. Close the Terminal Services window. A message appears informing you that the session will continue to run even after you close the window and disconnect the session. Click OK to clear the message.

12. Access your former Terminal Services session by repeating Steps 7 through 10. Notice that the window you left open in Step 10 is still there—your session continued to run while you were "gone."

13. To actually close the session, click **Start**, **Shut Down**, and log off the session. It is now truly closed.

Project 12-4

In this project, you will view the Windows 2000 Event Log.

1. Log on as Administrator.

2. Right-click **My Computer** and click **Manage**. The Computer Management console opens.

3. In the left pane, expand the **Event Viewer** underneath System Tools. You should see three or more log categories, depending on the role of the server. The server in Figure 12-13 is a Domain Controller and DNS server, so it has a few more logs than might otherwise be present. Otherwise, your screen should look similar to this.

4. Select a log category in the left pane. Then, double-click any event in the right pane. Use the up and down arrows in the Event Properties dialog box to move up and down the list of messages.

5. Most servers probably have a warning or error of some kind. Make a note of a particular Event ID, search Microsoft's support site to see if you can find any information about the event, and answer the following questions:

   a. Does the event seem to be critical to the operation or performance of the server? How?

   b. Is there a resolution or additional information for the problem displayed in the Event Properties dialog box? If so, what is the resolution or information?

6. Close the Event Properties dialog box, and then close the Computer Management console.

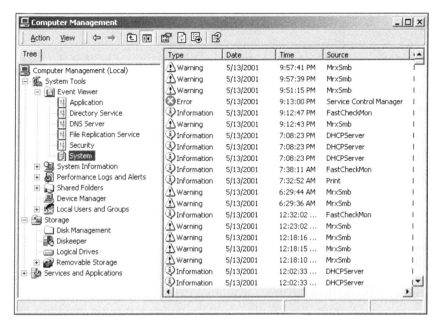

Figure 12-13   The Event Viewer categories with the System Event Viewer chosen

Project 12-5

In this project, you will search the Novell newsgroup to learn from others about Novell NetWare.

12

1. Using your web browser, access *www.novell.com*.

2. From the home page, click the **Get Support** link. Then select the Forums link from the support page.

3. On the Forums page, you can select the type of interface you want to use. If you have a newsgroup reader (such as Outlook Express), select **News Interface**. If you do not have a newsgroup reader or don't know, select **Web Interface**.

4. Select a link under support for **Operating System Products**, and then for **Server**, **NetWare 5.x**, and finally the **Utilities Forum**.

5. There are thousands of messages available, but only a few hundred have probably loaded into your newsgroup reader. Browse through messages of your choice and answer the following questions.

   a. What kind of troubleshooting problems had administrators been encountering?

   b. Were there responses that seemed to be incorrect? (This is a potential draw-back to newsgroup support; sometimes people just offer a best guess.)

   c. What appears to be the best solution?

6. Close the browser and any open newsgroup readers.

Project 12-6

In this project, your instructor has deliberately caused a hardware problem on the server. Work with one or more other students to diagnose and troubleshoot the problem server. Be sure to utilize the troubleshooting logic from the chapter. Also, have someone record every step you take. Finally, when you have finished diagnosing and repairing the problem, write down on a separate paper what you think would be a useful server log record for this situation.

CASE PROJECTS

1. Kramer has been the supervising network administrator at a company for several years. Recently, Kramer noticed that several users were surreptitiously playing a game downloaded from somewhere on the Internet. Later, Kramer noticed an unusually high number of calls from users who said their files have started to disappear both locally and from the file server, and Kramer assigns an administrator to restore as many files as possible from tape backup. However, it disturbs him that so many files are missing. What would you say is a likely cause of the missing files? What should Kramer do? Would a written policy regarding programs that users can install on their computers help?

2. Jana, the IT supervisor for a medium-sized organization, returns from a two-week vacation to find that one of the company's two clustered web servers failed shortly after she left. The other administrators did not know how to fix the failed web server, and knowing that Jana would be able to fix it, they just let the problem remain unresolved. Jana looks at the server log records to see what happened to the server, and finds the last action was performed by Chuck the day after Jana left for vacation. Chuck's note only says: "Applied update. Started 2:14, ended 2:22." What else could Chuck have included in the log?

Appendix

EXAM OBJECTIVES FOR SERVER+ CERTIFICATION

The following table lists the domains covered on the Server+ Certification exam and the weight assigned to each domain. The remainder of this appendix lists each objective covered in the exam and indicates where the objective is covered in this book. For more information about Server+ Certification see the CompTIA web site at *www.comptia.org*.

On the CompTIA web site, there is also a link for the Server+ Concepts and Skills. These are an expansion to the main test objectives, and provide more detail on some of the topics you should know. This book addresses both the certification objectives and the Concepts and Skills

Domain	% of Examination (approximate)
1.0 Installation	17%
2.0 Configuration	18%
3.0 Upgrading	12%
4.0 Proactive Maintenance	9%
5.0 Environment	5%
6.0 Troubleshooting and Problem Determination	27%
7.0 Disaster Recovery	12%

DOMAIN 1.0: INSTALLATION

Objective	Chapter: Section
1.1 Conduct pre-installation planning activities • Plan the installation • Verify the installation plan • Verify hardware compatibility with operating system • Verify power sources, space, UPS, and network availability • Verify that all correct components and cables have been delivered	• Chapter 2: Determining the Business Purpose, Anticipating User Demand, Planning for Interoperability, Server Placement, Creating the Network Diagram, Planning Physical Site Readiness, Power • Chapter 4: Uninterruptible Power Supply, Site Preparation • Chapter 6: Making an Inventory
1.2 Install hardware using ESD best practices (boards, drives, processors, memory, internal cable, etc.) • Mount the rack installation • Cut and crimp network cabling • Install UPS • SCSI ID configuration and termination • Install external devices (e.g., keyboards, monitors, subsystems, modem rack, etc.) • Verify power-on via power-on sequence	• Chapter 6: Avoiding Electrostatic Discharge • Chapter 4: The Rack, Cable Management, The KVM • Chapter 7: Network Cabling, How to Cut and Crimp RJ-45 Connectors, Networking with a Modem Pool • Chapter 4: Supplying Power to the Server, Uninterruptible Power Supply • Chapter 6: Upgrading the UPS • Chapter 5: SCSI Configuration, SCSI Termination • Chapter 3: CMOS, BIOS, and POST

DOMAIN 2.0: CONFIGURATION

Objective	Chapter: Section
2.1 Check/upgrade BIOS/firmware levels (system board, RAID, controller, hard drive, etc.)	• Chapter 3: CMOS, BIOS, and POST • Chapter 5: SCSI Configuration
2.2 Configure RAID	• Chapter 5: RAID
2.3 Install NOS • Configure network and verify network connectivity	• Chapter 8: Installing NetWare 5.1, Installing Linux, Installing OS/2, Installing Windows NT 4.0, Installing Windows 2000 • Chapter 7: Verifying TCP/IP Configuration and Connectivity
2.4 Configure external peripherals (UPS, external drive subsystems, etc.)	• Chapter 4: Uninterruptible Power Supply, Failover for the UPS • Chapter 5: Fibre Channel, RAID

Objective	Chapter: Section
2.5 Install NOS updates to design specifications	• Chapter 6: Pre-Installation Tasks, Test and Pilot • Chapter 8: Updating the Operating System • Chapter 12: Check Log Records
2.6 Update manufacturer specific drivers	• Chapter 6: Upgrading Adapters, Hands-on Project 6-7
2.7 Install service tools (SNMP, backup software, system monitoring agents, event logs, etc.)	• Chapter 9: Monitoring Protocols, SNMP, DMI • Chapter 10: Disaster Planning, Backup Software, SNMP Settings • Chapter 12: Server Messages
2.8 Perform server baseline	• Chapter 11: Establishing a Baseline
2.9 Document the configuration	• Chapter 12: Check Log Records

DOMAIN 3.0: UPGRADING

Objective	Chapter: Section
3.1 Perform full backup • Verify backup	• Chapter 10: Backup Software

3.2 Add Processors
  • On single processor upgrade, verify compatibility
  • Verify N 1 stepping
  • Verify speed and cache matching
  • Perform BIOS upgrade
  • Perform OS upgrade to support multiprocessors
  • Perform upgrade checklist, including: locate/obtain latest test drivers, OS updates, software, etc.; review FAQs, instruction, facts and issues; test and pilot; schedule downtime; implement ESD best practices; confirm that upgrade has been recognized; review and baseline; document upgrade. (This upgrade checklist applies to each hardware upgrade that follows. Note that not all updates require each item on the checklist. For example, hard disk upgrades do not usually require an updated driver.)
	• Chapter 6: Upgrading the Processor, Processor Slots and Sockets, Updating the BIOS
	• (Performing upgrade checklist items) Chapter 6: Most of the chapter
	• Chapter 8: Updating the Operating System
	• Chapter 11: Establishing a Baseline
	• Chapter 12: Check Log Records

Objective	Chapter: Section
3.3 Add hard drives • Verify that drives are the appropriate type • Confirm termination and cabling • For ATA/IDE drives, confirm cabling, master/slave and potential cross-brand compatibility • Upgrade mass storage • Add drives to array • Replace existing drives • Integrate into storage solution and make it available to the operating system • Perform upgrade checklist	• Chapter 5: ATA Cable, Master, Slave, and Cable Select, SCSI Configuration, SCSI Cables and Connectors, SCSI Termination, Drive Configuration (SCSI ID and LUN), Fibre Channel • Chapter 10: Hard Disk, Hard Disk Solutions, Add or Replace Hard Disks
3.4 Increase memory • Verify hardware and OS support for capacity increase • Verify memory is on hardware/vendor compatibility list • Verify memory compatibility (e.g., speed, brand, capacity, EDO, ECC/non-eCC, SDRAM/RDRAM) • Perform upgrade checklist • Verify that server and OS recognize the added memory • Perform server optimization to make use of additional RAM	• Chapter 3: Memory • Chapter 6: Upgrading Memory, Identifying Memory • Chapter 12: Memory
3.5 Upgrade BIOS/firmware • Perform upgrade checklist	• Chapter 3: CMOS and BIOS • Chapter 6: Updating the BIOS
3.6 Upgrade adapters (e.g., NICs, SCSI cards, RAID, etc.) • Perform upgrade checklist	• Chapter 6: Upgrading Adapters
3.7 Upgrade peripheral devices, internal and external • Verify appropriate system resources (e.g., expansion slots, IRQ, DMA, etc.) • Perform upgrade checklist	• Chapter 6: Verifying System Resources
3.8 Upgrade system monitoring agents • Perform upgrade checklist	• Chapter 9: Monitoring Protocols, SNMP
3.9 Upgrade service tools (e.g., diagnostic tools, EISA configuration, diagnostic partitio, SSU, etc.)	• Chapter 10: SNMP Settings, Server Management Software • Chapter 12: System and Hardware Diagnostic Utilities
3.10 Upgrade UPS • Perform upgrade checklist	• Chapter 4: Uninterruptible Power Supply, Site Preparation • Chapter 6: Upgrading the UPS

DOMAIN 4.0: PROACTIVE MAINTENANCE

Objective	Chapter: Section
4.1 Perform regular backup	• Chapter 10: Develop a Backup Strategy
4.2 Create baseline and compare performance	• Chapter 11: Establishing a Baseline
4.3 Set SNMP thresholds	• Chapter 9: SNMP
4.4 Perform physical housekeeping	• Chapter 2: Planning Physical Site Readiness • Chapter 10: Physical Care and Maintenance • Chapter 12: Come to Your Senses
4.5 Perform hardware verification	• Chapter 6: Test and Pilot
4.6 Establish remote notification	• Chapter 6: Notifying Users • Chapter 9: Monitoring Agents • Chapter 10: SNMP Settings

DOMAIN 5.0: ENVIRONMENT

Objective	Chapter: Section

5.1 Recognize and report on physical security issues
  • Limit access to server room and backup tapes
  • Ensure physical locks exist on doors
  • Establish anti-theft devices for hardware (lock server racks)
	• Chapter 2: Planning a Secure Location
	• Chapter 10: Storing Backups

5.2 Recognize and report on server room environmental issues (temperature, humidity/ESD/power surges, back-up generator/fire suppression/flood considerations)	• Chapter 2: Planning Physical Site Readiness, Power, Availability, Disaster Planning

DOMAIN 6.0: TROUBLESHOOTING AND PROBLEM DETERMINATION

Objective	Chapter: Section
6.1 Perform problem determination • Use questioning techniques to determine what, how, when • Identify contact(s) responsible for problem resolution • Use senses to observe problem (e.g., smell of smoke, observation of unhooked cable, etc.)	• Chapter 12: Troubleshooting Logic and Problem Determination, Investigation, Check Log Records, Exactly What Happens? How Does it Happen? When Does it Happen?, Come to Your Senses

6.2 Use diagnostic hardware and software tools and utilities
• Identify common diagnostic tools across the following OS: Microsoft Windows NT/2000; Novell NetWare, UNIX, Linux, IBM OS/2
• Select the appropriate tool
• Use the selected tool effectively
• Replace defective hardware components as appropriate
• Identify defective FRUs and replace with correct part
• Interpret error logs, operating system errors, health logs, and critical events
• Use documentation from previous technician successfully
• Locate and effectively use hot tips (e.g., fixes, OS updates, E-support, web pages, CDs)
• Gather resources to get problem solved
  - Identify situations requiring call for assistance
  - Acquire appropriate documentation
• Describe how to perform remote troubleshooting for a wake-on-LAN
• Describe how to perform remote troubleshooting for a remote alert
	• Chapter 12: Diagnostic Tools, Network Diagnostic Tools, Connectivity Utilities, Operating System Utilities, System Hardware and Diagnostic Utilities, Troubleshooting Specific FRUs, Check Log Records, Server Messages, Getting Help, Remote Administration,
	• Chapter 6: Upgrading the Processor, Upgrading Memory, Replacing the Power Supply, Upgrading Adapters

6.3 Identify bottlenecks (e.g., processor, bus transfer, I/O, disk I/O, network I/O, memory)	• Chapter 11: What is a Bottleneck? • Chapter 3: Bus Interfaces, Processors, Memory • Chapter 7: Star, Tracert, Network Adapters
6.4 Identify and correct misconfigurations and/or upgrades	• Chapter 12: Entire chapter
6.5 Determine if problem is hardware, software, or virus related	• Chapter 12: Troubleshooting Logic and Problem Determination, Troubleshooting Viruses

DOMAIN 7.0: DISASTER RECOVERY

Objective	Chapter: Section
7.1 Plan for disaster recovery • Plan for redundancy (e.g., hard drives, power supplies, fans, NICs, processors, UPS) • Use the technique of hot swap, warm swap and hot spare to ensure availability • Use concepts of fault tolerance/fault recovery to create a disaster recovery plan • Develop disaster recovery plan • Identify types of backup hardware • Identify types of backup and restoration schemes • Confirm and use off-site storage for backup • Document and test disaster recovery plan regularly, and update as needed	• Chapter 2: Do We Really Need this Server Right Now?, Disaster Planning • Chapter 5: RAID-1, RAID-5, RAID-0+1 • Chapter 4: Power Supply • Chapter 10: Spare Parts, Developing a Disaster Recovery Plan, Types of Backup Hardware, Develop a Backup Strategy, Storing and Securing Backups • Chapter 7: Network Adapters • Chapter 1: Storage
7.2 Restoring • Identify hardware replacements • Identify hot and cold sites • Implement disaster recovery plan	• Chapter 3: Processors, Memory • Chapter 6: Upgrading the Processor, Upgrading the Memory, Upgrading Adapters, Replacing the Power Supply, Upgrading the UPS • Chapter 10: Spare Parts, Hot Sites, Cold Sites

Glossary

802.11b Standard — An Ethernet specification for 11 Mbps wireless networks.

802.3 Standard — An Institute for Electrical and Electronic Engineers (IEEE) networking standard that defines the rules for configuring an Ethernet network as well as determining how elements in an Ethernet network interact with one another. By following 802.3, network equipment and network protocols can communicate properly.

"A" cable — 8-bit, 50-conductor SCSI cable.

Accelerated Graphics Port (AGP) — A high-speed graphics port that relieves the system bus and CPU of video-processing traffic.

accelerated hub architecture — Connects buses to the system bus independently through a dedicated hub interface to the PCI bus, yielding throughput of up to 266 MBps.

access time — The time it takes for the hard disk drive head to arrive at the location of the data. Access time depends upon the spin rate of the hard disk.

acknowledgment — In DHCP, a confirmation from the server to the client that the DHCP lease process completed successfully.

active cluster — A clustering method in which all nodes perform normal, active functions and then perform additional functions for a failed cluster member.

Active Directory — Microsoft's LDAP directory service for Windows 2000 that is a comprehensive database capable of storing millions of objects such as users, groups, computers, and more. In terms of functionality, Active Directory users can log on and access resources anywhere in the enterprise regardless of geographic location and where the user account was originally created.

active termination — A requirement for faster, single-ended SCSI, active termination adds voltage regulators to provide a more reliable and consistent termination. Another type of active termination is active negation termination, which uses a more complex circuit to stabilize the voltage supply level, further eliminating electrical noise from the signal.

actual power (also **true power**) — The power in watts delivered from the utility company.

actuator mechanism — A mechanism that physically positions the drive heads to the appropriate location on the disk platter to read or write data.

Adaptive Fault Tolerance (AFT) — Installing two or more server network adapters to provide an emergency backup connection between the server and the network. If there is any problem with a cable, NIC, switch port, or hub port on the primary adapter, the secondary adapter can kick in within seconds to provide transparent recovery for applications and users.

Adaptive Load Balancing (ALB) — A technique of guaranteeing a consistent level of high server throughput and transparent backup links by implementing multiple NICs and balancing the data transmission load across them. ALB is also known as "asymmetric port aggregation."

adapter teaming — Installing two or more network adapters in a server and then logically grouping them so that they appear to the operating system as a single network interface.

address (A) record — Also known as a host record, this is the actual record that resolves the host name to the IP address.

Advanced Intelligent Tape (AIT) — A Sony invention that uses an optional Memory in Cassette (MIC) chip on 8 mm tape that is able to quickly locate which of the 256 tape partitions contain the backed-up data.

Advanced Transfer Cache (ATC) — L2 cache located on the processor die and running at full processor speed.

AFS — Refers to Carnegie-Mellon's Andrew File System, a UNIX file system.

apparent power — The power delivered to a device after passing through the power supply.

arbitration — Determination of which of two or more devices has control over the bus.

ARP (Address Resolution Protocol) — Displays the resolution between the IP address and physical (MAC) address on the NIC by building a table as IP addresses resolve to MAC addresses. You can also modify the ARP cache and table entries.

ATA (AT attachment) — Drive technology that attaches to the 16-bit AT bus.

ATA-1 — An ATA standard that supports master, slave, or cable-select determination using jumpers and connecting to a 40-pin cable. The transfer rate is 3.3–8.3 MBps.

ATA-2 — An ATA standard supporting large drive support up to 137 GB. Also known as Fast-ATA-2 and Enhanced IDE (EIDE).

ATA-3 — An ATA standard that supports S.M.A.R.T. and transfer rates up to 16.6 MBps.

ATA-4 — An ATA standard that introduced the optional 80-conductor/40-pin cable and transfer rates up to 33 MBps. Also known as Ultra-DMA and Ultra-ATA. In reference to the transfer rate, you might also see UDMA/33 or Ultra-ATA/33.

ATA-5 — An ATA standard requiring the 80-conductor cable, also adding support for the IEEE-1394 (FireWire) specification and a 66 MBps transfer rate. Later implementations achieve 100 MBps and are also known as Ultra-DMA/100.

ATA-6 — The upcoming official 100 MBps ATA standard.

ATAPI (ATA Packet Interface) — A specification that allows other devices besides hard disks to plug into the ATA interface.

authentication — Verification of a person's identity based on their credentials (usually a username and password).

authorization — Verification that an authenticated user is permitted to access a network resource.

autoloaders — Robotics inside a tape library that automatically swap tapes in and out of drives.

backbone — A larger, common avenue through which data transfers take place from smaller lines connected to it.

back-end application — Application that run on the server on behalf of the client.

backprobing — Inserting the probe alongside the live connection.

back side bus — The data path used to access L2 cache.

Backup Domain Controller (BDC) — A Windows NT server that stores a read-only copy of the Primary Domain Controller's (PDC's) directory database, and is useful as an extension to the PDC for logging on users and computers. You must have a PDC before you can have a BDC.

backup window — The optimal period of time in which you can perform a backup, usually when most files are closed.

bandwidth — The transmission capacity of the network. For example, most Ethernet networks can transmit 10 Mbps or 100 Mbps.

baseline — A collection of data that establishes acceptable performance. You compare variances in performance against the baseline to determine if perceived performance issues are real.

bend radius — A limitation with network cable that impairs signal transmission when the cable is bent at too tight an angle. Typically, the cable should not bend more than four times its diameter to avoid signal loss.

bindery — A NetWare directory of users, groups, and network resources that provides network clients with the information that is stored on the NetWare server's local directory partitions. A bindery is restricted to the computer on which it resides, and users can only use resources managed in the same bindery to which they log on.

BIOS (basic input/output system) — A series of input and output configuration settings for peripherals, adapters, and on-board components.

blind connector mating — Refers to the fact that you can't see the SCSI hot-plug connection take place inside the chassis.

BOOTP — The Bootstrap Protocol; uses a BOOTP server that can distribute IP addresses to clients (similar to DHCP).

bottleneck — One or more system components that hinder the performance of the rest of the system. Other system components must wait for the bottleneck item to complete its task before resuming activity.

bridge — A network device that connects separate networks together. Bridges connect similar or different network types, such as Ethernet and Token Ring.

buffer (or **read cache**) — On a hard disk, memory that stores part of the data read from the hard disk. Later, the CPU can request the same data and it will be retrieved from the buffer, which is many times faster than mechanically retrieving it from the hard disk.

buffered memory — Re-drives (amplifies) signals entering the memory module.

bulk erase — Removal of data from magnetic tape using a large magnet. This is not a standard practice anymore, because most tapes require special markings that bulk erasure removes.

bus — Set of wires or printed circuits that provides the data path to and from the processor, memory, hard disk, adapters, and peripherals.

bus mastering — A technology that allows devices to bypass the processor and directly access memory, resulting in an overall increase in processor performance. Bus mastering devices can also communicate among themselves without processor intervention. Bus mastering is actually a form of direct memory access (DMA).

bus topology — A network topology in which nodes link together in a series where each node is connected to a common backbone cable.

bus queue entries — A Pentium Xeon technology that holds outstanding bus and memory operations.

bus width — The number of individual data wires that transmit data. The more wires the component such as the motherboard has, the more data it can transmit in a given period of time.

cable management arm (CMA) — Rack equipment that allows orderly arrangement of cables, and expands and contracts so that you can move equipment on the rack without accidentally unplugging it.

cable select — The IDE drive's position on the cable indicates whether it is a master or slave.

cache memory — A small amount of memory that stores recently or frequently used program code or data for fast access. Processors and hard disks use cache, and cache is separate from main system memory (RAM).

caching-only server — A DNS server that has no zone database, either of its own or copied through a zone transfer from a primary domain server. Caching-only servers mostly function to improve performance by reducing the number of forwarded queries.

centralized management — The ability to administer a given system from a single location instead of disparate locations.

Challenge Handshake Authentication Protocol (CHAP) — A flexible and common authentication protocol that supports encryption for a variety of operating systems. Microsoft also has two specific implementations: MS-CHAP for all Windows clients and MS-CHAP v2 for Windows 2000 clients.

chassis — The metal frame to which the motherboard is attached and that forms the case structure.

chipset — Circuitry that provides motherboard features and organizes the various buses.

client — A network workstation that requests and receives service from the server.

client-server — A network that begins with a LAN and one or more servers. The client-server network can also encompass a more complicated network configuration such as multiple, geographically distant LANs connected to one another across a relatively great distance, known as a wide area network (WAN).

clock speed — The number of instructions the processor can execute in a single instruction, measured in megahertz (MHz)—which is one million cycles per second. Instructions sent to the processor require a certain number of cycles, so the more cycles the processor can handle per second, the faster it operates, or "thinks."

clock speed — The number of times in one second that the electrically charged quartz crystal located on the motherboard vibrates (oscillates). Also known as clock cycle, clock frequency, frequency, or cycle.

clustering — Redundant servers hosting the same application for the purpose of fault tolerance. If one of the servers fails, the remaining server(s) continues to serve the application to the network.

CNAME record — Stands for a canonical name record and is an alias that points to another host.

cold site — A disaster recovery facility designed to receive computer equipment. All power, water, air conditioning, raised floor, and other items requiring a long lead-time to acquire, install, and house a computer center are in place.

collision—An event that results when two nodes transmit packets to the network at the same time.

collision domain — A network boundary in which multiple nodes could potentially attempt to access the network at the same time.

command queuing — A method that allows the host adapter to send as many as 256 commands to the drive. The drive stores and sorts the commands for optimum efficiency and performance internally before responding to the host adapter.

communities — A group of SNMP hosts that each use the same community name. You can name the community whatever makes sense for your organization. The community name is not so much a grouping as it is a small measure of security. When SNMP queries are issued to a community, only members of that community respond, and the community name functions as a rudimentary password.

CMOS — Complimentary metal oxide semiconductor that includes a small amount of memory, the purpose of which is to store the BIOS settings.

compiler — Translates high-level programming language into the lowest language the computer can understand, machine language.

compression — Data formatted to use less storage space than unformatted data.

console — An inclusive term for the keyboard video mouse (KVM) and all attached servers.

ConsoleOne — A central management point for performing NetWare 5.1 administration.

container — In Novell NetWare, a general term for an Organization or Organizational Unit, which are hierarchical components of the NDS tree. All network objects must reside in a container in the tree.

convergence — A state in which all routers connected to a network have the same updated information.

copy backup — A backup that copies all selected files, but does not mark each file as having been backed up. Copying is useful to back up files between normal and incremental backups because it does not affect other backup operations.

counter — In Windows NT and 2000 Performance Monitor, a subset of an object that measures a particular aspect of that object.

crosstalk — Intruding signals from an adjacent twisted pair or cable.

cyclical redundancy check (CRC) — A calculation used by the sending device based on the data in the packet. The data arrives at the destination target and another calculation is performed using the same "formula." If the calculation in the packet matches the calculation performed by the destination device, the data is complete and considered error free.

daemon — The Linux and UNIX name for a service.

daily backup — A backup that copies all selected files that have been modified on the day that the daily backup is performed. The backed-up files are not marked as having been backed up.

daisy chain — Connecting one device after another on a SCSI bus.

data bus — The pathway along which data passes between the processor and memory.

datacenter — A term with two meanings, depending upon the context. It can refer to a consolidation of the majority of computer systems and data into a main location, or it can refer to one or more very powerful servers optimized as database servers—sometimes configured with as many as 32 processors.

data rate — The actual quantity of data transferred within the limitations of the bandwidth.

DDR SDRAM (double data rate SDRAM) — Transfers data twice per clock cycle, similar to RDRAM, but at a lower cost because DDR SDRAM is an open standard charging no royalties.

dedicated application — A server running a single application or service and nothing else. This helps to assure that application performance is unhindered by interference from other applications or services and also contributes to the stability of the server.

density — A measure of the number of devices or servers within a given area of floor space. Higher density means more servers in a given area, usually accomplished by stacking equipment in racks.

Desktop Management Interface (DMI) — Similar to SNMP, except that it contains specific information about an actual device.

DHCP server — A server that automatically allocates IP address configuration to DHCP clients.

differential backup — A backup that copies files that have been created or changed since the last normal or incremental backup, which can reduce

the amount of time that is required to complete the backup process. It does not mark files as having been backed up.

digital audio tape (DAT) — Originally a high-fidelity digital recording format, now used on 4 mm and 8 mm tape backups. Uses helical scanning to record data.

digital linear tape (DLT) — A digital tape recording format that allows up to 70 GB of compressed data to be stored on one rather large tape, which, unlike 8 mm or 4 mm helical scan technology, passes linearly over a fixed head.

digital multimeter (DMM) — A device that measures AC voltage, DC voltage, continuity, or electrical resistance.

Direct Memory Address (DMA) — A resource that ISA devices use to directly access memory without first having to access the processor, both increasing device performance and reducing processor load. There are eight DMA channels, numbered 0–7.

directory service — A network service that identifies all of the resources on a network and makes them available to applications and users. Resources can include things like email addresses; user, group, and computer accounts; and peripheral devices such as printers.

disaster recovery plan (DRP) — A comprehensive plan designed to recover an organization to productivity after a disaster.

discovery broadcast — A broadcast initiated by a DHCP client that seeks a DHCP server.

discrete L2 cache — L2 cache located inside the processor housing but not on the processor die.

Disk Druid — A Linux disk partitioning utility.

disk mirroring — See RAID-1.

disk platter — A rigid disk inside the sealed hard disk enclosure. Magnetic media on the surface of the platter store the actual hard disk data.

disk striping — See RAID-0.

distributed application — The application runs on the server. The client can send requests to the server but does not run the application or perform processing.

Distributed File System (Dfs) — A Windows NT/2000 service that deploys what appears to be a single directory structure over multiple physical file servers.

DNS zone — A naming boundary for which a DNS server is responsible.

domain — In Windows NT or 2000, a security and administrative boundary. Not the same as a DNS domain.

Domain Name System (DNS) — A service that stores a record of both the node's IP address and host name, and uses these records to service name resolution requests.

domain validation — The determined SCSI transfer rate is tested, and if errors occur, the rate is incrementally reduced and again tested until no errors occur.

double transition (DT) clocking — SCSI technology that transmits data on both the rising and falling edges of the clock cycle. On a 16-bit, 40 MHz bus, this yields a transfer rate of 160 MBps.

drive head — A magnetically sensitive device that hovers over the hard disk platter and reads or writes data to the hard disk.

drive logic — The circuitry included in the floppy or hard drive that interfaces with the disk controller.

driver — A software interface that allows the hardware to function with the operating system.

duplexing — Two host adapters with one drive on each adapter.

Dynamic DNS — The ability to accept name registrations from DHCP clients automatically.

Dynamic Host Configuration Protocol (DHCP) — A protocol that allows its clients to lease IP address configuration automatically from a DHCP server.

dynamic RAM (DRAM) — Main memory referred to as dynamic because the information requires continuous electrical refresh, or else the data can become corrupt or lost.

EEPROM (Electrically Erasable Programmable Read-Only Memory) — A chip that stores the BIOS programming. EEPROM has been mostly superceded by a similar memory known as flash BIOS.

EIA (Electronic Industries Alliance) unit (U) — A rack unit of measure equaling 1.75 vertical inches (4.45 cm).

El Torito — A CD from which you can boot the computer, provided the BIOS supports this feature.

electrostatic discharge (ESD) — A discharge of electrical energy that occurs when two objects with differing electrical potential come into contact with one another because the electrical charges seek to equalize. ESD can damage, destroy, or shorten the life of the server's electrical components.

enterprise — A geographically dispersed network under the jurisdiction of one organization. It often includes several different types of networks and computer systems from different vendors.

error correcting code (ECC) — Circuitry on the memory chip that uses check bits to verify the integrity of memory and corrects single bit errors.

Extended ISA (EISA) — An evolution of ISA, the EISA bus provides backward compatibility with older ISA devices and provides maximum bus bandwidth of about 33 MBps.

extended partition — A partition that provides the ability to store logical drives.

failback — A clustering term referring to restoring resources to a node that has been offline when it comes back online.

failover — An alternate system that takes over for a failed system. If one server fails, the remaining server(s) continue to provide service.

Fast SCSI — SCSI operating at 10 MHz instead of 5 MHz.

Fast Ethernet — A 100 Mbps Ethernet implementation, also known as 100BaseT.

fault tolerance — Continued service despite failure of a server or component.

FAT/FAT32 — A Microsoft-based file system. FAT is capable of 2 GB partitions and FAT32 is capable of 2 TB partitions. Neither file system offers local security features.

FDISK — An MS-DOS utility used to create hard disk partitions.

Fibre Channel (FC)— A storage area network (SAN) SCSI technology that can use gigabit Ethernet networks, but is primarily intended for fiber optic cable as the name implies.

Fibre Channel Arbitrated Loop (FC-AL) — A connection of up to 126 devices on a shared bandwidth fiber hub.

fiber optic cable — Technology that uses glass (or plastic) threads (fibers) to transmit data using light pulses. The receiving end of the message converts the light signal to binary values. The maximum length is 25 km (15.5 miles) with speeds up to 2 Gbps.

field replaceable unit (FRU) — A system with replaceable CPU, CMOS, CMOS battery, RAM, and RAM cache.

File Allocation Table (FAT) — A Microsoft-based file system compatible with nearly any operating system.

file server — A server that provides a central location to store files for network clients.

Filesystem Hierarchy Standard (FHS) — A UNIX directory structure to which Linux complies.

File Transfer Protocol (FTP) — A TCP/IP protocol that manages file transfers. Usually used to download files over the Internet.

fill buffers — The interface between the CPU and main memory.

firewall — A hardware or software solution that protects internal LAN users from the public Internet.

FireWire (IEEE 1394) — An extremely fast bus allowing up to 63 connected devices and up to 3200 Mbps throughput in the latest version.

flash BIOS — BIOS memory that can be reprogrammed without having to remove the chip. Instead, you download and run a program that updates the BIOS.

forced perfect termination (FPT) — An advanced form of SCSI termination in which termination is forced to a more exact voltage by means of diode clamps added to the terminator circuitry. FPT is very clean, and it's the best termination available for an SE bus.

FORMAT — A command line utility that creates a Microsoft-based FAT file system.

Fox and Hound (or tone generator and locator) — A pair of network tools. The tone generator applies a tone signal to a wire pair or single conductor and, using an inductive amplifier probe (locator) on the other end will permit you to identify that conductor within a bundle, at a cross-connect point such as a patch panel, or even at the remote end.

front-end application — An application running on the client that retrieves information processed by a back-end application.

front side bus — A 64-bit data pathway that the processor uses to communicate with L1 cache, main memory, and the graphics card through the North Bridge chipset.

full-duplex Ethernet — The addition of another pair of wires (total of six wires) to Ethernet cable and removal of collision detection to double the connection speed. Hosts can simultaneously send and receive data similar to a telephone conversation in which both parties can speak at once. (Half-duplex would be more like a CB radio conversation.)

generator kick (also **kick** or **kickstart) —** The time required for the backup generator to come online.

Gigabit Ethernet — Supports data transfer rates of 1 Gigabit (1000 megabits) per second.

GNOME — A GUI for UNIX administration.

Grandfather-Father-Son (GFS) — A backup strategy that uses three sets of tapes for daily, weekly, and monthly backups, retaining three months of archived data.

Graphics Memory Controller Hub (GMCH) — Replaces the North Bridge in newer chipsets, providing higher data throughput.

gray code — A binary code that identifies physical locations on the drive. Gray code is written to the drive by the drive manufacturer.

handshake — The squawking noise that faxes and modems make when establishing a connection.

head crash — When the drive head contacts the disk platter during operation. This can result in corrupt data or damaged hard disk media, especially on older drives.

heat sink — An attachment to the processor that either dissipates heat through cooling fins or a small cooling fan in addition to cooling fins.

helical scanning — A tape recording method that uses a rotating tilted head to record at an angle, allowing a higher-density recording format on the tape.

hierarchical bus — Various portions of the bus running at different speeds, with the slower buses hierarchically structured beneath the faster buses.

Hierarchical Storage Management (HSM) — A storage management strategy in which infrequently used data is moved from expensive hardware (hard disks) to less expensive media such as optical disks or magnetic tape.

high byte — The dangling bits resulting from terminating only 8 bits on a 16-bit bus (also known as high 9). Use special terminators that will terminate both the 8 and 16 bits.

High Performance File System (HPFS) — The native file system of IBM OS/2.

high voltage differential (HVD) signaling — SCSI signaling circuitry that uses a comparatively high voltage to extend the length of the SCSI chain to as much as 82 feet (25 meters).

host adapter — The more accurate term for what is usually referred to as an IDE or SCSI hard disk controller. The host adapter is the physical interface between the hard disk and the computer bus.

host — A network device (usually a computer) in a TCP/IP network.

HOSTS file — A plain text file that contains static, manual entries of host-to-IP-address mappings.

host name ("A") record — A DNS entry that resolves a host's IP address to its host name, allowing users to access a server using the name instead of the IP address.

hot fix — A NetWare feature that verifies the integrity of all disk writes, and if a write fails this verification, the data is redirected to a hot fix area and the original destination is marked as unusable. The default size of the hot fix area is a small percentage of a partition's total size.

hot-plug (or **hot-swap)** — Add or remove a device without first powering down the computer.

hot site — A location containing computers and necessary peripheral equipment that may be occupied or utilized by a subscriber immediately after a disaster declaration to restore its own systems, applications, and data.

hot spare — A specific component (usually a hard drive) or a complete server that can immediately perform on the network and transparently perform the exact same function as the original.

hub — A network device that connects network cables together in a central, star configuration. Passive hubs simply make the connections, and active hubs (multiport repeaters) regenerate the signal to increase the distance it can travel.

HVD termination — High voltage termination for HVD signaling.

instances — In Windows NT and 2000 Performance Monitor, a subset of object counters that distinguishes like objects from one another. For example, instances would apply to multiple processors, hard disks, or NICs.

incremental backup — A backup of only those files that have been created or changed since the last normal or incremental backup, which can reduce the amount of time that is required to complete the backup process. It marks files as having been backed up by setting the archive bit.

Industry Standard Architecture (ISA) — A bus interface that connects ISA devices to the ISA bus, which is 16 bits wide and accommodates both 16-bit devices and older 8-bit devices. The ISA bus only operates at 8.33 MHz and is capable of transfer speeds up to 8 MBps.

inrush power — Temporary surge of power to the server when it is turned on.

Integrated Drive Electronics (IDE) — Refers to any hard disk with an integrated controller. Closely associated with the ATA standard.

intelligent hub (or **managed hub**) — A hub that allows administrators to monitor the traffic passing through the hub and configure each port in the hub.

Intelligent Input/Output (I2O) — An I/O design initiative that allows improved I/O performance via an I2O processor using the I2O driver model.

interface — The hardware connecting the drive to the computer motherboard.

interleaving — A process that allows memory access between two or more memory banks and/or boards to occur alternately, minimizing wait states.

Internet Message Access Protocol (IMAP) — In its current version (IMAP4), IMAP allows the email client to leave messages on the mail server even after logging on instead of downloading each one.

interrupt request (IRQ) — An electrical signal that obtains the CPU's attention in order to handle an event immediately, although the processor might queue the request behind other requests. There are 16 IRQs, numbered 0–15.

inter-site communication — Communication between hosts in different sites, such as over a WAN link.

intra-site communication — Communication between hosts within a single site, often over a LAN.

I/O Controller Hub (ICH) — Replaces the South Bridge in newer chipsets, allowing higher data throughput.

I/O port — A location in memory that the processor uses to communicate with the device.

IPCONFIG — A Microsoft utility that displays a wide variety of IP configuration data for a Windows 98/ME/NT/2000 system, including the IP address, subnet mask, and default gateway and other information.

IPX/SPX (Internetwork Packet Exchange/Sequence Packet Exchange) — The default Novell protocol implementation for all versions of NetWare until 5.x, which can also use TCP/IP.

iterative query — When a DNS server refers the resolver to another DNS server that might be able to resolve the request.

ISA bus — A 16-bit data pathway for slower expansion adapter cards and the floppy disk, mouse, keyboard, serial and parallel ports, and the BIOS via a Super I/O chip, which mitigates the need for a separate expansion card for each of the aforementioned items.

Journaled File System (JFS) — An OS/2 file system that contains its own backup and recovery capability. Using an indexing system and log to corroborate file changes, JFS can interoperate with the operating system to repair corrupt files.

keyboard, video, mouse (KVM) — A console that enables you to control multiple servers from a single keyboard, video monitor, and mouse.

L1 cache — A small amount of memory (usually 32–64 KB) that provides extremely fast access to its data because of its proximity to the processor and because it runs at the same speed as the processor itself—not at the speed of the motherboard.

L2 cache — Provides the same basic benefits as L1 cache, but it is larger, ranging from 256 KB to 2 MB.

lease — The length of time for which a client receives IP configuration from a DHCP server.

Level 2 Tunneling Protocol (L2TP) — A relatively new VPN protocol that requires an established certificate authority. Clients establishing a connection must download a digital certificate from the certificate authority. The certificate then validates the connection attempt over the VPN connection attempt.

Lightweight Directory Access Protocol (LDAP) — A directory service standard for enabling searches and queries to locate, identify, and utilize resources among networks.

line conditioner — A device that filters out power inconsistencies, temporarily bridges power in the event of a brief brownout, suppresses high voltage spikes, and provides overall buffering between building power and the system.

Linear Tape Open (LTO) — A collaborative technology effort headed up by HP, IBM, and Seagate to provide extremely high tape capacity and restore capability.

Linear Tape Open - Cartridge Memory (LTO-CM) — Memory in Ultrium tapes that transmits tape characteristics using radio frequency (RF) signals.

link aggregation — Combining multiple adapters into a single channel to provide bandwidth greater than the base speed of the adapter (10, 100, or 1000 Mbps). Link aggregation works only across multiple source address/destination address pairs.

Linux — A version of UNIX that operates on PCs as well as Alpha RISC and PowerPC platforms.

Linux Loader (LILO) — A Linux boot management utility that allows you to select from two or more operating systems at boot time.

LMHOSTS file — A plain text file that contains static, manual entries of NetBIOS name records.

load balancing — Distributing a network role between two or more servers.

local area network (LAN) — A collection of computers in close proximity to one another on a single network.

load equipment — Anything connected to the UPS that draws power, usually servers and possibly other network equipment.

logical drive — A section on the hard disk that appears to the operating system as if it were a separate hard disk, and that has its own drive letter.

logical unit number (LUN) — A subunit of the SCSI device, used to identify items within the device.

Logical Volume Manager (LVM) — An OS/2 utility that allows you to span a single partition across multiple physical disks, and partitions can increase in size without reformatting. You can also add or move hard drives without altering the drive letter.

low voltage differential (LVD) signaling — Similar to HVD except for use of lower voltage and shorter cable lengths (39 feet, or 12 meters).

LVD termination — Low voltage termination for LVD signaling.

MAC (Media Access Control) address — A globally unique identifier found on each NIC.

magic packet (or wake-up packet) — A packet consisting of 16 copies of the MAC address sent to the host system from a server system, which has a remote network management application installed. When the WOL NIC receives the magic packet, the server turns on.

Mail Exchanger (MX) record — Routes mail to the appropriate server(s) for members of the domain.

mainframe — The most powerful level of computer classification, mainframes are extremely large and powerful computers. Also known as "big iron."

Management Information Base (MIB) — A database of definitions for the specific SNMP device being monitored.

Management Information File (MIF) — A DMI database of information such as model ID, serial number, memory, and port addresses.

mapping — In virtual memory, copying virtual pages from disk to main memory.

master (drive) — The drive that receives the first drive letter assignment from the operating system and contains a boot record.

master server — An authoritative DNS server that transfers zone data to one or more slave servers. ("Authoritative" means that the server is configured to host the zone and return query results.)

mean time between failure (MTBF) — The anticipated lifetime of a computer or one of its components.

media access method — A method to place the data packets transmitted from the NOS software to the physical network device (such as a NIC) and then to the wire.

member server — A Windows NT server that is similar to a stand-alone server, but is a member of the domain.

memory address — Some devices reserve a dedicated region in system memory that is unavailable for use by any other device, application, or the operating system. This can help device stability by ensuring that nothing else trespasses the memory, which causes system errors.

memory core dump — Representation of the contents of memory in the event of a problem, also known as simply a "memory dump."

memory leak — A program that uses system memory but does not release it when finished. A memory leak consumes memory over time, and causes performance problems because more hard disk virtual memory is required. Eventually, memory leaks can cause a system to return out-of-memory messages or crash.

mezzanine bus — An add-on bus used to increase the number of processors in a single system.

midrange computer (or minicomputer) — A broad computer classification that lies somewhere between desktop workstation and mainframe computer.

modem pool — One or more external physical devices that represent several modems.

motherboard — The heart of the computer, which attaches to the chassis and includes slots, sockets, and other connections for server components.

mount — A reference to preparing a Novell NetWare volume for use. You mount or dismount volumes.

multihomed — Computers using NICs with multiple ports or multiple NICs to increase effective network throughput.

Multipurpose Internet Mail Extensions (MIME) — A protocol that adds the mail capability of attaching and transferring multimedia file attachments. To use MIME, you must also have an email client capable of decoding the MIME format.

multistation access unit (MAU) — A networking device that looks much like a hub except that it includes an RI (ring in) and RO (ring out) port. Tokens still pass from one host to the next in a logical ring.

multithreading — Two or more simultaneously running program threads. Multithreading is useful for improving performance. Multithreading requires an operating system that can support this, and programmers must be careful to write applications so that threads do not interfere with one another.

multi-user mode — The mode in which a Linux/UNIX server and its resources are available to network clients.

N+1 — A term that describes the expandability of a given server component or components, or space provided for expandable components. "N" is a variable that refers to the quantity of a given component installed in a system, and "+1" refers to a spare component.

Name Server (NS) record — Specifies what DNS servers are delegated servers for the domain, meaning that the server specified in the record can resolve queries authoritatively.

NetBEUI (NetBIOS Enhanced User Interface) — A small, fast protocol optimized for small networks.

NetBIOS — Broadcast-based name resolution scheme where a client simply broadcasts the NetBIOS name of the computer it wishes to reach to all of the computers on a subnet. The broadcast message identifies a computer that acknowledges the broadcast and establishes a communication link.

NETSTAT — A command-line networking utility that shows TCP/IP protocol statistics using any of several options. One of the most useful options is –r, which shows the routing table. This is useful in verifying the efficiency of the routing tables.

NetWare File System — Novell's file system that offers large volume support, efficient cluster size, and local security.

NetWare Loadable Module (NLM) — Programs that run on a NetWare server. An NLM might include a management utility or server-based applications such as a database engine.

network — A collection of two or more computers connected with transmission media such as network cable or wireless means, such as radio or infrared signals. Usually includes other devices such as printers.

network applications — Server-based programs that run in memory and on the processor on behalf of other servers or clients.

network attached storage (NAS) — One or more storage devices attached to a network, most commonly Ethernet. Simple to configure, you plug in the power, connect it to the network, and turn it on.

network device — Any device connected to the network for purposes of communicating with other network devices. (A network device is also known as a host in most networks.)

Network File System (NFS) — A UNIX file system that makes files accessible over a network.

network interface card (NIC) — The workstation's adapter card that connects to the network and through which network communication takes place.

network operating system (NOS) — Provides file and printer sharing, centralized file storage, security, and various services. Primary examples of a NOS include Microsoft Windows NT or 2000, Linux, IBM OS/2, or Novell NetWare.

network resource — An object users can access from across the network, such as printers, files, and folders.

network utilization — The percentage of bandwidth in use in a given period of time.

node — An active device connected to a network, such as a computer or printer, or networking equipment such as a hub, switch, or router.

non-maskable interrupt (NMI) — An interrupt that takes priority over standard interrupt requests. An NMI is useful to stop the system or issue a message in the event of critical events or failures such as failing memory.

normal backup — A backup that copies all selected files and clears the archive bit for each one.

North Bridge — A chipset element that divides the processor bus from the PCI bus and manages data traffic to and from the South Bridge, and components on the FSB and PCI bus.

Novell Directory Services (NDS) — A hierarchical database of network resources that allows users from anywhere in the enterprise to access resources throughout the organization, as opposed to logging on to a single server and accessing only resources available from that server.

Novell Storage Service (NSS) — Operates alongside the traditional NetWare file system to support large files, improve performance, and provide flexible storage management.

NT File System (NTFS) — A Microsoft-based file system designed for Windows NT/2000, offering large volumes and local security.

noncondensing relative humidity — Absence of moisture accumulation, such as on the outside of a cold glass.

null cable modem — A special cable that uses special crossed wires to simulate a modem presence, allowing data to travel between two hosts without an actual modem or network connection.

objects — In Windows NT/2000 Performance Monitor, resources such as Processor, Memory, PhysicalDisk, and Network Segment.

offer — The DHCP server's proposed IP address and configuration to the DHCP client.

online retention period (OLRP) — References how far back in time a tape library can restore from tape without manual intervention.

Open Shortest Path First (OSPF) — A routing protocol that builds its routing tables using a link-state algorithm, which calculates the shortest path to each host based on the network topology, not just the fewest number of hops (as with RIP).

optical disk — Any disk written and read by laser, including CD-R, CD-RW, DVD, and so forth.

overclocking — Increasing the speed of the motherboard clock and/or the CPU to accelerate the clock speed, which can yield a performance increase. Not recommended on servers because of the higher risk associated with higher temperatures and a reduction in overall stability.

oversubscribe — A network connection with network utilization that exceeds an acceptable baseline for the available network bandwidth. The network utilization has a direct relationship to network bandwidth: the higher the network bandwidth, the lower the network utilization.

"P" cable — 16-bit, 68-conductor SCSI cable.

packetization — A data transfer method that reduces the overall communication overhead. Previously, data was transferred over the SCSI bus using a series of phases to set up and transfer data. Packetization streamlines this process by combining the process into a packet, reducing overhead.

page fault — When the operating system requests a needed page of data or instructions that is not currently in memory.

paging (or swapping) — Copying virtual pages from disk to main memory.

paging file — Microsoft term for a Windows NT 4.0 or Windows 2000 swap file.

parallel bus — A SCSI reference meaning that multiple wires on the cable can transmit data at the same time.

parity — In SCSI, an encoding scheme that represents data appearing on other drives.

partitionless — Using an existing DOS or Windows partition instead of creating a partition manually during installation using FDISK or Red Hat's Disk Druid partitioning tool.

passive cluster — A clustered server with identical services as its failover partner. A passive cluster partner remains in an idle node state until such a time as the primary node fails.

passive hub — A standard hub that simply receives signals and repeats them out to all ports.

passive termination — The simplest type of SCSI termination, but also the least reliable. Passive terminators use resistors to terminate the SCSI chain, similar to the way terminators are used on coaxial Ethernet networks. Passive terminators usually work best on short, SE SCSI-1 buses. It is unlikely you will find many passive terminators in servers.

pass-through termination — If the last position on the SCSI chain is in use by a device that does not terminate itself, you can place a terminator over the connection, which allows signal transfer to and from the device while also providing the necessary termination.

Password Authentication Protocol (PAP) — A security protocol that sends logon information in clear text. Using a packet sniffer, an eavesdropper can analyze the packet and retrieve the logon data.

PCI hot swap (PCI hot plug) — The ability to add, remove, or replace PCI devices without first powering down the server.

PCI interrupts — Assignment of a designation to PCI devices that represent an actual ISA IRQ. The main benefit with PCI interrupts is that if no more IRQ addresses are available, PCI can use PCI steering to assign two or more PCI devices the same ISA IRQ.

PCI steering — Using PCI interrupts to assign two or more PCI devices the same ISA IRQ.

PCI-X (PCI-eXtended) — A 64-bit addendum to PCI 2.2 utilizing 64 bits and up to 133 MHz.

peer-to-peer (P2P) application — The server primarily exists to run software that allows peer computers to communicate with one another.

peer PCI bus — A bus architecture that increases available PCI bandwidth and expands the number of PCI expansion cards from the usual limit of four with a minimal impact on overall system bus bandwidth. This architecture usually involves dual peer PCI buses and two North Bridges, which connect to a primary PCI bus and a secondary PCI bus.

peer-to-peer network — A collection of networked computers with no logon server to verify the identity of users. Each network device has an equal (peer) level of authority.

Peripheral Components Interface (PCI) bus — A 32-bit data pathway for high-speed I/O for expansion adapter cards, USB, and IDE ports. The CMOS and system clock also connect to the PCI bus. The PCI bus connects to both the North Bridge and the South Bridge.

per seat — A licensing scheme that requires each client that connects to the server to have proper licensing.

per server — A licensing scheme that represents the number of concurrent connections allowed under the licensing scheme you purchased.

permissions — The configured level of access applied to a resource. For example, if a user can read a file but not change the file, then they have read-only permission.

Physical Address Extension (PAE) — Intel technology that allows the processor to utilize 36 bits to address up to 64 GB of memory.

pilot program — Isolating an upgraded server in a portion of the network that makes performance determination easier to determine and lessens negative impact should some part of a major upgrade fail.

Pin Grid Array (PGA) — An arrangement of pins on the underside of a processor. The pins fit inside a corresponding PGA socket.

Ping (packet internet groper) — An all-purpose utility for verifying that a remote host is accessible by sending small packets of data to which an accessible host responds.

plenum — The space between the dropped ceiling tiles and the actual ceiling, or the space between the raised floor surface and the concrete.

Point-to-Point Protocol (PPP) — A very flexible line protocol that interoperates with a variety of RAS software packages. PPP supports the NetBEUI, IPX/SPX, and TCP/IP protocols, data compression and encryption, and authentication protocols.

Point-to-Point Tunneling Protocol (PPTP) — A popular and easy-to-configure VPN tunneling protocol.

port aggregation — Similar to multihomed computers, port aggregation uses software to combine multiple ports from the server into a single logical connection to the network but with bandwidth that is multiplied times the number of ports.

positive pressure — The internal environment of a server case or cabinet that utilizes one or more filtered fans to supply main internal airflow throughout the server. Internal server fans draw only upon this filtered air.

POST (power-on self-test) — A BIOS verification of motherboard hardware.

Post Office Protocol 3 (POP3) — A line protocol that allows messages to be stored on the mail server for incoming email.

power distribution unit (PDU) — A device similar in function to a household power strip that connects multiple devices to a power supply, but it is capable of much higher power capacity.

primary domain server — The starting point of all DNS records. The zone database is readable and writeable on the primary domain server: You can add, remove, or modify DNS records.

primary partition — A bootable partition on which you can install operating system files.

process — A running program.

power factor — The difference between actual power and apparent power.

power supply unit (PSU) — The internal power supply powering a server or servers.

Primary Domain Controller (PDC) — A Windows NT server that stores the only read/write copy of the directory database. This database is a record of user and computer accounts, and is used for logging on users.

primary master server — There is only one primary master server per DNS zone, and it is the first and final authority for all hosts in their domain. Primary masters are the source for records that are copied to master or slave DNS servers.

PTR record — The actual record used in reverse lookups.

pull replication partner — In WINS, a replication partner that requests and then accepts changes from its push replication partners.

push replication partner — In WINS, a replication partner that responds to requests for changes from its pull replication partners.

Quick Arbitration and Selection (QAS) — Reduces overhead by reducing the number of times that arbitration must occur and by allowing a device waiting for bus access to do so more quickly.

Quarter Inch Cartridge (QIC) — A common tape format that is a quarter inch wide. A variant of QIC is the QIC Wide format, which is .315 inches (8 mm) wide. QIC cartridges are generally not sufficient for server purposes.

rack — A cabinet that houses stacked network equipment, storage, and servers. A rack can store multiple items in the same floor space.

RAID-0 — Also known as disk striping, a level of RAID that lays down data across two or more physical drives, benefiting from the combined performance of all drives in the array.

RAID-1 — Also known as disk mirroring, a level of RAID in which the controller writes the exact same data to two disks at the same time (redundancy).

RAID-0+1 — A level of RAID that offers the performance of RAID-0 and the redundancy of RAID-1. In this implementation, two channels and at least four drives are required. Data is striped across two or more disks in the first channel (RAID-0), and the data is mirrored to disks in the second channel (RAID-1).

RAID-5 — A level of RAID that offers the performance benefits of RAID-0 striping but also adds redundancy by use of parity with less overhead.

RAID cache — A high-speed memory cache that fills with data sequentially beyond the actual requested data in anticipation that the next data will soon be requested. If the data is indeed required, the RAID cache serves data more quickly than if data must be retrieved directly from disk.

RDRAM (Rambus DRAM) — Memory manufactured under license to Rambus. RDRAM is very fast, transferring data on both leading and trailing clock cycles.

recursive query — A query forwarded from one DNS server to another.

redundancy — The ability to continue providing service when something fails. For example, if a hard disk fails, a redundant hard disk can continue to store and serve files.

Redundant Array of Inexpensive (or Independent) Disks (RAID) — Utilization of multiple disks to improve performance, provide redundancy, or both.

registered memory — Memory that re-drives (amplifies) signals entering the memory module. Registered memory also enacts a deliberate pause of one clock cycle in the module to ensure that all communication from the chipset arrives properly. Registered memory is useful on heavily loaded server memory, and was designed for modules containing 32 or more chips.

remote access service (RAS) — The ability of a server to accept a connection from a client even when physically disconnected from the LAN.

remote monitoring (RMON) — An extension of the SNMP protocol, providing more comprehensive network monitoring capabilities. Instead of devices answering queries from the SNMP management system, RMON proactively sets off alarms for a variety of traffic conditions.

remote user — A user connected to the LAN from a geographically distant location, usually over a modem or virtual private network (VPN).

replication — Copying the database from one server to another, as in the case of a WINS server.

replication interval — The amount of time between WINS pull replication requests.

replication trigger — The WINS pull partner's message that initiates replication with the push partner.

request — The DHCP client's acceptance of the DHCP offer.

resolver — A host that requests DNS name resolution.

re-tension — A process that fast-forwards tape to the end without reading or writing data, and then rewinds all the way to the beginning again. This makes tension even throughout the tape.

reverse lookup zone (IN-ADDR.ARPA) — Useful for performing the reverse of a normal query: Instead of resolving a name to an IP address, it resolves an IP address to a name.

ring topology — A network topology in which all of the nodes are connected in a closed, single, logical communication loop.

RJ-45 (registered jack-45) — An eight-wire connector that connects Ethernet network devices.

round-trip time (RTT) — The time it takes for a Ping packet to reach its destination and return to the source.

router — A network device that connects multiple networks using routing tables and routable protocols. Routers use headers and a forwarding table to determine where packets go, and communicate with other routers to calculate the best route between any two hosts. Routers determine whether to forward or filter a packet based on the IP address and subnet mask, which identifies the network to which a host belongs. The router filters a message destined for a host on the same network, and forwards messages destined for a host on a different network.

Router Information Protocol (RIP) — A distance vector-based protocol that identifies the best route for a destination based on the number of hops.

run time — The number of minutes that batteries can power the system.

S-spec — An alphanumeric code printed on the processor that uniquely identifies the processor version and is more specific than processor stepping.

scalability — A server's ability to grow in terms of the number of processors.

scope — A range of IP addresses that the DHCP server distributes to DHCP clients.

SCSI-1 — The original SCSI implementation.

SCSI-2 — A version of SCSI that introduced Fast and Wide data transmission.

SCSI-3 — A compilation of several different documents, SCSI-3 can be mostly equivalent to SCSI-2 in its features unless several of the various SCSI-3 features are applied. At present, SCSI-3 can be as fast as 320 MBps under Ultra320.

SCSI-3 Parallel Interface (SPI) — See SPI.

SCSI ID — Unique numbering for each SCSI device to ensure proper SCSI operation.

SCSI Interlock Protocol (SIP) — The SCSI-3 parallel command set.

secondary domain servers — A DNS server that can receive a read-only copy of the zone database from a primary domain server. Secondary domain servers are useful for providing redundancy and load balancing.

segment — In reference to SCSI, dividing a SCSI bus. Each SCSI segment is electrically independent, and therefore capable of the maximum cable length as if it were truly its own bus. Each segment requires its own termination, and each device must still have a unique SCSI ID across all segments.

server — A computer with more processing power, RAM, and hard disk capacity than typical workstations. A server has a server NOS such as Microsoft Windows NT or Novell NetWare, and provides file and printer sharing, centralized file storage, security, and various services.

Serial Line Internet Protocol (SLIP) — SLIP uses only the TCP/IP protocol and is useful for UNIX connections. SLIP is very basic and does not support authentication protocols, encryption, or compression.

servo mechanism — Detects precise cylinder locations on the platter using gray code.

services — A function of the NOS that provides server features to the network.

shielded twisted pair (STP) — Network cable that consists of two copper wires, each encased in its own color-coded insulation, which are twisted together to form a "twisted pair." Multiple twisted pairs are then packaged in a metal (foil) sheath to reduce external signal interference.

Shiva Password Authentication Protocol (SPAP) — Shiva products (acquired by Intel) are a popular alternative to Microsoft RAS solutions. Shiva encrypts authentication credentials for Shiva LAN Rover software.

signaling — Transmission of data using electrical impulses or variations. These electrical transmissions represent data that the sender originates and the receiver translates based upon a mutually agreed-upon method.

Simple Mail Transport Protocol (SMTP) — A mail protocol that transports only basic text. SMTP is the protocol that transfers or forwards mail to an email server.

Simple Network Management Protocol (SNMP) — A network monitoring and management protocol. Its usefulness is comprised of several elements that work together with the ultimate purpose of informing the administrator of a changing trend in the use of an object or alerting the administrator of an error, failure, or condition.

Single Edge Contact Cartridge (SECC) — A slot format processor that stands upright inside a motherboard slot, similar to adapter or memory slots. The cartridge contacts are covered by the housing.

Single Edge Contact Cartridge2 (SECC2) — A longer form of the SECC slot that accommodates Pentium Xeon processors. The cartridge contracts are exposed.

single-ended (SE) signaling — The original signaling method used on the SCSI-1 bus, that uses a common signaling method in which a positive voltage represents a one and a zero voltage (ground) represents a zero, resulting in binary communication.

single sign-on — A single logon that allows transparent access to multiple servers. For example, a single sign-on might allow you to log on to a NetWare server and pass the logon credentials to an NT 4.0 server as well.

single-user mode — In UNIX/Linux, a mode in which user connections are closed, ensuring that there are no locks on open files. This is not a complete shutdown because the operating system is still running.

site — The LAN(s) on either side of a WAN connection.

six-cartridge backup — Similar to a GFS backup strategy, but with a two-week history.

slack — Hard disk space wasted when data does not fill a complete allocation of cluster space.

slave (drive) — Equal in every way to the master, except that it does not receive the first drive letter assignment nor contain a boot record.

slave server — An authoritative DNS server that receives the zone transfer from the master and is named in the zone by an NS record.

SMARTDRV.EXE — An MS-DOS-based caching utility that significantly speeds up file reads and writes.

SNMP agent — A service that runs on the actual object you want to monitor using an SNMP management system.

SNMP management system — Sends requests for information from the monitored system, known as the SNMP agent.

SONET — A fiber optic transmission medium that is self-healing. If a line is cut, traffic redirects to another ring.

South Bridge — A chipset element that divides the PCI bus from the ISA bus.

SPI — SCSI-3 parallel interface, defining SCSI-3 standards in SPI-1 through SPI-3 releases. The original SPI release has been renamed SPI-1 for clarity when comparing against other successive SPI versions. SPI-1 is also known as Ultra SCSI or Wide Ultra SCSI.

SPI-2 — Also known as Ultra2 SCSI and Wide Ultra2 SCSI, a SCSI-3 standard that introduced SCA-2 connectors LVD signaling, and Fast-40 40 MBps transfer rate on a narrow (8-bit) channel or 80 MBps on a wide (16-bit) channel.

SPI-3 — Still in draft stage at the time of this writing, a SCSI-3 standard that introduces CRCs for data integrity, domain validation, DT clocking, packetization, and QAS. Also known as Ultra3 SCSI.

SPI-4 — The latest SCSI-3 specification, still in draft form at the time of this writing. Most hard disk and host adapter manufacturers have products using the standard's 320 MBps data rate. This data rate is accomplished by doubling the bus speed from 40 MHz to 80 MHz and using DT clocking. Manufacturers are calling this standard Ultra320.

stand-alone server — A Windows NT server that is not a member of the domain and does not store the directory database, but is useful as a file, print, or application server, or provides one or more services.

standby power supply (SPS) — A power switch technique that detects an interruption in line power and switches to a large transformer that stores a small amount of power required to bridge the time it takes to switch to battery power.

static IP address — An IP address that is manually and permanently assigned to a network host.

static load balancing — A clustering technology in which a cluster member remains idle until a failure occurs.

Staggered Pin Grid Array (SPGA) — Same as a PGA processor or socket format, except in a staggered arrangement to squeeze more pins in the same space (as opposed to straight rows).

star topology — A network configuration in which all of the nodes connect to a central network device such as a hub or switch. All nodes receive the same signal, reducing effective bandwidth, and the central network device can become a bottleneck because all data must pass through it.

Start of Authority (SOA) server — The authoritative server for information about the DNS domain; the domain cannot function without it.

stepping — The version of a processor.

storage area network (SAN) — Generally refers to Fibre Channel and any other type of network-based storage solution that is not server-based.

subfloor — A space between the concrete floor and the floor tiles; also known as the plenum.

subnet — A division in the network useful for limiting network traffic to a particular location; also known as a segment in many contexts.

subnet mask — A series of network identification numbers which, when compared against the IP address, identifies the specific network to which the host belongs.

superscalar — A processor architecture that allows a processor to execute more than one instruction in a single clock cycle.

switch — A networking device that separates a network into collision domains so that network rules can be extended. Each of the segments attached to an Ethernet switch has a full 10 or 100 Mbps of bandwidth shared by fewer users, resulting in better performance.

switch — Similar to a router in that it segments a network, and similar to a hub in that it connects network cables together in a central, star configuration. Switches forward traffic at very high speeds.

switched fabric — A somewhat inexact reference to Fibre Channel storage connections. The connection can use any number of connection routes, depending on which one is deemed best at that particular moment.

switching hub — A hub that reads the destination address of each packet and then forwards the packet to the correct port.

symmetric multiprocessing (SMP) — The simultaneous use of multiple processors on the same server.

synchronize — The process of making data in one location consistent with data in another location. Synchronization is necessary to ensure that user accounts, for example, are consistent from one logon server to another. Synchronization also applies to items such as data files.

synchronous dynamic RAM (SDRAM) — Memory that operates at system clock speed.

Systems Network Architecture (SNA) Server — A Microsoft product that acts as a gateway between the client and the mainframe.

System Performance Monitor/2 (SPM/2) — Tool used to measure performance statistics in the OS/2 operating system environment.

tape library — A self-contained tape backup solution that is preloaded with several tapes. Most tape libraries include autoloaders to swap tapes.

TCP/IP (Transmission Control Protocol/Internet Protocol) — A suite of protocols in common use on most networks and the Internet.

terminator — A connector placed the end of a SCSI chain that absorbs the transmission signal to avoid signal bounce, making it appear to the devices as if the cable was of infinite length. Terminators also regulate the electrical load, and are therefore critical in establishing a reliable communications medium. Proper termination requires a terminator at both ends of the SCSI cable.

thermistor — A power supply thermostat that increases or decreases fan speed based on heat generated by the power supply.

thicknet — Based on the 10Base5 standard, which transmits data at 10 Mbps over a maximum distance of 500 meters (1640.4 feet). Thicknet is about 1 cm thick and has been used for backbone media because of its durability and maximum length.

thin client — A computer that receives its operating system environment, including applications and data, from the server.

thin-film — A magnetic medium applied to disks in a near perfect, continuous vacuum.

thinnet — Based on the 10Base2 standard (10 Mbps/Baseband transmission), networking cable that utilizes RG-58 A/U or RG-58 C/U 50 ohm coaxial cable with maximum segment lengths of 185 meters (606.9 feet).

threads — Program units of execution that can run separately from other threads. A thread is also the means by which an application accesses memory and processor time.

throughput — A measure of the quantity of data sent or received in a second.

time domain reflectometer (TDR) — A network troubleshooting device that measures the approximate distance to cable breaks.

time to live (TTL) — In DNS and WINS, the length of time a record is stored.

token passing — A method of collision avoidance that prevents two nodes from transmitting messages at the same time.

topology — The geometric configuration of devices, nodes, and cable links on a network. Topologies define how nodes connect to one another.

tower — An upright, free-standing computer case.

Tower of Hanoi backup — A tape strategy that requires relatively few tapes and backs up a daily history of 32 or more days.

TRACERT — A command-line trace routing utility that works like Ping but shows the actual router hops taken to reach the remote host.

traditional NetWare file system — Offers similar, competitive features to the NTFS file system, and allows you to create NetWare volumes.

transceiver — A device in a Token Ring node that repeats the network signal to move it around the ring.

transistor — An electronic device that opens or closes, or turns on or off to provide a logic gate or switch. Transistors provide the "thinking" capability of the processor.

trap — A message issued from the SNMP agent to the SNMP management system.

Travan — Created by Imation, a QIC-based standard capable of up to 20 GB compressed capacity.

Travan NS — A Travan format that can use hardware compression and fast data verification.

turnkey fax servers — Self-contained, freestanding devices in which the software and hardware are already installed. Except for some company-specific configurations, they are ready to fax right out of the box.

Ultra160, Ultra160+ — A collection of SCSI-3 standards that ensure compliance with a minimum level of SCSI-3 standards, offering speeds of 160 MBps.

Ultrium — A tape format that offers a native capacity of up to 800 GB and data transfer of 80–160 MBps. Ultrium tapes use a single reel cartridge that makes room for more tape and less mechanics. Ultrium cartridges can contain memory right on the cartridge that stores a redundant file log and user-defined information.

uninterruptible power supply (UPS) — A device that supplies power temporarily to allow administrators to perform a graceful shutdown of server equipment. Otherwise, the sudden loss of power to the server can be extremely damaging to the operating system, applications, and open data files.

UNIX — An open server operating system that allows vendors to specially modify it to their servers. UNIX usually operates on more expensive RISC-based processors.

UNIX File System (UFS) — The UNIX file system, which supports large volumes and local security.

unshielded twisted pair (UTP) — Network cabling that does not rely on physical shielding to block interference (as does STP), but uses balancing and filtering techniques to reduce signal interference. Noise is induced equally on two conductors, which cancel out at the receiver.

uptime — The continued operation of the overall server or specific components.

virtual console — A separate Linux context to which you can log on and perform various tasks while other virtual consoles or a GUI also run.

virtual memory — A portion of hard disk space that extends RAM memory.

virtual private network (VPN) — A communications session protected inside an encrypted virtual "tunnel" that is extremely difficult for intruders to breach. VPN is most commonly used over an Internet connection.

voice coil — A construction used by the hard disk actuator mechanism to move from one location to the next.

volume — In NetWare, a collection of files, directories, subdirectories, and even partitions.

wake-on LAN (WOL) — A technology that allows you to remotely wake a computer from its sleep mode. WOL works by sending a "magic packet" from a remote station to the WOL host. The "magic packet" contains 16 copies of the WOL host's MAC address.

WAN link — The telecommunications connection that links the various networks that comprise parts of a wide area network (WAN).

WebSphere — An IBM application for building and managing web-based applications.

web farm — Multiple web servers providing the same web content.

wide area network (WAN) — Multiple, geographically distant LANs connected to one another across a relatively great distance.

Wide SCSI — Utilizing 16-bit transfer instead of 8-bit (which is "narrow" SCSI).

Windows Internet Naming Service (WINS) — A Microsoft NetBIOS name resolution service.

WINS proxy agent — A WINS-enabled computer that listens on the subnet for WINS broadcast messages, such as: query, refresh, release, and registration. The WINS proxy then communicates with the WINS server to resolve or register NetBIOS names.

workstation — Desktop computer with only enough hardware to service the needs of a single user at a time. Synonymous in most contexts with PC, desktop computer, or client.

X.500 ITU — Originally a standard for searching email directories but has much broader application. The standard is so large and complex that no vendor complies with it completely.

X Term — A text-based terminal interface within the Linux GUI.

X Windows — A GUI for the UNIX administration.

Zero Effort Networks (Z.E.N.) or ZENworks — A NetWare tool that administrators use to manage the user or server operating system environment by automatically distributing applications and controlling the user desktop.

zero insertion force (ZIF) — A socket format that allows gravity alone to seat the processor. The processor is then locked into place with a locking lever.

zone transfer — A copy of the zone DNS database that is copied to another DNS server.

Index